Human Behavior in
the Social Environment

each of us arises from unique traditions
    that energize our lives
    lend us security
    and give us vision for the future

but traditions can only be guideposts
    to taking life's journeys
    dealing with relentless changes
    and fulfilling our destinies

and we complete the circle to discover
    that we are of the same family
    our differences are small
    beside the sameness of our experiences

peace to us all
                —Photographs and poem
                  by Duane Massing

Carel Bailey Germain

HUMAN BEHAVIOR IN THE SOCIAL ENVIRONMENT

AN ECOLOGICAL VIEW

Columbia University Press
NEW YORK

Columbia University Press
New York   Chichester, West Sussex
Copyright © 1991 Columbia University Press
All rights reserved

Library of Congress Cataloging-in-Publication Data

Germain, Carel B.
Human behavior in the social environment : an ecological view /
Carel Bailey Germain.
p. cm.
Includes bibliographical references and index.
ISBN 0-231-05404-1
1. Social psychology.   2. Environmental psychology.
3. Developmental psychology.   4. Family—United States—
Psychological aspects.   5. Minorities—United States—Psychology.
6. Social work education.   I. Title.
HM251.G3497   1991
302—dc20   90-47014
CIP

*To Adrienne
and Denise and Jonathan
with love*

Contents

Appendixes

Preface

This book is designed to help social work students build a theory foundation for their professional practice. Its content reflects what has been designated by the Council on Social Work Education as required for all social workers, regardless of their method or field of practice. It is also designed to meet the needs and interests of experienced practitioners. As Whitehead observed, knowledge keeps no better than fish, yet "keeping up" with new theoretical developments and research is difficult without a centralized source of information. This book is intended to be such a source. The book is also designed to provide social work educators (class and field) with a rationale for incorporating into the curriculum new theories and research findings as they appear, and for dropping those that are no longer valid or no longer pertinent to contemporary practice and social conditions. The rationale is consistent with social work's mission in society and its person(s)-in-environment emphasis.

Required Content

In its 1982 Curriculum Policy Statement (CPS), the Council on Social Work Education (CSWE) mandates, for all graduate and undergraduate curricula, specific content on ethnic minorities of color, women, and other groups (such as those with disabilities and gay and lesbian people) who are consistently affected by bias and oppression, with explicit attention to the patterns and consequences of discrimination and oppression. For the human behavior sequence in particular, the CPS requires all educational programs to develop a coherent approach to selecting research and theories in the social, behavioral, and biological sciences, and to present them in a way that will illuminate divergencies and interrelationships.

The CPS also specifies content on the relationships among the biological, psychological, social, and cultural systems that shape human behavior and are shaped by it. More specifically, it requires the inclusion of theories and research findings regarding the functioning of individuals, families, households, social groups, communities, and organizations and how individuals develop over the life course through membership in these collectivities. And finally, the CPS expects the curriculum to impart to students an understanding of the relationship between knowledge and social work practice, policies, services, and programs. This book aims to meet all these curriculum requirements.

The book is organized into two parts. The introduction to part 1 presents definitions of social work's function in society developed by the National Association of Social Workers (NASW) and the Council on Social Work Education and relates them to an ecological perspective. This is important because the definitions govern the selection of content for the profession's theoretical and research foundation. Following its introduction, part 1 presents the environmental arenas in which human development and functioning take place. Chapter 1 considers central concepts bearing on development and functioning in context, including culture and the social and physical environments. Chapters 2 and 3 examine the community as context. Chapter 4 analyzes varied family structures and functions as comprising the most intimate context of human development in today's world. Chapter 5 examines family processes and transformations, within particular cultural and societal contexts, as experienced by the members.

The introduction to part 2 presents the concept of *life course* that is used throughout in place of the traditional concept of *life cycle stages*. Part 2, the longer section of the book, is concerned with the biopsychosocial development of individuals in the context of family, community, and culture—taking account of the influence of expectable and nonexpectable challenges and stressors, life tasks, and other factors. Attention is given to love; work; women's and men's issues; cultural differences; health, illness, and death; the influence of the community's and the society's social, economic, political, health, and environmental policies and structures on the family and the well-being of its members; and the variations in development and functioning that arise from the richness of human diversity.

Most books on human growth and development begin with the individual's birth and infancy and proceed in a linear fashion to her or his old age and death. In contrast, this book assumes, first, that the development of all members of the family—children and adults—occurs in tandem (M. Bloom 1979), with each member influencing the development and functioning of the others. Individual processes merge into collective processes that result in the family's own development and functioning as a family. Hence, part 2 begins with two adults coming together to form a couple, and perhaps later becoming parents. Their young adulthood, middle adulthood, and older years are considered in tandem with their child's development through pregnancy, infancy, childhood, and youth. If the couple do not become parents, an acceptable option in our society today, their couplehood is still considered over the life course.

Second, this book assumes that social work's purpose in society—its historical commitment—is related to its historical person-in-environment perspective. Many books with a linear conception of human growth and development, however, find it difficult to incorporate environmental elements and their influence beyond the parents. Hence, I have elected to place the environment (community and family) first as the major context for individual and family development and functioning, shaping them in countless ways, with cultural variations, human diversity, and the impact of societal processes serving as continuing threads throughout the book. This means that individual development is not considered until part 2. Nevertheless, I hope that readers will pursue the content in the given order, for then the person and the environment are more likely to be understood and viewed as a unitary system in which each is influenced and shaped by the other. While readers are free to begin with part 2, later picking up with part 1, they risk having a fractured sense of person(s) and environment rather than an integrated one. I should explain that I use a colon rather than a hyphen in the unitary term *person:environment* in order to avoid that fracturing.

One other explanation: I struggled with the ambiguities in minority group designations and have decided—where a category term is indicated—to use the terms *blacks, Hispanics,* and American Indians inasmuch as these are the designations used by the U.S. Bureau of the Census.

I recognize that *African-American* has recently come into use, replacing the former *Afro-American*, but it appears so far to be less common than the designation *black*. For some Spanish-speaking groups, the term *Latino/Latina* is beginning to be used instead of the term *Hispanic*, but also less frequently so far. Also, many Spanish-speaking people prefer specific designations such as Puerto Rican, Cuban, Guatemalan, Argentine, and so on that are country-of-origin designations. I use these when more specific terms are needed. Some people of Mexican origin or descent prefer to be known as *Mexican-American* instead of the more politicized designation *chicano/chicana*. I use both, with *Mexican-American* as a more general designation. Furthermore, the Caribbean peoples include not only Spanish speakers, but French-, English-, and Dutch-speaking populations, who may be of varying races or ethnic groups. *Asian-American, Southeast Asian,* and *Pacific Islander* are general terms referring to race, while *Chinese, Japanese, Korean, Vietnamese, Laotian, Cambodian, Filipino/Filipina, Guamanian, Samoan,* and *Hawaiian* are ethnic and/or country-of-origin designations. Persons from other parts of Asia, as well as from Europe and Africa, are usually designated by their country of origin. These many ambiguities highlight the lack of clarity in distinguishing among the concepts of race, ethnicity, and national origin, and they also point to our limited understanding of the source of identity of each of our many diverse populations and cultures.

Acknowledgments

The book represents a twenty-year process of reviewing idea systems while teaching a course in human behavior and the social environment. During the last three years of that process, the course was enriched by the insights of my friend Professor Judith A. B. Lee, who taught a second section—to the delight of her students. I owe the conception of tandem development of parents and child to Professor Martin Bloom, who presented the idea in his book *Life Span Development: Bases for Preventive and Interventive Helping* (1980). I am grateful to him for the organizing power of his creative idea. As a reviewer of the manuscript, he provided many helpful suggestions, for which I thank him.

To John D. Moore, President and Director of Columbia University Press, I extend my thanks for his idea for the book and his continued interest. He makes writing for the Press a pleasure. I am grateful to Louise Waller, former Executive Editor of the Press, for her thoughtful solutions to knotty problems of organization. To former students and practitioner colleagues Kanani Bell, Laura Cohen, Sandra Boston DeSylva, Jane Fuller, Roland Haley, Joyce Hellerman, Karin Laakso, Mary Beth Langton, Jean Williams, and others, I owe a deepened understanding and respect of life forces. I appreciate their permission to quote from their unpublished materials. The bibliographical research of Mark Allard and Carolyn Forsyth in the initial planning of the manuscript was also helpful. Above all I treasure the loving encouragement of my husband, William.

I thank the following publishers for permission to adapt my earlier publications for use in this book:

Columbia University Press: "The Place of Community Work Within an Ecological Approach to Social Work Practice." In Samual Taylor and Robert Roberts, eds, *Theories and Practice of Community Work* (1985), pp. 30–55; "The Elderly and the Ecology of Death: Issues of Time and Space." In Margot Tallmer et al., eds., *The Life-Threatened Elderly* (1984), pp. 195–207.

Family Service, America: "Time, An Ecological Variable in Social Work Practice." *Social Casework* (July 1976), 57(7):419–426; "Space, An Ecological Variable in Social Work Practice." *Social Casework* (November 1978), 59(9):5–22.

The Free Press: *Social Work Practice in Health Care* (1984).

The University of Chicago Press: "Human Development in Contemporary Environments." *Social Service Review* (December 1987), 61(4):565–580.

I am also grateful to the following organizations, individuals, and publishers for their kind permission to reproduce materials:

American Association of Retired Persons: selected portions of "A Profile of Older Americans," copyright 1989.

Brooks/Cole: Irwin Altman, *The Environment and Social Behavior* (1975), diagram, p. 7.

Dr. Andy Farquharson, University of Victoria, British Columbia: diagram, "Model of the Helping Continuum," unpublished.

The March of Dimes/Birth Defects Foundation: *Genetic Counselling* (1987), boxed figures, pp. 12, 14, 15, and 16.

Duane Massing, MSW, Grant MacEwan College, Edmonton, Alberta: photographs and poem, frontispiece.

The Science Museum of Connecticut (Roaring Brook Nature Center), West Hartford.

Dr. Toni C. Antonucci, diagram, page 100, from T. C. Antonucci, "Personal Characteristics, Social Support, and Social Behavior," in Robert M. Binstock and Ethel Shanus, eds., *Handbook of Aging and the Social Sciences*, New York: Van Nostrand Reinhold, pp. 94–128.

Human Behavior in the Social Environment

I

The Contexts of Human Development and Functioning

Introduction: Professional Purpose; Perspectives on the Human Being

Part 1 is an introduction to the whole. It presents *selected* concepts and research findings from various disciplines that are designed to provide a coherent and integrated theoretical foundation for all social work methods, practice models, and fields of practice. Immediately, three questions come to fore. The first one is: Who rules on a theory's or a study's relevance to social work? I believe that the relevance of content can rest on two parallel definitions of social work's mission in society provided by the Council on Social Work Education (CSWE) and the National Association of Social Workers (NASW), the standard-setting bodies of the profession.

THE PROFESSION'S MISSION IN SOCIETY

In a profession as diverse as social work, the dominant challenge in defining its social purpose is to produce a conception of social work broad enough to engage the commitment of all social workers regardless of the method employed (casework, group work, community organization, generic, administration, research, planning, and policy) or the field of practice selected (for example, child welfare, public assistance, health, mental health, or corrections). Both the NASW and the CSWE definitions meet that challenge. Moreover, they are suffi-

3

ciently similar and have enjoyed a sufficient consensus among members of the profession to provide—for now, at least—a rationale for the selection of foundation theories and research. Both also convey an ecological perspective on people and environments that is used to integrate the theoretical and research content in this book.

NASW Definition

Within the practice segment of the profession, the work on defining social work is clearest in the efforts of Harriett Bartlett and William E. Gordon that began in the 1950s as a committee effort at the behest of NASW. The committee noted, "The [social worker] facilitates interaction between the individual and his *[sic]* social environment with a continuing awareness of the reciprocal effects of one upon the other" (Bartlett 1958); later, Bartlett (1970) used two concepts: *life tasks* to describe common, demanding situations that confront people; and *coping* to describe how people actually respond to these situations and how they master them. Together, the two concepts reflect certain interactions or exchanges between people and environments.

Working closely with Bartlett, and building on social work's traditional commitment to person-in-situation, Gordon (1969) advanced the notion that the social work task is to match people's coping patterns with the qualities of impinging environments. The purpose is to produce growth-inducing and environment-ameliorating transactions. The professional task and purpose require the social worker to maintain a dual, simultaneous focus on people and environments. Gordon suggested that, depending on the particular situation, client and social worker together seek to change coping behaviors or qualities of the impinging environment, or both, in order to bring about a better match between them. A problem arises in this conception insofar as it is unclear whose values are to be employed. Who is to decide what constitutes a good match? The client? The social worker? The agency? The profession? The community? The society? Today, social workers are more aware of the prevalence of value conflicts and ethical dilemmas than in 1969, when Gordon was writing. The profession is now more concerned about empowering people to make their own choices and decisions. Although this is a practice issue, it also influences the selection of content for foundation theory for practice—in this instance, inclusion of content to illuminate the political, economic, and social bases of the disempowerment of groups that are vulnerable because of color, age, ethnicity, gender, disablement, and sexual preference.

Nevertheless, the work of Bartlett and Gordon in defining the distinctive elements of social work contained the seeds of an ecological metaphor for social work. Their definitions require content pertinent to the life tasks, transactions between people and environments, coping, and environmental qualities in today's society. For the ecological frame of reference to serve its integrating function, however, additional organizing concepts are included, such as positive outcomes of people:environment transactions (adaptation, human relatedness, competence, self-direction, self-concept and self-esteem, and the capacity to attribute meaning to life experiences) and negative transactional outcomes (coercive power, social and technological pollutions, and life stressors).

CSWE Definition

The CSWE is responsible for developing standards by which master's and baccalaureate programs are evaluated for accreditation. Its 1982 Curriculum Policy Statement (CPS) defines the social work purpose or mission as the promotion, restoration, maintenance, and enhancement of the functioning of individuals, families, households, social groups, organizations, and communities. The profession carries out this mission 1) by helping individuals and collectivities to prevent distress and to use their personal and environmental resources for growth and development and 2) by planning, developing, and implementing the social policies, services, and programs required to meet basic needs and to support human growth and development. Influenced by the work of Bartlett, Gordon, and others, the CSWE definition in its Curriculum Policy Statement (1982) also states, "Professional practice thus focuses on the transactions between people and their environments that affect their ability to accomplish life tasks, alleviate distress, and realize individual and collective aspirations" (1982:4). The professional mission and the person:environment frame of reference (an ecological perspective) are similar in both definitions and were used as the basis for the selection of content presented throughout this book.

Neither the frame of reference nor the theoretical foundation is specific to any one method, field of practice, or practice model. They apply to all, insofar as methods, fields, and models reflect the mission of social work as defined by the CSWE and NASW. The breadth of the frame of reference and the theoretical foundation give rise to the second question: In borrowing selectively from a discipline or a body of theory, how can violation of the integrity of theoretical structures be avoided or, at least, minimized? I believe one answer lies in relating the borrowed concepts to assumptions underlying the particular theory wherever possible, and in integrating them one with another through an overarching frame of reference—in this instance, an ecological or person:environment perspective that is consistent with the social work purpose as defined by the CSWE and the NASW. Also, additional readings are provided at the end of this volume so that interested readers may pursue in breadth or depth the theories from which concepts are borrowed and/or may review additional research findings.

The third question is what distinguishes the social worker's acquisition of foundation theory in the curriculum area of human behavior in the social environment (HBSE) from study in the academic disciplines producing the theories and research findings? Here the answer lies in the explicit connections made with the requirements of the profession. It is neither necessary nor sufficient, for example, that social workers become experts in sociology, psychology, anthropology, political science, economics, biology, or other behavioral and life sciences. Rather, social workers need to understand and apply relevant concepts and findings from various disciplines and bodies of thought that will provide a base for professional decisions and action as filtered through the lens of social work purpose, values, and ethics. Hence, connections are made in this book between social work and most of the theories and research concepts presented.

Part 1 presents the environmental context of human development and functioning. But chapter 1 first sets the stage with 1) some assumptions about the nature of human beings and their environments derived from an evolutionary, adaptive point of view; 2) elements of foundation theory and knowledge required by the NASW and CSWE definitions; and 3) some organizing concepts of the ecological perspective as the book's frame of reference. I believe the perspective also has the capacity to integrate concepts and research findings from a variety of disciplines pertinent to social work's mission or purpose in society, including the experience of social work itself.

Chapter 2 presents the community as the environmental context for development and functioning of individuals and collectivities, including physical and social settings and the culture. Chapter 3 continues with the community, focusing on support systems ranging from formal organizations to informal affiliative relationships. Chapters 4 and 5 present concepts about families, the most intimate context of development and functioning across the life course. Chapter 4 considers the family as the most intimate developmental context and one of the community's support systems. Concepts include family forms, functions, and tasks. Chapter 5 continues with family development, dynamics, and cultural variations.

1

The Ecological Perspective

Before we take up the frame of reference and its specific concepts, several knowledge and value issues must be addressed.

An Evolutionary, Adaptive Point of View

In the neo-Darwinian or synthetic theory of evolution, *Homo sapiens*, the present species of human beings, is known to have peopled the earth for more than 100,000 years. The genus *Homo*, however, originated several million years ago in the semitropical savannas of East Africa. Early forms were *Homo erectus* and others. By 100,000 years ago, however, *Homo sapiens neandertalis* (Neanderthal people) were living and were replaced by *Homo sapiens sapiens* (Cro-Magnon people) about 35,000 years ago. The reasons for the disappearance of both are not known. But nearly all the characteristics that we consider distinctively human were present in both groups (Dubos 1981). Much earlier, the *Homo* line and the hominids and great apes are believed to have descended from a common ancestral line. Therefore, our species, *Homo sapiens*, is thought to have shared with primates this earlier common ancestor, and with the mammals a still earlier one, and so on back to the one-celled organisms.

We are now the only living species of the genus *Homo*, but just so we do not feel alone on the planet, it is well to remember that we retain our relationship to other members of the primate order (and indeed, to all forms of life if we go back far enough). This means that we display certain physiological and behavioral traits that are similar to certain traits of the great apes. Indeed, we now know that humans and chimpanzees share 98 percent of their genetic material (DNA); thus ends the controversy over whether the gorilla or the chimpanzee is our closest living relative (Sibley and Ahlquist 1984). The 2 percent makes all the difference.

In any case, Clarence Day, a well-known writer of an earlier generation, wrote a charming essay, "This Simian World" (1920), in which he poked fun at the very human characteristics that we share with apes and monkeys: our great curiosity, inventiveness, self-centeredness, general messiness, and laziness, and our endless interest in chatter, gossip, and self-expression. We have expanded the latter into numerous language systems, writing, printing, broadcasting, television, and now computer technology and other forms of electronic communication that wire us together around the planet as though we were one giant organism (L. Thomas 1974). Day observed that we are also insatiable inquirers into the news, especially news of the kind our species loved when they scampered and wrangled in the forest, because it stirs our most primitive simian feelings—news of love affairs, family quarrels, misbehaviors, accidents, and catastrophes. Day also played with the idea of what our behavioral characteristics might have been had we descended from the great cats, or elephants, or even eagles, instead of from simians.

In a more serious vein, one physical attribute that distinguishes us from the apes, the hominids, and the earlier apelike common ancestor is our large brain (two other differences are our small jaw and upright posture). That brain enables us to learn from experience and to transmit learning and experience down the generations—through the use of symbols, including language, knowledge, technology, belief systems, and meanings. Organic evolution in *Homo sapiens* has been replaced by cultural evolution, but nonetheless on a biological base (that is, the brain). We no longer change our physical and psychological structures by slow evolutionary processes of genetic mutation and environmental selection that require millennia for their operation. Instead, we change ourselves rapidly through new knowledge, technology, and social organization, and the meanings we attribute to them. In other words, cultural evolution has replaced organic evolution in human beings.

Why is this evolutionary hypothesis important to social workers?

From an evolutionary perspective, human beings are living today with ancient physical and psychological equipment that evolved in prehominid and early *Homo* experience in response to conditions in the African savannas (and perhaps to some conditions occurring as recently as the Stone Age period of 100,000 years ago). With the development of human culture, the species spread from a semitropical environment to all corners of the earth. We are able to survive under harsh climatic and other conditions because of cultural adaptations such as shelter and body covering, tools, varied forms of social organization, and the controlled use of fire. Today, human beings can survive in even harsher environments such as Antarctica, the ocean depths, and outer space because of technology, not because of organic (genetic) changes.

The development of cities, following on the invention of agriculture some 10,000 or more years ago, and the industrialization of Western societies in the nineteenth century, followed by today's technological mass societies, eventually resulted in environments that bear no resemblance to those in which humankind evolved. Our cultural efforts to adapt to them have sometimes created even more serious physical and psychological burdens. Some so-called adaptations are not so much adaptive as reflective of our species' evolved plasticity, which allows us to tolerate maladaptive conditions such as pollution, overcrowding, and the production of hazardous wastes. Individually and collectively, we pay for this plasticity with heavy physical, emotional, or social costs, either immediately or further along the life course. Dubos (1981) and other life scientists have noted that much of the chronic illness that continues to resist medical control (such as hypertension, certain cancers, some heart disease, and stroke), many emotional disturbances, and some social dysfunctioning are consequences of a poor fit between our ancient physiology and psychology, on the one hand, and the kinds of physical and social environments we have created, on the other. Contemporary biogenetics would add an inherited susceptibility to these conditions as well, which depend on environmental triggers for their appearance.

It is true that some organic evolution does take place at the level of individual organisms since species' gene pools contain untapped diversities that remain unrealized except where a newly manifested mutation fits a new environmental circumstance. But this kind of evolution appears to be now largely unavailable to humankind, given our long life course and the accelerating rate of social change. A new adaptive advantage cannot spread through a human population in time for a better fit. It would be very quickly overtaken by further social changes of great magnitude. It is nevertheless the case that, like the gene pools of other forms of life, the gene pool of the human species contains an untapped reservoir of diverse potentialities. For their appearance to occur at individual levels, a parallel diversity of "nutritive" environments is needed to release and support them. This is an optimistic feature of the human condition, for while the end of organic evolution means that we are probably limited to what is now contained within the gene pool of the species, we can explore and develop those potentialities far more than we have, especially the untapped potentialities in the human brain.

Thus an evolutionary view leads to a philosophical conception of human beings as continually growing, changing, and learning. They are goal-oriented and purposive in their behavior as they strive to achieve, individually and collectively, an adaptive balance with their environment. Such a balance promotes the innate human push toward growth and health and, ideally, protects and enhances environments. However, the evolutionary view also underscores the limited nature of our knowledge about what actually constitutes the responsive and nutritive social and physical environments that will support the diversity of human beings and cultures already exhibited, let alone diversity yet to be realized. Some of our ideas about nutritive environments represent culturally based beliefs and value preferences masquerading as knowledge. An example is the assumption that the nuclear family of father, mother, and children is the normal family, and that other family forms are unfortunate deviations from the norm. This assumption has been regarded in the recent past as firm knowledge. It is now coming to be understood as a culturally based belief that flies in the face of what is being learned about families in other times and places, and in our own pluralistic and rapidly changing society.

Determinism in Human Development

The distinction between knowledge and belief leads into the issue of determinism in respect to human behavior. Classical psychoanalytic theory, for example, rested on a belief in psychic determinism, which, in brief, assumes that all behavior, including cognitions and feeling states, is determined by antecedent conditions and experiences of the person (see the section in appendix 1 on Freudian theory). In contrast, early forms of learning theory supported environmental determinism, which, in brief, assumes that human behavior is caused, shaped, and influenced entirely by environmental reinforcement in a stimulus–response arc. Internal features such as feelings, conflicts, motivations, self-concepts, and cognitions (the so-called black box) are not accessible to direct observation and measurement; hence they are considered inferred states. Whether they exist or not, they are viewed as irrelevant. More recently, learning theories have moved toward an interest in internal states, as in operant conditioning and a cognitive emphasis in learning.

Sociobiology represents a position of genetic determinism, which assumes that human behavior is determined by the genetic program of the individual and of the species. It is the genes that reproduce themselves, not the individual. Hence behavior reflects or is the consequence of the efforts of an individual's genes to make sure that they will survive to be reproduced. For example, the altruistic sacrifice observed in many species, including humankind, represents the effort of "selfish genes" to survive in order to be reproduced. An animal or a bird will forfeit its own life to protect the survival of an offspring or a littermate or a fellow nestling because at least half the genes in the offspring or sibling are identical with half the genes in the sacrificing individual. From the perspective of the genes, it matters not which individual survives as long as at least one of them lives to reproduce those genes (Wilson 1978).

What is important in these three assumptions of determinism in behavior is that there is little or no room for probability and uncertainty, for continuous growth and learning, or for human resilience and emergent qualities. Each asserts that human behavior is fixed—by past intrapsychic phenomena, or by environmental stimulus and reinforcement, or by genetic programming. Each creates a reductionist view of the human being as a creature of primary drives, or as a set of conditioned and unconditioned reflexes, or as mainly a product of heredity. In each, causality in present and future behavior is fixed by prior conditions, and there is no escape from their influence.

These deterministic assumptions contrast with a very different view of determinism advanced by Theodosius Dobzhansky (1976), a geneticist and evolutionary biologist. His is the view adopted in the ecological perspective and in this book. Dobzhansky recognized that the old heredity–environment controversy is far from settled in the minds of many social and behavioral scientists, and of some segments of the general population. Disagreement is found in the relative influence of nature and nurture in the development of human traits, personality, and behaviors. In Dobzhansky's view, the extremes of the environmental, psychic, and genetic determinisms described above, as well as of the economic determinism of Marx and other reduction-istic views, falsely simplify the extreme complexities of the matter. As a consequence of evolution, all human beings (except for those suffer-ing aberrations such as birth defects) share certain species-specific features such as locomotor abilities, cognition, sensory perceptual capacities, educability, and the capacity for language. Beyond such common features, differences in behavior, abilities, traits, and person-ality are the outcome neither of genetic determinism (heredity) alone, nor of environmental determinism (learning and experience) alone. Rather, they are the outcome of a complex interplay of both genetic and environmental determinism, in which their relative weight in most features is still largely unknown.

The genotype (the totality of the genes carried by an individual) is a bundle of potentialities. Which of those potentialities will be re-leased as the phenotype (the observable expression of a gene or genes in the individual) is decided by the environment. The relationship between genes and environment is demonstrated in the case of hered-itary disorders, where the contribution of the genes is most clear. For example, the condition of phenylketonuria, which causes severe men-tal retardation, is due to a recessive gene (see chapter 7). The condi-tion was incurable until the discovery of its metabolic nature. Now, if the condition is treated early enough by an environmental measure (a particular diet), the retardation can be prevented. In using this dis-ease as a paradigm of heredity–environment interrelations, Dobzhan-sky underscored the fact that human physical and psychic structures are genetically variable, and that their ultimate character is influ-enced by the environment. Dobzhansky added:

> In principle, whatever stems from the genes can be enhanced or suppressed by environmental influences. In practice, this is far from always possible, because of our ignorance. Schizophrenia is a disorder found much more often than phenylketonuria. It is undoubtedly genetically conditioned, but neither the mode of its transmission nor its physiological basis is established. As a re-sult its control is uncertain. (1976:159)

The use of the term genetically *conditioned* instead of *determined* is notable. Elsewhere, Dobzhansky wrote:

> Intelligence, personality, special abilities, and other traits are susceptible to modification by genetic as well as environmental factors. . . . What actually develops is conditioned by the inter-play of the genes with the environments. . . . Heredity is not a

status but a process. Genetic traits are not preformed in the sex cells, but emerge in the course of development, when potentialities determined by the genes are realized in the process of development in certain environments. Similar genes may have different effects in dissimilar environments, and so may dissimilar genes in similar environments. . . . A genetic conditioning of the variations in intelligence does not necessarily mean that the intelligence of a person is irremediably fixed by his *[sic]* genes. It can be enhanced or stunted by upbringing, training, and disease. (1973:7–9)

Dobzhansky explained why the assumption that genes determine the upper and lower limits that traits can reach is not useful. Existing environments are almost infinitely varied, and there is no way of knowing what limits traits can reach because we cannot test gene reactions in all present and future environments. Moreover, humans have a certain freedom from the genetic and environmental determinisms: "A person to some extent makes himself *[sic]* what he wishes to be, of course within the constraints imposed by the external environment" (1976:161). Dobzhansky believes that equality is a political and social arrangement involving opportunity and socioeconomic status; it is not a biological arrangement. People are biologically diverse and are not the same; they are not interchangeable. Hence *equality* refers to the right of people to be unlike. Humans can follow freely chosen and different paths of self-realization. At the same time, however, equality, as an ethical maxim making such freedom possible, must be implemented by political means. Because people are diverse, the environmental conditions for releasing their diverse potentialities are not likely to be the same for all. Thus the importance to social work of participating in efforts to abolish poverty and oppression is clear. The profession has long been committed to helping create optimal social, physical, nutritional, economic, and educational environments for all, and we now recognize that the release of diverse potentialities in all people requires diverse environments.

THE ECOLOGICAL FRAME OF REFERENCE

Building on the earlier work of Bartlett and of Gordon, the ecological perspective is a more specific, and at the same time a more elaborated, base for integrating theories and research findings on people:environment transactions. Ecology is the science that studies the relations between organisms and their environments. In this book, it is used as a metaphor. It facilitates our taking a holistic view of people and environments as a unit in which neither can be fully understood except in the context of its relationship to the other. That relationship is characterized by continuous reciprocal exchanges, or transactions, in which people and environments influence, shape, and sometimes change each other.

At first glance, the notion of transaction seems simple. Yet it is quite complex and is made more so by the fact that our language and our education from elementary school on are geared to linear or simple cause-and-effect thinking (with the exception of the biological and physical sciences). Relationships between persons and their environments can indeed be linear; that is, a cause may precede an effect. One element is then understood to influence or change the other at a particular moment or in particular circumstances *but is not itself changed.* Such linear causality is useful in understanding some simple phenomena but is less useful in understanding the complex situations with which social workers are involved.

Transactional relationships, in contrast, are reciprocal exchanges between entities, or between their elements, in which each changes or otherwise influences the other over time (Lazarus and Launier 1978). Whereas in linear relations one entity changes the other, in transactional relations *both entities are changed with consequences for both.* Whereas linear causality is one-directional, proceeding from an observed or assumed cause to an observed or assumed effect, transactional causality is circular. It is like a circular loop, in which an event or process may be a cause at one point and an effect at another in the ongoing flow around the loop of social, cultural, emotional, psychological, biological, and physiological processes. This significant difference in the two kinds of thinking about human phenomena has an impact on how we view causality in people's life issues, how we act to help, what kinds of social work research are needed, how environments can be made more responsive to people's needs, and how we teach and learn the knowledge and theory, the values and ethical principles, and the skills of social work.

Rooted in the notion of transaction, the ecological perspective points to theoretical systems that yield the needed understanding of human beings (at all levels of organization from the individual to collectivities of various kinds and sizes) and their environments. Thus biological, physiological, psychological, emotional, environmental, and cultural knowledge and theory are required for the theoretical foundation of social work.

PEOPLE:ENVIRONMENT RELATIONSHIPS *

We begin with several sets of concepts, derived either directly from the science of ecology or from its use as a metaphor: 1) adaptedness and adaptation, and stress and coping; 2) withholding of power as oppression or prejudicial discrimination, and abuse of power as social and technological pollution; and 3) human relatedness, competence, self-direction, and self-esteem—self-concept. All are viewed as transactional in nature. That is, they do not refer to personal or environmental characteristics alone. Rather, they express particular kinds of relationships or transactions between people and their environments. It is precisely the transactional quality of these concepts that enables the social worker to maintain a dual focus on both person and environment and to carry out the professional purpose described earlier. In later chapters, we will draw on additional bodies of knowledge, theory, and research for additional concepts.

Adaptedness and Adaptation

The central ecological concept is adaptation, which is sometimes imperfectly understood, perhaps because in lay usage it is often confused with the notion of adjustment. But adjustment and adaptation are very different. Adjustment connotes a passive accommodation to the environment or the status quo, no matter how lacking it may be in health-supporting, growth-promoting qualities. In contrast, adaptation is action-oriented; that is, human beings strive throughout life for the best person:environment "fit" possible between their needs, rights, capacities, and aspirations, on one hand, and the qualities of their environment, on the other. If the fit is not good, or if capacities, goals, life conditions, and so on change, then people may actively decide to change themselves or the environment or both. Such changes are termed *adaptations*. These may be internal (physiological and psychological) or external (social and cultural). Adaptations may be directed to changing oneself in order to meet environmental opportunities or demands, or they may be directed to changing the environment so that physical and social settings will be more responsive to human needs, rights, goals, and capacities.

* The colon is used in the person:environment formulation to signify a holistic or unitary system. Its use seeks to repair the fractured connection caused by the earlier use of a hyphen.

For the most part, then, *adaptation* refers to an active process of self-change or environmental change or both, and not to passive adjustment. However, in extreme situations, people sometimes make an active decision to remain passive as a survival measure. What makes the critical difference in respect to the active-passive dimension is whether the individual is in control of the decision-making process or is controlled by either internal or environmental forces. A third type of adaptation is the search for new environments and includes moving, migration, religious conversions, and the like. Here, the issue of activity versus passivity is connected not only to whether the new environment promotes a better person:environment fit, but also, in some circumstances, to whether the person is moving toward something or away from something else (Hartmann 1958), that is, whether a life issue is managed by actively grappling with it or by passively avoiding it. A move, for example, can be either, depending on whether it is an attempt to avoid a predicament or to search for a better fit. Determining which is operative or uppermost in a given situation requires that many pertinent factors be considered in the assessment process. And finally, the content and direction of adaptations are shaped by personality, resources, experience, the nature of the environment, and culture.

Life Stressors and Subjective Stress

Adaptedness, by definition, expresses some degree of person:environment fit, that is, a positive person:environment relationship. Life stress, however, may express either a positive or a negative relationship (Lazarus and Launier 1978). It is positive when experienced as a challenge that carries with it positive feelings of zest, anticipation of mastery and growth, and a favorable level of self-esteem. Social work students, for example, may experience emotional and physiological stress as a result of demands made on them by their teachers and clients. But for most students most of the time, the stress of professional education is experienced as a challenge. It does not seriously lower self-esteem or prolong unrealistic fears of failure. Based on their previous successful employment or educational experiences, most students anticipate eventual mastery of the educational demands, buttressed by positive feelings of hope, by personal and professional satisfaction, and by the environmental resources of familial and peer support.

It is important, then, to keep challenge in mind as one of the perceptual and transactional forces affecting growth, development, health, and social functioning. But life stress can also express a negative or poor person:environment relationship when actual or perceived environmental demands or harms exceed the actual or perceived capacity for dealing with them. This kind of life stress is associated with a sense of being in jeopardy. It arouses negative and often disabling feelings, such as anxiety, guilt, rage, helplessness, despair, and lowered self-esteem (Lazarus and Launier 1978). Like challenge, it, too, is a perceptual and transactional force, but unlike challenge, it may lead to impaired growth, development, health, and social functioning unless it is managed effectively.

It is life stressors that most if not all persons who use social work services are experiencing. Stressful life events and issues propel them into social work services even though they do not necessarily present their situation in that form. Or in the case of those for whom social work services are mandated by the courts, the schools, or other social institutions, stressful circumstances may not be acknowledged to begin with, except, perhaps, for the stressor that the mandate or an unwanted referral represents.

In some theoretical formulations, stress is regarded solely as an environmental event. Numerous studies have attempted to relate physical and emotional disorders to a scale of life changes (Holmes and Raye 1967). The methodology tends to ignore individual perceptions and culturally based or personality-based attributions of meanings to various life changes, as well as the ways in which change can disrupt interpersonal relations and life tasks. Mechanic (1974b) noted that life changes clearly play a role in the occurrence of physical and emotional disorders, but that knowledge of the complex interplay between such changes and biological, social-psychological, cultural, and personality factors is essential in each instance.

Still other formulations regard stress solely as a physiological response, thereby ignoring emotional and environmental factors. For example, in behavioral medicine, biofeedback training enables patients to develop control over stress-related physiological processes in the laboratory. Yet this training does not ensure control when the person transacts with the same environment that generated the original response. What is also needed is change in the transactions themselves (Coyne and Holroyd 1982). Even when biofeedback training is effective in the treatment of stress-related physiological symptoms, the tendency is to attribute the improvement to the learned control and not to consider equally plausible alternative explanations related to psychological or environmental factors.

A third formulation was advanced by Lazarus and his colleagues (Coyne and Lazarus 1980) and has been adopted for this book. It conceives of stress as a transactional phenomenon. That is, like adaptedness, stress expresses a particular person:environment relationship. It is not just the environmental stressor or just the internal response (physiological or emotional stress), or a characteristic of the person. Rather, stress encompasses both the external demand and the internal (conscious and unconscious) experience of stress, including both emotional and physiological elements. Life stress is also perceptual as well as transactional in nature. What is perceived as stressful varies across age, gender, culture, physical and emotional states, past experience, and the perceived and actual nature of the environment. The same event or situation may be perceived as stressful by some but not by others, depending on the personal or culturally based meanings it has for the individual. Thus what is a stressor to one may be a challenge to another, or an altogether neutral event to still another. Misperceptions of stressors as present or absent, severe or not severe, lead to incongruity between an actual and a perceived stressor in a particular situation (Cox 1978).

According to the Lazarus group, two appraisal processes are applied by the individual to transactions that then determine the stress reaction, the feelings generated, and the adaptational outcomes. The first is a primary appraisal that answers the tacit question, "How am I doing?" The answer may be that the transaction is irrelevant or neutral, or that it is positive (a challenge), or that it is negative (stressful). If primary appraisal evaluates the person:environment transaction as stressful, then secondary appraisal must answer the tacit question, "What can I do about it?" The answer represents an evaluation of personal and environmental coping resources, options, and constraints. The two appraisal processes, separated here for purposes of analysis, are actually not separable. In fact, they interact with and shape each other. Primary misappraisal that overestimates the stressor (as in misperceiving a neutral event as a real harm or loss) may lead to inappropriate physiological, emotional, and behavioral responses. Primary misappraisal that underestimates a stressor (as in misperceiving a harmful stressor as benign) may lead to inaction and may increase the potential for harm. Secondary misappraisal that overestimates coping resources (as in the erroneous belief that further information or particular skills are not needed) may lead to coping failure and the increase of stress. Secondary misappraisal that underestimates coping resources (as in unrealistic helplessness or hopelessness) may lead to the persistence of stress because certain personal or environmental resources are not activated. It is often the social worker who helps people reduce the incongruence of the actual and perceived stressor (primary appraisal) or of the actual or perceived coping capabilities (secondary appraisal) for greater coping effectiveness.

Coping

The subjective (emotional) experience of stress evokes special adaptations called *coping*. When such measures are effective, the stressful demand or harm is eliminated or meliorated, or its effects are mastered. But if coping activity is not successful and severe stress persists, then physical dysfunction, emotional disturbance, or disruptions in social functioning may result. These conditions create further stress in a downward spiral that becomes harder and harder to interrupt or to overcome.

For example, grave physical illness, while viewed as a challenge by some, is appraised by many as a life stressor that can lead to severe subjective stress for ill persons and their family members. Some cope successfully with the biological, emotional, and social demands that the illness poses, so that the person recovers or learns to manage a chronic illness, and the family continues to support all its members in their life tasks much as it did before the illness struck. However, it often happens that the demands posed by the illness exceed the coping abilities of the ill person and/or the family members. The stress generated by the illness may then spread to spousal, parent–child, or other primary relationships, or to the school or work situations of the family members, thereby creating additional life stressors and increased stress and coping demands.

Coping capability, like adaptation and life stress, expresses a person:environment relationship, and it is transactional and perceptual in nature. Two major functions of coping are problem solving (what needs to be done to reduce, eliminate, or manage the stressor) and regulating the negative feelings aroused by the stressor (Coyne and Lazarus 1980). They are interdependent functions inasmuch as each is a requirement of the other, and each supports the other. Progress in problem solving leads to the restoration of self-esteem and to the more effective regulation of the negative feelings generated by the stressful demand. Progress in managing feelings and restoring self-esteem frees the person to work more effectively on problem solving.

However, problem solving is difficult until the negative feelings are brought under some control. Yet negative feelings are hard to regulate unless one has a sense that some progress is being made in resolving the issue or demands. What seems to take place in successful coping with severe stressors is a partial blocking out of negative feelings, and even enough blocking out of the situation's reality, so that hope is maintained and some problem solving can begin. As problem solving proceeds, self-esteem is elevated, hope is strengthened, and the defenses that were needed at the outset begin to relax. Thus reality perception clears bit by bit, the negative feelings are regulated, and problem solving continues in an upward spiral. Both problem solving and the management of feelings and self-esteem require personal and environmental resources to be effective. For example, problem-solving skills, although they are personal resources, require training by environmental institutions such as the family, the school, the church or temple, or the hospital. Similarly, the person's ability to manage negative feelings and to regulate self-esteem depends, in part, on social and emotional supports in the environment. Successful coping also requires additional personality attributes such as motivation, which depends on familial or community incentives and rewards, and self-direction, which depends on the availability of choices and opportunities for decision making and action as well as access to material resources (Mechanic 1974a; White 1974).

Traditionally, coping with life stressors has been distinguished from defense along the following dimensions: coping deals with externally generated stress, and defense with internally generated anxiety; coping represents flexible, reality-oriented, and often novel solutions to present and anticipated future demands, and defense represents stereotyped, rigidly patterned, unrealistic responses used in the past to avoid pain but unrelated to the present demands; coping is an active grappling with the unwanted condition, and defense represents passive avoidance of it; and coping is largely conscious or preconscious, while defense, by definition, is unconscious (Kroeber 1963). However, we are coming to realize that coping and defense are both efforts to deal with an external or internal stressor and the negative feelings it arouses. Some efforts are adaptive because they restore the previous person:environment relationship to an optimal degree, while others are maladaptive because they fail to restore the previous fit or may even make it worse.

In certain situations, for example, the defense of denial may be adaptive over the short run. A young person who has suffered a serious spinal injury in a diving accident may need temporarily to block out from awareness the full implications of what has happened in order to mobilize remaining strengths for what lies ahead. Avoiding the emotional pain may facilitate the beginning efforts to deal with the initial demands presented. However, if the denial persists, it may interfere with the needed participation in physical and vocational rehabilitation by distorting the reality of the injury's effects. If the person is to reach maximum rehabilitation, the denial will have to be gradually relinquished, so that bit by bit the horrifying reality can be admitted to awareness and the accompanying feelings of grief, anger, anxiety, despair, possible guilt, and low self-esteem are managed. Hence denial may be adaptive over the short run, but maladaptive over the long run.

In a different situation, denial may be maladaptive from the outset. Alcoholism or other chemical dependence will not yield to denial, even in the short run. In this instance, denial, from its very start, blocks the initiation of problem-solving efforts to relinquish the dependence. Resorting to alcohol and drugs is an effort to cope with painful life stressors, but the effort misfires and leads to further stress in other areas of life, including health, economic and employment status, and family life. It may be more useful, then, to regard coping with stress as adaptive efforts that fall along a continuum. At the negative extreme lie those coping efforts (related to the above description of defense) that are clearly maladaptive, and at the positive end lie those coping efforts (related to the above description of coping) that are clearly adaptive, with various gradations in between (as shown in figure 1.1).

This formulation must take into account the nature and extent of the particular stressor or the previous person:environment relationship, and whether the coping efforts restore the previous fit or, at least, improve the present person:environment relationship. Notably,

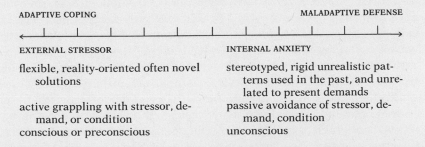

FIGURE 1.1. Variations in Responses to Life Stressors. A continuum showing the range from adaptive coping to maladaptive defenses.

certain life stressors, such as unresponsive school systems or undesirable conditions in nursing homes, are often beyond the ability of most individuals to change them. But sometimes they are amenable to collective action by small groups, neighborhoods, and communities. Still other stressors, such as structural unemployment, poverty, inflation, and nuclear dangers, are societal in nature and causation and require societal solutions. They are beyond the capacity of individuals or small collectivities to resolve them by coping measures. Nevertheless, individuals and small collectivities may enter into coalitions for political action that will affect at least the more tractable societal stressors. For the social worker, societal and institutional stressors become the subject of social policy analysis and legislative advocacy.

Power, Oppression, and Pollution

These concepts derive from the concept of dominance in the science of ecology. They denote person:environment relationships that are unequivocally negative. They impair human growth, health, and social functioning and are destructive of physical and social environments for all human beings and, in some instances, for other forms of life that share the planet with us. Dominant groups in society may withhold power from others and/or may abuse their political and economic power to exploit others.

Power may be *withheld* on the basis of various personal or cultural characteristics such as color, ethnicity, gender, age, sexual preference, religion, socioeconomic status, and physical or mental disablement, the result being the oppression (prejudicial discrimination against or disempowerment) of vulnerable groups. The *abuse* of power by dominant groups creates both social and technological pollutions. *Social pollutions* include poverty, structural unemployment, militarism and nuclear arms proliferation, and inadequate systems of housing, education, health care, and income distribution. *Technological pollutions* poison our air, water, food, soils, and oceans. They include the presence of toxic materials in workplaces, schools, and dwellings, and of hazardous wastes in communities.

Disempowerment and pollution are major stressors that afflict the entire population, including the oppressors. But their burden is heaviest on vulnerable, disenfranchised, and excluded groups. They form the conditions of life—the context—in which the development and functioning of members of those groups take place. They threaten health and social well-being, and they impose enormous adaptive burdens on the affected individuals and collectivities over the life course. Buttressed by greed and corruption in private and public life, disempowerment and pollution express person:environment relationships in which the social order permits some human beings to inflict injustice and suffering on other human beings.

The effects of oppression on people's physical and emotional health is considered further in many of the chapters that follow. For now, benign personal power, or what is termed *self-direction* in this book, is examined in the following section, along with human relatedness, competence, and self-esteem and self-concept.

Human Relatedness, Competence, Self-Direction, and Self Esteem

These next four concepts express positive person:environment relationships across the life course of individuals and collectivities. Together with the six concepts just described, they serve as major organizing themes in the chapters that follow. They refer to potentialities in the human species that depend for their release and continuance on the properties of people's past and present environments. The four are briefly described here, and their development is examined in detail in later chapters.

Relatedness, unlike the psychoanalytic concept of object relations (see the section in appendix 1 on Mahler), refers to the hypothesized innate capacity of the human being at birth to form attachments to other human beings, beginning with the relationship of infant and primary caregiver (perhaps this attachment is present at a biological level even before birth). Bowlby (1973) sees attachment as a biological and social imperative built into the genetic structure of the species over evolutionary time because of its survival value. That is, attachment behaviors in the infant, such as crying and clinging, and caregiving behaviors on the part of the parent ensured proximity between infant and caregiver as protection against predators in the evolutionary environment. Evidence is accumulating that human relatedness through attachments and social affiliations is essential for optimal functioning throughout the life course. Social affiliation refers to informal networks of kin, friends, neighbors, and others that often serve as positive support systems, protecting the person against life stress or enhancing the coping resources for dealing with it.

Competence (White 1959) is also thought to be an innate capacity that depends on the nature of the environment for its release and continuance. The infant has experiences with its caregiver that either release or inhibit the infant's sense of having an effect on the environment and of influencing it to meet her or his needs. As experiences of being effective in influencing one's environment accumulate, the young child develops a sense of competence, of being able to influence and control the environment, to explore it, and to learn in it and about it. Later social and physical environments, in youth and adulthood, may provide for the continuing development of competence or may hamper its further development and even stifle the innate motivation.

Self-direction is akin to the concept of ego autonomy but goes beyond it to include the social structure. In ego psychology, autonomy refers to the person's ability to maintain some degree of independence from the peremptory demands of internal forces (sexual and aggressive drives) and from the demands and pressures of the environment (see the section in appendix 1 on Hartmann). Without ego autonomy, the person is said to be at the mercy of tyrannical forces that may be internal or environmental. The concept of self-direction also connotes taking responsibility for managing one's life while respecting the rights and needs of others. Thus it is related to the concept of benign personal power (as distinguished from exploitive and coercive power). The concept of self-direction also recognizes that personal power and the freedom to be self-directing are very much functions of where one is located in the stratified social structure of society. That is, one's social position influences one's access to options, choices, and resources, and to opportunities for making decisions and taking action about one's life, the well-being of one's family and cultural group, and so on. Disempowered persons occupy positions that block such access. Hence empowerment practice in social work is designed to restore the positive personal power required for self-direction. It is the power to make choices, reach decisions, and engage in socially effective action on behalf of the self and the collectivity—to be self-directing, self-managing, and self-regulating.

Self-esteem refers to positive feelings about oneself acquired through experiences of relatedness, competence, and self-direction across the life course. One's self-concept begins to build in infancy through identification with and incorporation of the caregiver's perceptions, expectations, and affirmations of oneself, and through successful experiences of eliciting from the environment responses appropriate to one's needs. Later, in toddlerhood, the self-concept is reinforced by experiences in exercising one's beginning independence with the caregiver's approval and pleasure, as in feeding, playing, exploring, walking, and language. Self-esteem and the self-concept are subject to greater opportunities and greater threats as the child moves into larger circles of relatedness where her or his personal and cultural characteristics will be appreciated or rejected by others. Both self-esteem and the self-concept continue to develop over the life course. Sometimes, however, a person is her or his own severest critic; self-evaluation can diminish self-esteem or undermine the self-concept.

Three important points to be made now are: 1) The attributes of relatedness, competence, self-direction, and self-esteem are outcomes of person:environment relationships. While we think of them solely as personal qualities, they depend, in part, on the environment for their development and maintenance. 2) These attributes appear to be interdependent; each derives from and contributes to the development of the others. Nevertheless, relatedness appears first and remains central. It will continue to be enhanced by the development of the other three, just as it facilitates their development. 3) The four attributes appear to be relatively free of cultural bias. For example, every human society values relatedness, although kinship structures, definition of insiders and outsiders, and the rules for relating to them may vary across cultures. Every human society seeks to prepare its members for competent adult performance in its valued social statuses and roles. What constitutes competence may vary across cultures, but as a desired outcome of socialization, competence is probably universally relevant. Even within our own society, competence may be defined differently by different subgroups.

Every human society is concerned about respect or esteem and the sense of belonging. Social respect and identity may inhere in the collectivity (the family, clan, or tribe) rather than in the individual, but in either case, they are valued and carefully protected attributes. In some societies, the self-concept may be nonexistent or may not be reflected on, although the concepts of one's tribe, clan, or family are likely to be highly significant. The matter of self-direction is more ambiguous. Probably every human society recognizes in some form the issues of power and subjection, of control and influence over others and the self. In some cultures, however, self-direction and personal power may be lodged not in the individual but in the family or the tribal elders. Marriages, for example, may be arranged by family heads. The times for the planting of crops may be set by tribal elders. These observations lead to considering briefly some characteristics of culture and of physical and social environments as the arenas where the development and functioning of individuals and collectivities take place. Like the concepts discussed earlier, theories about culture and environments are part of the theoretical foundation of social work.

THE NATURE OF CULTURE AND OF ENVIRONMENTS

Culture

Included in the concept of culture are value orientations and the norms governing behavior; knowledge, technology, and belief systems; language; and the meanings attributed to objects, events, and processes, including the uses of and the responses to time and space. Values and norms are described in this section, and the other aspects of culture are presented in later chapters. Values are assumptions about the world, expectations of the self and others, and attitudes toward life events and processes. Family values derive from the family's various group affiliations, such as ethnicity, parental families of origin, social networks, religion, socioeconomic status, occupation, and geographic location. Values internalized early in life are usually out of awareness, yet they shape our thinking, perceptions, feelings, and behaviors. For example, values underlie and justify the gender-typed roles that many people assume are "natural."

Norms are rules of behavior, derived from value orientations. They are the ideas that people hold about what is proper, customary, and desirable behavior. Value and normative orientations must be understood on their own terms and not on the basis of an observer's own values and norms. Most of us tend to view our way of doing things as *the* way things should be done, and we assume that everyone holds, or should hold, that view. We fail to recognize that our way is merely a product of our particular values and norms. Thus social workers strive to become increasingly sensitive to their own norms, beliefs, and expectations, which are derived from their personal and professional values. Effective self-awareness enables us to be more sensitive to the differing values of those whom we serve and to understand patterned differences in behavior, expectations, and attitudes across different cultural groups.

By being careful to distinguish between the cultural traits, values, and norms attributed to a cultural group (such as the generalizations offered in this book and in anthropological theory), on the one hand, and the unique features of a specific family in that group, on the other, social workers are better able to avoid the danger of group stereotypes. Like all generalizations, group patterns are based on group data and may not fit an individual instance. It is also important to distinguish among traditional, contemporary, and transitional values and norms. Transitional orientations are a mix of the other two, and sometimes they lead to generational conflicts (Bernal and Alvarez 1983), particularly in immigrant groups. Similarly, at the societal level, massive changes in family structure and in sexual behavior and gender-typed roles in the recent past have weakened traditional values and norms. Yet new values and norms develop slowly. In the resulting normative gap, transitional values and norms, a mix of the old and the new, are useful for some families but generate conflict and ambiguity for others, frequently along age or gender lines. Value conflicts and normative confusions in family functioning may also arise from a difference in the cultural backgrounds of the adult partners, or they may be the result of a migration that confronts the family with a cultural transition, along with many other adaptational demands.

The functionality of a family's value system and normative structure is reckoned by how values and norms operate to achieve the family's objectives and to facilitate the members' growth, health, and development. However, Walsh (1983) noted that what may be functional values and norms at one system level (individual, family, community, or society) may not necessarily be functional at others. Examples are found in culturally based differences in how families relate to societal institutions such as social agencies, schools, and health care organizations; how families perceive, define, and cope with a life issue; what pathways they use for seeking and obtaining help; and what their expectations are of help and how they relate to a social worker. Unless cultural influences are taken into account in the organization's policies, practices, and procedures, the discrepancy between the expectations of a family and those of the organization or the professional will interfere with effective service.

The Physical Environment

Physical settings comprise the natural world of plants, animals, geographic aspects, climatic features, and the built world of urban and rural layouts, city squares and village greens, dwellings and other structures, aesthetic and utilitarian objects of all kinds, media systems, transportation systems, and electronic systems, as well as physical space and certain structures of time. The distinction between the natural and built worlds is artificial because environments constructed by humans are just as natural as those constructed by other forms of life, such as animal burrows and birds' nests. Nevertheless the distinction is useful for purposes of analysis, and it helps to clarify the dynamic nature of various aspects of the physical environment in transaction with one another and with the social environment and the culture (Germain 1981).

Dubos (1968) believes that some of the ills of civilization are due to our disregarding our relationship to the world of nature in which our biological and psychological equipment evolved. We tolerate conditions that we have created but that do not fit our evolutionary needs. And we have lost our essential connectedness with the natural world. Searles (1960), too, believes that human beings not only must respect the natural world, our life-sustaining environment, but must remain in touch with its restorative and healing forces. He specified four positive effects of relatedness with what he termed the nonhuman environment:

1. The assuagement of various painful and anxiety-laden states of feeling. Relatedness to the non-human environment assuages our existential loneliness in the universe. It alleviates the fear of death, facilitates a sense of peace, and counteracts feelings of insignificance.

2. The fostering of self-realization. Relatedness to the natural world helps us gain a deeper sense of personal identity and of the extent of our abilities and their limitations, and it stimulates creative capacities.

3. The deepening of our feeling of reality. Connectedness to the natural world enhances and sharpens our experiencing of our own existence and the existence of the world around us as *real*.

4. The fostering of our appreciation and acceptance of and our compassion for our fellow human beings. Through the sense of relatedness to the world of nature, in which we are individually and collectively alone, we come to value our self and others.

These ideas help explain the sense of serenity and wonder felt by those fortunate enough to experience mountains, seashore, and countryside—and the powerful influence of wilderness therapy and organized camping for persons of all ages and varying states of physical and mental health.

The Social Environment

Social settings comprise the world of other human beings. Its components include pairs (two-party systems such as friends or couples); families; neighborhoods and communities; natural groups and social networks; formal organizations, including systems of health care, education, and recreation, and workplaces, religious organizations, and political and economic structures at local, state, regional, and national levels; and social space and social time. A conceptual ambiguity reveals itself in this formulation insofar as families, groups, and communities, and occasionally organizations, may be the client units served by social work. They are then not environments in the strictest sense but need to be viewed as embedded in their own larger social and physical environments. For example, families, groups, and communities are environments for individual clients. But families and groups can be clients, and their environment is the community and beyond. When the community is the client, its environment is the larger city, region, state, or society. And these, together with community and neighborhood, are also environments for families, groups, and individuals but are further removed.

It is also artificial to separate physical and social environments in this way. For example, communities and organizations are physical and social settings simultaneously. Also, continuous, complex transactions take place between physical settings and social life. Physical settings and arrangements shape the nature of social arrangements and the interactions that occur in them. In turn, physical settings and arrangements are shaped by social patterns, needs, and goals. Such reciprocal relations, together with the influence of culture on both physical and social settings, must be kept in mind in a consideration of human development and functioning.

For example, problems of access for children and adults with physical disabilities appear mainly in the physical setting, but they act to limit participation in social settings as well. And, in fact, such life issues have their origin in the interplay of physical and social environments, culturally based belief systems, and attributions of meaning. Problems of access continue despite the passage of federal legislation requiring equal access.

Spatial Behaviors

Not only are people influenced by physical settings, but they actively use their physical environment, as in wilderness therapy or organized camping for children and families. Also, people use certain behaviors in the physical environment that then become part of the social environment. Such spatial behaviors are commonly used by individuals and collectivities to regulate social intimacy and distance. They serve to define and maintain status and role expectations, as well as authority and/or decision-making hierarchies in families, communities, and organizations. They include verbal, nonverbal, and territorial behaviors that are explored in later chapters.

Altman (1975) presented a helpful social-psychological framework for understanding people's spatial behaviors. This research-based model draws on concepts of privacy, interpersonal spacing, territoriality, and crowding or isolation. The focus is on the interaction between the internal processes of perception, cognition, motivation, and emotion, on the one hand, and the spatial features of the physical setting (as mediated by the social setting and the culture), on the other. The concern is with how individuals, families, and other collectivities regulate their desired level of social interaction and recognizes that the spatial behaviors are also influenced by age, gender, experience, emotional and physical states, the particular situation, the particular others involved, and the societal context.

Privacy is defined as the selective control of access to oneself or to one's group by others, and not merely aloneness. It is viewed as an interpersonal boundary process that regulates levels of social interaction for an individual or a collectivity. Regulation takes place by means of spatial behaviors (interpersonal spacing and territoriality) that actively use the physical environment. Figure 1.2 illustrates how the operations of these regulatory processes lead to desired states or stressful states of privacy or interaction and isolation or crowding.

Interpersonal Spacing

In his classic work on the anthropology of space, Hall (1966) developed the concept of personal distance, one of several zones of social space. Personal distance can be understood as a kind of protective imaginary shell in which one is encased. Cultural differences in the size and shape of this imaginary shell can distort communication and social interaction. What is regarded as proper distance for intimate relations and for impersonal relations differs across cultures: Latinos prefer smaller interpersonal spacing than North Americans. The difference can distort social interaction as the North American retreats from the Latino's advancing closeness. A Greek person gathers information from the way people use their eyes and look at her or him, but in the Navaho culture, one's eyes must never meet those of another person. Most New Englanders stay out of other people's olfactory range and avoid breathing on anyone, while Arabs have great difficulty interacting with others without being enclosed in their olfactory cloud (Dubos 1968).

Maladaptive flight-or-fight responses connected to the personal distance zone can also be observed. People described as schizophrenic, for example, often display flight responses to physical closeness, resisting even eye contact. They may also be unaware of other people's personal spatial boundaries and may intrude on others in unwelcome ways (Sommer 1969). Some evidence exists that persons prone to violent behavior have large spatial shells, misperceive intrusions into them as hostile actions, and react with fight responses (Kinzel 1970). In addition to differences in personal distance related to personality factors, there appear to be age differences (De Long 1970), gender differences (Moos 1976), and differences due to physical states (Spinetta, Rigler, and Karon 1974).

Territoriality

Territorial behavior in animals seems to be connected to patterns of social dominance that regulate access to food, mates, nesting sites, and so on and is genetically programmed. Whether it is also a genetic

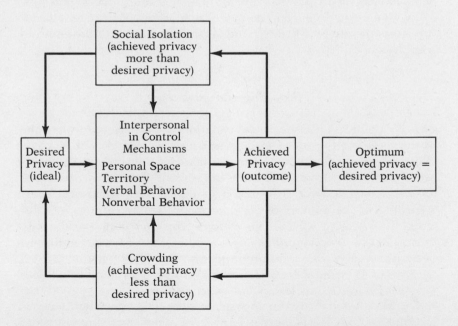

FIGURE 1.2. Overview of Relationships Among Privacy, Personal Space, Territory, and Crowding.

trait in human beings is open to question. Even if territoriality is not part of the genetic heritage in human beings, however, it is observable among individuals and collectivities. People display feelings of possessiveness toward space and objects. They mark spatial territories with nameplates, signs, doors, locks, and fences. They use uniforms and badges, gestures, threatening verbal and nonverbal behaviors, bells and buzzers, and in-group language and jargon to defend space.

In Altman's analysis (1975), territoriality can be a positive means of regulating social interaction, helping to reduce conflict and distorted communication in groups and between individuals. Territorial behaviors are important means of defining the individual or the collectivity and thus contribute to the sense of personal or group identity. They also provide important cues to others, help to make statuses and roles clear and explicit, and thus stabilize social organization in families, organizations, and communities. In upper-middle-class apartment buildings, for example, the residents tend to keep control over their shared territories of lobby, garage, laundry, stairwells, and elevators by employing doormen, television monitors, and maintenance personnel. In many public housing projects, however, the residents have no control over who enters their shared spaces, and they live with a sense of constant danger. The blocking of their territoriality affects the family's lifestyle and its transactions with the environment (Newman 1972).

Crowding and Isolation

Crowding and its opposite, social isolation, are experienced when the processes of interpersonal spacing and territoriality do not function effectively. Crowding results when a person's demand for space exceeds the available supply or when the amount of social interaction is greater than is desired. Crowding is an unpleasant psychosocial state regardless of the number of persons present in the setting. It is different from density, which is the ratio of people to space. Density may or may not be experienced as unpleasant and stressful depending on one's personality, one's culture, and who the other persons are, regardless of their number. One may feel crowded at any level of density, even when it is as low as one other person.

Social isolation is also an unpleasant state. It occurs when space is in excess so that one is more distant from others than one wishes to be. The amount of social interaction is less than is desired. Again, social isolation appears to be unrelated to density since one may feel painfully alone in a crowd, depending on who those present are. When others are not available or are lost through separation or death, or when one is fearful or otherwise unable to reach out to others, profound loneliness and social or emotional isolation may result (Weiss 1973).

Outcomes

When interpersonal spacing and territoriality are successful, the desired level of either privacy or social interaction is achieved. If the desire is for privacy, but boundary regulation by spatial behaviors is ineffective, then crowding is experienced. If the desire is for some level of social interaction, but boundary regulation is ineffective, then the subjective state of isolation or loneliness is experienced. Coping activity may be instituted to increase the level of interaction in the case of loneliness or isolation or to decrease it in the case of insufficient privacy. Loneliness and social isolation are widespread in our society and are often a major problem for those using social work services. Therefore they are examined further in later chapters.

Temporal Behaviors

Time, like physical and spatial aspects, is an important dimension of both physical and social settings. It takes time to grow and develop, and it takes time to learn. One must have time for solitude and time for interaction, as well as time to develop ways of coping with stress. Actually the experience of time has biological, social, psychological, and cultural dimensions. Like other forms of life, human beings have certain biological rhythms, or what are often called *biological clocks*. We are aware of some, such as respiration and pulse, while others are outside of awareness. All have been entrained in human beings over evolutionary time in consonance with rhythmical aspects of the physical environment. Hence some rhythms are entrained to day and night, or twenty-four-hour cycles (circadian rhythms), and others to monthly, seasonal, and annual planetary cycles. Many of our ways of life in contemporary society, such as the long flights made by flight personnel over a prolonged period (causing jet lag in bodily systems), as well as night or rotating shifts in workplaces, are life stressors. They violate biological rhythms, cause physiological and perhaps psychological stress, and may lead to dysfunction.

Social time refers to such matters as standard and daylight time; hourly, daily, weekly, semimonthly, or monthly pay periods; rental and leasing arrangements; work shifts and vacation schedules; organizational hours of service; travel schedules; and so on. Psychological time refers to differences in how the passage of time is experienced, depending on age, feeling states, and physical and mental condition. Time's passage is experienced by children as slow, stretching out endlessly, and by the elderly as accelerating rapidly. The elderly also tend to reckon time in terms of how much is left instead of how much lies ahead, as is the case with young adults. People who are physically ill and suffering from fever may experience short durations of time as long, so that it is hard for them to wait for attention or service.

Spiegel and Kluckhohn (1954) speculated that the temporal focus of human life is among the several universal problems to be solved by all societies. In their comparative analysis, they found that Spanish-Americans of the Southwest tend to emphasize present time, accepting each day for what it is. They pay little attention to the past and consider the future unpredictable. In the society of old China, ancestor worship and strong traditions tended to emphasize past time. Nothing new was expected to happen because present and future were only cycles of the past returning again and again. Middle-class Americans place a high value on change and the expectation of continuing progress, and thus they tend to emphasize future time. (This analysis, made in the 1950s, may be less accurate with respect to orientations today.)

Additionally, cultural attitudes toward time are often reflected in the language. In the English language, the clock "runs," but in Spanish, the clock "walks." "Such a simple difference as this has enormous implications for appreciating the differences in the behavior of English-speaking and Spanish-speaking persons" (Maxwell 1971:49), such as conceptions of punctuality, the sequence and pacing of events, and the rhythms of family life. English tenses build the linear structure of past-present-future into the language. Other languages may not use tenses at all, thus imposing a different temporal structure on their users. Speakers of English rely on spatial metaphors to describe time: time flows like a river, it unrolls like a carpet, it lies ahead or behind us, it is long or short. By contrast, some other languages use temporal metaphors to describe space: a village, for example, lies so many sleeps away from another. Freud, too, used temporal metaphors to describe the inner space of the psyche: repressed content, being unable to enter consciousness, remains unchanged over time; while the person moves on in time, elements of her or his inner space do not;

and in Freud's concept of fixation, time is frozen, whereas in regression, time goes backward.

People develop temporal behaviors reflective of the biological, psychological, social, and cultural dimensions of time, and these behaviors become part of the social environment. Like spatial behaviors, they may be used to regulate togetherness and separateness, intimacy and distance, in social relations in community and family life.

The External and Internal Environment

Adding to the complexity of context is the fact that human beings incorporate cultural orientations and aspects of their physical and social settings into themselves as part of their worldview and their sense of identity. They attribute symbolic meanings to their environments and to the activities in which they engage while in those environments. Such meanings may be derived from personality processes of cognition, perception, emotion, and action, and from culture and life experience.

Furthermore, not only does how people experience the environment differ because of social, cultural, and geographical influences, but variations depend on whether one is male or female, young or old, healthy or ill, newcomer or native, urban or rural dweller, rich or poor. People have differing sensory-perceptual thresholds to understimulating or overstimulating environments and differing psychological and physiological capacities for dealing with the stress that such environments may induce. Differences in experiencing the environment may also be generated by anxiety, fear, guilt, shame, rage, despair, or depression, or by the adaptive or maladaptive use of defenses against such feelings (Germain 1981).

Physical and social settings, as well as the culture, are context variables in human development and functioning throughout the life course. They provide security and shelter, symbolic identification, and opportunities for social contact, pleasure, growth, and feedback about the consequences of one's action. They can also be sources of pain, stress, and conflict. And through processes of internalization, environments and culture become "part" of the person's self-concept. Their properties, functions, and influences, as well as their interplay, are therefore part of the theoretical foundation of social work. Their operations through the life course of individuals and collectivities are considered in later chapters.

2

The Community as Context

Community is an ambiguous concept for several reasons. For community social workers, the community is the client unit served. For other social workers, the community is the environment in which individuals and families live who are being served. It is in the community that many of the society's social, economic, and political processes and events impinge on residents. And despite the transience of populations and the dispersion of residents' interests and affiliations to areas outside the community, the community influences the development and functioning of its residents in many ways.

Definitional Issues

Does the term *community* denote something actual and recognizable? It is used to refer to a unit of people, but it does not usually conform to units with discernible boundaries such as political subdivisions, school districts, police precincts, church parishes, and catchment areas. If the community is something real and recognizable, how should it be defined when it seems to cover many different kinds of entities? For example, the peoples of the world are coming to be viewed as a global village or community; social workers consider themselves a professional community; a university is often described as a community of scholars; and a rural village, an urban neighborhood, an ethnic enclave, and a large residential district in a city may all be termed *communities*. The latter four are attached to place, however, and it is that fact that singles them out as the principal focus of this chapter.

Although such place-associated units may not have discernible boundaries, people do live in localities where they are in physical proximity to one another. They display locality-relevant behaviors (Warren 1963): they depend on common social structures and services; they may share similarities of interest and concern; and they may even think of themselves as a community. Some communities manifest a psychological and perhaps a cultural or a social component in addition to the locality base. A locale-based community presents to its members physical settings in which primary group relationships, institutions, and organizations are created and re-created.

What is often seen in urban life are communities within a community, much like a nest of boxes, one within the other. Depending on the focus of observation or the level of analysis, the practitioner may work with the residents of a tenement, an apartment house, a city block, a housing project, or a neighborhood, each of which may view itself as a community within the larger community. Rural communities tend to be culturally homogeneous, while urban communities are apt to comprise several heterogeneous subcultures that may exhibit conflicted relationships. In addition, a community's cultural web of norms and values, knowledge, and belief systems may or may not be harmonious with the culture of the larger environment.

Certain communities of vulnerable groups are apt to be nonplace network communities that provide a safe communal haven to members. Two examples are the gay community and the lesbian community, in which the members may not live in proximity to one another. Yet they share the functions, structures, activities, solidary sentiments, and reciprocal support that other communities do. Nonresidential urban communities of gay men consist of bars, coffeehouses, restaurants, social and educational groups, and churches (Moses and Hawkins 1982). The gay bar is the community's major institution, where gay men can eat and drink together, sit alone or with friends, dance and, still "can" (and do) find sexual partners.

Nonresidential lesbian communities are structured quite differently. The bar is less important, and the personal community that enables lesbian women to relax with others who share the same lifestyle and to enjoy a strong network of support is more important (Moses and Hawkins 1982). The function of a lesbian community is to serve as an extended family or support network that provides approval, a sense of continuity, emotional and financial support in times of stress, shared experiences, and a common history and culture. Lesbian women are more engaged in lesbian culture and community than gay men are in gay culture and community, possibly because lesbian women are more apt than gay men to view gayness as something more than a sexual orientation. The gay and lesbian communities may join together in rallies, marches, and in organizations such as the National Gay Task Force, but for the most part they function as separate communities (Moses and Hawkins 1982).

The authors also note that living in a rural community may cause problems for gay and lesbian people because of their greater visibility in a place where everyone knows everyone else, and because of the conservatism of rural communities, which tend to be unaccepting of any difference. The social isolation of gay and lesbian people may be great, since other gay persons may not live near, and gay structures such as coffeehouses, restaurants, and activity and political groups are lacking in rural areas.

What do communities "do" that makes them important to the social worker? That is, how do they influence the development and functioning of their members? Warren suggested that all communities serve five major functions:

1. *Production-distribution-consumption* refers to local participation in producing, distributing, and consuming those goods and services, access to which is deemed desirable in the immediate locale. This function is carried out by small and large businesses, schools, churches and temples, governmental units, health and welfare services, systems of housing, and so on.
2. *Socialization* is the process by which the community's institutions, especially the family and school, transmit prevailing knowledge, social values, and behavior patterns to its individual members.
3. *Social control* is the process through which the community influences the behavior of its members toward conformity with its norms. This function is carried out by the police, courts, schools, families, religious organizations, and social agencies.
4. *Social participation* is provided by religious organizations, voluntary organizations, and informal groups of many kinds.
5. *Mutual support* is provided by primary groups such as family,

friends, neighbors, and other affiliations and by formal systems such as health and welfare organizations. (1963:9–11)

COMMUNITY ATTRIBUTES

Over time, human communities experience, to varying degrees, positive outcomes of their transactions with the outer environment and among their constituent parts. The outcomes include the emergence of a sense of identity and community pride (self-esteem in individual terms), competence, relatedness, and self-direction. As community dimensions, their weakness or strength in any given community is an empirical question.

Community Identity

Homogeneous, self-aware communities, such as American Indian reservations and Canadian Indian reserves, and those formed by ethnic, religious, lesbian, and gay groups manifest *communitas*, or solidary sentiments, based on similarity, intimacy, and reciprocity, and hence a strong sense of identity. However, in some locales, people live in close proximity but lack a sense of shared interests and concerns. For example, the residents of a condominium or an apartment complex may consider themselves a distinctive community and may separate themselves from the town or village in which they are located and on which they depend for such services as water, sewage disposal, and fire and police protection.

On the other hand, a public housing project, an SRO (single-room-occupancy) hotel, a nursing home, a residential facility for the elderly, a group home for society's outsiders (such as the developmentally disabled, the mentally ill, substance abusers, and released prisoners), or a shelter for the homeless is often viewed by surrounding residents as a community separate from the community in which it is embedded. That view may or may not be shared by the members of the facility in question. Such definitions are boundary-maintaining processes that determine who is inside and who is outside the "real" or desirable community.

In today's rapidly changing society, people frequently move in and out of local communities. What was once a homogeneous rural village becomes a "boomtown," attracting people of differing lifestyles and placing difficult demands on existing values, norms, and services. Generational and other changes in the community's demographic composition are prevalent in many rural areas. Young people depart for the cities, leaving the elders behind. Similarly, in cities, young adults may move out of the community while their aging parents remain behind, having to learn to accept, respect, and interact with newcomers who are often of a different race, ethnicity, or religion. In either the rural or the urban instance, conflict or anomie (lack of norms) may develop as old folkways and mores confront a multiplicity of lifestyles, values, and norms. Time is required for newcomers and longtime residents to develop a new sense of community identity based on recognition of and pride in the community's fresh and rich diversity.

Without a sense of identity, a community will find it difficult to develop commitment to its self-defined needs and goals. Cottrell suggested that people become genuinely committed to their community when "They see that what it does and what happens to it has [sic] a vital impact on their own lives and values they cherish; they find that they have a recognized significant role in it; and they see positive results from their efforts to participate in its life" (1976). That sense of identity and community pride is interdependent with community competence, self-direction, and relatedness.

Competence

The competent community is one that manifests a collective capacity for dealing with the wide-ranging needs and problems in communal life. Cottrell defined competence as the ability of the community's component parts to "collaborate effectively in identifying the problems and needs of the community; achieve a working consensus on goals and priorities; agree on ways and means to implement the agreed-upon goals; and collaborate effectively in the required actions" (1976). As an ideal type, a competent community values and seeks to mobilize the active participation of all members in matters that concern them individually and are pertinent to the collective well-being. Members help to maintain connections with the community's larger social, economic, and political environment so that needed resources can be located, obtained, and used, and they seek to acquire the technical skills for maintaining connections and seeking resources. The competent community also concerns itself with achieving and maintaining internal strengths, as defined by the residents, through developing and nourishing mutual aid and natural support systems. And it seeks to develop skills in managing intergroup conflict and in building or restoring mutual concern and respect among the community's component parts.

Self-Direction

Fully autonomous communities do not exist in mass urbanized societies, if, indeed, they ever existed. But in contrast to the so-called anomic community, a community that strives toward self-direction achieves and maintains beneficial connectedness to the outer environment. It is committed to, and engaged in, protecting itself against the loss of resources, self-direction, competence, and relatedness imposed by external or internal forces of coercive power.

Pinderhughes' transactional conception of disempowerment (1983) suggests that weak connections to the larger environment, or its failure to provide needed resources to a community, entrap the members and set in motion a malignant process by creating powerlessness in the community. The more powerless a community is because of denial of resources and services, the more its families are hindered from meeting their needs and from organizing to improve the community so that it can provide them with more support. The more powerless the family is, the more its members are blocked in their attempts to acquire skills, to develop self-esteem, and to strengthen the family, and the more powerless the community becomes. This process is an example of the circular causal loop described in chapter 1.

The issue of community self-direction, then, parallels issues of empowerment, and it is illustrated in the determination of American Indian leaders, parents, and children to see that their children are reared in Indian families:

> More American Indian groups, for example in Nevada, Washington State, and Minnesota, and Alaska native groups have taken over and are now administering their own social service programs. . . . The cornerstones of these successes were self-determination and opportunity rooted in tribal control. Indian people, working through tribal social services agencies and tribal courts, more quickly identified solutions to child-welfare problems in the rich resources visible to them in the lives of their

people. Historically, these strengths have been wasted by non-Indians, who ignored or misunderstood them. (Blanchard and Unger 1977)

Farquharson (1979) provided another example of the process on the Stony Creek Indian Reserve in British Columbia.

Without such self-direction, a community is in danger of internal disorganization, on the one hand, or of external tyranny and social neglect, on the other.

Human Relatedness

Community identity, competence, and self-direction rest on human relatedness, on the sense of belonging and being "in place." Relatedness is the essence of community. It is the base of *communitas,* or the reciprocity of caring for and being cared about. Many communities transcend the harshness of their conditions by the operation of their natural support networks (Stack 1974; B. Valentine 1978; J. Shapiro 1970; Myerhoff 1978a); their shared pleasure in music, language, laughter; and their shared commitment to religion, social clubs, or other affiliations (Valentine and Valentine 1970; Draper 1979; Mizio 1974; Moses and Hawkins 1982). A community laced with natural support systems is more likely to be a community with a firm sense of identity, competence, and self-direction.

Identity, competence, self-direction, and relatedness are the foci of social workers' practice in neighborhoods or communities. Participation in community life, which can be facilitated by the social worker, helps powerless people to develop some degree of community and personal self-direction and to experience a greater sense of relatedness or solidarity with others, thereby increasing their personal competence and self-esteem as well.

PHYSICAL AND SOCIAL SETTINGS IN COMMUNITY LIFE

Two concepts from ecology, when applied metaphorically, are useful in considering the physical and social settings of communities. These are habitat and niche (Germain 1985).

Habitat

In ecology, habitat designates where organisms are found in a living community, including their nesting places, home ranges, and territories. In the case of human beings, the physical and social settings of community, workplace, school, and so on constitute the habitat. Physical settings such as dwellings, buildings, rural villages, and urban layouts must support the social settings of family life, interpersonal life, work life, spiritual life, and so on in ways that fit the lifestyles, age, gender, and cultural patterns of the residents. The human habitat must provide a physical environment capable of supporting the full range of human needs and interests as they evolve biologically and culturally, including appropriate access to physical (and social) settings for the community's aging and physically disabled populations.

In poor communities, any dwellings may be in poor repair, may be infested with vermin, may contain lead paint and asbestos fibers, or may be otherwise dangerous to the health and well-being of children and adults. While residents may be dissatisfied with their slum housing, they may nevertheless be satisfied with their immediate neighborhood because of the supports it offers as a social setting. Following the redevelopment of Boston's West End, for example, Fried (1969) found that many lower socioeconomic and working-class residents of the predominantly Italian neighborhood experienced prolonged depression, symptoms of stress, helplessness, and anger, with tendencies to idealize the lost place. Social networks of kin, friends, and neighbors had been broken, and helpful relations with shopkeepers had ended. The short, narrow streets overlooked by windows and stoops were important to the residents' sense of belonging and as sources of friendship and informal social control. They had been lost forever.

The lack of any housing is the greatest threat of all—to life, human dignity, and the personal sense of self: "Add to that the experience of hunger, of ill health, of fear, of living in doorways and keeping warm on steam pipes . . . or endless walking with nowhere to go, or of finally finding shelter in a place that gives three square meals and a bed but is often as frightening and unsafe as the streets and more humiliating to the spirit" (Lee 1986:247).

The hobo and the tramp appeared in urban and rural America in the 1800s and early 1900s, street people in the 1960s, and bag ladies in the 1970s. Usually classed as vagrants, and regarded as a public nuisance by the rest of society, these persons were often arrested and confined to jail or held for psychiatric observation and then released back into the streets. In the 1960s and 1970s, large numbers of chronically mentally ill patients were "deinstitutionalized" and released from state hospitals into unready communities on the assumption that they would experience a more humane environment. Without services in place, however, some were unable to negotiate complex welfare, mental health, and housing systems and joined the ranks of those living in the streets. The numbers of homeless poor people continued to grow through the 1980s at an alarming rate in communities of various sizes across the nation. Today it is not only deinstitutionalized people (about 20 percent of the homeless), unattached men, street people, bag ladies, chronic alcoholics, and addicts who are homeless, but teenage runaways rejected by their parents, elderly persons, and young adult women, often victims of domestic violence.

Many of the "new" homeless had managed on limited social security incomes, Veterans Administration pensions, or low-paying jobs but, when evicted for any reason, could no longer find affordable housing. Families with children are increasingly among the homeless in our affluent society. For example, ten thousand families in New Jersey and over seven thousand in New York City were homeless in 1988, and an estimated three million children are homeless throughout the United States. The children live with their families in temporary public shelters, parks, automobiles, or welfare hotels, the latter a corrupting and dangerous environment for children. Their physical and mental health and overall development, self-concept, schooling, and peer relations suffer severe damage. Homeless children in some areas are barred from attending school because they lack a permanent address.

The increase in homelessness is associated with unemployment or low wages, as well as with the rising rents of an inflated economy. More salient is the lack of housing stock. In the larger cities, neighborhood gentrification, condominium conversion, and the destruction of unsafe low-income housing instead of rehabilitating it are examples of unsocial practices by developers and landlords. Other low-income housing is lost to highway development or is destroyed by accidental fires or arson and replaced by office buildings and housing for middle- and upper-income groups. Federal cutbacks in housing assistance have been severe and have been accompanied by widespread corruption.

Because very different groups constitute the homeless population, their multiple and heterogeneous needs require very different community services and programs. Many communities are struggling to meet those needs through shelters, food banks and cafeterias, and social services (Lee 1989), perhaps with some help from the state, but only a trickle of federal support. The public mass shelters provided in some communities are viewed by homeless people as more dehumanizing and dangerous than sleeping in bus terminals and subways and under bridges. The most humane services and programs are often provided by churches, religious groups such as the Salvation Army, and other private groups that may be staffed with social workers and volunteers.

Spatial Stressors

Cooper (1976) believes that the physical design and structure of high-rise public housing violate the self-image of the resident as a separate and unique person of worth and dignity. The vandalism seen in housing projects may be, in part, the residents' angry response to the blatant violation of the house-as-self and the consequent dehumanization and depersonalization that residents experience. Newman (1972) used the spatial concept of territory to help explain the prevalence of crime in high-rise housing projects. Crime takes place in semipublic spaces such as lobbies, stairwells, elevators, and grounds where surveillance by tenants is not possible. Boundary markers are not present, and intruders cannot be recognized as such, so these spaces become indefensible. Newman proposed architectural design (such as garden apartments) that would release latent territoriality and a sense of community among residents. But for the interim, he advocated the creation of intermediate territories such as a play facility for young children on each floor. Such a facility is apt to bring families out to use it and may lead to a shared effort to maintain the facility's security for children by screening intruders. Social workers can help project residents develop such informal arrangements and other social connections for the improvement of their shared physical and social environment.

Community territories may range in size from a stairwell to the entire housing project, from a particular park bench held by elderly friends to several blocks held by a youth gang against other youths. In some poor communities, however, the spatial dimensions of the physical setting may not even provide opportunities for positive territoriality to develop. Residents cannot then regulate the desired degree of closeness and distance in social relationships or render culturally based statuses and role relationships explicit. For example, constricted access to public spaces may lead to generational conflicts between teenage and elderly residents, or to conflict between racial, ethnic, or religious groups. Public space such as parks, streets, and sidewalks may be taken over by predators who adversely affect access by women, young children, and the elderly in particular. In such instances, territoriality is manifested by hostile aggression rather than by social organization.

Because of poverty, powerlessness, and other factors, home ranges (the areas of the habitat traversed by individuals and groups in daily life) may be severely limited, especially for youth, and the development of their full potentialities may thus be inhibited. For example, many children and youth in inner-city communities have much smaller home ranges than middle-class young people. Their circumscribed ranges furnish little exposure to the cultural attractions of the larger urban environment, and they are often intimidated by processes of social comparison when crossing the boundary of their own neighborhood into other neighborhoods. Inner-city children and youth have rarely seen farms and animals, mountains, or ocean. Conversely, rural children and youth of any socioeconomic status may have extensive home ranges within the area, but the poor among them have little opportunity to visit cities and to learn from and enjoy their attractions.

Temporal Stressors

In addition to spatial sources of stress, it is likely that violations of biologically based temporal rhythms, culturally based orientations to time, or psychologically based needs for time that are the effects of temporal arrangements of the community's institutions will also be stressful. The fixity of hours in community services and facilities may not fit the social needs of families with child-rearing, caretaking, and work responsibilities. The temporal arrangements of health and welfare services and community workplaces may not fit the biological rhythms of gender and age nor the cultural norms and values regarding time held by community residents. Even the social rhythms of the community may differ from those of "outside" employers and providers and purveyors of services and goods. Like spatial behaviors, temporal behaviors are evoked by a community's physical settings and contribute to the operation of its social settings.

Other aspects of the habitat in poor communities may be undesirable. Schools may be dilapidated, inadequately staffed, and poorly financed and may contain asbestos fibers. Health and social welfare services, child care facilities, garbage collection, street cleaning, police services, traffic control, and fire protection may be inadequate and/or characterized by hostile relationships between personnel and community members. Both public and private housing may be located far from public or low-cost transportation, while in rural areas transportation may be lacking altogether. In both instances, access to health care, shopping, workplaces, and so on is severely limited. Amenities such as parks, recreational areas, libraries, and museums may be missing, and therefore the quality of life in the community is lowered.

The absence of appropriate physical settings in the habitat may lead to difficulty in people's ability to work, play, provide or eat food, sleep in renewing comfort, mate, raise children, explore and protect territory, meet with peers, and make decisions and take actions that control the shape and quality of their social settings (Spivack 1973). Furthermore, what people do in a physical setting makes a place (a social setting) out of mere physical space, and identification with "place" is an important component of one's identity and self-esteem, sense of competence, relatedness, and self-direction.

Earlier in the chapter, we noted that one of the community's functions is the production and distribution of needed goods and services by the community's businesses and industries for consumption in and/or outside the community. Hence a central component of the community habitat is the workplace. Some worksites are located in the community; others are situated outside the immediate community but are sources of employment for community members. Workplaces depend on the community for a pool of workers having certain skills and for services such as utilities, fire and police protection, schools, and amenities. A workplace may or may not have connections to other organizations, such as labor unions, professional associations, the local university or vocational school, trade associations, and service organizations, but in one way or another, workplace and community are interdependent.

Some workplaces are oriented toward community service, acting to return corporate benefits to the community in the form of support to other institutions such as museums, symphony orchestras, public television, health and social services, United Way, and neighborhood development projects in the inner city. Others develop profit-sharing plans and entitlement programs for their workers, as well as structures to facilitate worker participation in decision making. Such workplaces seek to create for all who work there a sense of being a community-within-the-community, despite their bureaucratic form of organization and built-in controls of operations. Above all, workplaces are the prime source of economic security for the community and its families because they provide wages, tax revenues, and other resources. Hence plant closings are catastrophic to community life. But workplaces may create other kinds of community disasters, including toxic fumes and leaks, explosions, hazardous waste dumps, and fires. Some cause personal health and safety problems for the workers and their families that are also costly to the community. In some workplaces, entry, promotion, and equal pay for comparable work have been made particularly difficult for persons of color, women, those with disabilities, gay and lesbian persons, and the middle-aged, although barriers are slowly coming down through affirmative action and community demands. In all these and other ways, the workplace is a significant force in the life of the community, and its pertinence to social work will be taken up in greater detail in chapter 10.

Community social workers or face-to-face practitioners and their clients may direct their interventions to the many and varied habitat issues.

Niche

In ecology, niche designates the position a species occupies in the biotic community's web of life. In the case of human beings, niche is used as a metaphor for the status or social position occupied in the social structure of the community by particular groups. Hence it is related to issues of power and oppression. What constitutes a growth-supporting, health-promoting human niche is defined differently in various societies and in different historical eras. In our own society, the assumption is generally held that such a niche is shaped by a set of rights, including the right to equal opportunity (DeLone 1979). Yet, in our society, millions of children and adults are forced to occupy niches that do not support human needs and goals—often because of gender, age, color, ethnicity, social class, sexual preference, mental or physical disablement, or some other personal or cultural characteristic devalued by society.

Many communities are laced with such marginal or destructive niches as "deinstitutionalized patient," "hard-to-place dependent child," "AFDC (Aid to Families with Dependent Children) mother," "hard-core unemployed," "school dropout," "project tenant," "migrant laborer," "old-woman," "homeless person," and "AIDS patient." These and similar niches are shaped by political and economic structures, and by systems of education, health and mental health care, child welfare, juvenile justice, welfare, work, and the media. Such niches violate society's professed commitment to social justice, cultural diversity in communities, and enhanced quality of life for all people.

Social workers need to be aware of additional niches in some communities where so-called "new arrivals" of varied racial, ethnic, and national origins are living. They occupy a particular status or niche: 1) *refugees* such as Southeast Asian groups, Jews from the USSR, and others; 2) *entrants* such as Haitians and the Mariel Cubans; 3) *privately sponsored immigrants* under the quota system; and 4) *illegal immigrants*. Refugees receive considerable government assistance as needed, for up to three years. Entrants receive far less assistance than do refugees, although they have some of the same problems as well as different ones. The recent waves of Haitians—mostly of the peasantry, in contrast to earlier Haitian immigrants—have been held for some time in U.S. detention camps and then have had to report regularly to a court. Constant fear of deportation has dogged them, not only because of the poverty, repression, and terrorism they had escaped: because of having left Haiti without the government's permission, they were at even greater risk. Of the illegal (undocumented) aliens, some 70 percent are from Mexico. They are at a serious disadvantage; because of their illegal status, they can safely seek only irregular and part-time work, and they fear applying for welfare, Medicaid, and food stamps, lest they be reported to the Immigration and Naturalization Service for deportation *(Practice Digest* 1983). Some became eligible to apply for legal resident status in 1989 under terms of amnesty provided by the U.S. government.

SOCIAL POLLUTION

Destructive habitats and niches are the outcome of social pollution that arises from the withholding of power from vulnerable groups.

Color

Racism practiced against people of color encompasses the cognitive, affective, or behavioral processes of an individual, a collectivity, or an institution through which the advantages and privileges of society are dispensed differentially. Barbarin stated that through reaffirmation of the status quo,

> Prejudiced attitudes become institutionalized, and [their] discriminatory effects . . . create social conditions which substantiate the very attitudes which initiated the cycle. For example, confirming evidence of the inferiority of nonwhites is found in low academic achievement, low income, concentration in menial occupations, underemployment, and substandard housing— all products of discrimination. These phenomena provide the [discriminator] with validating evidence for distorted beliefs and feelings about nonwhites. In this way, the victims of discrimination are held responsible for the consequences of racial prejudice. (1981:7)

Institutional racism in a community takes the form of community and organizational processes such as formal and informal policies, procedures, and practices in community housing, schools, workplaces, health care, social services, and so on. These processes produce negative outcomes for people of color relative to those for whites. They encourage among whites passive, acquiescent, and ineffective responses to inequality. Together, individual racism and institutional racism create community environments in which people of color must live and establish a circular loop that traps them in powerlessness (Barbarin 1981). Institutional racism results in high infant mortality rates, high morbidity rates, low life expectancy among people of color, and high unemployment rates, especially for minority youth actively seeking work.

Gender

Like racism, sexual inequality based on gender differentiation is a major life stressor. Male dominance and privilege subordinate, devalue, and oppress women in family, work, and community life. Since the 1960s, the feminist movement has achieved progress on the road to gender justice. Some changes have occurred in gender ratios in some occupations, professions, and workplaces; elementary and secondary schools' curricula; political roles and voting patterns; the civil and legal rights of women; sexual reform, reproductive health care, and new social services for battered women and rape victims; family life and family roles; and the legitimation of women's natural closeness and affiliation with other women through proclaiming sisterhood (Lerner 1971). Despite valiant effort, however, little change has been achieved in the portrayal of women in the media, pornography, and advertising. Even where changes in laws have been attained, the community institutions that should support them still lag behind (for example, equal pay for comparable work, adequate child care arrangements for working mothers, and adequate law enforcement against violence toward women).

Since men possess power, status, and dominance, few men and fewer women would agree that men, too, suffer from gender-based oppression, but in fact, men also experience strain in filling gendered roles that do not fit contemporary realities in the community and family nor their own internal experience, feelings, and aspirations. For example, an extensive literature review (O'Neil 1982) yielded six adverse consequences for men of male dominance: 1) restrictive emotionality; 2) homophobia; 3) socialized control, power, and competition; 4) restricted sexual and affectionate behaviors; 5) obsession with achievement and success; and 6) health care problems.

These effects on men, as well as those on women, are examined in later chapters. For now, it is sufficient to note the observed movement toward a modest change in men's roles that may eventually complement some of the changes achieved by the women's movement. Stereotyped male roles in the family appear to be changing slowly among younger adult men in some communities—perhaps, in part, because of modifications of the socialization of male children that began in the early 1970s within educated middle-income families. The beginning change may also be due, in part, to the recognition among some younger men of the emotional and physical costs of competing for success in the workplace, which deprives them of time with their families and the pleasure of bringing up their children. Also, the number of profeminist men in some communities is growing. They include men whose own "consciousness of how men oppress women has grown from their relationships with women who confront their sexist behavior" (Tolman et al. 1986:63), as well as those who have attained such awareness through other avenues, including education, films, the media, religious teaching, and personal reflection. By 1987, 6 of 750 chapters of the National Organization for Women (NOW) had elected profeminist men as their presidents.

Disability

Like racism and sexism, able-ism (disempowerment based on disability) is a major life stressor for an estimated one tenth of all children and one fifth of all adults in the United States who suffer serious physical, sensory, or mental-health-related disabilities. Such discrimination in the community creates destructive, unjust differences in the resources and life conditions of those children and adults. It operates by the withholding of power, whereby the society assigns those with physical or mental impairments a stigmatized niche and a deviant role as handicapped and excludes them from the economic, political, and social processes of the community.

Gliedman and Roth (1980) showed how the characteristic medical-model approach to persons with disabilities magnifies the problems they face and obscures the societal forces and responsibilities that are often more important to their functioning. These authors proposed in place of the medical model an approach that views individuals with disabilities as an oppressed minority group, not because of a shared culture but because "society exposes most of them to a common set of socially produced hazards" (1980:4). Their oppression imposes a social identity on an otherwise heterogeneous group of children and adults who happen to have a physical or mental impairment. Able-ism results in prejudice, job discrimination, and destructive stereotypes and myths that exaggerate the true limitations of many disabling conditions.

Millions of adults with disabilities in communities across the nation are unable to find work because of employment practices and hiring procedures, and several hundred thousand earn minuscule amounts in sheltered workshops. They are underrepresented in the professions and the well-paying occupations. Although the technological community has shown increased interest in developing environmental adaptations and personal devices for those with disabilities, this interest is far less than that invested in the able-bodied. Researchers have shown little interest in studying the developmental and life experiences of children and adults with disabilities, regarding them as deviants from the norm (much as in nonfeminist views of female development), instead of regarding them as responding to their unique social context and their daily experience of discrimination. Gliedman and Roth (1980) observed that our society lacks a tradition for raising reasonably happy, reasonably self-fulfilling children who have disabilities. They suggested that some children with disabilities develop according to a healthy logic of their own.

Prejudicial discrimination that tolerates community barriers to those with physical disabilities is critical in determining personal futures. For example, the failure to develop and provide needed resources for optimal independent living in the community, including outdoor mobility and out-of-home activity, prevent those with disabilities from participating in the social and work life of the community. Physical and social barriers prevent them from participating in the political life of the community, thereby constricting their capacity as assertive consumers to influence policy, procedures, and practices regarding their civil rights and benefit rights. In these and other ways, they are disempowered by their community and are denied their right to full personhood (DeJong 1979).

The independent living (IL) movement among the physically disabled is a powerful and empowering influence in the lives of many physically handicapped persons, as well as a major force in societal change in public attitudes and in reducing environmental barriers and social obstacles. Rejecting the sick role and the impaired role for the physically disabled, the IL movement declares that "the disabled do not want to be relieved of their familial, occupational, and civic responsibilities in exchange for a childlike dependency" (DeJong 1979). Further, problems in living with a serious disability are located not in the person but in the physical and social environments. They "are as critical as, if not more so than, personal characteristics in determining disability outcomes" (1979). To cope with the harsh environment, many disabled individuals are assuming the consumer role. Increasingly, they participate in advocacy, peer counseling, self-help, consumer control, and barrier removal. The IL movement emphasizes the importance of living arrangements, consumer assertiveness regarding rights and entitlements, outdoor mobility, and out-of-home activity. It sees self-care as a less important outcome since assistance from a human helper does not necessarily mean dependence but may actually make employment, for example, more feasible.

Some improvements have occurred. Yet, as recently as 1986, and despite the laws in place, one state university had done nothing to make its social work school and environs accessible, even after several years of pressure, until the Organization of Students with Disabilities finally took their plight to the media and the public.

The mentally disabled include the mentally retarded and those with Down syndrome and other mental conditions such as severe epilepsy and severe psychiatric disturbances. The conditions may be genetic or congenital in origin, or they may be the result of accidents, disease, or toxic materials' affecting the brain and the nervous system. The mentally retarded also include those who were malnourished or seriously deprived of environmental stimuli over a very long time in early infancy and childhood without later enrichment. The retarded child or adult has often been regarded as a second-class person unwanted by society and of no use to it. Fortunately, this attitude is changing with new research findings that refute past assumptions about limitations. Indeed, many experts now believe that the concept of mental retardation should be abolished as having no scientific value. It is defined by arbitrary criteria regarding an individual's behavior at a particular time. Because it is a discriminatory label, it is gradually being replaced by the term *developmental disability*. This is not a synonym for *mental retardation* as is sometimes assumed. Strictly speaking, it refers to all physical and mental impairments that appear before the age of 22 years and are likely to continue indefinitely (Gelman 1983). To avoid the confusion generated by a broad definition, however, I will sometimes specify physical and sometimes mental disability in subsequent chapters.

Disempowerment is created by community attitudes that 1) stigmatize those with mental disabilities and their families and 2) prevent the establishment of group homes for children and adults, the recruitment of foster homes, the development of coordinated services and respite care to support the family's wish to provide home care, and the provision of appropriate educational and vocational training. Such disempowerment is a severe lifetime stressor added to the multiple stressors created by the disorder itself.

Sexual Orientation

The effects of oppression and disempowerment in community life are also demonstrated by homophobia, the irrational fear or hatred of homosexuality or homosexuals. This is a belief system that supports negative myths, misconceptions, and stereotypes about gay and lesbian people and that is a major life stressor. As a consequence of homophobia, an estimated 10 or more percent of the U.S. population, or approximately twenty-three million lesbian and gay persons, live under constant stress arising from deprivation of human and civil rights in the threatened loss of their work, housing, friends, and family, including their children. Other stress arises in making decisions about coming out, dealing with the prejudicial assumption of pathogenic causation of homosexuality, and feelings of powerlessness (Cummerton 1982). The fear of AIDS (acquired immune-deficiency syndrome, an incurable and terminal disease assumed to be spread primarily by gay men) can intensify homophobia and the associated stigma, stereotypes, and myths.

Lesbian and gay people, if they are open about their sexual preference or are "found out," face additional stressors such as loss of legal rights concerning visitation or custody of children; denial of visiting rights in hospitals when the partner is ill; discrimination in the workplace, in housing, and in some religions; and lack of protection of the law in some states and communities. A gay social worker wrote:

> It's taken the better part of my first 40 years of life to feel positive about my homosexuality and how this major aspect of my life has affected my personal and professional life. My struggles to survive in a heterosexually oriented society have certainly helped me to understand some difficulties encountered by the poor and ethnic minorities with whom I work. "Coming out" is a form of adaptation that gays and lesbians must face throughout their lifetime. This adaptation can have both positive and negative aspects and connotations, and I am continuing to strive to heighten the positive and eliminate the negative aspects within myself. As is true of any aspect of adaptation, there will always be risks, but we have all learned that life without risk is stagnant and unchallenging. I hope that my making an effort toward a healthier personal and professional adaptation will make me better able to help my clients do the same.

THE COMMUNITY AND THE LARGER ENVIRONMENT

Knowledge of the community's external relationships to its environment is also required by social workers. Social, economic, and political forces operate at national, state, regional, and metropolitan levels, and they may bear on the provision or the withholding of the resources that the community needs to carry out its functions. An example of negative impact on urban communities, in particular, lies in the lack of sufficient fiscal support from the outer environment for the care of patients suffering from AIDS and for public education on and biomedical research into the disease. This frightening, incurable disease was first recognized in the United States in 1981, the initial infections probably having occurred in the early or middle 1970s, since the disease seems to appear about nine years after infection. (*Surgeon General's Report* 1988).

By April 1990, the U.S. Centers for Disease Control had reported a provisional total of some 124,500 cases since 1981, with about 77,000 resulting in death (*HIV/AIDS Surveillance Report* 1990). By the end of 1991, ten years after the first cases were identified, an estimated cumulative total of 270,000 cases is expected with a cumulative total of 179,000 deaths. The cost of care for people with AIDS is expected to be more than $1 billion a year by 1991 (*Surgeon General's Report* 1988). Despite the existing numbers of infected persons and the projected increases in future years, the federal government has given very little financial support to the states and cities where the incidence and prevalence of AIDS are high, let alone elsewhere (cases have appeared in every state).

Although the rate of spread of the virus among gay men is leveling off because of changes to nonrisk sexual practices, the incidence will remain high for some time because of the long incubation period of the virus and also because of the continuing high rate of infection among intravenous drug users and their sexual partners, as well as the growing numbers of babies infected at birth. Most of these babies will eventually develop AIDS and die. Very small numbers of hemophilia patients and others requiring transfusions before 1985 also suffer from AIDS through having received contaminated blood. Donated blood and blood products are now considered safe, since appropriate procedures for testing and treating them were instituted in March 1985 (*Surgeon General's Report on AIDS* 1988).

The *Surgeon General's Report* was distributed free to all Americans through various community institutions. It clarifies the etiology and the modes of transmission of AIDS, describes high-risk behaviors, and emphasizes the need of all persons to be informed, and educated, and to use preventive sexual practices, since no cure or vaccine for the the disease is in sight. The report also underscores the economic and political changes that will affect our social institutions, educational practices, and health care in the 1990s, thus having an impact on all Americans whether or not they are touched by AIDS personally. The report is a useful resource for social workers in health care organizations, family services, schools, child welfare, community organizations, and so on. The ways in which all social workers can help prevent this tragic and deadly disease, which primarily strikes down young people, include providing information on AIDS to the individuals and collectivities whom they serve and to the staff in their own places of employment; becoming members of community task forces on AIDS; helping to involve minority-community organizations in AIDS prevention (the disease is disproportionately prevalent among blacks and Hispanics); counselling teens and others regarding sexuality; and making appropriate referrals for the voluntary testing of high-risk individuals. Social workers can help those already suffering from AIDS by advocating for the protection of patients' rights and needs; by serving as mediators to obtain housing, transportation, jobs, and health care for patients; and by providing support groups and supportive counseling to patients, lovers, and families, especially those who may be learning for the first time of their son's homosexuality in the context of a deadly illness or who feel stigmatized by the disease.

Another kind of community impact exerted by the larger political and economic environment is found in many rural areas. Some rural communities in Alaska and the western states have been changed drastically by the boomtown phenomenon as the search for new sources of energy continues. Other rural communities, once visited only by summer tourists, are now becoming suburbs of nearby cities, while others have acquired new residents who are "returning to the land." In the middle and late 1980s, rural farm communities suffered new forms of poverty as the result of several years of drought, falling farm prices, increased costs, and cutbacks in federal subsidies. Rates of farm auctions, foreclosures, and corporate takeovers accelerated to a dangerous degree. This is a poverty that exists side by side with the long-standing desperate poverty of migrant workers and low-income farmers, whose plight is now all the more perilous. In 1988–89, however, the federal government granted drought relief funds to farmers in those areas that suffered large losses in the 1988 drought, the worst since the 1930s.

Rural social workers are devising innovative ways to create more services with fewer and fewer resources. More services are needed because demands for them are increasing from migrant workers, farmers, dealers in farm implements and others who have lost their small businesses, workers in agricultural industries who have lost their jobs, and even bank personnel and their families, who are feeling the stress of having to foreclose on the farms of friends, neighbors, and relatives. Farming communities are in crisis, and no solution is in sight for those who have lost their land and businesses, who have no other marketable skills, or who are past the years of young adulthood.

"We got a crisis call from a 57-year old farmer whose farm was going to be sold at auction that day. He said he had been walking out in his fields in the morning, saying goodbye to them, and he didn't know if he could go on." [The social worker] explains that he was feeling suicidal, that he talked about his grandfather bringing the farm through the Depression and his father farming that same land all his life, and the shame he felt in not being able to keep it in the family." (Ashley 1985:4)

Despite the idyllic myth of rural life in America, rural communities experience many stressors. The incidence and prevalence of malnutrition, substandard housing, maternal and infant mortality, unemployment and underemployment, poverty, water pollution, and increase in divorce are greater than in urban communities. For example, rural communities tend to have higher dependency ratios (the percentage of people over 65 and under 18 in the population) than urban communities (Coward and Jackson 1983). Other stressors, such as social isolation, are made more severe because of the nature of the physical setting. Still others, such as crime, are less prevalent in rural communities.

Many rural areas are composed of residents having a sense of shared identity and of belonging to a recognizable system of social relationships that represent significant coping resources at the community level. These include natural helpers such as relatives, friends, and neighbors, and social networks of exchange such as church members, grange members, volunteer fire fighters, school-based parent groups, and adult-led youth groups. However, most rural communities have few social and health or mental health services provided at the state or county levels, and those few may present difficulties in accessibility. Also, a comprehensive federal policy has not been developed for rural communities, in contrast to the attention, programming, and fiscal support given to urban communities (Coward and Jackson 1983). Nevertheless, schools of social work in rural areas are developing specialized professional education for rural social workers. They prepare students to serve individuals and collectivities in rural areas where formal social services are sparse, to function in a context of rural values and customs, and to be competent in advocating at state and local levels for the extension of services.

In addition to technological disasters at some worksites, large national corporations, industrial plants, and U.S. military installations also produce life- or health-threatening conditions in a rural or urban community's habitat. Abandoned, uncontrolled toxic dumps and poorly controlled landfills used for hazardous wastes are found in or near some rural and urban communities, especially poorer ones. For example, a 1987 study by the United Church of Christ's Commission on Racial Justice reported that communities with the greatest numbers of toxic dumps had the highest concentration of black and Hispanic people. More than 15 million of the nation's 26 million blacks and more than 8 million of the nation's 15 million Hispanics live in communities with one or more uncontrolled toxic dumps (L. Williams 1987).

Abandoned toxic waste dumps exist at thousands of military installations and other federal facilities across the country. These were reported in 1988 by the federal Environmental Protection Agency (EPA) as continuing to pollute the soil and the underground water on which the surrounding communities depend. Sites at some fifty military installations were recently listed by the EPA as requiring immediate cleanup. The conditions were acknowledged by the military. In 1988, the U.S. Army and the Shell Oil Company were ordered by a federal court to pay up to $1 billion to clean up, by the year 2000, one of the most contaminated toxic waste sites in the country, the Rocky Mountain Arsenal, next to Denver's airport. The wastes have seeped into the underground water supplies in the area and have contaminated the soil. Both entities acknowledged responsibility and agreed to pay (Shabecoff 1988).

The federal Department of Energy has acknowledged the environmental contamination in thirteen states of deep underground water sources (aquifers) by radioactive wastes from its plants and laboratories for making nuclear weapons. The department estimated the cost for cleaning up the contamination at $100 billion (Schneider 1988). Local water supplies, including waterways and groundwater, are sometimes contaminated by improperly treated sewage, gasoline and oil spills, solvents, pesticides, fertilizers, radioactive materials, toxic chemicals, and heavy metals. By 1980, at least 44 cases of groundwater pollution had been documented in Massachusetts, 16 in Connecticut, 25 in Pennsylvania, 12 in New York, more than 200 in California, and 1 or more in each of twenty other states (Shabecoff 1981). Waste disposal in the ocean is affecting fisheries adversely, and potentially dangerous medical wastes such as vials of blood and untreated sewage despoil coastal areas and recreational beaches.

The bulk of low-level radioactive materials from medical sources is rapidly approaching maximum capacity at the three sites used for the storage of such materials in Washington, Nevada, and South Carolina. The sites must be capped after filling and must be monitored for at least two hundred years. At least four years are required to prepare an adequate disposal site, and five more sites are needed just to meet the country's needs to the end of the century. Otherwise, medically important radioactive materials may not be produced. But negotiation for sites is proceeding slowly (*Harvard Medical School Health Letter* 1986).

Clearly, all communities are at risk from technological pollution, and some social workers have or can have an important role in interdisciplinary efforts to help community organizations deal with the complex health, social, political, and economic issues involved, and to advocate at state and federal levels for better protection of the quality of life for all people. At the federal level, some progress is being made to protect communities through cleanup funds, disclosure requirements, bans on dumping hazardous waste into landfills, and the development of new means of disposal. The hope is to empower communities so that they can pressure government and industry to correct the unsafe practices that threaten their health and environment.

When working with disempowered communities, social workers require extensive knowledge of cultural and social groups other than their own, together with profound self-awareness, if they are to help people to improve their habitats, to reshape nonsalutary niches, and to improve the transactions between the community and its environment. Increasingly, social workers and social agencies are participating in efforts to influence the local, state, and federal policies, programs, and structures that empower groups and communities. These activities include 1) legislative advocacy by joining with professional associations and other concerned groups (Mahaffey and Hanks 1982), lobbying, giving expert testimony, and, for some, running for public office; 2) making skilled use of the press and other media (Brawley and Martinez-Brawley 1982) in order to heighten public understanding of human needs and to gain support in addressing the issues; and 3) other activity as individual, concerned citizens.

The community is a natural site for preventive social work practice and program development and for engaging community members themselves in planning neighborhood forums, workshops, and other psychoeducational experiences to help improve intracommunity relationships (Bloom 1979). In prevention programs, people need not be defined as clients, and nonstigmatized facilities, such as libraries and schools, can usually be used for such activities. Without the community's participation in developing and carrying out prevention programs, however, paternalism, disempowerment, and value conflicts will undermine community receptivity and program effectiveness. Whether engaged in preventive or interventive practice at the community level, the ecologically oriented social worker supports community strengths and promotes community empowerment.

3

The Community: Support Systems

In chapter 2, I noted that communities are made up not only of individuals but also of collectivities that represent varied levels of social organization in community life. Among the collectivities are those considered support systems, both formal and informal. The two types differ on several dimensions. Formal systems such as schools, workplaces, hospitals, municipal departments, and social agencies are created to achieve specific objectives. Most are characterized by 1) hierarchical levels of authority that govern decision making and communication; 2) specialization of functions as reflected in job titles; 3) organizational roles in which occupants are replaceable; 4) role relations based on what people do; and 5) rules, policies, and procedures that cover the operations of the organization and the work behavior of its personnel. Complex bureaucratic organizations typify formal systems that range from the highly centralized and hierarchical to those with lower degrees of formalization.

In contrast, informal systems develop spontaneously. They are networks of face-to-face personal relationships of an intimate and affiliate nature based on sentiment. Informal systems are largely oriented to personal and collective satisfactions, emotional support, and participation in the life of the society and culture. Roles are not specialized and interchangeable, and people in the system relate to one another on the basis of who they are, not what they do. The occupants of some roles are not replaceable (for example, a child who dies). Others are replaceable, but replacement may lead to changes in the system's activities and its internal and external relationships (for example, divorce and the remarriage of a parent). Families typify informal systems, which also comprise adult friendship groups, children's play groups, and informal support networks.

Figure 3.1 (Farquharson 1978) represents a continuum along which formal and informal support systems can be placed according to the degree of formality.

This diagram suggests the range of support systems in a community. Families, natural helpers, and kin–neighbor–friend networks are at the informal end of the continuum as purely informal systems. Self-help groups typically begin as informal systems, but over time, and particularly as they develop into large regional or national associations (such as those for the major diseases), some construct formal arrangements of organizational roles and job titles, hierarchical authority and decision making, formal policies, and so on. Hence some self-help groups may fall at the informal end of the continuum, some at the formal end, and some in between. Voluntary associations such as clubs, rural granges, churches, political groups, hobby groups, youth organizations, and formed social work groups are formal inso-

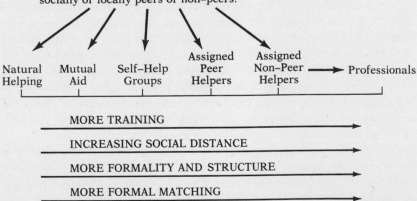

ONE MODEL OF THE HELPING CONTINUUM

VARIABLES: Primary concern self or social situation, duration of helping relationships, mutuality/reciprocity or one–way helping, short–term change for long–term maintenance; functionally, socially or locally peers or non–peers.

Natural Helping | Mutual Aid | Self–Help Groups | Assigned Peer Helpers | Assigned Non–Peer Helpers | Professionals

MORE TRAINING

INCREASING SOCIAL DISTANCE

MORE FORMALITY AND STRUCTURE

MORE FORMAL MATCHING

FIGURE 3.1. One Model of the Helping Continuum.

far as they are based in formal organizations and subject to organizational arrangements, purposes, and requirements. Such groups may elect officers, create committees, and develop rules. But they are informal insofar as they develop affiliate and intimate relationships and structures of their own. But such entities as these do not develop spontaneously as play groups do; they are created for specific objectives and are more formalized than self-help groups. And finally, the community's bureaucratic organizations are at the formal end of the continuum.

Social support, whether formal or informal, is transactional, mediated by what the person does and how receptive she or he is to the efforts of others, the behaviors of those others, and the environmental context (Coyne and Holroyd 1982). Hence, social support expresses a person:environment relationship. Empirical questions of whether a support system's impact is positive or negative; what meaning it has for the community, family, or individual being served by the social worker; and whether the focal unit is receptive and able to use social support—all are part of the process and content of social work assessment. Also, some people may lack the requisite social skills or receptivity to others and may be unable to use a support system. For example, the absence in early life of warm, responsive, affirming interpersonal experiences is thought to lead to later difficulties and fears in relating to others. Others may be subject to personal orientations or cultural proscriptions that interfere with the use of formal support systems, even in the face of need.

Nor are support systems necessarily always supportive. They may exert a negative impact occasionally or consistently, in which case a system may be viewed by clients and social workers as an object of change. A young mother, for example, may feel criticized and unsupported by her social network. An organization may be unresponsive to the cultural norms and values of the community it wishes to serve. In their operations, then, informal and formal systems may arouse stress instead of reducing it, may interfere with coping efforts instead of supporting them, and may undermine the individual's or the collectivity's sense of competence, relatedness, self-esteem–self-concept, self-direction, and construction of reality (worldview or meanings). A formal or informal support system may also be temporarily unable to be supportive, either because of a high level of stress within the system itself, because of environmental pressures, or because the focal person's relationship with a supportive figure may be conflicted.

This chapter examines both types of support systems, beginning with formal organizations, followed by formed groups, self-help groups, social networks, and natural helpers, in that order (families are considered in the next two chapters). All are significant elements of the community. Since they differ from one another, their influence on the community and the functioning of its residents also differs.

FORMAL, COMPLEX, BUREAUCRATIC ORGANIZATIONS

In our bureaucratized society, almost everyone is born and subsequently dies in a hospital, a formal organization. This pattern is shifting as home births and dying at home increase, and as homelike birthing centers and hospices develop. Still, most of us will continue to spend large portions of our youth and adulthood being educated in, working in, worshiping in, and dealing with formal organizations such as schools, workplaces, churches or temples, social agencies, public utilities, communication and transportation bureaucracies, corporate purveyors of goods and services, and governmental organizations at local, state, and federal levels—to name but a few.

Bureaucracy evolved in the nineteenth century as a consequence of urbanization and industrialization. It was a way of organizing collective effort to achieve greater productivity, efficiency, and profits through rational methods of management. The new form spread to other areas of endeavor, including charity organization societies. So-called scientific philanthropy bureaucratized alms giving by the use of management methods to control duplication and fraud. In today's society, most community systems of work, education, health and mental health, and social services structure their services and other activities in bureaucratic forms to some degree. Yet many poor and disempowered persons have not been provided by education or life experience with knowledge of how to negotiate with these bureaucracies for the services they need. Hence, social workers need to know precisely how organizations work and what their impact is on those served and on practice, policy, and program development as well. Equipped with such knowledge, social workers can

- help the poor and others negotiate organizations successfully;
- help make their own and other organizations more responsive to the needs of those served, through the use of internal and external advocacy, respectively; and
- help secure professional self-direction for the social work staff so that the value and knowledge commitments of the profession are implemented in the organization's social services.

These activities are in the realm of practice theory and will not be included here. Instead, our focus is on organizational theory as part of social work's theoretical foundation.

Formal organizations are created to achieve specific objectives and to solve problems that arise in their operations, including the management of internal strains and adaptation to the environment. As an organization develops, a planned arrangement of tasks and functions becomes necessary to ensure effective problem solving and goal achievement. Such planning brings complexity in its wake. Administrators must be hired to oversee operations, set priorities, and manage resources. They must coordinate the efforts of personnel who carry out specialized tasks and occupy positions with differing degrees of prestige. Cost effectiveness and financial accountability become prime organizational norms (Hage and Aikin 1970).

Rules and procedures are introduced to ensure uniformity and efficiency of production or services, to control employee behaviors, and to regulate the organization's relations with its environment. In highly centralized large-scale organizations, such arrangements tend to be hierarchical. Authority, decision making, and formal power are lodged in a few persons at the top of the structure. One danger of such centralized control in a community's social service organizations is that it tends to increase the distance between decision makers, on the one hand, and practitioners and those served, on the other, so that it is difficult to respond flexibly to individual need. This is particularly true in structures in which adherence to rules and regulations is strictly enforced (Hage and Aikin 1970).

Policies, rules, and procedures are originally designed to ensure uniform quality of services; equitable, fair treatment of all clients and staff; and efficiency of operations—all in support of problem solving and goal achievement. Because of their nature, however, rules and regulations may become more rigid over time, so the original intent is transformed into maintaining the status quo rather than serving the avowed goals, a process known as *goal displacement*. This usually means that the social and psychological needs of the clientele and staff are neglected in favor of observing the rules, and the organization becomes unable to adapt to changing conditions. Less formalized agencies with few rules are more flexible, permitting adaptive responses to social change and some individual discretion among staff for decision making, and enhancing responsiveness to community needs.

A common problem in bureaucratically organized social services is restricted job specifications or arbitrary or uniform implementation of policy and procedures so that social workers are not free to operate on the basis of professional values, knowledge, and judgment. An agency may even prescribe how people's life issues are to be defined, and where, when, how, and to whom service is to be provided. Thus conflict arises between professional norms and bureaucratic norms and between social work values and organizational policies. Staff turnover and burnout can be related to such conflicts as well as to large caseloads, poor working conditions, and low salaries. These matters affect practice adversely, reduce the quality of service to the community, and damage staff well-being. Since they tend to be more prevalent in large-scale public services, they play a part in the tendency of some practitioners to forsake the public bureaucracies that primarily serve the poor and to seek positions in private agencies. This is a serious problem for the community and the profession and is not likely to be easily overcome.

However, not all large-scale service organizations, public or private, operate in these ways. Some combine hierarchical and collegial aspects in the human relations type (Litwak, Meyer, and Hollister 1977): professional and administrative staffs develop structures that define and regulate the different tasks and responsibilities of the two groups. Examples are found in large social welfare organizations and community mental health agencies, whose administrators exert centralized control over financial policy and procedures and other structural aspects but leave professional decisions in case situations to professional staff. Yet financial policies do play a fundamental role in how professionals can operate on behalf of their clients, so that professional autonomy may sometimes be more apparent than real. In the rarer collegial model, some social agencies, especially those administered by and for women (Hooyman and Cunningham 1986), do encourage the real participation of professional staff as colleagues in policy development, program planning, and decision making.

Informal Systems in Formal Organizations

The description so far of formal structures and how they differ from the community's informal structures has ignored the fact that primary groups arise and develop in formal organizations and can have a marked influence on their operations. Such informal structures are networks of interpersonal relationships created by people working together. Complex organizations are not able to meet the individual psychosocial needs and interests of their personnel, even if they recognize that such factors are important in job satisfaction and hence in an organization's performance. The informal structure is a way of meeting these needs. It is shaped by the personalities, feelings, personal goals, motivations, attitudes, and professional commitments and ideologies of the members. Together, these features create a subculture within the organization as an adaptation to the stressors of organizational life. It is an important mutual aid system that provides social and psychological support to the members. Under certain conditions, however, informal systems may also create stress if they lack such elements as trust, mutuality, cooperation, and helpfulness.

Informal subsystems have certain properties parallel to those of the formal system (Hage and Aikin 1970). For example, informal power is gained through personal influence. Informal customs and traditions exist side by side with formal rules and regulations. Informal prestige, like formal status, has its distinctive rewards. At different times, the informal system may be congruent with and supportive of the formal system, or it may be incompatible with, disruptive of, or even subversive of it. Informal norms may support formal decision making, authority, and rules or may undermine them. The informal structure may be a positive or negative force in efforts to innovate or to increase the organization's responsiveness to community needs. Hence the operations of both the formal and the informal structures affect the organization's clientele and the community for good or for ill. The social worker must thoroughly understand both structures in order to practice effectively in an organizational setting and, where necessary, to help increase its responsiveness to community needs.

Community–Organization Relations

A social service organization must be familiar with the demographic characteristics of the community, including distribution patterns of age, race and ethnicity, religion, gender, family forms, and socioeconomic status. It must keep up with rates of unemployment and plant closings in a metropolitan community, or of farm foreclosures in a rural community, and with the community's epidemiological data on physical illness or disability, emotional disorders, and rates of mortality and morbidity by age and race. Services and programs can then be shaped to fit community needs and cultural orientations to the greatest degree possible in order to be effective and optimally used, and to elicit more positive than negative attitudes toward the organization and its staff and services.

The organization's spatial and temporal arrangements are important for access and utilization—especially by the poor, those with disabilities, and working parents. Public transportation, parking space, easy physical and social access, and flexible office hours are important to potential users of the service. Most agencies have not yet promoted community members' involvement in policy and program development that goes beyond token membership on advisory councils and the like. Yet this can be an effective way to secure community acceptance and to increase rates of utilization.

THE FORMED GROUP

Formed social work groups are located toward the formal end of the continuum. Unlike primary groups such as families and natural peer groups, they are created for a specific purpose, exemplified in treatment teams in various practice settings; structured groups (Middleman 1981) such as activity, support, task-oriented, or discussion groups fulfilling psychoeducational functions; therapy groups; youth groups in membership associations such as Scouting, Camp Fire, the Y's, and 4-H; and faculty committees in university and college governance. Authority is lodged in the sponsoring organization and in the group's leader as its representative. Formed groups usually have formal rules and a set of tasks, often structured by roles and stratified by status, for achieving the objectives for which the group has been formed. Indeed, Schwartz described the social work group as "a collection of people who need each other in order to work on certain common tasks, in an agency that is hospitable to those tasks" (1971:7).

Nevertheless, social work groups are not as formalized as bureaucratic organizations. In large measure, they depend for their effectiveness on developing a strong, positive informal system, and not only on the structure and resources provided by the sponsoring agency or institution. Over time, a network of relations among the members appears, characterized by the personal influence and prestige of some members, and by such informal roles as leader, scapegoat, and tension manager. Other informal processes include the operation of group norms, rituals, and customs. The formal structure is relatively clear and predictable at the outset, at least to the leader who helps make it clear to the group. In contrast, its informal structure will manifest emergent or unpredictable qualities over time.

Like the formal structure, the informal one affects the group's transactions with its environment. For example, informal operations may actually deflect the group from its purpose and tasks by using the group for socializing instead of work (not to be confused with the group's need from time to time to look at its own process in order to facilitate the work), thereby threatening its survival in the sponsoring environment. This happens frequently in children's groups, especially where the group's purpose has not been made clear. It can also happen in adult groups as a means of avoiding the discomfort posed by the work. If it persists, the leader uses her or his authority to hold the members to the work, or a member with informal influence may do the same.

Because it is sponsored by an organization, a group can provide the agency with information concerning its impact on its clientele or its community, as may happen in a foster parents' group. A group may introduce innovation or change into agency programs and procedures, as when a tenant council in a housing project proposes and achieves a new policy regarding repairs or security. A group may also affect intraorganizational relationships either for good or for ill, such as changed relations between teachers and administration as a consequence of group process in a teachers' group led by the school social worker, or between cottage parents and the youth who are served in a residential treatment center as a consequence of group process in a staff group formed by the agency's social worker.

Some formed groups may resemble a primary group at the outset, as do some school-based groups in which the children already know each other and must then work to formalize their structure. But whether that is the case or not, the process in all formed social work groups is expected to lead to the members' coming to feel close to one another and to the leader. The intimacy and reciprocal caring that develop in the informal system provide the forceful dynamic of mutual aid that serves the formal purpose and tasks for which the group was assembled. The emergence of mutual aid signals the effectiveness of the leader's work with the group and enables the sponsoring agency or organization to fulfill its own social purpose.

Group theorists suggest that formed groups experience specific, identifiable phases of development over their life course (Garland, Jones, and Kolodney 1965). Sarri and Galinsky (1967) specified three dimensions of group development:

1. Changes in the group's organization—its structure and patterns of participant roles and statuses—such as changes in the power structure at different stages of development.

2. Changes in activities, tasks, and operations of the group, such as changes in decision-making processes over time.
3. Changes in the group's culture, including its values, shared purposes, and its behavioral norms—such as changes in members' expectations of one another.

Hartford (1972) developed a framework of nine such phases. Phase 1 is a pregroup period during which preparations for the group's formation are made, including attention to group size, duration, location, and individual member characteristics. Then the potential members are informed of the plan for a group service. Phase 2 includes convening the group and the face-to-face beginnings of getting acquainted and defining goals, roles, focus, and direction. Phase 3 is marked by a beginning coalescence among the individuals as a group. In phase 4, members begin to respond to the actuality of the group's existence with ambivalence toward getting involved and possible resistance.

In phase 5, the members become reinvolved as a group and begin the work for which the group was established. In phase 6, the work continues both on the group's purpose and on the maintenance of its own interactions, norms, culture, cohesion, and control, all of which require the group's attention from time to time. Phase 7, pretermination, involves getting ready for ending and separation, as well as beginning to work through the group's meaning and process. This is followed by phase 8, termination itself. The group's ending is ritualized to underscore its significance to the members. Phase 9 is less usual, being a posttermination follow-up activity.

The phases are shaped by the characteristics of the group members, the patterns of group process (relationships and communication), the nature of the group's environment, and, to a lesser degree, the element of time and the duration of the group. The phases do not necessarily follow the sequence as outlined. A phase may recur, and several may appear in one session, as happens in single-session groups—though not exclusively. In long-term groups, single phases may extend over a number of sessions.

SELF-HELP GROUPS

Some conditions exist for which neither formal, professional systems of care nor the informal, nonspecialized, natural helping network are quite right. But, "There is another informal or natural system composed of 'self-help' groups which combines the specialized knowledge of specific problems along with the empathy, genuineness and warmth of the natural helping system" (Maguire 1979:12). The rapid expansion of self-help reflects the readiness (always present, but until recently not acknowledged nor recognized) of people in all segments of society to solve their own problems, in concert with others like themselves. The expansion process may be buttressed by distrust of professionals and organizations because of experiences with impersonality, inflexible policies and procedures, and the loss of personal control over decisions affecting one's well-being. Self-help groups are not a replacement for all professional services, but they are a preventive force and a stabilizing influence, and they can complement formal services.

Self-help groups are formed by people who come together in order to manage a shared life issue and to bring about desired personal or environmental change. Groups may be initiated by lay individuals, or professionals may bring the members together at the outset. Groups may continue with a professional as consultant (although many do not), while the members retain control of policy and resources. The largest category of self-help groups helps individuals to cope with their common life issue through peer support, role modeling, and the like. Such groups include certain populations with whom professionals have little success (such as addicted persons, the chronically mentally ill, and persons involved in sexual offenses), but who are helped effectively through self-help groups (Maguire 1979).

Health-related groups are particularly prominent in the self-help movement. Farquharson (1978) found thirty-five health-related self-help groups in Toronto with an active membership of some twelve thousand persons. Gussow and Tracy (1976) noted that in the United States, a self-help group exists for nearly every major disease listed by the World Health Organization. Many observers suggest that the importance of health-related self-help lies in the fact that once the need for acute medical care has been met, the management of chronic illness or disability is the task of patients and families. It is they who best understand the social and psychological consequences and can best teach other group members how to manage them.

This is clear in Farquharson's (1978:5) research: a member of the Lost Chord Club, a fellowship of people who have had surgical removal of the larynx to arrest cancer, stated, "I now have more understanding of the problems that my condition creates for other people and thus I'm able to relate to them more effectively." A member of the Crib Death Parents Group said, "I have much less guilt and I don't feel like a curiosity anymore . . . I realize that I'm not the only person in the world who has experienced the unexplained death of a child." Farquharson found that the aspects of the group experience that members felt were most helpful were sharing a common concern; having the opportunity to help others; hearing of both successful and less successful attempts to deal with the shared concern; and developing a sense of belonging.

Self-help also includes a second category of groups that are more oriented toward social change than toward personal coping. These groups carry out programs that educate the public, raise funds for research, and lobby for needed legislation on behalf of a class of individuals (Spiegel 1982). Some of these groups started out as small informal units, geared to peer support and experiential learning. As they grew in size, and as longtime members became less interested in personal concerns and more interested in social change, the groups took on some characteristics of formal organizations, such as hierarchical decision making and specialized roles and functions. Such associations often experience continuing tension, especially at the local level, between the need for formalized means of carrying out political advocacy, public education, and fund-raising tasks and the need to maintain informal supportive relationships for new members. A third category of self-help comprises resource-exchange networks, such as food co-ops, day care co-ops, neighborhood improvement associations, and groups that help members to explore new interests and learn how to be self-directing for greater fulfillment, such as feminist groups (Lenrow and Burch 1981).

Self-help groups and mutual aid associations not only fit the worldview of various cultural groups in pluralistic North American society but are a significant force for the empowerment of impoverished or devalued communities. No matter what the groups may later accomplish, most start out from a disempowered position. They lack needed resources, social respect, or opportunity or all three. Through group processes, the members are gradually empowered by gaining information and rediscovering their own capacities. As the individuals and the group are empowered, the community itself gains in power in the same circular causal loop of community–family–individual transactions identified by Pinderhughes and described in chapter 2.

SOCIAL NETWORKS

Social networks consist of relatives, neighbors, and friends. In a cross-cultural analysis, Litwak and Szelenyi (1969) found that each constituent serves different functions. Neighbors are nearby and are best able to provide short-term services and help in immediate emergencies, such as transportation. Kin have a permanent commitment and so are appropriate providers of long-term resources, such as help during a period of unemployment. And friends, unlikely to have permanent commitment or to live nearby, are best able to help in matters requiring guidance, affirmation, emotional support, and feedback. Persons of other statuses have since been included in the concept of network. They may be coworkers, coreligionists, or others who are defined by the focal unit as supportive, but they are not necessarily friends or neighbors. They may also be natural helpers (described below).

Social networks serve as coping resources for dealing with life stressors. They facilitate mastery of the twin tasks of problem solving and management of feelings by providing emotional support, information and advice, and tangible aids, and by undertaking action. They may also serve a primary preventive function in effectively staving off an imminent stressor. In carrying out these functions effectively, informal systems also contribute to the member's self-esteem and relatedness and may enhance the sense of competence and self-direction.

How do we know all this about social networks? Extensive studies have found a significant association between social ties and physical, mental, and social well-being. For example, a well-known long-term study (Berkman and Syme 1979) of 7,000 adults of differing ages found a significant relationship between deaths from all causes and a low social network index (the number of close friends and relatives, and how often they were seen each month). A widely cited study of pregnancy complications found that pregnant women who experienced life stressors but lacked support systems were more likely to have complications during delivery than those who were strongly supported by others (Nuckolls, Cassel, and Kaplan 1972). While there is evidence that unrelieved stress can lead to physical dysfunction, it is not yet equally certain that social support makes a difference. All that can be said so far is that social support does moderate the effects of stress and that it does appear to be positively related to health.

Most human beings know deep within themselves that social ties are needed across the life course. According to Bowlby (1969), we come naturally by that biological and social imperative. He observed that human beings tend to make strong attachments to a few other particular individuals at various points in life. As long as these attachments remain intact, we feel secure, but when they are broken by moving, unwanted separation, or death, we become anxious, even grief-stricken, and sometimes seriously depressed. Bowlby's theory and supporting research are described in later chapters. On the basis of observations by ethologists (scientists who study animals in the wild), we know that such bonding or attachment is also characteristic of many species of animals and birds. Therefore, it is likely that this need was built into the human genetic structure very early in evolutionary development, even before we were fully human.

Dubos (1968, 1978) pointed out that human evolution took place in the context of small bands in which the members knew one another personally. Within such bands, there was a strong pull among young and adults to remain in close proximity—the stray in any animal group is often the victim of predators. In contemporary life, most of us sustain personal relationships, characterized by intimacy and sentiment, with only a small "band" of others. Because our evolution prepared us for intimacy with a small number, we consciously or unconsciously experience urbanized mass society as stressful, despite its attractions and advantages. We protect ourselves by maintaining noninvolvement through depersonalized, detached interactions with those outside our own "band." Dubos based his view on available evidence from prehistoric human settlements, and on observations of existing "primitive" cultures, nomadic societies, and primate groups in the wild.

Wilkinson, a Cherokee, wrote: "For most of man's [sic] existence on earth, he was a tribal individual and he has only just begun to detribalize himself. One wonders whether those tribal institutions have really been adequately replaced or whether there is really something that is now missing that man [sic] needs. Perhaps those smaller communities are necessary and perhaps a holistic life that is built around kinship and similar kinds of things is really necessary for survival" (1980).

Hirsch (1981) views social networks as "personal communities" and suggested that they reflect 1) involvement in the major spheres of life; 2) the degree and manner in which these spheres are integrated or segregated; and 3) the values and choices by which human beings seek to achieve meaningful participation in their culture, society, and community. Personal communities also embed one's statuses and roles and hence support one's social identities in each life sphere. Hirsch suggested that developmental issues and stressful events over the life course demand new social identities and hence adjustments in one's personal community.

Antonucci (1985), like Hirsch, took a developmental view of social networks and conceived of them as "social convoys" within which social support is given and received over the life course, as shown in figure 3.2. As conveyed by Antonucci in figure 3.2, the determinants of the convoy's structure and functions are 1) *personal characteristics,* such as age, race or ethnicity, gender, socioeconomic status, abilities, and needs (arrow A), and 2) *situational characteristics,* such as life events and transitions, role expectations, financial and information resources, locale of residence, demands and opportunities, and organizational memberships within a given cultural context (arrow B). Together, personal and situational attributes determine the structure of the convoy. The *structural characteristics* of the convey include its size, stability, connectedness, homogeneity, symmetry, and complexity. These attributes are said to influence convoy functions (arrow C). Changes in structure over the life course are likely to affect the focal person's perception of the convey and its operations. *Convoy functions* are the support given, received, or exchanged by convoy members, as well as its distribution over time. The personal and situational characteristics and the convoy structure and functions determine the *convoy's adequacy* (arrow D). Antonucci suggested that adequacy is a subjective element dependent on the person's perception of the convoy and its operations. In turn, the perceived adequacy is a determinant of individual performance and well-being as *outcome* (arrow E).

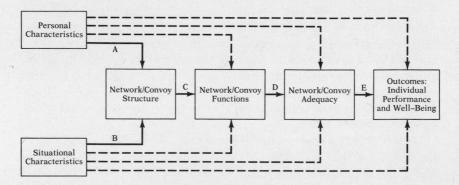

FIGURE 3.2. Hypothetical Determinants and Effects of Network/Convoy Properties.

Attneave (1976) suggested that both the various dyads and the connections among the network members are influential in the focal person's behavior. For example, the attitudes of members with whom the person has little connection may nevertheless exert positive support for or negative sanctions on the focal person as norms and attitudes flow through the linkages and across the circles. This point is illustrated in an early analysis of dropout rates in family service agencies (Mayer and Rosenblatt 1964). The analysis suggests that the norms and values of the network members may determine whether the focal person will initiate and continue contact with professional services. Referring to client dropout from service, these authors declared that the following questions should be considered before one finds fault with the person's motivation or the worker's skill: "Which members of the client's social network are aware that he [sic] is receiving professional help? What are their reactions? What effects do their reactions have on him [sic]?" (1964). It is also true that the network's negative attitudes may change as the service continues. And in other instances, members may actually serve as referrers to services and may strongly encourage continuance (Lee and Swenson 1978).

Hartman (1978) developed an ecomap related to both formal and informal supports, in which the conflicted or nonconflicted nature of the relationships and the direction of energy flow in the connections can be shown. The ecomap is a powerful tool in social work assessment and intervention, as it helps individuals or families to 1) visualize their relationships with informal and formal support systems in a way that talking about them cannot convey; 2) note changes in these relationships through the passage of time or as a consequence of life events and transitions; and 3) reach decisions about any changes they believe are needed in their present support systems, or about engagement with new ones.

Figure 3.3 illustrates an ecomap. Clarice is a 26-year-old single white woman who operates a small business she recently purchased, which is fraught with financial and help problems. She feels empty and lonely and is continually fatigued. Suffering from chronic anxiety, she has expressed the fear that she is going "crazy." The ecomap reveals few informal or formal supports. Only one relationship shows reciprocity; the rest are conflicted. This relationship is with a good friend, described as the one normal person in her life. Her former boyfriend has a college degree but works at an unskilled job. He is pressuring Clarice for reconciliation. Her one employee had been a friend. This young woman often fails to show up for work and, when

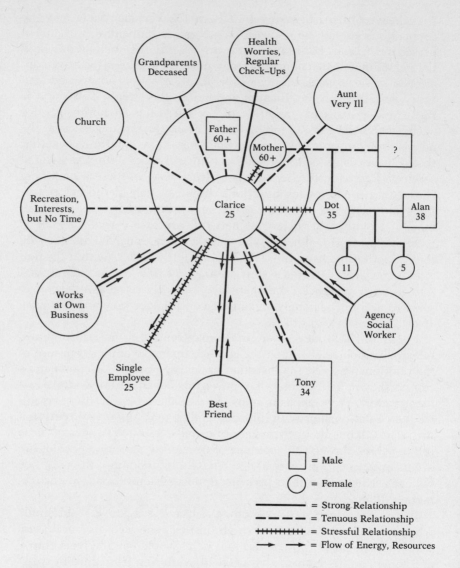

FIGURE 3.3. Ecomap for Clarice.

she is there, makes many errors. Clarice can't bring herself to fire this person because she fears hurting her.

Clarice's parents are divorced. Her father is described as a "jerk." Her mother is described as possessive and demanding but dotes on the young children of her daughter from an earlier marriage. This doting is difficult for Clarice as she felt neglected as a child by her mother. Clarice also feels hurt and rejected by her half sister. Her grandparents died about 12 years ago. She misses them very much as they were loving and supportive. Inquiring about the cause of death brought out the family history of diabetes. Her aunt is now severely ill with the disease, and her brother, Clarice's uncle, died of it. Clarice worries about becoming diabetic herself.

Natural Helpers

Pancoast (1980) and Collins and Pancoast (1976) have described natural helpers as central figures in a social network or in a neighborhood who have gained recognition for their unique wisdom, resourcefulness, and caring qualities. They have achieved centrality by "playing key helping roles and by matching resources to need" (Pancoast 1980:114). They have numerous and rich relationships with others in the network. They may link people together who were previously unknown to each other, and they may help coordinate the efforts of others to assist someone in the neighborhood. Not every network has such a central person, but Collins and Pancoast have demonstrated how, in those neighborhoods where a natural helper is present, she or he can provide preventive support to families at risk for child abuse or neglect.

Natural helpers are often crucial in the successful management of disease suffered by chronically ill individuals and in the provision of essential respite to their families. For example, Strauss and Glaser (1975) found that strategies of illness management require the assistance of family and friends and also, at times, natural helpers, who may be acquaintances or strangers. All these helpers, termed "agents" by the authors, fulfill different tasks. Some act as rescuing agents (saving a diabetic individual from dying when he is in a coma); protective agents (a wife agreeing to warn her husband, suffering from cardiac disease, when she senses his oncoming fatigue before he does); assisting agents (helping a kidney patient with home dialysis); or control agents (helping a patient comply with dietary, medicinal, or other regimens). We might add transportation agents, grocery-shopping agents, and so on.

Recognition is now being given to companion animals as significant natural helpers in physical illness and emotional disturbance. Pets have been used in the treatment of psychiatric patients and to relieve the loneliness of elderly persons. Horseback therapy is used for seriously physically disabled children, including those with muscular dystrophy, paraplegia, spina bifida, and cerebral palsy. Programs for bringing pets from animal shelters to visit patients in hospitals, nursing homes, and geriatric facilities are spreading (Curtis 1981). In addition to the services that dogs, cats, and monkeys perform for blind, deaf, and paraplegic individuals, pets of all kinds are reported to have a beneficial effect on the one-year survival rates of coronary heart disease patients (Friedman et al. 1988). These researchers found that pets may have a soothing effect: "They offer an unambivalent exchange of affection, attention, and contact comfort."

Patterson and her colleagues studied rural natural helpers in two rural communities in the Midwest and New England (Patterson and Brennan 1983; Patterson et al. 1988). The helpers, ranging in age from 16 to 83 years, were all white (only one was self-identified as American Indian), reflecting the racial composition of both communities. Findings included the following: rural natural helping is characterized by reciprocity; the helpers provide help to their friends, neighbors, and kin, and they themselves have been helped by those same individuals.

Men tend to be doers, for example, performing farm and garden chores in the case of illness. Women tend to be facilitators, inviting emotional expression and encouraging the person's own thinking and doing. Some women and men use both styles, especially older women. For the most part, helpers and recipients share similar worldviews. Usually they have known each other for a long time, often having grown up together. Helpers display almost total spatial and temporal accessibility. They also tend to reach out when they see the need, not waiting to be asked. These helpers use a range of techniques. A woman, age 77, reported on helping a friend:

> Her problem was a disastrous marriage. It had broken up once before and they had made up, and then the second round was it. He was abusive and very, very, very abusive of their son. When the divorce was finally completed, it made her very sad because it all started because of alcohol. She really still liked the guy, but she was determined this was it. As a result she was badly in

need of friends. And that's where I thought I helped her—more for listening than anything else because I couldn't do anything else. Just talking and listening to what she had to say. . . . When you're with somebody a lot you just communicate. It's communication, that's what it is. I like that word. (Taped interview)

A 37-year-old man described being helped by a neighbor:

He helps with my milking seventy-six cows on Tuesdays and he comes around on Saturdays and Sundays, too. He helps with the cleanup when he's here. He talks a little but he don't hang around to do anything other than just milk. . . . It originally started when he wanted to come to learn how to do it, and I was supposed to be kind of helping him. But it really worked out the other way. He was a whole lot better than doing it without him, and I said so. He kinda thinks it's fun and I kinda hope he keeps thinking it's fun. If you gotta do it all alone, it just takes twice as long. (Taped interview)

An example of an urban natural helper is found in a news report of Hetty Fox, a 47-year-old black woman in the impoverished, rapidly deteriorating South Bronx, New York City:

Residents of Lyman Place . . . have seen her save abandoned buildings earmarked for demolition, recruit dozens of families to move into buildings that would certainly have been torn down, turn vacant garbage-strewn lots into gardens, confront unsavory characters and run them off, [induce the city to] close off the street during summers for an all-day recreation program, teach classes for adults and children in abandoned buildings, and prod the city into pouring new sidewalks and planting trees on their block. [A resident comments,] "Instead of a dump . . . things are growing here now. We have eight new babies on the block." (Geist 1984:25)

CULTURAL PATTERNS OF INFORMAL SYSTEMS IN FOUR MAJOR GROUPS

Network structures and functions may vary within and across ethnic groups or racial groups because of individual, social class, religious, or national origin differences—and tribal and individual differences among American Indians. According to the Howard University psychologist Jacquelyne Jackson (1985), we confuse the terms *race, eth-*

nicity, national origins, and *minority group.* For example, not every ethnic group is a minority group, and a minority group is not necessarily limited to a single ethnic group. She cited Schermerhorn's definition of an ethnic group as having " 'real or putative common ancestry, memories of a shared historical past, and a cultural focus on one or more symbolic elements defined as the epitome of their peoplehood . . . such as kinship patterns, physical contiguity, religious affiliation, language or dialect forms, tribal affiliation, nationality, phenotypical features, or any combination of these' " (1970:12). Jackson added that ethnicity does not connote prejudice, discrimination, oppression, or power. It should be limited in application to culturally homogeneous groups and should not be applied to any group categorized only by race (Jackson 1985).

Citing another source, Jackson found that groups such as the Navaho, Zuni, Amish, and Hasidic Jews are highly distinctive ethnically from other groups. Asian and Hispanic Americans, Orthodox Jews, and certain black subgroups are moderately distinctive ethnically from other groups, and Italian-, Polish-, Jewish-, and Irish-Americans, for example, have a low level of ethnic distinctiveness (Trela and Sokolovsky 1979). A minority, on the other hand, is a vulnerable or a disempowered group with limited access to roles and activities central to the economic and political institutions of the society. From this standpoint, Jackson suggested, women and Hispanics are neither minorities nor ethnic groups (insofar as Hispanics include Mexicans, Puerto Ricans, Cubans, and Argentines, and many others of varied national origins). They do not have common ancestry nor shared historical memories. Similarly, blacks in the United States include, for example, Haitians, Jamaicans, and Nigerians who are foreign-born, immigrants, and of different national origins. Thus American blacks in the United States constitute a racial but not an ethnic group.

Black Networks

The study of an impoverished black community by the anthropologist Stack (1974) demonstrates the survival value of kin and intimate nonkin networks that draw on members' resourcefulness, resilience, and the swapping of money, food, child keeping, and other goods. For example,

> Cecil (35) lives . . . with his mother Willie Mae, his oldest sister
> and her two children, and his younger brother. Cecil's younger

sister Lily lives with their mother's sister Bessie. Bessie has three children and Lily has two. Cecil and his mother have part-time jobs in a cafe and Lily's children are on aid. In July . . . Cecil and his mother had just put together enough money to cover their rent. Lily paid her utilities, but she did not have enough money to buy food stamps for herself and her children. Cecil and Willie Mae knew that after they paid their rent they would not have any money for food for the family. They helped out Lily by buying her food stamps, and then the two households shared meals together until Willie Mae was paid two weeks later. A week later Lily received her second ADC check and Bessie got some spending money from her boyfriend. They gave some of this money to Cecil and Willie Mae to pay their rent, and gave Willie Mae money to cover her insurance and pay a small sum on a living room suite at the local furniture store. Willie Mae reciprocated later on by buying dresses for Bessie and Lily's daughters and by caring for all the children when Bessie got a temporary job." (1974:37)

Stack concluded that these networks of mutual aid are highly adaptive in conditions of unrelenting poverty, racism, and chronic unemployment.

Comer and Hamilton-Lee pointed to the importance to all black people of the family, the church, and the school, as support systems sustaining personal and community strengths from the period of slavery to the present day. The family and the school in black communities are considered in later chapters; in this section the significance of the black church within poor and middle-class black communities is underscored: "Shared child-rearing among black relatives and friends, shared housing, income, and services, and strong emotional mutual support systems—most often church based—were as necessary after as during slavery" (1982:124). Although churches are formal organizations, most congregations develop informal systems.

More than a church, the black church has been a "substitute society" that has served to bind the black community together in the face of oppression during slavery and after (Comer 1972). It has been a source of social control in the sense of maintaining values, setting directions, and supporting or censuring desired or undesired behaviors, as the case may be. The black church has also led the community in efforts first to survive and then to overcome oppression. It has provided the base for mutual aid and voluntary associations, and for identity formation, validation, and the sense of belonging. It has become a sanctuary from a hostile environment through emotional catharsis, music, oratory, and other expressive functions. The black church today continues to serve as a significant support system having these same functions, but like other religious institutions in North American society, it is being affected by forces of social change.

Hispanic Networks

Delgado and Humm-Delgado (1982) analyzed natural support systems in Hispanic communities, in particular Puerto Rican and Chicano communities. These systems comprise:

1. *The extended family*, including those related by blood and marriage as well as friends and special neighbors within ritual kinship systems of reciprocal support and obligation. These are considered in the next chapter.

2. *Folk healers*. In Puerto Rican communities these include four types: the spiritist and the *santero*, who focus mainly on emotional and interpersonal problems, and the herbalist and the *santiguador*, who focus mainly on physical ailments. "In Mexican American communities, the *curandero*, a fifth type, is the primary folk healer" (Delgado and Humm-Delgado 1982).

3. *Religious institutions* that serve as support systems for individuals in crisis: "Although the Roman Catholic Church traditionally has been regarded as the primary religion of Hispanics and in some instances continues to be so, its influence is not as great with some Hispanic groups, particularly Puerto Ricans, as with others." (Delgado and Humm-Delgado 1982). In a study of support systems among Puerto Rican migrant women in New York City, Garrison found that the missionary societies and the ministries of small Pentecostal churches "provide emergency financial aid, go to the airport to meet new arrivals and orient them to the city, and locate housing and employment for members through the Pentecostal grapevine. [They] support several Pentecostal programs to rehabilitate drug addicts, prostitutes, and other outcasts of society" (Garrison 1978).

4. *Merchants and social clubs*. These fulfill both formal and informal roles in a culture-specific framework. The most common are the *botanicas*, which provide herbs and healing paraphernalia; the *bodegas*, neighborhood grocery stores that also meet a variety of social needs; and the *social clubs*, found predominantly in Puerto Rican communities. They are hometown clubs that provide recreation, ori-

entation for newcomers, and linkages to housing, employment, and other social institutions.

Queralt (1984) observed that while Cubans, Mexicans, and Puerto Ricans are more alike than different, sharing similar versions of the Spanish language and of Catholicism, they vary in their demographic characteristics, cluster in different areas of the United States, have different immigration histories, and belong to diverse cultures. For example, on the average, Cuban-Americans are twelve years older than Puerto Ricans and Mexican-Americans. Their personal income is larger than that of the other two groups, but substantially lower than that of the general U.S. population, despite the stereotype of their prosperous condition. More than 50 percent of the one million Cuban immigrants live in Dade County, Florida, while smaller Cuban communities are found in New Jersey, New York, California, Illinois, Texas, and Puerto Rico.

Cuban immigrants have come to the United States in large numbers only since the Castro regime attained power. Those in the earliest group tended to be of the upper and upper middle class. However, each successive group comprised more people of lower socioeconomic, educational, and occupational status than the previous one (Queralt 1984). Progressive discrimination by the larger society accompanied these shifts. Also, Cubans came to this country as political refugees and tend to have a more conservative outlook than the Puerto Ricans and Mexicans, who came seeking better jobs and living conditions and hence have a greater interest in liberal activism than do the Cubans. Cubans, like Puerto Ricans, lack the Indian ancestry of many Mexicans because the Indian populations in Cuba and Puerto Rico were all but wiped out by the Spaniards, whereas the highly advanced Indian populations of Mexico were subjugated but could not be annihilated by the conquistadores (Queralt 1984).

Like other groups forced to leave their own countries, Cubans have experienced multiple losses and difficulties in adapting to a new culture, physical and social environment, and language. Many have suffered deprivation and health problems, sadness and depression, anger and despair, loneliness and estrangement, family disruption, and intergenerational conflict. Some have never become acculturated: "They remain in the Cuban communities of large cities and avoid contact with people who do not share their language and culture. [This tends to handicap them because] they need to function within both the Cuban and the American cultural contexts, each with its separate set of rules" (Queralt 1984).

The *santero* and *santera* are described by Queralt as important supportive figures in Cuban communities. They are consulted for various folk illnesses, such as the evil eye, fainting spells, lack of energy, and obsessive thinking. *Santeria* is a religion centered on the worship of gods and derived from a melding of Spanish Catholicism with the religious beliefs of African slaves brought to Cuba by the Spanish colonists. It is believed that *santeria* beliefs and practices, such as the sacrifice of sheep and chickens and lavish dinners offered to the gods, are widespread in U.S. Cuban communities (Queralt 1984).

American Indian Networks

In a consideration of informal systems of tribal and family networks among American Indians, important differences among a population of some million individuals must be kept in mind. Today there are 13 different language groups (and 200 mutually unintelligible languages), 130 major tribal groupings and an undetermined number of subgroupings, and different levels of sociocultural development among American Indians (Carpenter [Cherokee] 1980).

Despite these differences, common value orientations concerning the importance of tribal and family networks prevail. Blanchard (Laguna Yaqui) and Unger observed, "Indian people derive their identity from relationships to their families, relatives, tribes, and land base. Blood and clan ties are the strongest relationships between individuals. Every Indian person has the benefit of these two relational systems, and the responsibilities of persons to each other are as strong and binding in either"(1977). The family is considered in the next chapter. Of tribes, Wilkinson (Cherokee) wrote:

> A tribe is a collection of families in which everyone has accepted duties and obligations to different people, and people operate in that kind of context. . . . A tribe is certainly nothing less than a big self-help organization that is designed to help people and meet the psychological, spiritual, and economic needs of its members.(1980)

Asian and Pacific Islander Networks

Vast differences exist in the history, culture, religion, language, and appearance of Asian, Southeast Asian, and Pacific Island Americans.

The resulting complexity is increased by intragroup differences across generations, social classes, urban-rural origins and settlement, and the presence or absence in North America of family, extended family, and community support systems. These differences are overlaid by differing conditions of immigration and/or experience as war refugees and, for more than 110,000 Japanese-Americans (two thirds of whom were citizens), internment during World War II—now recognized as a racist violation of constitutional rights. The most populous groups are Chinese (from the mainland, Hong Kong, Taiwan, and Vietnam), Japanese, Korean, East Indian, Lao, Lao Hmong, Cambodian, Thai, South Vietnamese, Filipino, Guamanian, Samoan, and Hawaiian. There are many others, but in smaller numbers. Most groups live in ethnic communities and isolated ethnic ghettos, although some Chinese, Japanese, and those from India are financially advantaged and may live away from urban enclaves. These three groups, in particular, are plagued by positive myths and stereotypes of the "model minority," educational achievement, and financial success (true only of some). Such stereotypes overlook the realities of poverty, discrimination, high rates of physical illness and emotional disturbance, substance abuse, and poor services and low utilization rates that prevail among Asian and Pacific Americans.

The Vietnamese, under centuries of Chinese domination, display many Chinese cultural patterns, including Confucianism, Taoism, and Buddhism and traditional Chinese medicine. Interpersonal relationships are highly valued, regulated, and hierarchical yet reciprocal. Lao Hmong not only differ from other Asians but also from other Laotians: "Hmong culture is uniquely structured in corporate kinship groups. . . . The patrilineal clan system of the Hmong dominates their social organization, serving as a primary focus for their culture as a whole by tying together social, political, economic, and religious aspects of behavior" (Tou-fou 1981:79). Below the clan is the branch, persons who share the same distant paternal ancestor and are important sources of help, and below the branch is the extended family, which is the most important unit. It is described in the next chapter. In America the Hmong try to live next door not only to other Hmong, but to their parents, children, and close relatives, so that all may thrive. Cooperation among a number of families helps the whole group to become self-sufficient.

With respect to all Southeast Asians coming to America from such systems of identification with family and community, Wong wrote: "Enhancement of community systems through community development and community organization activities improves individual and family support systems (1981:202). Through social action, refugees learn ways to make their voices heard, to empower themselves, and to attempt to solve systemic problems in refugee programs" (1981:210–211). As in other cultural groups, religious personages (in this instance, Buddhist monks) often serve as significant natural helpers, and mutual aid associations (collectively among Southeast Asians or individually within Vietnamese, Cambodian, and Hmong communities) promote health and reduce the stress and loneliness of refugee life in America. However, the value placed on family and mutual aid networks is sometimes unrecognized by agencies and professionals, so that social services may violate cultural norms and patterns.

Pacific Islanders are less known to other Americans than the Asian groups, even though Guamanians and Hawaiians are American citizens, and Samoans are American nationals. Little research and few specialized services have been directed their way. Yet they suffer from the same general barriers and problems as the Asians. Far from home in an industrialized mass society, the Islanders band together for social survival. The primary group of friends or families provides social roots and an affirmation of cultural heritage and identity: "The various Islander peoples have their own clubs which [offer] social activities and economic assistance to members, but mainland family and friends remain the chief source of support for new arrivals" (Munoz 1976).

In light of the great significance of informal support systems to all people, social work services, policy, and practice need to be directed to strengthening and sustaining them. Services that draw on social networks in community life have greater cultural congruence than traditional services and are apt to be more effective. Considering the rich diversity of history, language, and culture among the new and older groups of Americans described here, social workers engaged in cross-cultural practice with individuals and collectivities require cultural sensitivity, culture-relevant knowledge, a bicultural training on an experiential base (Pinderhughes 1979). Those who serve a particular cultural group must become thoroughly familiar with the specific value orientations, norms, patterns, and social-cultural history of that group.

Dana (1981) specified three dimensions of cultural differences between middle-class white Americans and the four major groups of Americans of color that affect the utilization of services:

1. *The meaning of emotional distress and physical symptoms* within personal experience and the cultural milieu. Similar symptoms either do not merit similar interventions in different cultures or require

supplemental interventions such as spiritist, *curandero*, medicine man or woman, or herbs.

2. *The manner in which a group's worldview shapes feelings and perceptions about the self and society.* Americans of color "typically experience less personal power, feel less control over their own lives, and they may also feel that they should not be directly responsible for themselves or experience greater control over their own lives" (1981:353–354).

3. *The function and importance of family and community.* Extended-family structures have a wide range of influence over individual lives. However, the central value of autonomy in white middle-class America is not part of the cultural heritage of these groups. Thus the potential for generational conflict exists in the families and communities of all newcomers to America, as the children take on its values, norms, language, and teenage behavior, including autonomy and self-direction.

The extended family, referred to here and there in this last section as an informal support system, is further described in the next chapter. Throughout North America, the family is not only a significant aspect of the community's social structure but is the most intimate environment in which individual development and functioning take place. Hence the next chapter examines the family from the community or exterior point of view, including its forms, functions, and development over its life course. Chapter 5 describes the family from the context-of-development or interior point of view: how members experience the various processes involved in family life.

4

The Family as a Community Subsystem: Its Functions, Organization, Cultural Diversity, and Tasks

The family occupies a somewhat different position in this book from that of the other subsystems of the community. As the most intimate and influential environment in which human development takes place, it is examined in greater detail than the other community subsystems. First, in this chapter various definitions of the family are considered. Then certain functions and tasks that the family carries out for its members and for the community and society are examined. Last, various structural arrangements (organization) of the family as a community subsystem are delineated. The intimate interior life of the family as a system in its own right is considered in the next chapter.

WHAT IS A FAMILY?

In times past, the family was commonly regarded as a group of persons related by blood or legal marriage, living together, and cooperating economically and in child rearing. As recently as 1972, Ball pointed out that this definition rules out childless couples, unmarried cohabiting couples, same-sex partners with or without children, one-parent families, and some extended families where the kin are fictive ("pretend relatives" and ritual kin). Fictive kin include, for example, the *compandrazos* of Hispanic cultures, and parents' good friends known as "uncle" or "aunt" to the children across ethnic groups and socio-economic status. It is sometimes the case among all groups that an old person and a younger person (and perhaps the latter's child) live together yet are not related and do not have a sexual tie to each other.

In the face of definitional confusion among social scientists and others, Hartman and Laird (1984) presented a definition of the family that is consistent with social behavior and social organization in the ending decades of the twentieth century. Their definition runs minimal risk either of *exclusivity* that leads to the view of some living-together persons as deviant, or of *overextensiveness* to the point where the very term *family* becomes meaningless. These authors reminded us, first, of two categories of families. One is the biologically rooted family of origin, into which one is born; it may include adopted members and fictive kin. This is the "family of blood ties, both vertical (multigenerational) and horizontal (kinship), living or dead, geographically close or distant, known or unknown, accessible or inaccessible, but always in some way psychologically relevant"(1984:30).

The other category is the current family constellation (structure) in which people have chosen to live. This family

> consists of two or more people who have made a commitment to share living space, have developed close emotional ties, and share a variety of family roles and functions. This family may consist of a middle-aged married couple whose children are reared; two elderly sisters, one a widow and the other a spinster, who share an apartment in a retirement community; a group of biologically related and unrelated adults and children who have formed a group or communal family in which a range of commitments exist and in which instrumental and expressive roles are shared. (1984:30)

It may also consist of a same-sex couple with or without children from a prior marriage of one or both partners.

In their definition Hartman and Laird took "a phenomenological stance in saying that a family becomes a family when two or more individuals have decided they are a family, that in the intimate, here-and-now environment in which they gather, there is a sharing of emotional needs for closeness, of living space which is deemed "home," and of those roles and tasks necessary for meeting the biological, social, and psychological requirements of the individuals involved" (1984:30).

Whether or not this definition of the family meets the requirements of social science or the strictures of certain segments of the society, it does fit an ecological perspective and the practice reality of today. As these authors stated, "Indeed, future generations may discover that many of the emerging family forms are highly functional adaptations, *solutions* to problems in our changing and complex environment rather than problems in and of themselves"(1984:31; italics in the original). Having accepted this definition, we next consider the functions of the family. Like definitions, these also vary from theorist to theorist.

FAMILY FUNCTIONS

Most students of the family include in its functions some of the following: the legitimation and regulation of mating and sexual relations; the procreation of children and child rearing; the socialization of all members into gendered (or nongendered) roles and other social roles valued by the society or cultural group; economic maintenance and household management, including the division of domestic labor; structures for authority and decision making; the transmission of the culture, including language, norms, value orientations, and belief systems; and the provision of connective links to the larger environment needed for the optimum development and functioning of all members throughout the life course.

Given the variations among cultures and subcultures, the accelerating rate of social change, and the emergence of new theories and knowledge about the family, it is unlikely that wide agreement will be found on any one of the above items or on desirable additions and deletions. For example, the assumption that the procreation of children is a definitive function of the family no longer holds, given the growing numbers of young couples choosing not to have children at all. Among families with children, the function of early child rearing is being increasingly shared with community day care facilities as mothers of infants and of children under school age enter the labor force in growing numbers.

Some functions have been lost over time to other social institutions, although some were later reclaimed. For example, early in the twentieth century the family lost to the formal health care system its functions of birthing and of caring for the ill and the dying. In recent years, some families have reclaimed these functions: more births take place at home or in homelike settings with family members often present, and many terminally ill patients return home to die. Lost functions are sometimes replaced by new ones. The family's function of meeting the emotional needs of all its members arose in the middle of the nineteenth century in reaction to the depersonalization of the newly industrialized, urbanized, and bureaucratized mode of life. This function rests on a view of the family as a haven from a troubled and troubling world (Lasch 1977), and it poses difficult tasks for many who feel ill equipped, uninterested, or resentful.

A particularly interesting example of a lost function rediscovered is education. Early in this century, the family appeared to yield its function of educating the young to compulsory education and the public school. However, in the past several decades it has been recognized that the family continues to serve as a significant educator of all its members (Leichter 1974). Some families now teach their children at home, which is not against the law in most states. Also, the family influences, for good or for ill, the outcomes of schooling. But more important, it is now understood that all family members teach and learn from each other. Children learn from their parents in countless ways. And parents learn from their children about school, peer relations, child development, and even the postindustrial, rapidly changing society in which they now live (Mead 1970).

Immigrant and refugee parents may learn a new language and customs from their children, although such learning can also lead to unwanted role reversal, parents' loss of face, and so on. Siblings learn values, attitudes, knowledge, and skills from one another. And everyone in some families may learn from grandparents and great-grandparents—often the custodians of the family's history, cultural values, traditions, and rituals. Notably in some communities, the school and the family do not agree on which of them should be responsible for the sex education of children, or it if should be a shared task.

Whatever functions a particular culture assigns to its families, an arrangement of statuses and roles is needed for carrying out those functions and their associated tasks. Such arrangements are referred to in this book interchangeably as the family's *organization, form,* or *structure.* Probably the most striking feature of American families today is the remarkable variety of their forms. The next section describes several prevalent family forms present in American life in the ending years of the twentieth century.

FAMILY FORMS

Nuclear Families

Until quite recently many clinicians and students of the family assumed that a new type of two-generation family, consisting of two
parents and their children, had begun to spread with the start of the
industrial revolution in the early nineteenth century. It was further
assumed that before then agricultural or peasant families tended to
live in extended-kin households. Most also believed that by the twentieth century the family consisting of father-breadwinner, mother-
homemaker, together with one or more dependent children, was the
dominant structure in the Western world. This so-called nuclear family was assumed also to be separated from kinfolk by distance, upward mobility, or norms of autonomy and independence. The nuclear
family structure was presumed to be the dominant and "normal"
form by social scientists, human services professions, the media, other
social institutions, and the American public.

Myths abound in these assumptions. First, contemporary historians of the family have discovered that the nuclear form prevailed in
England and western Europe long before the onset of industrialization. Probably it was only the wealthy and powerful who lived in
large, extended households. The nuclear form was brought to America
by the first colonists. The assumption that agrarian Americans lived
in extended-kin families is unfounded, although it is true that at times
an elderly infirm parent might move back to the home or farm of an
adult child. This arrangement was not frequent because the life course
was much shorter than it is today (Demos 1974). However, extended-
kin networks currently serve as support systems to many so-called
nuclear families. Even when geographic distances are great, contact
is maintained by telephone and rapid transportation facilities. It is
said that today many of us are housed in nuclear units but live in
extended networks.

Second, the nuclear unit has been steadily declining in number and
percentage of total families. In 1987 two-parent family groups with
children under 18 represented 73 percent of all family groups with
children. Among white family groups, the percentage was 78.3, and
among black family groups the percentage was 41.5 (U.S. B.C. 1989:50,
table 67). From another perspective, married couples with children
represented only 47.8 percent of all households in 1987, down from

57.1 percent in 1970 (U.S.B.C. 1989:51, table 70). Third, while the nuclear family was prevalent even before industrialization, few such families then or later represented the idealized form of father-breadwinner and mother-homemaker. The fact is that in agricultural societies women and children performed farm labor along with the father. Changes in the social order due to industrialization and urbanization meant that many poor and working-class wives and mothers then worked in cottage industries or outside the home in sweatshops, domestic service, factories, and offices instead of in the fields. In middle- and upper-class households created by industrialization, however, many wives and mothers were freed from labor inside and outside the home. Instead, they were expected to be the source of emotional support for the other family members, and to make the home a refuge from the outside world. The nuclear family or father-breadwinner and mother-homemaker was a reality only in these classes.

Beginning in the 1880s and continuing through the 1950s, the few highly educated, married middle-class women who worked typically withdrew from the work force when their first child was born. If they returned to work, it was not until the last child was in school full time or out of the home altogether. For most wives, then, the husband's career took precedence, and the wife's was merely temporary until she took her "proper place" in the home and reared the children. This picture changed rapidly beginning in the 1960s. Growing numbers of middle- and upper-middle-class women entered the labor market as the expectations and roles of women changed, opportunities increased, and social pressure on mothers to remain at home lifted. Facing family needs in an inflated economy, many more working-class mothers of very young children entered the labor market as well.

By 1981 the Census Bureau reported both husband and wife worked in 62 percent of all married couples, up from 50.1 percent in 1970 and 40 percent in 1960. By 1986 only 29 percent of two-parent families had a single breadwinner *(New York Times,* June 26, 1986). By 1987 40 percent of all mothers of minor children were employed. The Bureau of the Census (Bianchi and Spain 1984) projected that the percentage would rise to 50 percent by 1990. By then it is expected that 75 percent of all children will have both parents working outside the home (Brazelton 1985:xviii).

Solo-Parent Families

The status granted in some quarters over the years to a mythical idealized nuclear family has been oppressive. It tended to suggest that other family forms are deviant from the norm, perhaps disorganized, and probably unable to carry out the functions of the family satisfactorily. For example, solo-parent black families consisting of mother and children were said by many observers to be responsible for the poverty and other stressors from which they suffered. By the 1980s, however, many social workers and social scientists came to understand that conditions of poverty, poor housing, poor health care, and inadequate education lead to the chronic unemployment of black men. This, in turn, discourages marriage and raises divorce rates. Also, welfare policies have forced men to leave their families in order that Aid to Families of Dependent Children (AFDC) for mother and children will continue. Family poverty and its attendant conditions encourage teenage pregnancy, school dropout, and consequent inability to find employment at high enough wages to establish a two-parent household and support a family. In this view the prevalence of black female-headed families mired in poverty is one consequence of institutional racism as described in chapter 2.

Regrettably, however, a residue of feeling that one-parent families are less functional than two-parent families appears to persist. A nonrandom anecdotal survey of 302 social work practitioners and administrators and 307 female solo parents was undertaken by the National Association of Social Workers (*NASW News* 1987). One third of the parents were poor, one half were minorities, and three quarters were from urban areas. Most were employed, primarily in jobs traditionally assigned to women. The survey found that the professionals "saw themselves as the primary support for these women, and also stated that they felt the women had very few strengths. [The parents] indicated that they thought they were survivors, that they worked under very difficult circumstances to keep their families together, and . . . thought they were doing pretty well" (*NASW News* 1987:1, 16). They reported that they reached out to their social networks for help and used them more than formal systems:

Many of the women cited "family harmony," spiritual beliefs and religious faith, "survival skills," and belief in oneself as strengths, and said the absence of abusive men made the home situation more peaceful. They also thought they were more in-

dependent than other women, had more stamina and persever-
ance, enjoyed a closer relationship with their children, and did
not take their children for granted (1987:1,16).

The report concluded that practitioners "should recognize and appreciate the strengths and resources of single-parent families and help
them build from these strengths rather than presuming weakness and
isolation"(1987:16).

There have always been some American families headed by a solo
parent because of death (especially during the seventeenth, eight-
eenth, and nineteenth centuries and the early decades of the twentieth
century), desertion, separation, or divorce. But in the 1970s and '80s
the number of solo-parent families in all segments of the population
increased at a rapid rate across racial, ethnic, religious, and socioeconomic groups. No longer is death the major cause of solo parenting;
rather, divorce, separation, desertion, and unmarried teenage parenthood account for most of it. In 1985 23 percent of the children under
18 years old lived with only one parent, compared with 10 percent in
1960 (*New York Times*, April 30, 1987, P.A.). In 1986, the figure was
24%. Of these, 89 percent lived with their mothers and 11 percent with
their fathers. Of the total, 42 percent were children of divorced parents, while 27 percent were children of parents who had never married; 24 percent had parents who were married but separated, and 7
percent had a widowed parent. Among white children, 18 percent
lived with a solo parent, compared to 30 percent of Hispanic children
and 53 percent of black children. The Census Bureau estimated that
60 percent of all children would spend some time in one-parent households (although some of those might later move into remarried two-
parent families) *(New York Times*, January 28, 1988:C-8).

These figures explain the "feminization of poverty," since women
raising families alone have more limited earning power and fewer
economic options than men. Women and their children are often
thrust into poverty as a consequence of divorce and separation, while
men often benefit financially. Some 60 to 80 percent of all fathers,
regardless of financial status, fail to comply with support orders,
which are woefully limited to begin with. Weitzman's (1985) study of
divorced families found that in the year after divorce, the standard of
living of the mother and children fell 73 percent and that of the
husband rose 42 percent. The most severe impact was experienced by
older homemakers and women with young children.

Most divorces occur relatively early in marriage (one half in the
first seven years). In 1982 the average duration of marriage was 9.4

years *(New York Times,* March 7, 1985). However, the National Center for Health Statistics reported that the U.S. divorce rate fell in 1986 to its lowest level since 1975 *(New York Times,* April 9, 1987). It is possible, then, that the U.S. divorce rate, while still among the highest rates in the world, is stabilizing. Contrary to the popular belief that divorce occurs mostly among the middle-aged, 40 percent of all divorces take place among couples in their 20s, a rate higher than that for any other age group (A. Yarrow 1987). However, it is easier for divorced women in their 20s to remarry. In that age group, 76.3 percent remarry, compared to 56.2 percent of those who divorce in their 30s, and 32.4 percent of those who divorce in their 40s. Across all age groups, divorced men are more likely than divorced women to remarry. According to the Census Bureau, five out of six divorced men, or 83 percent, remarry, while just under three out of four divorced women, or about 72 percent, do. Of first marriages 47 percent end in divorce and almost 49 percent of remarriages are terminated by divorce (A. Yarrow 1987).

Some part of the increase in female-headed families is also attributable to the numbers of pregnancies among unmarried white and minority women. According to the U.S. Bureau of the Census the mothers of 15.7 percent of all white infants born in 1986 were unmarried and mothers of 61.2 percent of all black infants born in 1986 were unmarried (U.S.B.C. 1989:66, table 93). A small percentage included decisions by nonpoor single women to be solo parents for a variety of reasons, including making up for delayed childbearing by many among the growing population of older unmarried women. The rest probably represented unintended pregnancies and some that may have been intended by teenage women living in poverty who may not have recognized nor understood the medical and social risks to themselves and their infants.

One-parent families, whether headed by the mother or by the father face the same tasks as two-parent families but without a partner to share them. Many of the women face additional exceptional tasks posed by poverty, racism, and sexism; by the solo parent's need both to work and to care for children; by the lack of jobs and equitable pay; and by the lack of adequate formal arrangements to support family functioning. Some without informal supports also experience social isolation and loneliness. Many social agencies have developed new counseling and ancillary services that reach some solo mothers or fathers to facilitate their meeting the life tasks of the family. These include self-help and support groups, parent–child play groups, divorce mediation services, family life education, and parent aide programs.

As important as these programs are, social workers recognize that to help solo mothers and their children escape from poverty requires new social and economic policies at the national level designed to support family functioning; adequate health care for mothers and their infants and children; family-oriented policies at the workplace; quality day care; enforcement of child support; and for those who cannot work, a redesigned program of welfare that will promote physical, emotional, and social growth and health instead of destroying them. In 1983 a single mother of two in Massachusetts had to earn at least $15,000 per year before she could afford to give up welfare for employment. Only that amount could make up for needed child care services, transportation, and clothing costs, and lost or more restricted Medicaid coverage (MHSC 1983).

However, by 1988, $15,000 led to increasing indebtedness because of increases in rent and food costs, loss of benefits if earnings go above the minimum wage, and increased taxes and health costs. Increased earnings were not enough to offset these losses. Findings of a recent study conducted by the Coalition (1988), are not encouraging, despite employment training programs. For example, "In 1986, a family which moved from full-time employment at the minimum wage to a salary of $10,400 would find, in spite of earned income growing by more than $250 per month, that their debt had increased from $263 to $338 per month" (MHSC 1988:Introduction).

Consider the situation of the hypothetical Ellen Peters and her two children. Ellen is 30 years old, and has been divorced for two years. Immediately after her divorce, with a four-year-old son and one-year-old daughter, she went on welfare. Her grant and other benefits never lasted to the end of the month, and she was forced to visit food pantries as often as she was allowed to try to feed her family. Her landlord threatened her with eviction when she was late with the rent and, terrified of homelessness, she delayed paying her electric bill as long as she dared and canceled her telephone.

Intent on making a better life, Ellen sought job training through the E.T. program, and got a job as a clerical worker in a downtown bank. In 1986, she earns just under $6.00 per hour, for a gross salary of $12,334. On the proud day when she started her job, she hoped her worries would be over. But as she wonders where she will find the money to pay for a pair of sneakers for her son, or to pay for the next oil delivery, her progress seems more like an illusion. Even though she lives in the same apartment as she did while on welfare, and scrimps just as much each month at the supermarket, there are still bills every month that she just can't pay.

The situation of single fathers is said to be qualitatively different from that of single mothers (Mendes 1976). Little attention is given to their plight in the literature, although it seems clear that they are vulnerable to special stressors that are different from those of the women (Nieto 1982). Solo fathers confront role ambiguity and the lack of norms, values, and environmental expectations for role performance. While single parents of both genders are at a disadvantage in regard to societal perceptions, solo-father families are frequently assumed to have been created by greater pathology in the mother than solo-mother families. And the solo-father is apt to be perceived as poorly prepared by his very nature for the performance of the necessarily expressive roles in child rearing.

Social workers have begun to provide support groups and educational programs for solo fathers, and a further development of services to meet their unique needs is essential. Also needed are theoretical frameworks for the analysis of single-father parenting; clarification of the unique roles, tasks, and stressors involved; and studies of the psychological, social, cultural, economic, and educational dimensions of the solo father population (Nieto 1982).

BLENDED FAMILIES

The blended-family form is also referred to as the *remarried family*, the *stepfamily*, or the *reconstituted family*. While it existed over historical time because of low life expectancy and early widowhood, its numbers have grown in recent decades in response to the increasing rates of divorce and the greater social acceptance of divorce and remarriage. By 1982 there were 35 million American adults living in blended families. About 1,300 new blended families with children under the age of 18 are forming every day. If those trends continue, the Bureau of the Census estimates that 60 percent of all children born in the late 1980s will live in a blended family or a solo-parent family for some part of the time before they are 18. About 75 to 80 percent of divorced partners remarry, and 44 percent of remarried persons divorce again (Wald 1981:8). It has been estimated that a substantial number of those divorced a second time will remarry again:

Typically, men are likely to be remarried seven times faster than women. Indeed, from 1970–80, there was a drop of 30 percent in the remarriage rate for women. Three quarters of women who divorce eventually remarry, but they spend longer periods of time as single parents, and compared to men, fewer divorced women are remarried. The chances for remarriage are significantly reduced as women age. Moreover, black women have fewer chances for remarriage than any other group (Wattenberg 1986).

Sometimes both partners bring children to the new family, or only one has children and either the other partner is childless or the children are in the custody of the other parent. Those children may visit the remarried family either occasionally or not at all, depending on custodial agreements, proximity, and so on. Children living in the new family not only have a new stepparent but may have stepsiblings, stepgrandparents, and other adult kin who may or may not accept the new parent or her or his children as relatives. To complicate the structure and relationships even more, the new parents may have a child or children together, who are then half siblings to all the other children. On the one hand, possibilities for individual and family identity confusion, jealousy, conflict, and divided loyalties are rife, and on the other, the potential exists for extended-kin support, loving relationships, a cohesive family life, and the emotional growth of all members.

Wald (1981) pointed out that such families are living through an experience without society's understanding of what that experience is like and what its consequences for the family and its members are apt to be. While the number of remarried families is increasing rapidly, knowledge of their special tasks is developing slowly. For the most part, research is limited to the study of remarried families who seek services because they are troubled. Less is known of such families who are making it without professional help. What is learned about the problems of these families may or may not be generalizable to families who do not ask for services. However, the findings of one exploratory study of 30 nonclinical remarried families (27 white, 1 black, and 2 Hispanic, of varying economic status) suggest that the families were doing better than had been anticipated. They did confront life stressors arising from complex, ambiguous relationships and uncertain social expectations. But after the first year most of the 60 adults and the 37 children interviewed reported positive feelings toward their new family. Many commented that it took time and work (Dahl, Cowgill, and Asmundsson 1987).

It is clear to many professionals that blended families differ. But it is less clear to the professionals and to the families themselves that the blended family is very different from the nuclear family described earlier. After all, both consist of two parents and children, so families coming together through remarriage expect no drastic difference. Yet they are often immediately plunged into problems arising from many significant differences. Wald (1981) identified some of these differences and their consequences as follows:

First, the image of the wicked stepmother is not only a pervasive theme in children's fairy tales but persists as a mythical stereotype in the culture, together with those of the helpless stepchild, the helpless or absent father who fails to protect the child, and the assumption that "step" is less. The continued existence of these themes and images can lead to conscious and unconscious fears in children and parents about the danger posed by the stepparent. It may also inhibit the stepparent from moving readily and effectively into the parental role.

Second, studies of children of divorce (see chapter 11) reveal that grief, anger, and persistent fantasies of reunion of the parents are prevalent among children and adolescents. Hence it is not surprising that some children in blended families resent the stepparent's assumption of the noncustodial parent's role, the perceived "loss" of the custodial parent to the new spouse, and the dashing of their hopes for the reunion of their biological parents.

Third, the kinds of spatial, temporal, and status conflicts that occur between some full siblings can be more intense between stepsiblings in the blended family. Decisions about where to live, who must move, and who must change schools are critical. Having to share one's room with a relative stranger, or having less time with one's own parent, or losing one's ordinal position in the birth family to an older stepsibling is a difficult challenge. Further, it is awkward, and sometimes conflictual, for children to use traditional role names for the new parent, grandparents, and other relatives, especially where children are loyal to or have maintained close contact with their own absent parent and other relatives. Similarly, the difference in the surnames of the child, the newly wedded parent, and the stepparent or stepsiblings can be embarrassing and troublesome for schoolchildren and youth.

Fourth, in the nuclear family the marital tie precedes the parent–

child tie. The children belong to the marital couple, and all generally live together until the children are grown. In the blended family each parent has had a relationship with her or his own children from birth, but the stepparent's experience in beginning a parental relationship with a school-aged child or a teen is very different from that of parents in a nuclear family starting out with their own infant and learning to parent that particular child as she or he grows. Thus there is a built-in structural imbalance in the ties shared by the newly remarried couple toward the children they are to parent.

Fifth, in the blended family, each parent has already developed rules, norms, customs, and routines that shaped each family's evolved patterns of relating, communicating, decision making, spending, and disciplining. Thus any aspect of remarried family life may have the potential for a clash in lifestyles. Structurally, steproles have no names, guidelines, or prescriptions for their occupants. As Wald pointed out, society and remarried families expect that role performance will be the same for steprelatives as for biological ones. Given all the differences between blended and nuclear families, the expectation is gratuitous.

Other complexities arise from each family's experience as a solo-parent family before the remarriage. For example, the financial condition of the new family may be better or worse, depending on whether one parent must continue alimony or support for noncustodial children, and whether additional new responsibilities for the other parent limit wage earning. Custody arrangements may mean that some children are absent but visit regularly and that some may be resident with the blended family but visit the absent parent regularly or irregularly. Previous divorces and remarriages may have created a train of in-law relationships having their own obligations or losses. Thus potential exists in all blended families for supportive resources and/or problem relationships as the numbers of participating members increase, and regardless of family strengths.

EXTENDED FAMILIES

Among immigrant populations in the late nineteenth and early twentieth centuries, extended kin tended to cluster together in one dwelling, as in the case of three generations living together, or in separate dwellings close by in the case of other relatives. To a degree, this pattern continues today among some Italian-Americans, Polish-Americans, and other white ethnic groups. American Indian and black families typically have extended-kin structures, as do more recent arrivals: Puerto Rican, Mexican-American, and Asian-American families. Unfortunately, these family forms are not recognized by the Internal Revenue Service, health insurance, Social Security, and public housing authorities. Their policies can undermine significant natural systems of support just when they are most needed for the tasks of cultural and geographic transition. This limitation is added to racism, poverty, unemployment, and limited culturally congruent formal resources (Mizio 1974).

Because independent living on the part of young unmarried adults became the norm in the white middle class beginning in the 1960s, ethnic families and families of color who still placed value on adult unmarried children (and sometimes married children, their spouses, and their offspring) remaining in the parental home were defined as raising problems. It is only recently that social workers and social scientists have stopped unthinkingly considering dependent the adult children in these groups who continue to live with their parents.

Spanish-Speaking Families

Puerto Rican, Mexican-American, and Central and South American Spanish-speaking groups are traditionally embedded in kinship systems (including kin and fictive kin) of reciprocal support and obligation. Cubans are less so. Such cultural patterns may be stronger in some families than in others, depending on how long they have resided in the United States (the mainland United States in the case of Puerto Ricans); on the nature of their experiences with its culture and its rewards and sanctions; their socioeconomic status, on their rural or urban origins; and on other variations. In Hispanic cultures, kinship consists not only of related kin but also of nonkin tied to the family through custom. For example, in Puerto Rico *Compadrazgo* refers to 'companion parents,' a ritual kin network

> Whose members have a deep sense of obligation to each other for economic assistance, encouragement, support, and even personal correction. Sponsors of a child at baptism and confirmation assume the role of *padrinos* ("godparents") to the child and *compadres* to the parents. Witnesses at a marriage or close friends also assume this role. *Hijos de crianza* ("children of upbringing") is the cultural practice of assuming responsibility for a child, without the necessity of blood or even friendship ties, and rais-

ing this child as if it were one's own. There is no stigma attached to the parent for surrendering his child or to the child who is given up. This may be a permanent or temporary arrangement. (Mizio 1974).

The Puerto Rican family values highly its unity, welfare, and honor, and there is a deep sense of family commitment, obligation, and responsibility: "Family ties and relationships are intense, and visits are frequent even if family members are not living in the same household. . . . The emphasis is on the group rather than on the individual. . . . The family guarantees protection and caretaking for life as long as the person stays in the system. Leaving the system implies taking a grave risk" (Garcia-Preto 1982:170).

Mexican-American families share traditional family values and the extended-family structure with immigrants from Puerto Rico, Cuba, and Central and South America, despite significant differences among them: "Migration and the process of relocation change the family's structure and disrupt the patterns of intrafamilial help and control. Yet there is a tendency among Mexicans in the United States to reconstitute, whenever possible, the original extended family group" (Falicov and Karrer 1980:386). Mexican-Americans are the second largest minority population in the United States, after the Puerto Ricans, and may soon become the largest. Some are members of families of Mexican descent and have lived in the American Southwest for several generations. The majority, however, were either born in Mexico or born to parents who were born in Mexico. For the most part, Mexican-Americans are from poor or working-class groups, usually rural or semirural, and are of mixed Spanish and Indian descent (Falicov 1982).

The generalizations that follow apply only to the poor and working-class families as middle- and upper-income Mexican families are markedly different in circumstances and value orientations (Falicov 1982). The family of parents and children is embedded in the extended-family network. This family of procreation usually lives in a separate household but near the extended family, thereby preserving their own boundaries and identity. The boundaries are flexible and may permit the inclusion of grandparents, uncles, aunts, cousins, and children whose parents are dead or divorced. Because young adults live with their parents until marriage, it is sometimes the case that boundary problems and loyalty issues erupt early in the new family's formation. Generally, however, the extended-kin network is characterized by both horizontal and vertical interdependence, with a sharing of child care, financial responsibility, companionship, emotional support, and problem solving. The *compadrazgo* system of *compadres* is also an important source of support to children and their parents and may be considered part of the extended family.

Despite proximity and the norm of interdependence, the hierarchical structure of the family is clear. Rules are organized around age and gender as the important determinants of authority in the patriarchal family (Falicov 1982). Because children reside with their parents until their own marriage and maintain an intense connectedness with their parents during adulthood, the parents continue parental and grandparental functions. Hence they may never experience the empty-nest phase of family life. Moreover, "The majority of Mexican families remain two-parent families throughout their lifetimes. The number of divorces is considerably smaller than for Anglo populations. However, common-law marriages and desertions are not infrequent among the urban poor" (Falicov 1982:140).

The terms *Chicano* and *Chicana* refer to those who are part of a social movement that is struggling to be free of oppression and to achieve opportunity and equality as a people. In addition, the Chicana is struggling to change the rigidly prescribed roles of women in the traditional culture. Fimbres (1982:94) described the Chicana as a woman who believes in self-determination and greater equality for Mexican-American women in the dominant society and in the Mexican-American culture. While bicultural and bilingual, she wants to retain her culture and language but eliminate the double standard between Chicana and Chicano. It is important that social workers be aware of differences within the Mexican-American population that arise from generation, education, socioeconomic status, gender, self-identity, and the attitudes and perceptions of the larger society.

Cuban-Americans are the third largest Hispanic group in the United States, numbering close to one million persons in 1982 (Queralt 1984). They, too, place great value on the family. Despite a tradition of paternal authority, derived from the Spanish influence, love of the mother is central. Pampering of children, overprotection, and overdependency are common. Respect for older and deceased family members is important (Queralt 1984). Provision of support by the extended family is probably less among Cubans than among Puerto Ricans and Mexicans. Nuclear families have been the norm among white Cubans since the 1930s, and the nuclear tendency has become more pronounced in the process of acculturation. Cubans may maintain closer ties to the extended family than some other groups, but the ties are evident mostly during crisis periods. The extended-family relationship of *compadrazgo* has lost most of its significance among Cubans in the United States, but friends are still occasionally referred to as *compadres* (Queralt 1984).

Women's status, always higher in Cuba than in other Latin American countries, has been elevated further in Cuban society since the 1959 revolution. But it is not known to what extent Cuban-Americans have been influenced by the changes. It appears that traditional gender-typed roles are still stronger among Cubans in the United States than among Anglos. *Machismo* (exaggerated masculinity) still prevails (Queralt 1984).

Black Families

Nobles (1974) believes that the extended-family form characteristic of black families reflects the African cultural heritage, which continued down the generations despite the horrors of slavery. The sense of Africanity, the hidden strength common to black families despite their diversity, rests on the ethos of survival of the tribe and "oneness of being." *Survival of the tribe* refers to the African definition of the family as including every member of the tribe. The individual was related to the tribal ancestors and to future generations (vertical relations), and to every living member of the tribe (horizontal relations). *Oneness of being* refers to the continuity and unity of people, functions, roles, relationships, and processes in African family systems. Because they are fluid and interchangeable, each element of the family system flows into other elements and is not distinct from them.

While Stack (1974, ch. 2) declared that mutual aid by kin is required for survival in a hostile environment, Nobles (1974:22) argued that kinship bonds and the extended family exemplify the sense of Africanity in black families and communities. Some suggest that both positions are valid: the extended-kin family structure and the values on which it rests have African roots and are also adaptive in the harsh environment of poor black families. Other polarities have been identified by both black and white analysts of the black family. For example, the behavior patterns of contemporary black families are the product either of slavery or of the so-called culture of poverty. In a critique of both positions, Solomon and Mendes (1979) concluded with Valentine & Valentine (1970), that black culture has three sources: shared African roots, the effects of domination by a white racist society, and an emergent black culture influenced most recently by black nationalism.

American Indian Families

In contrast to a Western view of extended families as three generations living together, Red Horse, a California Cherokee, described
Indian family networks as structurally open and village-like. They
include

> "several households representing significant relatives along both
> vertical and horizontal lines . . . accompanied by an additional
> bonding feature of incorporation by which significant non-kin
> become family members . . . through formal and informal pro-
> cesses. An individual, for example, may become a namesake for
> a child through formal ritual. This individual then assumes fam-
> ily obligations and responsibilities for child rearing and role
> modeling. . . . Structurally, naming ceremonies organize an
> obligatory, supportive network for children"(1980).

Attneave (1982) stated that among urban Indians, many still adhere to extended-family values and relationships, even though contemporary living conditions may change the actual structure. Red
Horse and Attneave agreed that these values continue even in those
instances where present family systems extend over several states.

The American Indian woman is expected to contribute to the cohe-
siveness and integrity of the family group and to the tribal group.
This expectation is in marked contrast to the general tendency toward
rigid gendered roles found in the patriarchal extended-family structures of other cultures (except black families). The socioreligious relational ties of the American Indian woman often place her in decision-making positions that affect the group. Her activities,
circumstances, and skills may also lead to her holding significant
leadership roles in traditional and contemporary tribal life (Blanchard 1982:100). In 1987, for example, a Cherokee woman, Wanda
Mankiller, was elected chief of the Cherokee Nation.

Asian-American Families

Despite fundamental differences among various nationalities, Asians
place high value on family obligations and responsibilities. The patriarchal extended family is the traditional structure among Asian
peoples. Both old and new Asian immigrants to the United States

place high value on a hierarchical organization of authority and responsibility, and on family obligations based on status and role within the extended family. Throughout Asia, the family supersedes the individual. Identity and other attributes derive from the family. One's position in the family "defines roles, governs behavior. . . . Each relationship carries different responsibilities and requires different responses" (Toupin 1980:302). Independence does not have the same value it has in Western society. Rather, interdependence and mutuality are the norms. However, as enculturation takes place, traditional social ties and interactional norms weaken among some younger cohorts.

Especially among adherents to Confucianism, Buddhism, and Taoism, reverence for the family's past and its ancestors, as well as concern for the family's future status and well-being, provides a strong sense of continuity and obligation. Thus, the individual is viewed as the product of all preceding generations. Individual actions reflect not only on the individual and the present family, but on past and future generations as well. Such a responsibility takes precedence over individual interest (Shon and Ja 1982).

Asian cultures in general prescribe the rules of behavior and conduct in family roles such as husband, wife, child, and in-law to a greater extent than in most other cultures. The extended family, the "clan," is responsible for maintaining the status of the family name or lineage. An individual's adherence to this code of conduct becomes not a reflection of the individual but of the family and kinship network to which he or she belongs. Male offspring are valued more than females, and the expectations of each sex are quite different (Shon and Ja 1982). Shon and Ja described the family form of the Chinese, Japanese, and Korean peoples. However, the extended-family structure also characterizes Southeast Asians and Pacific Islanders, with differences due to religion (e.g., Hinduism or Islam), social class, war and refugee experiences, and island life. The Hmong extended family, for example, includes all the people who share the paternal grandparents. Thus the extended family is a corporate kinship group that is based in a patrilineal clan system. It may consist of two to ten households in which mutual help is a salient feature (Tou-fou 1981).

Shen Ryan (1982) noted that the traditional values of the Asian cultures have provided the society with a social structure and a strong set of moral values. But they have also fostered great injustices against women, relegating them to a lower status throughout life. This heritage continues to affect the lives of many Asian-American women in

North America, even of third-generation native-born Asian-American women. They face gender stereotyping and racial discrimination in the society and in their ethnic group.

Many Asian-American women succeed in adapting to the new culture and in defining new roles for themselves. But the role strain taxes the coping resources of many others, adding to the life stress generated by poverty, dilapidated housing, poor working conditions, and so on. Role strain is also likely to affect adversely the Asian-American family's hierarchical structure and its gendered roles, increasing the stress on all members. Enculturation in the new country may weaken traditional social ties and norms of interdependence and mutuality, especially among young newcomers. In some instances, migrating entails a loss of the extended family and its resources, so that the immediate family of parents and children are alone emotionally, economically, and socially:

> While most refugees who have become separated from their family members dream of family reunion and make strong efforts towards that goal, the Vietnamese, due to a strong emphasis on family loyalty and relationship, may be particularly tenacious and persistent in pursuing such a reunion. . . . The loss of family support is particularly difficult for a sub-group of Vietnamese consisting of young, unmarried ex-servicemen who, by and large, escaped from Vietnam at the last moment with the crowd, leaving their entire family network behind. Over the years, these people have developed mutually supportive units that could be called "pseudofamilies." Three or four of them live together and work at the same factory or go to the same school. (Lin and Masuda 1981:43)

COMMUNAL FAMILIES

The communal structure appears to have more similarity to extended-kin structures than to other family forms, although some theorists, notably Kanter (1972), maintain communes are not families but groups, some of which may contain families. Others view communal families—that is, people living as families in a collective—as an experimental family form, different from other families in some important ways. In nineteenth-century America, utopian communes were quite prevalent. They included the celibate Shakers, the polygamous early Mormons, and the Oneida Community with its "complex marriage" (Demos 1974). Communal structures reappeared during the late 1960s with the student revolt, flower children, hippies, and other countercultural movements. Their members share resources, common facilities, household tasks, and sometimes child rearing. Some three thousand communes were estimated to exist in 1978 (*Newsweek* 1978). The present number of communes is unknown, but it is believed to have declined gradually since then *(State of Families* 1985). Most seem to last only about four or five years. Those that work "have a sound economic structure, shared activities, a supportive atmosphere, and often a strong father figure" *(Newsweek* 1978:90).

Urban communes tend to be easier to start and quicker to dissolve than rural communes. They also have a more fluid membership recruited mostly on a friendship basis, whereas rural communes seem to require a more serious commitment to communal living because of their social and geographic distance from the past urban environment of the members and the unfamiliar types of work required. Some communes are organized around an ideology, often religious or crusading in nature ("creedal" communes). They require adherence to their doctrines and submission to the authority of a guru or leader. They may have sacred books or documents as repositories of collective beliefs and rules of conduct. Membership is open—indeed some creedal communes are missionary in regard to recruitment. Noncreedal communes tend not to have formal documents but assume that certain beliefs are known and shared by the members. They rely on friendships as sources of membership and as a base for solidarity (Berger, Hackett, and Millar 1974).

Berger, Hackett, and Miller described value systems, worldviews, and lifestyles of rural noncreedal communes as these affected economic arrangements, family structure, sexual relations, and child rearing at the time they were writing. These facets of communal living are briefly summarized as follows: Economic arrangements included subsistence farming, barter, welfare (for the women with children), windfalls (such as gifts, and inheritances), and collective enterprises. Sexual relationships tended to be monogamous at any particular time. They were fragile, however, with a frequent change of partners associated with the mobility, or "splitting," of the men. In the 1960s, raising children tended to be shared by the members, but by 1974, child rearing and discipline were increasingly limited to the mother. Children belonged to their mother, but they did experience fathering despite the absence of norms requiring paternal attention. Children were considered autonomous persons, as part of the commune's egalitarian ethos and within the limitations of age.

Skolnick and Skolnick commented that while the commune challenges nuclear family ideology and imagery, some similarities exist. People join communes or form a nuclear family in order to find love, personal fulfillment, and a peaceful haven away from a harsh, impersonal society. They fail for similar reasons: "personality clashes, value disagreements, contradictions between individual desires and commitment to the group or family, and difficulties arising from the routine necessities of daily family life" (1974:437).

Little social work activity with members of communes has been reported in the professional literature. However, for ten years following her divorce, a social worker lived with her three young sons in a network of twenty communal houses with a total of 120 residents. She reported joyful successes, from the rotation of maintenance and child care tasks to sufficient time and energy for relationships, celebration, and spiritual development, from processes of conflict resolution to the freedom from traditional roles. But, she added,

Two areas where we fell short were the economic and a commitment to the group. Both were strongly influenced by the culture, which we were trying to change, and by our socialization to old roles. People needed to be in control of personal finances, which perpetuated class differences and thus access to such opportunities as education and travel. We did not have the perspective, or discipline, or preference to make the same commitment to the community as to ourselves. As people moved on, those who remained felt discouraged at starting the efforts over again with fresh recruits. Our community was a tremendous catalyst for casting off prescribed roles and values, but those same things got rechosen eventually. This not to say that there weren't small changes that perhaps were significant in the long run. For example, my three boys grew up in a household where they were fed and put to bed by every member of the household. They lived with heterosexual and gay couples. They are used to mothers running demonstrations while men provide child care. They are used to negotiating spatial needs, handling money, what food to buy, and the like. They are used to relationships changing, instability in family living, a valuing of assertiveness, self-respect, and egalitarian relationships over maintenance of structure. For all the freedom and personal responsibility we were willing to risk, and the instability we tolerated, I wonder if we created a next generation whose return to traditional roles will speak to the essential need in family life for stability above freedom and individuality. If we find ourselves back where my generation started, I hope the commitment will be accompanied by a greater awareness of shared leadership, flexibility of roles, and skills in negotiating needs so that rebellion to the degree we took it will not be necessary.

LESBIAN AND GAY FAMILIES

The number of gay and lesbian people living together as couples is unknown. Lesbian and gay families perform most of the same functions and tasks that other families do, such as household management, child rearing (in many), arrangements for decision making and role allocation, and meeting the emotional needs of the members and the sexual needs of the adult partners. They do not serve certain other functions, such as legitimizing sexual relationships or procreating children (except for lesbian women who choose to become biological parents, often by artificial insemination). Because they lack legal and social sanctions, they may not be able to provide environmental linkages for members to the same extent that heterosexual families do, except for connections to the gay or lesbian community when one exists. In some instances, life issues are created by the loss of relationships with families of origin and the denial of credit, insurance, licensing, the joint purchase of a home, inheritance rights, and joint tax returns. Those in urban areas may have environmental resources in the gay rights movement, in the Lambda Legal Defense and Education Fund, in their relatives and friends, and in the gay or lesbian community, including its churches and health and social services. In certain instances the American Civil Liberties Union may be an environmental resource. Its 1986 policy statement advocates recognition of gay and lesbian marriages and economic benefits for "life partners" similar to those enjoyed by partners in a heterosexual marriage, including employee benefits, insurance coverage, income tax benefits, and visitation and next-of-kin rights. In 1989, San Francisco inaugurated a policy providing for official certification of gay and lesbian relationships.

Lesbian and gay couples meet each other's needs for companionship, sharing, support, understanding, and love just as heterosexual couples do (Fairchild and Hayward 1979). The relationship involves commitment and mutual responsibility for each other's well-being, and not just sexual involvement (Moses and Hawkins 1982). Typically in lesbian and gay relationships, gender-typed roles are replaced by egalitarian roles based on personal interest or ability. Lesbian women have female identities and are socialized as women; gay men have male identities and are socialized as men. With understanding of these facts and the maturing of the gay community, the earlier butch– femme dichotomy modeled on heterosexual gendered roles began to diminish in the late 1960s, especially among lesbian women. This freedom from gender role expectations is experienced as a source of strength by both lesbians and gays. Usually both members of the couple work, so that economic dependency is not an issue, although differences in work status and income may pose problems for some (Moses and Hawkins 1982).

Long-term relationships have been more typical of lesbian women than of gay men. Many lesbian women live in a lifelong relationship until death takes one partner The reality of AIDS, however, is changing the former sexual promiscuity of many gay men, especially younger men who have not yet formed a long-term relationship. Even before AIDS, however, significant numbers of men maintained long-term and even lifelong relationships until parted by death. Issues faced by gay and lesbian families not faced by most other families—or not to the same degree—include reaching agreement on private and shared time and activities, monogamous or nonmonogamous sexual relationships, the coming out of one member that causes internal conflict and possible threats to employment and friendships for the other, separate or shared dwellings, and child-custody–child-rearing matters arising from a prior marriage.

Issues of child custody, fostering, or adoption by gay or lesbian parents have legal, emotional, and social aspects. In the case of divorce where one parent is gay or lesbian, the courts have tended to grant custody to the heterosexual parent on the basis of the sexual preference of the other parent and regardless of parenting ability or the wishes of the child. Generally, restrictions are also applied to visitation and other parental rights. In instances where custody has been granted and it is later found that the custodial parent is now gay or lesbian, custody has frequently been revoked and granted to the other parent. Some progress is being made in ruling out gay or lesbian lifestyles per se as cause for loss of custody, and appellate courts in ten states and trial courts in many states have found that "sexual orientation is not to be a factor unless it can be demonstrated to be harmful to the child" (Gutis 1987:C–16).

The prevalence of adverse rulings rests on three assumptions that arise from homophobia and associated myths, augmented by the irrational fear of AIDS contagion for the children: 1) The gay or lesbian parent or parent's lover will molest the child. This myth is countered by the fact that 97 percent of child molesters are heterosexual males. There is no evidence that gay parents are more likely than nongay parents either to seduce their children or to allow them to be seduced (Moses and Hawkins 1982). 2) Gay or lesbian parents will try to convert their child to their own sexual preferences. This myth is countered by the fact that sexual preference is not a matter of choice. Further, the majority of lesbians and gays have been raised in heterosexual families and not by lesbian or gay parents (Moses and Hawkins 1982). 3) Children of gay or lesbian parents will be ostracized and damaged because of the societal reaction to homosexuality. This myth is countered by the lack of evidence in research that children suffer disproportionately because of their parents' sexual preference. Moses and Hawkins pointed out that children of minority poor families, parents with physical impairments, and divorced parents also suffer from prejudice:

> The fact that a child's parents are different from the majority of white, middle-class, unimpaired parents is not usually considered an appropriate reason for removing a child from the home. We see no reason why sexual preference should be any different in this respect, unless it can be shown that there is some clear and consistent impairment because of this (1982:200)

The study of children in same-sex families is still limited, and longitudinal studies are rare. It has been said, however, that the possibility of a child's rejection of a homosexual parent increases with the age of the child (Shernoff 1984). In referring to her practice with lesbian parents, Goodman observed that "Teenagers who do not grow up in a lesbian environment but are introduced to this family style later in life seem to have much more difficulty regarding peer pressure and their own sense of self and natural fears of sexual self-statement"(1980:164). Moses and Hawkins suggested that very young children handle the knowledge most easily, while older children are likely to worry about their home life being different from that of their peers. They may be embarrassed in public and worried that their friends will find out. The authors provided guidelines that will help parents to talk with their children.

The exceptional child-rearing tasks for the lesbian and gay parent and her or his lover are similar to many of those of the blended family in terms of steprelationships and roles. However, they are made more difficult for same-sex families because of social intolerance. Exceptional child-rearing tasks include giving special attention to open communication, coming out to the children, dealing with difference and stigma, and negotiating relationships with the divorced parent and with grandparents who may be hostile to the lesbian or gay relationship (Goodman 1980). Many professionals believe that gay parents should come out to their children as soon as possible.

TWO-PROVIDER FAMILIES

"The money's good when you work full time. Mind you, you get bloody tired, working full time. It would be nice if you could just sit down to a meal when you get home instead of having to get it ready first. Then you could . . . get on . . . with the housework, the washing, the ironing."
—Gwen Wesson, *Brian's Wife and Jenny's Mum* (1975)

The life issues facing families when both parents work actually cut across all family forms. They apply even to the one-parent family because the solo parent carries many functions of two parents and may work besides. The major cost is in having too little time to meet the demands of both family and work. In a study by Moen and Dempster-McClain (1981), half of the working mothers of preschoolers reported that they would prefer to work fewer hours, and nearly a third of the fathers said that they would prefer a reduced work week in order to spend more time with their children.

Although traditional norms for gender roles are changing, in most two-provider families the overall responsibility for child care and household management still falls to the mother. Even though the father may help with some tasks, working mothers usually carry the major share at the expense of leisure and sleep time (Bianchi and Spain 1984). It would seem that for most men the work role still remains primary and the family role secondary, while the reverse is still the case for most women. Brazelton (1985) noted that working couples with small children have five careers between them: two nurturing jobs, two in the workplace, and their relationship with one another. He believes they can keep alive their sense of pleasure and their sense of sharing so that all five careers succeed only if both learn to do well the two jobs of nurturing and working.

In considering two-provider families, it is useful to distinguish between two-worker and two-career families because their motivations, benefits, and costs are markedly different. As we saw in the section on nuclear families, many working-class mothers work to make ends meet. Jobs for both parents are a necessity rather than an option in the blue-collar and lower-middle classes. These are the two-worker families. Since the 1960s their numbers have increased sharply as mothers of preschoolers have entered the labor market because of the rising cost of living and of raising children, and because opportunities in service occupations have increased with the advent of affirmative action.

In contrast, the two-career family with preschoolers is a relatively new phenomenon. Its development is associated with a changing perspective on the status and roles of women brought about by the women's movement. The change has resulted in greater numbers of women entering higher education and professional education; smaller family size; and women's awareness of their increased life expectancy and of their vulnerability arising from the high rate of divorce. A career presents a new and higher social status and role for middle-class women, many of whom now aspire to both a career and motherhood. Because of an inflated economy and costly lifestyles among young well-educated adults, many two-career families also feel a financial need for two incomes.

Moen (1983) reported that most research on the consequences of work in two-provider families has been done on two-career families, so less is known of the consequences for two-worker families. It is likely that the requirements of the jobs in two-worker families are less flexible regarding working hours and individual discretion than the work in two-career families; the result is less freedom to deal with family concerns. Two-worker families may have to make do with juggling schedules, compromising needs, or just letting things slide. Many such families attempt to solve the problem of child care by each parent's working a different shift. However, this solution reduces the time the couple have together, and parents who work the afternoon shift report they have less time with their children. In contrast, two-career families have the financial resources to purchase quality child care, housekeeping services, and dining out. It is also easier for them to make arrangements with their employer in order to cover unanticipated family emergencies. The implications of all this underscore the plight of the solo parent, who faces alone the difficult and challenging tasks of working and nurturing, while not having access to quality child care and other services because of low income and the lack of adequate subsidized services.

Among two-career families are spouses or partners who live apart at a geographic distance imposed by their worksite locations and who come together only on weekends or at longer intervals. They represent an extreme separation of work and family life that began with the industrial revolution, when the family changed from being a production unit to being a distributive unit. In their study of commuter families, Gerstel and Fross reported that the commuter couples missed most the taken-for-granted qualities [in family life]. They missed coming home at the end of the day and saying, "Let's jump in a cab and go see a film and go to a restaurant"(1985:60). They missed trivial sharing such as events at the office. Another spouse reported, "Now we don't have time . . . to do things together. You know, talking and going places"(1985:61). It is not known how many of the 20 million two-career families consist of commuter couples, but estimates range from 500,000 to 2 million.

Moen's (1983) review of the research suggests that for many mothers in both types of two-provider families, identity, self-esteem, and a sense of competence are significant plus factors. But in two-worker families, such satisfactions depend on the characteristics of the job, since some jobs lead to depression and dissatisfaction. The U.S. Department of Labor reported in 1980 that 90 percent of full-time homemakers do not wish to work outside the home (Bianchi and Spain 1984). In a 1988 letter to the editor of the *New York Times*, one woman wrote:

> It is upsetting that homemakers' work is so undervalued in this society, not only by men, but also by women who are unable or unwilling to stay at home themselves. . . . It is also insulting to women who choose to remain in the home. Has it occurred to anyone recently that the best people to raise children are their parents? I worry that women will be mentally coerced into thinking that childrearing is best done by "experts." My presence at home allows my children a break from the pressures and regimentation of school. . . . It used to take courage for a woman to go out into the work force. Now it appears to take more courage to stay at home.

Clearly, what is needed is maximum free choice and available options for all women and men. And social workers need to guard against assuming without evidence that a woman who is a homemaker would rather be working outside the home.

Moen (1983) observed that as two-provider families proliferate (because in most instances it takes two earners to support a family today), individual solutions to work–family strains will not suffice. Needed societal solutions include greatly increased provision of quality child care; options in work hours and schedules; job sharing in certain occupations; parental leave following childbirth (which is beginning to increase for both parents); reduced working hours and work responsibilities when children are small; and disability leave during children's illness or other family crises—without sacrifice of position, benefits, or status.

The acceptance of such changes toward an optimal balance between family and workplace will rest on continuing modifications in the gendered roles of women and men. What have been defined as personal troubles must now be redefined as public issues (Schwartz 1961). It is heartening that some larger employers are providing day care services to their personnel, either on-site or through financial subsidies. But the magnitude of the need also requires public policies and financing. Given 1) the growing prevalence of two-provider families and solo parents, 2) the risk to women of being without a profession, and 3) the need for two incomes to raise a family, a nation cannot afford to have more than half its young children in unsupervised, makeshift, or poor-quality substitute care as is the case today in the United States. Many Western societies less affluent than ours, as well as China and Japan, now provide maternity and paternity leave and subsidized day care for babies and young children on a universal basis.

These and other issues constitute a body of activity for social workers who are trained in social policy development and programming. Business and industry are increasingly involved in policy issues, and industrial social workers trained in social policy and program development are well equipped to assume responsibilities in such areas of the workplace as personnel and administrative policy development, issues management, government relations, employee relations, community relations, and wellness programs (Rotman 1983). Rotman also stated that social workers can work preventively in the workplace: "For it often takes only one, well-informed, well-researched, and well-communicated opinion to change the entire policy of an organization."

This chapter has presented a view from outside the family that considers how various family forms carry out their functions and tasks as subsystems of the community and society. The view from outside is only half the picture, however, and the next chapter presents a view of family life from inside the family itself.

5

The Family: A View from Within

While living always in a world that builds them, families live
also in the worlds they build themselves, as they always have.
—Gerald Handel

This chapter shifts the perspective from outside the family to its
interior in order to examine certain elements of family life as experienced by the members. The elements are shaped by the following
biological, psychological, social, and cultural forces:

1. The family's transactions with its social, economic, political,
   and physical environments, including a) the societal context
   of oppression and disempowerment; b) the community and
   its institutions, including the formal and informal support
   networks; and c) the mass media, especially television and its
   mythical images of family life;
2. The cultural values and norms of the family as influenced by
   race, ethnicity, religion, occupation and socioeconomic status, and urban or rural location;
3. The personalities of the family members, as well as the parents' earlier experience in their own families of origin;
4. The health status and biological maturation of the family
   members;
5. The internal organization or structure that the family evolves
   and transforms out of its unique experiences over time, including roles and tasks, boundary processes, levels of authority and decision making, and its worldview, myths, and rituals.

The interaction of these features helps shape the behaviors, relationships, and communication patterns that the family creates and recreates among its members over its life course. Their interaction serves also to regulate such common polarities in family life as the tensions between closeness and distance, constancy and change, and authority and self-direction. The chapter presents these matters within a general systems theory (GST), a systems framework of family functioning. That is, the family is conceived of as a system transacting with its environment. The system consists of transacting parts or subsystems, each within a metaphorical boundary. Family members are organized into three types of subsystems: the governing parental pair (or solo parent); the parent–child subsystem; and the sibling subsystem. The transacting parts or subsystems constitute the family, but each subsystem also functions one level down as a system of transacting individuals marked by a metaphorical boundary and transacting with larger environments, including the other family subsystems and the family as a family. (See appendix 2.)

The Feminist Critique of Family Systems Theory

Feminists in the family therapy field assert that the systems assumptions underlying work with families fail to include the societal (historic, social, economic, and political) context in which women are subordinate to men in regard to status, power, and access to resources in a patriarchal social order. They argue that assumptions in systems theory lead many family theorists and practitioners to an implicit acceptance and an explicit reinforcement of oppressive gender-typed family roles and a tendency to take a reciprocal-transactional view of causation that blames the victim in such women's concerns as battering, incest, and rape (Taggart 1985). The omission of the societal context is ironic insofar as one aim in the use of systems theory, at least in social work, was to achieve a conceptual wholeness of people:environment relationships previously fractured by personalistic models that emphasized individual change at the expense of needed social change.

I believe there is nothing inherent in systems ideas that prevents the integration of context. Rather, the absence of such a content may reflect a male bias in our language, thought, epistemology (ways of knowing), and social arrangements. To be true to its own aspirations, GST can and must emphasize that families, like all human systems, are inseparably embedded in the historical, social, cultural, economic, and political context in which they exist. So, too, are theory building and ways of knowing. Thus practitioners, theorists, and researchers, as feminist theory asserts, must examine and come to terms with their own gendered attitudes, beliefs, and values in order to be most effective in helping families recognize theirs. If it does not take context into account, family systems theory (and the practice based on it) will indeed violate gender equality, maintain gendered power relations, and "ignore women's issues, reframe them as something else, or recast them as women's fault" (Taggart 1989:104). Its practice will fail to educate families about the linkages between their own pain and the social order.

The ecological perspective is a systemslike view, but it is closer to the human condition and to people's perceptions of, and responses to, complex environmental forces than are the abstractions of GST. Seeking to understand and to deal with the reality and fullness of human life as inseparable from the environment, the perspective incorporates issues of dominance, power, and oppression. Therefore, in the sections that follow, selected prevailing concepts in family systems theory are presented within an ecological frame of reference that does not ignore issues of an oppressive society and of gendered roles, power relations, and actual or emotional father-absence (Luepnitz 1989) in family life. The perspective also values all family forms, the enlightened self-direction of family members, and the force of cultural difference. Meanwhile, we await the family field's own reconstruction of an integrated theory of family-in-environment that will be wholly free of gender bias.

BOUNDARIES: A METAPHOR FOR CONNECTEDNESS AND SEPARATENESS

In his analysis of the family interior, Minuchin (1974) emphasized that the metaphorical boundaries a family places around itself and its subsystems must be clear and firm but permeable. They must be firm enough so that 1) the family remains free from undue intrusiveness by outsiders, thereby maintaining integrity and self-direction in its own affairs; 2) the parents protect their relationship to each other from manipulation or interference by the children, thereby sustaining optimal parental unity on child-rearing practices; and 3) the sibling relationships are free from undue parental interference, so that the capacity of the siblings to learn from each other and to regulate sibling relationships is safeguarded.

At the same time, however, the metaphorical boundary or "skin" around the family must also be permeable enough to permit the reciprocal exchange of resources with its environment. The boundaries around the governing-adult, parent–child, and sibling subsystems must also be permeable enough to allow for reciprocal need-meeting and the exchange of love, respect, and emotional support within the family. If boundaries are too rigid around the family and/or its subsystems, the family may become disengaged (so that there is an excessive or unwanted distance between the members). If boundaries are too loose, the family may become enmeshed (so that there is excessive or unwanted closeness among the members). For example, in Minuchin's conception of an enmeshed family, the subjective stress experienced by one member is apt to spread rapidly across the diffuse subsystem boundaries, causing all members to experience stress. The family may then be immobilized and unable to provide support to the suffering member or to manage the stressor effectively. In a disengaged family, subjective stress in one member, unless unduly severe, may not reverberate across its rigid subsystems boundaries to the degree needed to generate protection and support from the other members and subsystems, or to deal with the environmental stressor.

Enmeshment and disengagement are relational styles. Most families experience some degree of enmeshment and disengagement that is appropriate at various points in the family's life course, such as early infancy and late adolescence, respectively. But enmeshment or disengagement that is at the extremes, or that is out of synchrony with individual or family transitions, can lead to blockages in need meeting and/or to maladaptive behaviors that interfere with the continued growth and development of the members. The family's relationships with formal support systems such as social agencies, schools, and clinics can also be understood in boundary terms. If the family's metaphorical boundary is too diffuse (as in extreme enmeshment), the family will not be able to develop and use its own internal resources to cope with stressors. It may then lose control over its own affairs and become increasingly involved with external controlling institutions:

When family-agency boundaries are diffuse, frequently the agency will define the family's problems for it [indeed, in patriarchal fashion, may reframe contextually-induced problems as the family's weaknesses or disorganization], become entangled in aspects of the family's life that are not the purview of the particular agency, and alternate between overprotecting family members and becoming exasperated with them. (Coppersmith 1983:89)

If the family's metaphorical boundary is too rigid (as in extreme disengagement), the family may not be able to seek or use needed outside information and other resources: "Rigid boundaries may be characterized by a family's stereotyped denial of entry to other systems, and isolation from extrafamilial information" (Coppersmith 1983:89). As important as this observation may be, it ignores the reality that formal support systems themselves sometimes have rigid boundaries, manifested in unrealistic, self-serving eligibility requirements; location and hours that restrict accessibility; cultural and language incongruences; and so on. These make it difficult for many families to obtain and use needed supports, information, and other resources. The ecological perspective also underscores the significance of who or what is drawing the family's metaphorical boundary. Is it the family itself, acting out of self-direction? Or is it an external force such as a social institution, a social value, or a community norm that presumes to define who is within the family and who is not?

The threshold of the family's dwelling is regarded as one actual boundary marking off its inner private space from the public world outside. Cooper (1976) suggested that the location of the threshold vis-à-vis the outside world may be symbolic of how the family members relate to the rest of society. For example, a social worker wrote of a home visit to explore alternatives to psychiatric hospitalization for Jane, the family's 18-year-old daughter:

> The house is the most forlorn in a remote lane of small houses. The bushes in front are overgrown, obscuring the number-plate and making the house difficult to locate. . . . The most striking aspect is that all interior doors are closed and locked. Mrs. Hall explained that Jane locks her door so they keep the others locked as well. To add to the air of isolation from the outside world, all the drapes on the front of the house are closed. Jane has chased her mother several times with a paring knife, so Mrs. Hall now leaves only the back door unlocked in order to get out and away from Jane if it becomes necessary.

The hidden threshold, the closed drapes, the locked doors, and the location of the only escape route at the back of the house mark an almost impregnable boundary around the family's territory. The thick metaphorical wall permits little or no nutritive exchange with the outside world of neighborhood and community. The locked doors in the interior suggest the emotional distance between the family members, as well as disturbed interactional patterns. Indeed, the total presentation suggests the family's image of itself as being in constant danger from within and without.

Cultural features are also found in boundary management. Sluzki (1983a) provided an example:

> In bilingual people, the choice of language has a symbolic meaning in and by itself—as languages are tied to contexts, memories, experiences, life periods, and relationships. They are clear markers of allegiances as well as reminders of many family rules. The choice of one language over another for a given transaction may automatically establish a boundary by means of including some and excluding other family members, according to their knowledge of the language. The choice of a language may define even the tone or climate of a given situation; for instance, bilingual couples may . . . show a tendency to fight in one language and to converse about neutral subjects in another; there are bilingual families in which discipline is imparted in one language and praise in another; in some of these families the choice of language will define the participants as engaged in a parent-child relationship or in a peer relationship (regardless of the present age of the participants.(1983a:75)

Draper (1979) described how a group of black teenagers succeeded in excluding their two white student group workers by the use of black English in group interaction. In a similar way, the formal vocabulary and construction of standard English used by a middle-class social worker may bewilder or even anger a poor black client. Language as an instrument of racism, sexism, and other forms of oppression is examined in chapter 9.

Triadic process is another kind of boundary issue. It refers to the formation of a two-person subsystem that excludes a third person, and it is usually characterized by inappropriate generational boundaries. In family life, triangles may appear briefly or may have a stable existence over time. For example, in a moment of tension a mother and son may move close and exclude father. But as the situation shifts and the tension subsides, the triangle may resolve or may be replaced by a different one. Should the triangle persist, however, it will become dysfunctional as the father–son relationship slowly erodes, and the parenting of the son is provided by the mother instead of being vested in both parents. In another example, a grandmother living with the family seeks to protect a child from the father's unwarranted scolding when he returns home one evening overly tired from his job. Grandmother and child form a momentary benign alliance against the father that may soon shift to an alliance between the father and the grandmother against the child in another matter, or between the father and the child against the grandmother in still another. But if the first triangle, for example, should remain stable over time, then parental authority and responsibility will be undermined, and the process will become maladaptive. Benign or neutral triangles shift depending on the situation, while maladaptive triangles are rigid and unchanging regardless of the situation.

A dysfunctional triadic process of scapegoating can be observed in some families. As described by Vogel and Bell (1968), the parents unite against the child as a way of deflecting their own and others' attention away from the disturbed marital relationship. The parents project their conflict onto the child, who acts it out in disruptive behavior. The focus on the child's behavior relieves the tension between the adult partners. This may help the family to continue existing, but it is damaging to the child's development. It is said that secondary gains sometimes accrue to the scapegoated child, such as increased attention from the parents and others in response to the behavior induced by scapegoating. Both the relief of marital tension and the child's secondary gains then help sustain the maladaptive transactional pattern despite the child's pain (perhaps an example of blaming the victim). Similarly, two siblings may align themselves against a third. Such temporary alignments happen among most siblings, but when the third sibling is systematically isolated, the triadic process becomes maladaptive. Members of a social work group may scapegoat one member who represents a feared or despised aspect of the members (Shulman 1967).

Families and external systems can also involve each other in triadic processes. These are sometimes seen in child welfare services where two parties in the multiparty system of agency, practitioner, child, foster parents, and natural parents may form a maladaptive coalition against a third. Coppersmith reported, "An examination of families who were chronically involved with public agencies over several generations revealed that such families were part of enduring triads, characterized either by conflicted relationships among the several systems 'helping' the family, or between the family itself and an agency" (1983:89).

Certain triangles that are maladaptive in nuclear families may not necessarily be so in extended families, because of the culturally based difference in the structure of the governing pair (Falicov and Brudner-White 1983). Nuclear families are characterized by a marital governing pair, while many extended families manifest a generational governing pair. In the latter instance, marital satisfaction and parental consensus are not essential to the family's continued existence. Hence triangles of mother and child excluding the father, for example, do not represent a hazard to the family. The child may feel somewhat distant from the triangled father but continues to respect his status, role, and authority. In contrast to the centrality of the marital pair as the governing relationship in the nuclear family, the significant or governing axis of the extended family may be father–son as in traditional Chinese and Middle Eastern families, mother–son as in traditional Hindu families, or brother–brother as in families in some African societies. In extended families, including some North American working-class and poor families, as well as ethnic families in transition, the central value is continuity between the generations, so the marital tie is not usually elevated over an intergenerational pair (Falicov and Brudner-White 1983).

This difference creates significant variations in subsystems and their boundaries, levels of authority, and patterns of relationship and communication. Thus a same-generational triangle, as when a husband supports his wife in her efforts to separate from her parents, can be functional for the marital pair but is likely to be very disturbing for families (and perhaps the wife) in those cultures where intergenerational ties are central. However, certain same-generation triangles in extended families can be beneficial. For instance, "In extended networks, the permeable boundaries around the nuclear [unit] allow frequent inclusion of adult siblings or other relatives. They can fulfill many instrumental functions, reduce tensions and diffuse conflict" (Falicov and Brudner-White 1983:60). Falicov and Brudner-White concluded that triangles are inherently neutral. They derive their adaptive or maladaptive character in part from their fit or lack of fit with the family's underlying "cultural code," which defines boundaries, authority levels, and power relations. Hence, understanding the nature of the governing pair in any given family is preliminary to determining the purpose and function of its triangular structures.

THE FEMINIST CRITIQUE OF THE BOUNDARY CONCEPT

The feminist position holds that boundary concepts reflect male values of separateness, power, and control and negate the female values of connectedness and intimacy (Hare-Mustin 1978). The notion of boundary is said to create a conceptual barrier that conceals from the family and the practitioner the family's and the practitioner's embeddedness in society. It also conceals from both how the family and the (nonfeminist) practitioner reflect the patriarchal context of sexist values, norms, and practices. I believe this obfuscation is not inherent in the boundary metaphor but is the consequence of unwitting and witting uses to which it is put and the fallacy of misplaced concreteness. In the ecological perspective, for example, a boundary is not a metaphorical barrier. It is conceived of as a metaphorical interface where inner and outer meet. It is at the interface where the family (or the community or individual) and the environment engage in reciprocal exchanges and interpenetrate each other (Gordon 1969). The family lives in environments and a culture, and the environments and culture "live" in the family members.

The interface, then, is a metaphorical arena of connectedness for individuals, families, and communities, including intimacy, attachments, and relatedness. It can also be an arena of separateness, either desired (as in privacy or solitude) or unwanted (as in loneliness and isolation). Sadly, it is also the arena where racism, sexism, and other forms of coercive power exert their sway as environmental aspects of the society. From the perspective on a boundary as an interface, it is difficult if not impossible to ignore the influence of historical, political, and societal structures and beliefs on family and individual functioning.

The feminist critique of the triangle or generational boundary metaphor is directed to practitioners' misreading of certain alliances that are related to the patriarchal context, as in "the alliance of the powerless mother and child against the powerful father or the father and child against the demanding mother," whose demandingness is likely to be related to her inferior status and subordinate role (Hare-Mustin 1978). Hare-Mustin's observation underscores the necessity to consider restrictive gender-role stereotypes and their psychological impact on family members in seeking to understand a family's patterns, including their shifting triangles. Triangles—dysfunctional and functional—are observable phenomena; the practice question is how the needs underlying dysfunctional ones can be met in a healthier way.

The feminist critique also views the metaphorical relationship styles of enmeshment and disengagement, as well as the alleged imputation of pathology, as mirroring a masculine bias, despite Minuchin's (1974) useful idea that degrees of either are actually appropriate at certain points in the family's life course. Common concerns among family therapists include enmeshed and fused family relationships. These relationships are viewed as pathological, while less concern is expressed about isolation and disengagement in family life. For example, Goldner observed, " 'Care' now becomes 'infantilization,' 'empathy' becomes 'intrusiveness,' and 'attachment' now is labelled 'enmeshment' " (1987:113)—which appear to me to be unwarranted exaggerations. Taggart suggested that the sexist values implicit in male theorists' naming of basic concepts that describe human relatedness leave few positive models of that relatedness. These criticisms are quite inappropriate, given the fact that male theorists developed the humane concepts of attachment (Bowlby 1969) and human relatedness (Sullivan 1953; Will 1959), while the theorist who was most responsible for the normative emphasis on separateness and individuation in human development, and who was most influential in the attribution of pathology to dependence, was a woman (see the section in Appendix 1 on Mahler). The concepts of interdependence, attachment, and human relatedness are significant elements of the ecological perspective in social work, and they receive detailed attention throughout part 2.

LEVELS: A METAPHOR FOR AUTHORITY STRUCTURES

Minuchin (1974) contended that the family must construct a structure of authority and decision making in which parents and children have different levels of authority, in contrast to former structures of unshared patriarchal power in family life. The family is not a society of peers. It is the parents' responsibility, based on their love, knowledge, and experience, to establish expectations for conduct and to make decisions for the protection and guidance of the child. By providing a structure of clear expectations, the parents actually prepare the way for the child's growth in self-direction. In toddlerhood, for example, many parents encourage and accept some decisions by the child that do not interfere with her or his health and safety ("Which sweater do you want to wear?"). Later, more leeway is extended to the schoolchild for age-appropriate decision making and responsibility in certain areas. At some points along the way, parents and children may undertake democratic decision making in family plans and issues. Kantor and Lehr observed:

> Conflicts over the extent to which the family should be allowed to control individual lives invariably arise. But if [family organization] is marked by either extreme freedom or extreme restraint, other potential problems arise. Thus if members feel totally free to do whatever they wish, anarchy can result. . . . At the other extreme, [total restraint] can produce conditions of tyranny, in which members are not allowed to do what they want, choose what they want, say what they think, or, for that matter, even dare to dwell on what they start to think. (1975:49–50)

Dysfunctional parental subsystems may manifest either insufficient or excessive control (authority) that stifles the child's development and growth in self-direction. But even in the best of situations, issues of authority and expectations may become difficult as teenage children engage in the age-appropriate quest for increased self-direction. In response, parents may impose excessive controls or may refuse to modify expectations of conduct that are no longer appropriate. The ensuing conflict requires negotiation and mutual accommodation by both the child and the parents for their mutual growth.

Explicit expectations regulating behavior within the family derive from the family's cultural values and norms, which define desirable or permissible conduct and proscribe other behavior. These expectations also derive from commonly accepted social and community norms. In this era of rapid social change, which is reshaping family forms and functions, new, more relevant standards are slow to evolve. The slow development of new norms leaves many families with uncertainty and confusion about what is right and wrong (Walsh 1983), especially in the case of gender roles and their underlying values and norms.

FAMILY WORLDVIEW

In contrast to explicit expectations that guide the socialization of family members and the organization of the interior life of the family, implicit family rules are more powerful regulators of behavior. They can result in self-perpetuating interactional patterns that limit variety and increase the chances that a particular problem-behavior sequence will occur. Not all implicit rules and repetitive sequences, however, are maladaptive. Actually, some regularities contribute to the sense of family identity and constancy. Implicit or covert rules that result in dysfunctional issues, relationships, and communications in the family include restrictive prescriptions for stereotyped gender behavior. Maladaptive behavior may also result from the family's worldview (Sluzki (1983b). Individuals develop personal constructions of their social realities, or worldview, in order to organize and explain their experiences. They project their constructions onto the social world, assuming them to be true copies of the actual social world, and use them as guides to action (Berger and Luckmann 1966). Families also develop worldview or explanatory systems. Indeed, the family worldview is the most important influence in shaping the personal explanatory systems of the family members.

Reiss (1981) termed the family's worldview "the family paradigm." He defined it as a framework of shared, out-of-awareness assumptions about the family's social world. It is held by the members despite their disagreements, conflicts, and differences. The family's basic patterns arise from its unique paradigm and may continue across generations of the same family or may be added to or modified over time. The paradigm also guides the family's transactions with its environment. In turn, the family's experiences in the environment determine which of the available social environments the family selects and the kind of linkages it establishes with the environment. For Reiss, these linkages include the family's conspicuousness in the community, the openness of its metaphorical boundary to relationships and experiences in the community, and the depth of its engagement in the community. The paradigm is created not only out of the family's transactions with its social world of kin, community or neighborhood, and formal organizations but also by disempowerment and oppression in the social, political, economic, and historical environments. And finally, family:environment transactions reinforce central assumptions of the paradigm that designed them in the first place.

FAMILY MYTHS

Family myths are a component of the worldview, and they, too, are influenced by the societal context. They may reinforce oppressive views of women or minority populations or may correct them and thereby transmit healthy values and behavioral norms to the children. It is out of real and fantasied experiences in historical and present time that families weave their mythical stories of the family's past and present, as well as its future destiny. Sluzki (1983b) suggested that family history itself is a mythology insofar as it represents agreed-upon meanings attributed to events and experiences.

In Hartman and Laird's (1983) multigenerational perspective, the family is linked to the parents' families of origin by the patterned elements in the family history over several generations. These include occupations and socioeconomic statuses; major moves; given names, identifications, attributions, and role assignments; health, illness, and causes of death; family villains and heroic figures; losses; emotional cutoffs; secrets; and disruptive life events. Data on such critical features in the family history and their impact on the current members are gained by the family and the practitioner together through the dynamic use of the genogram, an intergenerational map of the family similar to a family tree (Laird 1983:215). Mythical processes may be involved in several features of any family's genogram—most especially but not exclusively in stories of heroic or villainous figures, disruptive events, and identifications. Family myths provide a base for understanding a family's implicit rules and other processes. While the myths may be about events and processes that never actually occurred, their thematic content and process can play themselves out in the current situation—for good or for ill.

FAMILY RITUALS

Hartman and Laird (1983) pointed out that little is known about how families' meaning and belief systems are formed and transmitted and how they retain their power. They suggested, however, that the family paradigm and the concept of ritual connect with each other in ways that may shed light on how family themes develop and persist. By nature, rituals are stylistic, repetitive, ordered ceremonies. They prescribe the behaviors of the individual or the group, embodying the should's and ought's of its implicit rules. Rituals may make use of symbolic objects, action, music, drama, dance, or other evocative media. Rituals may be public, such as singing the national anthem at athletic events, or private, such as compulsive personal behaviors; political, such as presidential inaugurations; professional, such as national social work conferences; religious, such as sacred rites; or secular, such as rites of passage celebrated in public or private. Family rituals are part of the family's own unique culture derived, in part, from the partners' families of origin and the larger cultural group and, in part, from the family's own experience. Rituals help shape themes and transactional patterns in family life and may contribute to constancy in the family. They make manifest the worldview or family paradigm and its societal context. When rituals cover up distasteful facts, however, they may take on a hypocritical quality (Turner 1982). Mother's Day comes to mind as an example—if it represents one day off a year from domestic chores that a family considers the mother's exclusive responsibility.

Especially important in family life are rites of passage, those rituals surrounding critical life issues, individual transitions, and family transformations. They include ritualistic or ceremonial observances, religious and/or secular, of the biological processes of birth, sexual maturation, and death, as well as ritualistic recognition of social processes such as graduation, a new job, a promotion, retirement, an engagement, a marriage, anniversaries, a new home, an adoption, or a return from war. Thus rituals help families to cope with change or discontinuity. Negative or negatively perceived social transitions, with the exception of unwanted retirement, do not have rituals to help ease the associated anxiety, although some families are beginning to create their own rituals. Such transitions include separation and divorce, the establishment or discontinuance of gay or lesbian partnerships, departure from home in late adolescence, geographic moves, miscarriage and stillbirth, parents' loss of a child to foster care and the child's loss of parents in such instances, job loss, and prolonged hospitalization—all of which are marked by required changes in the family's organization of roles, functions, and tasks. Some may be associated with negative feelings, some with social stigma, and some with both. They are considered throughout part 2.

At the community level, rituals of celebration, such as a military parade and marching bands, or of degradation, such as admissions procedures in a public psychiatric hospital, carry significant social messages.

Laird pointed out that rituals can be destructive, such as drinking rituals and rituals "used to avoid contact, to suppress information, to forestall change, or to disallow the expression of feeling" (1984) She suggested also that in our society rituals appear to be losing their celebratory character and are taking on a cloak of avoidance—avoidance of communication, of connections with the past, or of valued meanings. She cited Bronfenbrenner's (1972) warning that ritualized television watching is an act of passive participation that substitutes for the games, spirited conversation, and shared activities that characterized some family life in the recent past. And she noted that many families now eat their meals in silence in front of the television.

Before the advent of this custom, not only did children learn eating etiquette and manners at the family dinner table, "but also the general roles, rules, and values of family living coalesce in this setting. The child is exposed to such things as age and sex roles [perhaps traditional or perhaps new], family membership roles, values centering about religious observances, bodily functions, sensuous enjoyment, and the expression of feelings" (Dreyer and Dreyer 1973).

And finally, family rituals can be adaptive or maladaptive: they may open closed communication channels, restore fractured relationships, and help reconstruct more salutary arrangements of the family's interior life; or they may defend maladaptive myths, reinforce illusions, reflect women's powerless status, and perpetuate dysfunctional rules. For example, in some families, holiday rituals contribute to pleasurable feelings and a shared identity among the members. In other families, they are dreaded for their rigidity, hypocrisy, and emptiness. And some families may even be underritualized (Hartman and Laird 1983).

SPACE AND TIME IN FAMILY LIFE

Space and Spatial Behaviors

Inside the family, territorial behaviors serve to regulate social interaction, thereby helping to reduce conflict and distorted communication. A family may stake out such territories as the father's chair, the children's places at table, and the mother's books and tapes. These territories provide important cues to others, help make role relationships and family expectations explicit (e.g., a younger sibling may not wear the clothing of an older sibling without her permission, or a child must knock before entering the parents' bedroom), and thus stabilize social organization. Territorial behaviors are also important means of defining the family and its members and so contribute to the sense of personal and family identity.

Kantor and Lehr observed, "Certain places tend to become more important than others for each subsystem of the family. The parent's bed, the children's treehouse . . . the T/V area . . . the dining room table, and the back porch can all become special gathering places for members; [becoming] regions in which the most intimate and meaningful activities of a family's life take place" (1975:42). Where dwelling space is constricted, togetherness at meals or in other common or overlapping activity may not be possible. Spatial conflicts can arise from unmet needs for privacy and solitude. In one study of the physical environment, the bathroom was said to serve some families as a library, a telephone booth, a think tank, a refuge from other family members, or even a locale for suicide, in addition to its original purpose (Kira 1966).

Kantor and Lehr (1975) noted that families develop spatial guidelines for organizing their shared space. They establish safety zones for their members inside the dwelling, its outside territory, the neighborhood, and the community. Spatial guidelines, part of the family's explicit or implicit rules, mark how far members of different ages and sexes may safely venture on their own. Without such guidelines, family members may manifest disturbed spatial behaviors and may lack a cohesive and coherent view of themselves and the family itself. For example, Henry (1973:36, 76) described how Mrs. Jones, despite her obvious love for her baby daughter, let her run toward the road and get into dangerous spaces repeatedly. In the house, there is a general tendency toward spatial disorder, with objects out of place and containers in a state of total confusion:

When Dr. Jones enters, space erupts: objects hurtle through space, children fling themselves at him, objects crash and sometimes break. Time, which hung empty, suddenly becomes crowded with events that burst like rockets on Dr. Jones and all around him, as the boys run from their room and "mow him down" on the stairs and the baby stands up in her crib and crows. Time, space, motion, objects and children are activated.

Time and Temporal Behaviors

Families—like individuals, organizations, languages, cultures, and societies—possess idiosyncratic orientations to time derived from cultural values. The temporal orientation shapes the members' temporal behaviors, or the ways in which they organize, use, and respond to time. The inner life of the family can be considered in the context of differing social cycles of time. Cycles of individual behavior are partly governed by biological rhythms, which provide the framework for daily routines. Individuals are also subject to such social rhythms as the weekly cycles, in which Monday, for example, is different from Saturday in terms of weekly activities; monthly cycles, in which bills are paid and the rent falls due; and annual cycles related to the seasons in which vacations and leisure pursuits may fall. Idiosyncratic cycles having to do with family or work life may be recurrent even though unrelated to the more standard periodicities. At any given moment, a person is locked into several different cycles with different periods, and his or her behavior is influenced by all of them as they operate simultaneously (Young and Ziman 1971).

In family life, "Individual cycles need to be synchronized or harmonized, brought into agreement, changed in phase or period, so that significant events may always occur simultaneously" (Young and Ziman 1971). This harmony is usually achieved by subordinating a dependent cycle to the more precise cycle or the more dominant routine. The work cycle, for example, governs the sleep–waking cycle of the parents, which, in turn, governs the sleep cycle of the children, who may have to get up for an early breakfast if a parent is to drive them to school. Meshing, however, can be difficult to achieve because of variations in members' biological rhythms. For example, infants and their mothers sometimes have difficulty synchronizing family schedules with the infants' sleep and hunger rhythms. An elderly relative in the home may find it difficult to adapt to slight changes in schedules or routines, and the result may be temporal conflicts. Also, night and swing shifts may damage health and restrict the worker's time with partner, children, and family friends. Cromwell, Keeney, and Adams citing Moore (1963) declared, "For policemen, hospital workers, firemen, watchmen, and other night shift workers, 'the problem of temporal coordination creates a kind of dilemma: either they must have a minimal relationship with their families and with other "normally" timed activities, or their families will be off-phase with the standard patterns of the community' " (1976).

Also, family members can be out of temporal phase with one another. Their intersecting temporal cycles of actions, feelings, and needs may not mesh. This lack of synchrony is seen when family members have differing orientations to time. One partner may be interested mainly in the past, the other in the future. Family members may have different responses to the pacing and rhythm of their shared life processes and events. For some, the tempo of family life may be too fast or too slow, too variable or too rigid. Some prefer routines, while others view the unexpected and the irregular as delights. Like all differences, these can lead to vitality and zest in family relationships, but at the extreme, they may become sources of conflict. Some family members may find that they have less time together than they desire because of overscheduling of events, while others find that they spend too much time together. In either case, preferences regarding private time and shared time do not coincide. Members may have differing definitions of what constitute good times and bad times, hard times and easy times, wild times and dull times. In all these and other ways, time is the "silent language" (Hall 1973) that speaks of potentiality and limits, as well as change and permanence, in family life.

FAMILY DEVELOPMENT AS SEQUENTIAL STAGES

Probably the first social work framework for examining family development was introduced by Pollack (1960). He viewed the family as a system of relationships that comprises three units with different relationship tendencies. In the long run, the spouse subsystem tends toward increasing closeness, while the parent–child and sibling subsystems tend toward decreasing closeness. However, these are temporarily blurred by short-run relationship tendencies that seem contrary. For example, Pollack believed that the adult partners must move apart somewhat in order to permit the necessary mother–child closeness during infancy. The healthy family was said to experience four developmental stages, construed as functions in marriage before the arrival of children, during child rearing, when the children leave, and after they have left. Constructed on the marital axis, the framework presents four sets of reciprocal need-meeting functions of the marital pair that differ at each stage: relatedness and security in care, as well as sharing; sexual functions; economic functions; and ego-strengthening functions.

A product of its time, this framework assumed a universal nuclear form of two parents and at least one child. It defined healthy families in terms of traditional gender roles and middle-class values and standards. Nevertheless, Pollack's (1960) ideas succeeded in moving many social caseworkers back to casework's original focus on the family and away from an exclusive focus on the intrapsychic difficulties of an individual member—even before psychiatry's "discovery" of the family in the 1960s. Two other social workers introduced similar family developmental frameworks (O'Connell 1972; Rhodes 1977). Both conceptions rest on Erikson's theory of individual development and functioning (see the section in Appendix 1 on Erikson) with adaptive tasks for the parental couple that parallel Erikson's individual tasks. Both adopted Erikson's epigenetic timetable and its assumption that the tasks of one stage must be successfully completed if those of the next stage are to be handled effectively.

A strength of the three frameworks lay in their purposeful efforts to consider the parallel development of adult and child members of the family as they negotiate their respective life tasks. But the absence of attention to differences that arise from ethnicity, socioeconomic status, religion, poverty, family form, and the historical context of male dominance and female subordination can lead to serious errors in understanding family development and change. Also, the frameworks reflected an assumption that the development of the family-as-system follows predictable, sequential stages in the same way that individual development in personality theories was construed. It is doubtful that universal, predictable family stages and tasks fit the complexities in family development today, if indeed they ever did. How, then, does the family as an emotional, social, and cultural system change and develop over its life course, while sustaining the necessary degree of stability?

FAMILY DEVELOPMENT AS NONSTAGE TRANSFORMATIONS

The position taken in this book is that a conception of family development based on the various common and unique *life issues* confronting a family over its life course is more dynamic and closer to contemporary families' experience than constructions based on universal sequential stages. Life issues may be generated by internal pressures arising from members' biological maturational changes; nondevelopmental status transitions; idiosyncratic troubles; external pressures arising from cultural imperatives and the societal context of racism and sexism and other abuses of power; or from other exchanges between the environment and the family or individual members. In order to cope effectively with such life issues as they come along, the family must modify its form or structure of roles and tasks.

Reiss (1981) presented a research-based model of how family change occurs. As mentioned earlier, families hold shared but implicit assumptions about themselves and their environment. A difficult life issue such as job loss, if it is to be managed successfully, may require a change in the family's worldview and in the family's accustomed patterns of behavior. At first, the family may try to cope with the issue in their accustomed ways. When these do not work, the family is apt to experience confusion. Implicitly understood rules that shaped family life may be lost as a result, and they are replaced by upsets in relationships, negative feelings and irritation, contradictory communications, and rigid systems of control. At that point, the family is said to be in acute stress. It may then disintegrate further or it may achieve self-healing by making qualitative changes. In the latter instance, the family restructures its belief system or worldview and thereby reshapes family roles, tasks, rules, and routines to integrate the life issue. A new family paradigm emerges: the family has changed itself. By such a "spontaneous evolutionary leap to a new integration . . . a set of new patterns appears that could not have been predicted from past functioning and that deal better with the new conditions" (Hoffman 1980:56). Examples are considered in part 2.

Terkelsen (1980) suggested that such a leap or family transformation is a process that includes 1) *insertion*—a new need (life issue) is recognized and validated by family members, thereby activating new behavioral sequences to meet the need; 2) *destabilization*—family behaviors become more variable and conflicted; and frustration, anxiety, and uncertainty appear; and 3) *resolution*—a new organization gradually takes shape as the novel element is integrated into the ongoing organization, which is now minus one or more former elements. It is this deletion of outmoded elements that generates the variability in family behavior during the change and the accompanying sense of loss and feelings of anger, hurt, sadness, and so on.

Terkelsen illustrated this process with a description of what might happen when a 5-year-old learns to dress herself:

> The elements of structure attached to the old need (mother dresses child, and simultaneously engages in reciprocal nurturing by giving attention, physical contact, verbal repartee) drop away. Child and parent seek out new behavioral sequences that allow the child to dress herself, and create an alternative format for reciprocal nurturing. For example: child enters kitchen, announces, "Mommy, I dress myself!" Mother praises her, helps her into a chair, brings her food, and straightens her dress. (1980:35)

Conflict and uncertainty now emerge, triggering behavioral trials in other members:

> Instead of dressing her child, mother now goes directly to the kitchen, and has more time to attend to her husband and two boys. Husband gets fed faster, but now finds himself criticized for reading at breakfast. The boys have more time for verbal repartee with mother, but simultaneously have acquired an increase in maternal supervision of their play. Father, in turn, may object to mother's supervision, initiating a discordant interaction between husband and wife. And so on. (1980:36).

While not mentioned by Terkelsen, this script can be written with the parental roles and actions reversed in whole or in part. As the author suggested, a series of such sequences takes place as the family searches for a new structure to meet the life issue posed by the little girl's growth, with minimal disruption to the meeting of the ongoing needs of other members. The search may be carried out unconsciously or by purposeful trial and error. The new structure will consist of the old structure plus the novel element and minus several now obsolescent elements. A change of operations also takes place in those areas of family life that lie close to the area where the life issue has arisen (in this instance, breakfast routines change).

Terkelsen made a valuable distinction between first and second orders of family change. First-order developments, illustrated by the 5-year-old's emerging ability to dress herself, involve increments of mastery and adaptation (a need to do something) leading to pride and satisfaction, despite the frustrations involved. The family's shared reality (worldview) does not require change. First-order developments occur very frequently over the life course, leading a family to experience itself as being in a state of flux. Second-order developments, such as loss and bereavement, involve changes in status and meaning (a need to be something new). Here, fundamental characteristics of the family must change because of an altered shared reality arising from a life issue that affects family loyalties, affectional and communication patterns, role assignments, worldview, and exchanges with the environment. Second-order developments go beyond mere insertion and deletion by setting in place a new assemblage of behavioral sequences and major changes in structure and meaning. In contrast to first-order developments, second-order developments occur infrequently, so that the family experiences itself as being in a state of constancy.

Reiss' (1981) model of family transformation appears to refer to what Terkelsen called second-order change, while Hoffman's idea of evolutionary leaps appears to refer to what Terkelsen called first-order developments. Terkelsen concluded that flux and constancy proceed together, transforming the family over its life course. Through incremental or first-order changes, the family is continually evolving, while through structural or second-order change, it is being re-formed episodically.

Life Issues, Stress, and Coping

Some life issues can best be understood as challenges and others as stressors. First-order developments, in general, are expectable, often challenging events and processes. For example, developmental transitions such as puberty and status transitions such as school entry are expectable in the life course of most families. Second-order developments are unexpectable, unanticipated events and processes such as grave injury or illness, job loss, family violence, and bereavement. Some life issues that are first-order developments for most people may be experienced as second-order developments by a few. For example, retirement is a challenging, first-order life issue in most families, but it can be a second-order development and major stressor for others, particularly if it is unwanted or comes too early because of illness or because it is forced.

Even the expectable life issues are not necessarily universal and certainly not sequential (except in the instance of biological timetables). Also, families define, experience, and handle challenging or stressful life issues differently according to the meaning that such issues have for a particular family. Meaning depends on many factors: the family's worldview; cultural features and individual personality features; the previous experience of the family; the nature of its environment, including the historical, economic, political, and social context; the family's internal resources, such as an integration of its values, norms, roles, affectional relationships, and resilience; and its external resources, such as adequate income, housing, health care, and other formal and informal supports for dealing with the issue.

Meaning is especially important because serious discrepancies may exist between the perceived and the actual life issue and between the perceived and the actual resources for dealing with it. Such discrepancies may account, in part, for families with seemingly adequate resources who fall apart when confronting a particular life issue, while others with fewer resources manage a similar issue effectively. Furthermore, what is defined as a stressor by one family may be defined as a zestful challenge by another. These are some reasons why ranked lists of so-called critical life-change events have been criticized for their omission of context, culture, and individual differences in meaning.

To summarize, the family copes with the stressful pressures of developmental and status transitions and other life issues by changing its form, structure of roles, tasks, expectations for conduct, routines, rituals, and organization of relationship and communication patterns. New ones must be developed that are more appropriate to the new situation brought about by the life issue. And while the changes are going on, family members must also manage the attendant pain, anxiety, ambiguity, and disruption that can accompany

any change. Successful transformations of the family's structure and organization usually lead to enhanced relatedness, competence, self-direction, and self-esteem in the members and therefore to enhanced functioning of the family-as-system. However, if the family resists needed first- or second-order change and continues outmoded behavioral patterns that now interfere with the needed adaptation and coping, it may become a troubled family in which individual and family development are blocked. At the extreme, it may become a disorganized family facing dissolution through separation, divorce, or the placement of children in substitute care.

A transformational position on family development accommodates more readily than a sequential stage position to variations in family forms, structure, organization, and the cultural and social variance among North American families today. The transformational position is an ecological, nonpathological view of change and constancy in family life as the consequence of complex internal and external life forces and their dynamic interplay. However, it is important to keep in mind throughout this book Reiss' caution about the shared construct of the family paradigm:

> [It] does not ignore the family as a seething cauldron of impulse and affect. But terror, pride, anger, and love—which ... are woven into the ... shared construct—are universals. They are both undifferentiated and undifferentiating because, as raw and unadorned motives of human action, they fail to account for why specific families behave in specific ways. A shared construct ... weaves these nonspecific affective elements into a more organized conception which is meant to account for action. ... It specifies that *this* family behaves in *this* way because, collectively, it is convinced that its social environment is (without a doubt) just *this* kind of a world. (1981:382; italics in the original)

Also, it is not necessarily the case that individual problem behaviors reflect a maladaptive family organization or that such behaviors necessarily serve to hold the family in balance. Too often the differences between pathology and a family's struggle with expectable or nonexpectable life issues—coping as best they can—are ignored. As Minuchin put it (1974:60), families today experience great difficulty in negotiating life issues under rapidly changing social conditions. Their difficulties do not necessarily mean disorganization. Indeed, many families are making adaptive efforts to cope with novel stressful life issues without the necessary societal supports in place. The development of supportive arrangements and institutionalized solutions often lags behind the social changes that make them essential. An example is the unmet need for quality child care despite the large-scale movement of mothers of young children into the work force.

Just as the family responds positively or negatively to individual members' coping efforts, so, too, does the community respond positively or negatively to the family's coping efforts insofar as they are publicly visible via connections to the school, health organizations, the workplace, neighbors, social agencies, and so on. Also, the community may hold certain norms and expectations in regard to coping styles by which family efforts are judged. Negative assessments by the community and its institutions are added stressors, especially if the assessments lead to ostracism and the social isolation of the family.

On what grounds does the community make such judgments? Reiss and Oliveri (1983) suggested that community judgments of the family are based on community perceptions of the degree to which a family is responsible for causing a certain event; of its duty to deal with it; and of its competence or capacity for doing so. Practice experience suggests that negative judgments are most often made about life issues or stressors viewed as being generated by the family's own internal patterns, such as wife battering, sexual abuse, or child neglect; marital conflict or parent–child conflict; criminal and delinquent behaviors; alcoholism or dependence on other drugs; and, in some conservative communities, even unemployment, poverty, physical illness, and emotional disorder.

However, the notion of the family as creator of its own stressful life issues is controversial. Croog (1970) pointed out that almost any stressor seeming to originate in the family actually has ultimate roots outside the family. For example, the above-mentioned internally generated stressors may represent maladaptive efforts to cope with earlier stress that originated in external arenas such as the school, the workplace, the social network, the economy, or the societal context of oppression. In recursive fashion, however, stressful life issues that originate in external arenas such as the workplace may have been generated by maladaptive behavioral patterns or interactions in the family. So the origin of family stressors is an empirical and theoretical question not yet answered satisfactorily.

Families that function at an optimal level have been found to buffer or mediate stress for their members. Such families demonstrate some combination of internal and external resources, including resilience and open communication; seeking and using information and financial or other resources; and drawing on informal supports (Lieberman 1982; Evans and Northwood 1979; Pilisuk and Froland 1978; Cobb

1976; Finlayson 1976). It is also likely that a family's ability to cope with stressful life issues depends on the efficacy of the institutionalized solutions provided by the particular culture, the community, or social institutions (Mechanic 1974a). In many instances, their absence is due to the social lag described above.

This chapter concludes part 1, which presented selected concepts and research findings about particular aspects of communities, social networks, formed groups, bureaucratic organizations, and various forms of the family and its organizing processes and transformations. Part 2 takes up selected theories and research findings on the tandem growth and development of all family members—infant, child, youth, adults, and elderly—and several family transformations over time. Chapter 6 sets the stage by considering the formation of a new family.

II

The Tandem Development of Family Members in Their Environment

Introduction: The Concept of Life Course

With the community, societal, and familial context of human development and functioning having been presented in part 1, we are ready to take up individual and family development and functioning in part 2. Its eight chapters make use of a "life course" model of psychosocial development in place of the more traditional "life cycle" models based on stages such as those of Freud (1953), Erikson (1959), Piaget and Inhelder (1969), Kohlberg (1969), Mahler, Pine, and Bergman (1975), Levinson (1978), Vaillant (1977a), and Gould (1980) (see Appendix 1 for a brief description of each).

Fashioned by the collaboration of psychologists, sociologists, anthropologists, and social historians, the "life course" model is transactional. It emphasizes life transitions, life events, and other life issues as outcomes of person(s):environment processes rather than as separate segments of life confined to predetermined ages and stages of experience. The concept of the life course is distinguished from the concept of the life cycle that is based on universal fixed stages of development. The term *life cycle* is meaningless since human lives are not cyclical. The life course is also distinguished from the concept of the life span, which is of limited usefulness because of its linear, one-directional character.

When new data emerge that cannot be explained by an existing model, a new theoretical model is needed. Newly discovered data

149

bearing on psychosocial development (or newly recognized meanings of older data) include cultural differences arising from race, ethnicity, religion, and socioeconomic status; differences in female and male socialization; variations in sexual orientation; the influence of disability; and the effects of powerlessness and oppression. The appearance of new family forms, tremendous shifts in community values and norms, and the critical significance of the environment and world peace to continued life on earth add to the need for a new model of human development.

The new data and new meanings cannot be explained by stage models because these models assume uniform pathways of development that lead to fixed, predictable endpoints, without regard for these powerful differentiating influences. In stage models, each stage must be negotiated at some optimal level during a critical period of development in order for the next stage to be addressed successfully. This is the epigenetic principle derived from embryological development and is inappropriate when applied to emotional and social development. Some stage models also have a limited conception of the environment as consisting merely of the baby's mother. The father becomes significant only toward the end of the first year of life or later, and the siblings later still. Hence, when there are problems in emotional and/or social development, the models have tended to fault the mother. This tendency is diminishing in the face of research findings on the genetic, biochemical, and neurophysiological aspects of some psychopathologies (e.g., Siever 1983; Yahraes 1978) and on the importance and influence of the father in early social and psychological development (e.g., Parke 1981).

In contrast, the life course model accommodates the new data and new meanings. In addition, it acknowledges the self-regulating, self-determining nature of human beings and the indeterminate nature of nonuniform pathways of psychosocial development and social life. In fact, diversity of life paths appears to be a prerequisite for social organization in complex societies such as ours (Freeman 1984). As described by Hareven (1982), the life course conception views life transitions and life events not as isolated, separable, fixed stages, but as ongoing processes, occurring and recurring at any point in the life course. They may be expectable or nonexpectable, stressful or challenging, depending upon uniquely combined influences of personal, cultural, and environmental features. The model also takes account of the merging of individual developmental pathways into collective processes in families, groups, and communities, so that it fits well with the principles of family transformation outlined in chapter 5.

A distinctive contribution of the life course model is its time perspective, that is, its notion that psychosocial development and functioning take place over historical, individual, and social time. For example, periods such as childhood or youth or old age are to be understood in the continuum of the entire life course, including 1) the effects of social change on individual and collective life experience (historical time); 2) the timing of life transitions within both the cultural context and the chronology of family and community life (social time); and 3) individual life history or life story (individual time). Just as anthropological research shows that human development and functioning are relative to different cultures, historical research demonstrates that it is also time-bound (Hareven 1982). Historical time and cohort theory serve as a backdrop for part 2, whereas social time and individual time are the central threads running through all its chapters.

HISTORICAL TIME AND COHORTS

A *birth cohort* is defined as all persons who were born at a particular historical time and thereby exposed to the same sequence of social and historical changes over their life course (Riley 1978). Members of a birth cohort experience the developmental process of growing up and growing older differently from the members of every other birth cohort because they live through different historical and social processes or through the same processes but at different ages. For example, people who were elderly in 1900 had been shaped emotionally, socially, and behaviorally by life experiences and historical forces totally different from those that have been shaping people who will be elderly in 2000.

Characteristics of the cohort itself affect individual life conditions. Cohorts differ in size and sex ratios. Smaller cohorts may have more productive educational experiences, more opportunities in the world or work, and a quicker rise in their economic status. Differences in sex ratios across cohorts affect pairing and parenting opportunities (Riley 1985a). As the members of the cohort grow up and grow older together, their collective lives can set off social changes that affect different cohorts differently. Riley (1985a) pointed out that the cohorts of young women in the late 1960s and early 1970s—responding to many shared experiences—developed common patterns of response, common definitions, and common norms. As a collective force, they pressed for change in social roles and social values. The next cohorts of young women and some young men brought the new ideas into the open, institutionalized them, and began the transformation of gendered roles and attitudes in the family and the workplace. This transformation led, in turn, to demands for new social policies and structures, such as expanded child care arrangements, flexible hours, maternal and paternal leaves, laws against sex discrimination and sexual harassment, and equal pay for comparable worth—all of which changed the life patterns of many of today's cohort of young women and men, as well as the developmental experience of their children.

The life patterns of each cohort are influenced by unique sequences of social changes in the family, the school, the workplace, and the community; in ideas, values, beliefs, science, technology, and the arts; and in patterns of migration, fertility, and mortality (Riley, 1985b). Within each cohort, however, there are individual differences due to personality and cultural features, as well as different life experiences and life conditions, that are more forceful influences on development than are cohort influences. Nonetheless, the latter add important social and historical dimensions to individual phenomena. Taking account of cohort influences prevents cohort centrism, analogous to ethnocentrism. Failure to do so can lead us to assume, erroneously, that each cohort follows the same developmental pathway of our own cohort (Riley 1978).

SOCIAL TIME, LIFE TRANSITIONS, AND COLLECTIVE PROCESSES

The traditional timetables of many transitions are disappearing. Neugarten recognized the crossover in traditional age roles when she wrote, "Ours seems to be a society that has become accustomed to 70-year old students, 30-year-old college presidents, 22-year-old mayors, 35-year-old grandmothers, 50-year-old retirees, 65-year-old fathers of preschoolers, 60-year-olds and 30-year-olds wearing the same clothing styles" (1978:52). Today, we must add to that list 65-year-old caretakers of their 85-year-old parents, as well as the particularly tragic crossover of child mothers rearing their infants. Clearly, the social timing of many transitions of adulthood is changing markedly. No longer is there a fixed, age-connected time for learning, selecting sexual partners, marrying or remarrying, first-time parenting, changing careers, retiring, or moving into new statuses and roles. Such transitions are becoming relatively age-independent.

Many persons are transcending traditional gender roles heretofore considered unalterable in our society (Giele 1980). Examples of gender crossovers include the actual exchange of traditional male and female roles in some families, solo parenting by fathers, single career women having their own children by various means and raising them alone, and the entry of women into previously male occupations and of some men into previously female occupations. Writing from a different stance, Gilligan, (1982) believes that human development must be reconceptualized to take into account the differing socialization and life experiences of women and men. She pointed out that women's socialization and life experiences are missing in the traditional stage models of development. When women are measured against criteria for developmental progression in stage models, they are found wanting because the models are based on the study of men and their life experiences.

These various age and gender crossovers are said by some to herald new potentials in the life course to be both young and old at the same time and to be both masculine and feminine—if one wishes. The changes are shaping the life transitions and psychosocial development of adults and transforming families. They are also shaping the development of children across the life course in ways that we cannot currently foresee.

INDIVIDUAL TIME: THE LIFE COURSE

Longitudinal research on healthy children and those with disabilities (e.g., Chess, Fernandez, and Korn 1980; Murphy 1974; Offer et al. 1988; Thomas 1975; Thomas and Chess, 1977) reveals the flexibility of development and the potential for change in children and adults. This flexibility defeats the assumption of fixed, uniform, sequential stages, which overlooks changing environmental influences. Thomas and Chess believe that the all-important status granted to early life experience in stage models of development does a disservice to human potentiality and resilience and to the significance of the developmental context across the life course:

> In our own New York Longitudinal Study . . . the evolving child-environment interactional process was affected by many emerging unanticipated influences—changes in basic function, new talents, new environmental opportunities or stresses, changes in family structure or attitudes, and possibly late-emerging genetic factors. . . . Early life experience may be important in getting a

good start in life, but does not fix subsequent development (Thomas 1981).

As we shall see in the chapters that follow, other researchers in a variety of disciplines also suggest that the emotional and social development of children and adults is not a uniform process. Instead, development reflects the complex interplay from birth to the older years of physical, biological, and cognitive-perceptual maturation; individual potential; cultural influences; environmental constraints and opportunities; and the historical context.

The life course conception provides a fresh vision of life transitions, life events, and other life issues. The emphasis is on human potentialities from birth to the older years and on the environmental "nutriments" needed for their release and continued development. In addition to reflecting the life course conception, part 2 also reflects the view that family members develop simultaneously in continual processes involving both generations, in which parents and offspring are active agents in their own and one another's development. Parents and children develop together, not in separateness. Martin Bloom (1980) referred to the tandem development of parents and child. This is a neutral concept of simultaneous, reciprocal influence by parents and children on the development of one another and on family transformation in *social time*. The family transformations brought about by individual, familial, and environmental processes, in turn, influence child and adult development in *individual time*.

6

Family Formation: Working, Becoming a Couple, and the Parenting Option

Freud declared that the major accomplishments of adult life are loving and working. Issues of working and the workplace, a realm of life from the start of adulthood or even earlier, are briefly introduced here and are considered in detail in chapter 10. Loving, becoming a couple, and deciding to parent or not are the major foci of this chapter.

THE WORLD OF WORK

Most, but not all, young persons enter the world of work upon leaving school and before assuming the responsibilities of couplehood and parenthood. Becoming a couple in today's economy usually requires that one or both partners be employed. For most people, the workplace will be the sole source of economic security, providing income and access to social security and unemployment compensation. Some will receive added benefits such as pensions, health and life insurance, and employee assistance and referral plans. If the workplace is unionized, workers may have access to other benefits and services as well. Work is also the main source of social status and psychological identity for workers and their families. In North American society, men, and recently many women, are defined by the work they do. That definition can raise or lower one's sense of competence, self-esteem, self-direction, and relatedness. The answer to the ever-ready question, "What do you do?" tells all.

Work can lend a sense of purpose in life and provide support to adaptive strengths, mental and physical health, and the social functioning of workers and their families. When it does, person–job fit is said to be good. The concept of *fit* refers to the degree to which a person's characteristics and skills match the requirements of the job, as well as the degree to which the person's abilities are used in the job, and to which her or his personal needs for growth and fulfillment are met (Cox 1978). Personal characteristics include age, sex, experience, education, goals, personality, and cultural features. Characteristics of the job include its physical and/or intellectual demands, its degree of complexity, its safety and health risks, its security, and its supervisory control. Jobs may be too stimulating or not stimulating enough. Either way, a poor fit between job characteristics and personal characteristics may create stress for the worker, while a good fit leads to job satisfaction.

LOVING: MULTIPLE OPTIONS

Young adulthood is the time of family formation for most couples as they come together to establish a new conjugal unit that may or may not be intended to include children. With the many social, economic, and political changes over the past two decades, options for young adults have increased to the point where many experience as stressors such multiple choices as getting married or living together or remaining single; having a child now or later or remaining childless; and for women, working or not. For example, a young social worker wrote:

> Maybe it was easier as a woman to grow up knowing what your role in life was and knowing what was expected of you. However, this has been only a fleeting thought, for I sincerely believe that the independence, power, and responsibility that come from having choices is well worth the stress that options create. . . . However, this stress is a luxury; it goes hand in hand with privilege. A well-educated white, middle-class woman like me has many life options, and therefore I experience stress. On the other hand, if I were poor and of color and had little education, that privilege would not exist. Instead, my stress would come with poverty, racism, and closed opportunities.

In 1985, the U.S. Bureau of the Census reported there were almost two million unmarried couples living together, almost four times as many as in 1970. Solo parenting is also being deliberately chosen—almost entirely by older, often professional, women. And the deliberate choice by married or unmarried couples to hold their family size to two adults without children is increasing. But legal marriage is still the dominant mode of coming together to form a family. In 1980, over 90 percent of women and 95 percent of men over the age of 30 had been married at least once (Bianchi and Spain 1984). Throughout the balance of this chapter, the term *marriage* is used whenever the legal institution of marriage is being referred to. Otherwise, all the content applies also to all couples in committed relationships, whether heterosexual or homosexual.

Factors in Partner Selection

American society subscribes to romantic love, including passion and sexual attraction, as the basis of marriage, in contrast to more traditional societies that view marriage as an institution arranged by the parents of both individuals for economic, political, and social reasons and benefits. It has been said by Freud and others that romantic love is akin to madness insofar as it leads to irrational views of the beloved, and it is believed by some therefore to be a poor base for a lasting marriage. Others assert that romantic love, passion, and sexual attraction do form an important base, but that they yield their salience gradually to a new kind of love that includes mutual affection, caring, respect, intimacy, and commitment—if the marriage is to be a lasting and fulfilling one for both. However, a lasting marriage is not necessarily a measure of fulfillment. For example, until recent decades the stigma attached to divorce, as well as women's lack of marketable skills, meant that marriages often lasted without romantic love or mutual affection and respect.

In all three forms of partnership (married, unmarried heterosexual, and lesbian or gay), being in love and having one's feelings reciprocated by the partner bring joy, elevated self-esteem, and a heightened sense of identity as a person who loves and is beloved. Rejection and disappointment in love can lead to loss of self-esteem, extreme upset, grief, or depression. However, in addition to falling in love, mate selection is thought to be influenced by sociological and psychological factors. The sociological factors include residential propinquity and shared settings of high school or college, church or temple, work, or recreation; congruency between the couple along the dimensions of race, religion, education, and socioeconomic status; and the expectations and requirements of some occupations.

Several sociological features, however, have declined markedly in significance because of widespread geographic mobility and the growing frequency of cross-cultural marriages. For example, 8 percent of Italian-Americans born before 1920 had mixed ancestry, but by 1970, the percentage had risen to 70 percent. In 1980, only 27 percent of white Americans of European ancestry were married to those of an undivided ethnic heritage identical with their own. Of these, 46 percent were married to those whose ethnic background was entirely the same as their own, and 26 percent were married to those whose ethnicity overlapped partially (U.S. Bureau of the Census 1985). However, formal marriage across racial lines, though increasing, is still infrequent for both black and white persons: 99 percent of black women and 97 percent of black men married within their race. Nearly 99 percent of non-Hispanic whites married other non-Hispanic whites. The 1980 census showed there were 613,000 interracial married couples in the United States, about 1.3 percent of all married couples. In 1970 there were only 310,000 such couples (Collins 1984). Also, 72 percent of Americans of Asian ancestry and 71 percent of Hispanic Americans married within their group. However, 53.7 percent of American Indians married persons who were not American Indians, mostly whites.

Interreligious marriages have also increased. Religion is not included in the U.S. Census, but according to the National Opinion Research Center, about a third of those Catholics marrying in large urban dioceses marry a non-Catholic. Since 1975, 40 percent of Jewish marriages have been to non-Jews. On the other hand, marriage between persons of quite different socioeconomic levels is less frequent and tends to occur only between adjacent levels and not between widely separated levels. Usually it is the female who marries upward. Statistics are nonexistent for relationships outside formal marriage.

The psychological factors in mate selection are both unconscious and conscious. In the psychoanalytic model, unconscious, often negative, motivations include a desire to escape an unhappy family situation; fantasies of rescuing the mate from alcoholism or other difficulties, or of being rescued oneself; revenge for a past rejection or unhappy love affair; a deeply felt, excessive dependence; a wish to dominate the opposite sex; and fear of one's own homosexual tendencies. Such motivations can create unrealistic perceptions and expectations of the partner. Hence, if one of these motives is the dominant factor in choice, the relationship is likely to be a conflicted one.

Conscious forces include the wish for children; a desire to conform to the prevailing norm of marriage or pressure to do so by friends and family; weariness with rapid changes in sexual partners and consequent loneliness; or the desire for a home of one's own. Sometimes marriage is precipitated by pregnancy. In most instances pregnancy merely determines the time for a couple who have already decided to marry. Where that decision has not been reached earlier, however, a forced marriage may fail because of built-up resentments or for other reasons.

THE NEW COUPLE

In the case of marriage, the wedding represents a formal joining of two families. But in all three forms of pairing, the new affiliation represents a critical life transition involving a change in status and roles for both partners. It is perceived by many as entering upon "real" adulthood. It may be experienced primarily as a desired challenge, or primarily as a stressful situation that generates undue anxiety, helplessness, or guilt. Becoming a couple is potentially an enriching arena of adult development, including deepened relatedness, sexual gratification, expanded competence in new social roles, firmer self-concept and self-esteem, and increased self-direction—in the company of another held dear.

At the beginning, new couples face a dilemma inasmuch as individual needs and the needs of the pair-as-unit are not always compatible. A major task for the pair is to balance individual patterns and traditions with the emerging sense of themselves as a couple. This requires developing a mutually satisfying sexual relationship; sharing responsibilities in household and economic management and trying out various ways of allocating roles and tasks; and becoming aware of the values, norms, rituals, tastes, and preferences that each brings from the past and deciding which will be retained and which discarded while beginning to form new ones as a couple. Other important tasks of beginning together include coping with the inevitable disillusions, differences, habits, and imperfections that tend to appear after a short time of living in close association; reaching agreement about closeness to or distance from the family of origin and the friends of each partner; reconciling the job demands of each partner and managing tensions between job and couplehood demands; working out ways to resolve or to manage conflict; and reconciling the idealized view of the partner, and of the relationship, with reality. How the various challenges and tasks are met will depend in large part on the mutuality of the couple's sexual relationship, the depth of commitment to each other, the level of intimacy, and the quality of their attachment—and on the personality and cultural patterns of each partner and the characteristics of their environment.

The Sexual Relationship

During the early months of the partners' establishing themselves as a couple, significant factors leading to a mutually satisfying sexual relationship include discovering, meeting, and becoming attuned to the partner's sexual needs and interests, and developing comfort in talking openly about one's own needs, anxieties, and preferences.

Sexual attitudes and behaviors have changed dramatically over the past several decades, especially in regard to greater sexual freedom and pleasure for women. Men and women now enter long-term heterosexual or homosexual couplehood having had previous sexual experience. Most therefore move easily as a couple into establishing mutually satisfing patterns of sexual activity, including issues of initiation, frequency, duration, accustomed and new behaviors, and shared feelings. However, despite their experience, some may lack accurate knowledge of sexual anatomy and functioning in both sexes, or early attitudes and feelings of fear, shame, or guilt about sexuality derived from families of origin, religious teachings, cultural factors, or previous sexual experiences of a disturbing nature (e.g., rape or having been a childhood victim of incest) may persist in one or both members of the couple and may interfere with mutual pleasure. These troubling inhibitions require of the partners special patience, sensitivity, and open communication if they are to attain a satisfying sexual relationship. More serious sexual dysfunctions that do not yield to the partners' efforts—often because of the interplay of physical and psychological factors—are now treatable by qualified sex therapists.

Depth of Commitment

Lauer and Lauer (1986) studied 351 couples with lasting marriages, of whom 300 said they were happily married. Among the common reasons that these 300 gave for their satisfaction was a strong sense of commitment based on religious, ethnic, or secular values. The survey described the happily married respondents as people who, among other things, were willing to endure troubled times by confronting problems and working through them.

Critics of the growing trend toward informal living together argue that formal marriage and the marriage vows tend to support the couple's commitment to each other and to the marriage over the long run. So, too, do gay and lesbian couples who seek the legalization of homosexual marriages. Critics of marriage, on the other hand, state that true commitment is not ensured by a marriage license and a wedding ceremony but is instead trivialized by them. Some also take the position that informal living together is a way of testing mutual commitment and the viability of a monogamous choice, before undertaking the legal and social responsibilities of marriage. It is implied that the process of living together before marriage is apt to result in a more enduring marriage. In a "His and Hers Panel Discussion" *(Hartford Courant)*, a 37-year-old man, married after he and his wife had first lived together for five years, stated,

> We specifically did not commit in our ceremony to "until death do us part" or anything that even resembled that. What we did try to commit to was to attempt to be emotionally present as much as we could for each other and for our child. Now if that meant that we would stay together, great. But it was no guarantee. The commitment was to continually evaluate the commitment to each other. . . . We've had some times when it's been shaky but I feel like I'm committed to work like crazy to make it go. (February 14, 1988:c-1)

Commitment develops gradually. Yet, for some couples, today's easy access to and acceptance of divorce—as important as these are—tend to inhibit the development or to lessen the force of a commitment to work on impasses and relationship problems. However, that tendency may be abating as the fear of AIDS and the emphasis on nonrisk sex appear to be inducing growing numbers of younger couples to work on barriers to their continuing relationship. Although commitment is essential to marital satisfaction, it is not sufficient by itself. Partners must continue to "work" on their relationship; otherwise, commitment tends to be hollow and devoid of intimacy and passion.

Level of Intimacy

Feminists and male profeminists note the difficulty of many men in achieving intimacy either in man-to-man or man-to-woman relationships. The gendered split between the expressive and instrumental functions makes it seem to many men—especially, but not exclusively, working-class men—that expressiveness and the intimacy it supports render them vulnerable and define them as weak and unmasculine. On the other hand, sharing intimate aspects of the self and expressing feelings are regarded by most women as essential to a love relationship; without such reciprocity, there can be no intimacy. The Canadian researchers Houle and Kiely studied levels of intimacy, using a Montreal sample of 125 women and men, ages 18 to 43. The women in all age groups achieved higher intimacy scores than their male counterparts. The authors reported that their analysis revealed that, compared to men, "Women are more accessible to their partners, more disposed to respond unconditionally to the needs of the other person, more open, and more committed to resolving problems that arise in the relationship. They also tend to share their emotions almost exclusively with the partner. . . . Men are open to their partners on a selective and conditional basis and are therefore less accessible." (1984).

O'Neil (1982) noted that self-disclosure, vulnerability, and trust are essential to the development of intimacy. Yet many men have been socialized not to admit human weakness nor to express intense feelings. Instead, they learn to rely on words, logic, and rationalistic explanations to control situations and explain reality, including the self. O'Neil stated that rigid gender specialization and differential treatment of females and males "has limited the sexes from developing all parts of their personality . . . needed to cope with the complexities of human experience. . . . The psychological, physical, and spiritual costs to humankind have been negative and great" (1982:39).

Balswick observed that the expectation that men be expressive, together with their early socialization to be tough and to avoid showing emotions, expecially tenderness or sadness, constitutes a discontinuity in cultural conditioning. Males are socialized to inexpressiveness as a valued masculine characteristic yet married couples are expected to share feelings and to show affection. Balswick adds, "The most serious and destructive effects of male inexpressiveness within marriages may be seen in accumulating evidence that links inability to express feelings to spouse abuse" (1989:6). The author also provided an alternative interpretation that this component of the gender-typed male role learned early in life leads not to an inability to be expressive, but to thinking that males are not supposed to be expressive. The assumption then is that in a committed relationship men can and do unlearn the constraints of earlier training and meet the partner's desire for reciprocity. Balswick gave greater weight to his first interpretation based on his and others' research.

A social worker recalled:

> The first two years of our relationship were filled with my being overly dependent and clingy and his being scared to death of getting too close. We had to work hard on these issues as individuals as well as a couple. When Hank and I used to have fights in those first two years of our relationship, I would get upset and depressed and angry and cry a lot, talk with friends, and not be able to get any work done. He, on the other hand, didn't talk to anyone and buried himself in his work. In those years it was always up to me to initiate the reconciliation talks, and I always did. He would have just let the relationship end. . . . Our neediness fit together: I clung too much, he distanced himself too much. But we learned together. We both very much needed a good dose of what the other's strengths were—mine of dealing with feelings and not being afraid of closeness, his of being able to keep getting the rest of life's tasks done when we were fighting, and being able to know his self separate from others, including me.

Quality of Attachment

Attachment is an important element in pair bonds, along with commitment and intimacy. Attachment theory, which differs markedly from object relations theory (see the section in Appendix 1 on Mahler), is presented in more detail in later chapters. For now, it is sufficient to note that Weiss (1982) found that adult attachments and infant attachments are expressed in similar and dissimilar ways. They are similar in 1) displaying a need for ready access to the attachment figure and desiring proximity in stressful situations; 2) displaying heightened comfort and diminished anxiety when in the company of the attachment figure; and 3) manifesting a marked increase in anxiety on discovering the attachment figure to be inexplicably inaccessible. These expressions of attachment are found regularly in well-functioning and some poorly functioning marriages (and other pair relationships).

Attachment in adults is dissimilar from attachment in infants in the following ways: Instead of attachment to parental caretakers, adult attachment is to peers of unique importance who are perceived either as sources of strength or as supporters of the person's own capacity for mastery. Adult attachment is usually directed toward a person who is also the object of sexual desire, and sexual contact may itself foster attachment. But it is also the case that adult attachments may not be accompanied by sexual desire. Weiss (1982) believes that attachment is more reliable than sexual desire in pair bonding because of its greater persistence, and it becomes increasingly persistent as the relationship becomes more established. In the face of threat, attachment becomes more powerful, while sexual desire is apt to be suppressed. And while attachment resists redirection to others, sexual desire seems less resistant to attraction to others.

Weiss (1982:174) emphasized that the adult attachment is not found in all the adult's emotionally significant relationships but appears only in relationships of central emotional importance. Earlier, Weiss noted that attachment is one component among many that may constitute love, including "idealization of the other, trust, and identification with the other so great that contributions to the other's well-being are felt to be immediately gratifying to the self . . . and perhaps seeing the other as completing the self by providing capacities or attributes that one lacks oneself" (1973:94). The various components of love, including attachment, are independent, and their varied combinations differ for different persons and perhaps in different experiences of love for the same individual. Thus attachment is not the same as love. It is also the case that attachment can be present in the absence of love. For example, divorced couples sometimes remain attached although they no longer love each other.

GENDER ISSUES

Role Structures

In the "modern marriage" (including informal living together), as contrasted with the "traditional marriage," the gender-based division of labor with the male as provider and the female as household manager is changing. The change has occurred in response to the feminist movement and interdependent social and economic trends, such as the growing numbers of women in the work force, the increased numbers of women having higher education, delayed marriage and childbearing, lowered birth rates, and the increased availability of inexpensive contraception, which gives women more control over their lives. However, only one half of the division of labor has really changed. Few if any men are demanding to do housework. Hence, in the "modern marriage," there is a limited reduction in male dominance or power, but little real change in household tasks despite the acceptance of gender equity as an ideal by many of those in such marriages and partnerships.

In contrast, the "egalitarian marriage" (including informal living together) accords equal status and power to the partners, both of whom are usually employed. Household and economic roles are not based on gender stereotypes. Instead, chores are shared equitably according to the partners' interests, abilities, and availability. Roles are interchangeable in the face of the situational needs of the moment, or they are rotated. In some instances, traditional gender roles are actually reversed by the deliberate choice of both individuals. The male partner may remain at home, taking on household and child-rearing tasks while the female partner works or obtains higher education. Egalitarian marriages and informal partnerships benefit from institutional supports (when available) such as part-time work for men and women with full benefits; the elimination of policies forbidding nepotism (relatives working for the same employer); paid maternity and paternity leaves; adequate day care arrangements for children or elderly relatives in the household, including round-the-clock emergency centers for temporary care during crisis, work-related travel, or need for respite; easily accessible medical and dental care, such as mobile neighborhood units; and recreation facilities located in schools-as-community-centers for children during after-school hours, for neighborhood forums, and for support groups. These institutional supports for egalitarian couples are equally essential for solo parents and two-provider families.

The egalitarian structure is designed to use the strengths and enhance the development of both partners by eliminating power and status differences. An egalitarian structure is probably found in most lesbian and gay relationships. But egalitarian heterosexual couples are found mainly among educated, liberal young adults, perhaps representing a small percentage of all couples. Even those subscribing to equality may wittingly or unwittingly fall back on more traditional roles when children are born.

During the 1970s, the concept of androgeny was emphasized as the means of achieving gender equality. But it turned out to be a concept fraught with difficulty. It is a " 'separate but equal' theory which attempts to affirm the psychological and social equality of men and women but perpetuates the association of personality characteristics with sex-linked differences between men and women" (Harrison 1978). Further, it does not eliminate gender stereotypes; it merely blends them, thus expecting both women and men to manifest both the so-called masculine and feminine qualities to a high degree. This expectation forces the individual to meet two sets of norms: "People can now be judged incompetent for two reasons not just one" (Matlin 1987:280). Also, developing an androgenous personality does not eliminate sexism nor lead to institutional change in the devaluation of women; instead, it emphasizes individual change. Hence Rebecca, Heffner and Oleshansky (1976) proposed a concept of gender transcendence to replace the concept of androgeny. Gender transcendence envisions going beyond traditional sex-typed roles to develop freely chosen individual styles, flexibly oriented toward shifting situations.

Nobles (1974) pointed out that black family organization has long been egalitarian. In intact black families (which constitute two thirds of all black families; Hill 1972), neither parent is dominant. In the remaining third, which comprise female-headed families for most part, Nobles disclaimed the myth of the black matriarch, distinguishing between strength and dominance. The black single mother has needed to be strong in order to maintain the survival of the tribe (family), and she is not necessarily domineering. A review of research findings regarding the socialization of black children reveals that the role behaviors usually defined in the Euro-American culture as feminine or masculine are encouraged in both boys and girls in black families (D. Lewis 1978). It is not surprising, then, that role flexibility between the parents in child care and household tasks has long characterized the black family (Hill 1972).

SOCIAL CLASS DIFFERENCES

Some of what has been said here about the new couple probably fits the white middle class more than it does poor and working-class groups. In addition to differences derived from ethnic and racial factors (chapter 4), important differences in the marital relationship are associated with socioeconomic status. These differences may be more significant than racial or ethnic differences. For example, the marital and child-rearing patterns of most middle-class black and white couples are similar, as are the patterns of most low-income black and white couples. Middle-class and low-income black couples are different from each other, and so, too, are middle-class and low-income white couples. In other words, poor whites and poor blacks resemble one another in these patterns more than they resemble either middle-class white or middle-class black couples. However, not every low-income couple fits the characteristics noted in this section, while any of those characteristics can be found among some middle-class couples.

In general, working-class or blue-collar marriages have reflected a strict division of labor; the roles and functions are allocated on the basis of gender, the authority for decision making is vested in the male, and there is little joint planning or activity. The middle-class value placed on love, intimacy, and companionship is less prevalent. In comparison with many middle-income marriages, many working-class marriages are characterized by emotional distance between the partners, reinforced by limited communication. Each spouse is likely to view the other as unpredictable, difficult to understand, and inconsiderate. The partners see themselves opposed to each other as though existing in different worlds. In fact, their lives are sharply segregated. What little leisure time exists is not often spent together, at least after children are born. Wives seek intimacy through motherhood, and their strongest emotional tie is to their children. Women remain close to their mother, their sisters, and their women friends. Men may stay in touch with their mother, but most of their time is spent with male friends and workmates. Thus some personal needs of both partners may be met outside the marriage, so that their relationship is relieved of the emotional demands made in the marital relationships of more affluent and educated groups (Bott 1972).

L. Rubin's 1976 study of 100 white working-class spouses in 50 San Francisco families bears out this bleakness. The couples had married early, and their experience was characterized by the presence of alcoholism and the absence of intimacy. The hope of moving upward had proved to be an illusion, but the struggle continued. The women were subordinate to their husbands and had little power in the family. Out of financial necessity, some had jobs but most were occupied at home in housework and child care. Their outside contacts were with relatives and neighbors. Few were aware of or had knowledge of the women's movement at the time of the study. However, changes in marriage and child-rearing patterns occurring in middle-income groups are often gradually taken up by blue-collar families. Hence many working-class couples may now be in transition, and some of these traditional patterns may be in flux.

OPTING TO BECOME A PARENT

Most heterosexual couples face another choice: to have a child now, or later, or to remain childless. The latter option now meets with less disapproval than formerly. Among couples opting to remain permanently childless or to have no additional children, reliance on female and male sterilization is growing (Shipp 1985). Although among young single women the pill remains the preferred contraceptive, the percentage of sterilized married women reached 26 percent in 1985, up from 7 percent in 1965, while those on the pill had dropped to 20 percent from a peak of 36 percent in 1973. Among married men, 15 percent had been sterilized by vasectomy in 1982, up from 5 percent in 1965.

This section considers the option of parenthood either by choice or by accident, since having a child is not always a matter of deliberate choice (adoption will be considered briefly in chapter 7). An unintended pregnancy that is also unwanted can be a problem for the child and for the parents, but many unintended or unwanted pregnancies do become "wanted" before or after the baby's birth. In any case, expecting a child can be predominantly a joyful challenge or predominantly a painful source of stress, depending on the couple's emotional and financial readiness, the quality of their relationship, their motivation for and their feelings about children, and the salience of other goals. Other influences are their health status, their cultural values and norms, and the available environmental supports. Some lesbian and gay couples—and some single, career-oriented women—choose to have a baby (through a sperm bank; a selected male friend, or a female friend in the case of the gay man; or a surrogate mother) although their numbers are not known.

Pregnancy

Different women have different emotional responses to their pregnancy experience. Their emotions may be primarily positive, with happy anticipation of motherhood and child rearing and pleasure in the attention and support of relatives and friends, or they may be primarily negative, with depressed feelings, especially in the first trimester, worries about bodily functions, and feelings of being fat and ugly:

> It is easy to understand negative emotions in an unmarried, pregnant 16-year old whose boyfriend and family have rejected her, and who must work as a waitress to earn extra money. It is also easy to understand positive emotions from a happily married 24-year old who has hoped for this pregnancy for two years and whose family income is sufficient to buy the new styles of "executive" maternity clothes that she can wear to her interesting, fulfilling job. (Matlin 1987:364)

If they are reasonably well, many pregnant women now remain in their jobs almost to the time of birth, in contrast to earlier decades when social disapproval of the practice prevailed. Whether the period is spent at home or at the workplace, being pregnant represents many changes for the expectant mother and many individual tasks. Physical and physiological changes occur that may be uncomfortable and/or pleasurable. She must give attention to her own and the expected infant's health, including possible changes to a more nutritional diet, increased exercise, and avoidance of tobacco, alcohol, and other drugs that can damage the child in utero or postnatally during breast feeding. The fetus depends on the mother for all its nutrients, and therefore her prenatal diet is important for the infant's later mental and physical development. There is some evidence that when the expectant mother is malnourished, fewer brain cells develop in the fetus, and stillbirths and premature births can also result.

Recognition is growing that the expectant father has his own set of adaptive tasks, including coming to terms with fatherhood and its personal meaning, especially in regard to early experience with his own father; making room for the baby in his relationship with his partner; providing emotional support to her during the pregnancy; and participating in prenatal classes and readying himself for his participation in the birth process if this is what the couple wishes. Joint tasks for the couple during pregnancy include anticipatory planning and preparation for the new roles of mother and father and for reallocating other roles and tasks; acquiring knowledge about pregnancy, childbirth, and parenting; securing the necessary equipment and clothing for the baby; selecting a name for either sex; and arranging for safe, consistent child care if the mother plans to return to work, or arranging for maternal and paternal leaves where available. A most important task is arranging for prenatal care and deciding on birthing arrangements.

Pregnancy and Fetal Development

Conception, pregnancy, and birth are parts of a continually unfolding relationship, first between mother and baby and, following birth, between baby and mother, father, and the environment (Macfarlane 1977). Even the relationship of mother and fetus from conception to birth, however, is influenced by the degree of support given to the mother by the father and by his feelings about having a child. It is also influenced by the environment in which the parents are embedded, including the presence or absence of the needed resources, services, and supportive networks and the presence of any noxious or toxic environmental features.

During the first two weeks after conception, the fertilized egg is termed a *zygote*. About the ninth day it forms two sacs. The inner one is filled with fluid and protects the zygote from injury. The outer one develops tendrils by which the zygote attaches itself to the uterine wall during the second week. Beginning in the third week, it is known as an *embryo*, and for the next six weeks, it develops all the major organs. The placenta, connected to the embryos's navel by the umbilical cord, develops from embryo and maternal tissue. By the eighth week, the embryo is about one inch long:

> It has a recognizable brain, a heart that pumps blood through tiny veins and arteries, a stomach that produces digestive juices, a liver that manufactures blood cells, kidneys that function, and an endocrine system. In the male embryo the testes produce androgens. The baby now has limbs and an enormous head with ears, nose, eyes, and mouth . . . it looks human. . . . It holds its hands close to its face; should they touch its mouth, the embryo turns its head and opens its mouth wide. (Newton and Modahl 1978).

From the ninth week, when bone cells appear, and until birth, the embryo is called a *fetus*. From here on it is provided a stable, protected environment by the amniotic fluid that fills the space between the two sacs that developed earlier around the zygote. By the eleventh week and the end of the first trimester, the fetus is able to swallow the amniotic fluid and urinates it back about every ninety minutes (Macfarlane 1977):

> Waste products travel from the fluid through the placenta, from which they enter the mother's bloodstream. . . . The fluid is completely replaced every two or three hours. By the end of the third month . . . the fetus has grown to a length of three inches and weighs about half an ounce. . . . It bends its finger when its palm is touched. . . . It has taste buds, sweat glands, and a prominent nose. By now it has eyelids, but they are sealed shut. (Newton and Modahl 1978).

The second trimester is generally a time of physical and emotional well-being for the expectant mother; the earlier discomforts of nausea, drowsiness, urinary frequency, and so on have disappeared or are diminished. Visible and internal signs of the pregnancy are now present. Quickening (fetal movements) is experienced by the the mother between the sixteenth and twenty-sixth weeks, although the fetus has been moving spontaneously and has been reactive to touch since the seventh week. The second trimester is also a time of rapid weight gain for the mother. Except for women who were very thin when they became pregnant, a total gain of about 24 pounds is considered desirable for most women at delivery. This represents the combined weight of fetus (7.7 lbs.), placenta (1.4 lbs.), amniotic fluid (1.8 lbs.), uterus (2.0 lbs.), water that enlarges the breast tissue (.9 lbs.), extra interstitial fluid throughout the body (2.7 lbs.), and extra blood for needed circulation (4.0 lbs.). The balance is stored as fat and protein to withstand the demands of the postnatal period (Newton and Modahl 1978).

By the sixth month, the fetus appears fully developed in many ways. Yet most fetuses this age would not be able to live outside the mother because their lungs and digestive system, though well formed, are not yet able to function. The fetus is now about 13 inches long and weighs about 1.5 pounds. By the end of the sixth month, the fetus is sleeping and waking; it can open its eyes, look around, and suck a finger; and occasionally it may hiccough or sigh. During the last trimester, the fetus makes heavy demands on the mother for nutrients, minerals, and vitamins. Its rapidly developing brain requires extra protein (Newton and Modahl 1978). Indeed, adequate nutrition is important all through the pregnancy.

The Uterine Environment

Macfarlane (1977:9) presented findings from his and others' research (using such instruments as scanners, microphones, and the experiences of observant mothers) that suggest the fetus lives and floats in a noisy, perhaps rose-tinted, and changing environment. Recordings from tiny inserted microphones reveal a constant, very loud swooshing noise in the uterus that pulses with the mother's heartbeat. It is due to blood flowing through the uterus. Noise also is produced by air passing through the mother's stomach. External noise is muted by the amniotic fluid, but extremely loud noises in the third trimester produce kicking and even violent activity in the fetus:

> The muscles for moving the eye and the actual system for seeing develop very early on in pregnancy, and in the uterus the baby makes eye movements both in response to his [sic] changing positions and—as he will through life—during dreaming sleep. . . . There is some evidence that toward the end of pregnancy the uterus and the mother's [abdominal] wall get so stretched that some light does get through to become diffused in the amniotic fluid. . . . If this is so, then the baby may go through periods of light and dark corresponding to the degree of light the mother is exposed to. (Macfarlane 1977:12)

Macfarlane (1977:7) pointed out that the fetus itself continually changes its environment by its very existence, and Hytten wrote:

> The fetus is an egoist, and by no means an endearing and helpless little dependent as his [sic] mother may fondly think. As soon as he has plugged himself into the uterine wall he sets out to make certain that his needs are served, regardless of any inconvenience he may cause. He does this by almost completely altering the mother's physiology, usually by fiddling with her control mechanisms.(1976)

Macfarlane also referred to evidence from several studies suggesting that prolonged severe stress in the expectant mother not only increases fetal movements but results in infant irritability, hyperactivity, and sometimes feeding problems in the postnatal period. However, to be valid, postnatal observations must be made before the baby has any postnatal contact with the mother.

Other adverse changes in the prenatal environment can occur because of damaging substances used by the mother that pass through the placenta to the fetus, such as tobacco, alcohol, and dangerous drugs. The significance of such a transfer was not recognized until the thalidomide catastrophe in the births of severely deformed infants during the 1960s. Not all pregnant women taking the sleeping pill at a critical time in the pregnancy gave birth to a deformed baby. Such variability in the effects of any teratogen (a substance that produces malformation) may reflect genetic differences in susceptibility. By 1977 over fifteen hundred substances had been identified as having an adverse effect on the fetus (Macfarlane 1977:6). In the first trimester the fetus is most vulnerable to dangerous drugs taken by the mother because all of the organs are being formed at this time. For example, the tranquilizer Valium is used by many people. Women who take it during the first trimester of pregnancy are four times more likely to have babies with cleft palate or cleft lip than women who do not take it. More recently, the drug Accutane, prescribed for severe, disfiguring acne and carrying a strong warning label, has been found to cause serious birth defects if used by pregnant women, most of whom use the drug before they become aware of their pregnancy.

The number of infants born drug-addicted because their mothers used heroin, cocaine, or crack during pregnancy is increasing at an alarming rate (Levine 1988). In New York City, for example, the number of such infants doubled during the 1987 fiscal year (from 1,325 to 2,521) and was increasing by an additional 50 percent, or 1,336 cases, during the first four months of the 1988 fiscal year (Grinker 1988). Such infants suffer severe withdrawal symptoms and even death. They show behavioral disturbances including irritability, sleep disorders, excessive and high-pitched crying, and tremors. These symptoms disappear within three weeks or earlier, depending on the drug. The long-range effects of infant addiction are not entirely known, however, although some of these babies have manifested hyperactivity and attention disorders by the time they entered school or pre-school programs.

Most of these infants are at severe psychosocial as well as medical risk. Some remain in hospitals for a long time as "boarder babies" because their addicted mothers are unable to care for them or have abandoned them. For example, at least one thousand boarder babies, ranging in age from newborn to 2 years, were in New York City hospitals during 1986, staying for months without individual mothering (Raske 1986). In some hospitals, volunteer foster grandparents give essential love and attention to these infants that busy pediatric staff cannot provide. Other babies are placed in foster care, but their difficult drug-induced behaviors render them vulnerable to frequent changes of foster parents. Even healthy infants who return home with their mothers are also at risk because the addicted parent(s) may not provide adequate care. The increase in the numbers of addicted babies is also associated with increases in cases of child abuse and neglect. In addition, it is now known that breast milk transfers cocaine and crack to the infant very quickly, causing immediate intoxication and even death.

Fetal alcohol syndrome, a serious disorder associated with heavy maternal drinking during pregnancy, has been recognized since 1970. Babies born with this condition are apt to be smaller, with lower birth weight than other babies, and to have slight malformations of the face, limbs, and cardiovascular system, and sometimes mental retardation. An expectant mother's occasional drink is probably not dangerous to the fetus, but because even moderate drinking can lead to some degree of low birth weight, abstinence is recommended by many authorities. Smoking one or more packs of cigarettes a day during pregnancy is associated with low birth weight, stillbirth, and early infant mortality. It is thought that these effects are due to a reduced blood and oxygen supply to the fetus, resulting in a deprivation of needed nutrients through the placenta. Smoking is especially dangerous during the second half of pregnancy.

Perhaps out of ignorance about the effects despite the dissemination of information, some women continue to drink, or to use other drugs, and/or to smoke during pregnancy. The question has been raised whether these behaviors during a pregnancy that is intended to go to term, when the mother has been advised of their danger, constitute fetal abuse (Mackenzie, Collins, and Popkin 1982). Does the fetus have a right to be protected from behaviors that threaten prenatal well-being, and that may result in postnatal disability or death? If so, should an expectant mother who does not respond with behavioral change to information, advice, and persuasion be made to do so? If so, by what means, given that she may be unable to stop drinking or smoking? This is a moral and ethical dilemma for health care providers and the society at large. What is sorely needed are effective ways to help expectant mothers give up their addictions.

Rubella (German measles) is a minor disease in the expectant mother, but if she contracts the disease during the first trimester, the effects on the baby can be blindness, deafness, mental retardation, and/or heart disease. However, not all babies of mothers contracting rubella are born with a defect. The AIDS virus in the bloodstream of expectant mothers with AIDS also passes through the placenta to the fetus, possibly dooming the infant to the disease and painful death in the first or second year of life or, in some cases, later. The presence of antibodies in a newborn's blood indicates that its mother is infected with the AIDS virus. In about 40 percent of those cases, the baby is believed to be infected as well. In the other instances, the baby has absorbed only the antibody, not the virus. Of the 1,605 babies who died during their first year of life in New York CIty in 1987, for example, 37 died of AIDS (Gross 1988).

Transfers of nutrients through the placenta to the fetus are essential and beneficial. Even antibodies in the mother's blood, resulting from certain earlier infections, are transferred. The baby is then immune for several months after birth to diseases such as colds, influenza, scarlet fever, whooping cough, measles, and mumps.

CHILDBIRTH

Childbirth was a woman-controlled, natural, biological process over the millennia, "a social rather than a medical event, managed by midwives and attended by friends and relatives" (Dye 1980). However, during the late nineteenth and early twentieth centuries, childbirth was gradually medicalized as though it were a disease process, and it came under the control of male obstetricians and hospitals. As late as 1920, almost 75 percent of American births took place at home, but by 1960, 96 percent took place in hospitals (Wertz and Wertz 1977). The change was accompanied by the mystification and medical monopolization of knowledge about birthing, or what Oakley (1979) pointed to as the claimed superiority of professional knowledge over the expertise of the mothers themselves. It was also accompanied by the psychologizing of such difficulties as multiple miscarriages, late attention to prenatal care, nausea and vomiting (early morning sickness), infertility, prematurity, and postnatal depression. Thus these phenomena were viewed as the result of the woman's "problem" with femininity and other intrapsychic issues. No attention was given to the social and economic contexts. Oakley (1979) commented that few studies of postnatal depression, for example, "consider the impact of sleep disturbance, exhaustion, social isolation, work over-load, etc., on a woman's feelings after the birth of a child."

Dye (1980) observed that since the 1920s, when hospitals took control of birthing, it has been viewed as a surgical process. Reliance on forceps, episiotomy (surgery to expand the opening to the birth canal), anesthesia, and the inducing of birth became common. More recently, an alarming increase in caesarean births has occurred and is thought to be associated with physicians' fear of malpractice suits. The expectant mother, now a patient, is expected to be passive and to submit to professionals' control of her body and the birth. Formal and informal studies reveal that women find the process alienating, isolating, and frightening. Childbirth in the hospital was believed to be safer than at home because the hospital offered an aseptic environment. But Dye's research review shows that mortality remained high until the late 1930s, largely because of the routine use of risky interventions.

Kloosterman, a Dutch professor of obstetrics, wrote, "Childbirth in itself is a natural phenomenon and in the large majority of cases needs no interference whatsoever—only close observation, moral support, and protection against human meddling" (cited in Macfarlane 1977:29). This view has been the basis of the organization of obstetrics in the Netherlands since the early 1900s. Oakley (1979) referred to Kloosterman's assertion that 97 percent of women are able to deliver babies safely and without problems. Macfarlane added, "A healthy woman who delivers spontaneously performs a job that cannot be improved upon. This job can be done in the best way if the woman is self-confident and stays in surroundings where she is the real center (as in her own home)" (1977:29). Macfarlane believes that only expectant mothers with signs of abnormalities belong in hospitals under the care of specialists.

The Lamaze model of prepared childbirth appears to eliminate the problems in the medical model of childbirth, at least to some degree. Mothers' and fathers' knowledge of the processes of pregnancy, labor, and birth, gained not only from the instructor but also from listening to the experiences of others, increases self-confidence in the mother and in the father if he assists at the birth. Most important, the model restores the control of labor and full conscious participation in the birth to the mother. The classes also include breathing exercises that are geared to the stages of labor and that reduce pain: "The informational aspects of the program and the rehearsals for labor seem to reduce the fear of the unknown and the sense of helplessness and isolation for first-time mothers and to give the father a more intimate role in the bringing forth of the child" (J. Williams 1983:286).

Birthing at home, assisted by a licensed nurse-midwife and, in some instances with backup hospital services if needed, is increasing in the United States. Birth then becomes a family event. Women deciding on this option report liking the informal, caring qualities of the midwife, who is also more apt than the physician to wait out nature's delays. The few available studies show that home births are just as safe as, and possibly more safe than, hospital deliveries for those with uncomplicated pregnancies and the expectation of uncomplicated births (J. Williams 1983). Some hospitals, interested in a more family-oriented birthing process, now provide support groups and programs for expectant mothers desiring natural childbirth or anticipating caesarean sections, their partners, and the expected baby's siblings and grandparents. The birthing rooms provided by some hospitals and by free-standing birthing centers combine the best features of home and hospital and offer a desirable option for many couples.

These alternative services are for the most part used by middle-class populations who have private health insurance, as not all centers accept Medicaid. Therefore mothers who are poor may not have access to birthing arrangements other than regular hospital obstetrical care. And, indeed, all the adaptive and coping tasks of pregnancy are far more difficult or stressful for poor and solo mothers, and even more so if they are without the support of relatives and friends. Royer and Barth (1984) emphasized the opportunities for social workers to participate in improving pregnancy outcomes and preventing fetal damage, infant disability, and death, through developing preventive and interventive programs for individuals, families, and groups. These programs include outreach to expectant parents and teenagers for skilled, knowledge-based educative and support services; effective referral and follow-up; and the mobilization of community resources. Such opportunities are available in any field of practice where social workers encounter families, youths, and young adults. All social workers can participate in policy advocacy to achieve equitable access to quality health care for all mothers and infants before birth and during the first five years of life.

The next chapter continues the examination of the parenting option in terms of the choices available to infertile couples and to those who are at risk of transmitting a genetic disease, together with the ethical dilemmas and legal-social issues that these options raise.

7

The Parenting Option Continued: More Choices

The 1970s and 1980s saw remarkable developments in reproductive technologies. Infertile couples now have more options beyond artificial insemination and adoption. Similarly, advances in the field of genetics allow for prenatal testing for certain genetic disorders. The patterns of inheritance of others have been identified, allowing for the expansion and helpfulness of genetic counseling for parents and prospective parents who are at risk of transmitting a genetic disease. Certain physical and mental disorders, previously thought to have only environmental etiology, are now understood to have genetic components that interact with environmental features and/or lifestyle, with implications for the treatment of the afflicted person, help to her or his family, and social policy development. Accompanying the new options for infertile couples and those at risk of transmitting genetic disorders, however, are new and very difficult ethical, legal, financial, and social issues for individuals and families. The issues also have an impact on medicine, social work, other professions, and society.

Services for infertile couples and genetic services represent a growing field of practice for social workers. It is also clear that all social workers now require as part of their biopsychosocial-cultural assessment, planning, and intervention the following types of basic information concerning 1) the new measures for overcoming infertility; 2) the genetic principles of inheritance; and 3) the impact of genetic diagnoses and disorders on individuals and families.

INFERTILITY: MORE OPTIONS

Demographically, fertility rates have declined since the early and mid-1980s. In 1986 births totaled 3,731,000, down 18,000 from 1985, a 2 percent drop, and the lowest rate (64.9 live births per 1,000 women aged 15 to 44) ever recorded by the National Centers for Health Statistics (*New York Times*, September 8, 1987). Women are having their first child later and are having fewer children than either their mothers or their grandmothers, as both women and men pursue education and careers. Canada is experiencing a similar phenomenon. In 1980, a little more than one fifth of all births were to mothers over the age of 30 (Schlesinger, Danaher, and Robert 1984). Despite the availability of safe and reasonably effective contraception, the increase in unwanted and teenage pregnancy is a major social problem, which will be taken up in chapter 12.

Infertility is a serious problem for many couples and appears to be on the rise. A couple is considered medically infertile after trying unsuccessfully for a year to have children. Learning of one's own or one's partner's incurable infertility can be a severe shock to both partners. Some respond to their lost hope for a child with grief, and others view the condition as evidence of impaired sexuality that damages their self-concept and identity as a male or a female. The effects of the news on some couples may require a transformation of the couple-as-family through second-order changes in their relationship, their communication patterns, and their worldview. The transformation may free them to undertake adoption or various technological options. Other couples manage the severe disappointment as a first-order challenge and move to other options without disabling, conflicted responses that require second-order changes. Adoption and artificial insemination were the only solutions to infertility until recent technological developments made available additional options: 1) in vitro fertilization, in which the mother's ova are extracted (a painful and expensive surgical procedure), fertilized in a laboratory dish with her partner's sperm, and then implanted in her uterus; 2) embryo transfers involving third-party contributions of ova and/or sperm; 3) surrogate motherhood, in which a woman impregnated through artificial insemination or an embryo implant carries the child for someone else; and 4) gamete intrafallopian transfer (GIFT), in which the ovum and the sperm are transferred to the recipient's fallopian tubes.

Excess embryos may be frozen, to be thawed later and transferred to the same or a different woman, and sperm, donated anonymously or otherwise, may be frozen and kept in sperm banks. Babies developed from frozen embryos have been born, although it is too early to know the possible long-term effects of freezing on genetic material (DNA). The accidental deaths of an American mother of two frozen embryos and her husband raised serious ethical and legal questions about the right of frozen embryos, such as whether unused frozen embryos have the right to be developed by implantation in another woman, and if so, whether the child has the right of inheritance to the natural mother's estate. Also, ethicists and others are asking if embryos and fetuses have the right to protection against being used in experimental research, including the use of tissues of aborted embryos in the treatment of adult disorders. Concern has been expressed that such efforts may lead to commercialized conception and pregnancy simply for the purpose of producing tissues for transplantation.

Central regulatory and monitoring structures, as well as medical and psychological screening procedures, are not uniformly in place for the medical, psychological, and legal protection of babies, donors, and donees despite the rapid growth of transfer programs. As a consequence, programs form their own policies, and most transfer centers and many sperm banks limit their services to married couples, thus discriminating against single women and lesbian women. In light of the many issues coming to the fore, social workers in family agencies, child welfare agencies, and medical and psychiatric clinics are, or will soon be, helping parents and children with the dilemmas and the unforeseen emotional ramifications arising from the use of the new technologies, as has been the case in adoption. Many adults adopted as children conduct a painful search for their biological parents in order to complete their sense of self and to secure knowledge of their cultural, familial, and genetic heritage. How will the children born of the new technologies respond to their situation? How will children react to the knowledge that they were conceived in a laboratory dish? In the case of anonymous donors, how will children respond to the fact that they can never know who their father was? What will be the impact on children born to surrogate mothers when they learn that they were given up for money?

The situation of Baby M in New Jersey exemplifies the unknowns for the child, the surrogate, and the parents. The baby was carried to term by a surrogate mother, Mary Beth Whitehead, who had been impregnated by sperm donated by William Stern. She was to be paid $10,000 upon delivery, with the stipulation that the child would be his and would be adopted by his wife, Elizabeth. Whitehead later changed her mind when the baby was born, rejected the money, and tried to keep the baby. The Sterns sued, and the court awarded custody to Stern, ruling also that his wife could adopt the child. Whitehead's parental rights were terminated.

She appealed, and the New Jersey Supreme Court overturned all decisions except the one of custody. Whitehead's parental rights, including visitation, were restored. She is now Baby M's legal as well as her natural mother, and the father's wife, Elizabeth, cannot now adopt the child. The court also ruled that surrogacy for pay (but not unpaid surrogacy) is illegal in New Jersey. Subsequently, the parties returned to the superior court for rulings on visitation rights for Whitehead (now Gould). Social work and psychiatric professionals and consultants to the parties disagreed on what the differing impacts on the baby would be if the natural mother's demands were granted, or if they were not. However, the court ruled that Gould might have the baby at her home one day a week for up to six hours, to be increased in five months by a second day every two weeks, and to be further increased six months later to include an overnight stay during the two-day visits. In the summer of 1989, the child was allowed to spend two weeks with Gould. The Court found

"no credible evidence or expert opinion that Melissa will suffer any psychological or emotional harm by continued and expanded visitation with her mother.... Melissa's best interests will be served by unsupervised, uninterrupted liberal visitation with her mother.... She and her mother have the right to develop their own special relationship. [She is] no less capable than thousands of children of broken marriages who successfully adjust to complex family relationships" (Hanley 1988:B-5)

From its inception, the case raised many legal, social, and ethical issues that, like legalized abortion, remain highly controversial, with well-intentioned arguments on both sides.

Two additional areas of controversy have appeared in regard to new reproductive technologies. Fertility drugs occasionally produce multiple fetuses. Moreover, embryo implantation involves the use of as many as four embryos as a means of ensuring against failure, yet sometimes all develop as fetuses. In both situations, some prospective parents have asked for and received abortion of the surplus healthy fetuses in order to ensure the safe development of one or two. This so-called pregnancy reduction is done by inserting potassium chloride by needle into the fetal chest cavity. The heart stops, and eventually the dead fetuses are absorbed. Ethicists and some physicians are raising ethical and moral questions about these procedures.

The second area of controversy concerns infants who survive a late abortion. Should not they have the same rights to neonatal care and support and plans for their future, if they continue to live, as other prematurely born but wanted infants? Fetuses that survive late abortions are usually between 20 and 24 weeks of age. Hence these infants not only are injured by the procedure itself but are at additional grave medical risk because of their extreme immaturity. Viability, or when the baby can survive outside the womb, is being gradually pushed back by technical advances from 28 weeks (cited in the U.S. Supreme Court's *Roe v. Wade* decision of 1973) toward 20 weeks. It now stands at about 24 weeks, but as technology improves, the age will undoubtedly be lowered further.

Some states have set the limiting age for legal abortion at 24 weeks (except where the mother's life is in danger), and some hospitals have set their own cutoff points for elective abortions at 20 weeks in order to prevent such a disturbing event and its emotional impact on the mother and the staff. At least one state (New York) requires that another physician be in attendance at the abortion of a fetus of 20 or more weeks of age in order to render care in the event of its survival. Some obstetricians, however, are replacing the saline method of late abortion after 20 weeks with dismemberment of the fetus in the womb (known as dilation and evacuation), thereby ensuring nonsurvival. Others believe that this is an unethical and inhumane action, even though it is not illegal.

Few as their numbers are so far, survivors of late abortion are generating difficult ethical, legal, social, and financial issues. The protection of their right to full supportive care and resuscitation is a matter of growing concern to many professionals and others (Kleiman 1984). Kleiman cites a 1984 Report of the U.S. Centers for Disease Control which stated that 90 percent of abortions are performed before the twelfth week. About 13,000, or 1 percent, are performed after the twenty-first week. Many of these may be carried out on teenagers who were not aware of their pregnancy until quickening (fetal movement), which usually occurs between the seventeenth and twentieth weeks. About 10 percent of late abortions, however, are performed because of serious fetal abnormality. Furthermore, amniocentesis, the most common means of fetal diagnosis for genetic and chromosomal disorders, cannot be performed until the fourteenth to sixteenth weeks of pregnancy. The results take up to four weeks to become available, so that an elective abortion following the diagnosis of severe defect may take place as late as the twentieth week. If problems occur in the culturing of the amniotic fluid, the abortion may be delayed still further (Kleiman 1984).

The reproductive technologies described in this section are viewed by many infertile couples, and by those of which one partner is at risk of transmitting a genetic disease, as preferable to adoption, even though only one parent or neither will be genetically related to the child. However, the new technologies are not options for the infertile male; his only choices are childlessness or adoption. Yet less than 1 percent of unwed black mothers and only 12 percent of unwed white mothers now choose adoption for their infants. Hence nonminority persons seeking adoption have turned to private and international sources. Meanwhile, many minority and disabled infants and older children, eligible for adoption, languish in long-term foster care, often with many changes of foster home, which lead to blighted futures. This tragedy is due, in part, to policies that do not permit financial subsidies to low-income minority persons interested in adoption and, in part, to a concern that cross-racial adoption deprives the child of her or his cultural identity, history, and context. Therefore, it is likely that infertile parents will turn more and more to the new technologies to satisfy their yearning for a child, despite the ethical issues and the possible impact on the children as they grow older.

"WILL OUR BABY BE NORMAL?"

Social Work and Genetics

Before and during pregnancy, many prospective and expectant parents wonder about the possibility of birth defects, miscarriage, stillbirth, or prematurity. This section presents briefly some basic information about genetic disorders, and the next section will consider miscarriage, stillbirth, and prematurity. While all such reproductive tragedies represent a large public health problem, burgeoning developments in medical genetics, prenatal testing, and fetal medicine now offer hope and some options to couples at risk of transmitting a genetic disease. Like those who learn of their infertility, learning that one or one's partner is at risk of transmitting a genetic disease may require first- or second-order changes that transform the couple-as-family, or the family if there are already other children. As with infertile couples, successful transformation helps to heal the blow to the affected individual's self-concept, to strengthen the couple's relationship and communication patterns, and to lead to a new family paradigm that reconstructs their view of the world based on their new reality.

Schild and Black pointed to the need for all social workers to acquire basic information on genetics and to understand the impact of genetic disorders on individuals and families. Social workers are likely to meet clients with genetic problems in "medical settings, family planning services, adoption and child welfare agencies, family service agencies, child guidance clinics, public health programs, agencies serving the mentally retarded and their families, and even welfare departments that now serve many developmentally and physically disabled clients" (1984:5). Social workers who possess basic genetic information are able to help individuals and their families with the special stressors and psychosocial ramifications of genetic disorders or diagnoses. They can also perform an important preventive service by referring to genetic counseling those clients who are planning to have a child but are at risk of transmitting a genetic disease, or who have been exposed to environmental teratogens (substances causing physical or mental malformations), or who have had three or more miscarriages. Genograms in which illness and mortality data are obtained across three generations can yield genetic information important in the social work biopsychosocial-cultural assessment (Hartman and Laird 1983) as well as provide the basis for referral.

In her survey of 88 graduate schools of social work, Black (1982) found that only 24 of the responding 56 schools reported at least some genetic content in their curricula. But many of these indicated that such content was represented by brief units or guest lectures. Only 8 of the 56 schools offered an elective related to genetic issues, and no school required such content for all students. By 1985, the Council on Social Work Education had recognized that all social workers, regardless of their method and field of practice, do indeed require a basic knowledge of genetics, especially in light of the rapid developments in biogenetics that are transforming our understanding and clarifying the influence of genetic factors in human development and functioning (*Social Work Education Reporter* 1985). The council announced plans to prepare modules of genetic content for the social policy, methods, and human behavior areas of the curriculum. Meanwhile, in some parts of the country, seminars and workshops designed for graduate social workers and students—and conducted by trained ge-

neticists, genetic counselors, and social workers in genetic services—
are now offered by continuing-education programs, public health departments, and university research centers. The outlook is encouraging.

Some Genetic Principles

Genetic disorders can be inherited just as physical traits can be. The
hereditary information is transmitted by the parents to the child by
thousands of gene pairs located on 46 chromosomes, the normal number in the human species. The chromosomes occur in 23 pairs, 22 of
which are known as *autosomes;* the 23d pair are the sex chromosomes,
XX in the normal female and XY in the normal male. For purposes of
diagnosis and research, chromosomes can be seen and photographed
under a microscope and then mapped. The photograph is enlarged,
and the chromosome pairs are cut and pasted in order of their size
and are numbered according to established convention. The resulting
"portrait" of a person's chromosomes is called a *karyotype.* Copies of
each chromosome with the genes located on it appear in all cells of
the body except the sex cells, which have just half the normal number,
23 instead of 46 chromosomes each. Thus, when the sperm and egg
unite, the fertilized egg receives its necessary complement of 46 chromosomes, or 23 pairs. The child's genetic makeup is determined by
the particular mix of chromosomes and genes received from the two
parents: "Every gene for a particular structure or function from one
parent is matched with a gene with the same function on the matching chromosome of the other parent. The actual function controlled
or directed by the two genes is a reflection of their combined action"
(Milunsky 1977:54). The odds that a child will inherit a particular
trait, characteristic, or disorder, and to what extent it will be expressed, depend on many interacting factors, including whether the
trait is dominant or recessive, the degree to which either parent has
the trait, and the impact of the environment.

GENETIC DISORDERS

Genetic diseases comprise structural, functional, metabolic, and blood
disorders. Their causes include defective genes; environmental factors, including mutagens (substances causing gene mutation or change);

a mix of genetic and environmental factors; and nonhereditary chromosomal abnormalities.

According to the geneticist Riccardi:

> Genetic and congenital disorders are important at all levels of health care because they can involve all body parts and functions and because they are so common. Major congenital malformations, defined as those which interfere with normal livelihood and/or require surgery, occur in two to four percent of all newborns. The incidence is even higher when assessed at one year of age, since by that time previously occult problems, such as urinary tract anomalies and deafness, have become manifest.... Up to the age of fourteen years, congenital malformations are the third most common cause of death in both sexes. From ages 15 to 35, they are the ninth most common cause of death in both sexes. Chromosome abnormalities account for at least twenty percent of all spontaneous abortions, as well as a significant amount of infertility. The incidence of chromosome aberrations among liveborn infants is at least 0.5 percent. Diseases inherited as Mendelian traits, [see below] though often rare when taken singly, have a collective incidence of about two percent. (1977:4)

The continued growth of knowledge and of technical developments in biogenetics during the 1980s led to increasing diagnoses of genetic disorders. Thus the incidence of genetic disorders, as contrasted to the declining incidence of infectious diseases, is now a major medical and public health concern. Because of their chronicity, genetic disorders require a disproportionate share of health care expenditures. Many common chronic diseases of adulthood are entirely genetic in nature or have a major genetic component. They include, for example, late-onset diabetes mellitis, rheumatoid arthritis, and peptic ulcer. Some diseases, such as hypertension, coronary heart disease, and certain forms of cancer, are the consequence of a complex interplay between one or more genes and the environment.

Genetic counseling is considered advisable for persons who have a suspected or confirmed genetic disorder in their family background, couples who already have one child with a birth defect, and members of particular populations known to be at high risk for specific disorders (e.g., among Ashkenazi Jews, Tay-Sachs disease, which is a neurological disorder causing early death; sickle cell anemia among blacks and Greek people; thalassemia, a blood disorder, among southern Italians. Genetic counseling is also advisable for women in their late 30s and their 40s planning to have their first child). Geneticists and genetic counselors also see those who are infertile, those who have experienced three or more miscarriages, or pregnant women who have used harmful substances. These counselors provide information and diagnosis, define the odds of having a child born with a particular genetic disorder as precisely as possible, and offer nondirective counseling services. The objective is to enable couples to make informed childbearing decisions with which they can be comfortable.

Genetic and chromosomal disorders have several types of causes: 1) chromosomal disorders may arise from an addition, a deletion, or a structural rearrangement of a chromosome; 2) single-gene disorders may be either autosomal-dominant or autosomal-recessive; the term *single-gene* is a misnomer since all genes work in pairs, so that these disorders are the result of an interplay between a pair of matched genes; 3) X-linked disorders are single-gene recessive disorders transmitted on the sex chromosomes; and 4) other disorders arise from multiple genes with small, additive effects (polygenic disorders) and between genes and a presumed or known environmental factor (multifactorial disorders). Each of these four types is described in the next section.

Principles of Inheritance

The principles of inheritance are as follows:

1. Chromosome disorders occur during a specific pregnancy, with only a small chance that the accidental "error" will recur in other children in the family or in subsequent generations. In a small percentage of cases, however, a structural chromosome defect is inherited. Chromosome errors occur particularly during the formation of reproductive cells. The zygote may then have an extra, a deleted, or a rearranged chromosome. Such errors are repeated in the millions of cells that form the child, and they can affect many body structures and functions.

The most common chromosomal disorder in living persons is Down syndrome, with an estimated incidence of 1 in 650 births to 1 in 1,000, depending on the age structure of the population (Berini and Kahn 1987:57). The affected individual has 47 instead of 46 chromosomes in each cell of the body, the extra one being located in chromosome 21. Because there are three instead of the normal two chromosomes in number 21, Down syndrome is called *trisomy 21*. Children with this condition have characteristic facial features that make them look more like one another than like members of their own families. They also suffer mental retardation and often a functional defect of the heart, the eyes, or the ears. With good health care, these children now have an average life expectancy of twenty years. They are usually sociable youngsters and with proper stimulation and education are able to function on a higher level than was formerly thought. Besides trisomy, there are two other types of Down syndrome, both rare. They are known as *translocation* (in which extra 21 material is attached to another chromosome in all body cells) and *mosaicism* (a mixture of trisomic and normal cells in an individual, noninheritable, usually causing milder symptoms).

Errors involving an extra chromosome may also occur in other chromosomes. These usually cause early miscarriage or multiple, severe defects in the newborn, who dies soon after birth. In addition to trisomy conditions, which arise from one too many chromosomes per somatic (body) cell, there are also monosomy conditions arising form one too few chromosomes per somatic cell. Both types of accidental errors can also occur in the sex chromosomes. For example, a male may have an extra X chromosome and will manifest the Klinefelter syndrome (in which the victims are feminized and infertile), a trisomy condition. A female may be missing an X chromosome and will manifest Turner syndrome (in which the victims are masculinized and infertile), a monosomy condition. The causes of chromosomal disorders involving too many or too few chromosomes are still not clear. Trisomy 21 (Down syndrome) is associated with births to women 35 years or older. However, it is estimated that 20 to 30 percent of this disorder is due to the father's sperm (Holmes 1958).

In addition to trisomy and monosomy, chromosomal disorders can be caused by structural defects or rearrangements in a chromosome: "These occur in approximately one in every 500 live births and result from breakage and rearrangements of one or more of the chromosomes. Breakages can occur spontaneously or result from known (e.g., viruses) or unrecognized causes. The tendency for breakage sometimes is transmitted in a family" (Schild and Black 1984:26). The nature of the disorder depends on which chromosome is involved and the size of the missing piece. Radiation of various types (medical, atomic, and nuclear) is hazardous to chromosomes, but the cumulative amounts, timing, intensity, and effects on male and nonpregnant female gonads and on pregnant women are not yet definitive enough to predict the effects on the fetus. Nevertheless, diagnostic and therapeutic uses of X rays and radioisotopes are avoided for pregnant women unless absolutely necessary. Also, some viruses are known to cause transient chromosome breakage (Riccardi 1977:134–137).

2. Single-gene, autosomal-dominant disorders follow Mendelian patterns of inheritance. If one parent has a dominant gene for an autosomal-dominant disease there is a 50 percent risk (a 50/50 chance) that each child will have the disease. There is also, of course, a 50 percent likelihood that a child will not receive the abnormal gene. That child and his or her children will be free of the disease. Dominant disorders are often milder than recessive disorders. Among the 1,914 confirmed or suspected autosomal-dominant disorders now cataloged (McKusick 1986) are achondroplasia (a form of dwarfism), some forms of chronic simple glaucoma (an eye disease), and polydactyly (extra fingers or toes). Some autosomal-dominant disorders do not appear at birth but have a late onset, and hence they pose special problems to the affected individual and the family. Huntington's disease, for example, usually appears in middle age. Figure 7.1 shows the mode of inheritance of autosomal-dominant disorders.

Single-gene recessive disorders also follow a Mendelian pattern. In these instances, one of a pair of genes in one parent is defective, but the other, normal gene protects against the disease. This is the reason that while all of us carry several defective genes, we are free of the disorders they can cause. In the case of a child affected with an autosomal-recessive disorder, both parents carry the recessive gene even though each appears normal and may be unaware of being a carrier. Each of us carries between four and eight recessive genes for serious defects, so all of us are at risk of transmitting a genetic disorder if our mate carries the same mutant gene. The probability that two individuals with the same mutant gene will produce affected offspring varies with the frequency of that mutation in the population (Schild and Black 1984:31). Thus the risk of certain recessive disorders is higher for persons of particular ethnic and racial groups among whom a given mutant gene is more frequent.

Tay-Sachs disease, for example, has an incidence of 1 in every 3,600 conceptions among Jews of Ashkenazi descent: "Screening for carriers in this group coupled with the availability of prenatal diagnosis and therapeutic termination has substantially reduced the incidence at birth" (Berini and Kahn 1987:222). Sickle cell anemia has an estimated incidence of 1 in 625 births in the American black population, and approximately 1 in 10 black Americans are carriers. Prenatal diagnosis is now available through amniocentesis and chorionic villus sampling (Berini and Kahn 1987:119). Both procedures are described in the next section. Cystic fibrosis is the most common genetic disease among whites. Its incidence among American whites is 1 in 2,000 to 1 in 1,600. The rate of carriers is assumed to be 1 in 20 (Berini and Kahn 1987:158).

As in all autosomal-recessive diseases, when both parents do carry the mutant gene there is a 25 percent risk that each child will have the disorder. Each child also has a 50 percent risk of receiving only one defective gene and therefore of being a carrier of the genetic trait while being free of the disorder, like her or his parents. Should such a child happen to marry a similar carrier, their children would be at the same degree of risk described. The chance of inheriting a recessive disorder is increased in a child whose parents are of first- or second-degree relatedness. Children born to victims of incest by a carrier

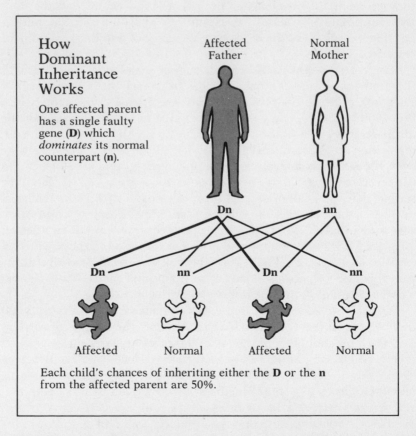

FIGURE 7.1. The Mode of Inheritance for Autosomal Dominant Disorders.

parent are at particular risk, with significant implications in child welfare and adoption (Black 1983).

These disorders tend to be severe, and many may cause death in infancy or early childhood. Among the 1,277 confirmed or suspected autosomal-recessive disorders cataloged (McKusick 1986), in addition to the three mentioned above, are phenylketonuria (a metabolic disorder leading to mental retardation) and thalassemia (a blood disorder). Infant autism also now appears to be a single-gene disorder that follows a pattern of recessive inheritance (Ritvo et al., 1985), a striking shift from the former assumption of environmental etiology due to parental functioning. Figure 7.2 shows the mode of inheritance of autosomal-recessive disorders.

3. X-linked disorders are usually manifested only in male children. However, female children may be carriers because normal females have two X chromosomes, while normal males have one X chromosome from the mother and one Y chromosome from the father. The recessive gene causing these disorders is found on one of the two X chromosomes of the mother. The only Y-linked trait is maleness, so there are no Y-linked (male-to-male) disorders. Baldness and hairy ears were formerly believed to be Y-linked traits, but it is now recognized that they are determined by the particular locations of autosomal genes (Kelly 1986).

In the case of X-linked disorders, the mother has a normal gene on her other X chromosome which protects her from the disorder, although she does function as a carrier. But when a male carries a harmful gene on his one X chromosome, he does not have a normal gene to counteract its effects and will manifest the disease (Schild and Black 1984:34). If the mother carries the mutant gene on one of her X chromosomes, each male child has a 50 percent risk of inheriting that gene and will manifest the disorder regardless of whether the father is genetically normal. Each daughter has the same level of risk of becoming a carrier like her mother. New genetic mutations are important additional sources of the disorder in families having no history of these diseases. Among the 253 confirmed or suspected X-linked recessive disorders now cataloged are hemophilia, muscular dystrophy, and color blindness. Figure 7.3 shows the mode of inheritance of X-linked recessive disorders.

Normally, male or female genitalia, determined by the presence or absence of the Y chromosome, are the basis for sex assignment. But various forms of genital ambiguities arising from a variety of genetic and environmental factors may make sex assignment a problem: "For example, a chromosomal male with ambiguous genitalia may be brought up as a female, if genital reconstruction is not clinically feasible. In other cases, gender of rearing may have been assigned before a disorder is recognized" (Berini and Kahn 1987:169). Genital ambiguities may arise from genetic factors such as sex chromosome abnormalities and autosomal and X-linked recessive disorders, and from intrauterine exposure to certain hormones. Recurrence risk estimates depend on the specific disorder. The treatment involves newborn surgical care, surgical reconstruction, hormone replacement

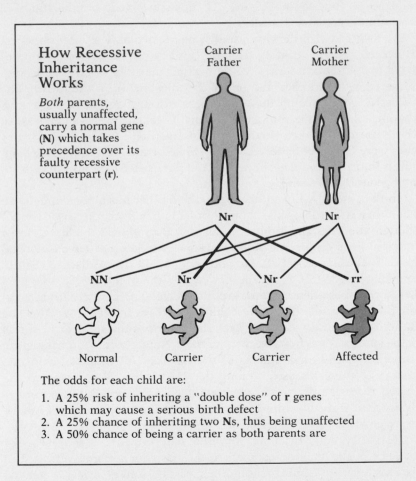

How Recessive Inheritance Works

Both parents, usually unaffected, carry a normal gene (**N**) which takes precedence over its faulty recessive counterpart (**r**).

Carrier Father   Carrier Mother

Nr   Nr

NN   Nr   Nr   rr

Normal   Carrier   Carrier   Affected

The odds for each child are:

1. A 25% risk of inheriting a "double dose" of **r** genes which may cause a serious birth defect
2. A 25% chance of inheriting two **N**s, thus being unaffected
3. A 50% chance of being a carrier as both parents are

FIGURE 7.2. The Mode of Inheritance for Autosomal Recessive Disorders.

therapy at puberty, and long-term counseling (Kelly 1986). Ambiguities represent either excessive masculinization of the female or insufficient masculinization of the male:

> [Their presence in the newborn] represents a true genetic emergency. Not only may such abnormalities trigger recognition of other potentially serious birth defects ... but the failure to promptly resolve the question of gender may lead to a major family psychosocial crisis. Nevertheless, precipitate and poorly

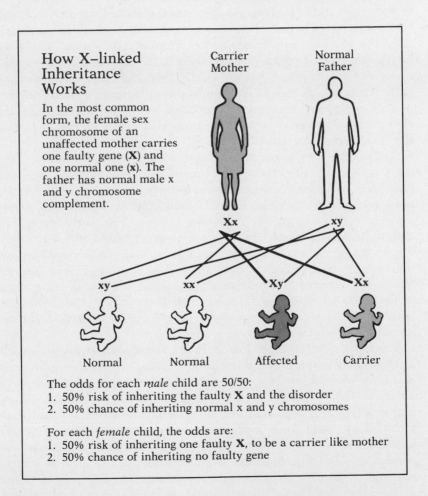

How X–linked Inheritance Works

In the most common form, the female sex chromosome of an unaffected mother carries one faulty gene (**X**) and one normal one (**x**). The father has normal male x and y chromosome complement.

Carrier Mother

Normal Father

Xx   xy

xy   xx   Xy   Xx

Normal   Normal   Affected   Carrier

The odds for each *male* child are 50/50:
1. 50% risk of inheriting the faulty **X** and the disorder
2. 50% chance of inheriting normal x and y chromosomes

For each *female* child, the odds are:
1. 50% risk of inheriting one faulty **X**, to be a carrier like mother
2. 50% chance of inheriting no faulty gene

FIGURE 7.3. The Mode of Inheritance for X-Linked Recessive Disorders.

thought out comments or actions can have even more disastrous consequences. Prompt evaluation and careful planning by a qualified team of consultants, including open discussion with the family, are the key to successful management. (Berini and Kahn 1987:167)

4. Polygenic disorders are due to the additive effects of a number of genes having equal input (Kelly 1986:159). They include neural tube defects (e.g., spina bifida), cleft lip or palate, clubfoot, and congenital heart disease, congenital scoliosis (curvature of the spine), and urinary tract malformations. Multifactorial disorders are those caused by the combined action of several genes (each of which has a small, similar, and cumulative effect) and environmental factors: "This may be considered as a *genetic predisposition* to the environmental triggering of the expression of a trait" (Kelly 1986:159; italics in the original). The terms *polygenic* and *multifactorial* are often used synonymously whenever there is a presumed or known environmental component. The distinction between them is one of emphasis rather than exclusion (Riccardi 1977:89).

Kelly (1986:160) noted that the vast majority of malformations are not the result of single-gene and chromosomal aberrations. Rather, they occur as isolated defects caused by polygenic and multifactorial phenomena. They may also occur in malformation syndromes of single-gene and chromosomal causation, but less frequently. Polygenic and multifactorial disorders do not have exact, well-defined risk factors as the single-gene disorders do. Hence their risk is estimated on the basis of epidemiological data and family histories rather than on Mendelian patterns of inheritance. In general, the risk of recurrence of these disorders is low (5 percent or less), but it rises with the number of affected family members, the degree of severity, and consanguinity (especially in incest).

The multifactorial disorders include common adult diseases such as essential hypertension and late-onset diabetes mellitis, certain types of mental retardation, schizophrenia, and some forms of cancer prevalent in a family. Recent evidence suggests that depressive disorders and about half the reported cases of Alzheimer's disease are multifactorial. They result from a genetic component that interacts in unknown ways with environmental factors. The remainder of the reported Alzheimer's cases have no known affected family members, although "There is increased risk for first-degree relatives of index cases in these families of approximately four times that of the general population, that is, eight percent to twelve percent" (Berini and Kahn

1987:85). This finding contrasts with a risk for first-degree relatives in the familial cases that approaches 50 percent. Regarding depressive disorders, Berini and Kahn stated that the mode of inheritance is unknown but the evidence for strong genetic predisposition is "overwhelming" (1987:262).

Alcoholism (distinguished from heavy drinking) is recognized as occurring in families, but the reasons are not fully understood:

> A growing body of evidence indicates that, at least in some cases, a genetic susceptibility may underlie the addiction. Other individuals may become alcoholic through environmental stimuli. . . . Most family studies show a risk of 25 percent, or more, for first-degree male relatives of alcoholics and five percent to ten percent for first-degree female relatives to become alcoholic, too. (Berini and Kahn 1987:268)

Figure 7.4 explains the meaning of percentages in the risks for all types of genetic disorders.

---

a common mistake

When risks are stated in percentages or fractions, parents unfamiliar with genetic mechanisms often interpret them incorrectly.

For example, those with one child affected by a disorder due to recessive inheritance may think that a 25 per cent—or one-in-four—risk means that the next three offspring are not endangered. *This is not true.*

The risk of genetic disease is the same for every child of the same mother and father.

FIGURE 7.4. The Meaning of Percentages in the Risks for Genetic Disorders.

PRENATAL TESTING FOR GENETIC DISORDERS

Amniocentesis and Chorionic Villus Sampling

Amniocentesis, the most widely used prenatal test, can detect the presence of well over one hundred defects (including neural tube defects, all known chromosomal abnormalities, and more than seventy metabolic defects). Other tests include sonar technology (ultrasound); fetoscopy; and blood, biochemical, and cytogenetic studies. The blood studies include an effective blood test of the expectant mother (high serum alpha-fetoprotein, or AFP) for the presence of neural tube defects in the fetus. It has the advantage over amniocentesis of presenting no risk to mother or fetus It is available at various research centers across the country. Mass screening for AFP has not been instituted in the United States, although it has been offered to pregnant women in various areas of Great Britain since 1974.

A more recent prenatal test is chorionic villus sampling (CVS), which has the advantage over amniocentesis of being performed in the eighth to eleventh week of pregnancy, with results available in hours or days. Thus a decision to terminate the pregnancy based on the results may be made by the twelfth week or earlier. It is done by inserting a slender tube through the vagina and the cervix to secure a fragment of placenta. CVS can reveal the same genetic disorders as amniocentesis except neural tube defects. Its disadvantages include a slight degree of increased risk, a higher rate of diagnostic error, and the fact that its timing requires the identification of at-risk pregnancies before many women have sought prenatal care. CVS is still an experimental procedure while safety studies continue, but it is offered at many genetic centers (Kelly 1986:372).

Inevitable conflicts and difficult decisions for the parents result from prenatal testing. In amniocentesis, for example, the long wait for test results (three to five weeks) is usually highly stressful for the parents. Emotional support before the test, during the wait for results, and after they are received is provided by a master's degree genetic counselor or a social work member of the genetics team. When a test is positive, the geneticist provides information on the prognosis and the management of the child's condition. Many parents whose tests are positive for the disorder in question elect to terminate the pregnancy, especially when the condition is severe or irremediable.

While the decision to abort is implicit in the earlier decision to undergo amniocentesis, it is nonetheless an agonizing choice for many couples to make about a wanted infant (Duncan and Weston-Smith 1984), and one that may cause lifelong pain for some. The parents' dilemma is intensified by the fact that the degree of physical and mental disability in many conditions is not always predictable before birth (or even after birth) because of variations in the expression of the disorder.

Some parents who receive positive test results for the disease in question, but for whom abortion is unacceptable, report the joys they experience—along with the difficulties—in raising a child with Down syndrome, spina bifida, or other disorders, as well as the remarkable developmental progress that some affected children can make. Such progress is due to the care given by accepting, loving, and supportive parents and siblings as well as to advances in health care, education, and other services. In some instances, it may also be related to less mental or physical impairment than the prognosis for the disorder suggests.

Testing at Birth and Population Screening

Routine testing at birth for the genetic disorder of phenylketonuria (PKU), for example, is successful because the disease can be accurately diagnosed, and a specific environmental treatment (diet) is available. Newborns with positive test results are placed on a restricted diet that prevents mental retardation. It is a complex, difficult regimen for child and parents, but it can be relaxed by the school years. However, little girls treated in this way may, as adults, give birth to mentally retarded babies (because of the presence of toxic phenylalanine in the mother's bloodstream) unless they return to the diet during pregnancy.

On the other hand, feasible population screening for several genetic diseases known to be associated with particular population groups presents a number of difficult issues. Well-meaning programs in the recent past produced serious problems because of their failure to include counseling services. A case in point is sickle cell anemia, a painful, life-threatening autosomal-recessive blood disorder. Both parents must carry the mutant gene for the disease to be expressed in their offspring. If the child receives the gene from only one parent, she or he will be a carrier of the *harmless* sickle cell trait:

"Many carriers of the sickle cell trait, because they were not informed otherwise, came to believe that they had a mild form of, or a tendency to, sickle cell anemia. Social stigmatization, occupational discrimination, uprating of insurance premiums ... were among the results of these programs. In addition, there was a lessened choice of marriage partners for the many people who mistakenly believed that a sickle cell trait carrier was a less desirable mate" (Motulsky 1974).

Motulsky and other geneticists have pointed out that before people are asked to participate in a screening program, they must be fully advised of all the possible social and medical consequences of being diagnosed as a carrier. Counseling services must be included as an essential part of the program because truly informed consent can be ensured only if there is adequate time for a thorough discussion of the technical information and for help with the psychosocial impact of the information (Schild and Black (1984:131). Population screening for Tay-Sachs disease, affecting mainly those of Ashkenazi Jewish descent, had several early problems somewhat similar to those of the sickle cell programs. Fortunately, prenatal testing is now available for both diseases, and it is hoped that one will soon be developed for cystic fibrosis, a disorder associated with the general white population.

In other situations, a conflict can emerge between the patient's right to confidentiality and the right of relatives to know of their genetic risks. It is a conflict that bears heavily on the social worker's ethical behavior. Schild and Black presented the following hypothetical example of a female patient whose son has hemophilia:

What if, following the genetic counseling, the woman refuses to contact her sisters, who are of childbearing age, and will not allow the genetic counselor to warn them of their risks for having affected sons? Even more to the point, what if a social worker in a community agency later sees the woman and becomes aware of this situation. Does that social worker have any responsibility, ethically and/or legally, to pursue actively attempts to get the genetic information to the sisters who unknowingly are at risk for having sons with serious health problems? As clinicians, social workers must weigh their ethical concerns for the rights of these sisters and their unborn children against a primary professional responsibility to their designated client. (1984:134)

Treatment of Genetic Disorders

Fetal medicine and perinatal medicine are developing rapidly, and some researchers anticipate a breakthrough in gene therapy and enzyme replacement (for inborn metabolic disorders) in the next decade or two. For now, treatment in utero is possible for a few rare conditions, and postnatal surgical correction is available for cleft lip and palate, clubfoot, various heart malformations, some instances of spina bifida, and many other structural defects. Chemical regulation by drugs, hormones, vitamins, and dietary supplementation or restriction is available, for example, for diabetes (insulin), inherited rickets (phosphate and Vitamin D metabolites), and PKU (protein substitute). Prostheses include hearing aids, artificial limbs, ostomies, shunts for hydrocephalus, and transplants of corneas, kidneys, bone, and, most recently, hearts and livers. Rh-factor babies can be saved by a complete blood exchange transfusion soon after birth. And habilitation services can help affected children to reach their full physical, mental, sensory, and social potential.

PREMATURITY, MISCARRIAGE, AND STILLBIRTH

Prematurity, miscarriage, and stillbirth may or may not be the consequence of genetic disease, but their incidence is higher in pregnancies involving genetic disorders.

Prematurity

Prematurity is a function of weight, not of length of gestation. Babies under 4 pounds, 6 ounces at birth are considered premature, and 5.5 pounds is considered the dividing line between normal and low birth weight. Low-birth-weight babies are frequently born to poor, undernourished mothers and very young mothers: "Underweight newborns have a higher death rate because of problems with breathing, heart action, and control of temperature and blood sugar. These difficulties can lead to long-term physical and mental impairment, though prompt medical care can help" (*Birth Defects* 1979:no pagination).

Modern medical technology enables many low-weight babies to survive who would have died a short time ago. With good pediatric care many of them will develop normally. The lower the birth weight, however, the more likely is the baby to suffer from serious respiratory disorders, mental retardation, cardiac problems, and other severe conditions (including those resulting from genetic disease in affected babies). Low-birth-weight babies, like those with genetic disorders, may have to be in neonatal intensive care for weeks, even months. Generally, hospitals with such units encourage parents to visit and telephone at any time during the day and night. They encourage the parents to touch the baby, and later to hold their infant and participate in its care and feeding, so that the baby and the parents become attached. For parents who live at a distance, which is frequently the case in regional neonate units, and for parents who are poor, who work, or who have other young children, frequent visiting may be difficult or impossible.

The birth of a premature, gravely ill baby or a baby with a serious genetic or other disorder induces deep shock and grief in the parents. They experience a tragic loss and dashed hopes. Where the baby's life hangs in the balance, the parents confront two conflicting demands: to begin to love and bond with their baby and at the same time to engage in anticipatory mourning in order to prepare for the possibility of the baby's death. The empathic support and provision of information by medical, nursing, and social work staffs are critical if the parents are to begin their grief work, support each other, cope with the multiple demands, and make informed decisions. The support of relatives and friends is also an important environmental resource if the child dies, or if the child lives and is handicapped.

When the baby does go home, the long separation and the baby's condition may make the attachment process difficult. The baby, even if on the way to recovery, may not be able to recognize and respond to the parents' caregiving, depending on the particular condition. The infant may not yet be able to cue the parents to his or her needs, and they may find it hard to satisfy the baby. Over time, they may become anxious, disappointed, guilty, or even angry at the baby. Perhaps it is not surprising that premature babies are overrepresented in the population of physically abused infants and children.

If the child survives, the parents will still mourn the loss of the healthy child they expected while they make plans for the baby who was actually born. They are involved in the same life transition and its tasks as other new parents, but the tasks are much more difficult and complex. They face many dilemmas and difficult decisions regarding their baby's continuing care, needed medical or rehabilitative procedures and attention, and crushing financial demands. Their emotional responses, and how they cope with them and with the exceptional adaptive tasks they face, will determine how they function in their relationship to each other, and how they attach to their baby, develop competence in caring for her or him, and maintain their self-esteem and self-direction.

Baby and parents are likely to confront occasional medical crises and even life-threatening issues that may require further family transformations during infancy and as the child grows. However, Darling (1979) pointed out that as difficult as the parents' adaptation to their child's handicap is, most parents, during the first year or so, do find helpful physicians and social workers, parents' associations or self-help groups, enlightening literature, physical therapy, behavioral training, and other helpful services and programs. With such resources they manage the needed family transformation. Earlier studies had suggested that the birth of a handicapped child was likely to result in family breakdown, but according to Darling, more recent research indicates that marital difficulties or separation in these situations is largely attributable to problems in the relationship before the child's birth.

Miscarriage and Stillbirth

Miscarriage (spontaneous abortion before the twentieth week of gestation) and fetal death (after the twentieth week of gestation) in a wanted pregnancy are also traumatic, although they are not always recognized as a grievous loss by well-intending relatives and friends, who may say to the parents, "It wasn't a person" or "You can have another." Fetal death is sometimes marked by the parents with a burial and ceremony, whereas the miscarriage rarely is so marked. It may, therefore, be less adequately grieved and may leave emotional scars (Callahan, Brasted, and Granados 1983). Social workers will do well, in genogram work with families, to be alert to possible miscarriages and stillbirths inadequately mourned.

A stillbirth is likely to be an even harsher loss. Because of their youthful years, the parents may not have had an earlier encounter with death, and now they face a most significant one. The grieving is supported and the shock somewhat eased when hospital staff and/or family encourage the parents to see and hold the stillborn baby, name the baby, accept a photograph of her or him, and hold a funeral service—if those are their wishes. These rituals affirm the personhood of the lost baby, sanction and release the grieving process, and help the parents and family members to support one another in their mourning (Stringham, Riley, and Ross 1982).

All these experiences with the death or disability of an infant are severe stressors involving loss, grief, and even anger ("Why did this happen to me?"). Sadly, it is sometimes also the case that guilt feelings of having been responsible or anger and projection of blame by the parents onto each other accompany the grief and shock. Such negative feelings may intensify if the grief work and the coping demands in caring for the child with a disability are not handled effectively. The feelings are an additional stressor that must be managed. If they are not, the cumulative effects may lead to the dissolution of the marriage or relationship, even where it was satisfying before the birth. In some instances, environmental resources may be insufficient to facilitate the parents' coping tasks, and this insufficiency, too, can create added stress with similar consequences.

For various reasons, not all parents are able to undertake the care of a severely afflicted infant. Society and the community must provide quality arrangements for the care of these children, respite services for parents who do raise their disabled or chronically ill children, and support groups for parents experiencing the tragedies described in this chapter. All social workers, regardless of their field or method, can work toward supportive social policy and the programmatic development of such resources, and for sensitive, responsive genetic services and programs for all who need them.

Clearly, the sad losses experienced in infertility, genetic disorders, miscarriage, fetal death, stillbirth, or the birth of a severely handicapped child—whether due to genetic or other causes—are extremely painful, unexpected second-order developments for the parents. The disorganization that accompanies the shock and sorrow can lead ultimately to second-order changes and to the family's transformation and reintegration. If changes and ultimate transformation do not take place, disorganization may continue, with ill effects on the family and its members. Outcomes depend on what personal and environmental resources are available, how the members use them to cope with the loss and its many meanings, and how they reconstruct their family paradigm, often with the help of a social worker.

Dilemmas and Issues

Frequently, a lag can be observed between developments in one realm of social life and society's responses to the unforeseen consequences of these developments. A lag is now apparent in the medicoscientific realm, especially in biogenetics and reproductive innovations. Progress in knowledge and techniques has forced agonizing decisions upon families, professionals, and society's judicial and legislative institutions because of unanticipated issues that still lack consensual guidelines for decision making by parents and professionals. Well-intentioned lay and professional individuals and groups can be on opposite sides of the many ethical and social questions coming to the fore as new technologies permit more and more severely handicapped infants to survive who, only a short time ago, would not have lived.

For example, decisions about forgoing treatment of newborns with multiple severe defects may be difficult to make because of uncertainty about prognosis at birth and assumptions concerning quality of life, about which reasonable people can differ. With aggressive treatment, a dying baby's suffering may only be prolonged. Or such an infant may survive only to exist in a vegetative state and as a never-ending emotional and financial tragedy to or burden on the parents, with a possible adverse impact on siblings. On the other hand, a baby with severe defects may, with aggressive treatment, improve enough to live a relatively satisfying life. In still other cases, a disastrous outcome is certain, and the parents and their physician may decide that the baby is to be kept as comfortable as possible while being allowed to die naturally without the use of modern heroic measures.

The issues were brought to public attention by the federal government's efforts to interfere in the cases of two such babies, charging that withholding treatment from them constituted discrimination against the handicapped, under section 504 of the Rehabilitation Act of 1973. The courts ruled that the section was not intended to cover medical decisions regarding the treatment of newborn infants. Two regulations of the U.S. Department of Health and Human Services that encouraged people to report to federal officers any situations of withheld treatment that seemed discriminatory were also invalidated (Schmeck 1985).

The infants involved were Baby Doe, born in 1982 in Indiana, and Baby Jane Doe, born in 1983 in New York. Baby Doe was born with Down syndrome and heart defects, and without an opening to his stomach. The latter defect, without surgical repair, would cause his death by starvation. The parents decided against surgery, the baby was sedated, and he died of starvation in six days. The case, termed *passive infanticide* by some, caused considerable public outcry. Some physicians, ethicists, and others take the position that a painless lethal injection is more humane than allowing an infant to die slowly of starvation and dehydration. Others hold the view that active killing is not morally acceptable. Many such cases had occurred earlier in other hospitals and medical centers, but without publicity.

Baby Jane Doe was born with spina bifida, hydrocephalus, and an abnormally small head. The doctors believed that she would be paralyzed, permanently incontinent, and severely mentally retarded and would probably not live beyond two years, even with surgery to close the spinal opening and to drain fluid from the brain. The parents and the doctors decided against the surgery. However, word of the case leaked out, and Lawrence Washburn, an antiabortion activist, sued unsuccessfully to force the doctors to operate. Then the federal government filed suit as described above, and a long delay set in. Meanwhile, the spinal opening closed naturally, and the parents gave permission for surgical reduction of the hydrocephalus. Baby Jane Doe returned home with her parents at age 6 months.

Her parents were interviewed on her first birthday and reported that she has taken " 'quite nicely to life. She's not in pain, is comfortable, and happy, but can't do anything on her own,' " and they are saddened by her helplessness. She lacks most of the cerebral cortex, is paralyzed from the waist down, and must be catherized six times a day because her urinary system is paralyzed. She is taken twice a week for physical therapy, and once a week a therapist comes to the home. Her parents are devoted to her care, and to paying the $50,000 in legal fees they owe for their daughter's case (*New York Times*, October 14, 1984:56).

The following year, the nation's Roman Catholic bishops and the American Jewish Congress released an unprecedented agreement supporting the rights of parents to make ultimate decisions regarding the treatment of handicapped newborns. The document declared, "Handicaps, in and of themselves, do not justify withholding of medical treatment when such treatment offers reasonable hope of benefit and does not impose excessive pain or other burdens on the patient. . . . What is best for the individual child should take precedence over any conflicting interests of parents or society." (*Washington Post*, July 24, 1985, p. H-20). One criticism of the Reagan administration's effort to force the aggressive treatment of all critically ill newborns was its apparent lack of interest in providing funds to help with the tremendous costs for the lifelong care of severely affected individuals saved by aggressive means.

Some observers hold that social priorities should be part of decision making. For example, keeping a severely affected infant alive by very costly professional attention and medical equipment over a long period of time, possibly to endure a life of pain, paralysis, sensory defects, mental retardation, chronic severe organic problems, and so on, means that limited medical resources will be even less available for other patients having less serious, more correctable conditions. In his discussion of the issues, Milunsky noted, "Parents and doctors working together with the best interests of the child at heart are undoubtedly best equipped to make these extremely trying decisions" (1977:296). Callahan, an ethicist, commented that the communal task is to support free choice, "allowing parents to make their own choice without penalizing them socially for the choices they make, or condemning them for those choices which will increase the financial costs to society. Part of the very meaning of human continuity . . . entails a willingness of society to bear the social costs of individual freedom" (1973:89).

The next chapter considers the tandem development of child and parents, as well as the family transformations, that take place over a baby's first year of life.

8

Family Transformations in Infancy

With every child who is born, under no matter what circumstances . . . the potentiality of the human race is born again.

—James Agee

Chapter 8 and the remaining chapters continue the theme of life transitions and family transformations as introduced in chapters 5 and 6. The major focus will be on the transitions and developmental changes of the individual family members that, together with other momentous events and processes, are the sources of family transformations within the context of community and society. This chapter begins with a brief review of studies of the impact of their baby's arrival on the parental pair, followed by research findings on infant capacities. Next it examines the processes of attachment that take place between infant and parents, including new conceptions of fathering. The transactional origins of competence, self-esteem and self-concept, and self-direction are also considered, along with an analysis of some environmental circumstances that may lead to developmental difficulties for the very young child.

FIRST-TIME PARENTING AND FAMILY TRANSFORMATION

Research on the impact of the baby's birth on the parents has shifted since the early 1970s from a crisis orientation to a view of the event as a normal life transition. The corresponding differences in findings lead one to wonder if research, like practice itself, tends to find whatever its theory base assumes is there. The crisis-oriented studies (for example, Hobbs 1965; Dyer 1963; LeMasters 1957) found that normal first-time parents of a healthy, wanted baby typically experienced a severe crisis, regardless of the quality of their own relationship. Although the crisis abated for most parents by the time the baby was about 6 months old, 83 to 58 percent reported that they had suffered disruptions in companionship patterns and routines, chronic fatigue, diminished social contacts, and (among working mothers) loss of the gratifications of employment.

Studies that assume that first-time parenting is a normal life transition (e.g., Cowan 1978) report that despite expectable initial confusions, doubts, anxieties, and unaccustomed tumult, most parents quickly settle down and cope effectively with the transition. They become more realistic about their baby and their own parenting, and they begin to sense a new kind of partnership between themselves as a couple. It is now generally recognized that the life transition of becoming a first-time mother and father not only results in personal changes within the parents as they gradually become socialized to their new status and roles but also requires a significant family transformation as the couple make room for the new member and become a three-party system.

They must undertake elaboration of the family structure or organization, incorporate the new roles of mother and father into the reorganization, and integrate these roles with their mate or spousal roles. Some shift in their relationship away from their preoccupation with couplehood and toward shared parenthood is required. Their usual patterns of functioning as a couple are likely to be disrupted. Roles and household tasks will need to be reassigned, temporal and spatial arrangements restructured, and the bases and means of decision making realigned. They must learn the principles of infant care and the tasks of child rearing; they must develop the ability to read their baby's signals and to respond sensitively. They may need to develop new familial values and norms associated with their new status as parents, and to manage new relationships with their parents as grandparents and with other network members. In these and other ways, the family achieves a new view of itself and its new reality—a major transformation.

Most parents regard this life transition as a challenge and a first-order development and meet it with readiness and positive feelings of confidence and anticipated mastery. The family changes go smoothly. Others experience the transition as a stressor that exceeds their coping resources, and they respond with negative feelings of anxiety, resentment of the child or of the partner, low self-esteem, and lack of confidence in their own parenting abilities. Among this group, however, some couples may have environmental resources to deal effectively with the stress of the transition, such as financial security and the social support of friends and relatives. Adaptive shifts in roles and tasks are eventually worked out, care of the infant is eventually more gratifying, and some degree of family transformation is eventually achieved. The new baby is integrated into the family's view of itself and its world. What emerges is a different family paradigm, with changed conceptions of relationships within the family and to the environment.

Others who are stressed by the transition may lack the environmental and/or personal resources to regulate their increasing anxiety or other negative feelings, or they may have financial or relationship problems so great that their coping with the new and stressful demands is less than optimal. The transition to parenting their infant is neither pleasurable nor smooth, and the family transformation is not accomplished. That does not always mean, however, that their parenting will remain a problem. Internal resources may be regenerated later, new external resources may be found, financial problems may be resolved, and so on, and the transformation may take place. If it does not, more serious consequences are apt to follow, such as marital breakdown, failures in infant–parent attachment, or abuse and neglect.

FINDINGS FROM INFANT RESEARCH

The Significance of Temperament

In the introduction to part 2, brief reference was made to the longitudinal studies of Chess and Thomas (1986). Based on their thirty-year longitudinal study of a large sample of white middle-class children, the researchers identify nine temperamental traits: 1) activity level; 2) regularity in biological functions; 3) approach to or withdrawal from new stimuli; 4) amount of adaptability to new or changed situations; 5) threshold of responsiveness to new social situations, external objects, and sensory stimuli; 6) intensity of reaction regardless of its quality or direction; 7) quality of mood; 8) distractibility; and 9) attention span and persistence. These characteristics can be observed in the first month of life and tend toward continuity in many, if not most, instances.

Further, Chess and Thomas specified three constellations of children's temperaments: easy, difficult, and slow to warm up. Easy children comprised 40 percent of the sample. The temperamentally easy baby responds positively "to the first bath, to most new foods, to new places and people, and her regular sleep and feeding patterns lighten the burden of caretaking routines. The easy child's quick and frequent smile evokes a pleasurable response from the parents, older children, and other adults" (1986:27). This baby usually makes new parents feel competent.

The difficult group comprised 10 percent of the sample. The temperamentally difficult baby fusses and cries frequently and loudly and shows "intense negative reactions to new situations and slow adaptability, as well as irregular sleep and feeding patterns" (1986:33). This baby "places special demands on parents and acts as a stress for them" (1986:30). Some parents may blame themselves for these behaviors and feel guilty and incompetent; others may blame the child as having some kind of defect. Some parents may consistently try to appease the difficult baby, thus creating a child tyrant; others may become hostile to the baby, and life together is experienced as an ongoing struggle for control and domination.

The slow-to-warm-up children comprised 15 percent of the sample. Temperamentally slow-to-warm-up babies present a "combination of negative responses of mild intensity to new stimuli with slow adaptability after repeated contact. . . . In contrast to the difficult children, [they] are characterized by mild intensity of reactions, whether positive or negative, and by less tendency to show irregularity of biological functions. . . . If given the opportunity to re-experience . . . new situations over time and without pressure, such a child gradually comes to show quiet and positive interest and involvement" (1986:280).

The three constellations claimed only 65 percent of all the subjects. The remainder were not readily categorized because of the many various combinations of temperamental characteristics in the individual children. Even those children who constituted the three temperamental constellations showed considerable variation in degree. Chess and Thomas emphasized that temperament is only one of the many variables influencing development and functioning. They also emphasized strongly that the three constellations represent variations within normal limits and are not predictive of emotional disorder, although particular environments—parental or otherwise—in which there is a poor fit with the child's temperament may, in their responses to the child over time, jeopardize her or his healthy development.

Chess and Thomas also showed in useful detail how parents and teachers can be helped to understand the child's unique temperament and how to respond constructively in day-to-day living—important knowledge for social workers who work with children or families. The researchers' position is an ecological one: parents need to learn how to respond to the individual temperament of their baby rather than to preconceived notions of how a baby should be. Such responsiveness creates a goodness of fit between baby and parents that fosters the baby's optimal development and the parents' pleasure and gratification in caregiving. Admittedly, the temperamentally difficult baby presents an inordinate challenge. But out of their empathy, love, and resilience, and/or with guidance from others and assurance that the baby is indeed normal ("Some babies come that way"), parents do begin to respond appropriately to their baby and develop optimal methods of caregiving. If for any reason they do not achieve this task, a consistent poorness of fit can lead to a pathological exaggeration of a temperamental attribute or a constellation.

Infant Capacities

It has always been recognized, intuitively or otherwise, that all newborn infants must cope with the stress of birth and its aftermath (for example, breathing, eating, and regulating their response to warmth and cold on their own) in order to achieve smooth organic functioning for survival and a sense of well-being. Very soon, young babies must cope with discomforts of all kinds through motor solutions such as wiggling to achieve a more comfortable position in the crib, perceptual-cognitive solutions such as stretching to be held in a more vertical posture for greater visual stimuli, and later, social solutions such as smiling and vocalizing to elicit interaction (Murphy and Moriarty 1976).

New findings in infant research are expanding our knowledge about infant capacities and are reshaping the thinking of clinicians and developmental theorists about the subjective life of infants and their emotional and social development (e.g., Bower 1976; Lichtenberg 1981, Sander 1980). Since the early 1970s, infant researchers in North America and abroad, using new techniques and ingenious instruments, have demonstrated that newborn and very young infants are remarkably capable human beings. They are not blank slates passively waiting for the environment to etch in their individuality, nor are they mere bundles of biological drives requiring gratification for the relief of tension. The distinguished infant researcher and practicing psychoanalyst Daniel Stern (1985) discussed particular findings that bear directly on two hypothesized developmental stages in object relations theory: the so-called "normal autistic" and "normal symbiotic" stages of Mahler (Mahler 1979) (see the section on Mahler, Appendix 2):

1. *"Normal autism."* We now know that infants arrive in the world well equipped with sensory-perceptual and cognitive capacities, including memory and learning, to participate in shaping their own experience. During periods of alert inactivity, infants direct their eyes and ears to the environment, actively taking it all in and even working to evoke stimulation. For example, newborns will engage in nonnutritive sucking on an electronically bugged pacifier that operates a slide carousel and projector. They will suck long and vigorously to keep the carousel presenting them with new and different slides to look at (Stern 1985:39). While it is true that young infants have less tolerance of stimulation than they will have later, there are optimal levels of stimulation below which infants will seek more stimuli and above which stimulation will be avoided (Stern 1977).

Stern also reported (1983) that evidence shows that human newborns have an innate predisposition to be exquisitely tuned and responsive to the human voice, face, and body. Caregiver and infant together regulate their interaction, shape each other's behaviors, and seek specific stimuli from one another. For example, the visual apparatus is almost mature at birth, and mutual gazing behaviors in infant and mother have been found to be important in attachment and bonding (Stern 1977). Infants 12 to 21 days old can imitate both manual and facial gestures, such as a protruding tongue or a widely opened mouth. What is so astonishing about the infant's sticking out his or her tongue after the mother or the experimenter sticks out hers? It indicates that infants not only can imitate the action but know that they have a tongue and know where it is even though they have never seen their own tongue. That is, very young infants can equate their own unseen behaviors with gestures they see others perform (Meltzoff and Moore 1977).

Brazelton (1979), an infant researcher and pediatrician, reported that at a few weeks of age, the baby can distinguish its mother's voice and smell from the voice and smell of another woman. By 2 or 3 weeks of age, babies display an entirely different attitude toward their father than toward their mother—being more bright-faced, wide-eyed, and playful in response to the father. These various abilities do not have to be learned; they are built into the way cognition and perception work in the human species from birth. Stern (1985) cited many studies showing that young infants do learn very early and very fast in the newborn period, in addition to those capacities they are born with. He concluded that they are able to perceive their distinctness from the environment and to use their capacities to affect their environment. They can discriminate the caregiver as a recognizable, specific entity in a world of other such potential entities. In the light of the extensive evidence, then, Stern suggested that Mahler's concept of a normal autistic stage is no longer tenable. At about 2–3 months the infant becomes more social, but that is not the same as becoming less autistic. "If by autism we mean a primary lack of interest in and registration of external stimuli, in particular human stimuli, then the recent data indicate that the infant is never autistic. Infants are deeply engaged in and related to social stimuli" (Stern 1985:234).

(Primary autism, a rare disorder, appears before the age of 3. A child so afflicted is unable to relate to people and social situations. Recent research reveals the presence of brain abnormalities in the cerebellum and the limbic system. The abnormalities are said to occur in early brain development and not through deterioration after development. Such a biological base of autism is likely to shift treatment from emphasizing parental causation to helping parents cope with the difficult behaviors.)

2. *"Normal symbiosis."* Extensive research indicates that human infants arrive in the world with an innate ability to transfer knowledge from one sensory modality to another. For example, a newborn moves her or his eyes to the right when a sound is on the right, and to the left when the sound is on the left, demonstrating an expectation that there will be something to look at, a source for the sound. This is a simple form of intersensory coordination already present at birth. Similarly, very young infants, blindfolded and given a nubbed nipple to mouth, will, when the blindfold is removed and they are shown the nubbed nipple and a smooth one together, give preferential attention to the nubbed nipple. In many such experiments, infants demonstrate their ability to coordinate information across different sensory modalities. This ability is now considered a predesigned human capacity built into the infant's cognitive and perceptual processes (Stern 1985). It is not a learned capacity inasmuch as the infants, in order to prefer the nubbed over the smooth nipple, did not have to first see and mouth both nipples and to form visual and tactile schemes of each as Piaget suggested (see the section in appendix 1 on Piaget).

Experiments (Kuhl and Meltzoff 1982) show that infants 18 to 20 weeks old can detect the correspondence between auditorially and visually presented speech. They manifest some of the elements related to the adult ability of lip reading. Infants look significantly longer at the one of two faces whose mouth movements match the sound. Kuhl and Meltzoff believe that this cross-modal perception of speech has implications for social development (coordinating joint actions between infant and caregiver), cognitive development, and linguistic development. Stern (1985) concluded that the presence of cross-modal capacities makes it highly improbable that the infant consistently confuses self and other through a long stage of undifferentiation that Mahler termed normal symbiosis (Mahler 1979) (see the section in appendix 1 on Mahler). Rather than having to individuate from an initial symbiotic position, it appears to Stern, the infant simultaneously forms various mental representations of self and self-fused-with-other from nondifferentiated (as distinguished from undifferentiated) experiences. He added:

> Many of the phenomena thought by psychoanalytic theory to play a crucial role in very early development, such as delusions of merger or fusion, [object] splitting, and defensive or paranoid fantasies, are not applicable to the infancy period—that is, before the age of roughly eighteen to twenty-four months—but are conceivable only after the capacity for symbolization as evidenced by language is emerging, when infancy ends. (1985:11)

For Stern (1985) the evidence from infant studies suggests the need to reconsider the concept of normal symbiosis and the extent of its explanatory power in childhood psychosis, borderline states, and other regressive phenomena. In his opinion, continued research may reveal that some of the earliest deviations in social and intellectual functioning are traceable to deficits in cross-modal and other innate infant capacities rather than to supposed distortions in the mother–infant relationship. Stern suggested that if this proves to be the case, we will have new explanations of, and interventions for, developmental disorders, primary autism, learning disabilities, attention deficits, and various difficulties in social functioning and competence.

In addition to implications for social workers in mental health services, these and other findings from infant research are important to social workers in family agencies and child welfare, especially in helping young people to prepare for parenting, and in developing family life education programs, parent support groups, foster parent groups, and so on.

PARENT–INFANT INTERACTION

The pediatricians Klaus and Kennell (1976), in their observations of mothers presented with their babies following hospital delivery, reported the following: all the mothers, including additional women whose infants were in incubators, uniformly took the *en face* position in an effort to achieve eye contact with their infants.[1] This report is noteworthy because at birth the infant's visual-motor system (looking at and seeing) is immediately operable:

> The newborn cannot only see but arrives with reflexes that allow him [*sic*] to follow and fixate upon an object. Without any previous experience he can follow a moving object with his eyes and head and can hold his gaze upon it. . . . He is endowed with the tendency to seek out stimulation. . . . So long as the stimuli do not overwhelm him, he goes about his momentous task with intensity and pleasure. (Stern 1977:34–35)

Korner and Grobstein (1966) were also interested in the newborn's visual capacities. They reported that ordinary good mothers being observed in a newborn nursery attempted to soothe their crying babies in varying ways. Some stroked their babies while they lay in their bassinets. Some picked up their babies and rocked them in their arms. Still others picked up their babies and held them to their shoulders. Most of the babies were comforted, but in the last instance, the babies also opened their eyes wide and scanned their environment from their mothers' shoulders. The researchers concluded that inadvertently, the last group of mothers had provided their babies with many more visual experiences than the other babies had received. In addition, those babies experienced upright body contact, with the attendant stimuli of warmth, containment, and olfactory and tactile-kinesthetic experiences. Korner and Grobstein suggested the possibil-

---

1. Klaus and Kennell contended that there is a sensitive period in the first minutes and hours of life during which it is necessary that the mother and the father have close contact with their newborn if later development is to be optimal. The studies were widely accepted initially. They were responsible, in part, for allowing fathers to participate in the delivery, and for the rooming-in of mothers and newborns, or at least extended contact, which were all to the good.

Subsequent controversy over theoretical and methodological flaws, however, led Klaus and Kennell (1982) to moderate their claims in a revised edition. They acknowledged that parents who did not have such a hospital experience can bond successfully with their infant. Having extended contact, however, may indeed ease the parents' transition from hospital to home and their full-time care of the baby.

ity that this particular soothing technique, by including environmental stimulation, contributes to cognitive and perceptual development.

Even more convincing is the research Stern (1977) conducted in the natural setting of the subjects' homes. He and his colleagues demonstrated that babies play an active role in their relationship to their mothers, and hence in their development into social beings. They do this through particular behaviors—in which gazing is a most important element—over the first six months of life. The importance of gaze in early human relatedness is supported by other formal studies and by clinical observation. For example, it is well established that infants prefer looking at pictures or drawings of a full face front, compared to profiles or to other objects. The crucial features accounting for the preference are two eyelike spots correctly placed in a larger oval. For Stern, "This implies that some scheme or 'picture' of a human face is encoded in our genes, reflected in our nervous systems, and ultimately expresses itself in our behavior without any previous specific learning experiences" (1977:36).

The mother's repertoire of infant-specific behaviors in the interaction includes gazing into the baby's eyes much longer than the usual normal length of eye contact with others; positioning herself in a relation to the baby that exceeds usual "intimate distance" boundaries; baby talk and other high-pitched sounds; head and body movements; exaggerated facial expressions; and the timing and rhythm of these behaviors. A mother performs these actions in an integrated display and in her own unique way. Many of these actions appear to be out of her awareness. If she is asked to perform just one alone, or to perform the display out of sight of the baby, she is likely to feel embarrassed and "silly" and to be unable to do so. Stern noted that the behaviors are not observable in any other interpersonal situation except possibly in lovemaking. He took an evolutionary view, holding that these maternal behaviors are at least partly innate and are elicited by the infant in some complex and not yet fully understood way. They are assumed to rest on a biological base, having developed over evolutionary time because of their survival value to the species, that is, ensuring care of the young.

The assumption would explain why it is that most human adults of any age and either sex, and even adolescents and older children without younger siblings (therefore the behaviors are not learned), tend to respond stereotypically and predictably to an infant. It is as though the infant's very appearance and expressiveness (what the baby does with features of her or his appearance) elicit partly innate behaviors, although some variability may be seen across cultures and societies.

Stern (1977:29–30) concluded that men, children, and adults past child-rearing age can be secondary caregivers and potentially primary ones if a group or society so chooses. We will return to this last point later, in connection with fathering.

Just as these behaviors are used by the caregiver to engage the infant in social interaction and to regulate the exchanges, so, too, does the baby have a reciprocal repertoire for engaging with and disengaging from the caregiver in play interactions. The repertoire is in place by 3 months of age at least and includes head movements and facial expressions as well as gazing. In what Stern (1977) described as the biologically designed choreography of mother and infant, the infant invites the mother to play, initiates interaction with her, modulates the flow of their exchange, and acquires signals to terminate or avoid their exchange or to place it temporarily on hold. Again from an evolutionary perspective, Stern argued that these infant behaviors are also expressions of a genetic predisposition and represent the unfolding of partly innate capacities. While they are unlearned in the beginning, they are soon shaped by learning. Together with the baby's appearance, they are the stimuli to which the caregiver and others respond in specific ways.

By 6 weeks of age, the infant is able to fixate the mother's eyes; as the infant does this, her or his own eyes widen and brighten. It is at this point that the mother feels her infant is looking at *her* and *into* her eyes and that she and the infant are now really connected. By the end of the third month, the infant's visual apparatus is virtually mature, and now the two partners have essentially equal control and use of the visual modality. For example, the baby's fixating the gaze, raising the head forward, and tilting the face upward signify an invitation to interaction. But the baby can also avert the gaze, signaling a wish for a temporary time-out. Averting the gaze and slightly turning the head are a somewhat mixed or ambivalent signal. Eye contact is still maintained, but the mother senses that the baby is uncomfortable about something. Other head movements, such as a full turning away of the head that breaks eye contact, signal an aversion to over-stimulation or an avoidance of something disliked. Lowering the head is a more definitive avoidance measure, leading to temporary disengagement. These observations on the importance of gazing underscore the difficulties experienced by blind infants and their caregivers and the impact on the beginnings of relatedness for them.

Facial expressions include the smile, the frown, and the full "cry face." Stern (1977) recalled Darwin's findings that in all higher animals the infant of the species is equipped with basic, species-specific forms of expression that contribute to survival. Darwin concluded that in the human infant, facial expressions, which later communicate basic emotions such as pleasure, displeasure, anger, fear, joy, sorrow, and disgust, are either present at birth or appear a few months later as an unfolding of innate tendencies. However, Darwin did not believe, nor do present-day researchers, that the baby is experiencing the emotions that these expressions signal in the older child or the adult.

The infant's smile follows an innate timetable of development. An endogenous or reflexive smile appears early in life, usually during dreaming sleep and drowsy states. It is not a response to environmental events or processes but is internally triggered by neurophysiological excitation and brain discharges. At about 6 weeks, the reflexive smile becomes exogenous as a response to external events, such as pleasurable sights and sounds, particularly the human face. It has become a social smile (Stern 1977:44). At about 3 months, the smile, looking just the same, now becomes an instrumental behavior designed to elicit a social response such as a return smile from the caregiver. At about the fourth month, the smile appears simultaneously with other facial expressions for more complex communications. These developments of the smile parallel those taking place in sensory perception and cognition; they are uniform across cultures, a fact attesting to their innateness (Stern 1977:45).

The cry face also follows a developmental course. It is the end point of a patterned sequence of facial expressions that show an increasing degree of displeasure. The sequence progresses from a sobering of the face, to a frown, accompanied by increasing knitting of the brows, to a quiver of the lower lip, followed by the lips pulling back as the mouth opens. Next the mouth turns down, and the full cry face is seen. Fuss noises may occur early in the sequence, but the actual cry occurs with the full cry face. The individual behaviors and the full sequence are present at birth as reflexive activities, and they change little over the life course. They become exogenous earlier than the smile does and may become instrumental as early as 3 weeks of age (1977:46–47).

Toward the end of the sixth month, the baby, having learned the fundamentals of social interaction with the humans in her or his life, now becomes fascinated with physical objects to reach for, grasp, and manipulate. Social interactions continue as the baby begins to learn about objects with the caregiver's help and participation. Sometime near the end of the first year, the social interactions culminate in what we can now call a relationship, a specific attachment. While

Stern relied on Piagetian ideas to account for the development of relationship, I will take up a different explanatory framework of ideas known as *attachment theory*.

ATTACHMENT THEORY

In contrast to his early work in object relations theory, Bowlby, a British psychoanalyst, came later (1969, 1973) to view affectional ties in humans as an innate need and capacity built into the genetic structure of humankind's earliest ancestors because of its survival value. Drawing on evolutionary biology and ethology (the study of animals in the wild), Bowlby construed attachment behaviors as having developed as an adaptive protection in the evolutionary environment. Attachments served this function not only for mother–infant pairs, but for all members of the small human bands traversing areas occupied by dangerous predators. Attachment is both a biological and a social imperative in the human being. In contrast, object relations theory views human relationships as arising from the infant's need for food and for relief of bodily tensions aroused by the oral drives. When object relations theorists use the term *attachment*, they appear to regard it as a synonym for *object relations*. They do not use it in Bowlby's restricted sense of an innate capacity and set of behaviors.

Precursors of attachment behaviors in the infant include calling, crying, clinging, and following. They serve to maintain proximity to the caregiver. True attachment behaviors are seen by the end of the first year but are especially striking in toddlers. Bowlby classified them as 1) signaling behaviors that bring the attached person to the child, such as crying, smiling, vocalizing, and raising the arms, and 2) approach behaviors that bring the child to the attached person, such as following, seeking, embracing, hugging, climbing on the lap, and other motor skills available to a child of this age and used to make contact. Reciprocally, the parent manifests what Bowlby termed *caretaking behaviors*. Together, these two sets of behavior constitute the concept of *affectional bonding*.

Initially, Bowlby (1969) held that attachments form only during a critical period from about 8 months to 10 to 12 months of age. If an attachment is not formed in the first year, he believed, it will not be formed at all. Rutter (1972), a British child psychiatrist and researcher, reviewed the available research and concluded that attachments can form as late as the second or even the third year. It appears indisputable that true attachment is in place by 8 months, and sometimes earlier, since it is readily observable in the infant's way of relating to the attached person(s). Bowlby originally maintained that infants form only one main attachment, usually to the mother. He later agreed (1973), on the basis of many studies and anthropological data, that infants are able to form more than one attachment, but he maintained that the primary bond differs from others. Rutter (1979:129) disagreed, contending that although the primary bond is important because of its strength, most young children develop similar attachments to several persons. While he acknowledged that in most families the mother is the person to whom the child is most attached because she has the most to do with the baby, Rutter added that the primary attachment does not have to be with the chief caretaker, the biological parent, or a female.

Babies benefit from attachments to persons of both sexes. Also, having more than one attachment is a protection for the baby against loss. Until recently, most research on parental attachment centered on mothers, except for at least three important studies. The first (Schaffer and Emerson 1964) found that almost one third of the children studied had formed their main attachment to the father. The second (Kotelchuck 1976) found that infants aged 12 months (observed in the laboratory) had formed attachments to both parents. The third study, of 7- to 13-month-old babies (observed at home), yielded a similar finding of attachment to both parents (Lamb 1977a).

FATHERING

As recently as 1972, Rutter deemed it necessary to remind the research and clinical communities that children also have fathers. Prevailing assumptions about fathers had held that they are not interested in infants, that they are less important and less competent than mothers, and that they prefer noncaregiving roles. Whether large numbers of fathers ever exemplified such stereotypes is doubtful (Parke 1981). Parke added that by the 1980s, variations were seen among fathers: some were uninvolved, some were active participants, and some were raising their child alone. The numbers of involved fathers are unknown, but Pleck (1986) estimated that 20 percent of fathers have substantial independent relationships with their children and spend a significant amount of time with them. Those who share equal time and responsibility with the mother, however, comprise only 5 percent of all fathers at the most. The rediscovery of fatherhood in the 1970s and 1980s by researchers and theorists was due, in part, to the rapidly growing number of mothers in full-time employment and the need for fathers to share child care tasks; to feminist and profeminist critiques of gender-typed roles; and to men's growing consciousness of the losses they suffer as a consequence of gender-typed limitations on their participation in child rearing.

Such influences were reinforced by the growing participation of fathers in childbirth classes and attendance at the delivery, and by the appearance of books, movies, and television sitcoms focused on fathering or shared parenting. Some consequences of these developments include the growth of paternity leave programs in industry (so far used by only a few of the eligible fathers) and the appearance of men's support groups, fatherhood education groups, custody mediation services, and vastly increased studies of fathering.

Prior to 1970, most studies of fathers were limited to the effects of the father's absence on the sex-role identity of boys in the oedipal period (see the section in appendix 1 on Freud). By 1980, however, many studies of fathering had established clearly the significance of the father from infancy on (e.g. Lamb 1981; Pedersen 1980; Parke 1981). Traditional fathers who are secondary caregivers are the subject of most studies rather than nontraditional fathers who are primary caregivers or shared caregivers. Also, American studies appear to rely on samples of white middle-class and blue-collar fathers. Variations across cultures and subcultures in North America have received minimal attention, although studies of father behaviors in other Western societies (Parke and Tinsley 1981) and in some African and Asian populations (Katz and Konner 1981) have appeared. North American studies cover father–infant relationships, father–infant play, the role of the father in daughters' and sons' social and cognitive development, the father's influence on the gender-role development of sons and daughters, and the effects of the father's absence. Excellent summaries are available (Parke 1981; Parke and Tinsley 1981; Lamb 1981; Pedersen 1980), so only highlights from a few studies in the first three categories will be given here. The father's influence on gender-role development and the effects of the father's absence are presented in the next chapter.

1. *Father–infant relationships.* In the infancy period, both middle-class and low-income fathers are as nurturant, affectionate, and stimulating with the baby as mothers (Parke and O'Leary 1976). Fathers, like mothers, adjust their speech to baby talk with their newborns; fathers are more apt to respond to infant vocalization by talking, and mothers are more apt to react by touching (Phillips and Parke 1979). Fathers spend less time than mothers in feeding and caregiving (Ko-

telchuck 1976), but when fathers do feed the infant, they are as competent as mothers in responding sensitively to the infant's signals of distress and in altering their feeding behavior (Parke and Swain 1976).

2. *Father–infant play*. Fathers spend a higher proportion of their time with the baby in play than mothers do, except for mothers who work outside the home (Kotelchuck 1976). This temporal difference persists beyond infancy (Richards, Dunn, and Antonis 1977). With young infants, fathers' play is more tactile and less verbal (an apparent reversal of the way they respond to the infant's vocalization) and elicits greater pleasurable excitement from the infant than mothers' play does (Yogman et al., 1977). With babies from 8 months of age to 2 years, fathers engage in physical rough-and-tumble play and more unusual games than mothers, who tend to engage in conventional peek-a-boo and pat-a-cake, jiggling a toy, and reading (Lamb 1977b). While both boys and girls respond more positively to play with fathers than to play with mothers (Clarke-Stewart 1980), girls 2 to 4 years old appear to shift to a preference for the mother in play (Lynn and Cross 1974).

Parke and Tinsley (1981) reminded us that the full reversal of primary and secondary caregiving roles and even shared caregiving, new definitions of masculinity and femininity, the kind of birth (e.g., premature or caesarean), and the child's temperament and other characteristics can alter the common patterns of caregiving and play.

3. *Fathers and intellectual development*. Fathers affect the cognitive development of young male infants, but not of infant daughters (Pedersen, Rubenstein, and Yarrow 1979). They influence the cognitive growth of their daughters only at a later point. At 30 months of age, both boys' and girls' cognitive abilities are affected by both parents, but the parents influence their sons and daughters in different ways. Fathers' physical play with sons relates to their intellectual development, whereas fathers influence their daughters through verbal stimulation. Mothers influence their daughters through verbal and intellectual stimulation, and their sons through social play and social responsiveness (Clarke-Stewart 1980).

Four-year-old boys of nurturant fathers (kind, praising, and helpful) had higher cognitive scores than boys of nonnurturant fathers (cool and aloof). Restrictive behavior by fathers was associated with boys' low cognitive scores (Radin 1976). Radin also found few consistent relationships between the cognitive scores of girls and their fathers' behavior. There is some evidence, however, that fathers influence their daughters' intellectual development through their support of the mothers. Radin also observed that intellectual growth in daughters may be influenced by their emulation of their mothers' styles of problem solving and thinking.

Fathers and mothers also differ in how much freedom of exploration they permit their babies and toddlers, the fathers being more permissive of exploratory behaviors and the mothers more cautious. As development proceeds, fathers tend to encourage exploration both inside and outside the home more than mothers do and are especially encouraging to their sons. From his review of the research, Parke concluded that fathers are fathers: "They are not simply substitute mothers; mothers and fathers have distinct styles of parenting. Fathers' physical and robust approach complements and contrasts with mothers' verbal, paced style. Children profit from this diversity of experience. These patterns are not fixed, however, and they are likely to evolve as social and work roles for men and women continue to change"(1981:114).

ATTACHMENT AND THE CONCEPT OF COMPETENCE

Bowlby (1973) linked attachment with the young child's ability to explore the environment. That link is central to numerous studies by Ainsworth (1974) and her colleagues and by Sroufe (1978, 1977) and his colleagues. The quality of the baby's or toddler's attachment (secure or anxious) is defined in terms of the balance between attachment and environmental exploration. The balance is reflected in the child's use of the attachment figure as a base for exploration and a source of comfort when distressed, and in the child's effectiveness in reestablishing contact following separation in strange situations. Marked differences in these behaviors differentiate consistently between securely attached and anxiously attached babies at 12 months and again at 18 months, as measured by Ainsworth's (1978) Strange Situation Instrument.

At age 2, when presented with problems to solve, those children assessed earlier as securely attached show much greater enthusiasm, motivation, and persistence than do the children assessed earlier as anxiously attached. The securely attached children also demonstrate the ability to use assistance effectively in a problem designed to require help. In other words, when under stress, securely attached children do not lose the sense that they can affect their environment, despite their individual differences of personality and temperament. Sroufe (1978) linked secure attachment to the self-concept and to the young child's belief in her or his own effectiveness: "The infant who uses the caregiver as a base for moving out into the world, and as a haven when threatened or distressed, develops motor skills and a sense of self as effective. In sharing his play with the caregiver at a distance, the baby evolves a new way of maintaining contact while operating independently" (Sroufe 1978). Hence self-direction is also connected to attachment, competence, and self-esteem.

The young infant begins to develop a sense of effectiveness in the environment (that ultimately leads to a sense of competence) as she or he experiences prompt, ungrudging, and accurate responses by the caregiver to signals of discomfort, hunger, cold, loneliness, and so on. Such responsiveness also contributes to the development of a positive self-concept and to beginning self-esteem as the baby learns that she or he is lovable, and that her or his needs are important and acceptable to the caregiver. As the baby's sensory and motor abilities increase (see appendix 3), she or he is able to explore the environment through looking, then creeping, and then walking. The sense of effectiveness, self-esteem, and self-direction also increases provided 1) the environment is appropriately stimulating and safe for exploration, and 2) the baby's explorations and actions in the environment are acceptable and pleasurable to the caregiver.

Sroufe's studies validate his hypothesis that the 1-year-old who shows a secure attachment will also be competent and self-directing in toddlerhood in terms of approaching problems and making an emotional investment in solving them. However, the children in these studies were from two-parent families in stable environments and were observed in the laboratory. Additional studies of children in their natural settings and living in different family forms and cultural groups are required before firm conclusions can be drawn about the hypothesized connection between attachment and competence. Nevertheless, the findings so far are congruent with White's theories of competence, to be examined next.

Effectance, Efficacy, and Competence

Dissatisfied with the psychoanalytic drive models of development, White (1971) viewed the human being as a system that is alive, growing, self-expanding, and itself a source of influence as well as being shaped by external influences. Like Bowlby and Stern, he drew on an evolutionary perspective. His observations of babies, children, and adults, together with reviews of ethological studies, led him to assume that all forms of life are motivated to have an effect on their environment or they wouldn't survive for long. Most advanced in human beings, this motive is independent of the drives of hunger, thirst, libido, and aggression. White believes that the motive operates most strongly when these other drives have been satisfied. He called this inborn human urge *effectance*. It is satisfied by exploration and action, and it leads to learning about the environment and to competence in acting upon it. Satisfaction of the drive lies in a considerable series of transactions—in a trend of behavior rather than a goal that is achieved (White 1959). Even in the first year of life the baby reaches out to the environment, tests it, explores it, finds out what can be done with its various elements, and takes an active part in learning about her or his world (White 1971). When the effectance motive is satisfied by effective actions in the environment, by making desired things happen, the child (or adult) experiences a state of *efficacy*. As experiences of efficacy accumulate, the child acquires a sense of *competence*, a sense of being effective and able to produce effects.

Competence is clearly an essential component of self-esteem and the self-concept. For White (1971), self-esteem depends upon the confidence, based on experience, that one can make desired things happen, together with the respectful recognition of this competence by others: "You have a strong bastion of self-esteem if you feel confident you can do the things that matter most, that in these ways you can affect your environment and thus influence the course of your own life. People who feel this way are unlikely to wonder about their identity" (White 1979:9). It also seems likely that, reciprocally, self-esteem is important in the development of competence.

Given the self-initiating and self-rewarding nature of effectance, competence also arises from and contributes to self-direction. That is, as the child becomes more effective in transactions with the environment, she or he moves toward greater self-direction and self-regulation, which in turn supports competence. It is reasonable to conclude that competence, self-esteem, and self-direction are interdependent. Since competence has its origin in secure attachments, and the other two also depend, at least in part, upon the nature of the individual's relationships with others, then relatedness is central.

The developmental experience of a chronically ill or disabled child may follow a different course, depending on the extent of the condition, the child's temperament, and the ability of the parents to construct alternative avenues to self-esteem, competence, and self-direction in a safe environment.

White's hypothesis lends an optimistic vision to social work. Given the inborn nature of effective motivation, the practitioner can assume that even if a person's life experience has lacked opportunities for experiencing efficacy and for competence development, the innate effectance motive remains despite the helplessness that the person may feel. It can be reawakened if we have a knowledge of and the means of aiding the process. Often we can help develop opportunities for successful experiences in real-life problem solving, decision making, and action that promote competence where it has failed to develop or has been undermined. In other situations we and other professionals fail because of limited knowledge and skill among the human service disciplines in promoting competence in certain situations. Also, the value issues of how competence is defined and who is defining it add to the difficulty. Although competence is prized in all cultures, what constitutes competence varies from culture to culture. White's concept is a biological, evolutionary one and not a moral one, but social values do affect definitions of competence.

In an urban youth drug culture, for example, definitional and value issues pose a difficult challenge to the social worker. Youth who are highly skilled in pushing drugs may feel a sense of competence and may be viewed by their peers as competent, but the larger society and the social work profession define competence very differently. Social work does not always have the knowledge and skill to help youths replace antisocial goals, which are supported by the external rewards of money, excitement, and peer respect, with prosocial goals and activities that will promote an internal sense of competence as it is defined by the society. This is especially the case where the opportunity structures of society are closed to vulnerable or powerless young people. Thus, issues of competence, self-esteem, and self-direction are also connected to issues of power and, in some circumstances, will require social change instead of, or together with, personal change. Engaging adults and/or youths in even modest social change efforts as individuals or as members of groups or of the community is often effective in altering social conditions and promoting the growth of relatedness, competence, self-esteem, and self-direction in the participants (Grosser and Mondros 1980).

A challenging research question for social workers arises from the observation that most children who are said to be at social risk do develop prosocial competence, self-esteem, self-direction, and relatedness. What is it that makes the difference? What protects them from the hazards of powerlessness and grossly harsh environments? Few studies have investigated the nature of the support, protection, or amelioration experienced by some children reared in harsh environments, which might yield clues to effective help for others. Rutter

(1979a, b), who has done as much work in this area as anyone, suggested that a number of elements may account for differing outcomes of adversity and disadvantage. First, predisposing genetic variations in vulnerability and temperament may interact in complex ways with the number and intensity of environmental stressors. For example, a child's temperament helps shape the nature of his or her social environment and its responses to him or her, and genetic factors influence how a child responds to the environment. Second, the presence of a strict but loving parent, other adult, or inspiring teacher with high performance expectations appears to protect some children against the effects of pervasive stressors. Third, the scope and range of the compensating experiences available outside the home can lead to self-esteem and the acquisition of coping skills in spite of environmental circumstances that defeat other children. Rutter reminded us that invulnerability and overcoming adversity are relative terms. Well-functioning children do not necessarily emerge from their harsh experiences completely unscathed. Some may be vulnerable later to similar stressors, may suffer inner insecurity, or may labor under the weight of rigid defenses. Nevertheless, there is a very great difference between these resilient children and those in similarly harsh environments who are beset by emotional disturbance, deviant behaviors, educational difficulties, or addictive disorders.

Resilience and Vulnerability

The psychiatrists Chess and Thomas were mentioned briefly in the introduction to part 2 and earlier in this chapter in connection with their thirty-year longitudinal study of 141 white middle-class children from birth to age 20. They have also carried out longitudinal studies of working-class minority children and of children with physical, neurological, and intellectual disabilities (e.g., Thomas and Chess 1984; Thomas 1975), and they have reviewed similar studies by others (e.g., Fraiberg 1977). On the basis of these studies, Chess and Thomas (1986) pointed out that the human brain is characterized by a plasticity that imparts a special human capacity for learning across the life course. They concluded that this plasticity enables children with disabilities to find alternate developmental pathways congruent with their capacities and limitations. Thomas (1981) added: "By the same token, the environmentally handicapped child is not inevitably doomed to an inferior and abnormal psychological developmental course. Whether the handicap comes from social ideology, poverty, and pathological environment, or special stressful experiences, the plastic potential of the brain offers the promise for positive and corrective change."

Murphy (1974) and Murphy and Moriarity (1976) conducted longitudinal studies from infancy to adolescence of thirty-two normal middle-class children living in Topeka, Kansas. The researchers identified resilience as a critical quality among young children who cope successfully with stressful situations, including life-threatening illness. Effective coping efforts to manage "threats and dangers, frustrations and defeats, obstacles, loss, strangeness and the new or unknown, and demands from the adults or others in the environment" (1974:71) yield increments of competence as well. No child in the sample was truly invulnerable to stress; all manifested some reduction in their best functioning. Some children, considered resilient, typically recovered quickly, however, and regained stable and smooth functioning. Others, regarded as vulnerable, did not recover easily and had difficulty in coping with the environment or in maintaining internal integration to support optimal functioning.

For Murphy (1974), resilience is not the same as coping. She defined resilience as an inner push toward self-healing that rests on positive feelings about oneself, reserves of energy, flexibility in actions and feelings, and a self-initiating, self-directing orientation. Resilience also requires the capacity to elicit and accept help or support from others, plus cultural or familial expectations and rewards for resilience. Clearly, the quality of resilience is a significant personal resource for children in coping with acutely or chronically stressful situations. Since Murphy's (1974) study was of children living in relatively secure middle-class environments, the findings cannot be generalized to children living in dire poverty who function well despite their grossly stressful environments. The findings are suggestive, however, and do fit well with Rutter's (1979a, b) work with children from poor families, and with the work of Thomas (1981). What Murphy called resilience may be due to the plasticity of the human brain as described by Thomas (1981). Research is gradually yielding specific information about what it is, environmentally and personally, that imparts protection to some children against the enormous stressors they experience. Happily, this information can assist social workers to develop improved prevention and intervention programs in behalf of those children.

DEVELOPMENT AND THE ENVIRONMENT

As we have seen, most babies come into the world equipped with remarkable sensory-perceptual capacities and a beginning memory, together with genetically based potentials for attachments, intellect, learning, and motor abilities. Innate potentials require certain "nutriments" from the environment in order to be released and further developed, just as physical growth and survival require appropriate food. Likewise, capacities present at birth require certain "nutriments" from the environment for continued development. Social workers are often called upon to provide services in situations where such nutriments are or have been missing. Several such situations will be briefly described, beginning with the deprivation of food. But first, some cautions are in order:

A lack of the required nutriments (real in the case of food and metaphorical in the case of deprivations of relatedness or of intellectual, sensory, motor, and linguistic stimulation) presumably places a child at biological, psychological, or social risk. However, the matter is more complicated than that. Cultures differ widely in child-rearing practices that prepare children for adulthood in that culture, so what is considered a nutriment in one culture may be meaningless in another. What is considered a lack in one culture may never be missed in another (Kagan 1984). Because children differ in biological, physical, and psychological makeup, they have differing degrees of sensitivity to environmental deficits. Context is also important, such as parental alcoholism or other substance abuse, severe discord between the parents, family violence, mental illness, criminality, and unsafe housing (including the presence of lead paint). Moreover the many biological and psychosocial factors in the child and the environment interact in as yet unknown ways to produce varying effects. It is therefore difficult to know which personal and which environmental factors, alone or in combination, are associated with observed developmental difficulties.

While the following discussion treats environmental lacks and assaults as though they fall into discrete categories that have discrete and specific effects, most of the time they probably do not. Developmental difficulties may instead represent varying mixtures of unique personal features interacting with different environmental circumstances.

Nonorganic Failure to Thrive

This syndrome is seen in babies who are of normal size and weight at birth but who do not gain weight or grow. They may even lose weight, sometimes to the point of death. Parents who bring the child to the hospital may maintain that they feed the baby adequately, yet in the hospital the baby gains weight rapidly, a result suggestive of something wrong in the home setting. Those parents who do seek medical care for their child are showing concern, but in some instances the recovered baby is soon brought back to the hospital in precarious state because severe weight loss has recurred. The cause is often attributed to the mother's assumed or observed hostile or rejecting attitudes toward her baby. Recently a more transactional view was advanced (Alderette and deGraffenried 1986), suggesting instead that something is awry in the family-as-system. In this view all members are disengaged from one another, so that neither parent establishes a relationship with the baby. The baby, in turn, withdraws. The treatment of choice is said to be family therapy. However, this approach may still not capture transactional totality.

For example, many, but not all, parents of failure-to-thrive babies (and abused babies) are socially isolated without supportive networks and beset by environmental stressors such as unemployment, financial problems, inadequate housing, poor health, and marital discord. In regard to environmental stressors, for example, studies suggest that marital satisfaction is associated with maternal competence, and marital discord is associated with mothers' having problems in nurturing (Pedersen, Anderson, and Cain 1977). Pedersen (1980) reviewed research linking the parents' own relationship and parent–infant relationships and found that the father's emotional support of the mother maintains effective mother–infant interaction. Adaptation in feeding appears to be facilitated by the father's encouragement and positive evaluation of the mother. The facilitating elements in the father's emotional support consist in making the mother feel competent, secure, and self-confident by easing her doubts and anxieties (Lewis, Feiring, and Weintraub 1981).

Some parents may know very little about infant needs, behavior, and care. From birth, some infants are less responsive to the parents' attempts at caregiving, thus setting off a spiral of failure of mutuality in parent–infant interaction. Some babies may cry a lot and may be difficult to soothe. The parents then feel even less competent and withdraw from the baby and from their nurturing role. The baby's discomfort may also have a negative impact on the parents' relationships, reducing their mutual support of each other in managing the transition to parenthood.

Commenting on the nonorganic label given to the syndrome, Berman (1986) rejected the organic-nonorganic dichotomy. She pointed out that organic and nonorganic features interact in complex ways. Even where environmental factors appear to be causal, malnutrition becomes an important organic factor leading to irritability, listlessness, sleep disorders, intestinal malabsorption, and other disruptions in the baby's bodily and mental processes. These conditions, in turn, intensify the original difficulty in establishing mutuality in the infant–caregiver relationship.

Clearly, failure to thrive is a life-threatening and complex condition. The social worker involved with the parents needs to understand it as the outcome of parent–child interaction that is strongly influenced by the mother–father relationship, in which the possibility of stereotyped gender-role assignments and power abuses needs to be examined. Additionally, all the family's interactions are embedded in an environment that may present stressors exceeding the parents' coping resources. Understanding this complexity, the practitioner can help infant and parents by teaching about infants and their care, eliminating stressors or reducing their impact, and mobilizing personal capacities and environmental supports to strengthen family functioning, including more equitable division of labor, power, and resources where pertinent—while keeping the protection of the baby in the foreground of her or his attention.

The biological effects of the syndrome appear to be reversible inasmuch as growth accelerates when the feeding is corrected. Still, there are indications that the stature and weight in adulthood of failure-to-thrive babies are below standard norms, depending on the duration and severity of the syndrome, and on the child's age at the time of correction. The reversal of any emotional and social ill effects will be considered later, in the section on unrelatedness.

Malnutrition and Mental Development

Early and prolonged malnutrition, when coupled with the minimal stimulation that may accompany it, is thought to impair brain growth and to lead to intellectual impairment. Malnutrition alone, however, has less a marked impact on mental development. Winick, Meyer, and Harris (1975) hypothesized that enriching the environment of previously malnourished children may result in improved development. They studied the current status of 141 Korean orphans who had been adopted before the age of 3 from a Korean orphanage by middle-class American families. All had entered the orphanage before the age of 2 years. The children were divided into three groups according to their nutritional status at the time of entry into the orphanage: well nourished, moderately malnourished, and severely malnourished. The researchers found that all surpassed the expected mean of Korean children for height and weight. They had all attained normal or above normal intelligence and school achievement levels by age 10, with statistically significant higher scores found in the well-nourished group over the malnourished group. Further, the school achievement of the severely malnourished group equaled that expected of normal American children. The well-nourished group attained a mean IQ and achievement score higher than that of middle-class American children. The researchers attributed the findings to the change before the age of 3 to a considerably enriched environment of love, attention, good nutrition, and appropriate stimulation. The question still remains whether there is an upper age limit beyond which the effects of malnutrition on mental development are no longer reversible given present knowledge.

This study is not entirely relevant to children suffering from the failure-to-thrive syndrome because other psychosocial factors are involved in their situations. But the study does underscore the tragic plight of American children who live in dire poverty and in whom undernourishment begins before birth and is likely to continue through childhood and, for many, into adulthood. Also, in some situations of malnutrition, minimal stimulation may be operating as well and will be examined next.

Developmental Retardation

The lack of sensory-perceptual, cognitive, and linguistic stimulation has grave consequences. It takes the form of motor, sensory, cognitive, and language deficits, language and verbal intelligence being the most seriously affected. The condition is seen in young children raised in those institutions where environmental stimulation of all kinds is minimal. It can also occur in home settings, often in the homes of the very poor, where the parents do not have the time, energy, or ability to read to their babies and young children, talk to them, play with them, help them explore and play with household physical objects, and so on. The upper age limit at which a reversal of the ill effects of the lack of such stimulation can be achieved is still uncertain. The following example illustrates the complex interplay among biological, psychological, social, cultural, and contextual factors and environmental circumstances:

A Head Start program referred Carl, a 4-year-old black child, to the state health department for a developmental assessment. He had been attending the program for three months. At first, he did not talk and made animal-like sounds, but he now uses a few words. He does not sit, respond to directions, nor reach out to the other children. He does not use paste, scissors, pencil, or spoon. Carl lives with his grandparents, and the staff believes he has very little stimulation at home. The staff feel that Carl cannot be helped in a group setting and doubt that he can be ready for school entry.

Data gathered by the public health social worker from medical records and home visits to the mother and the grandparents include the following: Carl was born prematurely to a 14-year-old mother. He was cyanotic (a morbid condition in which the skin turns blue because of insufficient oxygen to the blood) and had difficulty nursing. He remained in an incubator and was tube-fed for two weeks; he then returned home to his mother and her parents. His follow-up attendance at the pediatric clinic was very irregular. A year ago Carl was seen in the hearing clinic; his hearing was normal, but he was referred for speech therapy because of serious language deficits. Few appointments were kept. His mother moved out of the home about a year ago and now lives with a boyfriend and their infant son. She says she has no interest in Carl because she had not wanted him, her parents raised him, and so he belongs with them. His grandmother works as a domestic, and his grandfather is currently unemployed. They say that Carl has been left with a succession of baby-sitters while they work. They also say they love Carl and wish to continue caring for him.

A developmental assessment examiner reported as follows:

Carl is a child who shows severe problems in nearly every sector of development. His relationships with people, emotional organization and expression, play with toys, self-help skills, and verbalization are at a very immature level and primitive in quality. Language functioning in particular reflects very serious difficulties. Cognitive functioning showed sporadic successes close to age level. While they do not establish Carl's intellectual level, they suggest that his potential is certainly higher than his present functioning. Carl is also capable of sustained interest and a variety of play with at least one toy. He also gives evidence of a desire and capacity to form a relationship with adults. Causes of Carl's difficulties are not altogether clear. Birth history and his difficulties in gross motor functioning suggest the possibility of organic damage. In addition, it appears that Carl's environment has been markedly understimulating and lacking in appropriate guidance. The combination of organic damage and lack of stimulation can have devastating effects.

The examiner recommended a neurological examination, speech therapy, and help for the grandparents so that they can provide appropriate guidance and stimulation. Also recommended was an intensive one-to-one educational experience so that Carl can learn to focus and attend and can gain the benefits of a close and caring relationship. Sharing the process with the mother and the grandparents, the social worker made arrangements for these services. The grandparents could not carry through despite the supports provided, and protective services—already active—decided that Carl should be moved to a therapeutic foster home. The plan was shared with his mother and his grandparents, and they seemed to understand and accept it. When arrangements were completed, however, it was learned that Carl's mother had sent him out of the state to live with his father.

Unrelatedness

Some as yet unknown amount of togetherness is required for an attachment to form, but the quality of interaction appears to be more significant than constant availability. For example, babies' secure attachments are associated with the sensitivity, responsiveness, and emotional involvement of the attached persons (Schaffer 1977; Lamb 1981). Insecure, anxious attachments may follow disruptions in continuity, ambivalence in the caregiver that leads to frequent shifts in the quality and quantity of caring, and insufficient sensitivity and responsiveness to the baby's needs and signals. Rutter (1979) added the caregiver's inability to experience pleasure from the baby's reciprocity and to initiate interaction.

Several different environmental circumstances bear on the question of the nutriments required for relatedness. The most serious circumstance is the lack of an opportunity to form an attachment. The condition is seen in young, not yet attached infants who are placed in poor-quality institutions, which are characterized by multiple, shifting caregivers, each of whom has a number of babies under care, and the resultant impossibility of individualized responsiveness to the babies. In a book that is painful to read, Provence and Lipton (1962) described such an institution.

Babies can suffer this way in their own homes if the caregiver is consistently unloving, outright hostile, and rejecting. If no alternative person is available for attachment, the baby does not become attached. This condition may also obtain in some failure-to-thrive, abusive, and neglectful situations, or in distorted infant–caregiver interactions associated with the adult's serious depression or other emotional disorder—again with no other available person. Long-term ill effects are thought to include some of the following: deviant behaviors, emotional disorders, a poor self-concept, and difficulties in loving and attaining love and intimacy, or even in cooperating with others. Studies of late adoptions of institutionalized infants who had no attachments have shown that attachments to the adoptive parents can form as late as 6 years of age. Whether ill effects can be reversed by environmental change after that age is still unknown. One possible reason for the absence of evidence is given at the end of this section.

Breaks in the continuity of an attachment already formed may be detrimental to the child's development, depending on the age when the disruption occurs and its duration, the child's own sensitivities, the quality of the attachment prior to the disruption, the ensuing circumstances, and the interplay of these factors (Yarrow 1964). Not all separations result in disruption, since the connection with the attachment figure may continue during a period of separation, as when a parent or a very young child is in the hospital but can be visited. Also, the outcome is mediated by the presence of another attachment figure, such as the other parent or an older sibling. The acquisition of language may help older children understand and accept separation more easily.

An already attached baby may respond to disruption of over a week's duration with the grief response of protest followed by despair. If the separation is prolonged, the sequence can end in detachment. Upon the child's or the parent's return, the child may be unsettled for a time, continuing to be detached and treating the parents as strangers. Subsequently there may be a period of overdependence and clinging behavior (Schaffer 1977:97). The severe grief reaction to loss or separation from the attached person—if another attached person is not present for the baby—may leave the child vulnerable to later losses and may trigger an innate (genetic) predisposition to depression. Rutter (1972) believes, however, that such depressions are associated with adolescent bereavement rather than with loss in early childhood.

The plight of a baby with a chronic illness or disability who must undergo periodic hospitalizations is highlighted by theoretical work on attachment and separation, which also underscores the need for hospital policies that liberalize parental visiting and overnight stays. The brief, continuing separations associated with multiple mothering, as in day care, are considered in the next chapter.

The question, "Is it better to have loved and lost, or never to have loved at all?" reverberates throughout studies of lack of attachment, on one hand, and loss or disruption of an attachment, on the other. In an absolute sense, the possible consequences of never forming an attachment are more dire than those of the loss of an attachment. But in a relative sense, gradations of quality in insecure attachments lead to ambiguous answers to the question. For example, some researchers and theorists suggest that loss and breaks in continuity have a different meaning to the child who has received indifferent caregiving and to the child who has experienced a protective and gratifying relationship. The better the relationship, the more severe the impact of loss. Others take a different position: the stronger the attachment, the better able the young child will be to form a new relationship, given the opportunity. Although the reactions of the securely attached child may be more severe at first, her or his long-term adaptation is likely to be more adequate than that of the insecurely attached child who experiences loss or disruption (L. Yarrow 1964). Rutter observed that "children with the most favorable home environments are least affected by [loss of the attached person,] and . . . those who have the least to lose are most affected when they love even that little" (1972:107).

Conclusions

Until more is known about the reversibility of the ill effects of insufficient or missing environmental nutriments after a certain age, it is imperative to keep in mind the evolved human trait of plasticity (although we are not infinitely plastic) and the positive impact of later enriched environments found in the Thomas and Chess longitudinal studies described earlier. Also to be kept in mind are the differences in children's vulnerability and resilience, which interact with environmental circumstances in varying contexts. Rigorous research is needed to validate what are still mostly hypotheses about the upper age limits for reversibility. Except for the work of Thomas and Chess, most studies of the reversibility of the environmental deficits discussed in this chapter have necessarily been carried out with clinical populations on a retrospective basis. Yet it is reasonable to assume that there are adults in the general population who suffered the ill effects of environmental deficits, including unrelatedness, and who then, *after the age of 3 or 6 years,* experienced a change to a loving, enriched environment. Such adults would be unlikely to come to the attention of clinicians or researchers if their changed environment, coupled with their personal characteristics, had brought about a reversal of the ill effects. And so we do not know of them.

Clarke (1982) added several pertinent observations. She hypothesized a biological trajectory from which individuals may deviate in the face of severe environmental deprivations, but to which they return when the stressors are removed or significantly diminished, and a social trajectory governed by accident of birth, yet changeable by chance or design. The idea is helpful in understanding spontaneous recoveries from environmental deficits—a kind of self-correcting tendency that pushes children toward continued growth whenever the environment permits.

Chapter 9 takes up the child's development in the preschool years, the continued development of the parent(s), and certain family transformations.

9

Family Transformations in the Preschool Years: The Socialization of Child and Parents

This chapter describes the reciprocal nature of the child's and the parents' ongoing development as the baby becomes an actively mobile child who acquires language, first friendships, and gender identity. Attention is given to the child's socialization into gendered roles and their consequences in adulthood and to temperamental differences and common early fears. Extrafamilial sources of socialization in day care and preschool education are then presented. The chapter concludes with a consideration of the parents' development and the family transformations brought about by the child's life transitions as the family struggles both to change itself and to maintain constancy.

LANGUAGE DEVELOPMENT IN THE SOCIAL CONTEXT

> Thomas Carlyle [the famed historian] was only eleven months old and had never spoken a word when, hearing another child in the household cry, he sat up and said, "What ails wee Jock?"
> —John W. Gardner 1961:59

Surely the story is apocryphal, since the acquisition of language is a slow and complex process, not to emerge fully developed overnight. How it takes place is still a mystery. To examine the conflicting types

237

of theories engaging linguists currently would take us too far afield. But when put together, the biological, cognitive, and social theories developed in linguistics over the 1970s and 1980s suggest that the ability to speak and understand a language is somehow related to the following:

1. A genetically based structure or process of the human brain is sufficiently mature at about age 2 to enable all human beings everywhere to learn and speak a language. Chomsky (1965) believes that the child innately knows and can recognize the deep underlying universal grammar or rules of language. Thus the child is able to utter a sentence that he or she never heard before and to construct it in an orderly, syntactical way. Not all linguists agree with Chomsky. Some adhere instead to Piagetian ideas about learning (see the section in appendix 1 on Piaget). Whether one part of the brain determines all cognitive activity or is specific to learning a language, the relation between language development and the child's mental representations of reality is still an issue (L. Bloom 1983).

2. Environmental stimuli are required to release the biological predisposition. These stimuli include, for example, the verbal responses that parents make to the infant's cooing and babbling, the older baby's vocalizations, and, later, the first words. Talking to the baby and later with the young child and asking questions and waiting for replies, rather than talking at the child, appear to advance language skills. It is not necessary to teach a child to speak (except for the small number who suffer language disorders). Children acquire language when the particular brain structure or process has matured and in response to having been talked to.

Bruner (1983), a cognitive psychologist interested in language acquisition, blended 1) and 2). He suggested that children's access to language begins in the social interactions of caregiver and infant and continues in their later play and word games, which serve the partners as ways of communicating and of sharing meaning. For the first eighteen months, the child is organizing his or her mental representations of the world of people, objects, and action by means of certain cognitive structures. The structures are prewired in the human brain so that certain distinctions in the real world are noticed and it is possible for the child later to pick up corresponding linguistic distinctions. These include distinctions between specific and nonspecific events, between state and process; between episodes and continuous events, and between causative and noncausative actions (Bruner 1983:30). The recognition of distinctions and of their linguistic counterparts enables the child to understand syntax (the rules of grammar), a lexicon (the meaning of words), and the intent of a communication (how to use language).

None of this could take place were it not for a genetic predisposition to acquire a language, similar to Chomsky's idea but requiring the adult's willingness to negotiate with the child about the three aspects of speech. Bruner believes that the most important negotiation involves making intentions clear and making their expression fit the conditions and requirements of the culture. Of less importance is involvement with the semantic scope of the child's lexicon, and of least importance is involvement with syntax. These involvements are stimuli that activate the genetic predisposition and make it work, transmitting the culture to the child at the same time.

Stern (1985:174–182) noted that while significant gains come with the acquisition of language, a great deal of the force and wholeness of original experience is lost or made latent by language. For example, with language, young children become estranged from their own direct experience. With language, a split in some preverbal or nonverbal experience of feeling, sensation, perception, or cognition occurs, transforming it into an experience separate from the original. A split in some experiences of self and of some experiences of relatedness will be imposed henceforth by the abstractness of language. Now a verbal version of an experience exists as well as the original nonverbal version. The two do not always get along well. Some nonverbal experiences may be poorly represented and "wander off to lead a misnamed and poorly understood existence"(1985:175). Some may not be accessible to language and therefore do not undergo linguistic transformation. They continue underground, nonverbalized, to lead an unnamed but very real existence.

Stern (1985) also suggested that something similar happens to the baby's cross-modal perception (chapter 8). Cross-modal (also termed amodal) experience is fractured by the specificity of language, which anchors an experience to one particular sensory modality. The language version of an experience then becomes the official one, and the cross-modal or amodal version (the totality of sensations in the experience) goes underground, not to reappear except in certain contemplative or emotional states or aesthetic experiences. For example, the words, "yellow sunlight" close out all the other preverbal, global experiences of sunlight. The cross-modal perceptual unity is shattered. Also, specific episodes of life-as-lived are lost because generalized episodes (an averaging of specific episodes) are the only ones named by language, such as "bedtime," "play with Daddy," "walking with Mommy," and "peek-a-boo." Specific episodes cannot be verbalized until language is very advanced and sometimes never. Meanwhile, no name exists for specific episodes, thus creating misunderstandings of meaning if the child says, "Bedtime" and is referring to a particular episode, but the mother infers the generalized ritual of going to bed. This misunderstanding leads to frustration for parent and child, but it also motivates the child to learn language better. In both childhood and adulthood, misunderstanding of meanings can arise from differences between what is said and what is meant—as in double-bind messages or in the incongruities between nonverbal and verbal communication.

According to Stern (1985), the ability to narrate one's own life story begins with language acquisition. The child now begins internally to build a story of what her or his life is like and continues the building through the life course. The connections to what actually happened may not be clear and may not even matter. The story is the way one's life is and feels, and it is a metaphor for actuality. (The child's narrative-building gradually forms a life story that later may be presented to a social worker). It is not clear how, when, or why the child begins to construct a life narrative, but Stern hypothesized that narrative making, a universal human phenomenon, may prove to be related to how the human brain is designed—an interesting observation in light of the rising interest in family stories and narratives among social workers who work with families (Laird 1989; Riessman 1989).

3. Linguists recognize that language is also shaped by the social context (L. Bloom 1983), the aspect of linguistics of most interest to the social worker. The influence can be either negative or positive. One positive feature is the impact of language acquisition on the 2-year old's sense of self and relatedness (Stern 1985). Not only does language provide the child with a new level of relatedness at age 2, but as speech continues to develop, relatedness expands with it. And language can lead to new levels of competence, self-esteem, and self-direction as well. Stern also took up the assumption in object relations theory that language acquisition is a major influence in the achievement of separation and individuation, second only to acquiring locomotion. In his view:

The opposite is equally true: language acquisition is a powerful influence in union and togetherness. With each word children solidify their mental commonality with the parent, and later with other members of the language community, when they discover that their personal experiential knowledge is part of a larger experience of knowledge, that they are unified with others in a common culture base. (1985:172)

At about the age of 3, if playmates are available, friendships become significant features of the social context of language. They provide resources different from but complementary to those provided by the family. For example, friendships shape the social skills of talking, gaining entry into group activities, exercising tact and sensitivity, and extending approval and support to peers. Friendships also shape the sense of identity and foster the sense of group belonging (Z. Rubin 1980). Language, then, is a most important facilitator of social interaction and friendships. They, in turn, contribute to the continuing development of language.

Language thus empowers the child along many dimensions. However, negative influences exerted by the social context operate to make of language a means of disempowering large segments of the population and reinforcing oppression. Disempowerment through language begins in the school years, or earlier, and continues through adulthood.

Speakers of Spanish

For example, Sotomayer (1977) described the consequences of political, social, and economic degradation of the language, culture, and ethnicity of minority groups. These consequences include severe damage to the self-concept, the sense of identity, self-esteem, and self-direction. When a group's language is devalued by the larger population, the group is disempowered. For Chicano and Chicana adults in this country, "social participation is not a matter of available choices, but rather whether the Chicano is allowed to participate due to his or her low ranking position. Language in this situation is utilized as a means of social control." Demanding that groups give up their native language for English is disempowering since the language is part of relatedness and provides a sense of community or solidarity in the face of oppression. This is not to say, however, that native-language speakers should not also learn English. It is a means of entry into the society's opportunity structures and is therefore empowering.

To provide educational, social, and health services to limited-English or monolingual Spanish-speaking groups is said to be difficult because different varieties of Spanish are used by different groups

(Puerto Rican, Mexican-American, Cuban, and various South American groups). This may be true where these groups coexist in large numbers in a given area, which is not ordinarily the case, or if written or broadcast materials are to be used across regions.

Speakers of Asian Languages

The observations regarding Spanish speakers hold true for speakers of Chinese, Japanese, Korean, Filipino, and other Asian languages. The elderly or recent immigrants may speak only limited or no English, and thus they face serious problems: "The lack of trained personnel who can understand their unique situations, language, and cultural barriers prevents them from participating in the health and welfare system of the United States in an informed manner"(Owan 1978). The result is an underutilization of services that leads to health and social problems for individuals, families, and the community. Owan pointed out that all ethnic groups have the right to share fully in the benefits of American society while retaining pride in their cultural heritage, their distinctive religion, and their language.

Speakers of Black English

Speakers of Black English face similar and different difficulties because Black English is a separate language and not merely poorly spoken English. Its speakers, like any other speech community, share a set of social conventions about verbal communication and rules about the use of metacommunications (how things are said) to signify intent, hidden messages, and emotionality. Although it shares some words with Standard English, leading most whites to assume that it is the same language, Black English actually has its own complex history and autonomous rules of syntax, as described by the linguist Dillard (1975).

Viewed ecologically, any language serves to relate its speakers to one another and to their environment. This is particularly clear in the case of Black English, which serves to strengthen the relatedness among its speakers, to enhance their sense of identity and self-direction, and to keep firm the boundary between its speakers and the oppressive social context. Draper analyzed the functional aspects of Black English for its speakers as they cope with racism and disempowerment and concluded, "As a boundary-strengthening or distancing device Black English enables its speakers to communicate safely within the group while effectively shutting whites out of the communication process" (1979:271). Draper's work demonstrates the importance of white social workers' respecting and understanding Black English as a separate language and not merely a distorted version of standard English.

Speakers of American Indian Languages

American Indians have been disempowered in many ways that threaten the survival of their cultures by the denigrating of their native languages and by being forced to give them up in government boarding schools. One example is the renaming of tribal landscapes and sacred places by the larger society. For three hundred years, a succession of explorers, missionaries, American soldiers, and the federal government have left linguistic and cultural footprints on American Indian lands (Rasky 1988). An anthropologist Keith H. Basso who has lived and worked among the Apache for thirty years declared in an interview with Rasky (1988) that superimposing an Anglo language on an Apache landscape is a subtle form of oppression and domination. He is collaborating with Apache leaders in a linguistic remapping that will restore the ancient names used by the Apache ancestors. In "Reflections of an Unremembered Past," Kanani Bell, a social worker, wrote:

> Cheyenne, Crow, Arapaho, Blackfoot, Sioux. From days never known and sights glimpsed only indirectly the names crowd my mind more than things merely remembered. Pawnee, Kiowa, Apache, Cree. The names are not reducible to history. They dwell in a different yet not unreachable region. Ogalala, Chiricahua, Cherokee. The names speak within me of the dimly understood. They crowd my world, my being, to the very corners until only the names remain. Or I am the names. . . . In the Navaho, who moved onto the vacated Anasazi lands and named them the Old Ones, the Anasazi live. I am Anasazi. . . . Kansas, Iowa, Wichita. . . . Dakota. Names by the tens and hundreds of thousand live through me. Or I live through them and I am the names. (1986)

Language Change

J. Rubin described the language and communication inadequacies encountered by limited-English and monolingual speakers in the domains of health, medicine, law, employment, communication, citizenship (census forms and voting information), social welfare, and education. She suggested four questions to be asked about the inadequacies:

> 1) What language/communication *inadequacies* have been identified, and by whom? 2) Who are the *planners* who have the authority and power to make and influence language-related decisions? 3) What *plans* or *goals* have been set out to attend to the communication inadequacies identified? 4) What attempts have been made at *planning;* that is, in what situations has a real effort been made toward implementation of or feedback to the plan? (1984:154; italics in the original)

Since social workers function in many of these domains, the questions serve as guidelines in advocating clients' rights. Practitioners can define the language-related difficulties experienced by their clients, determine who are the decision makers and planners, provide information to them for making a plan, participate in the planning, define the criteria for effective implementation, and monitor the process and outcomes. Owan (1978), a social worker, described how successful language change in a Social Security Administration office in New York City's Chinatown provided more satisfactory services for clients. It also increased productivity and reduced work load pressures on the staff.

Issues of Linguistic and Cultural Diversity

In 1988 three states, Arizona (Article 28), Colorado (Article 2, Sect. 30A), and Florida (Art. 2, Sect. 9) passed state constitutional amendments declaring English to be the official language. California had passed a similar constitutional amendment in 1986. All four are states with large Spanish-speaking populations. While not applying to bilingual education, which is mandated by the federal government, the measures apply to state government documents and proceedings, from which Spanish translations are excluded. Such efforts have been criticized by many as racist. Others welcome such efforts on the grounds that the universality of English will help the United States to achieve its "melting-pot" ideal and thereby to defeat the trend toward cultural pluralism, which values cultural and language diversity.

The Canadian experience is pertinent to this controversy. Despite many historical and contemporary similarities between Canada and the United States, they differ markedly in policies regarding language diversity. Equality of English and French has been official Canadian policy since 1867, although English was dominant over French in most situations. In the 1960s, a Royal Commission on Bilingualism and Biculturalism was established in response to political violence and a rising consciousness among French-speaking Canadians. The commission documented great inequality between the languages, whereupon the Canadian parliament, reaffirming Canada's bilingual status, initiated a series of changes to overcome inequalities in services and opportunities for French-speaking Canadians. The Province of Quebec then established greater cultural and linguistic autonomy within provincial affairs and pressed for greater equality for French- and English-speaking Canadians in national life (O'Barr 1984). O'Barr noted:

Official bilingualism was questioned ... by other disenfranchised groups (i.e., non-native speakers of either English or French, including both immigrants and Amerindians). By the end of the decade, national concern with bilingualism and biculturalism had shifted to discussions of the appropriateness of multilingualism and multiculturalism. The 1980s, although different in their specifics, have witnessed no abatement of the concerns about language rights among the Canadian population. (1984:263–264)

OTHER FORMS OF LANGUAGE-BASED DISCRIMINATION

Sexist Language

Language has been used as an instrument to disempower girls and women and to reinforce gender typing. The term *sexist language* refers to the generic use of the male noun and pronouns to denote both males and females (but not the specific use of them to denote the male sex alone). A gradual reduction in sexist language occurred in the 1980s in the publications of the professions, the academic disciplines, government agencies, and, to a far smaller degree, the public media.

Despite this small advance, sexist language persists in both spoken and written forms, and its significance as an instrument of disempowerment is trivialized by being treated humorously or being ridiculed by men and even by some women. Martyna (1980) observed that when the situation is reversed and the female pronoun is used generically, as in the teaching profession, male teachers have argued for change on the grounds that the female noun and pronouns have resulted in a poor public image and low salaries.

Opponents of eliminating the generic use of the male noun and pronouns claim that the generic and specific intent in their use is easily established by context. However, Martyna's research shows that ambiguity occurs even when the context is clearly generic, as in examples from her study: "When someone is near a hospital, he should be quiet" and "Man, being a mammal, breast-feeds his young"(1980). In addition to the sexism built into English grammar, it is found in the vocabulary, as in the widespread use of derogatory and obscene terms to denote woman, and in the use of masculine values, such as leadership, authority, and historic significance, as the norm. Examples of the latter include "the fathers of modern science," "the courageous pioneers crossed the plains with their wives and children," and even "Neanderthal man," when many of the skeletal remains of prehistoric human beings are of females (Farb 1974).

Deaf Speakers

Disempowerment through language follows the deaf over their life course. Shut out from the world of the hearers and speakers of language, they inhabit a world that is the culture of deafness, with its own language and codes of behavior, and deaf friends, organizations, groups, media, sports, commerce, and even street gangs (Walker 1987). Walker and her two younger sisters, all with total hearing, were born to parents who had been profoundly deaf from infancy. Having attended the Indiana State School for the Deaf, the parents were trained in speaking and lip reading. American Sign Language, which has its own syntax, structure, and grammatical rules separate from English, was not taught, but the children at the school taught each other and learned from the few teachers who were deaf. Walker's parents were proficient in signing, but their verbal speech was unintelligible to all but their children.

The children were their parents' guides and interpreters, as they had learned to sign before they learned to talk. Although the father and mother conversed with each other in American Sign Language, they communicated with their children by simultaneously speaking and signing: The children did learn to speak through contact with many relatives living nearby and through television.

Walker described her parents as extremely private people because of staring, insults, and hurts from others all their lives. But name calling is only a small part of being deaf. Walker explained that many people regard deafness as a simple affliction. They assume that the deaf can write notes, pass their leisure time reading, and can converse by talking and reading lips. But it is all much more complicated for, as we saw earlier in this chapter, the first two years of life are critical for language acquisition. If a baby is deprived of those years of hearing speech, she or he can never make up the loss:

> Using the basics of English becomes a task as difficult as building a house without benefit of drawings or experience in carpentry. Writing a grammatically correct sentence is a struggle. Reading a book is a Herculean effort. Nor is lip-reading the panacea. . . . The best lip-readers in the world actually "read" only 25 percent of what's said; the rest is contextual piecing together of ideas and expected constructions. The average deaf person understands far less. (Walker 1987:19)

Such piecing together is a slow process and often results in errors of understanding, leading the speaker to assume a lack of intelligence in the deaf person. The extreme social isolation and lack of acceptance and understanding of their disability experienced by deaf people are disempowering because they limit participation in community and political life on the basis of a separate language (signing) and/or hearing (lip reading). Nevertheless, pressure is growing for a return to teaching sign language to the deaf and to using deaf teachers and administrators in residential schools for the deaf. Mainstreaming deaf children in the public schools is believed by many to be ineffective because instruction is given in oral and written English, although 80 percent of deaf children have become deaf before language acquisition.

Among the deaf and educators of the deaf, the issue of whether to teach sign or lip reading continues to be controversial. Most schools for the deaf now teach only lip reading and speaking, and they rely primarily on nondeaf teachers. A very few schools rely on signing as well as speaking. To add to the complexities, different forms of sign language exist. The native language of American deaf persons is American Sign Language (AMESLAN). Deafened persons who lost their hearing in adulthood may prefer Signed English (SIGLISH), which follows the syntax and linguistic structure of English (Luey 1980).

A report by the United Nations Educational, Scientific, and Cultural Organization (UNESCO) on the education of the deaf concludes:

> We must recognize the legitimacy of sign language as a linguistic system and it should be accorded the same status as other languages. . . . Now that the importance of the national sign languages for deaf education is better understood, it is no longer admissible to overlook them or to fail to encourage their integration into deaf education. The old idea that the use of sign language interferes with the acquisition of spoken and written language is no longer considered valid. (Lane 1987:35)

The Poor

A group on whom professional language and jargon have a severely negative impact is the poor. Lee (1980) showed that, in describing the poor, many human services professionals use words that disempower, depersonalize, and dehumanize individuals and families. By labeling people and using value-laden generalizations and negative symbols, we fail to individualize people and their particular life situations. From the literature of several helping professions, including social work, Lee culled words and phrases used to characterize poor persons who are served by health, mental health, and social agencies.

Her list includes the following: "lower class"; "apathetic"; "serious deficits"; "poor therapy patient"; "poor verbal ability"; "nonverbal"; "lack of introspection or emotional responsiveness"; "lack of self-awareness"; "abstract reasoning considered inappropriate with lower-class patients"; "emotionally deprived"; "lack of parental interest and stimulation"; "disorganized"; "multiproblem family"; "preoccupation with survival issues"; "disadvantaged"; "inadequate parents"; "dysfunctional"; "uneducated"; "unmotivated"; "hostile to any approach"; and "resistant." Lee noted the frequency of the prefixes *un*, *in*, *dis*, *non*, and *mal* and the use of terms such as *deficits* and *lack of*. This is defining by negative symbols that provide no definition. It transmits a negative view of the poor through articles, case records, diagnostic statements, and other written and oral reports.

Lee (1980) argued that what is needed are descriptions of positives instead of negatives; of what we see instead of what we don't see; and of what *is* rather than what is *not*. Strengths must be identified and described, for they are the bases for growth and change. Anything less than these descriptions further disempowers a group already oppressed by poverty.

The Illiterate

And finally, many social workers observe every day the disempowering effects of widespread illiteracy in reading and writing language in the United States, and they are committed to help in the work of overcoming such handicaps. We need also to monitor the differential access of children (and adults) to learning new and increasingly important language technologies, such as computer languages and programming, that are apt to lead to differential access to knowledge and opportunities that empower.

THE PRESCHOOLER'S FRIENDSHIPS

In the first year of life, infant's play centers on objects such as toys. Two infants put together tend to regard each other as physical objects to be explored. Early in the second year, however, babies begin to interact. They smile, vocalize, extend objects to each other, and exhibit negative feelings and actions when angered by the other. By age 3, their interactions display in an early form the basic elements of social interaction of older children and adults; sustained attention, turn taking, and mutual responsiveness in which each takes responsibility for maintaining the exchange. Usually conversation is part of the interaction, although it does not always make sense to the adult listener. Three-year-old partners may talk past each other, each in his or her realm of interest (Z. Rubin 1980).

Until age 5, the friendships of preschoolers differ along several dimensions from those of school-aged children and adolescents. For the preschooler the important features are physical presence, physical rather than psychological elements in forming friendships, and the conception of a "best friend" as the one with whom you do more of whatever it is you do with a friend, a quantitative rather than a qualitative assessment (Z. Rubin 1980).

GENDER-ROLE TYPING

Before examining gender-role typing and childhood socialization into gendered roles, definitions (largely derived from Money and Ehrhardt 1972) of biological sex, gender identity, and gender role itself are in order. Whereas sex is a biological attribute of persons, gender is a social attribute in terms of behaviors regarded by society as appropriate to the person's sex. Sex is biologically defined; gender is socially designed.

Biological sex refers to the physiological and anatomical attributes of male or female derived from genetic factors. XY chromosomes in the male determine the formation of testes, and XX chromosomes in the female determine the formation of ovaries. Biological sex sets off fetal-neonatal endocrine function (hormonal mix), which organizes the internal and external structural and functional differentiation of male and female. A most controversial issue still being investigated is whether the sex hormones (androgen, estrogen, and progestogen) and/or other mechanisms acting on the brain before birth produce sex differences in ways of thinking, feeling, and behaving. Biological sex also includes the secondary sex characteristics distinctive to each sex; sex differences in the fat–muscle ratio, height and weight, the contents of bodily fluids, and the levels of androgens and estrogens; and irreducible features such as female menstruation, gestation, and lactation and male impregnation.

In addition to these innate biological differences, various psychological differences between males and females have been declared innate (they are discussed in the next chapter), sometimes as justification for rigid gendered roles, but a biological basis of these behaviors has not been established. More important, even if they should prove to be innate, they can be, and indeed are, modified by culture, society, and parents.

Gender identity refers to the subjective sense of the individual as a male or a female, masculine or feminine, or both male and female and masculine and feminine. Gender identity is a core part of the total body image and self-concept, is evident as early as 18 months of age, and is fully attained by the age of 2 or 3. Once in place, it is thought to be unchangeable. It is manifested by the individual's behaviors in gender roles. Money and Ehrhardt (1972) showed that precisely timed interactions between genes, gonads, hormones, brain structures, and early socialization are the basis for gender identity acquisition, early socialization being the most influential.

In their studies of hermaphroditism, Money and various colleagues worked with children who were genetically male but had been raised female and those who were genetically female but had been raised male. The "errors" in sexual identity were due to the ambiguous or improperly differentiated external genitalia at birth. In many instances, with corrective surgery and hormonal therapy in some, the genetic males (XY chromosomal pattern) grew up to be normal women and the genetic females (XX chromosmal pattern) to be normal men. They experienced themselves and acted (including in intercourse) in accordance with the gender in which they had been raised, irrespective of chromosomal, gonadal, or hormonal sex.

If the ambiguity is not thoroughly evaluated, and should the sex assigned at birth need to be changed later, Money believes that the reassignment should be made before the age of 18 months. If reassignment is made in early infancy, only the responses of others must be changed. But if the reassignment comes after about 18 months of age, the baby's own responses, made on the basis of her or his emerging gender identity, must be changed. This change can lead to serious difficulties in gender identity, but forced sex change after the age of 3 or 4 without consideration of the child's gender-identity status is likely to result in iatrogenic (physician-caused) emotional disorders.

Money's studies over the years have led him to conclude that a major part of gender-identity differentiation is accomplished postnatally: "It then takes place, as does the development of native language, when a prenatally programmed disposition comes in contact with postnatal, socially programmed signals" (Money and Ehrhardt (1972:18). These authors believe that it is essential that the child grow up knowing that sex differences are primarily defined by the reproductive capacity and having a sense of pride in her or his own genitalia and their ultimate reproductive use.

Gender role refers to the behaviors, expectations, beliefs, attitudes, values, and norms defined by the society as male or female. In contrast to the term *sex role, gender role* refers to the total woman and her femininity or the total man and his masculinity. The sex role is part of the gender role but refers only to the person's sexuality and sexual behaviors. Despite this useful distinction, the two terms are used interchangeably in much of the literature. Gender roles are typed; that is, they are restricted on the basis of sex. What are defined as the male role and attributes are restricted to males, and what are defined as the female role and attributes are restricted to females. In a patriarchal society, the male role and its attributes are invested with power and status, and the female role and its attributes are without power and status and are considered inferior and less desirable. Gender-role typing accords a wide range of options and opportunities to males and severely restricts the options and opportunities of females. It ignores individual interests, talents, and abilities and hence limits the realization of all individuals' full potentials. These generalizations about the male role refer only to the men of the dominant groups. Even so, men in powerless groups often hold power over women in their own group, and they also enjoy higher status.

Gender role, like gender identity, is internalized. Thus we feel and act as though the role were innate and are blind to its social and cultural origins. However, gender roles are more easily modified than gender identity, particularly as the roles become less typed, a process that is beginning in North American society, although it has always been the frequent case among American blacks. Being less typed means being less restrictive. To the degree that gender typing abates, gender roles become more flexible. Presumably, gender roles, their behaviors, and their attributes would become interchangeable were gender typing to disappear altogether.

Gender Schema Theory

Gender theories include the following (Bem 1983): 1) Psychoanalytic theory views identification with the same-sex parent, following the oedipal resolution, as the mainspring of gender identity and gender-typing; 2) social learning theory emphasizes the environmental rewards for gender-appropriate behaviors and the environment's aversive responses to gender-inappropriate behaviors in gender typing, together with learning through role modeling by parents and others and the child's own observations; and 3) cognitive-developmental theory emphasizes the need for cognitive congruence, which, following upon the child's acquisition of gender identity, motivates the child to prefer peers and behaviors associated with it and thereby leads to gender typing.

Bem (1983) argued that 1) psychoanalytic ideas about the acquisition of gender identity are not borne out by empirical research; 2) social learning theory views children as passive recipients of environmental forces rather than active agents who seek to organize and comprehend the social world; and 3) cognitive-developmental theory assumes that children spontaneously develop self-concepts and value systems even without environmental pressure to behave in gender-stereotyped ways but fails to explain why sex has primacy over other possible ways of categorizing the self, such as color, caste, and religion.

As a replacement for inadequate theories, Bem advanced a "gender schema" theory that draws on some features of the social learning and cognitive-developmental theories. It assumes that gender typing is learned and is therefore neither inevitable nor unalterable. However, in addition to learning about sex differences such as anatomy, reproductive function, division of labor, and personality attributes, the child also learns to encode and organize new information in terms of an evolving gender schema. Bem defined a schema as "a cognitive structure, a network of associations [sex-linked in the gender schema] that organizes and guides an individual's perception" (1983). Schemas provide a readiness to categorize stimuli on the basis of a particular dimension, and therefore they determine what is perceived.

As children learn the contents of their society's gender schemas, they learn which attributes and behaviors are linked with their own sex and hence with themselves. The child learns to apply this selectivity to the self, and to choose only the dimensions applicable to her or his sex for organizing the contents of the self-concept. In this way, the self-concept becomes gender-typed. Bem called this gender-schematic processing. The child also learns to measure her or his behaviors, characteristics, and preferences against the particular culture's gender schemas as a behavioral standard and a regulator of self-esteem.

Childhood Socialization and Gender Typing

Studies cited in chapter 8 found that fathers and mothers treat sons and daughters differently from birth, and Parke concluded:

> [The] pattern of fathers expressing affection for their daughters and stimulating their sons may be the earliest form of sex-role typing. Fathers, as we know from other research, want to encourage the physical and intellectual development of their sons. For daughters, the fathers' aim may be to encourage femininity. . . . Mothers contribute significantly to their girls' intellectual development; the mother's early stimulation of her infant daughter may be an antecedent of later intellectual encouragement. (1981:44:45)

Other differences are noted. Both parents play with their male and female infants, but fathers touch and vocalize more with male infants, and mothers are more active stimulators of girls. Some studies have found that parents tend to cuddle girl infants more than boy infants and to let males cry longer, so that strivings for bodily contact, nurturance, and relief from emotional discomfort are discouraged in male babies but reinforced in females. Yet many, but not all, parents believe that they treat their children "just the same." Most commonly, child-rearing practices result in a dichotomy between male and female roles and behaviors beginning at birth.

The descriptions of socialization processes that follow are generalizations and apply to some individuals in North American society to varying degrees, and to some not at all. Traditionally, the sex of most infants is immediately and publicly assigned by the parents through the differential use of pink and blue, the choice of a name, and the gendered pronouns that will govern the gendered responses of others across the individual's life course. Biological traits and temperamental qualities that fit traditional gender roles tend to be reinforced or extinguished, depending on the child's sex (e.g., size and strength in boys, petiteness in girls, activity in the male infant, and passivity in the female). Most people are unaware that their responses to the baby are actually shaping her or his gendered behavior. Adults take for granted that their own behavior is a no-option response to gender-appropriate behavior in the young child, and it is assumed to be innate (Money and Ehrhardt 1972).

During the preschool and early school years, boys are given sports equipment, toy guns, and other active toys that require movement and manipulation, while girls are given dolls, sewing kits, miniature kitchen equipment, and dollhouses. Young boys are expected to play games that require competitiveness, aggression, and violence, while young girls are expected to play house or shopping and quiet games such as jacks and hopscotch. Boys are expected not to cry but to be strong "little men." They may be taught not to fight but are encouraged to defend themselves in violent ways. Boys are taught to avoid all female-typed behaviors and interests. Although in some families girls may be permitted male-typed behaviors and interests until puberty, many are taught from the outset to avoid them.

As a consequence, children grow up preferring same-sex peers and the activities, attributes, behaviors, and self-concepts that are assigned by society to their sex. It is not surprising that by the age of 3, clear-cut behavioral differences are in place, boys are under continuous pressure to maintain and develop them. Girls may be less pressured until after puberty. Internalized gender roles continue to be reinforced by school materials and routines, movies and TV, advertising, peer activities, and stories of male heroes and female spectators—

all of which are present images of how men are supposed to act and how women are supposed to act.

The Gendered Role of Women

Feminist inquiry into the status and roles of women has extended to most if not all the humanities and sciences, and to many professional disciplines. In traditional psychology, for example, ideas about female development and traits used studies of male development and traits as the standard. Differences in male and female behavior were considered the consequences of differences in physiology and anatomy, women's behavior being regarded as a deviation from the male model. Masculine values such as achievement and autonomy, as well as male behaviors such as competitiveness and abstract thinking, were regarded as abnormal in females. The social context that shapes behavior was ignored.

Since the early 1970s, a separate psychology of women has been produced by feminist scholars who reject traditional male-centered psychology and argue that women must be considered on the basis of their own experience and not in comparison with men. Whether in the future the two psychologies will remain separate or will be integrated into a human psychology is not yet clear. Gilligan (1982) developed a model of differences in female and male moral development. Building on Chodorow's (1978) psychoanalytically derived ideas that masculine identity is defined by separateness and autonomy, and feminine identity by relationships and community, Gilligan took issue with Kohlberg's stages of moral development based on male models and experiences, in which women are found to be wanting (see the section in appendix 1, on Kohlberg). What are regarded as deficits in women are simply differences from men that have resulted from differences in their upbringing, especially in the experience with their mothers.

In listening to women talk about their lives and in considering their responses to Kohlberg's moral dilemmas, Gilligan inferred that the moral issue for most (but not all) women is conflicting responsibilities, arising from a web of relationships and caring. The female issue requires contextual and narrative thinking for resolution. This is sharply different from the moral issue for most (but not all) men: competing rights, arising from a reliance on abstract principles of justice, rules, and hierarchical values. The male issue requires formal, logical modes of thinking for resolution. Gilligan concluded that women order their experience in different terms than men do, and that their responses to the dilemmas posed in Kohlberg's studies provide an alternate conception of maturity.

Gilligan's (1982) book is extremely popular among women, including social workers and other professional women, to whom it rings true. For example, a female social worker wrote:

> Looking at how children play, I found my own experience to be exactly what Gilligan described, both as a child myself, as a camp counselor, and in two years as a full-time worker with over seventy children, ages 5 to 11. In the latter experience I noticed that girls adapted rules to suit the situation. The boys didn't do that—it violated their sense of justice. For example, a second-grade boy sat talking with me as two fifth-grade girls played "two square" nearby. The girls, rather than calling it "losing" when one missed the ball and started over, changed the rules so that they could keep playing one long continuous game with no winner or loser. Jamie looked at me and said, "How can they do that? They're breaking the rules!"

Several feminist social scientists recently joined in a negative critique of Gilligan's work (Kerber et al. 1986). Kerber (a historian) pointed to Gilligan's use of a psychological explanation for what is a consequence of socialization in a patriarchal social order. She also asserted that Gilligan's position gives support to traditional gender stereotypes and ignores the historical and social context of women's status in a sexist society. Strong criticism of the research methodology is expressed by Maccoby and her student (who are psychologists) and Luria (a sociologist). Stack (an anthropologist) reported that her own research of black migrants' returning to the rural South reveals a convergence between women and men in their construction of themselves in relationship to others; in their vocabulary of rights, morality, and the social good; and in their configuration of gender differences and similarities. She noted the absence of race, class, consciousness, and cohort in Gilligan's theory building and the construction of gender, and she added:

> Gender consciousness emerges from a negotiation between material conditions and cultural ideologies, from a negotiation between what is out there (historical conditions, class- and race-specific experiences, age, and generation, the ecology of life course) and what we see with it (the assumptions and interpretations that we have in our minds, our shared models of the world, our

visions and dilemmas of adulthood). . . . Gender is a construct shaped by the experience of race, class, culture, caste, and consciousness. (Kerber et al. 1986)

Gilligan's (1986) rejoinders to the critiques notwithstanding, such experience factors are indeed missing from her work. It may be that her material feels right to many middle-class and professional women because it matches the internalized gendered role. In any case, research with diverse populations will be welcomed by Gilligan's critics and believers alike.

Cole (1986), an anthropologist, is also concerned about the issue of diversity. She has opposed the assumption in much of the feminist literature that all women share the same female experience, whether in their family, parenting, working, or sexual, spiritual, social, economic, or political lives. While all women share some aspects of what unites women, nevertheless women of color, poor women, European ethnic women, and women with disabilities have very different histories, statuses, and resources from those of white middle- and upper-class women, who are the feminist leaders, researchers, and theorists. Class, race, ethnicity, age, religion, sexual orientation, rural settings, and physical disabilities create the specific content of oppression and cannot be covered over by a notion of sisterhood and its assumption that the oppression of all women is identical.

Feminist activism calls for women's greater participation and power in electoral politics, equal pay for comparable worth, reproductive rights, and effective law enforcement in matters of sexual exploitation and violence. But, Cole wrote, women of color, while not negating the importance of these goals, would place them in the societal context of racism. Women of color are twice as likely to be unemployed as are white women; their life expectancy is years less than that of white women; they are fifteen to twenty-nine times more likely to live in substandard housing and to receive no or inadequate health care; and their children are far more likely to receive a substandard education: "Thus their struggle against sexism cannot be divorced from their struggle against racism" (Cole 1986:25). Further, some feminist positions on women's sexuality, the family, and religion, for example, rub up against deeply held culturally based value preferences of some women of color, some rural women, some working-class women, and some older women that are very different from the value preferences of middle-class white feminist women.

For a profession and its members to participate effectively in achieving gender equality and social justice in North American society and elsewhere, the diversity of race, ethnicity, religion, culture, age, sexual orientation, and physical ability must be in the foreground of attention along with gender.

The Gendered Role of Men

The beginning recognition that men, too, experience gender-role strain because of rigid gender roles appeared during the sixties with the critique of traditional masculinity among many younger men of the counterculture. A well-developed analysis of a masculine mystique came to the fore during the 1970s. The mystique reflects a complex set of values and beliefs that define the traditional male role and optimal masculinity (O'Neil 1982). The extent to which these gendered values and beliefs are held by any man will vary, depending on his early gender-role socialization, his age, his race, and his socioeconomic status. O'Neil believes that the mystique is rooted in the fear of femininity that arises early in boys' socialization. The gender-role socialization of boys is more intensive than that experienced by girls, perhaps because of parents' particular concern about their sons' conformity to the masculine role. Gender-role deviance is more severely punished in boys than in girls. The term *sissy* is more opprobrious and evokes greater anxiety among boys than the term *tomboy* does among girls.

The socialized fear leads to aversion to any feminine quality, constant striving for masculinity, an inexpressive male image, and an emotional and physical distancing between men because of feared homosexuality. Men who desire to express their full potential for the values and behaviors traditionally ascribed to female gender roles risk devaluation for nonconformity to the stereotypes male role. O'Neil also suggested that the fear of femininity is a base for the persistence of sexism and is the major source of gender-role strain among males in family and in community life. Drawing together many studies of men's lives (and acknowledging a white middle-class bias in most of them), he identified six patterns of gender-role strain that aid in understanding men's behavior and their common health problems:

1. *Restrictive emotionality.* Many (but not all) men have been socialized not to admit human weakness or to express intense feelings. Instead, they learn to rely on words, logic, and rationalistic explanations to control situations and to explain reality, including the self. Yet self-disclosure, vulnerability, and trust are essential to the development of intimacy. Both instrumental and expressive communica-

tion are necessary for full human relatedness, but both sexes have been restricted to the style defined for their gender.

2. *Control, power, and competitiveness.* Many (but not all) men are socialized from boyhood on to compete for power and dominance. Sensitivity to others may be subordinated to winning at sports, work, relationships, love, and sexuality, and to gaining autonomy, power, and control over others.

3. *Restrictive sexual and affective behavior.* The potential restrictions on many (but not all) men's sexuality include a conception of sex and orgasm as goals and conquest rather than as an intimate communication between two persons; the use of sex as a means of measuring performance and masculinity; a view of sex as an objective, impersonal process rather than as a subjective, intimate process; the separation of sex from the interpersonal, loving, affectionate, and intimate parts of a human relationship; and a view of sex as a situation requiring male control, dominance, and power for mutual gratification.

4. *Obsession with achievement and success.* Some (but not all) men's persistent preoccupation with work, accomplishments, and success as a means of demonstrating masculinity involves elements such as distrust, control, manipulation, and repression of human needs. These behaviors turn a man's life into a competitive struggle that leaves little time or energy for a healthy nonwork life.

5. *Health problems.* Most men have been socialized to ignore physical symptoms that may lead to acute or chronic health problems. The masculine mystique supports men's views of themselves as tireless and invincible. When men are socialized to ignore feelings and internal bodily signs, they may suffer serious illness, stroke, heart disease, exhaustion, and early death. Even when such signals are recognized, some men do not heed them and continue at the same pace and level of stress.

6. *Homophobia.* Most (but not all) men fear that they will be considered homosexual if they break the rule that a "real man" never resembles a woman nor shows vulnerability and openness. O'Neil observed that although it is an irrational fear, homophobia is not so much a phobia as a socially determined oppression similar to racism and sexism. Men fear their own sexual or interpersonal attraction to other men. This homophobia is likely to prevent interpersonal and emotional intimacy between heterosexual men, and it is a probable barrier to male self-disclosure, companionship, and touching.

Following childhood socialization into the male gender role, many men find it difficult to experiment with new roles in adult life. The accompanying behaviors can be costly, leading to job loss or social ostracism. These dangers are diminishing, however, as more and more younger men modify the male gender role in their emotional, work, and interpersonal lives in response to the changes wrought by the women's movement. Indeed, an extensive literature in men's studies now exists, much of which advocates either male liberation from restrictive, dysfunctional gendered roles or actual profeminism in men.

Tolman et al. (1986) distinguished between liberated and profeminist positions. The liberated position of men focuses 1) on men's rights in divorce and custody issues that obscure the mistreatment of women by the legal system and 2) on the negative aspects of the male gender role while ignoring institutional sexism and the privileges that men derive from their status in society. In contrast, the profeminist position of men reflects a feminist analysis in which men are viewed as oppressors benefiting from the subordination of women and having the responsibility to work toward the elimination of institutional sexism (and other oppressions), and to change gendered roles in their personal lives.

Tolman et al. specified eleven principles for men's profeminist commitment: developing a historical, contextual understanding of women's experiences; being responsible for oneself and for other men for their part in sexist injustice; redefining masculinity; accepting women's scrutiny without making women responsible for ending male power and oppression of women; supporting the efforts of women without interfering; struggling against racism and classism; overcoming homophobia and heterosexism; working against male violence in all its forms; taking responsibility for sexism; and acting at the individual, interpersonal, and organizational levels to eliminate it; and attending to process and product in men's groups and other collective struggles to end sexism. Further, like Cole and Stack on diversity among women, Tolman and his colleagues pointed to the issues of race and socioeconomic status that influence men's commitment to gender equality. They cautioned against assuming that all men, regardless of race and socioeconomic status, have the same responsibility and resources for ending male privilege. They cited Staples (1978) who contended:

"The problems caused by the legacy of racism are paramount. Although many middle-class black males will have to concentrate on the changing role of women, black males of the working class must continue to confront the challenge of economic survival. It is questionable how much emphasis should be placed on re-orienting their concept of traditional sex roles when they, in many cases, have not been allowed equal access to those roles."

Returning now to the child's development, the next section takes up day care and preschool education.

EXTRAFAMILIAL SOURCES OF CHILD SOCIALIZATION

Day Care Arrangements

According to 1981 U.S. Department of Labor statistics cited by L. W. Hoffman (1984), 45 percent of the mothers of preschoolers in families with the father present and 59 percent of the mothers of preschoolers in father-absent households were employed in 1980. Therefore quality day care for infants and children of working parents is one of the pressing changes required for the well-being of families. It is also a controversial issue because of the still widespread but not always verbalized view that mothers of young children and especially of infants should be at home full time to nurture them, and also because of research findings. Many studies show that *quality* day care does not damage preschool children and may even enhance their development, provided such care begins after age 24 months (Clarke-Stewart 1982; Gamble and Zigler 1986). Studies of children entering day care before 12 months of age have found a negative impact on the attachment of infants to their mothers (e.g., Owen et al. 1984; P. Schwartz 1983). All such studies, however, were of populations at high medical or psychosocial risk, and/or some day care settings may not have been of high quality. Hence a recent investigation (Barglow, Vaughn, and Molitor 1987) was purposely designed to study a low-risk sample of fifty-four middle- and upper-middle-class mothers and their firstborn infants. All mothers had worked full time for at least four months prior to the infant's first birthday. All were living with the infants' fathers. All infants were cared for in their own homes by a nonrelative (an arrangement generally considered superior to group care for infants during the first year of life).

The infants were assessed at age 12–13 months by means of Ainsworth's (1974) popular Strange Situation Instrument (SSI) (see chapter 8). A significantly greater proportion of the infants were found to be insecurely attached to their mothers than infants in a comparable sample whose mothers had remained at home. The authors concluded that the repeated daily separations of infants from their mothers constitute a risk factor for anxious attachment. However, they also noted that the majority (53 percent) were securely attached, thus implying that factors not identified in the study may have had moderating effects on the daily separations. Kagan (1984), another well-regarded developmental theorist, disputes the power of the SSI to reveal the quality of the attachment, and he points to the significance of differences in temperament and in coping skills that may often account for observed differences in babies' responses to the strange situation.

In contrast to the conclusions of these researchers, the widely respected pediatrician Brazelton (1983) has taken a different position based on his extensive clinical and research experience. He believes that ideally the longer the parent who is the primary caregiver can remain at home with the new baby the better. But at least and if possible, he recommended not returning to work until the baby is well into the fourth month of age. By that time, parent and infant have learned much about each other, and the reciprocal attachment is in place (note the different timing for attachment from Bowlby's or Rutter's timing, reported in chapter 8). Also by that time, the mother is apt to be more ready to share her baby with another caregiver, and the baby is ready to relate to a new caregiver (Brazelton did not discuss fathers). Other "good" times for returning to work are when the baby is 9 to 10 months old and at 18 months to 2 years of age.

Although Brazelton focuses on the mother, he does believe that the father also should have a period in which to have the same learning experience with his baby even if he is not the primary caregiver. Brazelton therefore supports the need for paternal leave for those fathers who wish it. By interacting with and learning more about their new baby together, the parents reinforce each other's nurturing capacities.

Finding an acceptable substitute caregiver is a conflicted task for many working parents because of possible guilt feelings and anguish in leaving the baby. Brazelton believes that the best solution is a paid sitter in the parents' own home (not an option for low-income working parents or most solo mothers), provided the sitter is capable of 1) being responsive to the baby's signals and needs; 2) being pleased with her or his development; 3) feeling connected to and noncompetitive with the parents; and 4) being supportive of their role. Brazelton's second-best alternative is family day care provided by a mother with a child who takes in several other children. This is an especially good solution because by the end of their first year babies are able to enjoy, play with, and learn from one another. Brazelton suggested talking with the other parents for their appraisal of the caregiver and observing her during mealtimes, morning leave-taking, or evening reunions.

As difficult as the decision may be to place one's child out of a home setting, Brazelton believes that a good day care center can be rewarding for both child and parents. It provides appropriate experiences for the child and becomes a community for working families. The support of the other working parents is important to the parents' well-being, especially since grandparents are less available now because of their own work or geographic distance. Brazelton included criteria for evaluating a day care center that are also useful guides to the social worker whose client faces this task.

Early Childhood Education

Quality preschool programs are effective vehicles for primary prevention and growth promotion for children living in poverty. By facilitating later school achievement, the programs enhance children's self-concept, feelings of worth, and sense of competence, which support continued learning. An example is Head Start, established in 1965 for low-income children. It provides two-year preschool programs for 3- and 4-year-olds. Many studies have found that the participating children do better through high school than nonparticipating children. The most effective Head Start programs are those that engage parents' participation through home visits. The visitor models and teaches the mother linguistic skills and how to play together, and how to read aloud to the child. Such programs are also good for mothers; many of them go back to school, get jobs, and participate more in community life. Where the parents are not involved, gains in IQ scores tend to wash out in the early school grades. Preschool education programs for young children with severe physical and/or mental disabilities are also more effective when they include teaching the mothers how to help their children learn (Phillipp and Siefert 1979). Sadly, there are too few such programs for chronically ill children and those with disabilities.

Benefits and losses are illustrated in a major study of eleven quality programs of early childhood education, serving mostly black preschoolers, toddlers, and infants, the latter through home visits to teach mothers how to teach their children (Consortium for Longitu-

dinal Studies 1983). Gains were made in IQ scores and superior reading and math achievement (as compared to well-matched control
groups). The gains began to diminish in the first and third grades,
respectively, and disappeared by the sixth grade. Nevertheless, by the
end of the twelfth grade only 13 percent of the participating children
had at some time been placed in special-education classes, compared
to 31 percent of the well-matched control children—an impressive
long-term gain. Reviewers of the report (Glass and Ellwein 1984)
raised the possibility that the findings may not have reflected better
school-related skills. They suggested that the elevated IQ scores and
school officials' knowledge of the children's participation in preschool
programs were enough to keep the children from being labeled, sorted,
and referred for special education, with the attendant damage to the
child's self-concept and lowered expectations by teachers, parents,
and the child herself or himself.

Weikart (1984) reported findings from a study of one of these programs that served sixty Michigan 3-year-olds from impoverished families. By age 19, the children had done significantly better than the
control children on such measures as high school graduation, further
education and jobs, less lawlessness, and fewer teenage pregnancies.
The fact that these effective programs operated in the early 1960s
leads some to hope that today's programs will be even more successful. Some experts recommend that early childhood education not
push any preschoolers into a formal study of reading, writing, and
numbers. The best programs are those that provide social, intellectual, and language stimulation, such as being read to, playing, singing
and listening to music, talking with each other and with the teacher,
and simple crafts.

Perhaps most exciting of all is the report that minority teenagers'
scores on the Scholastic Aptitude Tests (SATs) and American College
Testing improved in 1988 for the third year in a row, while overall
scores remained substantially the same. Blacks and Mexican-Americans made the largest SAT gains. However, large ten-year increases
were also scored by American Indians, Asian-Americans, and Puerto
Ricans. The testing services attribute the improvements to the positive impact of Head Start and other early education programs (Carmody 1988).

RECIPROCAL SOCIALIZATION OF CHILD AND PARENTS

The Child

Toddlerhood has been described as the terrible 2's and the negative 3's. Erikson (1959) characterized this period as the struggle for autonomy and control of the self, with the negative outcome being shame and doubt. Fraiberg (1959) declared that parents of toddlers are missionaries who must civilize the savages during the few short years before school begins. What lies beneath these observations is, first, the rapid advances in the child's locomotor, cognitive, affective, perceptual, and language capacities from age 2 to 5 years. Second, these capacities combine to enlarge the concept of the self as someone who can do things, manage herself or himself, say "no," and participate in an expanding social and physical world. And third, these new capacities result inevitably in struggles with the parents side by side with their shared pleasure in new accomplishments. For their part, the parents find they are now interacting not with a docile, relatively helpless baby, but with a little person with a mind and will of her or his own.

With their biological, psychological, and language systems maturing and empowering them, most toddlers and preschoolers naturally struggle to exercise their new powers and to do things their own way in their own time. Thus parents have a narrow path to tread. Most North American parents want their child to grow in self-direction (this may be less true of many parents in working-class groups and among minorities of color). At the same time, parents need to maintain sufficient control in order to provide the child with the necessary protection and with productive learning experiences. Most of the time, most parents try to keep unpleasant interactions from escalating by being firm when needed and more flexible when the issue is not a life-and-death matter. They maintain as much of their sense of humor as they can. Above all, most of the time, they are loving rather than hostile in the face of the inevitable frustrations and conflicts. Children generally respond positively to parents' age-appropriate expectations in exchange for parental love and approval. They identify with and want to become like the loving and loved parent.

In contrast, when young children are consistently forced to relinquish their own wishes and impulses by physical punishment, verbal abuse, harsh authority, or withdrawal of love, they may comply with the demands, but this compliance is often obtained at the price of later rebelliousness or overconformity. The child's anger, sense of helplessness, and even feelings of hate toward the parents are buried. In the psychoanalytic view, the accumulated negative feelings continue to operate in disguised ways, and the child's identification with the parents is apt to be a negative one. Ambivalence, normal at this age, may persist instead of diminishing, and the problem issues of control and authority may continue in adulthood.

Most parents, most of the time, distinguish intuitively between criticizing the whole child and criticizing a behavior. Parents who encourage their children and avoid labeling the child as bad, stupid, and so on are helping her or him build a positive self-concept and feelings of worth and self-esteem. The preschooler with a positive self-concept is eager to explore the social and physical world and to risk failure, bounding back to try again and gaining in competence, self-esteem, and self-direction along the way.

The initial child–parent struggles reflect the introduction of socialization by the parents to prepare the child for social functioning in a given society and culture. Whereas Freud placed major emphasis on toilet training and the achievement of bowel and urinary control in toddlerhood, most clinicians and theorists now agree that the range of required learning is much greater. Numerous parental demands involving emotional, social, and biological elements go far beyond toilet training and sublimating anality (appendix 1). As the child grows, the parents guide, encourage, model, and expect the child to conform more and more to the values, attitudes, beliefs, behavioral norms, and customs of their family and culture. This is commonly a time of tantrums, food fads, nightmares, and occasional ambivalence toward the parents. At issue may be matters of general obedience, continence, table manners, nutritional rules, bedtime rules, and the child's having to wait for something he or she wants. Other demands are likely to include playing "nicely" with siblings and playmates, being polite to grandparents and other adults, conforming to the family's temporal routines and the rules for indoor and outdoor spatial exploration, and managing preschool educational experiences. The cultural variations in child rearing are many in North America. Hence not all these expectations will be exerted on all children, and others not mentioned perhaps will be.

The Influence of Temperament

Temperamental traits, noted in the previous chapter, continue, and parents need to carry out their caretaking and socialization functions with sensitivity to their toddler's and preschooler's distinctive temperament. The Chess and Thomas (1986) goodness-of-fit model of child rearing means that the demands and expectations of the environment must fit with the needs, capabilities, and temperamental characteristics of the individual child. "Temperamentally easy" toddlers adapt most of the time to new demands and new situations happily and even with zest. "Slow-to-warm-up" toddlers usually require more time and repetitive experiences with new demands and situations in order to adapt, and their responses of pleasure or displeasure will be low-keyed. They are shy and tend to stay on the sidelines. If not pressured, they eventually engage themselves pleasurably in new situations or gradually accept new demands and expectations. "Temperamentally difficult" toddlers are apt still to have trouble with irregularity of functions such as bowel control and sleep times. They may react with intense negativity to new behavioral expectations and demands. They may complain about the actions of peers and may be easily angered by them.

Chess and Thomas (1986) described two combinations of temperamental traits that may reveal themselves or become clearer during toddlerhood. For example, high persistence and low distractibility are often associated, as are low persistence and high distractibility. In the first combination, depending on the context in which the persistence occurs, parents and teachers will be pleased or upset by the persistence. For example, parents value the ability of a toddler to keep herself busy with her toys for a time. But if it is necessary to interrupt a persistent child, and she or he won't be distracted but instead protests loudly or throws a temper tantrum, some parents become angry and eventually come to view the child as stubborn.

The child displaying the second combination (low persistence and high distractibility) is not likely to displease the parent during infancy because of the parent's ease in distracting the child's attention in order to deflect her or him from dangerous explorations, resistance to being dressed, and so on. However, in the preschool years and beyond, this combination can lead to failure to carry out household tasks or homework because other activities continually beckon. Over time parent or teacher may assume that the child lacks a sense of responsibility or is defiant, especially if the child also has a low level

of persistence. Chess and Thomas cautioned that distinguishing between temperamental constellations and traits, on the one hand, and
motivational and defence patterns, on the other, requires an observation of behavior across different settings. They also provided suggestions on how parents can be helped to modify their adverse responses.

The parents of a chronically ill or disabled child continue to face
additional challenges or stressors in helping their child to develop her
or his potential to the fullest extent possible during early childhood.
The child's temperament, among many other factors, will continue to
influence both the child's own development and the parent–child
relationship. Chess and Thomas (1986) suggested that a persistent
child with a chronic illness or disability may succeed in many efforts
to achieve inner-impelled development and to respond to parental
encouragement more often than a child who tends to give up more
easily. The child who is prone to negative mood reactions may exhibit
tantrums or other severe frustration responses in the difficult struggles with developmental tasks. Severe frustrations can interfere with
the child's coping abilities. Another child who has the same disability,
but who tends toward positive mood reactions, may experience only
minor frustrations that do not interfere markedly with task mastery.
The authors pointed out, however, that temperament is only one
factor in development. Other factors include the parent–child relationship, sibling relations, the meaning of the chronic illness or disability to the parents, and the presence or absence of financial resources, network support, adequate housing, and so on. These are
discussed in more detail in chapter 11.

Sibling Relationships

Siblings also play a role in childhood socialization. Until now this
chapter has assumed that the child whose development is being described is a firstborn and hence an only child. From about age 2 on,
however, the average firstborn child will experience the birth of at
least one sibling. This is a momentous event and may come as a total
and possibly unwelcome surprise to the toddler or preschooler, who
may request the mother to return "it" to the hospital. Or the child
may have been part of the talk and plans during the later months of
the mother's pregnancy and may have been looking forward happily
to a new playmate. In this instance, the child may soon discover that
the noisy newcomer not only is too small and delicate to play with
but also demands what feels like the total time and energy of the

parents. Psychoanalytic theory emphasizes the rage and rivalrous feelings generated by the birth of a sibling as the elder child finds herself or himself cast out of paradise.

In many instances, and depending on the quality of parenting and situational factors, the negative feelings wane, or at least they become part of occasional ambivalence, perhaps rising to the surface in the face of hurt or frustration. As positive feelings come into ascendance, they lead the older sibling to become mentor, protector, and perhaps even caregiver to the younger during their shared childhood and adolescent years, and sometimes into adulthood. Occasionally these roles may be reversed, but either way, siblings serve as socializing agents to each other, although secondary to the parents.

Researchers and clinicians have identified many more aspects of sibling relationships than conscious and unconscious jealousy and rivalry, as significant as those emotions are. For example, Dunn (1985) reported on U.S., Canadian, and British studies of nonclinical populations of siblings, including her own longitudinal research. Many differences in the quality of sibling relationships are found across families in the preschool and school years and adolescence. They range from characteristically negative and hostile relationships to those that are characteristically playful, affectionate, and supportive. Evidence suggests that what produces such differences are not the factors of birth order, age gap, and gender, as is widely assumed, but the children's personalities and each child's relationship to the parents. The emotional quality of the sibling relationship is more apt to be positive in families where the parents engage in "talking to each child about the other, explaining feelings and actions, emphasizing in a consistent way the importance of not hurting the other" (Dunn 1985:167).

Nonetheless, as Dunn pointed out, birth order does influence power relations and dominance between siblings; the age gap does influence caregiving behaviors toward each other; and hostility in the early years is more commonly seen between siblings of different sex. Also, most firstborn children feel at least some ambivalence toward the sibling. Hence quarreling is common in many families, and the parents are not necessarily responsible. Dunn also found that by 16 to 18 months of age, children are able to grasp the feelings and intentions of their siblings and to show empathy and concern. Their social understanding can also be seen in their ability to participate in fantasy play with the older sibling and to take on "pretend" identities much earlier than has been thought.

Bank and Kahn (1982) view the sibling relationship, whether posi-

tive or negative, as one of life's most enduring and influential relationships through the life course. It is critical in childhood and youth,
may or may not diminish in importance during the busy years of
adulthood, and is likely to intensify again in the elderly with the loss
of spouse or partner and friends, and with the preoccupations of adult
children with their own affairs.

EARLY CHILDHOOD FEARS

Many studies indicate that healthy children suffer certain fears related to their age. For example, infants are easily startled by loud
noises and later may fear strangers and looming objects. Toddlers and
preschoolers may fear imaginary lions and tigers, monsters and witches,
the dark, and thunder. Through the first six years of life, children fear
separation from their parents. In healthy children, most fears tend to
appear at a particular time and to disappear at a particular time. In
the psychoanalytic view, some fears and worries arise out of the
child's unconscious oedipal and sibling conflicts, aggressive wishes,
and separation anxiety. Thus children's fascination with fairy tales
and heroic myths or folk stories is said to derive from their addressing
such conflicts and the attendant violent emotions, and their resolving
them at a latent and symbolic level (Bettelheim 1976).

Even very young children are aware of death, as they hear about it
in fairy tales and on television and see dead animals or birds. Before
the age of 5, most children do not view death as irreversible but
picture it as sleep or a journey from which the person (or pet) will
return. They may ask, "What do they eat in heaven?" or "How do
they sleep underground?" And parents can explain that a dead person
or pet no longer breathes or eats or talks and feels no pain. Child
development experts suggest that parents encourage their young children to express their questions, anxieties, and sadness when a death
occurs. Parents can explain their own tears and sadness and answer
the child's questions simply and briefly. By doing so, they actually
help their young children in a lifelong task of coming to terms with
the inevitability of death as part of life.

Children also need to know that death is a result of a very unusual
accident, a very serious illness, or great age, while being reassured
that it will be a long time before they or their parents will die even
though they become ill now and then. Usually, children also need
reassurance that they did not cause the death of a parent or a sibling
or other person close to them by their own behavior or wishes, and

they need acceptance of their natural feelings of anger and abandonment about the loss *(Caring About Kids* 1979). Child specialists suggest that preschoolers can participate in the healing process of family mourning and should be present at the funeral *if* they wish to be and if they are well prepared for what they will see and hear. Never should they be coerced.

THE SOCIALIZATION OF THE PARENTS

We tend to assume that socialization is a process limited to childhood, the social control of deviance, and the society's demand for conformity. In fact, socialization is a lifelong process experienced by all human beings. Confusion arises because social control has become linked with socialization, creating a pejorative view of the latter as well. Yet both socialization and appropriate social control contribute to social order and the continuity of a society. At the covert level (and sometimes overtly), both may harshly impose rigid conformity as an ideal. Thus the potential for individual creativity in the family and for social change in the society and culture, which may lie in diversity and even deviation from established norms, can be lost.

Socialization designates a process of training for, and induction into, new roles throughout the life course. It occurs throughout adulthood because childhood socialization in no way prepares us for all the adult roles we undertake in an increasingly complex society. The family and the community (especially the workplace) are major arenas of adult socialization. They are where we acquire new statuses and their associated roles and where we learn to carry them out. For example, during the first five years of their child's life and beyond, not only are the parents socializing their child, but in effect, the child is socializing the parents to their parental roles. The child helps shape the parents' continuing development as young adults, as a pair, and as parents through her or his responses to their caring and love, just as the child's development is shaped in part by the parents' responses to his or her growth, learning needs, and love. In addition, each parent helps the other learn the parenting roles, just as they helped each other learn the roles associated with the status of wife, husband, or committed partner.

People usually move into new statuses and roles by choice and because of the pressure of maturity, such as establishing a relationship of intimacy and commitment, becoming a parent, entering an occupation, and affiliating with community groups and institutions as a child, a youth, and an adult. All are rich in socialization experiences. For example, when one takes on the status of social work student, multiple roles follow, and different levels of demands are associated with each. The student occupies a colleague role with agency staff members, a practitioner role with clients, an advisee role with the adviser, a class member role with instructors, and a trainee role with the field instructor. The varied socialization demands in the status of student and its accompanying roles are heavy. They include acquiring new knowledge, skills, values and norms, beliefs and attitudes, and a professional self-concept. When this status is combined with the status of family member and all its roles, and perhaps with the status of employee in the case of work-study, the socialization demands are enormous.

People also move into new statuses and roles involuntarily as a consequence of such exigencies as widowhood, grave illness or disability, job loss or job changes, separation or divorce, and retirement (this can be a choice rather than an exigency). Whatever their source, major changes in status and the associated roles require a reorientation to life, often including a new self-concept, new relationships, new knowledge and skills, and new behaviors, attitudes, values, and norms. The demands and their impact vary according to the nature of the statuses and roles, and to the expectations and prescriptions of others and of oneself. They may also differ across race, ethnicity, socioeconomic level, religion, sexual orientation, gender, personality, physical and mental states, environmental supports, and previous experiences. Family and friends often give supportive help in the person's acquiring the required attributes, knowledge, and so on. And aids are found through self-initiated education, books, practice in the behaviors and observation of others, as well as in the community's self-help and support groups, professional helpers, and the media.

In addition to unexpected statuses and roles, certain stigmatized statuses and roles exist, having their own demands and sanctions that affect negatively the self-concept and relationships with others. They include criminal offender, alcoholic, addict, welfare mother, and even ex-offender or ex-addict.

The expectable life transitions to toddler and preschooler, with their changing statuses and roles for child and parents, commonly present a series of life issues throughout the period that result in cumulative changes. As the child develops, the parents must modify their image of the child and their own self-concept. They need to develop new relationship and communication patterns between themselves, with the child, and perhaps with the grandparents. From time to time, they may need to develop new temporal and other arrangements that restore the balance between the worlds of work and family, especially if the mother returns to work during these years. They may need to learn how to relate to the shifting personnel with whom they share their child's care.

The child's own self-concept, status, and role in the family change, so that she or he must also develop new ways to relate to and communicate with parents and other relatives, new peers, child care personnel, and so on. She or he may not be responsive to the parents' mode of socialization because of physical illness or developmental disability, or because the parents have not been able to respond appropriately or consistently to their child's new needs.

The increasing demands on the family resulting from these expectable transitions of the child may be a source of zestful challenge or of painful stress, depending on the meaning of the changes to the family members and on the adequacy of the internal and external resources for handling them. Whether challenging or stressful, the psychosocial demands of the transitions typically give rise to uncertainty, anxiety, and negative feelings from time to time in both parents and child. The parents may attempt to cope with the new demands in accustomed ways, but when these do not work, most parents sense the need for change in their assumptions and behaviors, with perhaps periods of confusion and even an occasional sense of failure. As tension mounts, most parents seek new information, try out new ways, support each other in the new tasks, and draw on external supports. Also, these are usually the years when the family develops celebratory rituals that support the mutual identification of family members and a sense of family solidarity, bringing added strengths to the tasks of transitions.

Over the toddler and preschool years, shifts in the family organization emerge that reshape roles, routines, images, and behaviors. Such first-order changes present new requirements and new opportunities for mastery and adaptation by the parents and the child. Ordinarily they do not involve second-order changes or modification of the family's worldview. By the time the child enters school, if these processes have gone well, a new integration has been achieved by the family, with increased relatedness, competence, self-esteem, and self-direction accruing to both parents and child.

Second-order change was illustrated in chapter 8. It is illustrated again in chapters 10 and 11, although the events evoking it, such as job loss, grave illness or disability, and divorce, as well as others, can and do happen during the toddler and preschool years and at any later time as well. Whenever they occur, they carry potentials for further growth or for bringing about family disorganization.

In this period of early childhood, as in infancy, middle childhood, and adolescence, the demands of parenthood are likely to be far more difficult for solo parents without help or support and for parents living in stressful situations such as poverty and chronic illness. The social isolation of parents, whether solo or not, is thought to characterize some situations in which children are abused or neglected. The lack of connectedness can induce negative images of one's child and of oneself as a parent and can adversely affect health and family functioning. Having a supportive social network, however, promotes the parental competence, self-assurance, and feelings of self-worth essential to a confident, assertive involvement in child rearing. Day care and preschool education, formal and informal parent education for all community residents, specialized services for chronically ill or disabled children and their families, neighborhood drop-in support and learning centers, and support and educational groups for solo fathers or mothers are in place in urban and some suburban areas, although perhaps less than the need requires. They may be missing altogether in many rural areas.

In the next chapter, child and family move into the middle years of childhood, with the school and the workplace receiving major attention.

10

Family Transformations in the School Years: The School, the Peer Society, and the Workplace

Following a brief overview of middle childhood, this chapter takes up the impact of school and the child's peer and sibling relationships on the family and on the child's development. Continuing the adulthood themes of loving (conjugal and parental) and working, the chapter next considers the influence of adult attachments, social networks, community affiliations, and work and the workplace on family life and the development of parents and children. First-order changes arising from the smooth developmental transitions of child and parents continue in the school years. However, in its final section, this chapter focuses on the unexpected life event of job loss followed by prolonged unemployment, which requires second-order changes in the family.

MIDDLE CHILDHOOD

For many children, the middle childhood years are indeed the carefree, golden age of childhood—at least in our adult memory. The social and physical worlds of school-aged children expand rapidly and become exciting and challenging arenas of mastery. The physical world exists to be explored, and the sense of adventure is high; the social world of peers is a source of pleasure and sometimes of hurt. Fantasy and daydreams help with feelings of inadequacy, and they stimulate renewed effort through envisioning a competent future. Some of the important influences on the child's ongoing development are family and school; friends, play, and games; collecting and trading treasured objects; identifying with heroes and heroines in sports, entertainment, and storybooks; creating secret clubs, rites, and rituals; and participating in the spiritual life of church or temple and in community youth organizations, settlement houses, and the like.

For many other children, these are not happy years. They face exceptional adaptive tasks imposed by family or neighborhood violence, abuse and neglect, chronic illness or disability, parental alcoholism or illicit drug abuse, the loss of a parent by death or divorce, and other griefs. For millions of our children, these years are filled with the horrors of poverty and societal neglect based on color, socioeconomic status, and gender. In a society that believes itself to be child-centered, we do little to ensure all our children safe housing in a safe neighborhood; a loving, economically secure home, free of abuse and exploitation; adequate health care; and uniformly excellent schooling.

As has been the case since birth, children bring to the experiences of middle childhood differences in temperament that, depending on the environment, will affect how they adapt to the multiple and simultaneous challenges and stresses. Freud viewed middle childhood as a universal period of latency of the sexual drive following a universal oedipal conflict (appendix 1). Anthropologists who disagree with Freud report that in other societies with different family structures and kinship systems, neither the Oedipus complex nor the latency period is found. Some suggest that a latency period doesn't exist in Western societies either, as most children continue their sexual play and interests, but away from the observation of adults.

In middle childhood, boys and girls grow in physical stature, musculature, and coordination. Facial structure changes as permanent teeth erupt. The pace of cognitive, perceptual, and knowledge development is striking. Socially and emotionally, too, this is a time of change. By now the child has a recognizable and unique personality, that is, relatively predictable ways of behaving and of responding to the environment, as well as characteristic motivational patterns, talents and abilities, and vulnerabilities or limitations. The accustomed ways of coping with stress or challenge that worked in toddlerhood may not suffice in the new environments of school and peer group. Hence, through trial and error, expanded facility with language, exploration of the social world, and parental guidance, the child learns new coping methods and new ways of interacting with others and achieves new levels of relatedness, competence, self-esteem, and self-direction.

Moral development is also discernible, and many cultural, familial, and personal values and ideals become part of the self through identification with loving and beloved parents as well as with teachers and peers, and through the cultural environment of rituals, religion, and the media. However, whether moral development proceeds in Piagetian stages with inferior outcomes for women is controversial (see the section in appendix 1 on Kohlberg) and was discussed in chapter 7. Pressure toward conformity, however, is exerted by the peer group and by the child's internal need to be like her or his peers and to be accepted by them. Thus some of the child's family, cultural, and religious values and norms may conflict with peer standards of behavior, but most parents help their children begin to take responsibility for their own behavior and impart elements of decision making useful in meeting peer demands. This is a time when parents also have an opportunity to teach respect for difference and the rights of others—aided by the child's growing capacity to empathize with the feelings of others. Similarly, it is an opportune time for parents to provide age-appropriate teaching about sex and reproduction. In many families this began during toddlerhood through the parents' simple answers to the toddler's and preschooler's questions, now posed at a higher cognitive level.

Other learning that takes place in the family during these years includes that gained from participation as a responsible family member through assigned chores, and from managing an allowance that is unconnected to chores. In many middle-class families, children receive special lessons in dance, art, music, and the like that can enrich their life experience. However, some observers believe that children can be overburdened by too many adult-scheduled activities that leave little or no time for creative child-initiated activity and spontaneous group play free of adult control.

WORRIES OF MIDDLE CHILDHOOD

Over the centuries children have devised their own ways of handling fears through games about witches and monsters, chants and rituals, and talismans (Opie and Opie 1969). However, when an irrational fear persists long after its "proper time," causing pervasive anxiety and interfering with the child's functioning or family life, the child may need professional help. A so-called school phobia, for example, can have the crippling effects of the adult phobias.

In middle childhood, earlier fears give way to very real worries, including concerns about parents' and grandparents' health; school issues; peer friendships; personal appearance; and how babies are made, how they are born, and what abortion means. Many worry about nuclear accidents and a nuclear war and about being kidnapped, injured, or killed—stimulated to some degree by media reports and TV programming about violence, drugs, and explicit sex. Childhood is no longer a time of innocence, if indeed it ever was. Parents in today's world feel that they must teach protective behaviors to children. Thus children are burdened with precocious knowledge without a mature capacity to deal with it. This circumstance creates confusions, fears, and feelings of incompetence in some children. The parents' dilemma is how to make their children feel safe and protected, while teaching them to act safely.

The golden haze through which adults view their own childhood veils the worries and concerns that most school-aged children experience. Hence parents are usually unaware of the pervasiveness and intensities of their children's fear. Indeed, Yamamoto, a psychologist who has conducted large cross-cultural studies of children, and his colleagues stated, "For two people who have lived side by side for such a long time, the adult and the child appear to know amazingly little about each other! . . . An upshot of this general orientation has been the relative lack of information on how the world actually appears to youngsters themselves"(1988).

In these studies of 1,814 mostly middle-class schoolchildren from the United States, Canada, Australia, Japan, the Philippines, and Egypt, the subjects were asked to rank twenty undesirable events. Their rankings were similar, with high correlations across cultures. All ranked the death of a parent as the most upsetting event and having a baby sibling the least upsetting. School issues ranked high among all. Variations among the grades, sexes, and personal histories of the children were statistically nonsignificant: "Because they are children in a contemporary world, their perceptions and experiences of more or less upsetting life events seem to reveal much that is common, regardless of where they are growing up and/or how" (Yamamoto et al. 1988). Still, these are middle-class children. Children in other circumstances might rank undesirable events differently.

Of interest is the authors' report of large differences in the actual experience of parental death, from 2.8 percent of the Japanese children to 42 percent of the Egyptian children. In the two American groups, the percentages were 20.2 and 21.6, and in the Canadian group, 11 percent had experienced the death of a parent. In the Australian and Philippines groups, the percentages were 16.8 and 16.0, respectively. At first glance, it is surprising that the percentages in the U.S. groups were so high. However, social work studies (Ewalt and Perkins 1979; Cho, Freeman, and Patterson 1982) reveal that growing numbers of schoolchildren and adolescents are experiencing parental death, yet have little or no opportunity to talk about it.

Few American families talk together about death or dying or encourage their children's questions about dying. In former times, when most deaths occurred at home, children and adults were involved together in the care of the dying. They grieved together when death occurred. But when hospitals and nursing homes took over the care of dying members from families, death became a taboo subject. Talking about death and talking with dying persons became very difficult for most adults, and parents tended to shield their children from the pain of loss and grief, so the taboo carried over to the home.

Since the early 1970s, a change to greater familial and institutional openness about death has begun. Classes in death and dying are offered in colleges, and bereavement groups for adults and for children are provided by social workers. Clinicians now recommend that when the death of someone close occurs, school-age children be encouraged to express their grief, to ask questions about dying and death, and to have their questions answered to the degree possible. Parents can acknowledge that they don't know all the answers *(Caring About Kids* 1979). Children's responses to the death of a parent or a sibling are considered in chapter 11.

THE SCHOOL AND SCHOOLING

Beginning School

Every society, through the elders, prepares its youth for the adult roles that it considers necessary to its functioning and survival. Schooling, however, represents learning and socialization processes that take place outside the family in a special, formalized setting and, in the case of public schooling, provided by the community. Starting school is a momentous event for child and parents. For the child, school is a new and unknown world that she or he is excited about and eager to enter. A few are initially reluctant to leave the safety and protection of home and family. For parents, the school represents the first real exposure of their parenting abilities—via their child's behavior—to a major community institution. Indeed, developmental and behavioral disturbances are often first recognized by the school. Parents may hold positive expectations and may be pleased about the new transition of school entry for the child and themselves, or they may be fearful of the school's judgment of their parenting and about their child's abilities and deportment.

Parents may have concerns about their child's exposure to values, norms, and lifestyles that vary from their own religious and ethnic values. The caretaking parent may welcome the relief that school entry can bring or may dread the "loss" and loneliness. Poor and minority parents may have had unhappy learning and social experiences in their own schooling and may fear similar experiences for their child. For these and other reasons, first-time school entry is an important life transition for all families with children, and in most instances, it is a smooth and even a happy one. To ease the transition, some school social workers conduct "early prevention" programs, such as discussion groups for parents whose children are beginning school.

The school is an environmental force in the life space of its children and their parents. It is also an extension of the family in terms of its educational and socialization functions, but it also differs from the family in important ways. The school relates to children on the basis of organizational function and what the child does and achieves, while family members relate to one another on the basis of who one is in terms of kinship, age, and gender. Role relations between teacher and student are formalized and impersonal (less so in kindergarten and the primary grades), while relations in the family are highly personalized and affectionate. School life is pervaded by competitiveness in which the child's performance is continually compared to that of peers by himself or herself, the teacher, and others, while family life is not ordinarily conceived of as an arena of competition among the members, although personalized competitiveness may develop between siblings or even between the adult partners. Regular and systematic evaluation is part of the school experience but not of family life. Norms of punctuality, promptness in completing assigned tasks, and compliance with rules are emphasized to a far greater degree in school than in most families.

Coming to terms with these differences is part of the child's adaptive task in the transition to school life. They represent preparatory socialization for adult roles in bureaucratic work settings that are formalized, hierarchical, competitive, and achievement-oriented, and in which worker performance is evaluated. Such settings are also impersonal in that employees are expected to relate to one another only in terms of their formal roles and to restrain the emotionality and spontaneity typical of family roles. The school's norms are geared to the workplace norms of punctuality, promptness, compliance with rules, diligence, regular attendance, and so on. One consequence is that when the school is unable to keep some students coming, not only do they miss out on knowledge acquisition, social experiences, and cognitive development, but they are not prepared for adult working life.

SCHOOL AND SOCIETY

Perhaps at no other time since the introduction of public education have the schools been subject to as much criticism as they now experience from all sides. Keniston (1977) sees the schools as arenas of injustice based on race, ethnicity, and socioeconomic status. Today, we add gender as still another arena. Keniston acknowledged that schools alone cannot create equality of opportunity, but he added that they can be expected to contribute to the goal instead of perpetuating the status of birth. They can teach all children, regardless of background, the basic cognitive skills for participating effectively in the adult world of jobs, social relations, and civic responsibility. Boyer, President of the Carnegie Foundation for the Advancement of Teaching, warned:

> Unless we find better ways to serve minority students and help those who already have dropped out, the social and economic fabric of the nation will be greatly weakened. . . . The even larger issue is whether this nation can embrace a new generation of Americans and build a renewed sense of national unity while rejoicing in diversity. Our response to this urgent and persistent challenge will have an impact far beyond the classroom and will reach into the future as far as anyone can see. (1984: Sect. 12, p. 63)

Many low-income and minority-group parents feel alienated from and apathetic toward the school as still another impersonal and coercive bureaucracy that dominates their lives. Most are critical of and deeply concerned about the school's failure to educate their children. Some suburban middle-class parents are also dissatisfied with the public schools, believing them to be stifling children's curiosity and creativity. Many are actively working toward improving the school and the educational processes. Others withdraw their children from public schools. An estimated 10 percent of all schoolchildren now attend private and parochial schools. Some educators argue that middle-class white children in private schools or all-white suburban schools miss out on multicultural experiences that will help prepare them for the multicultural character of the real world.

Still other parents teach their children at home. It is estimated that about a million children are taught at home, although the practice is legal in most states. Even though parents may be capable of giving their children an enriched education at home, some educators believe that the children may suffer from lack of peer contact, of formal credentials for college entry, and of exposure to ideas other than those of their parents.

The bilingual education of limited-English-speaking children (LES) and non-English-speaking children (NES) is rapidly becoming a political and emotional issue in a nation that has long been hostile to bilingualism. For example, a growing "English-only" or "English-first" movement now threatens to undermine the educational programs serving LES and NES pupils. Controversy surrounds the question of how the federal government should carry out its charge to educate our non-English-speaking children. Should the government finance programs that teach children the basic academic subjects in their original language while English is phased in progressively until the children are ready to join regular classes? Or should education be bicultural, preserving the native language and other cultural elements throughout the school years while the children also learn English?

Some opponents of bilingual education attack it on the basis of the myth that it produces cognitive deficits. In fact, the academic skills initially taught in the language of origin transfer to English as it is acquired. The children do not need to learn the same subject twice, once in each language (Hakuta 1988). Hence bilingual education actually advances the learning of LES and NES children instead of defeating their learning at the outset by imposing the unknown English language as the sole vehicle of instruction. Other opponents claim that bilingual education prevents pupils from learning English. Although recognizing that very few bilingual persons ever have nativelike control of both languages, Hakuta demonstrated that quality bilingual programs can produce students who are able to speak their native language and also "produce complete meaningful utterances" in English (1988:4).

Hakuta believes that bilingual education is desirable for all English-speaking American schoolchildren—not only for cognitive, linguistic, and cultural enrichment but also to prepare them as citizens of today's world: "Speakers of immigrant languages would then be seen as holders of a valuable national resource to be developed, and they in turn would help in the efforts of monolingual English-speakers" (1988:229–230).

Meanwhile, some issues remain. Certified teachers, especially for new immigrant and refugee children (e.g., Laotian- and Arabic-speaking) are in short supply. Another issue arises from the fact that the educational system often regards poor black children as unteachable because they do not speak standard English and have trouble learning to read it. The consequence is school failure and dropout, which result in the effective closure of society's opportunity structures of higher education and rewarding work to young blacks. Since the children come to school with a rich language of their own, which does not prepare them for the expectations and tasks of the school, many linguists have suggested they be taught standard English as a second language, just as Spanish-speaking children receive bilingual education. Stewart (1969), for example, contended that it is important for poor black children to learn to read black English first so that what they see on the printed page corresponds to the speech they hear in their family and community. The transition to learning to read standard English will then be comparatively easy (Smitherman 1984).

As the smallest minority, American Indian schoolchildren number about 400,000 from 305 tribes in the lower forty-eight states. The Bureau of Indian Affairs educates about 10 percent of the children or some 38,000, and the rest attend public and parochial schools under bureau contracts. The bureau's boarding schools and educational policies have a sorry history of stripping American Indian children of their language, culture, and spiritual values. As this is being written (1988), the bureau is trying to turn over its 181 schools to Indian control, along with continued federal aid: "The idea here, advocated by the Government and supported by many Indian councils, is that tribes can better educate their children than administrators sitting at desks in Washington" (Norman 1988:B-9). An example of the new drive for self-direction is the Santa Fe Indian School, a boarding school operated by the governing board of the nineteen Pueblo Councils in New Mexico with a Pueblo educator as superintendent. It seeks to educate its students for today's world while preserving the tribal past through the use of Indian modes of learning, Indian history, and books by Indian authors.

CHILDREN WITH SPECIAL NEEDS

A physical illness or disability may contribute to learning difficulties. For example, limited alertness and stamina, the side effects of medications, prejudice or overprotection on the part of teachers, rejection by peers, inappropriate expectations, excessive illness-related absence, and problems in psychosocial adaptation may create difficulties that aggravate the concerns that all schoolchildren have about their competence and self-worth. On the other hand, high levels of motivation, resilience, persistence, intelligence, and ability to cope with stress contribute to positive educational outcomes for many children with a disability or chronic illness.

Since 1975, the schools have been required to provide appropriate education to children with a functional impairment due to chronic illness or physical and sensory disabilities, and to those who suffer from mental retardation, from severe emotional disturbance, or from the so-called learning disabilities. In 1975, a federal law (P.L. 94-142) mandated equal access to education for these children, including individualized educational programs and related services to meet their unique needs. Parents have the right to participate in the evaluation and placement decisions for their special-needs child and the right to due process in their native language. Children are to be provided with the least restrictive learning environment in a range of alternatives from a regular classroom to special classes, and from part- or full-time to residential treatment, depending on the severity of the problem. Each child is to have a written individual learning plan. Many school social workers, trained in the due process procedures of P.L. 94-142, are serving as mediators in disputes between school and parents regarding the need for special education and the types of services required.

Learning disabilities are not widely understood. The most common one is dyslexia, or the impaired ability to read and write. With appropriate instruction in how to compensate, dyslexic children can succeed academically. Many go on to higher education and the professions. Other learning disabilities are impairment in the ability to speak and in the ability to handle numbers, attention deficit, and hyperactivity. All are thought to be neurological disorders, and some apparently have a genetic base. Learning disabilities are not due to intellectual deficit, although learning-disabled children are sometimes mistakenly assumed to be mentally retarded. Because they may manifest emotional and social distress, they are also frequently misdiagnosed as emotionally disturbed. Their distress, however, is usually due to frustration and low self-esteem as the result of frequent academic failures and social difficulties—before their condition is properly diagnosed. When the diagnoses is accurate and the educational plan sound, beneficial results may accrue. However, the concept of the learning disability is becoming increasingly controversial—most especially in regard to hyperactivity.

LABELING CHILDREN AS HYPERACTIVE

For several reasons, controversy is growing over the use of labels by the school. First, labels do not include social and contextual variables. For example, the label *learning disability* is hazardous to the child if it is applied without a skilled, knowledgeable study of the child, the family, and the school. Locating the trouble in the child or the family without considering the impact of the school and the nature of teacher–child transactions can result in viewing a child's unique ways of learning, and even her or his creativity, as a problem. Rist and Harrell (1982) contended that social contingencies, such as the time, place, situation, and the professional attributes of the labeler, together with the race, sex, socioeconomic status, religion, and personal attractiveness of the child, operate to bring about the application of a label and the associated segregation and stigma.

The unfortunate negative consequences of labeling include less positive interaction with the teacher, increased levels of peer rejection, and the emergence of "learned helplessness" on the part of the child. Teachers and parents expect less, and eventually the children may come to expect less of themselves. Once labeled, children usually retain the label and stigma throughout their school careers, and improved behavior and academic work tend not to be noted in school records. Controversy is especially heated on the issue of labeling children *hyperactive* because the potential for injustice is clear. Several million schoolchildren are so labeled. They are said to be impulsive, noisy, rude, fidgety, sometimes clumsy and accident-prone, and unable to follow directions or to focus on a task. They may show poor judgment, low self-esteem, labile moods, and temper tantrums and are usually avoided by other children (Johnson 1988).

Hyperactivity is attributed to "minimal brain dysfunction," or to the newer "minimal neurological dysfunction"—often on what many claim is flimsy evidence. The suggested causes range from genetic factors to prenatal, congenital, and postnatal accidents and conditions. Other observers point to the possibility of gender bias on the part of teachers, who, preferring the docile and conforming behavior believed to be typical of girls, refer many more boys for treatment because of their behavioral styles (estimates range up to twelve boys for each girl referred). Little boys are socialized to reject so-called feminine behaviors. Yet, when they enter school, they face behavioral expectations of a feminine cast (for example, submissiveness, neatness, and quietness). It is not surprising, then, that many boys are more likely than girls to manifest the male-gendered behaviors experienced by some teachers as a problem and to end up with a label of "bad" or hyperactive. Most of those referred are black males, a circumstance that raises the even more disturbing question of institutional racism.

A variety of treatments have been advanced, including drug therapy, behavioral modification, family treatment, diet, cognitive therapy, and psychotherapy. Johnson (1988) stated that stimulant medication (principally the drug Ritalin) is the most effective single treatment, decreasing "motor activity, fighting and provocative behaviors, negativism and argumentativeness, and increase[s] attention span and ability to listen." The use of Ritalin is increasing at an alarming rate, raising another question: Is it a prescribed treatment for an actual disorder or a means of sedating disruptive students, whose culture and behavior are not understood by teachers? Critics assert that improved learning from the use of Ritalin has not been proved. Yet the drug is viewed by teachers as a magic cure-all for management problems in the classroom and is overprescribed by some physicians in response to school pressure. There is some evidence that doses high enough to calm hyperactive children are high enough to inhibit learning capacity. However, Johnson (1988) stated that if the correct dosage is prescribed, the lethargy, apathy, overcompliance, and lack of spontaneity reported by many observers do not appear.

A different phenomenon, yet somewhat related to the above discussion, is the continuation of corporal punishment in many schools. The *National Coalition of Advocates for Students* reported that 5 percent of black children and 2 percent of white children in the United States are physically beaten by their teachers (legally) (*New York Times*, December 12, 1988). The findings were based on analysis of biennial data published by the federal Department of Education's Office of Civil Rights in 1986. The fact that the rate for black students is more than twice that for white students again reflects institutional racism.

We are a society that permits its children, in the thirty-eight states without laws against corporal punishment, to be abused by the very institution designed to educate, protect, and nourish them. Almost all other Western nations and the Soviet Union have laws prohibiting the corporal punishment of children by teachers, parents, and others.

Homelessness

A newly identified vulnerable group of children are the homeless, who, with their families, form a large segment of the homeless population. In 1987 The National Coalition for the Homeless (Hechinger 1988) estimated their number at about 700,000. Of that number, more than 200,000 attend school irregularly or not at all. Some are placed in suburban motels and must commute long distances by county-paid buses or stigmatized "welfare taxis" to whatever school district agrees to take them, or to their former city district. They must try to do their homework in one crowded motel room. While the children fall in the same general scholastic range as other pupils, many are fatigued and depressed, and understandably, some present academic and behavioral difficulties (Schmitt 1987).

In the cities, homeless families and their children live in temporary shelters or welfare hotels, and the children move from school to school as their families move from shelter to shelter. Some school districts refuse to admit homeless children on the grounds that they enroll only children with permanent addresses. Most homeless children already feel stigmatized and ashamed and suffer further damage from living in miserable, even corrupting environments. Being denied school admission is a final blow. School is a lifesaver for these children, who desperately need to spend at least part of their day in an ordered, nurturing setting (Hechinger 1988).

In July 1987, the Stewart B. McKinley Homeless Assistance Act was passed by the U.S. Congress, largely because of efforts by the National Coalition for the Homeless. It established a national policy and limited funds for the education of homeless children, and it eliminated the residency requirements that exclude homeless children from school. Hechinger (1988) commented that if the children's right to an education is to be protected, progress under the act must be carefully monitored. This is a task that social workers working with the homeless, school social workers, and those involved in policy analysis and program development are in a position to carry out at family and community levels.

Family Forms

Some teachers refer to one-parent families as "broken homes" in considering behavioral and learning difficulties that children may present. They assume erroneously that neglect, lax discipline, and lack of interest in the child's schoolwork typify such families, producing poor grades, delinquency, and so on. Furthermore, most schools do not adjust their procedures to the needs of one-parent families. Solo mothers or fathers must often take time off from work if they are to appear at the times that teacher–parent conferences are scheduled, and not all schools notify noncustody or joint-custody parents about school activities or their child's progress, although the parents have a right to this information under federal law. Also, textbooks tend to show only the two-parent family as "normal" and ignore the growing numbers of other family forms. The implication for the children in a one-parent family is that there is something wrong with their family, as though love and academic success are possible only in two-parent families.

Some teachers hold stereotyped views of maternal employment and attribute poor school performance to the mother's work outside the home. When income level is controlled, many studies show that the children of working mothers do as well as those whose mothers are at home. Etaugh (1984) reported research findings that maternal employment is unrelated to academic achievement for elementary-school females and is either unrelated or negatively related for white males but positively related for black males, including those in low-income one-parent families. In a study of 10-year-old French-speaking Canadian children, no relationship was found between maternal employment and school grades, IQ, or academic achievement (Gold and Andres 1980). Some school staffs may reflect societal homophobia, thereby placing the children of lesbian or gay parents at educational risk because of myths about and negative stereotypes of their family life, leading to biased expectations of social and academic performance. The effects are similar to the school experiences of many children in one-parent families.

The School and Sex Differences

The Federal Education Act of 1972 (Title IX) prohibits sex discrimination in federally supported schools but has been poorly enforced. Hence many schools have not yet discarded labeling and other practices that discriminate against either sex. Gendered-role socialization by the school is carried out not only through behavioral expectations, but by the content of readers and texts, classes in cooking and sewing for girls and in shop and woodworking and mechanics for boys, play and games, hair and dress codes, and so on—all of which are educational barriers based on sex. In addition to behavioral preferences and labeling that discriminate against boys, rewarding docility and passivity in girls is restrictive of their full potential and hence is also discriminatory. Moreover the general absence of male teachers in the primary grades results in less access to role models of competence for boys and deprives girls of the option of not identifying with the teacher (Allen-Meares, Washington, and Welsh 1986).

A vast literature on the psychology of sex differences exists that can be only briefly summarized here. Maccoby and Jacklin (1974) reviewed hundreds of studies and concluded that there is no difference between girls and boys in total cognitive abilities such as problem solving, concept formation, memory, learning ability, reasoning, and creativity. Further, the evidence supported only three sex differences in specific cognitive skills: a greater verbal ability in girls, and greater spatial and mathematical skills in boys. However, Hyde (1981) reanalyzed the relevant studies and concluded that these differences in boys and girls were so small that the average male's and the average female's scores are likely to be only a few points apart.

It now seems likely that girls' superior verbal skills are related to faster female maturation; boys catch up with girls as they, too, mature (Henley 1985). Also, boys tend to regard verbal skills such as writing, reading, and spelling as feminine and so may have less investment in learning them. The hypothesis that boys do better than girls on mathematics tests presents two problems. First, no account is taken of environmental and cultural factors. For example, formal training may be the same for boys and girls, but who helps with homework, what sort of toys and games the children play with, and the expectations of teachers and parents are a few overlooked factors. Second, it has not been established whether test scores measure innate mathematical ability or simply developed ability (Schafer and Gray 1980). Schafer and Gray asserted that environmental factors that act as barriers to the full realization of female students' potential must be removed. Most researchers now agree that children of either sex should not be discouraged from pursuing particular interests and careers on the basis of disproved assumptions about very small sex differences in cognitive areas.

NEW DIRECTIONS: EDUCATIONAL REFORM

Since the publication in 1983 of the report of the National Commission on Excellence in Education, *A Nation at Risk*, some improvement has begun. Many state legislatures have appropriated money to raise teachers' salaries. School districts have set new standards in curriculum and teacher competence and have introduced systematic curriculum reviews and teacher training. In an interview (Fiske 1988), former Secretary of Education Terrel H. Bell stated that such reforms have benefited about 70 percent of schoolchildren, but not the remaining 30 percent, consisting of low-income and minority children. Even so, the public is now more aware of the plight of minority and low-income children and of the threat of growing illiteracy and ineffective education to the nation's future. Hence a reform emphasis in the 1990s on modifying the fundamental structure of public education is likely to be supported by a more enlightened citizenry (Fiske 1988).

Educational experts declare that urban schools must be restructured, the control of education being returned to the schools by overgrown, centralized educational bureaucracies. Schools must be smaller or at least must consist of smaller units to foster personal bonds between teachers and children. Teachers must be personally responsible for their students' progress, and principals must share educational decision making with their teachers, while providing educational leadership. Some urban school districts have already moved toward a new management model.

Some observers believe that schools must enhance their contribution to the community by serving also as community centers for 1) after-school and vacation-time play, study, and other activities for all children, especially those who return to unsupervised homes after school because their parents work, and 2) evening educational, cultural, and civic programs for parents and other community members, especially in poor neighborhoods. Many school districts have already begun such programs.

School social workers can make important contributions to achieving the needed reforms. The ecological nature of the school makes it a potent site for social work programs, services, and child advocacy to help 1) prevent negative educational and socialization outcomes among children with a range of vulnerabilities; 2) promote personal capacities for successful learning and socialization for all pupils; 3) restore adaptive social and educational functioning in situations where a good child–school fit is absent; 4) facilitate needed policy and procedural changes; and 5) encourage parents' participation in school policies and educational matters. For social workers engaged in policy formation and analysis and in research, school systems are an important arena for policy and program development, and for studies that will contribute to a public understanding of the need for structural change in public education.

PEER RELATIONSHIPS IN MIDDLE CHILDHOOD

Learning not only takes place in the family and the school but is also imparted by peers. Age-appropriate social behaviors learned from peers are as essential as those learned from parents and teachers (Hartup 1979). Children are gradually empowered not only by successful learning but by successful social relationships as well. The achievement of friendship and peer group acceptance strengthens the child's self-concept and self-esteem, relatedness, and competence and, following a long period of conformity, contributes to self-direction. Hartup suggested that the egalitarian give-and-take of peer relations, as well as the freedom from constraints imposed by family attachments and hierarchical authority, are responsible for their valuable and unique contribution to the child's social development. The lack of good peer relations in middle childhood is associated with discomfort, anxiety, and a general hesitancy to engage the environment.

The Peer Group

Being part of a peer group provides "a variety of resources that an individual friendship cannot—a sense of collective participation, experience with organizational roles, and group support in the enterprise of growing up. Groups also pose . . . some of the most acute problems of social life—of inclusion and exclusion, conformity and independence"(Z. Rubin 1980:94). Rubin pointed out that peer groups are generally homogeneous and tend to exclude the child who is different in appearance, skills, or temperament. Until the recent past, groups also practiced exclusion on the basis of race and sex. To the degree that racism abates in society and children have more cross-racial experience in school, peer groups may show a trend toward less exclusion on the basis of race. Similarly, to the degree that parents encourage cross-sex friendships in their preschoolers and schools observe the rights of girls to join boys on athletic teams and in "male" courses (and of boys to join girls in "female" courses), peer groups may show a trend toward less rigid exclusion on the basis of sex. The other bases, particularly that of mental or physical disability, are apt to persist until parental and school efforts to convey acceptance and to teach understanding become more effective. Children fear what they do not understand.

Across age and culture, boys more than girls tend to congregate in large groups; girls more than boys tend to form pairs. Boys tend to view the group as an entity and to emphasize loyalty and solidarity. Girls tend to view the group as a network of intimate two-person friendships. Boys also have friendships, but they tend to be less expressive and intimate than those of girls. It is probably still accurate to say that, typically, school-aged boys and girls tend to shun and tease each other, to invite and resist attraction, and to express stereotypical taunts such as "Girls are silly, "or "Boys are disgusting." Individual cross-sex friendships occur, but generally the cross-sex friend does not become a member of the other's peer group. In late childhood, as puberty approaches, a less ambivalent interest in the opposite sex appears, although interaction is still strained. These nascent interests help prepare children for romantic interests among teenagers and for the mixed peer groups of adolescence (Z. Rubin 1980).

Typically, elementary-school children have played gender-typed games and sports. Probably the majority still do, despite the integration beginning to occur in organized school sports, Little League, Camp Fire, and the like. Girls' games, such as jumping rope, jacks, and hopscotch, tend to be played with one or two well-liked persons. Boys' game are likely to be played in large groups, and they require cooperation whether or not teammates are well-liked persons. Such differences help to explain the different models of social relations of boys and girls. That is, boys learn to operate within systems of rules and to cooperate with persons they may not like. They acquire social skills that prepare them for the workplace, but peer socialization for most boys does not lead to an ability to form intimate friendships. On the other hand, peer socialization teaches girls social skills related to intimacy and emotional expressiveness that fit the requirements of personal and familial relationships but not those of the workplace. Thus sex-typed play and social patterns will continue to deprive each sex of learning other important skills for today's world until both have the opportunity to share in the learning experiences of the other (Z. Rubin 1980:109).

Peers are important sources of social comparison; "How am I shaping up?" reflects the universal human need to evaluate oneself by comparison with others. In addition to exclusiveness, peer groups tend to expect conformity as the base for acceptance and evaluation. The tendency is often troublesome to parents because it can stifle individuality. It is especially troublesome when the group's norms, values, beliefs, and expectations differ from those of the parents, and this difference may also be distressing for the child. Pressure toward conformity intensifies in adolescence and is even present to some degree in adulthood (Z. Rubin 1980).

Peer group structures are sources not only of great pleasure but sometimes of pain. Based on their studies of thirty-nine elementary classrooms, Lippitt and Gold (1959) found that the social structure of the classroom becomes a dominant aspect of the child's environment and total life situation. The pupil's location in that structure influences his or her status, learning, emotional well-being, motivation, and ability to participate in classroom interaction. Being highly liked or being perceived as expert in valued activities is a significant pathway to social power in the classroom. Teachers were observed to respond more positively to popular children who enjoyed social influence among the other children. Most important, the social structure of the classroom forms rapidly and remains fairly stable throughout the school year. Lippitt and Gold hypothesized that the low-power children's continuous experience of social failure and rejection by peers is created and maintained by a circular social process involving the individual child, her or his classmates, and the teacher.

Although Lippitt and Gold's study is more than thirty years old, classroom peer structures continue, with varying mixes of benign and undesirable features. School social workers have devised preventive interventions in the form of classroom meetings with the teacher present. They use mental health principles in modeling and teaching problem solving, empathic relationships, and communication skills that help develop supportive peer structures in the classroom (Winters and Easton 1983; Allen-Meares, Washington, and Welsh 1986).

Given the significance of peer relations in middle childhood, it is not surprising that social workers find that troubled school-aged children respond well to experience in social work activity groups, "talk" groups, and mixtures of the two (e.g., Lee and Parke 1978; Gitterman 1971; Middleman 1968). Social work groups are also important vehicles for promoting growth for all school-aged children in school, at camp, and in neighborhood settings.

Friendships

For most individuals, peer friendships are important throughout the life course from toddlerhood to old age. The school-aged child who wants to make friends but does not is likely to be unhappy and distressed, while the child with close friendships is apt to be a happy child (Z. Rubin 1980). By the age of 11 or 12, most children view a close friendship, the "chumship" (Sullivan 1953), as a special, reciprocal relationship of intimacy that develops over time. The preteen's emphasis on psychological compatibility builds on the toddler's emphasis on physical accessibility and the primary-grade child's one-way conception of a friend as a person who does things that please one (Z. Rubin 1980). For the preadolescent, friendship comes to mean appreciating each other's abilities and experiences, trusting each other with one's innermost feelings and private facts, being concerned about the well-being of the other, and accepting reciprocal obligations to each other. Patterns of friendship do vary among individual children: some prefer to have a number of friends, and others concentrate on one or two. Also, conceptions of friendship may differ across societies and across subcultures within North American society.

Parents and others generally view cross-age friendships and groups as undesirable, or at least inappropriate, perhaps because age segregation begins with school entry. Nevertheless, as Rubin (1980) pointed out, the assumption that segregation by age is the only right way is negated by the fact that children in non-Western cultures play and socialize in mixed-age groups.

However, mixed-age relations can have negative aspects, such as bullying of the younger child by the other, rejection of the older child by his or her own age-mates, a younger child's engagement in activities for which he or she is not yet ready, or an older child's sudden loss of interest in and dropping of the younger one. An exclusive preference for older or younger friends may indicate emotional or social difficulties. On balance, however, Rubin suggested that the potential advantages outweigh the negatives. Hartup (1979) cited research findings that younger peer therapists can help withdrawn youngsters. Older peer tutors contribute to the competence and self-esteem of both tutee and peer tutor.

The ending of a friendship because of geographic moves, or because one of the pair loses interest, is a painful stressor. Children differ in how they cope with it. In the case of a move, some respond to the loss of friends and place with sadness and even depression, while others are excited by the newness and opportunity for new friends and experiences. In later childhood, making friends in a new setting is difficult because cliques are already in place. Z. Rubin (1980) believes that most children ultimately succeed in managing the loss and making new friends. Very frequent moves (as in military families), however, appear to have more persistent negative effects on the ability of some children to make lasting friendships. Rubin noted that parents sometimes underestimate the impact of the loss of friendship. They may minimize it with statements such as, "Don't worry, you'll find another friend," as though a friend is like a standardized, replaceable part. It is more helpful to encourage the child to express the attendant feelings and for the parent to verbalize an understanding of how hard the experience is. These important guidelines can also be followed by social workers who work with children.

SIBLING RELATIONSHIPS

Campbell (1964) suggested that sibling relationships influence the child's orientation to and interest in peers and the way she or he relates to them. Whether children are in the primary grades or well into middle childhood, some report that they play frequently with their siblings, and others report that they rarely play with them, preferring to play with other children (Dunn 1985). In one very large study, the researcher asked the children, " 'Would you be happier . . . if you didn't have a sister or brother? One/third of the children said they would prefer not to have a sibling. " 'Yes, I would be happier without her. Could you make her disappear?' " But most preferred to have the sibling, although not without some ambivalence: " 'Oh, I'll keep him. He's bad, but not that bad"(Dunn 1985:44).

Another large study found that the 6-year-olds interviewed used more emotional terms in speaking of their siblings, both positive and negative, than in speaking of their friends. Those who made very positive comments were the same children who three or four years before had been particularly friendly to their younger sibling, despite having been in school, making friendships, and going through a range of new experiences since then (Dunn 1985). Dunn concluded that "conflict, jealousy, sharing, companionship, and ambivalence between siblings continue as the children grow into middle childhood. . . . In some families, at least, the sibling relationship remains an intensely important one throughout childhood"(1985:48).

In a large study of 10- to 13-year-olds and their sibling relationships, the researchers found that the consistent behavior of each sibling can be very different. For example, one child can be consistently hostile and disparaging, while her sister consistently responds in a neutral way, even attempting friendly overtures that are ignored consistently. Dunn suggested that such mismatches show that "children can make the same family environment very different from each other, and thus may directly contribute to the development of individual differences between siblings"(1985:55). Other processes leading to difference (in addition to personal temperaments) include role assignments by the family such as the "friendly one," the "shy one," the "real student," and the "lazy one." These may become self-fulfilling prophecies. Some siblings respond by developing different interests and achievements from those of the sibling holding the more positive role. Others respond by withdrawing from efforts to compete, accompanied by lowered self-esteem and a lowered sense of competence. In these and other ways, differences become more marked as the siblings reach middle childhood and adolescence. However, evidence is meager on a clear connection between the quality of the sibling relationship and a child's self-esteem and social behavior in school and with peers.

THE FAMILY AND THE WORLD OF WORK

Social workers sometimes overlook the influence of work and the workplace on the lives of individuals, families, and communities. Yet the family and the workplace interpenetrate each other for good or for ill. What goes on in the family may support or interfere with job performance; what goes on in the workplace may enrich or interfere with family life. Failing to take account of the influence of work can lead the practitioner to errors in assessment and intervention. For example, what is defined as marital conflict may have its origin in job stress that needs to be ameliorated if the conflict is to be resolved. Or the strengths indicated in a woman's work history, if they are explored and affirmed, can be enlisted in helping her bring order into what may be a chaotic personal life.

A second-year social work student wrote:

> My client is an elementary-school teacher who is clinically depressed and on lithium. I was ineffective, trying to treat her by talking about childhood, marriage, kids. After our class discussions and the readings, I started talking with her twice a week about work—a subject we hadn't touched on in our three months together! We learned that her work feeds into all her negative feelings about herself: her low self-esteem, lack of confidence, feelings of incompetence, and lack of self-direction. She and I are now doing well, and she is thinking about securing an M.A. in teaching reading, which would lead to positions that would allow her more control and autonomy at work. It would be simplistic to say that it's a cure or even that work is the only element in her depression, but it's an important key to working with her.

Wetzel (1978a, 1978b) demonstrated that the antecedents of depression may be found in the environmental features of work that interact with features of the personality. Her study of working women supports her hypothesis that women socialized to a dependent orientation are vulnerable to depression if their job requires them to be assertive and self-directing. Conversely, women having an independent orientation are vulnerable to depression if their job does not provide an opportunity for self-direction, major problem solving, and decision making. In each instance, the person–job fit is poor.*

Person–job fit may be good until it is upset by family processes such as divorce or serious illness or by community processes such as a change in day care arrangements. Or the fit may be poor to begin with, as in Wetzel's examples. Occasionally, the fit is too good, so that absorption in the work role engulfs the person's family roles and reduces the quality of life for family members. In other situations, the person–job fit is good, but the family–job fit is poor. For example, the

---

*Wetzel pointed out that, to a lesser degree, the same relationships hold true for the family as an environment. For example, a woman who is socialized to an independent orientation, and whose partner maintains rigid control over the family budget and other major decision areas, is more likely to be depressed than a woman with a dependent orientation in a similar partnership. However, the woman with a dependent orientation whose partner expects her to manage finances or participate in major decisions is more likely to be depressed than a woman with an independent orientation in a similar situation.

uprooting of corporate families may be difficult for the spouse and the children, as important social ties are left behind and the sense of place that forms part of one's identity is lost. The worker, however, moves into a new ready-made network of coworkers and the demands of the new position and so may not be aware of the stress for the spouse and the children.

Families that face the periodic absence of one parent, often the father, due to such work as long-distance trucking, submarine service, and frequent business travel have the special tasks of dealing not just with the father's absence but with the father's return. Borders reported a new clinical category devised by a psychiatrist, called the "intermittent husband syndrome." It was said to be found in wives of oil riggers, military and diplomatic service personnel, and others. One woman was quoted as saying, " 'I can't keep on making this transition, at two-week intervals, from being completely dependent on him to running the whole show by myself' "(1980:B12). This so-called clinical disorder is manifested in such symptoms as headache, moodiness, and uncontrolled weeping. Such psychologizing appears to be an example of blaming the victim, who is said to require psychiatric treatment for what is actually an environmental stressor.

In sharp contrast to this approach is a preventive social work program for U.S. Navy submariners and their families (Gerard 1985). It is a psychoeducational group program designed to help submariners and their family members cope successfully with the stressor of periodic separations of five to six months' sea duty followed by reunions. The program provides information on, and opportunities for the discussion of, the emotional, practical, and social role changes involved. It seeks "to reach people affected by stressors before they define themselves as suffering from those stressors. . . . to make the private experiences of anxiety, loss, family friction, and stress feel normal and bearable rather than unexpected and pathological" (Gerard 1985:85). The program is supplemented by individual consultation if desired.

Work as a Developmental Force

The world of work has a significant impact on the development of all family members and not just the working member(s). The socioeconomic status of the working parent(s) (in combination, perhaps, with ethnic or racial factors) influences the child's access to education, health facilities, and adequate nutrition. It determines the nature of the child's physical environment, including housing and neighborhood, and it influences the kind of child-rearing practices and peer relations that she or he experiences (L. W. Hoffman 1984). The schoolchild soon perceives the segregation of occupations by race, class, and gender; the concentration of males or females in certain occupations; and the gap between the earnings of whites and people of color and between women and men in American society.

Although some barriers are coming down, limited access to male-dominated occupations and professions and upper-level positions, together with the lack of job-protected maternity leave and unequal pay for comparable worth, continues as a life stressor for most working women despite the laws in place. For the first time since records began in 1979, the U.S. Bureau of Labor Statistics reported in February 1988 that full-time working women earned 70 percent of what men earned in 1987. The figure was 62.5 percent in 1979. Even so, this is still less than the percentages reported for women in many other Western countries. The difference is greater at executive, administrative, and managerial levels: women earned only 61.6 percent of what men earned in 1987. It is smaller at the professional level: women earned about 75 percent of what men earned in 1987. Additionally, "Educational improvements for blacks [over the 1980s] were offset by lower earnings at the same educational level, higher rates of unemployment and underemployment, and a much larger share of female-headed families" (Rosen, Fanshel, and Lutz 1987:24). Unemployment rates for Hispanics fell between those for whites and blacks but were closer to the black rate. These discriminatory processes affect children's motivations and their own life chances.

The nature of the work of the parent(s) affects the lives of all family members. For the infant, it makes a difference in the time and energy available to the parents for pleasurable interaction with their infant and the resources they have for adequate infant care. It makes a difference in the life of the schoolchild as she or he becomes aware of the above-mentioned racist and sexist (and able-ist) processes and of who works and is paid for it, and who works but is not paid for it (as in homemaking, child rearing, care of elderly family members, and the unpaid work responsibilities of the spouses of clergy, corporate executives, politicians, small business operators, farmers, and physicians).

Working parents are important role models for their children. Studies show that the daughters of working mothers are more likely to want to work, to plan to work, and to have higher career aspirations than the daughters of nonworking mothers (Moen 1983). Moen added that since fathers take a more active role in child rearing when the mothers work, the gender-typed socialization of boys and girls may diminish, and the development of independence and achievement in girls may be facilitated.

The world of work also affects adolescents in direct ways, since some teenagers work part time while in school; others not attending school look for work; and still others are engaged in occupational or career planning. For young parents, work can be a major source of challenge, socialization, and continuing growth and development, or it can be a severe life stressor. For example, parents who work but receive too little to support their family learn that they are neither needed nor valued by society. Underpaid work creates severe problems for families and interferes with developmental processes throughout the life course. Underpaid work is most often the lot of people of color, migratory laborers, and those who perform the "dirty," unskilled but necessary work of society.

And finally, retirement from work roles affects the aging family in various positive and negative ways, including reduced income (see chapter 13).

For all family members and not only the working members, then, the world of work is a developmental context of singular importance and a potent force in family life.

The Workplace as a Social Environment

As a social setting, the workplace is often an arena where friendships are made, thus expanding the worker's and the family's social support network and enhancing their relatedness. When jobs are lost, many workers report losing their network of friends at a time when emotional support is needed most. The presence of informal support systems has been found to ameliorate the health effects on blue-collar workers of stress generated by job loss due to plant closings, with differences noted between rural and urban workers (Kasl and Cobb 1982). In the city, the men lived all over town, so the plant itself conveyed a sense of community and social support. When it closed down, this sense of "community" was lost. But in the small rural town, the inhabitants were the major source of the sense of community and of social support. When the rural plant shut down, the community was still intact, and the social interaction among the former workers continued.

Although many workers experience supportive relationships at the workplace, others find their relationships with workmates, supervisors, or supervisees difficult because of job stress or because of personal and interpersonal factors such as anxieties, ambivalences, problem attitudes toward authority and control, high performance expectations held by oneself or others, and the sexual harassment of working women by male supervisors or coworkers (the reverse is thought to be rare). Sexual harassment is a severe psychological stressor still experienced by many working women despite the laws in place.

The Workplace as a Physical Environment

The spatial and temporal aspects of the physical setting affect the social environment of the workers. For example, the worksite may or may not be accessible by public transportation and may or may not provide such amenities as parking spaces, lunch facilities, areas for privacy as well as social interaction, rest areas, or child care facilities—all of which help mediate work-generated stress. Temporal characteristics such as irregular hours, overtime, night shifts and rotating shifts, travel requirements, and take-home work, in the case of professionals, can be major stressors. They violate the worker's biological needs and limit the amount of energy and social time for family activities and responsibilities. Also, many women and men in managerial and professional employment work very long hours, while blue-collar workers often hold down two jobs in order to support their families. These various temporal arrangements can have adverse consequences for the mental and physical health and social functioning of the worker and the other family members.

SAFETY, HEALTH, AND THE WORKPLACE

As a physical setting, the workplace may create health problems that are a major source of severe stress to workers and their families, undermining the developmental potentials of all members. The extent of injury, chronic disease, disability, and death caused by the workplace makes it one of the most dangerous of human environments.

Occupational Accidents

The rates of accidents due to fire, explosion, electrocution, unsafe machinery, falls, moving and lifting equipment, and so on are still high. The Occupational Safety and Health Administration (OSHA); established in 1970, estimated that from 1955 to 1984, more U.S. workers were killed in the workplace or died from occupational disease than in any modern war. Every year approximately sixteen thousand workers die in industrial accidents, and two and a half million more are injured, according to estimates made by the U.S. Public Health Service (*NASW News* 1985). In effect, these are minimum estimates, since many workplaces pad their safety records and disguise job accidents.

Until 1987 mining jobs were the riskiest, with an average of 315 mining deaths from accidents per year in the period 1980–1984. Construction was the second most dangerous industry, with an average of 252 on-the-job deaths per year during the same period. However, in 1987, farming, an unregulated industry, became the most dangerous occupation. The farming death rate in 1987 was 49 per 100,000 workers, while the rate was 38 deaths per 100,000 in mining, 35 per 100,000 in construction, and 6 per 100,000 in manufacturing (U.S.B.C. 1989:413, table 680). Wilkerson (1988) cited a 1988 report of the National Safety Council that 1987 saw 1,600 adults and 300 children killed in accidents involving farm equipment, and 160,000 more adults and 23,000 children disabled.

Of all on-the-job deaths, 95 percent occur among males, who represent only 52 percent of the labor force:

> More than any other group, black men die from personal injuries on the job. Because of the racist structure of the labor market, black men work in some of the dirtiest, more dangerous job situations in this society. For example, a disproportionately high number work near open hearth furnaces and in industries that produce toxins and contaminated wastes. Davis (1977) [has shown that blacks] face a 37 percent greater chance of suffering occupational injury and a 20 percent greater chance of dying from a job-related injury than do whites. (Gary and Leashore 1982:57)

Of on-the-job deaths of women, 42 percent were due to homicide and 5 percent to suicide (the comparable figures for men were 11 percent and 3 percent). On-the-job homicides among women are highest among grocery clerks and waitresses. On-the-job homicides among males are highest among taxi drivers, followed by police officers and detectives.

Occupational Disease

Occupational accidents are far easier to control than health hazards because the latter are more difficult to recognize, and their consequences may not appear for many years. Approximately 100,000 die of industrial disease each year, 340,000 more are disabled by it, and about 390,000 new cases appear annually, according to estimates made by the U.S. Public Health Service (*NASW News* 1985). Other estimates of yearly deaths from occupational disease are far higher, ranging from 200,000 to 300,000. Miners, construction and transportation workers, farm workers, and blue-collar and lower-level supervisors in manufacturing and industry suffer the bulk of occupational disease.

White-collar workers, executives, and professionals are not exempt from occupational hazards. Dentists have high rates of nervous system disorders, leukemia, and lymphatic cancer, as well as the highest rate of suicide of any professional group. They are being studied for the possible effects of contact with X-ray, mercury, and anesthesia. Administrators have higher rates of cardiac disease than do scientists and engineers. Operating-room personnel have several times the number of defective newborns and higher miscarriage rates than other women. Beauticians are said to have high rates of cancer and of cardiac and respiratory disorders.

In 1973, OSHA listed over twelve thousand toxic materials in workplaces, including harmful fibers, dusts, gases, heavy metals, chemicals and their vapors, and radiation. With the continuous development of new industrial technologies, new substances appear at the rate of about three thousand a year (Stellman and Daum 1973). The effects of some are immediate, but the effects of most will not be known for years. It was not until 1985, for example, that OSHA set standards for the carcinogens benzene, formaldehyde, and cotton dust. In January 1989, OSHA put new limits on 164 substances, including grain dust and gasoline fumes, and strengthened the existing limits on 212 other substances. Until these new regulations, the agency had issued limits on only 24 substances in the previous seventeen years. Toxic materials enter the body through the eyes, the ears, the mouth, and the skin, and by inhalation or ingestion. In some instances, materials and fibers unwittingly carried home on workers' clothing have resulted in the contamination of family members.

Although some improvement has occurred, OSHA has insufficient resources for the real enforcement of laws and standards regarding safety and health at the workplace. In 1988, it had only about one thousand one hundred and twenty-five inspectors to cover four million workplaces on a regular basis (Trost 1988). Since it is currently able to conduct seventy thousand inspections a year, it would take sixty years to inspect all workplaces just once. Also, setting standards for workers' exposure to potentially dangerous materials takes years. Since 1987, the agency has been pursuing a more aggressive policy in industrial record keeping in matters of health and safety. Since 1985, chemical industries and, since 1986, manufacturers and importers have been required to inform workers about toxic substances present in the workplace. In 1987, the requirement was extended to all non-manufacturing industries under the jurisdiction of OSHA.

During the first half of this century, the Women's Bureau and the Children's Bureau in the U.S. Department of Labor reported regularly on the occupational health of working women and the effects of working during pregnancy on the health of mother and newborn. But since the 1950s, health studies of working women have not been conducted: "Currently, we do not know if there are occupations where women are the most or the least vulnerable, or whether somatic effects are associated with their particular female characteristics" (Hunt 1975). Hunt suggested that the lack of studies is due to several false assumptions, such as 1) women are usually in a safer work environment than men, an assumption that ignores the existence of millions of blue-collar women workers; 2) women do not show features of illness or death that are different from men in the same work environment, an assumption that ignores the different hazards for women because of their reproductive capacities; and 3) women are in and out of the labor market, an assumption that overlooks the many blue-collar and skilled women who work consistently over several decades.

With the introduction of new technologies and new substances, a conflict has arisen between concern about equal opportunities for women and concern about protection from special health risks for pregnant women and their expected infants, such as miscarriage and birth defects from exposure to radiation and to toxic substances. Also few companies restrict the work of men whose partners are trying to conceive.

In their study of 54 Massachusetts electronic and chemical industries in which workers were exposed to toxic substances hazardous to reproductive health (out of a total sample of 198 companies), Paul, Daniels, and Rosofsky found that some policies overprotected women workers. Policies restricted them from work which does not represent a significant threat specifically to women as a class.

For instance, one company restricted all women from any heavy lifting. . . . Women only (including pregnant women, women of childbearing age and all women) were restricted from work with lead and radiation even though these exposures may present a risk to adults of both sexes as well as the conceptus. (1989:40)

In contrast some restrictive policies were "under inclusive" on the assumption that only pregnant women were at risk.

Pregnant women and women trying to conceive were restricted from work with glycol ethers, which are also strongly implicated as male reproductive hazards. In sharp contrast, none of the 54 companies with glycol ethers in use had policies or practices that restricted men from work with these substances. While such policies may protect the health of pregnant women in the short run, they cannot address the risk posed to the reproductive health of men and women before conception. (p.40).

A different, yet in some ways similar, issue has arisen in connection with proposals for gene screening at the workplace in order to determine the presence in workers of hereditary hypersusceptibility to the toxic effects of hazardous substances. Those who support the idea believe that it will protect workers from illness and death through guiding employers' placement of their personnel in safe jobs. Those who oppose the idea believe that it is racist, antilabor, an invasion of privacy, interference with free choice, and a means of outright or, at the least, de facto discrimination. Some suggest that it is being supported by industry as an alternative to cleaning up the workplace.

Drug Use at the Workplace

Other kinds of health problems at the workplace are alcoholism and illicit drug use. According to the National Institute on Alcohol and Drug Abuse (NIDA Capsules 1988) one in every six workers is impaired by alcoholism or the abuse of illicit drugs. Sixty percent of the nation's top firms now have alcohol and drug abuse programs, reporting a reduction in accident claims, workers compensation claims, and health-related absences. By 1985, over eleven thousand corporations had established employee assistance programs (EAPs) for referral and counseling for familial, personal, and drug-related problems. Many are staffed by social workers, and some are operated by hospital social work staffs. Family service agencies also contract with industry to provide counseling under a company's EAP. It was estimated in 1984 that roughly 10 percent of Canada's workers were also covered by EAPs (Santa-Barbara 1984).

Fine, Akabas, and Bellinger (1982) described the social and structural characteristics of worksites that induce or support the norms and values of "cultures of drinking" on the job (as in the construction industry, or in the routine, prolonged liquid lunches of managers and professionals, often sanctioned by company policy). Such cultures create an occupational endorsement of drinking and protect or hide the vulnerable problem drinker and even exacerbate the disease of alcoholism in those afflicted. These authors described interventions that industrial or union social workers can use in helping to modify such drinking cultures.

AIDS and the Workplace

As a new health problem at the workplace, AIDS raises many issues to be faced by employers, workers, customers, and patients. Because of the extreme variability of the disease across patients, no single answers can yet be given. The issues range from the legality of firing employees with AIDS, or terminating workers who refuse to work with, treat, or serve people with AIDS, to the ethical issue of whether employers should advise workers, customers, or patients that they have an employee with AIDS (Banta 1988). Gradually, many of the legal questions will be resolved by the courts, but it is likely that ethical issues such as the patient's right to privacy and the public's right to know will remain. For now, potential conflict exists (in such occupations as food handling and such workplaces as hospitals) between protecting the applicant or employee with AIDS, or AIDS-related complex from discharge, deprivation of insurance, or other discrimination, and the legitimate business concerns and health interests of other employees (a growing concern of unions) and the public.

According to Banta (1988), the number of legal challenges of employer decisions by workers with AIDS is small, perhaps because of the reluctance of workers to declare their condition publicly, the absence of statutes, and the desire of many employers to reach equitable solutions. On the other hand, a gay rights lawyer reported that job discrimination against AIDS patients and those who are carriers of the AIDS virus is prevalent in New York City: "People are fired, asked to take the antibody test, ostracized to lower posts, or not allowed back after a hospital stay" (James 1988:3R). In contrast, exemplary AIDS health and information programs for the workplace have been developed by some employers.

Discrimination is believed to be rampant also against employees with cancer, heart disease, and other disorders who wish to return to their job, or who are applying for a job, after surgery or other treatment. No federal laws protect all workers from discrimination based on health, although federal workers and others paid from federal funds are protected by the 1973 Rehabilitation Act. That legislation was originally designed to protect only persons with physical disabilities, but it is now extended to certain diseases. It is hoped that these provisions will cover those with AIDS as well. Additionally, a number of states have enacted laws protecting private-sector workers against discrimination because of illness.

Despite the extent of occupational mortality and morbidity, few educational programs of any of the health care professions, including social work, include the issues of occupational health and safety in their curricula. The possibility that many illnesses coming to the attention of social workers in health care, union and industrial settings, family services, and so on are occupational in origin is therefore not considered. However, some sixty occupational health clinics have now been established across the country, mostly at university medical centers. In some of them, new roles are developing for social workers as the skilled gatherers of pertinent work history and workplace data, as workers' compensation advocates, and as collaborators with labor organizations, lawyers, and government officials (Shanker 1983).

The ecological nature of the workplace makes it an important site for industrial social work services, program development, advocacy, and research. Social work contributes to occupational health and safety, occupational disease clinics, union welfare programs, community support activities of business and industry, corporate programs in management and organizational development, EAPs, and so on.

SUDDEN JOB LOSS AS A SECOND-ORDER DEVELOPMENT

At the societal level, the economic-industrial structure affects both family life and community life. Lack of work arising from acute job loss due to plant closings, corporate takeovers, and major layoffs, as well as chronic unemployment and the steady loss of unskilled jobs since the 1960s, have grave economic, emotional, and social consequences for the worker and all family members and for communities where unemployment is widespread.

Having less seniority, young adults with growing families are vulnerable to job loss when the local or national economy is in trouble. New economic forces are now causing many skilled and professional persons in middle adulthood to lose their jobs as well. Another position, especially at the same level, is not easily found despite laws against age discrimination. Little is known, however, of the impact of job loss or chronic unemployment on women workers, an area that awaits study. Beginning in February 1989, federal law requires employers with 100 employees or more to give their workers sixty-day notification of plant closings. It also provides federal aid to the states for job training and counseling services for workers as well as for displaced homemakers and others without a place in the occupational structure.

Job loss followed by prolonged or permanent unemployment is a nonexpectable second-order development in family life, triggering emotional turmoil in even well-functioning families. The sense of competence, self-esteem, and self-direction is damaged not only in the worker member but also in the other adult family members and the children. Hence the quality of relatedness in the family, and between family members and their social worlds, may also be strained or even damaged. If a new job is not found soon, the average family also faces economic problems. Many do not earn enough to have savings, and those that have savings may soon exhaust them. The family may face a severly reduced standard of living, loss of its home or its rented dwelling (because the rent is now beyond its means), ultimate impoverishment, and even homelessness. The worker's feelings of guilt, rage, shock, despair, and shame may not be easily assuaged by supportive family members, who may gradually succumb to their discouragement and fear. These, in turn, increase the worker's negative feelings, which then increase the family's, in a recursive loop.

Individual efforts to cope with this major stressor and the feelings it arouses affect how the family reorganizes itself. For example, widespread job loss and unemployment are associated not only with higher rates of suicide, physical illness, depression, and infant mortality, but with increased rates of substance abuse and family violence (H. Brenner 1984). These maladaptive attempts to cope with the stressor intensify the pain felt by all family members. Also, the children and teenagers in the family may act out their anxiety in troublesome

ways, ranging from lowered academic performance to antisocial behaviors. The various maladaptive coping efforts by the adults and the
children interfere with the family's needed transformation of its
structure and, if not halted, can lead to family disorganization and
even dissolution.

Fundamental changes in the family's structure and processes are
required. The family's social reality and image of themselves as individuals and as a family are severely threatened by the loss of work,
income, and status. Family loyalties, relationships, communication,
role allocations, transactions with the environment, and worldview
are all affected. As the tension mounts to a crisis point, the family
may draw on its self-healing processes, of which the members may
have been previously unaware.

In so doing, the family begins to restructure its internal world: role
assignments may need to shift, so that another adult becomes the
wage earner or one or both undertake job training. Others may reach
a creative solution such as beginning a small business that requires
little start-up money, or undertaking a career change. Routines of
daily living, including the use of time and space, may need to be
rearranged to accommodate to new demands imposed by the stressful
event. The parents will need to strive for open communication between each other and with the children. Efforts to draw all the family
members into the restructuring process in age-appropriate ways may
be required to help the children actively manage the difficulties during the period of reorganization.

Similarly, the family's view of its external world may need to
change in response to economic and industrial realities at the societal
or community level. Certain expectations of the parents for themselves and for the children may need to be placed in abeyance, at least
temporarily, and other, more limited goals may have to be adopted to
give a more positive meaning to the struggle for reorganization. The
family must also restructure its relations with the environment: a
move to another location may need to be carefully weighed. Financial
counseling and job counseling may be helpful. Reaching out to network connections for emotional support and for assistance in job
finding is necessary. Public assistance following the expiration of
unemployment benefits may be required. And perhaps the school will
need to be made aware of the child's home situation, so that the
teacher will handle the child's upsets constructively. These last three
changes may first require the resolution of conflicted issues such as
shame and damaged pride.

In making these or other second-order changes in their internal organization and in how they view and use their environment, the family create a new paradigm and worldview oriented to a new reality that enables them to survive intact and even to improve their position. Without such changes, the family may become more and more demoralized and even disorganized, so that meeting the developmental needs of the members become extraordinarily difficult or impossible.

ADULT DEVELOPMENT

Family life (except for those who live alone), parenthood (for those with children), and work (for those employed) are major sources of continued development in adulthood. Other sources include community activities and affiliations.

The middle years of childhood and beyond usually free the parents for a variety of growth-promoting and rewarding activities in the community, depending on their interests and work schedules. These may include participation in neighborhood and block affairs, church or temple affairs and spirituality, clubs and service organizations, the rural Grange, and service as a volunteer leader of youth groups or other community-based organizations. Such activities lead to social learning and may require a reappraisal and reorientation of one's attitudes, values, and beliefs regarding oneself and others, leading to further psychosocial growth.

The attachment and caretaking behaviors of infancy are supplemented in adulthood by pair formation and sexual bonding, as well as by affectional bonding with a few others, such as best friends or relatives who are considered best friends. As Bowlby put it:

> Attachment behavior is in no sense confined to the young; in illness or emergency each one of us seeks the comforting presence of those we know and trust—and moreover feel troubled, unhappy, and anxious if for any reason they are not available. So far from being regressive, as is sometimes suggested, attachment behavior is a normal and healthy part of human nature from the cradle to the grave. (1973:46)

One consequence of the difference between object relations theory and attachment theory, discussed in the previous chapter, is a changed view of dependency. Being attached to another is not the same thing as being dependent on that person. One may be dependent on someone without being attached or may be attached to someone without being dependent on that person. Bowlby's work suggests that human beings as they mature are able to be dependent or independent, to care for others and be cared for, to take care of and to be taken care of, as circumstances demand. All human beings need both attachments and social ties from birth to old age.

The next chapter will examine the effects of the life issues created by divorce, illness and disability, and death and bereavement, as well as the family transformations they require.

11

Family Transformations: Divorce, Chronic Illness and Disability, and Death and Bereavement

Miscarriage, stillbirth, and premature birth (chapter 7) and sudden job loss followed by prolonged unemployment (chapter 10) are only a few of many unanticipated life events that may arise in families. This chapter takes up three additional second-order developments that can occur at any point in a family's life course: 1) divorce, which is relatively common; 2) chronic illness and disability in adults and children, which is less common; and 3) death and bereavement, which are universal and yet are profoundly painful second-order developments for children and adults. Sudden death is clearly unanticipated, but in many respects, death is experienced as unexpected and unacceptable even when an illness is known to be terminal.

All three belong to a class of nonexpectable life events and processes characterized by grievous loss. Because of space limitations, they will also serve here as examples of many other second-order developments, such as family violence, rape, and psychiatric disorders. The issues they create pose difficult individual and familial tasks if the family is to integrate them into a reorganized structure, functioning, and view of itself and its world. These and other second-order developments contrast sharply with expectable developmental transitions, such as toddlerhood (chapter 9) and adolescence (chapter 12), and with nondevelopmental ones, such as retirement (chapter 13), which in most, but not all, instances require only first-order changes,

312

leading more or less smoothly to the family's transformation and continued development.

SEPARATION, DIVORCE, AND CUSTODY ISSUES

After almost doubling since 1965, the U.S. divorce rate fell for the first time in 1986, to its lowest level since 1975. Although it is still one of the highest in the world, the rate appears to be stabilizing (chapter 4). Remarriage rates are also high, but many remarriages also end in divorce. Indeed, some observers note that the United States may no longer be a monogamous society. Instead, it may be trending toward a polygamous society, but practicing plural marriages sequentially rather than concomitantly. The high divorce rates notwithstanding, separation and divorce are painful experiences for every member of the family, and their emotional, social, economic, and legal issues create severe stress. How long the stress continues depends on how well the family restructures itself. Throughout this section the focus is on divorce in families with children. The section begins with separation, usually the preliminary step in the divorce process.

The Separating Family

For many, securing a divorce may take a year or more because of crowded courts, as protracted disputes over child custody and property settlements clog court calendars. Whatever the duration, however, life is on hold for separating spouses, and work, finances, parenting, and plans for the future are permeated by emotional upheaval and uncertainty. On the basis of their research, Bloom, Hodges, and Caldwell (1983) concluded that the separation experience is far more stressful than the actual divorce, which finally comes almost as a relief to the spouses. The research subjects were fifty newly separated white men and women from a nonclinical population, some with and some without children, and a matched group of nonseparating persons. Both groups were well educated, some being in graduate school. The incomes ranged from $1,077 and $863 monthly spendable income for male and female parents, respectively, to $727 and $533 for male and female nonparents. The average length of marriage was 8½ years, ranging from 4 years for male nonparents to 15½ years for female parents.

The data were derived from initial in-person interviews about two months after the separation and a telephone follow-up six months after the initial interview. Most of the subjects reported their marriages had been generally good except for a six-month period prior to the separation. During this period, slightly more than 25 percent of the subjects had experienced changes in the relationship with the spouses, and in sleeping and eating habits, finances, work responsibilities and hours, and social and recreational activities. Also reported were sexual difficulties, in-law troubles, and physiological and psychological symptoms, such as weight loss, headaches, upset stomach, fatigue, and feelings of an impending nervous breakdown.

The three most frequent marital complaints were communication difficulties, differences in values, and lack of love reflecting "the slow distancing that takes place within a couple as their relationship deteriorates" (Bloom, Hodges, and Caldwell 1983:224). Complaints of physical abuse were rare, while verbal abuse was common. It was reported more frequently by women than by men and more frequently by parents than by nonparents. The most frequent precipitating events were infidelity; events outside the relationship, such as completing school, changing jobs, taking a trip without the spouse, or the expiration of the lease on the home; and some version of the "last straw," such as prolonged drinking, a second suicide attempt, or continual delays on the part of the spouse in completing graduate school.

The subjects drew readily on formal and informal supports. Nineteen persons had received couples' counseling and twenty-five had obtained individual counseling prior to separation, and almost all the subjects reported having someone—a supportive friend or relative—with whom they could talk about their marital problems. However, loneliness was a problem for many, and for some it predated the separation. At the time of follow-up, loneliness was reported as frequently as it had been originally, but the degree of severity had lessened.

Seventeen separation-related problems were reported in the initial interviews. Three were more severe at follow-up: child rearing, career planning, and relationships with parents. At follow-up, the males reported significantly less severe problems than the females in four problem areas: guilt and self-blame, feelings of incompetence, homemaking, and relationships with parents. Three problems were less severe among parents than among nonparents: mental health, self-blame, and feelings of incompetence.

In comparison to men, women, prior to separation, have greater dissatisfactions with their marriages and more symptoms, and more commonly initiate the separation. They seek more help and have stronger social supports. . . . At the time of the initial interview, women perceive more benefits from the separation. . . . Women's initial adjustments to the separation appear to be more positive and to be made more easily. (Bloom, Hodges, and Caldwell 1983:236)

By the end of the first eight months, the men had caught up with the women and tended to perceive fewer problems with the separation. For both the men and the women, attachment to the spouse appeared to weaken during the early months of separation.

Custodial parents felt that the problems associated with marital disruption were made greater because of having children. Parents reported changes in their children since the separation; 40 percent of these changes were viewed as positive. About half reported that their children were having interpersonal difficulties in school but felt that these were unrelated to the separation. In regard to work and the workplace, forty-two of the fifty subjects were employed at the follow-up. Fifteen percent of the subjects at the initial interview reported work-related difficulties, such as absenteeism, loss of effectiveness, or conflict with coworkers. At follow-up, 90 percent reported such problems.

Initially, the parents were more opposed to separation than the nonparents, but they had fewer postseparation problems—perhaps because they were older than the nonparents. Also, the parents experienced far more and longer lasting anger in response to marital disruption than the nonparents. Regardless of their sex, the parents tended to blame their spouses for their difficulties and saw as little as possible of the spouses during the separation. The authors concluded that acceptance of the reality and permanence of the separation was at least partially achieved. Other aspects, such as physiological and psychological problems, were just as disturbing at follow-up. Work-related and child-rearing problems intensified as time went on.

The Postdivorce Family

Most of what was noted in Bloom, Hodges, and Caldwell's study of separation also characterizes the first year or two after divorce. Divorce itself, while a major life stressor, is not as important as the postdivorce family environment in determining the mental health of the family members (Goldsmith 1982). The postdivorce family must carry out the same functions as the married family but does so in altered ways. Divorce does not necessarily result in the family's disintegration, nor is it the end of the family. Rather, the family continues but must reorganize its structure of roles, tasks, and relationships following the loss of an adult member. Factors affecting the restructuring process include "the predivorce family situation, sex and age of adults and children, postdivorce quality of family relationships, custody arrangements, and prior mental health of adults" (Goldsmith 1982:298).

The prominent divorce researchers Hetherington, Cox, and Cox (1982) view divorce outcomes as different for each family member. Stressors, supports, and coping abilities vary for the spouses, the parents, and the children. These authors regard divorce not as a single event, but as a complex social, psychological, and economic process over time that imposes different stressors and elicits different responses at different points. During and immediately following divorce, conflict, loss, change, and uncertainty are likely to be prominent. These are usually resolved within a few years if additional, multiple stressors do not appear. The long-term adaptation will depend in large measure on the nature of the custodial family as an environment for its members.

Mourning a death is aided by religious and other ceremonials, but society has not developed rituals, customs, and support systems to assist divorcing parents and their children to move through this second-order development (Elkin 1987). Each family must find its own way of integrating the divorce into its new paradigm. Beal (1980) suggested that couples who work toward maintaining friendly relations during and after the divorce are apt to have a less intense experience of loss. They will also be better able to dissolve the marital relationship while maintaining the relationships between each parent and the children that are so important to the children's well-being. The family transformation is easier to achieve.

Goldsmith (1982) also found that positive feelings toward the former spouse are associated with more effective coparenting, particularly when the feelings are mutual. She declared that positive feelings toward the former spouse should not be confused with continued attachment and inability to separate. Divorced persons who are unable to separate emotionally will be unable to mourn the loss, work through the separation, and move on in their separate lives. In Goldsmith's study, most parents who held positive feelings did not experience themselves as being unable to separate, as is often assumed by clinicians when they observe positive feelings between former spouses.

Effects of Divorce on Children

In reviewing the research on the impact of divorce on children in maternal custody (still the most prevalent and hence the most studied), Warshak and Santrock (1983) concluded that the factors responsible for the variability of children's responses to divorce include the child's personality, developmental status, and sex; the personality and parenting styles of each parent, as exhibited in the mother–father, mother–child, and father–child relationships; the child's degree of access to both parents; and the custodial parent's economic condition and use of social supports.

Hetherington, Cox, and Cox (1982) studied seventy-two white middle-class children, who lived in mother-custody homes and attended nursery school, and their divorced parents over the two years following the divorce. A matched group of children from nondivorced families and their parents were included for comparison. Data were gathered through interviews, structured diaries of the parents, observation of the parents and the child interacting in the laboratory and at home, checklists of the child's behaviors, parents' ratings of the child's behavior, personality scales on the parents, observation of the child in nursery school, teachers' ratings of behavior, and measures of the child's sex-role typing, cognitive performance, and social development.

Many differences in parent–child relations were found between the divorced and intact families. The divorced parents exhibited poor parenting when compared with the still-married parents. They communicated less well with their children, made fewer demands for mature behavior, tended to be less affectionate, and were much less consistent in their disciplining. The parenting difficulties were especially marked one year after the divorce but diminished somewhat by the end of the second year. The relations between divorced mothers and sons were less positive than those between mothers and daughters. The fathers were more successful in obtaining compliance from the children and used half as many commands as the mothers.

The children, especially the boys, exhibited many more negative behaviors than their counterparts in the nondivorced families. During the first year, the mothers were harassed by their children. Compared to the children in the intact families, the children didn't obey or attend. They nagged, whined, and made many more dependency demands. The boys were more oppositional and aggressive toward their mothers, and the girls were more whining, complaining, and compliant. After two years, such behavior had all but disappeared in the girls and was greatly diminished among the boys—but was still higher than that of the boys in the intact families: "The second year appeared to be a period of marked recovery and constructive adaptation for divorced mothers and children" (Hetherington, Cox, and Cox 1982:258).

The researchers found certain similarities in the home and school environments of those children in divorced families who showed more rapid and satisfactory adaptation. When the home and school environments manifested clear and consistently enforced standards, roles, and responsibilities, as well as a responsive and nurturing climate, the children showed more adaptive behavior. The authors suggested that young child under the severe stress of divorce may not be able to structure their own world or to muster self-control and are therefore more dependent on a stable environment than children under less stress.

In both the intact and the divorced families, the parent–child relationship was more effective when support and agreement existed between the parents. In the divorced families, the frequency of father visitation was associated with more positive mother–child relations, less stress for the mother, and a more positive adaptation by the child, provided the father was emotionally mature and had a positive attitude toward the mother, and conflict between the parents was low. Otherwise, visitation was associated with poor mother–child functioning and disruptions in the child's behavior. Grandparents, siblings, close friends of the parents, or a competent housekeeper was also associated with the divorced mother's effectiveness. The grandparents, if they lived in the area, were helpful with finances, child care, and emotional support. The grandfathers were especially significant in regard to the sons in the divorced families, imparting skills and participating in activities with them.

In a well-known five-year longitudinal study of 131 middle-class children of divorce, aged 3 to 18 at the time of the divorce, Wallerstein and Kelly (1980) found that parents and children were still suffering severe turmoil and stress at the end of the first postdivorce year. But by five years after the divorce, half the fathers and two thirds of the mothers reported being more content with their lives, while one fifth of the adults regretted the divorce. In contrast, only one third of the children and adolescents were doing well. One third were moderately to severely depressed; they were still angry at both parents, intensely lonely, and feeling deprived and rejected despite their normal functioning before the marital disruption. The remaining third exhibited a mix of strengths and negative features. The authors stated that childhood or adolescence had been a sad and unhappy time for all the children.

Reporting more specifically on thirty-four preschoolers who were 3 to 5 years of age at the time of the divorce, Wallerstein (1984) stated that at the five-year follow-up they had seemed to be more disturbed than the older children. Yet, by the ten-year follow-up, they had actually managed better than the older children. They had fewer memories of conflicts and seemed more settled than the older children. Ten years later, those who were 9 to 18 years of age at the time of divorce still harbored memories of suffering, were concerned about the unreliability of relationships, and feared betrayal. A "sizable percentage" of all the children continued to have problems ten years after divorce because of diminished parenting, "a widespread phenomenon" that consisted of: "Decreased availability of the parent to the child, a sharp decline in emotional sensitivity and emotional support for the child, decreased pleasure in the relationship, decreased attentiveness to the child's needs and wishes, less talk, less play, less interaction altogether, and a steep escalation in the expression of anger" (Wallerstein 1985).

While such lapses in parenting are time-limited in most families, "many parents remain profoundly troubled or continue to be disinterested in their children" (1985). As a result, "a large group" of children, ranging from toddlers to adolescents, had had to take the responsibility for their own upbringing. A second group in the same age range had assumed the responsibility for maintaining the psychological functioning of one or both parents. A third group of children had become the objects of protracted conflict and litigation between the parents. And a fourth group had experienced a second parental divorce and could not cope with two disruptions (Wallerstein 1985). No numbers or percentages of such "overburdened children" are given. Contrary to studies finding that girls suffer less than boys as a result of divorce, the ten-year follow-up also revealed a "sleeper effect" in which 66 percent of the girls, as they entered young adulthood, began to experience serious effects of the divorce (Wallerstein & Blakeslee 1989).

Wallerstein's findings on divorce outcomes for children of all ages and both sexes are far more bleak than those of other researchers.

Hers is the only longitudinal study, so perhaps we are to assume that 30 to 60 percent of middle-class white children of divorce do remain emotionally and behaviorally disturbed or become so over time. Such an assumption would suggest that the recovery or improvement by two years postdivorce, reported in other studies, might have shown deterioration after the second year if the studies had continued. The inference does not seem reasonable. The assumption also does not jibe with the work of Rutter (1979a, b), Chess and Thomas (1986), and Murphy (1974) on children's resilience (chapter 8). We are left with a sampling issue to consider.

Wallerstein and Kelly (1980) began their research by establishing a divorce-counseling service for divorcing families with children. The sixty research families came voluntarily for psychological help and for social and educational recommendations for the relief of acute stress. In return, they willingly entered the research project. The authors stated that by providing psychotherapy they had research access to the inner worlds of the children and the parents not otherwise available. However, the sixty families represented a clinical population that sought help with unmanageable stress. Moreover no control groups—either of intact families or of divorced families not seeking psychotherapy—were used. The researchers acknowledged the lack of a control group and the confounding of the findings by clinical aspects. Altogether, it is not wise to generalize these findings to the larger non-clinical universe of divorcing parents and their children. Also, conclusions, from all studies must be tempered by an awareness that no research has yet been carried out with divorcing families in social and cultural groups other than the white middle class.

Custody Issues

During the twentieth century, most custody decisions have been made almost automatically in the mother's favor, probably because of cultural stereotypes that view mothers as uniquely suited to provide care. Today, maternal custody still prevails, although more and more fathers are being granted custody, not necessarily on the grounds of the mother's unfitness, but often because both parents wish it for financial reasons or because of the mother's need for education and career planning. Goldsmith (1982) reported that the issues for a custodial parent of either sex are generally identical, and there is no evidence that custodial fathers do any worse or better than custodial mothers. But many noncustodial mothers feel stigmatized by friends and relatives because of the cultural stereotypes of motherhood.

In one of the few studies of father custody, Warshak and Santrock (1983) studied sixty-four white, mostly middle-class families with children ranging in age from 6 to 11. Half the children were boys and half were girls. Approximately one third of the children were in their father's custody, one third were in their mother's custody, and one third were living in intact families having no history of separation. The three types of families were matched for the age of the children, for family size, and for socioeconomic status. The two groups of children from divorced families were also individually matched for sibling status and for age at the parents' separation (which, on the average, preceded divorce by ten months). Most custody arrangements had been agreed upon prior to the court hearing, and relinquishment of custody by both fathers and mothers appeared to be a matter of not wanting custody or of having no preference rather than issues of unfitness.

The assumption that children of divorce will function less well than children of intact families was not borne out in this study. However, there were differences between boys and girls in father custody; the girls did less well. In general, when children in maternal custody were compared with children in paternal custody, the researchers found that children living with the same-sex parent uniformly scored higher than children living with the opposite-sex parent on measures of demandingness, maturity, sociability, and independence. Whether psychoanalytic, social learning, or other theories are used to explain these results, Warshak and Santrock declared that "there is something very important about the ongoing, continuous relationship of a child with the same-sex parent" (1983:259). They added that the findings should not be used to advocate dividing the custody of siblings along sex-related lines, since the importance of the sibling system in postdivorce adjustment is unknown.

The authors also found that in both forms of custody, parental warmth, a clear setting of rules, and extensive verbal interaction were significantly correlated with six of the nine child observation scales: self-esteem, maturity, sociability, social conformity, anger, and demandingness. Custodial fathers used support systems more than custodial mothers did, and children in paternal custody had more contact with the noncustodial parent than children in maternal custody. The most frequent drawback of the divorce mentioned by the children was their reduced access to the noncustodial parent. Eighty-four percent of the children expressed ongoing reconciliation wishes. Two thirds of the children were positive about the possibility of their custodial parent's remarriage: "Taken together—the focus on parental loss, the reconciliation wishes, and the remarriage endorsement— these findings suggest that children of divorce want to live in two-parent homes, despite the conflict, turmoil, and failure of the predivorce family" (1983:257).

According to Goldsmith, "In any family, there will be a 'decider system'—that part of the system that maintains control and order" (1982:304). In married families, this is determined internally; in divorced families, it is determined externally. However, in the latter, the legal arrangement is less important than the actual control structure that develops. In maternal or paternal custody, coparenting may vary from little or no sharing of control and decision making to almost equal sharing. In either case, the former spouses, despite the end of their marriage, continue to be the parents of their children for life. Hence, in any custody arrangement, the parents' cooperation and shared decision making in regard to the children are necessary for the children's continued development. The structure of the divorced family, then, consists of the coparental, custodial parent–child, noncustodial parent–child, sibling, and individual subsystems. In the event of the remarriage of one or both parents, the children and their parents actually remain a continuing interdependent subsystem of a total system that is now much larger. Some problems experienced by the new system may indeed derive from continuing difficulties in the relationships among the original family members, as described in chapter 4.

To ascertain the intrapersonal and interpersonal factors that contribute to successful coparenting, Goldsmith (1982) studied eighty-five divorced couples with children under 18 years of age. The couples had been separated for from two months to two years prior to the divorce. Their names were randomly selected from the court records of Cook County, Illinois. The subjects were white, and all the mothers had legal custody. Interviews took place one year after the divorce and again three years later. Wherever possible, the former spouses were interviewed individually. Only those couples in which the father had seen the child at least once in the two months preceding the interview were included, since the focus of the study was coparenting.

The majority of the couples experienced some conflict or stress in the coparenting relationship, the fathers being more dissatisfied than the mothers. Eleven couples reported a cooperative, supportive, and satisfying coparental relationship. Many others who reported stress as a characteristic of the relationship also said their relationships involved cooperation and mutual support. Most of the couples had maintained direct communication with each other, and this tended to increase in connection with a special occasion or a problem with the child, such as school or medical issues. The majority also reported that they occasionally spent time with each other and the children during birthdays, school events, church functions, visits to grandparents, or outings. The parents generally felt more satisfied and supported when there was a sharing of responsibility and interest: "The noncustodial fathers in these cooperative coparenting couples are more likely to stay actively involved with their children and to achieve emotional separation from their former wives" (Goldsmith 1982:321).

A friendly, cooperative coparenting relationship supports the custodial parent's effectiveness in child rearing and the child's continued development: "Many former spouses . . . were able to relate in friendly ways without becoming involved with one another sexually or romantically, and while continuing to develop new relationships" (Goldsmith 1982:317). Those who did not establish clear boundaries around their parental interaction experienced enmeshment and distress. These contaminated the coparenting, and the couple's ability to separate and develop new relationships was inhibited. Goldsmith suggested that substituting the term *coparent* for the term *ex-spouse* may identify and validate this ongoing, important subsystem of the divorced family. It may also help an enmeshed couple clarify their status vis-à-vis each other.

With a million or more children experiencing divorce each year, their emotional and developmental needs require greater public and professional attention. Joint custody has come to the fore as a means of ensuring children's access to both parents: "Sole custody too often results in the father feeling disenfranchised and divorced from his child, and the mother being overwhelmed by having to assume most of the parenting responsibilities" (Elkin 1987). Some thirty-four states now have joint custody statutes, although there are many differences among them. Some courts oppose the notion of joint custody; others impose joint custody on parents who do not wish it and who will be unable to coparent because of extensive reciprocal hostility.

Elkin pointed out that in joint custody "both parents are empowered by the court to retain *equal legal rights, authority, and responsibility* for the care and control of their child, much as in the intact family" (1987; italics in the original). Joint custody does not determine physical custody but allows the parents to work out the residential arrangements that will best suit the child's needs. It is an option that is not right for every family. For example, joint custody is not appropriate in the presence of any of the following negative factors: family violence, including child abuse; child neglect; mental pathology; a family history indicating parental inability to agree on child rearing; the parents' inability to distinguish their needs from those of the children; children who are likely to be unresponsive to joint custody or to rebel against it; a family history of severe disorganization; the unalterable opposition of both parents to joint custody; and logistics militating against a joint custody plan. Elkin's analysis of the assumptions, benefits, and pros and cons of joint custody can be helpful to social workers involved with separating and divorcing families.

Elkin described a kind of divorce mediation that, like joint custody, represents a focus on what is best for the children in divorce. (The mediation process is used to resolve all divorce-related issues, and not only custody.) As in joint custody, the aim is self-determination: the right of the divorcing families to define the postdivorce structure and rules in accordance with the needs of each individual and the family as a whole. Mediation is neither therapy nor arbitration. Rather, it is a short-term, goal-directed problem-solving process in which a trained divorce mediator tries to reach goals that will help the couple to disconnect emotionally and to reconnect as parents.

Luepnitz (1982) carried out an early study to compare the three types of custody. She conducted a one-evening structured interview and a family task with each of 50 volunteer families in which separation had occurred at least two years earlier, together with their 91 children. There were 16 custodial mothers, 16 custodial fathers, and 18 parents with joint custody. The children in the first two groups experienced avuncular relationships with their noncustodial parents, while those in joint custody enjoyed filial relationships with both parents. The joint custody parents did not report more parental conflict than the single custody parents.

Only eight children scored a low self-concept according to standardized norms, and those eight had problems antedating the divorce. Luepnitz acknowledged that studying each family for only four to six hours may have led to an underestimation of maladaptive functioning (also, these were volunteer, nonrandom subjects). She concluded that, although each form of custody has its advantages and disadvantages, joint custody in this study had more advantages and fewer disadvantages than either paternal or maternal custody. She observed that among those who were successful in coparenting, the mothers took on budgeting, finances, and work responsibilities and experienced new levels of self-confidence. The fathers took on house-

keeping, including cooking and sewing, and lessened their involvement in the workplace in order to spend more time with their children. The children assumed new household tasks and greater
participation in decision making. The families' relationships to their
environments expanded to include formal and informal supports.

Second-Order Changes

The process of marital disruption, separation, and divorce represents
a second-order development that requires a major family transformation so that the developmental needs of all members will be met
to an optimal degree. The marital disruption throws the family and
its members into a state of crisis marked by conflict and the eruption
of powerful negative feelings; that "derive from the experiences of
emptiness, uncertainty, and aimlessness, all of which are in the ascen-
dancy during second-order developments" (Terkelsen 1980:39). As a
result of the crisis, reciprocal or competing needs of the members are
not met. The relatedness, competence, self-esteem, and self-direction
of both the child and the adult members begin to diminish. Tension
and strain mount (sometimes to the point of violence—not usually a
good prognostic sign). As recognition of the impact grows, efforts to
resolve the crisis may begin.

The studies reviewed in this chapter and the literature in general
suggest that to resolve the crisis and achieve a transformed family
structure, both spouses must begin to 1) work through the marital
conflict by ceasing to blame each other and recognizing and acknowledging their own contributions to the failure of the marriage (Beal
1980); 2) reevaluate the marriage and its strengths and weaknesses
and what has been learned from it (Beatrice 1979); 3) end the spousal
relationship and relinquish the attachment, while working to maintain the child(ren)'s relationship to both parents (Beal 1980); 4) mourn
the loss of the marriage and its hopes and expectations, which were
part of the family's view of itself, and let go of the past; 5) cope with
new roles and reality demands and take responsibility for their own
lives (Beatrice 1979); and, eventually, 6) move on to new relationships
and new directions in their lives. The process appears to take at least
two to three years, although not all families succeed in all tasks. Some
achieve the family transformation through their own self-healing processes, and some seek out and are responsive to mediation services
and/or social work help.

From the outset, both parents must allow the children to express their anger, sadness, fears, and despair and must accept their feelings while helping them to understand and manage the feelings. In the best interest of the children, the former spouses must build and maintain a coparental subsystem in the transformed family structure, sharing responsibilities and decision making to the greatest degree possible, regardless of custody type. Such a subsystem continues whether or not the parents remarry. Through reasonably effective work on these painful and stressful tasks, both parents and children can come to accept and integrate the divorce into the family's view of itself and its environment. Family functions, roles, and responsibilities are reorganized in ways that are appropriate to the social, emotional, and physical needs of the individual members in the changed circumstances. The parents each seek to expand positive relationships with their informal and formal community of relatives, friends, and others, thus reducing loneliness, gaining needed support, and widening the social worlds of both adult and child. Ideally, the capacity for relatedness, a sense of competence, self-concept and self-esteem, and self-direction of all members is gradually restored: "Ultimately the family's prior system of meaning [the family paradigm] gives way under the advance of a new shared reality" (Terkelsen 1980:39). The new paradigm will now shape the transformed family's interpretation of its world, its daily routines, and its actions in the environment (Reiss 1982).

CHRONIC ILLNESS AND DISABILITY: FAMILY TRANSFORMATION

Chronic Illness and Disability in Adulthood

Chronic illness and disability can occur in adulthood at any point over the life course of any family. And "In many chronic conditions, patients receive less than a total of one day per year in direct contact with doctors and nurses. The rest of medical care is provided by self, family, and friends" (Coyne and Holroyd 1982:118). As Coyne and Holroyd pointed out, chronic illness and disability are home care problems, since only 4 percent of those suffering from these conditions live in institutions. Hence family members are crucial in the management of the illness or disability, while having to deal with their own emotional pain and the relentless caretaking demands at the same time.

Today's major illnesses include AIDS and chronic, degenerative illnesses such as heart disease; hypertension and stroke; cancer; kid-

ney failure; diabetes and its sequelae; emphysema and other respiratory diseases; rheumatoid arthritis; the neurological damage to perception, emotion, language, thought, memory, or action inflicted by
illness or injury; disabilities caused by serious accidents and injuries;
and impairments of hearing and vision. Contrary to a general miscon-
ception, chronic illness is not solely a geriatric problem, although the
elderly are more likely to have chronic conditions and more of them
(Strauss and Glaser 1975:2). About 18 to 20 percent of young and
middle-aged adults have one or more chronic conditions, with some
or total limitation in a major activity. Over two million are profoundly deaf, including those born deaf, those whose hearing was lost
before language acquisition, and those deafened in adulthood, who
constitute about 78 percent of all deaf persons and whose needs and
adaptive tasks are different from those of the prelinguistic deaf (Luey
1980). According to the American Foundation for the Blind, almost a
half million persons in the United States are legally blind.

The life issues created for the patient, the partner, and their children by chronic illness or disability are often permanent as well as
persistent and unrelenting. The spouse may need to prepare a special
diet, create a stress-free environment, control her or his own anxiety
and allay the children's fears, supervise helpers, operate complex
medical equipment, conduct speech or physical exercises, avoid making the ill person feel helpless, and perhaps hold a job needed for
income. For example, a social worker began to visit Mr. and Mrs.
Gaines. She wrote:

> Mr. Gaines has suffered from lupus for years. He is bedridden
> now and helpless. He is depressed, and his coping efforts are
> limited to expressing anger at his family and the world. He is
> physically very uncomfortable, and his physical care requires
> time, nursing, and extended effort on the part of his wife and
> other family members. Nurses are assisting, but the added ex-
> pense is a growing problem. . . . Mrs. Gaines cooks all natural
> foods, gives Mr. Gaines large amounts of vitamins, and reads all
> the latest medical literature for possible "cures." She, too, is
> under enormous stress, as she must assume the roles of house-
> hold head and decision maker, nurse, comforter, and therapeutic
> liaison, as well as carry out her customary roles of wife and
> mother.

In serious illness, or injury leading to permanent disability, the
afflicted person and the family can be expected to respond first with
denial of the gravity of the condition. This is needed temporarily for

sheer emotional survival. Gradually, however, they must relax the denial, allowing themselves to experience the painful reality and the accompanying periods of depression. These enable the patient and the family members to begin to mourn the losses involved and to move toward coping with them and managing the illness. And the patient can begin slowly to construct a new identity, not as a sick person but as a different person, still with a sense of competence, self-esteem, self-direction, and relatedness within the limits set by the condition— an awesome achievement.

The interaction of personal, cultural, and social factors affects the course of the illness or the management of the disability, the patient's compliance with medical regimens, and strategies for coping with the illness or disability. Personal factors include personality, temperament, gender, the age of onset, the meaning attributed to the illness or disability (for example, fate, punishment for sin, or one's own or another person's negligence), the self-concept, coping skills and defenses, excessive dependence or independence, and activity–passivity orientation.

Cultural factors include culturally shaped attitudes and values about health and disease, definitions of illness and its treatment, illness behaviors, and the meanings attributed to the symptoms—according to race, ethnicity, religion, and socioeconomic status. Access to health care is often blocked by language barriers.

Social factors include the disruption of family roles and responsibilities, possible problems in sexual functioning, loss of work and income if the illness or disability strikes an adult member, the social stigma of AIDS and some other diseases, and the presence or absence of formal supports in the environment. Other social factors are the behavioral expectations inherent in the sick role, the complexities of the U.S. health care system, the use of advanced medical technology, and the ethical, moral, and legal issues that technology creates for families and staff. Social factors also may include disempowerment and poverty, which limit access to quality medical care and result in wide differences between whites and people of color in life expectancy and infant mortality rates.

In the latest available figures, the life expectancy of whites at birth was continuing to rise in both sexes (U.S.B.C. 1989:71, table 106). The life expectancy of black male Americans dropped from the high of 65.6 in 1984, probably because of rising death rates from homicides, accidents, AIDS, tuberculosis, and other infectious diseases, which have a disproportionate impact on black Americans, especially males.

In 1986 whites had a life expectancy of 75.5 years, (72.1 and 78.8 for males and females respectively) and black Americans had a life expectancy of 69.7 years (65.4 and 73.6 for males and females respectively). The pattern is similar in the rates of infant mortality. In 1986 the rate for all Americans was 10.4 deaths in the first year of life per 1,000 live births, the lowest ever recorded in the United States. For blacks, the rate was 18.0, a decline from 18.2 in 1985. The rate for whites was 8.9, a decline from 9.3 in 1985 (table 113. p.76). The differences in life expectancy and infant mortality rates between whites and American Indians are even greater than between whites and blacks. Comparative data for Hispanic and Asian groups are not available. Rates of cancer and hypertension in adults and of lead poisoning in children are much higher among blacks than among whites.

The continuous coping tasks in chronic illness identified by Strauss and Glaser (1975:7–8) include the following:

1.–*Normalizing social interaction and lifestyle to the degree possible.* Strauss and Glaser's concept of "identity spread" describes powerfully intrusive symptoms that cause others to view the sick person only in terms of symptoms. Identity spread is similar to the experiences of deaf, blind, and physically challenged persons who are regarded by others as being incapable of self-management, and being unable to work, act, or be like others (Jeppsson-Grassman 1986a, 1986b). The symptoms are overgeneralized and thus dominate the social interaction. The chronically ill or disabled individual and his or her family members may work hard to develop normalizing tactics that will keep a symptom invisible, enabling the individual to "pass" as a well person or, if the symptom can't be hidden, to reduce it to minor status by maintaining composure, dignity, and control of interactions.

2.–*Complying with painful or difficult medical regimens.* What is labeled *noncompliance* includes failure to enter or continue in a treatment program, to keep follow-up or referral appointments, to take prescribed medicines, or to change one's activities or give up smoking, alcohol, certain foods. Noncompliance may be the result of financial problems; transportation problems; combinations of medicines and complicated medication schedules; the length of the treatment; a prolonged denial of the illness because of anxiety, anger, and humiliation at the loss of self-direction; lack of sufficient information from, or poor rapport with, the physician or treatment team; and other factors. Noncompliance cuts across socioeconomic groups, types of persons, and medical settings (Noble and Hamilton 1983); these authors also suggested ways in which social workers can help in cases of noncompliance).

3.–*Juggling time*. Family and patient must establish flexible temporal arrangements as needed, including the management of too much time (resulting in boredom, loss of social skills, and physical deterioration), not enough time (used up by symptom control and regimens), complicated schedules, and the timing of family events and processes. Arrangements must be flexible because they are often disturbed by changes in symptoms, regimens, the illness, family relationships, and finances.

4.–*Developing and accepting emotional and social support*. A positive network of relatives, friends, and neighbors provides emotional and social support in the management of problems in living with chronic illness and disability. A spouse operates the home dialysis machine and checks blood pressure for the person who suffers from end-stage kidney disease. Friends and neighbors provide respite for the family by staying a few hours or over a weekend with the ill person. Others provide transportation for trips to the medical center or do the family's grocery shopping. Sometimes a friend helps the ill person comply with difficult or painful procedures. Establishing, coordinating, and maintaining a social support system requires interpersonal skills, trust, and network resources (Strauss and Glaser 1975).

Support systems are especially important for those chronically ill or disabled adults who live alone. They are extraordinarily burdened, yet many manage well with the aid of relatives, friends, neighbors, community services, seeing-eye dogs, signal dogs for the deaf, monkeys trained to help those with paraplegia, and newly developed technological and electronic aids and protheses of many kinds, such as the telecommunication devices for the deaf (TDD).

Sadly, having symptoms or disfigurements that are repelling or frightening to others may impel an ill or physically handicapped individual to withdraw from social contacts other than those with family members. Or the network members may withdraw. Mr. Gaines' social network shrank as his disease progressed because his speech was increasingly affected. His friends and former associates found communication too difficult to continue visiting.

5.–*Managing medical crises and adapting to changes in the course of the illness, such as remissions, unpredictable relapses, or downward progression*. Some chronic diseases confront the individual and the family with the dire possibility of premature death. A social worker, suffering from Hodgkin's disease, a form of cancer, recalled:

When I was in the acute stage and close to death, I made peace with myself and the significant others in my life. And I discovered I wasn't afraid to die, but afraid to be alone at that time and afraid to be in pain. After surviving the acute stage, it took me several years of preparing myself to stay alive and to *live*. Being chronically ill is a lot to handle, but with the right help it can be done, especially if social workers stress the importance of keeping one's life as normal as possible despite the illness. Even when I was most sick, we accepted all social invitations—some I couldn't attend, some I could, but the normality of being involved was at least as valuable as the chemotherapy.

Second-Order Changes

As with other life issues, how family members carry out the tasks of coping with adult chronic illness, the devastating emotions aroused, and the many life issues it generates will vary somewhat according to the age, gender, and personality of the patient and the other family members; the developmental point in the family's life course; environmental circumstances such as work, finances, housing, and network support; cultural factors; and the nature of the illness or disability. The coping tasks that will facilitate second-order changes are cognitive, emotional, and social in nature. The *cognitive* tasks include learning and applying as much as possible about the illness, its usual course, and the rationales for the treatment processes through reading, the skillful gathering of information from health care personnel, and the use of familiar as well as newly developed problem-solving efforts of all kinds. The latter may include preparing for any eventuality through mental rehearsals of alternative outcomes, as well as modifying personal and familial expectations and aspirations or developing new, more appropriate ones. Intellectual mastery in itself is empowering: the individual and the family members feel that they have some control over their situation or, at least, are made less helpless by it.

The *emotional* tasks include the support that patient and family members give to one another in their mutual efforts to manage the difficult emotions of sorrow, anxiety, guilt, anger, and resentment that are inevitably aroused throughout the course of the illness, the multiple demands it imposes on all members, and unexpected medical crises. Such emotional support requires active and continual work on keeping communication open among all members. Mutual support and open communication between the spouses help the patient with difficult issues such as regression in the face of inordinate stress, dependence–independence conflicts, sexual problems, loss of other bodily functions, damaged self-concept and self-esteem, and preparation for an uncertain future. For some, faith in a divine purpose, or a spiritual or existential philosophy of life and its meaning, imparts emotional strength and sustains hopefulness. With or without faith or philosophy, people cope successfully from a position of hope rather than of despair.

Children may suffer anxiety, resentment, or guilt when a parent is severely ill. They worry about what is going to happen to them and their family, whether their parent will die, and whether they were responsible for the illness. Both parents need to be sensitive to unexpressed feelings and to encourage their expression, accept them, and answer questions truthfully at the child's cognitive level.

The *social* tasks include seeking and accepting appropriate social (and emotional) supports from friends and relatives and from formal systems of care, medical and otherwise. These tasks include active efforts to prevent social isolation or, if isolation is inevitable for whatever reason, working out ways to live with it. Planning simple, shared experiences of pleasure or joy in family life strengthens morale for the difficult times. An essential means of effective second-order change that is at once social, emotional, and cognitive is the flexible reorganization of family roles and tasks as needed from time to time, including the participation of the ill or disabled member in decision making, problem solving, and family activity to the greatest degree possible and of the children at age-appropriate levels.

Through second-order changes brought about by these coping efforts, the family begins gradually to 1) modify its assumptions about the world and its place in it and 2) integrate into its worldview the illness and its consequences, so that 3) a new paradigm emerges that is congruent with the new reality. In achieving these changes, the ill or disabled adult and her or his spouse or partner may feel that the experience has brought them closer together. Each may feel loved by the other in ways they never felt before. They may discover capacities that they did not know they had. And the children may gain cognitively, emotionally, and socially as well. Relatedness, competence, self-esteem, and self-direction are preserved at optimal levels in the patient and all family members, despite the inevitable ups and downs. Family myths concerning health, illness, and death—based on real and fantasized experiences—may color attitudes toward the chronically ill or disabled adult (or child), facilitating adaptation or interfering with it. If the attitudes are negative, the family's successful management of the illness or disability through second-order changes is likely to reshape the myths for the better.

In contrast, failure to reach an adaptive balance of the family members' needs because of unsuccessful coping with the illness, the life issues it generates, and the accompanying negative emotions can exacerbate the illness and undermine the members' relatedness, competence, self-esteem, and self-direction, making continued coping efforts still less effective and the achievement of a modified family paradigm impossible. For example, a failure to relinquish the early coping strategy of denial when it is no longer adaptive may result in a resistance to proper self-care and to noncompliance with medical regimens. In other instances, the family or the individual may persist in an overestimation of the severity of the illness or disability, which will lead to overprotection by the family and/or overdependency in the patient. The family and/or the ill individual may also persist in an underestimation of the severity, which will lead to insufficient support by the family or to the ill persons's refusal to accept the needed help.

These and other failure in adaptation, in turn, can lead to the dissolution of the marriage, emotional disorders in either partner or in the children, and further family disorganization that will confirm mythical irrationalities. However, it is important to note that before this point is reached, the family may be thrown into crisis by the mounting of tensions, leading them to reach out to professional services, including social work. The family may then be helped to rediscover its own capacities and to redesign its coping efforts. A family crisis can serve a positive function: "Though filled with risk, it ultimately opens the family to new experience, altering its sense of itself and the outside world and thereby transforming a paradigm that may have guided it for years or even generations" (Riess 1982: 1419).

Chronic Illness or Disability in Childhood

Among adults, chronic illnesses are few in number but are fairly common. "In contrast, the chronic illnesses of children are relatively rare, and there is a tremendous variety of conditions" (J. Perrin

1985:3).* Despite their rarity, the illnesses do affect a sizable population. About one million American children, or 1 to 2 percent of the total child population, suffer severe chronic illness, and another ten million, or 10 to 15 percent of the total child population, are less severely involved (J. Perrin 1985:1, 3).

Some conditions are genetic or congenital in origin, and others are the result of disease or accident. Some childhood illnesses and disabilities, such as spina bifida, missing or deformed body parts, heart disease, Down syndrome, brain damage, blindness, and deafness, are apparent at birth or during infancy. Others, such as diabetes, cystic fibrosis, leukemia and other cancers, asthma, sickle cell anemia, and chronic kidney failure, may not appear until early or middle childhood. Common issues face all chronically ill children, whatever their particular illness or disability. However, a few differences can exist within a single condition or across conditions that have different impacts on the child's school attendance, peer relations, and adaptation to the illness or disability—just as personal, social, and cultural differences do.

Among such differences are the following: 1) limited mobility in some conditions affects access in the physical environment and may prevent participation in sports and other activities with peers and siblings; 2) the course of any condition may remain stable or may change over time: some conditions may progress toward improvement (as in controlled diabetes) and others toward decline (as in muscular dystrophy), and some are characterized by unpredictable ups and downs (as in asthma) that may be more stressful for a child than a stable yet more severe condition; 3) children with cognitive or sensory impairments have different adaptive patterns and service needs from those without such impairments; and 4) the visibility of the disorder (as in facial or limb deformities) has a significant negative effect on peer relations, with social and developmental consequences for the child (Pless and Perrin 1985).

Chronically ill and disabled children are at higher risk of emotional and social disorders than healthy children. The available evidence suggests that children with mild disabilities suffer as much as or more than those with severe disabilities—perhaps because of the invisibil-

---

*J. Perrin (1985) specified eleven childhood diseases that serve as marker diseases in considering matters of policy, services, the impact on child and family, and so on. That is, they have characteristics that make them representative of all childhood chronic conditions. The eleven are juvenile-onset diabetes, muscular dystrophy, cystic fibrosis, spina bifida, sickle cell anemia, congenital heart disease, chronic kidney disease, hemophilia, leukemia, cleft palate, and severe asthma.

ity of the symptoms, which enables a child to pass as "normal," and to keep the illness secret. Peers then expect her or him to behave in all respects as others do. When, for medical reasons, the child cannot, a difficult conflict arises for her or him (Pless 1984).

"Diagnosis of a chronically ill child is one of the most severe stresses that a family can sustain, because it involves not only the sudden shock and grief experienced when the child is diagnosed but also years of multiple traumatic events, constant medical treatment, and continual worry and anxiety" (Stein 1983). Where the chronic illness or disability of a child is severe, it has serious consequences for the family's development and well-being. Indeed, "family members are burdened with caring responsibilities, affected by anxiety and sometimes by guilt, strapped by unpredicted expenses and possible economic ruin, and facing an uncertain future that may include the premature death of the child" (J. Perrin 1985:2).

Limited finances complicate the situation. One parent, usually the mother, may have to leave employment for full-time care of the child, and the other parent may have to work at two jobs. There may be no money or time for recreation and vacations. Stein pointed out that insurance policies vary, and that eligibility for public aid is often inconsistent and meager: "There are also hidden costs; lost opportunities, lost work time, lost chances to advance in one's career or to go back to school." The parents may not have the time or energy to maintain their social ties or affiliations with self-help groups, which can be very helpful, even essential, to the family's well-being. The scarcity of community services or difficult access to them also makes life more difficult. These and other consequences of childhood illness or disability become enormous burdens for a solo parent.

The late onset of illness or disability implies different developmental and service needs of the child from those for a child having an early onset:

> Children born with a condition affecting their functioning appear to adjust to it more readily or to develop in the context of their illness in different ways from those able-bodied children who, having gone through typical developmental phases, develop permanent conditions later in childhood. Children born with spina bifida, as an example, have different patterns of adjustment from children rendered paraplegic from injury in adolescence. Children who have once had an ability react to its loss differently from those who never had it. (Pless and Perrin 1985:47)

The tasks faced by the parents and the family during the school years are somewhat different in the two groups, since the parents in the first group have had to deal with a grave condition for all of the child's life. If they have been relatively successful in meeting the life issues involved and the feelings engendered, the child and the parents will be relatively ready for the transition of school entry and the many adaptive tasks of the school years. In contrast, the parents in the second group may still be mourning their child's lost health and may still be caught up in life-threatening aspects or life issues that the illness creates for them and the child. In the face of the painful and relative newness of the illness or disability, they and the child must now meet the demanding new challenges of school entry and all that follows upon it.

For the school-aged child, growing up different takes its toll psychologically and socially: "Handicapped children want a chance to grow, to have freedom and fun, training and education, and to progress to the extent of their abilities with help from their family, school, and community" (Berns 1980). Their interests, goals, and concerns are the same as those of other children, and this is a particularly difficult time to be different from one's peers. The restrictions imposed by disability or chronic illness, such as limited mobility, pain and discomfort, arduous treatment, or parents' or teachers' well-intended but excessive efforts to protect the child from medical crises, can unduly inhibit her or his desired participation in the play and academic activities that are so important in sustaining relatedness, competence, self-esteem, and self-direction. Weitzman (1984) noted that the school provides "chronically ill children with numerous opportunities to address issues [of independence and social skills. It] is the logical setting in which overdependence can be diminished, negative social behaviors can be unlearned, and social conventions can be assimilated into the child's behavioral repertoire."

Despite the hazards of growing up different, a serious illness or disability does not rule out successful adaptation by the child and family. For professionals such as social workers, "there are many ways to help in the adaptive process, by being available and supportive, by anticipating, and by advocating for the needs of children with physical health problems" (Stein 1983). And families themselves develop successful adaptations through second-order changes and family transformation.

Second-Order Changes

Darling (1979) identified three types of long-term adaptive styles in families with a chronically ill or disabled child: the normalizing, crusading, and resignation styles. They are pertinent to family transformation and can incorporate the pertinent coping tasks identified by Strauss and Glaser (1975) in the previous section.

Darling believes that most successful parents adapt to the child's condition by creating a near-normal life for themselves and the child. This normalizing adaptation is possible, however, only where the needed medical and other services have been found. It can be thought of as embracing the cognitive, emotional, and social processes for second-order change. In the cognitive area, for example, parents can impart knowledge and accurate information about the illness or handicap to the child that will give him or her some sense of power over the condition. Through anticipatory guidance, rehearsal, and role play, they help the child learn how to talk about the condition with other children. Parents can also teach their child acceptable social behaviors, possibly through praise and developing opportunities for the child to experience success in appropriate activities.

In the emotional area, parents support each other in managing their chronic sadness and occasional anger or guilt feelings, so that they can freely encourage their child's optimal independence, relatedness, self-esteem and self-direction. Additionally, the child's condition often requires a disproportionate amount of emotional investment by the parents, as well as time and finances, leaving less for the other children, who may feel, and perhaps are, emotionally neglected by the parents. They may be expected by the parents to take on some of the burden of care; some may resent it and may feel guilty about their resentment. They may even worry that they will "catch" the illness or that they may pass it on to their own children in later years. The siblings of a developmentally disabled child may feel shame and stigma in their peer relations. The parents' acceptance of the negative feelings of their other children helps the siblings to know that their feelings are normal and understandable (Bloch and Margolis 1986).

In the social area, the family strenghtens or begins to build a network of supportive neighbors and friends; they seek and accept financial or child care help from relatives as needed. Loving grandparents can support and enhance the emotional resources of both child and parents and can help keep hope alive. They provide "an emotionally healthy, tension-free circle of security . . . for their children and their children's children" (Berns 1980). Normalizing parents try to establish a mutually helpful relationship with their child's school. They provide the teacher with the necessary information about the illness or disability and encourage the teacher to take a normalizing approach to the child consonant with the nature of the condition. They seek out organized youth groups that can provide important normalizing activities. They help their child to develop special abilities, interests, and skills as a substitute for athletic prowess that can make a difference in peers' perceptions and acceptance, and in attracting and keeping a special friend or chum (Weitzman 1984).

Families who adapt the normalizing style have a sense of control over their lives much as parents with healthy children do. They make second-order changes through these cognitive, emotional, and social processes and achieve a new family paradigm. The transformation involves reorganizing family roles, tasks, and so on, as described for adult illness. This adaptive achievement allows the needs of all family members to be met at an optimal level, despite the many demands made by the child's condition, and allows the illness or disability to be slowly integrated into the way the family views itself and its world.

In the crusading style, parents become assertive and effective advocates and lobbyists for services and programs for their children and themselves. Others write books and articles about their experiences. Many become active in parent groups, self-help groups, and national voluntary associations that address themselves to their child's particular handicap. These are empowering activities that give additional meaning to the parents' lives. Probably many normalizing parents incorporate elements of the crusading style into their new paradigm and its worldview.

Darling believes that only a few parents adopt the third style: resignation. These parents become fatalistic and resign themselves to their powerlessness. Many develop neurotic symptoms, and some may even fail to cope effectively and break down. In most instances these parents are socially isolated and do not become integrated into self-help and voluntary associations. Some may live in isolated rural areas, and some may have had family problems predating the child's condition. In our frame of reference these families are probably unable to make second-order changes in order to achieve a new family paradigm. They fail to integrate the illness or disability adaptively into their lives and worldview; the developmental needs of some or all family members are not met.

In some instances, however, such families may find their way to social work services. The practitioner in health care, schools, family agencies, or child welfare can help the family and the child to reach toward an improved adaptation by mobilizing and supporting their strengths rather than focusing on deficits; by teaching effective coping strategies; and by making connections to formal and informal supports. In particular, social work groups for patients, for parents, and for siblings are powerful supports.

Much remains to be done for chronically ill and handicapped children and their families. The needs include specialized services related to the specific condition and the generic services that all afflicted children require; better organization and coordination of services through the use of case managers; regionalized services; more extensive training for all health care disciplines in the skills of managing chronic conditions in children; and further research (Pless and Perrin 1985).

FATAL ILLNESS, DYING, AND DEATH: FAMILY TRANSFORMATIONS

> You would know the secret of death.
> But how shall you find it unless you
> seek it in the heart of life?
> —Kahlil Gibran (1923:90)

Death, like life itself, is an ecological process involving the interaction of biological, social, cultural, and psychological forces. Death that comes at its expected time, at the end of a long life, and death that comes in infancy, childhood, youth, or young and middle adulthood pose coping tasks of differing orders of difficulty for both the dying person and the bereaved. Whether the time of death is right or wrong will depend, in part, on the individual's age and roles, his or her self-concept and conception of death, the nature of the illness or other cause of death, the cultural context (particularly ethnic patterns, religion, and spirituality), and the presence or absence of supportive relationships.

For example, the needs and responses of a dying child or teenager (discussed in the next chapter) are different from those of adults. Differences also exist between dying in old age (discussed in chapter 13) and dying in young or middle adulthood, when one is likely to occupy many statuses and roles on which family functioning depends. The meaning of the loss to the dying person and to the family is apt to be different, the coping tasks are different, and the pain of grief may be of differing intensity. For the young adult at the threshold of life, embarking on new roles in the world of work and in a newly created family, dying means the loss of cherished hopes and plans. It means having to cope with rage, frustration, and disappointment. In middle adulthood, the dying adult faces the same issues and may also experience guilt about leaving her or his spouse, children, and even parents, with deep concern for how the family will manage. Frustration may also arise from thwarted efforts to achieve in one's work or with one's special talents (Pattison 1977b).

Stages of Dying

The widely known work of Kübler-Ross (1969) on the sequential stages of dying—denial, anger, bargaining, depression, and acceptance or resignation—freed many health care practitioners to be more open with the dying person, so that death could come with optimal dignity, humaneness, and a sense of closure to one's life and affairs. At first, professionals assumed that open communication as a right made it automatically desirable for every patient and family member to be aware of the terminal nature of the disease. That position has been tempered by the realization that not everyone wants to know the truth, and the positive expectations of some may be dashed by the truth, so that the power of hope is undermined. And denial in some others seems to serve important functions right to the end. The readiness of the patient or the family members to hear the truth, to want to hear it, and to deal with it must be carefully assessed.

Many health care professionals now believe that the shifts that occur are phasic, rather than that they occur in sequential stages. This is probably a more accurate view of the twists and turns, the overlaps, and the going forward and back observable in patients and families as they move through the period of living with dying. Glaser and Strauss (1968) conceived of death as a trajectory with temporal dimensions. The trajectory may be long, as in a chronic illness, and may or may not be punctuated by periods of remission followed by further deterioration. It may be relatively short, as in rapid downhill course, or it may cover only a few brief hours or days. Each dying person's trajectory has its own duration and tempo and its own element of certainty and ambiguity.

Pattison (1977a) suggested that different dying trajectories require different strategies on the part of patient, family, and professionals, and that they vary in their evocation of stress:

1.–*Certain death at a known time,* which provides the dying person, the family, and the social network with a relatively specific time frame in which to order their responses. Such situations, however painful, are generally easier to cope with than those in which there is ambiguity.

2.–*Certain death at an unknown time,* as in chronic illness where the living–dying interval may continue for several years. The family and the patient live constantly with dying and can best be helped with a focus on what is certain, that is, on the predictable daily issues of life.

3.–*Uncertain death, but a known time when the question will be resolved,* a trajectory likely to be pervaded by intense emotion on the part of all involved. There is an acute phase of uncertainty, as in "waiting for the pathology report after surgery, waiting to see if the organ transplant will work, waiting to see if the severely injured person will survive, waiting to see if the malformed infant will survive" (Pattison 1977a:306), followed by intense reactions when hopes are dashed.

4.–*Uncertain death and an unknown time when the question will be resolved,* in Pattison's opinion, appears to be the most difficult trajectory because of the double load of uncertainty. It creates a high level of anxiety that cannot be resolved and may therefore generate maladaptive efforts to deal with it. An example is the patient maintained on renal dialysis who lives with chronic uncertainty and "with the ever-present possibility of an untimely death" (Beard 1977:275).

We must add still another trajectory: *sudden, unexpected death.* In this instance, the family has been given little or no warning. The death of a loved one comes suddenly and unexpectedly, perhaps through accident, homicide, suicide (see chapter 12), heart attack, or stroke. The hospital emergency room (ER) is often the setting of such catastrophic situations, although these events occur also in hospital surgeries and intensive-care units. Because ER medical staff are involved with medical lifesaving procedures, they are not available to respond and care for the members of the family as they arrive in the ER. That becomes the task of the ER social worker or the intensive-care-unit social worker, where the patient may have been transferred only to die later (Germain 1984).

Families of homicide victims suffer particularly devastating emotions of despair and nihilism connected to a violent, "unacceptable death" (see chapter 12). Such feelings affect the grieving process, family relationships, and reintegration into a society, now perceived as relentlessly dangerous (Getzel and Masters 1985). Any sudden, unforseen death presents an excruciating burden of shock and grief and other emotions, unsoftened by a preparatory period of anticipatory grief as in the case of lingering illness.

When an illness reaches the terminal phase, the family and the adult patient together must manage a host of new issues, including anticipatory mourning and practical matters such as financial planning. For the fatally ill adult, the major coping tasks are to secure and receive permission to die from significant others if death is to be peaceful, and then voluntarily and gradually to let go of every person and possession held dear, finding completion and freedom. Permission to die is granted in open and honest interaction between the patient and the family members or other significant persons and reflects their mutual recognition of the reality and of the differing needs of each other. The patient will then be able to die without blaming herself or himself or others; family members and friends demonstrate their ability to go on living without blaming the dying person or threatening irremediable anguish. With permission thus gained, the individual can let go:

> He [sic] can begin to release his hold on life, then gently, with growing decisiveness, unlock the chains that bind his heart to all earthly treasures, to valued persons, and to every possession. He begins with the outer circle of important acquaintances and business associates now rarely seen, extending to close friends and family. . . . Internally, the dying individual agrees to allow the world to go on without him. (Kavanaugh 1979:418)

The coping tasks of family members include staying involved with the dying person while remaining separate from her or him; adapting to role changes; bearing the emotions of anticipatory grief; coming to terms with the reality of impending loss; and saying good-bye (Lebow 1976).

Out of concern about providing more humanized environments for the dying, which acute care settings are not organized to provide, the hospice concept was developed in England during the 1960s and spread to North America in the 1970s. The hospice provides interdisciplinary care to dying persons and their families. It includes both emotional support; control of symptoms such as nausea, weakness, and difficulties in breathing; and prevention of pain without sacrificing the patient's alertness. Hospice care may be provided in free-standing facilities, in specially designed inpatient facilities in hospitals, or only at home, with no central facility as backup (*HEW Secretary's Task Force on Hospice* 1978). As of 1987, there were about two thousand hospices, and two hundred of them provided outpatient and hospice care to children and their families.

The two greatest fears of many dying persons are the fear of pain and the fear of dying alone. Many fatally ill patients prefer to die at home in familiar surroundings and in the midst of their families. Many parents wish to have their terminally ill child die at home, where they can comfort and reassure the child. By providing the needed services that will enable such patients and their families to carry out the wish for care at home, hospice service in home care meets an important need. For the patient who can no longer remain at home, for whatever reason, or for the patient for whom home care is not appropriate, hospice inpatient care also meets an important need. In both instances, the quality of life for the dying person and for the family is enhanced. Most hospices provide social work counseling for the family and the patient.

For each family member, accepting the loss when death comes and relinquishing the ties will take time as they grieve and eventually come to terms with a world in which the loved one is no longer present. In addition, family members must cope with new statuses and roles, such as widow or widower, fatherless or motherless child, or childless parent, and with the social and financial consequences of the loss. To lose one's spouse in the early years of family life is particularly grievous—with young children still to be raised, plans and expectations of what might have been now never to be realized, together with the pervasive sense of loss of all that the relationship meant.

For the school-aged child, the loss of a parent evokes sadness and grief, anger at the perceived abandonment, and guilt about negative wishes or behaviors in the past. These feelings need to be handled wisely by the surviving parent despite her or his own grief. For the grandparents who have lost their adult child, grief is intense. The tragedy, shock, and unnaturalness of outliving one's child make them inconsolable. They are often left to grieve alone, while major supportive attention is given to the spouse and the children (Rando 1985).

For the family, death is a second-order development of major proportions, requiring profound second-order changes in family life. The family may have to reorganize family functions, roles, tasks, and relationships; to establish new connections to the social environment, including the world of work or school and social networks; and to modify their view of themselves and the world. These changes are extraordinarily difficult because the work of transformation goes on in a context of grief, followed by a period of mourning and resolution of grief. Mourning is helped by rituals such as sitting shivah in the Jewish religion, the Roman Catholic wake, and many other rites in differing cultures and societies. In most segments of Western society, mourning begins after initial shock and possible denial. It is a spontaneous process of reviewing the relationship to the dead person, calling up memories of the relationship and mulling them over in dreams and fantasies, and tolerating the feelings of sadness and yearning stimulated by the memories:

> Mourning is one of the most profound human experiences that it is possible to have. Even if it is not possible for an individual to conceptualize his [sic] own death, it remains undeniably true that a person can actually experience the death of another—and to feel the sense of emptiness, loss, fear and bewilderment. . . . The deep capacity to weep for the loss of a loved one and to continue to treasure the memory of that loss is one of our noblest human traits. (Shneidman 1988:179)

The literature, in general, has presumed that "normal" mourners experience an initial period of severe stress that gradually subsides. By the end of a year or so, the bereaved adult gradually accepts the loss and returns to a world in which the loved one is no longer present. It is at this point that some may begin to consider the possibility of a new relationship, a new attachment. However, recent studies dispute these views. The new evidence suggests that there is great individual variation in the length of "normal" mourning (Wortman and Silver 1989). The length appears to be associated with the type of death. Mourning a sudden, untimely, or accidental death of a loved one may take as long as four or more years to complete. The death of a child appears to be the most difficult, characterized by everlasting grief. Moreover not every mentally healthy bereaved person goes through the initial period of acute depression that is presumed to lead to a more balanced adaptation later. Some show psychological strength, or resilience, that enables them to manage their lives effectively from the outset, even though their sorrow is great. The conclusion being reached is that there is no one right way to grieve and no one correct length of mourning.

A more important indicator of troubled behavior than length of mourning is the degree to which prolonged grief interferes with other life tasks. For some, mourning goes awry and persists for years. Known as *pathological grief*, it interferes with work, relatedness, and other aspects of personal and family life; inhibits the needed second-order changes in the family; and can block the development and well-being of other family members. The periods of depression and feelings of apathy, numbness, inertia, and self-hatred that are often part of normal mourning are considered pathological if they are prolonged or very intense. It also appears that mourning is much more difficult when the relationship was a conflicted one.

The social network, social work bereavement groups for children and for the surviving spouse, and widow-to-widow programs are important sources of support during the long effort to recover from the loss and to work gradually toward the needed family transformation.

Dying in Childhood

Dying in infancy, childhood, and youth is a particularly anguished experience for the dying young person, the parents, and the siblings. Not only is it regarded as unfair and inappropriate, but the unique issues in losing a child make parental bereavement an overwhelming assault (Rando 1985). This is true at any age of parent and child, as outliving one's child is tragic, untimely, and unnatural: "No matter what the age of their child, [the parents] have lost their hopes, dreams, and expectations for that child, have lost parts of themselves and their future, and suffer the terrible ordeal of outliving their child." Parents who have other children must somehow continue to carry out the parental role that they are grieving for and having to relinquish. Additionally, "Parents must 'grow up with the loss.' It is not uncommon for them to mark [birthdays and] the times when the child 'would have' graduated, 'would have' gotten married. The grieving process is continual. . . . Their grief may continue longer and have more upsurges in it because parents demarcate their lives by events in the lives of their children, whether the children are alive or dead." (Rando 1985).

Rando observed further that because both parents are simultaneously confronted by the same overwhelming loss, the most therapeutic resource—the spouse, to whom one would usually turn for emotional support—is not fully available. Friends who are parents sometimes avoid the bereaved for various psychological reasons, so that social supports may not be available. Survival guilt is generated "because this is an era, in comparison to centuries past, when infant and child mortality is at the lowest rate ever, leaving parents unprepared to deal with the loss of their children" (Rando 1985). Grandparents suffer a double loss, for they grieve for their children's loss as well as their own. Self-help groups, such as Compassionate Friends, for parents whose child has died of any cause, and Candlelighters, specifically for parents of children who die of cancer, can be very helpful. Hospital social workers also offer parent support groups.

For the very young dying child, the fears of separation and abandonment are uppermost; hence the parents must try to assuage those fears in their child at a time when they are dealing with their own fears and grief. A preschooler has similar fears plus the fear of annihilation or mutilation through painful diagnostic and treatment procedures. The school-aged child possesses an intellectual comprehension of death to some extent, yet an endless future had seemed to stretch ahead for the pleasures of doing and achieving. Dying at this age is therefore an interference with the sense of self and an assault on relatedness, self-direction, and the sense of competence. Some believe that the older schoolchild knows intuitively when she or he is dying and is deeply worried about dying alone. Reassurance that she or he will not be alone is extremely important. While many terminally ill children die in hospitals, more and more families arrange for their child to die at home surrounded by the family, with parents holding her or his hand or holding her or him in their arms.

Throughout the mourning process and beyond, the work of integrating the loss of the child into the family paradigm goes on. The work can be hampered by a deteriorating relationship between the parents, even though their relationship was satisfying before the death. One or both parents may displace feelings of blame and anger on the other. They may misinterpret each other's grieving behaviors as hostile or uncaring. They may engage in incompatible grieving styles that keep them from comforting and supporting each other. Gender typing can impede the expression of grief in men or the expression of anger at the loss in women. If the mother is a homemaker, she encounters numerous reminders of the child continually, while the father, who is at the workplace, may be distracted by his job activities and may experience some relief.

The fear of losing another child may inhibit sexual intimacy, or the depression experienced by one partner may lead to sexual problems for both. The parents may be unable to respond to the questions, fears, and sadness of their other children, so that further tensions may develop. Families with these or preexisting difficulties are at risk of physical or emotional disorders, divorce, or disorganization. Social work services, if they are sought or if the family accepts referral, can help to prevent such outcomes by providing emotional and social support in the tasks of reorganization. (Rando, 1985, listed helpful suggestions to social workers who may be working with bereaved parents.)

Some families, given sufficient time and adequate personal and formal supports, slowly transcend what is likely to be a permanent sense of loss and anguish, and they turn their attention to meeting the needs of the surviving members. Physical activity; rituals and ceremonies, including anticipatory planning for anniversary phenomena each year; open communication and expression of feelings, including acceptance of the periodic ups and downs of individual members' emotions in response to the loss; flexibility in roles and tasks; sharing decision making; and making opportunities for recreation—these appear to be a few of the self-healing processes that families draw on for the work of reorganization. Eventually, they achieve a new view of themselves as a family in which the lost child is now present only in memory. They attain a new view of their relationship to the world, in which they may help other parents facing or experiencing loss, may work with a voluntary health association to raise funds for research, and the like.

ISOLATION AND LONELINESS

Most of the studies reviewed in this chapter comment on the salience of loneliness and on the significance of social supports. Loneliness is found in divorced parents with or without custody, among their children, and in the chronically ill, disabled, and bereaved. It is examined briefly in this concluding section of the chapter. "Loneliness seems to be such a painful, frightening experience that people will do practically everything to avoid it" (Fromm-Reichmann 1959:339). The psychiatrist Harry Stack Sullivan, himself a loner (Perry 1982), believed the "quintessential force" of loneliness to be so great as to defy description.

Weiss' (1973:29) distinction between social and emotional isolation is a useful assessment tool for social workers in planning with lonely children, youth, and adults, whether the loneliness is caused by divorce, death, or other environmental stressors. *Social* isolation and loneliness are produced by the absence of an accessible social network (due to moving, migration, aging, job loss, stigma or ostracism, or lack of relational skills). *Emotional* isolation and loneliness are produced by the absence of an emotional partner or the loss of a person to whom one was emotionally attached (as in the separation from, or the death of, one's child, parent, or spouse or lover):

> Except for the unusual "empty shell" marriage, the marital state tends to fend off the loneliness of emotional isolation irrespective of the extent to which the marriage is satisfying. It is for this reason that the loneliness of emotional isolation seems to be a risk almost peculiar to the not-yet-married and to those whose marriages have ended by death or divorce. It perhaps should be stressed that this does not mean that the married are necessarily happier than the unmarried; only that they are much less likely to be lonely. (Weiss 1973:94–95).

Either emotional or social isolation can lead to the painful, inexpressible experience of loneliness. One element of the loneliness of emotional isolation is restless anxiety, and elements of the loneliness of social isolation include feelings of intentional exclusion, marginality, and boredom (Weiss 1982). The person's situation interacts with personal characteristics (such as shyness and introversion), but little is known of how they jointly produce loneliness. Some shy people are not lonely, and some extroverted persons are. There are indications that poor people are more lonely, perhaps because of a restricted social life, but again this possibility has not been investigated. Loneliness is more widespread and intense in adolescence than in the older years, although conclusive evidence is lacking. It is not known if there is reduced vulnerability to loneliness as people age, but it has been noted that younger widowed and divorced persons are more likely to report being lonely than older widowed and divorced individuals (Weiss 1982).

Weiss suggested that there is a greater urgency in the response to the loneliness of emotional isolation. It may appear all at once in contrast to the loneliness of social isolation, where the reaction develops slowly as isolation continues. The "corroding effects" (Will 1959) of social isolation and loneliness can be relieved only by reconnecting to the former network or connecting to a new set of social ties in which one is valued and esteemed, and in which mutual interest and support are experienced by the members. In contrast, the loneliness of emotional isolation can be relieved only by the formation of another primary attachment following completion of the mourning process (Weiss 1973).

The difference is illustrated by the summertime plight of a school-aged child whose friends have all gone off to summer camp, leaving her or him without playmates (adapted from Weiss, 1973:148). The unwanted social isolation and loneliness will not be relieved by playing with the mother, at least not for long. The child will feel lonely until the playmates return. On the other hand, if a parent dies or is otherwise lost to a child, playmates cannot relieve the child's anguish of emotional isolation and loneliness. If the child does not have another attachment, or does not form one when mourning is completed, emotional isolation and loneliness will continue. Weiss believes that "Children need both friends to play with and parents to care for them, and adults need both a social network for social connectedness and an attachment figure for emotional relatedness. Positive network support does help the bereft adult avoid the pain of social isolation and loneliness that would otherwise be added to the excruciating emotional loneliness. Many who are widowed or divorced and without network support do suffer from both types of loneliness, which compound their anguish.

Weiss contended that some persons who isolate themselves from others seem to be rejecting in order not to be rejected, a reactive-defensive stance rather than an adaptive one of actively searching for others. Will observed about such isolates that "humans must develop ties with their fellows in order to become human, but in doing so frequently learn to fear their attachments, recognizing in them the possibilities of dreaded hurt and loss as well as support" (1959). Hence, in some instances, reducing the fears and thus relaxing the reactive-defensive stance may become a useful shared aim of the social worker and the individual.

Another few people, described as loners, appear to prefer a life unconnected to others. This is a different condition from the occasional need of most people for privacy or solitude. Those who are loners by choice seem to have a capacity to be alone, perhaps out of commitment to spiritual beliefs and needs, for example, or of wanting to live close to nature and to be solely dependent on it for all their needs. This capacity to be alone differentiates loners by choice from those who hunger for human attachments or social ties but are unable to form them. Thus, whether or not one feels a sense of isolation and loneliness may depend on how one defines the situation. The practitioner needs to make sure that the disconnected person really wants to be connected and is ready to participate fully in the decision to connect or reconnect. In considering connecting and reconnecting persons or families, much will depend also on their possessing or learning the social skills needed to enter into and maintain supportive relationships. That is, network support is not simply an environmental feature; more accurately, it is a person:environment or family:environment transaction.

Networks vary in their capacity to render support because they differ in their demands, constraints, and conflicts, as well as in the benefits that their relationships provide (Coyne and Holroyd 1982). Their behaviors may vary across cultures as well. The parents' social network can also influence the child's development for good or for ill, depending on the characteristics of the members and their interactions. Network influence is direct when the child has recurring contacts with network members. When such contacts are positive, they may provide the child with cognitive and social stimulation, opportunities to learn networking skills, support, and models of workers, friends, and good neighbors (Cochran and Brassard 1979).

Network influence is indirect when its influences on the parents bear on the child, such as providing emotional support and material assistance, encouraging positive parent–child interactions or discouraging negative ones, and serving as parental role models. Having a supportive social network promotes parental competence, self-confidence, and feelings of personal worth that can lead to growth-promoting parent–child relationships.

The next chapter returns to the progression of the life course and examines the impact of the adolescent years on the continued development of the child, the parents, and the family.

12

Family Transformations in Adolescence

After the preceding chapter's detour through several second-order developments, this chapter begins with a return to first-order developments. Puberty and adolescence are major expectable transitions, generally calling for moderate and usually nonconflicted changes in most families' organization and worldview. In a relatively small number of young persons, however, the biological and nonbiological transitions may precipitate or may be accompanied by one or more nonexpectable second-order developments, such as "coming out," substance abuse, unintended pregnancy, grave injury, suicide, chronic illness, or terminal illness. These require major family transformations and are addressed in this chapter. Similarly, the developmental transitions of the parents as they leave young adulthood and enter the middle years may represent first- or second-order developments inducing mild or major changes in the family. These, too, will be considered.

PUBERTY, ADOLESCENCE, AND THE ENVIRONMENT

Puberty and Entering the Teens

Puberty is a biological process that results in the transformation of the child into an adult. The process is crucial for the survival of the

351

species and momentous for the individual. Puberty begins in most girls at about the age of 10 or 10 1/2, and in most boys at about 12 years, and it takes about two years to complete. It involves hormone changes, which, in interaction with the hypothalamus (a part of the brain), lead to increased physical size and muscular development, the redistribution of body fat, changes in facial contour, the growth of internal sexual organs and external genitalia, and the appearance of secondary sex characteristics (the female breast and pubic and axillary hair; lowered pitch of the voice and facial hair in the male). Ovulation and menarche in females usually occur at about 12 1/2 years. Early cycles are frequently but not necessarily infertile. In males, the ability to ejaculate may occur as early as 12, but the production of mature sperm usually occurs later, at age 13 or 14.

The rapid physical and physiological changes in both sexes lead to youngsters' preoccupation with body image and physical appearance. Hamburg (1974) noted the different effects on girls and boys of early entry or late entry into puberty. Some individuals complete pubertal changes before other individuals have begun. This is a serious disadvantage and a life stressor for many late-developing boys. They continue to look like elementary-school boys at a time when it is important to look grown up. They have a four-year developmental lag as compared to the average girl of their age, and perhaps a two-year lag in relation to the average boy their age. They most likely do not know or believe that they will later catch up with their peers. Hence their self-esteem is low and their anxiety is high. Their compensatory behaviors may be maladaptive and may tend to continue even after puberty has been completed.

Early-maturing girls are at some disadvantage compared with late-maturing girls: they may be self-conscious and feel "different" from their classmates because of their physical development. As a result, they may lack poise and ease in social interactions. Petersen and Spiga (1982) concluded that while early puberty is better for boys, being on time is best for girls. For both boys and girls, how puberty and its changes are experienced varies according to the timing of the developmental changes, the preparation for them, the meaning attributed to them, individual vulnerabilities, and the nature of the environment, especially the family, the school, and the peer group. Hormonal treatment is now available for children who enter puberty prematurely and for those whose entry is abnormally delayed, thus preventing trauma. Either condition is usually defined medically as being out of average range by a year or more.

Entering the teens represents the acquisition of a new status and social identity as an adolescent—the badge of entry into teenage culture. This can be pleasing or stressful, or both, depending on how the individual responds to the need for new behaviors, standards, and role models. Drugs, drinking, and sexual activity now reach down to the junior high school, exerting new pressures on the "new" teenager to act wisely, often without preparation or support. Hamburg (1974) contended that youngsters entering the teens and for the next few years want and benefit from the guidance and support of their parents (especially the same-sex parent) in their efforts to cope effectively with this major life transition.

Adolescence

In contrast to puberty which is a biological process, adolescence is a cultural phenomenon, which, in effect, is an "artificial" postponement of adulthood. It is a comparatively recent invention that arose out of late-nineteenth-century changes in the economic and social structures of American society (Kett 1977). With industrialization and its growing need for universal education at higher and higher levels, and with the reformist definition of child labor as morally wrong, children's dependence on their parents began to lengthen. Gradually, the period between puberty and the time when the individual achieved economic and social independence as a young adult became formally defined and institutionalized as adolescence. For a time, it was assumed to end about age 18 at the completion of high school. Now, with many women and men completing college and graduate or professional education, often with continuing financial dependence on the parents, the period has lengthened to include the years from 19 to 22 and beyond—at least in the minds of some parents and psychologists, if not in the minds of the young themselves. As the columnist Ellen Goodman once observed, "Adolescence isn't a training ground for adulthood now. It is a holding pattern for aging youth."

In nonindustrial societies, after a childhood of practicing increasingly adultlike tasks, formal ceremonies and rituals mark the smooth transition of the pubescent child into the rights and responsibilities of adulthood. But in Western societies, the invention of adolescence segregates youths from the world of adults for a decade or more. Thus adolescents form a separate society, having its own subcultures of norms and values, dress codes, leisure activities, music, food, and language. Some adult activities are permitted the older adolescent, however, such as driving, voting, serving in the armed forces, and drinking alcohol. These lead to ambiguity and contradictions in the definition of adolescence. In the absence of alternative rituals, sex, drinking, and drug use become the rites of passage for many youths.

During the past century, psychoanalysts and others viewed adolescence as a time of personality disorganization, severe mood swings, bitter rebellion against the parents, and maladaptive behaviors. The emotional upheaval is said to derive from the upsurge of libidinal and aggressive drives, which weaken the defenses against earlier oedipal strivings. The turmoil is considered necessary, as it propels the youth toward separating from the parents, establishing her or his own identity, and becoming a mature healthy adult. These assumptions were based on generalizations made from studies of clinical and correctional populations.

Coexisting with this view is a normative position that youth is a period of physical development, psychological growth, and the development of life plans. It holds that most teenagers and their families cope successfully with the adaptive tasks of puberty and adolescence. These adaptive tasks in the life transition from childhood to adulthood include:

1. Creating an expanded self-concept (including a new body image), which draws on identifications with one's gender, family, and cultural group that began in childhood and became part of the self, and on past experiences and aspirations for the future. The self-concept may now expand to incorporate new feelings of pride, or it may contract with feelings of shame.
2. Increasing self-direction and independence from the parents while maintaining mutually satisfying relations with them.
3. Establishing same-sex and opposite-sex friendships, and preparing for adult commitment to a sexual partner.
4. Maintaining group affiliations and learning social interdependence.
5. Defining vocational interests and readying oneself for pursuing them.
6. Building on values absorbed from the parents, and developing one's own set of moral values, spirituality, and philosophy of life.

Despite occasional tensions and discontents, the successful completion of these tasks and the parents' reciprocal tasks lead to first-order changes in family roles, responsibilities, and relationships consonant with the adolescent's increasing maturity. This is not to deny that among some adolescents and their families, the adaptive tasks exceed the resources for coping with them. Rather, it is to say that social, emotional, and behavioral difficulties are neither inevitable nor universal in all adolescents and their families. For some, adolescence may pose stressful life issues, depending on genetic, familial, cultural, societal and other environmental factors. Before we consider these stressors, the next section considers what is known about normal adolescents.

STUDIES OF NORMAL ADOLESCENTS

Throughout the 1960s, 1970s, and 1980s, Offer and his colleagues studied what normal adolescents think and feel about themselves in psychological, social, familial, sexual, and coping areas (e.g., Offer, Ostrov, and Howard 1981; Offer and Offer 1975). *Normal* was defined not as psychological health, but as random groups of adolescents who were representative of a school's student body. Large samples were drawn of male, and later of female, high school students in the United States, and later in the United States, Australia, Ireland, and Israel. The researchers also compared younger teenagers (13 to 15 years of age) and older teenagers (16 to 18 years of age), as well as two different cohorts experiencing adolescence in two different decades and comparison groups of physically ill, delinquent, and disturbed youth.

The vast majority of those in the normal samples functioned well, maintained satisfying relations with peers and family, accepted the values of the larger society, and were not wracked by emotional upheaval. Most had adapted to their bodily changes and emerging sexuality without undue conflict and were making a relatively smooth transition to young adulthood. About 20 percent, however, reported feeling empty emotionally, being confused most of the time, or hearing strange noises. A major cohort difference was found in greater self-esteem among the 1960s normals than among those of the 1970s. The difference was attributed to experiences of growing up in the affluence of the 1950s versus growing up in the 1960s with the turmoil of the Vietnam war, Watergate, and economic distress.

The differences between normal and delinquent, disturbed, and physically ill adolescents were significant in many areas. Delinquent adolescents showed lower self-esteem and were much more hostile, unhappy, suspicious, empty, confused, ashamed, and pessimistic than the normals; their reports about their families were especially negative. The disturbed adolescents were significantly lower in self-esteem than the normals. Disturbed affect, pessimism, poor body image, and interpersonal difficulties were prominent. They felt as negatively toward their families as the delinquent youths did, but instead of rebellion and hostility, they reported deep self-doubt and emotional upheaval. They also felt sadder, lonelier, and more rejected by their parents than the delinquents did. The physically ill were similar to the normals in many ways. Where they differed was where they could be expected to differ. They expressed "sadness, loneliness, and negative feelings about their physical well-being, yet they retain a sense of optimism and commitment to values and family" (Offer, Ostrov, and Howard 1981:117–118). They felt they were a burden to their families, and they denied the importance of sexuality. The authors suggested that the latter attitude was an adaptive response, inasmuch as its opposite, yearning for the unattainable, would only bring on great pain and despair.

In the early 1980s, the researchers (Offer et al. 1988) studied 5,938 middle- and upper-class teenagers from the United States, Australia, Bangladesh, Hungary, Israel, Italy, Japan, Taiwan, Turkey, and West Germany. The findings were similar to those described for the normals in the earlier studies. The authors claimed to have found a "universal adolescent," based on agreement (75 percent or higher) across countries in the areas of positive familial relationships, vocational and educational goals, superior coping, satisfying social relationships, and, to a limited extent, individual values.*

Rutter (1979b) and Thomas and Chess (1984) also rejected the idea of adolescence as a time of emotional turmoil, maladaptation, or identity crisis:

> Most young people go through their teenage years without significant emotional or behavioral problems. It is true there are challenges to be met, adaptations to be made, and stresses to be coped with. However, these do not all arise at the same time and most adolescents deal with these issues without undue disturbance. (Rutter 1979b:86)

* A commentary at the end of the book by Harry C. Triandis, a cross-cultural psychologist, notes that a questionnaire limits responses, so "there is no opportunity to inquire about aspects of the subject's world that are specific to particular cultures." Moreover, all the subjects were literate, urban, middle-class, and exposed to the mass media. Thus they may have thought alike, but they may have been "diverging progressively from teenagers in their cultures who are less affluent. Without representative samples we cannot say much about a 'universal adolescent' " (Offer et al. 1988, 128).

Interviewing the white middle-class subjects in their New York City sample, Thomas and Chess (1984) found that for teenagers with a healthy childhood developmental course, the teen years were a challenging period of psychological growth. They entered adolescence with an optimal level of self-esteem, healthy behavioral patterns, positive relationships with family and peers, and effective coping resources. Others mastered the demands and expectations of adolescence but did so less smoothly. There were, perhaps, rebellious or negativistic, but without social or legal difficulties or evidence of psychopathology. For them, too, it was a positive and healthy developmental period with a successful outcome.

Among those who had suffered behavioral disorders in childhood, some found new coping resources as a consequence of maturation, environmental opportunities, and a supportive family situation that enabled them to master the earlier psychological problems. But among them were a small number in whom the new demands of adolescence were experienced as very stressful, exceeding their resources for coping with them. The result was a behavioral problem or the exacerbation of a previously existing disorder.

These studies are largely of white middle-class groups, except for the study by Rutter, (1979b) who reported on disadvantaged youth in Great Britain. Few studies of nonclinical populations of minority and poor adolescents are available. However, over a four-year period during the 1960s, Ladner (1971:77–108) studied 100 low-income, urban, black female children and adolescents in the United States. Despite the stressors of growing up black and female in a racist society, most of these youngsters showed adaptive strengths of self-esteem, awareness of the societal sources of their oppressive circumstances, resourcefulness, supportive kin and peer networks, and a generalized hope for improving their life chances through education that would ensure employment.

SOCIETAL ISSUES AFFECTING ADOLESCENTS

We have seen in earlier chapters that society itself has certain tasks and responsibilities in the support of all its families at points of transition in the life course. In the case of teenagers, however, American society has done little. Instead, we create and tolerate environmental conditions that adversely affect many of our youth. These include intense, pervasive sexual stimuli across all media formats;

high levels of violence in families, the streets, and the schools; militarism and the settlement of international political conflict by violence; readily available alcohol, illicit drugs, and guns; a steadily widening resource gap between impoverished and affluent families; and corruption in high places. These environmental conditions are societal issues and not psychological ones. If they exceed the coping resources of many teenagers today, the solution is not individual change but societal change.

Junior, Middle, and Senior High Schools

Junior high schools, consisting of the seventh, eighth, and ninth grades, were introduced in the 1930s as a means of putting together children who were similar biologically and intellectually and separating them from younger and older children. Concurrently with the biological changes of puberty, youngsters leave the elementary school and the security of a self-contained classroom and a single teacher. They enter the larger, more impersonal junior high school, where classes rotate, each with a different teacher and perhaps different students. Academic pressures increase, and there is an emphasis on achievement and an increased threat of failure. This setting is similar to the high school, so that what was expected to result in a smooth transition later simply displaced the transition downward by two years, increasing the stress on the 12- or 13-year-olds (Hamburg 1974).

As a means of reducing such stress, middle schools were introduced, offering the sixth, seventh, and eighth grades. Students then go on to junior or senior high schools. While larger than the elementary school, the middle school seeks to maintain personal relationships by the use of teaching teams and small units of students.

What was presented in chapter 10 concerning discriminatory practices in the elementary school applies also to the high school experiences of many minority adolescents. Unresponsiveness to cultural diversity, the prevalence of stereotypes, and lowered expectations based on color and/or language continue. Males, especially, are disproportionately represented in high school dropout rates, placement in non-college-bound tracks, school suspensions, and so on. Urban high schools are often old, poorly maintained, dilapidated, and vandalized. They are usually much too large, often with as many as five thousand students, and the result is extreme depersonalization, anonymity, and a prisonlike atmosphere. Even with systems of guards and ID cards, many schools are plagued by violence from outside.

They also suffer from inside violence because some students carry weapons to protect themselves while on the way to and from school and once inside as well. Drugs and drug dealers are easily accessible both inside and outside some schools.

In some suburban districts (and urban ones), parents, colleges, and employers complain that high schools no longer prepare students to meet successfully the demands of higher education or of the world of work. Researchers and academicians report a disturbing degree of illiteracy in one subject after another among the nation's teenagers. Enlightened school districts are initiating changes. Some high schools stimulate the aspirations of minority students through the participation of community experts in the life of the school. Some high schools collaborate with local colleges and universities to improve their teaching content and methods. Others interest local corporations in supporting high school enrichment programs to strengthen curricula and stimulate student motivation and interests. Many high schools offer community service programs, believing that helping others builds students' competence and self-esteem and provides important community roles for adolescents.

ADOLESCENT WORRIES

Most teenagers are apt to worry about their physical appearance and sexual attractiveness; their relationships with peers, including finding a romantic partner; their athletic prowess; their relationships with their parents; their academic performance, their future academic or vocational goals, and the financial means for achieving them; and the social pressures toward alcohol or illicit drug abuse and sexual activity.

Nuclear Dangers

Part of normal growing up in the 1970s and 1980s was coming to terms with the ever-present threat of nuclear annihilation by war, accidents involving nuclear energy plants, and life-threatening environmental contamination by both military and civilian nuclear activity. The remarkable emergence of freedom throughout Eastern Europe is in full sway. Assuming that these almost unbelievable events, together with Russia's *glasnost*, promise peaceful Soviet–U.S. relations, I have deleted content on research into the effects of the fear of nuclear war on children and youth. Despite the decreased likelihood of nuclear war, we may nevertheless need to consider the potential of the ongoing psychosocial consequences for children and youth of their having lived in fear of the earth's total destruction. For many adolescents, this meant a loss of the stability and the confidence in the parent generation that are crucial for developing values, ideals, commitments, and a philosophy that give meaning to life and death (Beardslee and Mack 1982). Other researchers and clinicians believed that nuclear fears contributed to the cynicism, disillusionment with family relationships, reckless behaviors, and immersion in sex, drugs, and alcohol observed among some adolescents.

Even as the threat of nuclear arms recedes, nuclear-related anxieties will continue, although it is not known if they will affect psychosocial development in the same way. For example, the growth of nuclear capacity in weapons and in energy production in some Asian and Middle Eastern countries remains a cause for concern about possible accidents, unintended errors, or irresponsible conduct in their development and use. The nuclear power industry in the developed countries has created continuing profound concern after the accidents at the Three-Mile Island (Pennsylvania) and Chernobyl (USSR) nuclear power plants, as well as the catastrophic gas leaks in the Union Carbide plant at Bhopal, India. The potential for such disasters, or worse, persists. Like the unsolved problems in nuclear waste disposal in all the developed countries, continuing nuclear accidents have potential for causing death, sickness, and genetic disorders to human beings and other species of life around the world.

L. F. Williams reminded us that the aging of many reactors poses serious problems:

> Retired reactors . . . must be cleaned up, dismantled, and buried, all in such a way as to keep their wastes from contaminating the soil and water for tens of thousands of years. At present, no country is prepared for this job, let alone ready to assume the staggering costs. These precautions also apply to old nuclear weapons, cruise missiles, submarines, and the low-level radioactive material used in scientific, medical, and industrial settings. (1987)

There are also some hopeful signs. A growing number of voluntary groups advocate alternate forms of energy, major cuts in military spending, and a return to supporting social and other domestic programs. Paradoxically, our best hope may lie in the growing worldwide interest in preventing the ecological collapse heralded by acid rain, climate changes, shortages of fresh water, accelerating rates of species extinction, depletion of the planet's rainforests, and the spreading destruction of the protective ozone layer. It is conceivable that cooperation among nations and peoples to save the planetary environment on which all life depends could transcend the economic and military competition that destroys human and other resources—particularly since this is an interest shared by youth around the world.

Sexual Orientation

Most, if not all, teenagers worry about who and what they are and will become. A significant element is one's sexual orientation. Moses and Hawkins (1982) distinguished between sexual orientation and sexual preference, which, together with gender identity and gender-role behavior, constitute one's sexual identity. Sexual orientation refers to 1) the *physical;* that is, one's past and present gender preference in sexual partners and sexual relationships; 2) the *affectional;* that is, one's past and present gender preference in primary emotional relationships; and 3) one's past and present gender preference in partners in sexual *fantasy.* These elements of sexual orientation exist on a continuum from exclusively homoerotic to exclusively heteroerotic. Being homoerotic does not imply a confused gender identity. Most gay and lesbian persons, like most heterosexual persons, have a gender identity that matches their sex.

Some persons may have no gender preference (bisexuality). Others may have a gender preference only in the physical activity, or only in emotional relationships, or only in fantasy, or in two or all three. The preference of some is realized, while others may experience life conditions in which their preference is not realizable, although their underlying sexual orientation is not affected. Also, the physical and the emotional components of the sexual orientation may not match. Various differences and similarities can be true of past preferences as well, and there may be differences or similarities between past and present preferences.

Probably many teenagers experience some initial confusion in sexual orientation. Some develop "crushes" on older same-sex peers or on same-sex adults whom they admire. Same-sex chumships and relationships, characteristic of late childhood and early teens, may give rise to homoerotic feelings. And some young teens may have had occasional homosexual experiences, actual or in fantasy, that may have been pleasurable or, instead, may have stimulated feelings of shame or guilt. None of these varied experiences necessarily reflect a homoerotic orientation, although they may. But they can lead the teenager to worry, "Is there something wrong with me?"

A small number of teens do become aware of their homoerotic orientation when dating begins. They find that dating the opposite sex is not enjoyable, and they are attracted instead to members of their own sex. This attraction may lead to concerns about their mental health, their gender identity, and the visibility of their difference, in the light of societal attitudes. For adolescents or others who are aware of but conflicted about being different, acknowledging their gay or lesbian orientation to themselves may be a painful struggle. Such acknowledgment to oneself and possible disclosure to others, known as *coming out,* is a long and difficult process. It may take place at any point in life, from the early teens to young, middle, and older adulthood. Indeed, many adults struggle against self-labeling and even marry and have children—perhaps to prove to themselves and others that they are heterosexual.

Moses and Hawkins (1982) specified four steps in coming out: 1) coming out to oneself; 2) identifying oneself to other gay people; 3) identifying oneself to heterosexual others, such as parents, other family members, and friends; and 4) going public at the work, school, community, and political levels.

1. *The self-labeling of gayness,* which seems to require one or two years to accept, means taking a step into a world of rejection, stigma, and isolation. For gay adolescents, the step is fraught with additional problems. Teenagers may not know quite what their homoerotic orientation means, but they do sense that they must not talk about it. Hence they are unlikely to obtain positive information or support, or to find positive role models, and may develop a distorted image of gay people and of themselves. Adolescence is the time when, regardless of one's sexual preference, one searches for a romantic partner and prepares for an adult commitment to a partner in living. These tasks are apt to be much more difficult for the gay teenager. And gay teenagers with physical disabilities face even more difficult tasks in a society that still discriminates against those with disabilities.

2. *Coming out to others.* The risks in this and the next two steps are very great for most teenagers, but they are included here in order to present the complete process as it may unfold among adults. Moses and Hawkins believe that the wisest course for teenagers is not to come out to others until they are of age—as painful as it is to pretend to be something one is not. Parents will be shocked and may react by punishing the teenager or by taking him or her to be "cured" or

"saved." Even in late adolescence or early adulthood, parental responses may be harshly negative. Similarly, the adolescent should be cautious about coming out to peers. They may subject her or him to severe ostracism, a painful experience to face without a supportive network. Adult gays can not be helpful to teenage gays because they are under age, and the probability of there being a teenage gay network is low.

Among adults, coming out to others is often less a matter of telling than it is of going to places where gay people are found and showing interest in persons of the same gender.

3. *Coming out to nongay persons.* Coming out to the wider social environment means communicating one's sexual preference and lifestyle to family members and friends (Lee, in press). The desired outcome is to have friendly relationships with both gay and nongay people. But such disclosures can be painful because of rejection or insincere acceptance by loved ones—generated mainly by negative societal attitudes. Rather than take this risk, an unknown number of gay men and lesbian women remain forever silent—also a painful state: "Being in the closet is depressing, exhausting, anxiety provoking, and time consuming. It necessitates continual efforts to dissemble . . . and produces anxiety over the prospect that one will be found out in spite of all that one can do" (Moses and Hawkins 1982:90).

Moses and Hawkins suggested that coming out to one's parents, especially, requires much thought and preparation—and in many instances, it may not be necessary or wise to tell them. In other instances, one or both parents do react positively, or at least they restore their positive relationship with their son or daughter after their initial shock, anger, hurt, and disappointment subside. For the gay or lesbian person, coming out to nongay friends may be less stressful than disclosing to parents because the risks are lower.

4. *Going public.* This step is the process of coming out publicly to all or most persons in one's life, taking political positions, and being part of the gay movement. Acknowledging one's homosexual orientation publicly and politically is an expression of courage and pride and may also reflect the presence of a strong supportive network.

A fifth step is identified by Lee as *self-acceptance and identity synthesis.* This refers to the attainment and continued strengthening of a positive, proactive self-concept as a gay person that is integrated with all other aspects of the self. She noted, "There is an externalization of the feelings of oppression . . . . a sense of settling down, being one's self, having a community of friends and chosen family, and a special committed loyal relationship" (in press).

ADOLESCENT HEALTH

The selected health-related problems in adolescence discussed in this chapter are death or disabling injuries incurred in accidents; suicide and homicide; chronic and terminal illnesses; alcohol and drug abuse; sexually transmitted diseases, including AIDS; and teen parenthood.

Adolescent Death by Accident, Suicide, and Homicide

Adolescence is a period of relatively good health as measured by illness and death rates. The death rate is substantially lower than in all other age groups except childhood, being 2.5 times the rate for children. The overall death rate in the United States dropped 20 percent from 1960 to 1978. Yet it grew by 11 percent for young people 15- to 24-years old. The death rate of young men is almost three times that of young women. Seventy-five percent of teenage deaths are caused by accidents (involving automobiles, motorcycles, and farm vehicles; swimming, diving, and other sports; fires, explosions, and firearms), homicide, and suicide. Teens represent two thirds of all accidental deaths (*Healthy People* 1979).

Fatal accidents in adolescence are attributed to errors in judgment, aggressiveness, and in some instances, ambivalence about wanting to live or die. Alcohol is implicated in about half of the fatal driving injuries. Teenagers also place themselves at greater risk while driving under the influence of marijuana and other drugs. Excessive speed is a factor in vehicular fatalities in almost half of those involving teenagers 15 to 19 years old (*Healthy People* 1979). Greater risk taking is present during adolescence than during other times of life. It may be a reflection of teenagers' normal striving for independence and exploration of novel experiences and situations. Recent studies provide evidence of the inability of many adolescents to evaluate risk realistically and the limited capacity among younger teenagers to understand the concept of probability. Other adolescents feel invulnerable and may hitchhike or refuse to wear helmets when riding motorcycles. Still others feel that the real risk lies in losing status with the peer group if one goes not submit to its pressure to engage in what adults define as risky behaviors (*Healthy People* 1979).

Suicide cuts across all age, racial, occupational, religious, and social groups. But the greater frequency with which it occurs in some groups suggests that social and cultural factors are significant. While the overall rate of suicide remains the same (it is the tenth leading cause of death in the United States), the rate has soared for adolescents and is the third most common cause of death in that group. For college students, it is the second most common cause. In 1970, the total suicide rate for the 15- to 19 year-old group was 5.9 per 100,000 (U.S.B.C. 1989:84, table 125). By 1986, the rate had jumped to 10.2. Since 1977, over 5,000 youths, aged 15 to 25, have killed themselves every year—about 20 percent of the total number of suicides. The actual numbers may be higher, as some suicides may be unrecognized or may be unreported because of the stigma or for religious or insurance reasons. The number of teenage attempts per year is estimated at 400,000.

Across all age groups, males comprise approximately three fourths of all who commit suicide, and white males account for 70 percent of that total. Males tend to use the deadliest weapons: firearms (over 50 percent) and hanging. Women used less lethal methods such as drugs and wrist slashing until recent years, when over half of the 15- to 24-year-old females who have killed themselves have used guns. In some urban areas, sharp increases in suicides among young black males have outdistanced the rates for white males in the same age group. This is a startling increase, since the overall suicide rate for blacks is traditionally about half that of whites. Blacks aged 15 to 24 now account for 26 percent of all black suicides, a greater proportion than that of whites in the same age group for all white suicides (A. Berman 1986).

The extent of suicide among other racial groups is not clear because in suicide statistics Hispanics, American Indians, and Asians and Pacific Islanders are subsumed under "Other." However, the suicide rate is believed to be high among new immigrants. And young American Indian males are killing themselves at a rate more than twice the average for their age group. The U.S. Indian Service states that the reasons include drug and alcohol abuse, economic distress, and unemployment. But tribal leaders believe that suicide, as one of the leading causes of death among native Americans ever since the development of reservations, reflects broad despair among Indian youth. On the Wind River Reservation, Wyoming, nine Indians aged 14 to 25 years killed themselves in a five-week period in 1985. A year later, eight Eskimos aged 17 to 29 killed themselves in a sixteen-month period in a village of 550 persons. During two months in 1988, six young people on the Warm Springs Reservation, Oregon (population 2,800), killed themselves, and sixteen others attempted suicide (Egan 1988).

Such suicide clusters also appear among white high school youth of both affluent and working-class families. Clusters are defined as three or more completed suicides closer together in time and space than would be expected by chance in a given community. The federal Centers for Disease Control reported in 1988 that about 5 percent of the five thousand teenage suicides a year are believed to be a part of clusters. Hearing about a suicide may induce adolescents already at risk to kill themselves, viewing the act as romantic or even heroic.

The trend toward increasing suicide among the young may be linked to:

1. *Environmental factors* such as the increased availability of fire-arms, changing family patterns, the declining influence of tradition-ally stabilizing institutions such as organized religion, the dissolution of a sense of community, rapidly changing social norms that aggra-vate the developmental tasks of adolescence, and the intensive pres-sures of competing for limited educational and employment opportu-nities.

2. *Personal factors* such as the loss of a parent, the loss of a family member to suicide in the past, a loss of self-esteem because of per-ceived failure or rejection, and the loss of a sense of security due to disorganized or abusive family situations, including sexual abuse (Pfeffer 1987). Nuclear anxieties may have contributed through creat-ing a sense of hopelessness.

According to Ryerson (1987), suicide-prone teenagers may show signs of feeling sad, hopeless, and worthless and may appear lethargic and withdrawn. But some may be verbally aggressive and physically assaultive and are apt to be viewed as being sullen or troublemakers rather than being suicidal. Suicidal adolescents often show less in-volvement with school and poor academic performance or under achievement. They may cut classes, be rebellious, and fail to prepare for classes. Those who do well academically tend to perceive their performance as inadequate, a perception that increases their despair. Suicidal adolescents may show changes in peer relationships and may become argumentative or disruptive with peers. They may give away treasured belongings. They report receiving little affection from their parents and little enjoyment from spending time with them. Berman (1986) speculated that this may be the reason why suicidal adolescents have deficient problem-solving skills and lack the needed personal resources for meeting the psychosocial demands of adoles-cence.

Youth who exhibit accident-prone or excessive risk-taking behav-iors, or who talk directly or indirectly about suicide, or who show sudden changes in patterns of school or familial functioning, are at high risk for suicide. Contrary to popular belief, those who make multiple attempts are at very high risk for a completed suicide. The suicidologist Berman (1986) believes that preventing teen suicides will require approaches that address vulnerabilities, impulsiveness, and the adolescent tendency to view suicide as the only possible solution. Many school social workers, as well as those in community mental health centers, offer suicide awareness and prevention programs. These may include training teachers in how to discuss the subject with pupils, to recognize the warning signs, to inform parents, and to refer suicidal students to knowledgeable staff members. Other social workers believe that it is also important to train teenage peers in recognizing warning signals and making referrals to staff, because a suicidal teenager is more apt to talk to peers than to parents or professionals.

Murder accounts for over 10 percent of all deaths among adolescents and young adults—just under 7 percent for whites but almost 30 percent for blacks in this age group (*Healthy People* 1979). While automobile accidents are more likely to occur among whites, young blacks of either sex are about five times as likely to be murdered. Among young black males 15 to 24 years of age, homicide is the second leading cause of death, and it is the leading cause of death for black males 25 to 44 years of age (Rice 1980). Most black homicides are related to drugs or alcohol (Gary 1980).

Disability and Chronic Illness in Adolescence

Although fatal accidents are the leading cause of death among adolescents, many accidents result in prolonged or permanent disability (including brain damage) in adolescents (and others). Superimposed on the developmental tasks, concerns, and interests of adolescents, disabling injuries cause severe biopsychosocial losses and require new behavior patterns. They represent particularly traumatic second-order developments for youths and their families.

Adams and Lindemann (1974) compared the medical data and life histories of two adolescents, 17- and 18-year-old males, who suffered similar severe spinal injuries and permanent paraplegia. Both young men no longer possessed the range of physical capacities taken for granted in human behavior. They had lost permanently the ability to walk, grasp and release, and many other sensorimotor functions. Despite their similarities, their responses to the physical, social, and psychological rehabilitation processes and those of their families were extremely different. One established a new and apparently quite satisfactory life for himself, while the other made little progress.

The latter regarded himself as sick and was regarded by his environment as sick. He therefore exhibited illness behaviors and expected to be cured. He was unable to come to terms with the real issue of being different, which requires a change in the self-concept, including a changed body image and changed feelings about oneself, one's world, and one's future. He clung inflexibly to his original vocational goal, no longer realizable, and was reinforced in this inflexibility by his family. Suggestions of more realistic aims by the treatment team were serious threats to his self-esteem, and he angrily rejected them, as did his family. Ten years later, despite all the efforts of the rehabilitative team, he remained seriously depressed, excessively dependent, and inactive.

The other teenager, after mourning his massive losses, gradually exhibited awareness and then acceptance of his difference. Despite recurring, severe medical problems and occasional depression, he developed a new self-concept and ways of adapting. He conceived and carried out new plans and new, realistic goals for the future. From the beginning, his family and friends accepted and supported his new self-concept, his changed expectations, and his independent orientation. He subsequently graduated from college and secured a position teaching in a high school.

Similarly, chronic illness is a difficult second-order development. It can undermine adolescent strivings and impose unwanted dependence on the parents and others. It may alienate peers insofar as the adolescent "differs" from the acceptable in appearance, diet, physical stamina, and activity levels. The illness may require a new body image and new feelings about oneself and one's future. It may make dating difficult or impossible or may induce feelings that the illness renders one unattractive as a potential romantic or sexual partner. Chronically ill adolescents face two dangers: "1) overstressing the limitations and potential interferences of the illness and succumbing to a sense of futility and despair, or 2) denying their realistic limitations, often setting themselves up for great disappointments when their unrealistic goals cannot be achieved" (Perrin and Gerrity 1984).

Failing to follow medical regimens and exacerbating the illness are another hazard. The teenager's opinion about regimens that might interfere with her or his lifestyle need to be listened to and each point addressed. Adolescents must be allowed to make decisions about their illness so they can gain some sense of mastery and control. The particular decisions should be appropriate to the individual's developmental level, and their range should be increased as the teenager continues to develop. Such self-care can help ready the adolescent to function as a competent adult with a chronic illness, even though it may lead to occasional errors or short-term marginal control. The process is more difficult for teenagers who have been chronically ill from early childhood and who have not been encouraged to strive for self-sufficiency. They are at risk of becoming dependent, unproductive, and unhappy adults (Coupey and Cohen 1984). Coupey and Cohen identified chronically ill adolescents who are in need of special counseling:

> Those with visible deformities that might interfere with the expression of their sexuality—for example, paraplegic adolescents, those with ostomies, amputations, or abnormal genitalia. The issues of physical sexual expression and reproductive capacity should be addressed during the adolescent years by an informed and sensitive counselor in order to correct misconceptions and avoid unrealistic expectations and later disappointments.

Teenagers with asthma, sickle cell disease, diabetes, scoliosis, or hemophilia, for example, go through the process of coming to terms with their new teenage bodies just as healthy teens do—wanting to be tall, slim, sexy, beautiful, and strong. Since some part of their body is already different, they often experience an intolerable blow to their idealized body image. Coupey and Cohen continued:

> It is bad enough to have scoliosis, but then to have to wear a body jacket that flattens your new, normal breasts and makes you look like a shapeless lump is difficult to accept. . . . We assume that the adolescent with scoliosis shares our concern over the progression of her deformity and possible future deterioration of her respiratory function and [we] fail to understand why she will not wear the corset as prescribed.

Terminal Illness in Adolescence

Typically, the older adolescent begins a lifelong process of developing a religious and/or philosophical position on the meaning of life and death that becomes the foundation for optimism about the future. The task of infusing the future with hope is more difficult now because of the increasing complexities and problems of modern life, and because of society's attitudes toward illness and death. What is it like, then, for a terminally ill adolescent to confront the imminence of his or her own death? Terminal cancer, while not common in adolescence, symbolizes the quintessence of the teenager's confrontation with an untimely death:

> The prospect of one's body killing one presents the patient with a most cruel paradox. It is this tragic quality that predominates or stifles the reactions of a majority of dying adolescent patients, their parents, and the caretaking staff. In our experience most dying adolescents deny their fate, while a more remarkable minority adjust best within the realistic context of their despair. (Schowalter 1977:195)

Schowalter believes that the young person's temperament shapes her or his illness behaviors—along with the type, extent, and rapidity of the disease process. Those teenagers who do not acknowledge that they are dying keep their thoughts and feelings vague. They defend equally against telling or being told about themselves. This reaction contrasts with the rage or the calm seen in those who either actively grapple with or passively submit to the idea of their death. While adolescent patients in general are inquisitive and demanding, teenage cancer victims are typically passive, probably because they know they have a fatal illness or because they have picked up cues that discourage questions, or both (Schowalter 1977).

Among teenagers who acknowledge that they are dying, the most common response is "Why me?"

> It is usually inconceivable to the patient that such an unspeakable horror as their cancer is not the fault of something or someone. . . . Self-blame [is] very common. Sexual fantasies or experiences, arguing with parents, getting bruised in fights, and poor physical hygiene have all been suspected by our patients as causing their malignancies (Schowalter 1977:196–197).

Schowalter added that if blame is missing, the patient must face the awful fact that his or her death makes no sense. Also, many fatally ill teens are haunted by the realization that they are dying before fulfillment. They not only mourn the loss of a future but lament that their time spent in growing up was wasted. And finally, being able to grasp the finality of death, teenage patients commonly express anticipatory mourning for the self and for those whom they will lose at death.

Substance Use and Abuse

The use of alcohol and illicit drugs becomes abuse when it interferes with an adolescent's social and psychological functioning. Substance abuse disrupts the family, leads to poor school performance and dropout, affects cognitive and social development adversely, and can lead to delinquency. It also has a potential for creating chronic illness and increases the risk of accidents, suicides, and homicides among teenagers. Some experts suggest that abuse is a symptom of severe emotional disorder and is a way of avoiding the pain of the emotional stress created by depression, emptiness, rage, and so on. Others believe that alcohol and illicit drug abuse are outcomes of complex transactions among biological, emotional, and such environmental factors as family, peers, school, and societal influences (including availability and easy access). In this view, substance abuse is a maladaptive effort to cope with the stressors that these systems and their interplay present. In turn, substance abuse creates new stressors.

Alcohol Use and Abuse

Although teenagers may drink less regularly than older persons, they tend to drink larger quantities and are more likely to become intoxicated. The latest statistics on alcohol use by youths 12 to 17 years old (National Institute on Drug Abuse—NIDA 1988a, 1988b) show that slightly over half that age group and 92 percent of high school seniors have used alcohol at least once. Among the 12- to 17-year-old group, 7.8 percent (during the prior four days) and 37 percent of the seniors (during the prior two weeks) had had five or more drinks at one sitting.

Cigarette Use

Sizable proportions of adolescents continue to establish cigarette habits. Cigarettes constitute the class of substance most frequently used on a daily basis by high school students. NIDA (1988b) suggested that almost a third of high school seniors apparently do not believe that cigarette smoking presents a serious health risk.

Illicit Drug Use and Abuse

The use of illicit drugs (alcohol and tobacco are legal substances) was virtually unknown among young persons until the 1960s. By the late 1970s, both experimental and frequent use of illicit drugs had spread to teenagers (*Healthy People* 1979). Except for alcohol and marijuana, the rates among youth were low compared to those among adults. Marijuana has been and continues to be the most widely used illicit drug in the United States. In one study, of the 12- to 17-year-old group, 23.6 percent had used the drug at least once, and 12 percent had used it in the prior thirty days. The corresponding figures for high school seniors were 36.3 percent and 21 percent. A strong relationship exists between current use of marijuana and the use of other drugs (NIDA 1988a).

NIDA (1988a) reported that 4.9 percent of the 12- to 17-year-old group have used cocaine at last once. But a sharp downturn in cocaine use by high school seniors occurred in 1987: 15.2 percent of high school seniors had used it at least once, whereas in 1985 the figure was 17.3 percent (NIDA 1988b). NIDA suggested that the decline in the rates occurred as youths began to perceive experimental and occasional use of cocaine as dangerous. However, high school dropouts were omitted from the coverage of alcohol and drug use among high school seniors and the 12- to 17-year-old group because they are not easily identifiable.

The use of *crack*, a low-priced, readily available, easily administered, highly addictive, free-based form of cocaine, apparently leveled off in 1987 to relatively low prevalence rates among high school seniors (5.6 percent). NIDA (1988b) cautioned, however, that crack use may be disproportionately located in the out-of-school youth relative to most other drugs.

Among 12- to 17-year-olds, in 1985, 9.2 percent used inhalants (gasoline, glue, amyl nitrites, etc.) at least once, 3.3 percent used hallucinogens (mainly LSD) at least once, and less than 0.5 percent used heroin at least once (NIDA 1988a). With respect to high school seniors, the illicit drugs having a major impact, along with marijuana, are the stimulants (mostly amphetamines). In 1987, 21.6 percent of the seniors had used stimulants at least once, and 12 percent had used them during the previous twelve months. Use is higher among females than among males. Next are the inhalants, used by 19 percent of the seniors at least once, followed by the hallucinogens and tranquilizers (11 percent) and opiates other than heroin and sedatives at 9 percent (NIDA 1988b).

Regular use of illicit drugs by adolescents leads to school dropout, unemployment, and street crime among all ethnic, racial, and economic groups (Fraser and Kohlert 1988). It is important to keep in mind, however, that among the 12- to 17-year-olds in 1985, 70.5 percent had never used any illicit drugs at any time in their lives, and 86.1 percent had not used any illicit drugs within the past month (NIDA 1988a). The findings of Thomas and Chess (1984) on adolescent drug use and those of NIDA appear to be congruent with the percentage of problem-free teenagers found by Offer and his colleagues. Nevertheless, even though the rates of current use of illicit drugs by high school seniors are also small (except for marijuana and the licit drug alcohol), they are not inconsequential. Just 1 percent of the nation's high school senior class of 1987 represented about twenty-six thousand individuals. The use of illicit drugs by high school and college students (and other young adults) remains greater in the United States than in any other industrialized nation (NIDA 1988b).

Newcomb and Bentler (1988) found that light alcohol or drug use (once a month or less) by adolescents at social gatherings does not lead to lasting negative effects. In fact, in later years such teenage users cannot be distinguished from those who had abstained. Heavy use (weekly use or more) by teenagers, however, is associated with serious personal, social, and economic problems in young adulthood whether or not the young person is still taking drugs.

Adolescent Sexual Activity

Sexual norms have changed drastically over the past several decades in the wake of social developments that led to more and earlier sexual activity in male and female teenagers. Estimates suggest that approximately 50 percent of those from 13 to 19 years of age have engaged in sexual intercourse (Gilchrist and Schinke 1983), with most initial activity occurring at the upper age range. Yet, like alcohol and drug use, sexual activity is a major threat to adolescent health. Sexually transmissible diseases such as syphilis, gonorrhea, and genital herpes are increasing among teenagers. In 1985 one out of four persons with gonorrhea or syphilis (25 percent) was between 10 and 19 years old. Those 15 to 24 years of age account for 75 percent of all cases of sexually transmitted diseases (except AIDS) *(AIDS and the Education of Our Children 1988).*

Sexually active teenagers (both heterosexual and gay) and those using drugs intravenously are at risk of contracting and transmitting AIDS. A 1989 study of 16,861 U.S. college students who had their blood tested as part of normal medical treatment found that 0.2 percent carried the virus that causes AIDS (Bacon 1989). If that rate were applied to all 12.5 million students, it could indicate that 25,000 college students may already have been infected with AIDS (Leary 1989). The incidence among students is slightly higher than the 0.14 percent for military recruits, and about half the 0.4 percent to 0.6 percent rate for the U.S. population as a whole. Out of the nineteen institutions across the country involved in the study, ten showed no cases, while five had rates of 0.4 percent or higher. The highest rate was 0.9 percent or 9 per 1,000.

Parents and schools share the responsibility for teaching teenagers about AIDS, how it is spread, and how risk of the disease can be avoided. Most adolescents do not know the basic facts: "A study of young people in San Francisco in 1986 revealed that 30 percent believed that AIDS could be cured if treated early. One third did not know that AIDS cannot be transmitted by merely touching someone who has AIDS or by using a friend's comb. In addition, a study of 860 Massachusetts adolescents aged 16 to 19 found that 22 percent did not know that AIDS can be transmitted by semen and 29 percent were unaware that it can be transmitted by vaginal secretions" *(AIDS and the Education of Our Children* 1988, p. 7). Knowledge does not always offer protection. In a survey of 458 University of Maryland students, 77 percent said they knew that condoms reduce the risk of AIDS, but only 30 percent reported increased use of condoms. Eighty-three percent of those males who said they were gay and sexually active also said they had made no changes in their sexual behaviors *(AIDS and the Education of Our Children* 1988).

However, using new data from the 1988 National Survey of Adolescent Males, Sonenstein, Pleck, and Ku reported:

> While sexual activity has risen, condom use, measured at last intercourse, also appears to have increased 176 percent during the same time period [1979–1988]. Conversely, reliance on ineffective methods of contraception or no methods at last intercourse has dropped 60 percent. The net result is that even though more teenage males are sexually active in 1988 than in 1979, proportionately fewer males may be at risk of the negative con-

sequences of unprotected sexual intercourse in 1988. This includes AIDS as well as unintended pregnancy and other sexually transmitted diseases. (1989:10)

More than half of sexually active teenage males reported using a condom at last intercourse. Sonenstein, Pleck, and Ku believe that the dramatic rise in condom use in 1986 and 1987 (condom sales as well, doubled in those years) was due to increased knowledge about and awareness of AIDS. The rates of utilization were significantly lower, however, among adolescent males who used drugs intravenously (IV) or whose partners were IV drug users, among those who had had sex with a prostitute, and among those who had had more than five sexual partners in the past year. These authors stated that efforts must be made to raise condom utilization rates for protection against AIDS. While less than 1 percent of AIDS cases involved adolescents, the authors cited research showing that prevalence was much greater among the 20- to 29-year-old group. The majority of these individuals had probably contracted the diseases during adolescence inasmuch as the average length of time between infection and onset is eight years.

Adolescent Pregnancy and Childbearing

More than one million American adolescents become pregnant each year. A little over 400,000 obtain abortions, about 470,000 give birth, and the rest miscarry (Hayes 1987). While teenage childbearing affects only a small percentage of adolescents each year (6 percent of the 12 to 19 age group), the cumulative numbers of adolescent parents and their children represent a major social problem. The human costs are high for the parents and their babies, and the social and economic costs affect society as a whole. Burt (1986) estimated that families begun by teenagers constitute 53 percent of all families receiving Aid to Families with Dependent Children (AFDC), food stamps, and Medicaid benefits. Babies of young mothers are at high medical risk of low birth weight, prematurity, mental retardation, and various physical disorders. If their mothers suffer from malnutrition, as many impoverished black teenagers do, the infants are at risk of physical and mental disorders and even death. They are also at the social risk of growing up in impoverished one-parent households.

Racial differences in sexual activity and unintended pregnancy rates have long existed, but premarital birthrates among white teenagers are rising, while the rates among blacks are declining. However, the rates are still higher among the latter (Moore, Simms, and Betsey 1986). Teenage mothers are at social risk of disrupted schooling, dropout, repeated pregnancies, limited employment prospects, and poverty. Adolescent mothers are also at medical risk because sexual intercourse, pregnancy, and childbirth in very young mothers are positively correlated with cervical cancer and with uterine disease requiring hysterectomy. Compared with older groups, young teenagers suffer a higher incidence of anemia, toxemia, labor complications, and maternal and infant death (Gilchrist and Schinke 1983). Black teenage mothers who are poor may not obtain prenatal care or may seek it late in the pregnancy.

The rates of adolescent pregnancy, abortion, and childbearing are higher in the United States than in other industrialized nations, although the age of beginning sexual activity and the rates of frequency are comparable. In 1987, the Alan Gutmacher Institute calculated the number of pregnancies and births for each 1,000 teenagers 15 to 19 years old in major Western countries as follows: USA—96 pregnancies, 54 births; England and Wales—45 pregnancies, 31 births; Canada—44 pregnancies, 28 births; France—43 pregnancies, 25 births; Sweden—35 pregnancies, 16 births; and The Netherlands—14 pregnancies, 9 births. The report concluded that the increasing availability of contraception and sex education had helped reduce the rates in other Western countries. The contrast was even greater for girls under age 15: "The USA rate, at five births per 1,000 girls of comparable age, is four times greater than that of Canada, the only other country with as many as one birth per 1,000 girls under age 15" (Hayes 1987:16).

Canadian policy and programs are instructive. Henshaw and Jones (1988) reported four major differences from the United States that appear to contribute to lower rates of unintended pregnancy: 1) Canada's lower economic barriers to contraceptive services; 2) the provision in family planning clinics of up to one and one-half hours of individual counseling on sexuality and sexual relationships for women when they become sexually active (with an emphasis on avoiding unintended pregnancy), and how to use a particular contraceptive method; 3) encouragement to use oral contraception as the most effective reversible method, although others are available; and 4) the referral of high school students for contraceptive services by school nurses placed by public health units in most public schools and many Catholic schools. The clinics also seek to educate the public about contraception and reproductive health. As a consequence of these differences, Canadians appear to be more effective users of contraception than are Americans and therefore have lower rates of unintended pregnancy and abortion.

Despite their extent, family-planning services in the United States are not easily available and accessible to young low-income teenagers. Contraceptives are difficult for young female adolescents to use, especially over the long run. Embarrassment in discussing them with the partner and in using them, together with lack of accurate information about pregnancy risk, interferes. For teenagers living in poverty, accurate information is harder to come by than for middle-class adolescents (Moore, Simms, and Betsey 1986). Public opinion about what needs to be done is not unanimous. Hence, a rational policy has been difficult to establish.

Also: "Sex saturates American life—in television programs, movies and advertisements—yet the media generally fail to communicate responsible attitudes toward sex, with birth control remaining a taboo subject. In addition, a deep-seated ambivalence toward sexuality has prevented Americans from responding to the problems of unintended pregnancy as rationally as have other Western nations" (Westhoff 1987).

Despite group and individual differences among teenagers, the National Research Council's Panel on Adolescent Pregnancy and Child Bearing (NRC Panel) observed:

For every young person, the pathway from sexual initiation to parenthood involves a sequence of choices: whether to begin having intercourse; whether to continue sexual activity; whether to use contraception and, if so, what method to use; if a pregnancy occurs, whether to seek an abortion or carry the pregnancy to term and give birth; whether to marry, if that is an option; and, if a child is born outside marriage, whether to relinquish it for adoption or raise it as a single parent. Whether consciously or unconsciously, actively or passively, all adolescents make choices about their sexual and fertility behavior. (Hayes 1987:27)

Teens themselves tell researchers and pollsters that peer pressure is the principal reason for opting to begin and then to continue sexual activity. In respect to the third choice, 60 percent of sexually active teenage girls reported that they did not use any contraception on a consistent basis, and almost 40 percent of young women and men reported that they never used any birth control at all. Most said that they did not intend to and did not believe that they would become pregnant.

The NRC Panel (Hayes 1987) found that two very different beliefs have existed in the United States over the years: 1) unwanted pregnancy and childbearing are due to a lack of individual responsibility, maturity, knowledge, and values, and 2) they are the result of pervasive problems associated with poverty, including limited education and employment opportunities and the likelihood of growing up in a fatherless family that is poor. The panel came down on the side of policy efforts to eliminate poverty, strengthen family ties, and enhance youths' perceptions of their future.

With respect to perceptions of the future, Moore, Simms, and Betsey (1986) found from their review of the research that youths with high educational aspirations are less likely to engage in sexual activity and to become parents. Black and white Americans hold equally high educational aspirations, but blacks are more apt than whites to drop out of school (for reasons shown in chapter 10 and earlier in this chapter). Those who drop out are more likely to become pregnant. The need, then, is to help young black people to remain in school and to achieve their educational goals.

The NRC Panel's report stated that the highest priority must be given to preventing unintended pregnancy among teenagers. For those who will nevertheless experience unwanted and untimely pregnancy, and who choose to raise their children, supports and services must be available to ensure the children's healthy development. Also, the panel stated that alternatives to childbearing and child rearing should be available. The report noted that abortion is a legal option for all women including teenagers, but it acknowledged that abortion is a highly controversial issue and is considered inhumane and/or morally reprehensible by many people in our society.

Adoption is also an option for those who choose to continue their pregnancy but do not wish to raise their child. However, adoptive parents are often difficult to find for minority children and children with disabilities or serious illnesses, and public policy usually does not approve low-income applicants for adoption or provide subsidy payments to them. Among the more than one million teenage girls who become pregnant each year, only about 7 percent relinquish their infants for adoption. Consistently, studies show the negative psychological consequences of the relinquishment decision. While some mothers do experience long-term grief and other adverse effects, the studies are flawed by the self-selection of the subjects, and by the lack of comparison groups of adolescent mothers who have opted for parenting. A recent, more careful study surveyed 146 adolescent mothers who had rejected abortion and had chosen adoption for their children and a control group of 123 mothers who had parented their children (McLaughlin et al. 1988). Those who had relinquished their children were found to be more likely "to complete vocational training, delay marriage, avoid a rapid subsequent pregnancy, be employed after the births, and live in higher income households" than the parenting mothers. "On several measures of self-esteem, satisfaction with life, and satisfaction with the decision, however, there were few differences between the two groups."

This was a surprising finding, given the widely held assumption that the psychosocial consequences of relinquishment are more severe than those of parenting. McLaughlin et al. concluded that there are no significant negative effects on teenage mothers who relinquish their children when they are compared with those who parent their children. The authors cautioned, however, that their findings cannot be generalized to all pregnant adolescents because 1) the subjects were clients of a pregnancy counseling service; 2) more than 80 percent were white, reflecting the racial composition of the area; and 3) the service was affiliated with an adoption agency and was therefore apt to attract adolescents who wished to relinquish their babies. These limitations, however, do not affect the conclusion regarding the relative well-being of both groups.

An unfortunate omission in the literature, and therefore one that probably exists in practice and research as well, is attention to the sexual developmental needs of adolescents in foster care or of physically or mentally disabled adolescents in institutional care. Although undocumented, there are strong indications that teenage child welfare clients are at high risk for early, unintended pregnancy. Many are in foster care because they are victims of sexual abuse, and many are from groups that have high rates of early sexual activity and low contraceptive use. Most face difficult obstacles to obtaining sexual guidance and counseling, including access to contraception. Foster parents, group home and institutional staffs, and child welfare workers in protective services have no clearly defined responsibility, legal right, roles, or training in these tasks (Polit, White, and Morton 1987).

Adolescent Fathers

Early studies (e.g., Ladner 1971; Stack 1974) found that the young fathers were usually unable to offer financial help to their partners and babies because of unemployment. But most acknowledged paternity and provided emotional support during the pregnancy. Following the birth, many couples continued their relationships. Some fathers visited regularly, and others lived with the mother and the infant. More recently, Sander and Rosen (1987) cited studies showing that "an adolescent father's involvement in his partner's pregnancy increases the young mother's sense of confidence in her nurturing skills, heightens her sense of security after delivery and raises the father's self-esteem."

McCluskey, Killarney, and Papini (1983) found a tendency for teen parents to marry within the first two years following the birth, usually because the father now had a job. If marriage did not occur within those two years, it was less likely to occur at all. The researchers also reported that the reactions of teenage fathers to pregnancy and birth are similar to those of older fathers when economic and social factors are not overwhelming. When compared to controls, teenage fathers are psychologically normal. However, it is not yet known if teenage fathers influence their children's development and, if they do, whether this influence is similar to the influence of older, married fathers in their children's development—especially that of their sons.

Brown (1983) studied 33 expectant black teenage couples whose pregnancies were unintended. The young women were 12 to 17 years old and had completed 9 to 10 median years of schooling. The young men were 16 to 21 years old and completed 11 to 12 median years of schooling. At the time of the interview 20 of the 33 expectant fathers were unemployed. Nearly two thirds of the young women and half of the young men were 13 to 14 years old when they first had sexual intercourse. Most knew that intercourse could result in pregnancy, but few knew the more effective methods of contraception. Most couples perceived their relationship as being based on love, and they wanted to marry. Brown concluded that services should be provided to both expectant parents. Both should be involved in decision making regarding the pregnancy, methods of contraception, and child rearing. Relationship counseling and employment counseling are also essential.

All adolescent males, including fathers, have been seriously neglected by sex education programs and family-planning services. The NRC Panel (Hayes 1987) underscored the need to include teenage males in the concept of the at-risk population. Unwanted childbearing is not a problem only of teenage girls. Boys' attitudes, motivations, and behaviors are as central to the problem as those of girls. Shapiro noted that, contrary to widespread assumptions, not many fathers or mothers talk with their sons about premarital sexual activity, nor do they communicate values that counteract the influence of the media and the erroneous information imparted by peers. As a result, adolescent males need accurate information about the "use of birth control, avoidance of exploitation, respect for the relationship, protection and checkups against sexually transmitted diseases, and consideration for one's sexual partner" (1981:14). Shapiro advocated sex education that includes values and ethical guides, communication skills, decision-making skills, and knowledge about sexuality, parenting, and family life.

Increasingly, schools across the country are providing sex education, but often as an elective. Many programs focus on reproductive information and do not include the content recommended by Shapiro. Few community agencies such as family-planning services and health care services reach out to adolescent males, and few have male staff members.

PARENTS' DEVELOPMENT DURING THEIR CHILD'S ADOLESCENT YEARS

The focus in this section is on parents in their 30s and 40s. Some parents are younger, having become parents when they themselves were adolescents, and many more are older, depending on their age at the birth of the child who is now adolescent. Adult development from age 50 on is considered in the next chapter.

We will assume that the 1990 cohort of parents of adolescents was born in the early 1950s. As part of the baby boom generation, they were young children in the mid to late 1950s and finished high school in the late 1960s. Some went on to college or technical schools, others learned a trade, and still others performed skilled or unskilled work in the tight job market of the early 1970s. As adolescents, the cohort experienced the social changes of the early 1960s, including the continued struggles for civil rights; the assassinations of President John Kennedy, Martin Luther King, Jr., and Robert Kennedy; the rise of the counterculture; the Vietnam war; the spread of drug use; the women's movement; the availability of the pill—and, in 1973, legalized abortion; and Watergate.

In addition, the low-income and minority segments of the cohort saw the resource gap between them and the middle class widen still further. The cohort, in general, had smaller families than those before them. Many more mothers in this cohort entered the world of work than ever before, and many more parents in this cohort divorced each other than ever before. Thus, like cohorts before them, they too created social changes that then shaped family life and the childhood and adolescence of their offspring.

Their children's teenage years are busy ones for most parents, filled with demands of their work or careers, keeping up the household, perhaps managing the needs of younger children, maintaining ties to extended-family members and friends, and participating in community affairs, including religious affiliation, the children's schools, other voluntary associations, and recreation. Except for those pertaining to children, these activities are also pursued by childless adults. Such activities contribute to the parents' ongoing psychosocial development. Many community roles give rise to first-order developments that are experienced by the parents as challenges leading to growth and lending a sense of continuity, stability, and definition to their lives.

The first-order developments of adolescence require the parents' recognition of their adolescent's growing intellectual capacity and their acceptance of the developmental importance of independent strivings, peer friendships, dating, and activities away from the family. They must gradually relinquish the kind of parental control exerted during childhood and must rely more on discussion and mutuality in establishing expectations for conduct. The occasional tensions created by defiance or arguments over peer norms and the negative feelings they generate are apt to subside gradually through patient negotiation and compromise, depending on the parents' ability to distinguish the important (the dangerous and socially unacceptable) from the insignificant. Even if the tensions spark occasional rebellion, parents and teenager will survive the struggles as long as the parents continue to show that they love their child and really care. Such first-order changes are easier for some parents and their teenagers than for others. The outcomes depend on personalities and culture, the past history of the parent–child relationship, the support of each parent by the other whether they are living together or apart, financial and network resources, and the nature of teenage norms and patterns in the particular school or community setting.

In a classical social work paper, Scherz (1967) identified the tensions that arise in some families from the tandem development of teenager and parents. These tensions have the potential to become second-order life issues, occurring in the realms of 1) sexuality;

2) education and vocation; 3) values; and 4) emotional separateness and connectedness:

1. Parents may be apprehensive about what middle age and the menopause will mean in terms of their own sexuality—such as loss of sexual vigor and activity—just at the time the adolescent son or daughter exhibits a budding sexuality and attractiveness: "Parents who have not clearly established their sexual identity or are in severe conflict about it . . . may unconsciously inhibit or inappropriately encourage the adolescent's sexual strivings" (Scherz 1967).

2. One or both parents may be experiencing stress in their work. Uneasily, they may recognize that their present level of achievement is as far as they will advance in their work. Or the mother may now be preparing herself for reentry or first-time entry into the world of work but may meet discouraging rejections because of age or lack of recent experience. Or she may be deeply engaged in developing new skills by returning to school. These and other work-related stresses can occur just as the teenager is making future vocational plans, or is already working and anticipating success, or is in college preparing for a professional career. If the parents are especially unhappy about their own work, they may subtly communicate that the child should not exceed the parents' own vocational achievements, and out of fear of competition the teenager may settle for less than her or his potential or may fail altogether. Unconsciously, some parents may seek to experience success through the child, defining her or his vocational goals and directing the educational process through which the goals are to be reached. This pressure denigrates the teenager's own vocational interests and deprives her or him of self-direction.

3. Scherz believed that a clash in the values of adolescent and parent is inevitable because of the adolescent's need to establish his or her own values (contrary to Offer's research reviewed earlier in this chapter). It is common, of course, for periodic tensions to arise between parental and peer norms of conduct that may stimulate adolescent negativism. If the parents retaliate, the conflict may escalate, and the relationship may deteriorate. In their longitudinal studies, Thomas and Chess found:

> Disputes arose over many issues—dress, hairstyle, curfew rules, tidiness in the home, manners, handling of money, school functioning, sexual behavior, and the use of alcohol and drugs. In the great majority of cases, these conflicts were resolved without disruption of the basic stable positive relationship between

youngster and parents. Often it was a matter of an agreement to disagree. (1984:242)

4. The issue of achieving separation while remaining emotionally connected presents particularly difficult interlocking life tasks for parents and adolescent. Probably, in most families, some ambivalence occasionally arises in the parent–adolescent relationship, generated by the conflict between letting go and holding on. Most parents are pleased to see their child growing toward maturity and independence. At the same time, they fear the coming "loss" that the independence will ultimately create for them, even as they look forward to regained freedom from child rearing. In a parallel way, teenagers are eager to be accepted as near-adults, yet they are also fearful of the responsibilities of adulthood. Also, most teenagers need or want from their parents closeness and help while simultaneously struggling against both needs. In general, families manage these ambivalences, as well as the hostile feelings they can produce, as some of the expectable ups and downs of living. The issue is experienced as part of the first-order development that adolescence presents and to which the family responds gradually, and more-or-less smoothly, with first-order changes. By the end of adolescence, ideally, the child becomes "an independent adult, connected by affectional ties to parents who have grown closer to each other" (Scherz 1967). He or she is ready for the challenges of work and love, and perhaps of starting a new family.

However, if the parents have not worked out their own separation issues or have not created a new balance in their own relationship, they may infantilize the adolescent, keeping her or him overly dependent and close. Or they may detach their teenager from the family prematurely. Such expulsion often underlies the phenomenon of runaway and throwaway youth. Runaway youth are defined as children from 10 through 17 who leave home without permission, are in need of services, and are without shelter. Throwaway youth are those "pushed out of their families when they would not otherwise have chosen to leave" or "because their parents have subjected them to intolerable levels of abuse and neglect" (Levine, Metzendorf, and VanBoskirk 1986).

FAMILY TRANSFORMATIONS IN ADOLESCENCE

This concluding section describes some changes in family organization required by the second-order, nonexpectable, and often sudden developments during adolescence described in earlier sections: homosexual orientation; teenage deaths caused by accident, suicide, and homicide; adolescent disability and chronic and fatal illness; substance abuse; and adolescent pregnancy and childbearing.

Sexual Orientation

In a homophobic society, an adolescent's disclosure of a homosexual orientation is usually a second-order, nonexpectable development in the family. When an adolescent comes out to the parents, or when the parents become aware indirectly of their son's or daughter's homoerotic orientation—whether adolescent or young adult—their responses are likely to include shock, disbelief, sorrow, anger, and fear of a difficult life for their child because of societal attitudes. They may be frightened by the spector of AIDS and their child's vulnerability. They may cling to the hope that it is a passing phase, or they may rush the child off to be "cured," not understanding that sexual orientation is not a matter of choice. They may wonder if they are at fault and may feel ashamed. They may hide themselves in their own "closet," fearing the questions or suspicions of their friends and relatives. The family's deeply held view of itself and its world can be shattered.

For the family to continue its development, second-order changes will be required, and a new view of the adolescent, the family, and a now threatening environment must be constructed. Meanwhile, family members are likely to be in a state of acute stress and will tend to rely on customary behaviors. These only heighten their confusion, add to the tension, and block communication. At the point at which the crisis becomes unbearable, some families do begin a process of self-healing. They grieve the lost aspirations linked to their heterosexual image of the child, including dreams of a wedding and the expectation of grandchildren. They seek knowledge from books and articles and from their child to help them move beyond the myths, stereotypes, fears, and homophobia engulfing them. They develop new expectations and new modes of communication, which can be difficult if, for example, one parent or some other family member "must not be told." The process, if successful, culminates in the family's reconstruction of its reality, through which they restructure their belief system, reintegrate the child into the family, *and* accept her or his lover as well.

In a sense, the family processes parallel the child's coming-out processes, including initial negative responses and denial of the reality, followed by gradual acknowledgment and beginning acceptance. But some families do not move beyond the initial negative response, and they reject their child totally. They institute rigid controls over their feelings, communications, and actions, restricting their own continued growth and preventing the integration that second-order changes could produce. Other families may seek and accept professional help in achieving the family transformation. Social agencies, whose staffs include gay social workers and/or nongay social workers who have dealt with their homophobia successfully, can be helpful to gay and lesbian adolescents or young adults and their parents in working on acceptance and second-order changes.

Supportive self-help groups for the parents of gay men and lesbian women are growing across the country, such as Parents of Gays and the Federation of Parents and Friends of Lesbians and Gays (P-FLAG). These can be helpful to parents as sources of information, emotional support to ease the stress, and help in dealing with environmental hostility and in managing negative feelings.

Sudden Death of an Adolescent

All that was said in chapter 11 about the impact of the fatal illness and death of a young or school-aged child on her or his bereaved parents and siblings applies to the loss of a teenage child as well. The excruciatingly difficult, sorrowful tasks of mourning and of creating a new family paradigm are the same. They are especially poignant for the parents of teenagers, who have glimpsed the beginning realization of the potential in their child and of what she or he was becoming.

In contrast to fatal illness, deaths by accident, suicide, or homicide occur suddenly and without warning. Parents and siblings have no opportunity for the emotional preparation and anticipatory mourning that are possible in fatal illness. This lack of opportunity aggravates the stress of loss to an all but intolerable degree, and it prolongs the mourning process, perhaps for years. Some parents of teenagers who die in accidents find comfort in their religious faith, but some who had been religious feel angry and bitter because their child was not protected by their God. In their anguish, they may ruminate for a very long time about what they might have done or should have done to prevent the accident. Social work services in the hospital or in community agencies, including bereavement groups for parents and siblings, are helpful to families in the long and hard tasks of transforming and integrating the family paradigm in the face of this overwhelming loss.

For the survivors of a completed suicide, especially the parents of an adolescent, grief may remain unresolved. Mourning may be difficult and prolonged because of irrational self-blame. Parents and siblings, as well as the teenager's friends and the school personnel, often feel that they should have been aware that something was wrong so that they could have prevented the death. Some may believe that their acts or failures to act were responsible for the suicide.

Similar feelings to those of the parents of accident and suicide victims are experienced by the parents of an adolescent who is the victim of homicide. But in addition, those parents suffer intractable grief, devastating rage, feelings of impotence, and alienation from society itself: "One common but dangerous reaction is self-blame; another is to see society as utterly anarchic and menacing" (Getzel and Masters 1985:8). The family may be preoccupied with thoughts of vengeance and retribution and may move only slowly to a concern about justice. However, when the assailant is apprehended, brought to trial, and sentenced, the original shock, rage, and alienation are reawakened and painfully reexperienced. From their work with over 350 families (as of 1982) in specialized victim services to families, Getzel and Masters concluded that with appropriate social work help, including family treatment and adjunct support groups, "the pain, rage, and isolation of families of homicide victims can be mitigated. . . . Survivors can find hope and meaning in the face of dreadful and overpowering events" (1985:16).

Clearly, sudden deaths by accident, suicide, and homicide at any age are devastating and severely disorganizing to the family. The tasks of mourning and then of reorganizing the family through second-order changes are extremely difficult and prolonged. With supportive help through natural networks, religious faith, cultural beliefs, social work services, and specialized bereavement groups, the parents and siblings of an adolescent victim can begin slowly to move through the grief, horror, rage, and guilt associated with the three types of untoward deaths. Some may even find an acceptable meaning or purpose in the death. Over time, many will be able gradually to reorganize family roles, responsibilities, relationship patterns, and to integrate to some degree their grievous loss into the family's view of itself and its now very different social reality. The family can then continue to meet the developmental needs of its members.

Chronic Illness and Disability in Adolescence

The issues arising from chronic illness are the same for the adolescent and the family as those described for the schoolchild and the family in chapter 11. Preventing or at least managing difficulties in physical, social, sexual, emotional, educational, and vocational development are critical tasks for the youth, the family, and the health care team, including the social worker. Family and team must support the ill or disabled adolescent in his or her efforts gradually to achieve a new self-concept, new life goals and plans, and new behavior patterns. At the same time, however, the parents need to manage their own sorrow and possible guilt feelings or anger about the disabling accident or the illness—especially difficult if the outcome of the illness or the disability is uncertain or has a downward course. They need also to deal with the loss of their original hopes and expectations for the youth, without forsaking their other children and their needs. Fundamental characteristics of the family must change because the family's shared reality has been changed.

Family loyalties, affectional and communication patterns, role assignments, worldview, and transactions with the environment are affected. Responsibilities in keeping up the household, shopping and cooking, paying bills, fulfilling transportation requirements, arranging for happy family times together, and earning an income may need to be redistributed. Managing a serious illness or disability and the inevitable contingencies require a new body of knowledge about the condition, its severity, its potential course, the associated complications, the limitations it imposes, and the regimens involved. Also required is a whole new assemblage of behavioral sequences on the part of the adolescent and the family members, such as controlling symptoms; monitoring, preventing, and managing crises; carrying out regimens; and dealing with physical limitations (Corbin and Strauss 1988). Such major changes in structure and routines take time, struggle, and pain to develop and set in place. Successful changes depend not only on whatever else is going on in the family's life, but also on whether the family's and the teenager's perceptions of the condition are realistic, denied, or accepted, and on the availability of supports and resources, especially for the times when the caregivers become emotionally drained or overwhelmingly fatigued.

When these processes go reasonably well over the long period that they require, the youth and the other family members gradually develop a new image of themselves as a family and a sense of their joint strengths and purpose, and they may even experience deeper ties to one another as well as acceptance of a changed future. Personal and family development can proceed from such a painful family transformation. However, if coping with the many stressors and reorganizing the family exceed the family's capacities and resources, family and individual functioning deteriorate. The adolescent and/or the parents may become depressed and overcome by despair and hopelessness, and the family itself may become disorganized or may even disintegrate.

Once home from the hospital or the rehabilitation center, many adolescents and their families benefit from social work help with problem solving, setting priorities, and developing skills in managing the condition that fit the family's particular situation, their usual interactional styles, and their culture. Social workers are skilled in mobilizing and coordinating community resources, such as home health care, respite and day care services, environmental aids and helpful devices, financial assistance, and the social support of neighbors and friends. Social work counseling at times of stress is an important resource. Social work groups and camping experiences for chronically ill and disabled teenagers and for their parents can be especially helpful. They provide emotional support and experiences in relating to peers and in learning together about the particular disease or disability and management of its biopsychosocial aspects.

Alcohol and Drug Abuse

Substance abuse is a troubling second-order development at any point in life, and perhaps no more at any time than in adolescence. Alcohol and illicit drug abuse are associated with school dropout, family conflicts, alienation from peers, malnutrition and health problems, difficulties in adolescent psychosocial development, crime, driving accidents, and lost potential. Because many adolescent abusers exhibited behavioral or emotional disorders or negative worldviews and school problems before becoming addicted, and because many are the children of abusers, second-order change and family transformation often require long-term professional help.

Residential, outpatient, day care, and halfway house programs are the treatments of choice. Meeks (1989) suggested that outpatient services are appropriate for youths who have no acute medical and psychiatric problems or chronic medical problems, who are willing to abstain from illicit drug use and to submit to urine testing, who have had past success in outpatient treatment, who are genuinely motivated, and who have family members who are interested and willing to participate. The various residential programs are appropriate for all others. Practitioners and researchers agree that continuing supportive help is needed for those who complete programs, and that developing means of reducing dropout rates is also necessary.

Given the diversity in age, education, patterns of drug abuse, and psychological, social, and cultural characteristics, no one approach will suit the needs of all young abusers. All programs should provide individual, family, and group counseling. A variety of treatment settings and options within an agency or in the community increases the possibility of successful treatment (Meeks 1989:337). Programs must take account of contemporary youth cultures. The problems and needs of youthful drug abusers are different from those of adult abusers, and therefore the treatment programs must be different. Fortunately, the families of young abusers are usually less resistant to becoming involved than are those of adult abusers.

Given the intransigent nature of substance abuse, Fraser and Kohlert (1988) believe that the most useful approach is community-, family-, and school-focused prevention programs. These are designed to help youth resist peer and other pressures to use drugs, aided by media campaigns and community action groups such as cocaine hotlines, "how to quit" clinics, "say no" programs, and Mothers Against Drunk Driving (MAD). Few data are available yet on the effectiveness of these and other preventive projects. Family-focused programs for high-risk families where drug abuse is already a problem include 1) parenting and family-skills training that involves parents and children together in attachment-building exercises, communications training, and child management training (Fraser and Kohlert 1988); 2) family self-help groups such as Young Peoples Groups in Alcoholics Anonymous, Cocaine Anonymous, Narcotics Anonymous, and Ala-Fam, which offer social support and clearly defined methods for dealing with the problems of chemical dependency; and 3) family therapy (Fraser and Kohlert 1988). From reports cited by Fraser and Kohlert, it appears that some high-risk families, with skilled help, do make second-order changes that support the psychosocial development of the adolescent and the other family members, and that perhaps lead to family transformation.

Teenage Pregnancy and Childbearing

This second-order development in a family differs from the first-order life issue of childbearing discussed in chapter 8 because it is unexpectable, comes too early in the life course for both mother and child, is fraught with characteristic dangers for both, and is a relatively uncommon event. Within the teenage parent's family, pregnancy and childbearing require major second-order changes, beginning with the pregnancy, for the young unmarried mother, her family, and, ideally, the teenage father and his family. The adolescent's health care, and that of her expected infant, must be given top priority. She now occupies a new status with new responsibilities and demands.

Many families, including those who are impoverished, achieve a positive resolution of the tensions and stress and carry out a successful family transformation. Furstenberg, Gunn, and Morgan (1987) conducted a longitudinal study of over three hundred primarily urban black women who had given birth as teenagers in the late 1960s. These authors found that a substantial majority had finished high school and had found regular employment. If they had been on welfare, they eventually managed to escape it. The women who had more economically secure and better educated parents were more likely to succeed. Also, those who had done well in school and had high aspirations at the time of the first birth were more likely than others to succeed later. According to McCluskey, Killarney, and Papini:

> Our stereotype of the teenage mother is usually one that involves the images of promiscuity, little ambition for education or job attainment, reliance on welfare, and neglectful parenting. This profile, however, is representative of only a small minority of these women. When provided with educational opportunities, emotional and financial support from family members and the baby's father, the adolescent mother and family form a viable familial system. (1983:107–108)

The NRC Panel (Hayes 1987) advocated three policy goals at the national level. The first is particularly helpful to adolescent mothers, their infants, and their families in achieving the needed family transformation. Just as important, the other two goals are geared to the prevention of early pregnancy and childbearing:

1. Promote positive social, economic, health, and developmental outcomes for adolescent parents and their children by providing appropriate health and nutrition services; preventing subsequent un-

timely and unintended births; ensuring the economic well-being of the teenage family, including educating young men about their child support obligations, enforcing those obligations over time, and encouraging grandparents to assume responsibility for the support of their minor children and the children of these minors; and enhancing life options for teenage parents through educational, employment, and child care programs.

2. Reduce the rate and incidence of unintended pregnancy among adolescents, especially among school-aged teenagers by a) enhancing the life options of those living in poverty, including life-planning courses, programs that improve school performance, employment programs, and programs that provide role models for high-risk youth; b) delaying sexual initiation, an approach that includes family life and sex education, assertiveness and decision-making training, programs that provide role models to young adolescents, and efforts to influence the media treatment of sexuality; and c) encouraging diligent contraception by sexually active male and female teenagers, a strategy that includes, for example, dispelling myths about the safety of the contraceptive pill; securing public support for contraceptive services to adolescents, and, at little or no cost, incorporating information on contraception into sex education programs; developing school-based clinic models for implementation in schools with large high-risk populations; and developing condom distribution programs.

3. Provide alternatives to adolescent childbearing and parenting. At present, these include adoption and legalized abortion services, although the council recognized that abortion is a controversial issue. Many successful programs, advocated in these two policy goals, are in place, staffed by skilled social workers and other practitioners. Many more are needed.

The next and final chapter considers the aging family and its transformations.

13

The Elderly Family and Its Transformations

"How old would you be if you didn't know how old you was?"
—Satchel Paige

Growing older is neither a social problem nor a disease, but a process of biological and psychosocial change that begins at birth and continues through life. In 1935, with the passage of the Social Security Act, mandatory retirement from the work force at age 65 became the American marker of old age. Yet there is nothing magical about that age. It had been set arbitrarily by Bismarck in pre–World War I Germany when a system of social insurance was instituted. Until 1935, most Americans worked as long as they could. With current laws against age discrimination in the workplace, the new reality is that some now work into their 70s at a high level of productivity, often higher than that of younger colleagues. A few may work productively into their 80s. Some affluent others in their 50s retire voluntarily to enjoy their leisure and good health as long as possible.

Being elderly today is partly a matter of self-definition. Given the extension of the life course and the improved health maintenance during the twentieth century, many people do not consider themselves middle-aged until their mid-50s, and they do not consider themselves old until their mid-70s or even their 80s. Self-definitions may derive from cultural influences, as some cultures define when one is an elder based on chronological age. On the average, blue-collar groups go through expectable life transitions such as leaving school, first job, marriage, and first child about five years earlier than those in middle-income and professional groups. It is not surprising, then, that working-class persons tend to define themselves as middle-aged and elderly earlier than middle- and upper-class individuals do. Those engaged in hard physical labor, for example, may feel middle-aged at 30 and old at 50.

Neugarten (1978) constructed the categories of young-old (55 to 74), old-old (75 to 85), and the very old (over 85). Such classifications underscore the great diversity among the elderly. What people in their mid-60s enjoy, require, and can do—and their adaptive tasks—are quite different from the needs, activities, and life tasks of those who are in their mid-80s. When individual differences in health and self-definition are added, the diversity becomes great indeed, requiring careful attention from policy and program developers and practitioners (Miller and Solomon 1979). The three age categories will be examined later in the chapter.

Genetic factors operate in biological aging. The timing of such processes as graying hair and skin changes, bone loss and decreasing stature, and diminishing visual and hearing acuity, muscle mass, vigor, and heart and respiratory function is related to genetic inheritance interacting with lifestyle and the environment over the life course. Thus the changes begin earlier in some people than in others. Race and poverty play important roles in aging because the longevity rates among people of color are much lower and the illness rates are much higher than those of middle- and upper-class persons and all whites.

Ideas about declines in cognitive capacities such as intelligence, memory, learning ability, and judgment are controversial. Myths and stereotypes view deterioration in these capacities as inevitable in the elderly. It is more the case that some persons show declining intellectual abilities beginning before age 60, while some show none at an advanced age. A recently reported study of 1,000 people age 51 to 92 years in thirty Florida cities found that when 450 of the subjects were retested ten years later (the rest had died or moved away), their verbal comprehension showed no significant change. Basic arithmetic skills showed only modest declines (Cunningham 1986). The researcher stated that educational level was a better predictor of test performance than age. He, like other investigators, believes that depression, substance abuse, alcohol, and lack of exercise, rather than aging itself, account for some diminished intellectual skills. Other studies have found that developing new means to solve problems is more impaired than knowledge learned in the past. Similarly, memory of the distant past tends to be better than that of the recent past, although this discrepancy may merely reflect the older person's interest in thinking and talking of the past as a means of maintaining self-esteem and a sense of identity and continuity.

The advice "Use it or lose it" applies to intellectual just as it does to physical capacities. Recent brain research has shown that brain cells are stimulated by use. Also, the brain of a healthy older person maintains its circuits and repairs them if they are damaged (Cotman 1987). Thus the effects of disease should not be confused with normal aging. For example, certain organic conditions, such as stroke, can lead to brain changes due to a gradual loss of cells in the cortex, which affect intellectual capacities. Alzheimer's disease and other forms of senile dementia result in gradual intellectual deterioration to a profound degree. Several of these abnormal conditions are considered in a later section on health.

This chapter begins by considering the middle years from age 45 to 64, followed by the young-old period from age 65 to age 74. Neither of these periods coincides with Neugarten's earlier age designations, but they seem to fit better with today's self-definitions, improved health, and increased longevity. The chapter concludes with the old-old (from age 75 to 84) and the very old (beyond age 85). Considerable individual variation and overlap of upper and lower limits will be found among the four age groups. The chapter also examines transformations in the family, now reduced to the parental pair or, in other instances, the widowed, divorced, or never-married elderly, who may live alone, as well as older gay and lesbian couples and individuals. Other areas examined include work and retirement; grandparenthood; societal attitudes; adult children and other social supports; health and illness; and racial, ethnic, and gender differences.

THE MIDDLE YEARS, AGES 45 TO 64

The last chapter ended with the development of the adolescent and the parent(s), presumed to be in their early 40s, and the associated family transformations. This section picks up with the departure from home of the last or only adolescent child, now a young adult. He or she may have departed for marriage, higher education, employment, the armed forces, independent living arrangements and self-support in whole or in part, and so on. The departure may occur at any time from about age 18 years on, depending on circumstances; physical, mental and emotional capacities; cultural, ethnic, and class patterns; and the like.

For many middle-aged parents today, the years from the time of the last child's departure until the death of the spouse may last thirty or forty years and, in some instances, may be the longest segment of the partners' life together. As the term *empty nest* implies, the parents now reoccupy the earlier status of childless couple. They may welcome or may need to rediscover and renew their love for, interest in, and attention to each other. Many enjoy their freedom from child-rearing responsibilities and provide support to each other for the "losses" involved. They may feel relatively comfortable in their work roles. Some women who began careers after children were in school may find that the pace of the career and their interest in it now pick up. Many men, with a diminished need to succeed, become interested in recapturing the warmth and intimacy of the early marriage years before the arrival of children. Some others, who have gone as far as they can in their work, may weigh carefully the idea of career or work changes as a now-or-never possibility. They will face barriers to overcome, such as covert age discrimination, the changing economy, financial risk, and the comfort of the status quo. To some extent, such changes are limited to those at the upper levels of the occupational structure. Also, such a change by either partner entails extra time and energy that may require shifts in the roles and responsibilities of each partner (Entine 1984).

But for most couples, these years mean that they have time at last for each other and for individual and shared activities and friendships. Many, if not most, parents and their young-adult child work out a different, but loving, adult-to-adult relationship. With the child's marriage or other committed relationship, the parents incorporate the partner into the family system and into their own psychic structures as a loved person—not always easy, depending on the circumstances. Also, they are now no longer the next of kin, a wrenching recognition. They must again modify their relationship to their adult child, who from now on will be more allied to her or his partner. The parents are no longer needed in quite the same way. But many begin to look forward to new statuses as grandparents. Meanwhile, they assume as best they can any new responsibilities as the middle-aged children of their own aging parents. Neugarten (1968) found that very few middle-class, middle-aged persons wish to be young again, although they do want to feel young and to have youthful attitudes. Many in their 40s and 50s feel that they now know how to manage their lives and to take whatever the future may bring.

Menopause

Earlier theory, bolstered by folklore, suggested that middle age is especially difficult for women because 1) their major function of child rearing is over, and 2) fertility is lost with the menopause, at the mean age of about 47 years. It is likely today that neither issue is a significant concern to many middle-aged women. First, almost 50 percent of mothers are in the work force, and over half of all women between the ages of 45 and 64 are employed, so child rearing has not been the only or the major function of most of today's middle-aged women. Many who did remain at home with their children until the last one departed look forward to returning to work, or to education for new work roles, or to taking on community responsibilities. Second, in contrast to the views of male physicians, recent studies indicate that most women experience menopause as a relief. Sexual activity is more pleasurable because the couple are freed from worries about pregnancy or contraceptive use:

> There is no age limit for female sexuality (that special sense of self through which we express passion, warmth, closeness and affection). Many women in their middle and late years enjoy satisfying physical and emotional intimacy. Many others do not because of poor health, negative attitudes, or because they have difficulty finding an appropriate sexual partner; still others choose a celibate life style. (*Hot Flash* 1984)

Some women may experience menopausal discomforts such as hot flashes, palpitations, and vaginal shrinkage and dryness because of hormonal changes, but hormone replacement therapy relieves these symptoms in most instances. Hormonal replacement therapy is believed also to protect older women from heart disease and osteoporosis, a bone-thinning disease that leads to fractures. Replacement of estrogen and progesterone in combination is thought to protect against the risk of uterine cancer posed by estrogen replacement alone, but it may increase the risk of heart disease for some. Because of the risks, the matter of hormonal replacement is still controversial within the medical profession.

Although most women don't suffer from the menopause or regret the end of child rearing to any great degree, others do find the middle years stressful. Troubled middle-aged women may suffer from depression, loneliness, reduced life satisfaction, lowered self-esteem, or alcoholism or drug abuse. Housewives are believed to be particularly vulnerable, especially those who have not been involved in activities outside the home. Some women seek professional help; others do not because they blame themselves for their problems. The gynecologist Notman (1981) observed a tendency among physicians to connect everything that occurs in women's middle years to menopause. Agitation, depression, insomnia, and so on are treated as "simply menopause" rather than as symptoms that need to be understood in the context of a woman's lifestyle and the stressors she is experiencing. Largely as a function of interactional patterns between a woman and her physician, women use more prescription and over-the-counter drugs than men do (Lisansky-Gomberg 1981). Women who drink heavily may also be on self- or physician-prescribed light tranquilizers, a potentially lethal combination. One cross-national study (of the United States, Canada, and other Western societies) reported a two-to-one ratio of psychotropic drug use among women as compared to men:

[These women] tend to be age 40 or above, in poor health, and to have less education than non-users. Higher use was found among housewives as well as women who were unemployed but who were looking for work. These women tend to show higher levels of anxiety and depression than men. . . . Women receive a greater number of prescriptions for psychotropic drugs . . . generally as a result of nebulous or vague complaints to general practitioners. The seeking of this type of medication to solve a medical problem is inappropriate since the real problems may be social or economic. (Drezen 1985)

Little information is available about the extent of alcohol abuse among midlife and older women, but we do know that "many of the ten million alcoholics in the U.S. are women who began drinking late in life, and, unlike their male counterparts, are closet drinkers" (Blume 1985). Notably, the highest proportion of problem drinkers in men is found in the 21- to 34-year-old group, while in women the highest proportion is found in the 35- to 49-year-old group. Many experts today agree that alcoholism is not willful misbehavior but an illness that has genetic, biological, emotional, and social roots. Yet all alcoholics, including women, bear a stigma. Additionally, women suffer a special stigma because they are expected to follow high moral standards. It is sometimes assumed that women who drink are sexually loose because of the historical assumed link between alcohol and sexual promiscuity. The triple nature of stigma and the shame women feel make it difficult for them to seek help for alcohol abuse, although there are now many self-help groups available.

The male climacteric is less clearly delineated. Males' gonadal function does not usually stop as abruptly as it does in the female. Rarely do males suffer symptoms of hormone decline such as hot flashes: "More typically, there is a gradual decline in testicular function, with concomitant loss of fertility and potency, beginning in middle age. Nevertheless, males, too, can remain sexually active (and some even fertile) into old age" (Katchadourian 1976). What has been noted by several researchers across different cultures, however, is a certain personality change in men and women that begins in the middle years. Men tend to become more nurturant and expressive and to shift from active to passive mastery. Women tend to become more active, assertive, and independent. Gutmann (1977), who developed the hypothesis, explained the shifts as "a return of the repressed." That is, early gender-role socialization erases one side of each gender's total humanness. Cross-cultural studies bear out the tendency among older people to become androgenous (Livson 1980; Sinnott 1980). Riley (1985a) suggested that this capacity to combine traditionally masculine and feminine traits, replacing earlier gendered roles, may be the best means of coping with aging. She believes that if these ideas are corroborated by further research, such a generic role in later life may contribute to the social adaptation of older persons.

Neugarten (1969) noted that the self-concept of middle-aged adults has elements of the past within it. Adults think of themselves in the present in terms of where they have come from, what they have become, and how content they are at 50 compared to when they were 40. For most men and many women, the middle years are a time of stock taking, of coming to terms with what has been achieved in contrast to what was hoped for. It is also a time for self-introspection and couple reflection, with consideration of possible changes to ensure a satisfying life ahead, and rejoicing in the freedom to enjoy it. Neugarten showed that for most people this period is accompanied by a changing time perspective: "Life is restructured in terms of time-left-to-live rather than time-since-birth" (1968:97).

Middle-Aged Children in the Middle

In addition to the departure of the now young-adult child, the couple (and childless couples or single individuals) may be faced with the declining health of their own parents. Given the extended longevity and the growing prevalence of four-generation families, they and their aging parents may even be faced with the care of their very old grandparents. They are part of what is called the *sandwich generation*, squeezed between attention to their children and grandchildren and the needs of their own elderly parents and very old grandparents. The problem has become a women's issue because most caregivers are women. A study by the National Center for Health Research of the U.S. Public Health Service (*NASW NEWS* 1987a) found that in 1986 caregiver relatives were 72 percent female, of whom 29 percent were daughters and 23 percent were wives, and the rest were other relatives (siblings, nieces, etc.) or friends. Their average age was 57 years; 25 percent were 65 to 74 years of age; and 10 percent were over 75. Three quarters of the caregivers shared living arrangements with the recipient relative, one third also worked, and one fourth reported their own health as poor. One third of the caregivers were poor, one third provided care without any assistance, and only 10 percent purchased formal services. Of the 28 percent who were male caregivers, 13 percent were husbands, and 9 percent were sons; the remainder were other relatives or friends.

On one hand, the need for caregiving is growing because elderly parents or other relatives are living longer. The fastest growing segment of the aged population is the over-85 group, who are more likely to suffer chronic illness or mental impairment and to need care. On the other hand, fewer caregivers are available because more women are working outside the home. The study just cited found that 44 percent of the daughters were employed and had to juggle the demands of working and those of caregiving, perhaps becoming themselves vulnerable to severe stress and consequent physical illness. Also, 14 percent of the wives and 11 percent of the daughters had left their employment to become full-time caregivers. Others had rearranged their work schedules or had changed to part-time jobs.

A Canadian occupational therapist (C. Hill 1984) studied a nonrandom sample of 50 people (2 men and 48 women) providing care and shared living arrangements to elderly relatives who were unable to live alone. The typical caregiving situation was that of a woman in her late 80s being cared for by her daughter, a married woman in her late 50s. The situation had arisen from the need of the parent for physical care and emotional support and had continued for five years or more. When the caregivers were interviewed alone, most commented spontaneously on their experiences. Some were predominantly positive or predominantly negative, but many spoke of both difficulties and mutual benefits. They took on extra activities by choice, such as efforts to maintain the relative's interest and awareness and to facilitate her contributions through appropriate tasks helpful to the family.

Some caregivers expressed guilt and resentment out of fear they had neglected their spouse and children, or because they could not do enough to satisfy the elder's demands. Even in instances where the arrangement had not worked out, mostly because of the relative's deteriorating health, the caregivers expressed satisfaction that they had tried rather than immediately choosing institutional care. Others wept as they spoke of the forced decision to find an alternative arrangement. The researcher concluded, as many clinicians have, that unpaid caregiving relatives must have specialized supports to sustain them so they can continue to provide care (Hill 1984). Recognition of this need is growing in North America, and services are being developed such as respite for the caregiver, day care for the elderly, nursing and homemaker services, and referral and information services. Many are staffed by social workers.

Grandparenting

It is widely recognized that grandparents have all the joy that children bring, without the responsibilities and pressures of child rearing. In the same way, grandparents bring a special joy to their grandchildren that some observers may call spoiling, but that to the children means gentleness, patience, love, and unrushed time (Christian 1984). Grandparents are living longer today, and many are lucky enough to know their grandchildren as teenagers and even as adults. Some live near enough for frequent visiting; others may live across the country but keep in touch by telephone, mail, and vacation visits. Still other grandfathers and grandmothers today may be employed full time beyond age 65 and are unable to be with their grandchildren as much as they would like to be. Many parents of adult children who have delayed childbearing in favor of careers feel that their anticipated grandparenthood is being suspended. For some, the suspension is likely to be permanent, as more young people come to prefer to remain childless. It may represent a troubling interruption of the emotional transition in the aging process—already labeled "grandparent anxiety" (Brody 1984). The basis for such anxiety is not simply the fear of the lost opportunity of the fun of cuddling a baby. Grandchildren are a reassurance to the older couple that their adult children will have fulfilled, secure lives. Even if the suspension is not permanent, delayed childbearing means that the grandparents will have less time to watch the grandchildren grow up, despite extended life expectancy. On the other hand, when hoped-for grandchildren are finally born, they will arrive closer to the grandparents' retirement. They may then have more time together (Christian 1984).

One of the few studies of grandparenthood is already over twenty years old (Neugarten and Weinstein 1968), but it remains pertinent. The authors interviewed both grandparents in seventy white, middle-class Chicago families; these grandparents lived in separate households from their adult children. (The authors acknowledged the need for studies of variations in grandparenting among various ethnic and socioeconomic groups.) The age range of the grandfathers was the mid-50s through the late 60s; for the grandmothers it was the early 50s to the mid-60s. Forty-six of the couples were parents of the wife, and twenty-four were parents of the husband. Each member of the couple was interviewed separately, usually in two sessions. The focus of the open-ended questions was on the relationship between grandparent and grandchild. The majority expressed comfort, satisfaction, and pleasure in the grandparental role. However, one third of the sample (36 percent of the grandmothers and 29 percent of the grandfathers) admitted discomfort, disappointment, or lack of positive reward in the role. The role was alien to the self-concept, or conflict with the parents over their child-rearing practices existed, or the grandparents were indifferent to caretaking or responsibility in regard to the grandchild.

Five major styles of grandparenting were identified: formal, fun seeker, surrogate parent, reservoir of family wisdom, and distant figure. Age differences are of particular interest. The formal style, following the prescribed role of grandparenting and not interfering with the parenting function, occurred significantly more often among those older than 65. The fun-seeker and distant-figure styles occurred significantly more often in those under 65. These represent new, nonauthoritarian styles that may be the consequence of the youthfulness (in actual age and in self-definition) of the grandparents and of their cohort experiences as they grew old in times of changing values: "They may also reflect processes of aging and/or the effects of continuing socialization which produce differences in role behavior over time" (Neugarten and Weinstein 1968:285).

FAMILY TRANSFORMATIONS: LIFE AS A COUPLE

Many middle-aged couples (or single parents) perceive the many adaptive tasks as challenges or opportunities. These center on the child's departure and subsequent marriage; the couple's new relationship to their child as an adult, to each other, and to in-laws; the new status of grandparent; and the recognition of their own middle age and the old age of their own parents as first-order developments. Most middle-aged couples make smooth first-order changes in statuses, roles, relationships, household routines, and other activities. The family's paradigm may shift so that their worldview includes new goals and reasonably happy expectations of the future.

Others dread the anticipated developments in advance, and their worst fears are realized when these developments actually occur. Perhaps the partners have been estranged for a long time, so that reconciliation and reciprocal support are now impossible. One or both parents may miss the child to a painful, even intolerable degree. Either or both may resent the signs of aging in self or spouse. They may experience their work as unsatisfying, or they may feel overwhelmed by the emerging needs of their elderly parents. The future stretches ahead as aimless, lonely, and dreary. The so-called empty nest, now a trap, represents a second-order development to these couples that leads to mounting tensions, depression, despair, and sometimes to declining health in one or both partners. Some may respond to the intensifying stress by seeking marital or personal counseling and/or informal support from relatives and friends. They may, with support and professional guidance, redefine their life situation. Some may be helped to recall what attracted them to each other originally, to reflect on earlier happy times, and to make use of environmental resources to bolster their self-esteem and to find some pleasure in their present relationship. As a consequence, they may undertake joint efforts to achieve second-order changes. Over time, they may gradually make modest yet useful changes in the family organization and worldview.

Others respond to the stressor differently. One or both partners may look elsewhere for a sense of fulfillment in a new love, or may resort to alcohol or drug abuse, or may undertake hasty, unthinking, disastrous changes in job or lifestyle. These steps can push the family toward disorganization. Divorce is not uncommon among such couples, often leaving the woman bereft not only of a mate but of a home and financial support as well. As a "displaced homemaker" in her 50s or early 60s, she may need to find work—a dismal prospect if she lacks skills and experience or has neither the money nor the energy to pursue training. She may be cut off from her husband's pension, health insurance, and even his Social Security if he elects to work beyond 65. If he remarries, the new wife can claim inheritance of his assets. If the divorced wife is receiving alimony, it is taxable, but it is tax-deductible for the former husband.

Older displaced homemakers are members of a birth cohort who were raised to believe that marriage was a life commitment. Many feel ashamed and humiliated by their perceived failure and the loss of their primary identity. They may lose married friends they had shared with their spouses and may suffer isolation and loneliness. They experience a double assault of being too old to start over and too young to give up, as one woman put it. Only about 11 percent of women who are divorced when they are over 50 years old remarry. They outnumber men their age by four to one, so many continually hope for reconciliation with the former spouse. Some believe that the death of the spouse would have been easier (Displaced Homemakers Network 1989). Widows receive better treatment, and there are also rites and rituals to guide their behavior.

This may be the last cohort to suffer such devastation, as women's attitudes and the norms surrounding marriage and divorce change, and as women's presence in the work force continues to grow. Meanwhile, displaced homemakers are a large proportion of the estimated 11 million women who have lost their source of support through divorce (30 percent), widowhood (67 percent), or the disability of their husbands, and who are unprepared for work outside the home. About two thirds have inadequate incomes, 70 percent are over 55, and 54 percent are over 65 (Displaced Homemakers Network 1989). Fortunately, some social agencies have established individual and group services for these middle-aged women, including mental health and financial counseling, job referrals, legal assistance, and referral service for shared and alternative housing. Some programs are currently offered under the Vocational Education Act of 1984.

The adult children of the divorcing couple also suffer. They may wonder if the parents stayed together for their sake, and their family life was a sham. They may feel disillusionment and shame and may even begin to question their own marriage. Some may side with one parent against the other, or may resent the loss of cherished family traditions and holidays, or may fear that they will now have to look after the bereft, lonely parent. On the other hand, some may develop more satisfying relationships with each parent separately, particularly if open tension between the parents has been long-standing. Conversely, older parents also suffer when their adult children divorce, and they worry about the impact on their grandchildren. Some may experience the divorce as a mark of their own failure as parents. Others may be resentful because divorce is against their religion. Still others, who became genuinely fond of their child's spouse, are saddened by the loss, especially if their adult child is angered by their wish to remain in contact with the former partner. Grandparents have feared the loss of their grandchildren if the custodial parent moves away or is too angry to permit visiting. However, as a consequence of grandparent activist groups, all fifty states now have laws establishing grandparent visitation rights, recognizing how important grandparents are to their grandchildren and how the maintenance of the tie can improve the child-rearing environment and help lessen the trauma of the divorce for the children. Breaking the tie is destructive and devastating and is a tragedy for both children and grandparents.

In sharp contrast, some grandparents may be physically and emotionally overburdened by the full-time care of grandchildren because of the custodial parent's employment or, more recently, because of parental drug abuse and neglect of the children. Instances of the latter kind of case are growing rapidly in the nation's inner cities. Most of these grandmothers are poor and infirm. Many of their grandchildren are physically, emotionally, or neurologically impaired because of their mothers' addictions, so that the grandmother's tasks are even more difficult.

GROWING OLDER IN AMERICA

> We dread becoming old almost as much as we dread not living
> long enough to reach old age.
> —Froma Walsh (1980:197)

Societal Attitudes Toward the Aging

In general, we are a youth-oriented and agist society. As Simone de Beauvoir noted (1972), we look on old age as a shameful secret that will never happen to us, only to other people. If older persons manifest common human needs for love, security, sexual expression, and acceptance, they are looked upon as absurd and ludicrous—the dirty old man and the little old lady in tennis shoes. In the aged persons that we must become, we do not recognize ourselves. Almost none of us foresees becoming aged until it is upon us—nothing is more expected, but nothing is more unforeseen. But as the birthday cards declare, growing old is better than the alternative.

We cling to myths and stereotypes of elderly persons as senile, infirm, destitute, unattractive, lonely, a burden to society, and unwanted by their families, who dump them in nursing homes as quickly as possible. Of course, there are many older people who are chronically ill or mentally impaired and far too many who live in poverty. We need more humane policies and programs for their proper care and for the elimination of poverty in all age groups. But the greatest number of older persons have relatively good health, are active in mind and body, and continue to develop and to participate in and contribute to their communities.

Demographics

The rest of this section draws on the *Profile of Older Americans* (1986), except where otherwise noted. From 1900 to 1985, the percentage of Americans 65 and older tripled (4.1 percent in 1900 to 12.0 percent in 1985), and the number increased nine times (from 3.1 million to 28.5 million). The older population is expected to continue to grow in the future. By 1987, 29.8 million persons were 65 or older (U.S.B.C. 1989:13, table 13). Growth will slow somewhat during the 1990s because of the relatively small number of babies born during the Great Depression of the 1930s. The most rapid increase is expected in the years from 2010 to 2030, when the baby-boom generation reaches age 65. By the year 2000, persons 65 and over are expected to represent 13.0 percent of the population, and this percentage may grow to 21.2 percent by 2030. The older population itself is getting older. In 1985, the 65 to 74 age group (17.0 million) was nearly eight times larger than in 1900, but the 75 to 84 group (8.8 million) was eleven times larger, and the group 85 and over (2.7 million) was twenty-two times larger.

In 1985 there were 17.0 million older women and 11.5 million older men, or a sex ratio of 147 women for every 100 men. The sex ratio increased with age, ranging from 122 for the 65 to 69 group to a high of 251 for persons 85 and older. In 1985, older men were twice as likely to be married as older women (77 percent of men; 40 percent of women. Half of all older women in 1985 were widows (51 percent). There were over five times as many widows (8.0 million) as widowers

(1.5 million). Five percent of older men and of older women had never married. Although divorced older persons represented only 4 percent of all older persons in 1985, their numbers (over 1 million) had increased nearly four times as fast as the older population as a whole in the preceding ten years (3.4 times for men, 4.0 times for women).

In 1985, slightly under 90 percent of persons 65 years of age and older were white, 8 percent were black, and about 2 percent were American Indian, Eskimo, Aleut, Asian, and Pacific Islander. Hispanics, who may be of any race, represented 3 percent of the older population in 1985. Research is still limited, but a few studies with an ethnographic emphasis will be reviewed. It is important to keep in mind 1) Jackson's (1985) distinctions among the terms *race, ethnicity,* and *national origin* as discussed in Chapter 3, and 2) the general caution that findings arise out of group data and do not necessarily apply to a particular individual, family, or community.

The hypothesis that advancing age is a leveler of racial inequalities that existed in midlife and the concept of double jeopardy arising from the interaction of race and age are mentioned frequently in the gerontology literature. There is some research support for the leveling hypothesis. Several life satisfaction studies of black elderly and white elderly indicate that they have similar levels of satisfaction, a surprising finding given the differences in their life circumstances over the life course. Some studies have not been controlled for socioeconomic status, however, and some have relied on subjective rather than objective reports of health status in measuring life satisfaction. Hence, the results are questionable (Jackson 1985). However, Schaie, Orchowsky, and Parham (1982) used life satisfaction data from whites and blacks, aged 30 to 73, from the 1973 and 1977 surveys of the National Opinion Research Center. Their analyses showed that the scores of black elderly were significantly lower both years, than those of the younger blacks while the white scores remained substantially the same. But the scores of blacks increased over time, and this increase supports the notion of leveling in the later years.

The idea of double jeopardy was first developed with respect to blacks but has since been expanded to include other oppressed groups and the notion of multiple jeopardies. While the concept of double jeopardy is important, the Schaie, Orchowsky, Parham study demonstrated that the double jeopardy concept must be supplemented by the interaction effects of race with cohort and historical period effects. For example, because marital history affects income status, the higher level of income of elderly white women than that of elderly black women is due not just to racial differences, but also to cohort differences in the marital stability and the occupational and wage histories of both women and men at different periods of time (Jackson 1985).

Economics

The median income of older persons in 1985 was $10,900 for males and $6,313 for females. Families headed by persons 65 years of age and over reported a median income in 1985 of $19,162 ($19,815 for whites and $11,937 for blacks). Elderly persons living alone or with nonrelatives were likely to have low incomes in 1985, with nearly half (46 percent) reporting $7,000 or less. One fourth (24 percent) had incomes under $5,000, while only 20 percent had $15,000 or more. The major source of income for older families and individuals in 1984 was Social Security (35 percent), followed by asset income (26 percent), earnings (23 percent), public and private pensions (14 percent), and "transfer" payments such as Supplemental Security Income (SSI), unemployment benefits, and veterans' payments (2 percent).

About 3.5 million elderly persons were below the poverty level in 1985. Another 2.3 million, or 8 percent, of the elderly were classified as "near-poor" (income between the poverty level and 125 percent of this level). In total, over one fifth (21 percent) of the older population were poor or near-poor in 1985. Almost two thirds (61 percent) of aged American Indians live below the poverty level, the greatest proportion among all groups (Crowley 1988). Almost one third (32 percent) of elderly blacks and almost one quarter (24 percent) of elderly Hispanics were poor in 1985, compared to one ninth (11 percent) of elderly whites. Poverty was probably more extensive among aged Mexican-Americans (and the fewer Central Americans and South Americans) than among Puerto Ricans and Cubans because many Mexican-Americans were undocumented aliens who could support themselves and their families only by part-time work. They are not eligible for Social Security or Medicare and are afraid to apply for welfare because of being reported to the Immigration and Naturalization Service and being deported (Salcido 1979). These constrictions have changed for some who were eligible and who applied for legal resident status under the 1986 Immigration Reform and Control Act. But the act makes it even more difficult for those without legal residence to secure employment because of employer sanctions or to obtain health care and social services because of lack of federal reimbursement and the fear of discovery (Gelfand and Bialik-Gilad 1989).

Living Arrangements

The majority (67 percent) of older noninstitutionalized persons lived in a family setting in 1985. Of these, 77 percent of the men and 40 percent of the women lived with their spouses. About 14 percent (7 percent of men; 18 percent of women) were not living with a spouse but were living with children, siblings, or other relatives. An additional 3 percent of the men and 2 percent of the women, or 650,000 older persons, lived with nonrelatives. About 30 percent (8.1 million) of all noninstitutionalized older persons in 1985 lived alone (6.5 million women; 1.6 million men). They represented 41 percent of older women and 15 percent of older men.

Of the 18.2 million households headed by older persons in 1985, 75 percent were owners and 25 percent were renters. Older male householders were more likely to be owners (83 percent) than were females (66 percent). The housing of older Americans is generally older and less adequate than the balance of the nation's housing. About 36 percent of homes owned by older persons in 1983 were built before 1940 (21 percent for younger owners), and 8 percent were classified as inadequate (6 percent for younger owners). About 83 percent of older homeowners in 1985 owned their homes free and clear.

Researchers find that about 80 percent of the elderly have children, and 80 percent of those see at least one child once a week (Dobrof and Litwak 1977; Weeks and Cuellar 1981). Most older persons do not want to live with their children and fear being a burden to them. Most like to live near their children but wish to maintain their independence as long as possible. We saw in the prior section that most families regard the nursing home only as a last resort in the case of the older person's severe impairment or the depletion of the adult child's personal resources needed to carry on the tasks. The myth that elderly dependent parents are financial drains on their adult children is false. Although their incomes are limited, most elderly are twice as likely to give regular financial assistance to their children than they are to receive it (Weeks and Cuellar 1981).

Many older rural and urban black and Hispanic persons live in unsafe, dilapidated housing because they are poor. A recent report (*After the Harvest* 1987) reveals that 15.2 percent of all farm laborers aged 65 and over live in housing without plumbing (18.3 percent of Hispanics and 33.8 percent of blacks). There are relatively few specialized housing projects for farm workers in this country. Among elderly American Indians, the situation is even worse: 42 percent of this population have no toilets in their homes and 65 percent have no telephones. Asian and Pacific Islander elderly, in general, do not experience such dire poverty, but many must live in unsuitable housing (Crowley 1988).

In addition to traditional "retirement homes" or "homes for the aged" supported by fraternal and religious organizations, a variety of alternate living arrangements have appeared in recent years, often subsidized by public and private funding. These include cooperative group or extended-family-type homes established and perhaps managed by community organizations, or established independently by five or six older people of one or both sexes who want to try shared living. Others are small apartment buildings especially designed for elderly individuals and couples, some of which develop strong mutual aid systems that promote relatedness among the tenants and enable frail individuals to avoid institutionalization (Hochschild 1974). Unused college dormitories have been converted into apartments for the elderly and offer a new way of life to them, including taking tuition-free courses if they wish and developing friendships with students, to their mutual benefit. In return, the college earns needed income. Such innovative housing developments are still in short supply, although the numbers of elderly needing them are growing rapidly.

Affluent older persons who live alone or with spouses or partners may reside in retirement communities of various types, depending on their income, leisure interests, and personal preferences. Some prefer continuing-care communities that are similar to retirement communities but that have medical, nursing, and infirmary care on-site. Others may reside in congregate housing that consists of private apartments with central dining areas, housekeeping services, and transportation by vans. Options also include elaborate mobile home parks.

RURAL LIFE AND AGING

In general, rural people are fiercely independent, resist outside intervention, and place high value on self-reliance and natural helping provided by kin, friends, and neighbors. Today, these values may be truer of rural elderly than of younger residents. While the elderly comprise 12 percent of the U.S. population, they account for more than 25 percent of the rural population. About 30 percent of all persons over 65 years live in rural areas. They include many members of racial and ethnic minorities, especially blacks, Chicanos, American Indians, Eskimos, and Aleuts. The conditions of life of rural older persons vary markedly across North America. In the rural Northeastern U.S., elderly persons who live alone and outside a village or town, and who are without transportation, may be extremely isolated during the snows of winter and the deep mud of springtime. In the Upper Plains, the Far West, and the Southwest, where distances are great and rural towns are far apart, the lack of transportation for health care, shopping, banking, visiting friends, and so on is a very serious problem for older people, especially if they are poor or disabled or both.

In some respects, the plight of older people in rural areas may worsen. For example, a 1988 report by the U.S. Senate Special Committee on Aging found that during 1986 and 1987 more rural hospitals than urban hospitals closed. Eighty-three percent of the hospitals that lost money during the first three years of Medicare's prospective payment system (DRGs) were located in rural areas.* As many as 600 additional rural hospitals may therefore have to close in future years (*NASW News* 1989). While these events will have an impact on all rural residents, the elderly, having more health problems, may suffer the most: "Rural aged are found to have poorer physical and mental health, more chronic disease, smaller incomes, poorer diets, and homes that are deteriorated and unsanitary than the aged living in urban residences" (Weber 1980:208). At particularly high social and medical risk are older farm laborers who are no longer able to work because of age, illness, or disability. The concept of retirement does not apply to them: most simply work as long as their physical condition permits. They may not qualify for Social Security, or if they do, they receive a small amount.

Social, health, and mental health services and skilled practitioners (physicians, nurses, and social workers) have always been in short supply for all age groups in many of the more isolated U.S. rural areas. What services exist often are located centrally in the nearest large town or city. Fortunately, in many rural areas, older persons are embedded in close, supportive relationships with kin, neighbors, and friends, who fill part of the gap and whose help also fits rural values. A sample of eighty older rural natural helpers, within a larger study, were found to be significant sources of relatedness, support, and tan-

---

*In this system, fixed rates are set by diagnostic category regardless of length of stay; therefore hospitals are encouraged to discharge patients as early as possible—sometimes before their condition warrants discharge.

gible assistance to their elderly, middle-aged and younger relatives, neighbors, and friends (Patterson 1987). Of the sample, forty-two were in their 60s, thirty-four were in their 70s, and four were in their 80s.

An example of more formalized help is found in a two-part program established in ten rural counties in the mountainous country of northeast California, where services were sparse or missing (*Practice Digest* 1979). It was operated by the Senior Information and Referral Center and funded by the State Department of Aging. The program consisted of 1) an information and referral service with a central toll-free telephone number to answer callers' questions and requests for information and 2) an outreach and educational service, employing local people as community service advisers (CSAs) in each county, to help senior citizens with more complex needs or issues not resolvable by telephone. In addition, a question-and-answer column was published weekly in most of the area's newspapers. The topics covered included wills, prescription drugs, Social Security, car repair, small claims court, and mobile homes. Often the CSAs sought out neighbors who could provide transportation to visit a specialist or who could coordinate home care for a convalescent. The following sections will take up the differentiating characteristics and needs of various age categories of older people.

THE YOUNG-OLD: AGED 65 TO 74

Let us assume that in 1990 members of the current group of young-old were born between 1916 and 1925. They represent a different cohort from the old-old and the very-old, with different formative experiences. The 65 to 74 cohort is better educated than the two older cohorts. Its members are more healthy and vigorous than the members of the two older cohorts were at their age. They are also more active politically and form an important age bloc in local and national politics because of their numbers, interest, and active participation. Many of them constitute a pool of wise, experienced, and caring people who make important social contributions through community activities and volunteer work and feel self-fulfilled in return.

Nonetheless, societal attitudes toward, and perceptions of, older people do reflect a loss of the dignity and meaning that characterizes older people in traditional societies. On the other hand, far greater opportunities for leisure, cultural, and educational activities, health maintenance, and self-realization exist for today's elderly, especially the young-old (Achenbaum 1985) and those with sufficient incomes.

Neugarten and Hagestad (1976) proposed that a large proportion of the young-old cohort provide a more attractive vision of aging, and that they may allay the fears of the young about growing old. They may help change prevalent myths and stereotypes about the elderly as "old-fashioned, rigid, senile, boring, useless, and burdensome" (Walsh 1980:197). Also, for many in the upper range of the young-old, role models for their age were not widely available in their earlier years, so they may have to develop new styles, roles, and self-perceptions that will be helpful to the cohorts of older persons who follow them. Neugarten (1978) also observed that, in general, the young-old are distinguished from the middle-aged primarily by retirement and from the old-old by continued vigor and social involvement.

Retirement

Before the legislation prohibiting forced retirement on the basis of age, many retirees, especially men, found adaptation to a life without work difficult. With the various options now open, and with improved health, men and women can undertake retirement when they are ready. Even some who are financially secure prefer to keep working as long as they can. Others mark a particular age as their retirement time. Many with very limited resources, however, need to work to supplement their small incomes from Social Security, and some of them may be unemployed and seeking work. Among that group are some black men who see themselves as "unretired." They have not held regular jobs and have no pension income. They believe they will always need to work, but it is difficult for them to find employment (*AARP News Bulletin* 1988).

Retirement had, until about the early 1980s, been viewed mostly in terms of loss—the loss of status, work role, health, spouse, and friends. In particular, retirement was a transition in which the worker exited from the "socially respectable, clearly defined status of work to the amorphous, ill-defined, and rather negatively perceived 'roleless role' of old age" (Nowak and Brice 1984:107). In their extensive review of the research, Nowak and Brice referred to a 1968 study (by Reichard, Livson, and Petersen) that proposed a typology of personality styles predictive of men's responses to retirement. The typology identified three adaptive styles: the mature, who find satisfaction in activities and relationships; the "rocking-chair men," who welcome freedom from the activity that has interfered with their passive orientation during their working years; and the "armored," who ward off their dread of physical decline by keeping active. Two maladaptive styles were also identified: the "angry men," who have histories of blaming others for their difficulties and are unable to accept their aging, and "self-haters," who feel depressed, lonely, and worthless in retirement.

Nowak and Brice also found research support for the following predictors of the quality of the retirement years: health, income, the characteristics of the occupation, willingness to retire, and the marital relationship. Atchley (1976) described retirement not as an event but as a process involving the interplay of many factors in the preretirement and retirement years. He presented a model of the process that is of particular interest to social workers in practice, programming, planning, policy, and research. It consists of six interrelated phases of adaptation to retirement: preretirement, honeymoon, disenchantment, reorientation, stability, and termination. Two subphases constitute the preretirement phase: In the remote subphase, one has a vague vision of retirement in the distant future that may encourage financial and other planning well in advance. The near subphase is oriented toward a specific retirement date. Workers may then begin to decrease motivation or performance, and employers may decrease expectations. Workers may also develop preretirement fantasies based on visions of expected health, income, and activity level. Such visions provide a kind of anticipatory socialization. If they are realistic, they are helpful in identifying issues that require advanced decision making. If they are unrealistic, they may contribute to disenchantment with the reality of retirement.

In active retirement, during the honeymoon phase, those with positive outlooks are likely to experience euphoria for a short or long while, keeping busy in valued activities that they previously had no time for. Depending on personal style, leisure-time options, and degree of flexibility in the face of change, the rapid tempo of activity gradually yields to a more reasonable, stable retirement routine. After this "high," some may experience disenchantment, a letdown, even depression—particularly those who had unrealistic preretirement visions. Even if the visions were realistic, however, the exigencies of fate may bring about changes in health, income, or family status. In this instance, if flexibility is absent, or if alternatives are not available, the disenchantment may continue indefinitely. When disenchantment sets in, it is necessary for retirees to reappraise their situation and their personal and environmental resources, to reorient themselves, and to reorganize their behaviors and expectations accordingly for a more satisfying life in retirement.

In the stability phase, the retiree has reached a point where criteria are developed for dealing routinely with physical and social changes. Some individuals move into this phase directly after the honeymoon phase, while others may never stabilize or do so only after repeated efforts at appraisal and reorientation. The ending or termination phase is part of retirement in Atchley's view. Because retirement is a status, it can be fulfilled only if one has the financial, social, psychological, and health resources for carrying out the retirement routine established in the earlier phases. Without the needed resources to be competent and independent in retirement, the individual transfers into the status of sick person and the role of patient, which have their own set of requirements for reconstituting the lifestyle. This process need not be overwhelming, because in most instances dependence and/or illness occurs gradually.

Studies of retirement have been done primarily on males; hence there is less knowledge about the impact of retirement on the female worker (except for teachers), or on the couple if both are employed and retire at the same time or at different times. The percentage of men 65 and older still in the labor force dropped from 50 percent in 1950 to 16.3 percent by 1980, while that of older women dropped from 10 percent in 1950 to 7.5 percent in 1980, a much less dramatic drop. The reasons for the proportionately longer delay in women's retirement are not entirely clear, but they appear to be related to women's poorer economic status and their more varied employment and life patterns (Matlin 1987; Szinovacz 1982, 1983). For example, most women in the present cohorts of retired persons are believed to receive much lower benefits, income, and pension protection than men. It is estimated that about 70 percent of the elderly poor are women who are subsisting on minimal Social Security payments. Future cohorts may see improved pension and Social Security benefits as more women pursue careers comparable to those of men and all working women earn equal wages for comparable worth.

Older Homosexual People

Older gay and lesbian persons are subject to the same culturewide stereotypes and societal attitudes concerning the elderly as other elders are. They also have the same interests and concerns that all older persons have, including love, health, financial security, and acceptance. How these interests and concerns are handled is not entirely clear because of limited research. Most of what is reported in this section is taken from Moses and Hawkins (1982), except where otherwise noted.

The few studies so far available and reviewed by Moses and Hawkins suggest that gay men and lesbian women may have a more successful response to aging than do many nongays. In a survey of 962 lesbian women under the age of 50, only one quarter expressed negative attitudes about aging (Jay and Young 1979). Lesbians holding negative views were concerned about physical appearance (mostly obesity rather than the physical changes due to aging) and loneliness in the later years. Most of the women were more interested in personality, intellect, and health, a finding suggesting they may have had less concern about being older than do nongay women, who face a constant emphasis on physical attractiveness and youthful appearance. The minority who worried about loneliness seemed to be expressing concern about being alone rather than being lonely. The small number may reflect a difference between lesbian and nongay women: lesbian women may have less difficulty finding partners in their older years than nongay women who are widowed or divorced.

The majority of younger gay men do not report worries about aging, although they do place more emphasis on youthful appearance in their choice of a sexual partner than do lesbian women. Saghir and Robins (1973) reported that, 44 percent of the men indicated that they expected to remain involved and interested as older persons. An additional 28 percent expected to grow old in a stable relationship. Among the small number of gay men apprehensive about aging, fears were related to inability to attract a sexual partner because of physical appearance, as well as loneliness and being alone. Moses and Hawkins believe that as long as the gay community emphasizes youthfulness and the "body beautiful," gay men will continue to worry about physical attractiveness. This worry is positive if it supports interest in maintaining fitness as gay men grow older. It is negative if the preoccupation with physical attractiveness leads to concern about being old.

The few studies of small samples of older gay men reveal that they are neither lonely nor alone. Berger (1984) indicated that in most urban areas gay rights organizations, social clubs, and gay churches are important places for meeting other gays. While dominated by younger men, these civic and religious organizations attract many older gay men and lesbian women. Berger also mentioned bathhouses, bars, parks, and beaches as sites for meeting others. However, in light of the AIDS epidemic, such places are probably no longer of interest to most gay men, young or old. Very little is known of the impact of AIDS on older gay men. Federal statistics on AIDS, so far, do not distinguish between adolescents and adults, or between adults of different ages. It has been said that many of the elderly do not consider themselves at risk, yet some older gays do have more than one partner (Waltner 1980). It is also conceivable that some older gays may not practice no-risk sex. Older gays with AIDS may also suffer from emotional and social isolation. Informing children or grandchildren, for example, may be traumatic.

Moses and Hawkins (1982) suggested that one predictor of the successful aging of gay men and lesbian women may be their leisure-time pursuits during young and middle adulthood. Saghir and Robins (1973) found that gay men are more interested in individual sports and artistic activities and less interested in group sports, while the opposites are true of nongay men. Gays are also more interested in intellectual activities. Similarly, lesbian women are significantly more involved in artistic pursuits and individual sports than nongay women (Saghir and Robins). To Moses and Hawkins, these findings meant that the leisure activities of early and middle adulthood will serve gay men and women well in their older years because they are more appropriate for older persons than the activities of young or middle-aged heterosexual men and women. No research has yet been undertaken to see if these differences in interests are maintained into the older years. The observational experiences of Moses and Hawkins suggest that they are.

These authors also presented evidence that the successful transcending of the stigma for sexual orientation, the presence of many friends, and retirement's freedom from worry about losing the job are factors in gays' easier adaptation to the aging process than that of many nongay elderly.

Berger (1982) identified unique problems that confront older gay men and lesbian women: The policies of hospitals and nursing homes may refuse to recognize the relationship to one's ill partner when visiting regulations and relatives' consent are at issue. Older homosexual persons may not have wills, so their property may go to emotionally distant, even hostile, kin rather than to the long-term partner. Social agencies may not provide bereavement groups for older gay and lesbian persons who have lost their partners. Many senior citizen centers, day care centers, and the like fail to provide appropriate groups and services to older homosexual people. Services specific to the needs of older gay people, however, are slowly developing in both traditional and new agencies and in churches. One landmark organization is Senior Action in a Gay Environment (SAGE), which encourages active participation by gay seniors (*Practice Digest* 1984).

HEALTH AND THE ELDERLY

As Neugarten (1978) pointed out, the young-old are distinguished from the old-old by continued vigor and social involvement. As we have seen, this is only partly the case, insofar as health, vigor, and social involvement vary according to income levels and race. So, while it is true for many, others at all income levels do suffer from poor health and often from multiple chronic conditions. Some suffer crippling falls and may incur fractured hips and limbs, especially women who suffer from osteoporosis. Blacks suffer the highest rates of hypertension, with its life-threatening wake of heart disease, stroke, and kidney failure. Among those aged 45 to 64, the loss of kidney function associated with hypertension is ten times greater than among whites the same age. The incidence of cancer is twice that for whites, and death from asthma is three times the rate of that for whites. American Indians rarely seek health care, and 80 percent of noninstitutionalized Hispanic elderly report at least one chronic illness.

Many married ill persons are cared for by their elderly spouses. The spouse is not compensated for home care by public or private insurance. Extra costs beyond what Medicare pays for services at home can rapidly drain away the couple's resources. To receive services from Medicaid, the couple must meet a means test that sets very low limits on income and assets. Each state designs its own Medicaid program, so there are many variations in the aspects of home care that are included. Corbin and Strauss related the accounts of sixty ill persons and their spouses, some of whom were young-old, as they struggled together to manage severe illness at home twenty-four hours a day, every day of the year. In addition to the struggles and pain of the ill spouse in managing the psychological and physical aspects of the illness,

> The well spouse, while indirectly weighing such concerns, also has personal concerns: balancing the value of live-in help against the invasion of privacy that comes with that help; responding to the mate's need for assistance and care yet feeling somewhat resentful that as the caretaking spouse, one can never become tired or ill because there is no one else to take over; willingly using one's life savings for the medical care of the ill person,

while at the same time wondering what lies ahead for one's own future once all that money is gone. (1988:6)

Another group of older persons, generally neglected, are those who are caregivers for their dependent adult children (Jennings 1987). Estimates of older retarded persons range from 50,000 to 315,000. Some are in institutions, but many live at home, where family members are the principal caregivers. Presumably, many caregivers are old-old or very-old parents, who have had the care of their developmentally disabled children from birth or early childhood. They continue to deal with the issue of "perpetual parenthood," often in the context of social isolation or declining social supports. Jennings pointed out that the emotional and physical care of the adult child are combined with the stresses the parents may be experiencing as they deal with their own declining strength, especially if one or both suffer from chronic illness. The elderly parents face added health costs for themselves and special expenditures for the child in the face of reduced income at retirement. An added persistent worry is the matter of who will provide care and protection after the parents are no longer able to do so or after their death.

Brody observed, "Most older people are not sick and dependent. . . . Most do not need any more help than the normal, garden variety of reciprocal services that family members of all ages need and give each other on a day-to-day basis, and in times of emergency or temporary illness." Adult children (mostly daughters and daughters-in-law) "shop and run errands; give personal care; do household maintenance tasks; mobilize, coordinate and monitor services from other sources; and fill in when an arranged care program breaks down." Nonetheless, with advancing age, impairments do increase and lead to a greater need for help from adult children or other relatives. Brody pointed out that while the amount of help needed by noninstitutionalized older persons varies, about 8 to 10 percent are as functionally impaired as those in institutions. Another 10 percent are bedfast or housebound. In addition, 6 or 7 percent can go out, but only with difficulty. These groups, for the most part, live with or are cared for by adult children or other relatives.

Because people are living longer and impairments increase with age, more and more adult children in their late 60s and early 70s will need to provide care and services to their very-old parents. Those young-old children themselves may be experiencing lowered energy levels, interpersonal losses including widowhood, the onset of chronic ailments, reduced incomes, and other pressures. They may have unfulfilled expectations of retirement opportunities such as leisure, freedom, pursuing new interests, and moving to a new climate. As demographic trends continue and inappropriate assumptions about filial responsibility persist, society must provide supports to the family because it is the only informal support system for old-old and very-old parents. Brody asked, "At what point does the public and professional expectation of 'filial responsibility' become social irresponsibility?"

The situation is even more difficult for people of color. Between 1970 and 1980, American Indian, Hispanic, and black elderly increased 65 percent, 57 percent, and 34 percent, respectively, compared with an increase of 25 percent of white elderly (Wood 1987). Wood stated:

> The situation for middle-aged and older minority caregivers is clearly alarming: Their parents and grandparents suffer more health problems and have fewer financial resources than nonminorities, yet they're often excluded from existing support services or aided only cursorily. As a result, the burden of caring for minority elderly rests primarily on their families—a population that is itself struggling with many of the same problems.

Also, for poor families dependent on public housing, regulations regarding the number of persons in an apartment often make it impossible to share living arrangements with an aged parent. Despite these factors, the extended family serves as a significant support to elderly blacks. Familial support is often reciprocal, as many elderly women and some men help in child rearing and in other ways. On all socioeconomic levels, "extended kin will 'squeeze blood from a turnip' to provide assistance" to aged members (Sussman 1985:431). Generational ties are strong, and elderly members are viewed as having legitimate claims for help. Mexican-Americans and Puerto Ricans have a high degree of culturally based family interdependence. A New York study found that Puerto Rican elderly had more social interaction with their adult children than did whites and blacks (Cantor 1979).

A few studies suggest that the traditional Chinese value of filial piety and veneration of the aged may be eroding in some families as young American-born Chinese are influenced by American culture. Chen (1979), for example, found desperate poverty, as well as loneliness, language barriers, physical isolation, and a sense of familial dislocation, in a small sample of elderly Chinese-American women and men residing alone in hotel rooms in the Los Angeles Chinatown. In her review of anthropological studies, Keith stated:

> In Boston, for example, traditional kinship and inheritance patterns affect care of the elderly Irish and Chinese. In both groups, the child living nearest is likely to become the major caretaker when one becomes necessary. However, among the Irish, this is likely to be a daughter, among the Chinese a daughter-in-law (1985:247)

Nevertheless, Keith cautioned us that overgeneralizing leads to the false assumption that all elders with obvious ethnic identities are valued and cared for by their extended family. That is no longer the case for many. She suggested that one generalization is appropriate: when younger members of an ethnic group value their ethnic identity, the position of older members as symbols and/or specialists is likely to be strengthened.

The need to provide outreach and information to elderly refugees, and to other older persons who do not speak English, about their eligibility for programs, services, and benefits is a pressing one. Lack of information is a significant barrier to medical care and social services. Unaware of their eligibility for government assistance up to three years, many refugees are very dependent for a variety of services on their adult children, of whom they disapprove because they are taking on strange American ways (Eastman 1988).

THE OLD-OLD (75 TO 84) AND VERY-OLD (85 AND OVER)

"People now, regardless of their age, have more parents, grandparents, and great-grandparents than has ever been true before" (Brody 1981). The grandparent generation is providing care for the great-grandparent generation. The squeeze will be even greater because the baby-boomer cohort, when they become young-old, will have fewer children to assist them as they enter the ranks of the old-old (probably many baby-boomer couples today have more parents than they have children!). And with the upward trend in longevity, there will be more old-old and very-old surviving and needing to be cared for. For example, between 1974 and 1978, the number of people 100 years old or over increased 43 percent. The numbers went from 8,317 to 11,922 (*Modern Maturity* 1979). By 1983, the latest figure, those people 100 years old or over numbered 32,000 (*Guinness Book of World Records* 1990, p.15).

Persons 85 and over constitute the fastest growing segment of the population. The well-known Framingham (Massachusetts) Heart Study has followed a large sample of "normal" men and women over many years. Extensive research into disability among the now older participants was reported in 1983 (Briley). The researchers found that men and women aged 75 to 84 were somewhat more likely to need help with social and physical tasks than the younger participants. Nevertheless, 77 percent of them were able to walk half a mile or more, 85 percent could climb stairs, 50 percent could perform heavy housework, and more than 90 percent were fully capable of carrying out activities of daily living. The researchers believed the group was fairly representative of persons aged 75 to 84 and reflected the better health of contemporary cohorts of the old-old.

The researchers also remind us that at any given time about 5 percent of the elderly are patients in long-term-care facilities, and that another 10 percent living in the community have comparable levels of disability and require assistance. It is these two groups who are of concern to social workers. The first group is considered in the next section. Among the second group are those who live alone. They are mostly women, very old, frail, and living on very low incomes. Older persons living alone constitute 55 percent of all those over 75 and 52 percent of all those over 85. A study of the problems faced by this group, conducted for the Commonwealth Fund Commission on Elderly People Living Alone (1987), found that among the national sample of 2,506 persons, 25 percent were childless, and another 20 percent did not have a son or daughter living within an hour's travel. Because of lack of social supports, the very-old living alone are at high risk for institutionalization. Half of all the respondents had lived by themselves for ten or more years. Nearly 86 percent of them said they preferred living alone to any alternative they were aware of.

It appears that many of the very-old, who are mostly women, outlive their assets and struggle along on small Social Security benefits based on unskilled work or on their being widows of eligible workers who may have received only small benefits to begin with because of low earnings. Also, half of the women over age 75 and eligible for SSI and Medicaid are not receiving benefits, being unaware of the programs or of their eligibility for them. Both the old-old and the very-old cohorts grew up in the early years of the twentieth century with an ethos of independence and self-sufficiency, and many prefer to struggle along on whatever income they have.

Despite their own poor health and poverty, over one third in the Commonwealth Fund study responded affirmatively when asked if they would accept a 5 percent cut in their Social Security income so that other elderly people would be guaranteed paid medical and nursing-home costs, home health services would be provided for all elderly people in need of such care, and no elderly person would live in poverty. This altruistic theme was also heard in a study of the elderly residents of a Veterans Administration domiciliary, an ambulatory self-care facility, intermediate between a hospital or nursing home and a supervised or independent dwelling in the community (Ewalt and Honeyfield 1981). Of the 720 veterans, 90 percent, or 646, participated; 40 percent were 55 to 64, and 25 percent were 65 or older. Of those desiring to remain at the domiciliary (almost 40 percent), one third said their first-priority need was for opportunities to be of help to others. This was the highest ranked need, although it was more frequent among those 64 and younger than among the older residents.

Health and Care Issues

From the standpoint of the old-old or very-old parent no longer able to live independently because of infirmities, the move to the adult child's home and family may be perceived as relinquishing her or his independence and self-direction. Sometimes, former tensions between parent and child may resurface; more important, most older persons dread being a "burden" on their children. The literature frequently refers to a "role reversal" assumed to occur between elderly parents and their adult children as the parents become increasingly dependent. This is now regarded as an injustice both to the parents and to the adult children, overlooking the complex development of relationships and roles over time. It is questionable "whether a child can, psychologically, ever really be a parent to his or her parent or that an older adult can renounce or even wish to renounce the parental role" (Harbor Area Geriatric Program Staff 1984:1152). The adult child needs, rather, to separate her or his relationship to the parent from what it was before and to establish a new relationship with new responsibilities. The Harbor Area staff suggests the use of the term *role change* to signify the new responsibilities.

For frail elderly (those at physical and/or mental risk) who, while unable to be fully independent, continue to live alone, as well as for many of those living with their adult children, some fourteen hundred day care programs around the country are a boon. Most must be funded by community sources (and sliding fee scales), and therefore not many communities provide day care. Exemplary day care centers provide van transport to and from the center (usually for a small fee), a nutritious lunch, and recreational programming such as painting, crafts, gardening, poetry and music, games, movies, guest lecturers, and field trips (Penney 1976). The staffs usually consist of nurses and social workers. Programs operated by hospitals may make medical and rehabilitative services available, including physical, occupational, and speech therapists. Day care programs provide a stimulating, health-oriented environment to their members, and like home health care services, they serve to prevent premature institutionalization. They also provide needed relief to family caregivers, even permitting them to work full time. While nursing-home costs average about $50 to $90 per day, "national estimates for the cost of one-year stays in a nursing home currently average about $22,000," (*Research Dialogues* 1989). The average cost of adult day care is about $30 per day and may be met by private or Federal insurance programs.

Another positive development for older persons with physical disabilities is that they, like younger people with disabilities, can benefit from increasing numbers of products and housing adaptations designed for their needs. Some products and adaptations are minor and inexpensive, and some are major and expensive. Home health care agencies may be able to pay for minor adaptations, and various catalogs of products are on the market. For practitioners working with older persons, hospital social workers and occupational therapists and area agencies on aging can be helpful informants on products, adaptations, and the availability of possible loans and grants.

Mental impairment may accompany physical illness or be disabling in itself. Alzheimer's disease, named for the physician who first described it in 1906, is an irreversible, progressively deteriorating mental disorder. Usually considered a disease only of older persons, it also strikes some in young and middle adulthood, and its course is more rapid and severe in such instances. The cause is still unknown, but the early-onset cases are believed to have genetic roots, because the disease seems to run in families who also frequently have children with Down syndrome or other chromosomal disorders. To distinguish between early and late onset, the disease that appears in the older years is referred to technically as SDAT (senile dementia, Alzheimer's type). Definitive diagnosis is possible only at autopsy, when the presence in the cerebral cortex of disease-specific neurofibrillary tangles can be established. Hence, differential diagnosis is difficult in cases of senility. The diagnosis of SDAT is made by ruling out other dementias through history, physical and mental examination, laboratory tests, and high-technology testing, which can be inaccurate. Some who are diagnosed as having SDAT may actually be depressed but not demented or may be suffering from fever, infection, cardiovascular conditions, or drug reactions, all of which can affect brain function and are treatable (Butler 1982).

As research into the cause continues, it is taking several directions. Some scientists are investigating chemical changes in the brain, since SDAT brains show a marked loss of an enzyme associated with the neurotransmitters responsible for memory. Others are studying the controversial link of SDAT to excessive trances of aluminum found in the tangles. Whether the metal is causal or not, it does seem to be associated with the disease, and it may be responsible for some of the symptoms. Still others are investigating the possibility of a slow-acting transmissible virus that takes twenty or more years to bring about the disease, and some are considering the possibility of age-related changes in the immune system (Kerson and Kerson 1985).

Approximately 1.5 million Americans over 65, or 5 percent of the elderly population, are thought to suffer from SDAT. The disease is devastating to patient and family, and at least until the final stages, most SDAT patients are cared for at home because Medicare does not pay for long-term care. It is estimated that about half the patients over 65 in nursing homes suffer SDAT (most are on Medicaid). The onset is insidious, with beginning forgetfulness and occasional confusion, depressed mood, or disordered sleep. Many patients recognize that they are functioning less well and may be terrified, or they may deny what is happening. As the months go by, deterioration may be slowed by a stimulating, but not too stimulating, home environment and by keeping the person involved in useful tasks, physical exercise, and social contacts. If still continent and able to leave the house, the person's participation in a day care center is also helpful for both patient and family.

As the tangles and areas of brain degeneration (termed *plaques*) increase over time, the symptoms worsen. The cognitive and memory dysfunction and disorientation gradually increase to the point where the individual cannot remember what occurred a few minutes before and does not know where she or he is. Hostile and uncooperative behaviors, wandering, incontinence, failure to recognize spouse or children, and a loss of awareness of the changes in oneself may be exhibited. The rate of decline and the extent of such losses vary in individuals. In the advanced stage, afflicted persons are totally unable to care for themselves and ultimately die. SDAT is now said to be the fourth leading cause of death among the elderly. While incurable, the condition is helped by environmental means to improve the quality of life, as described above, and counseling for the family. Keeping patients safe by changes in the home to facilitate their functioning and keeping them healthy by careful personal hygiene and treatment of any other conditions are important (Butler 1982).

Sacks noted, "In Korsakov's [an organic brain disorder due to alcoholism], or dementia, or other such catastrophes, however great the organic damage . . . there remains the undiminished possibility of reintegration by art, by communion, by touching the human spirit, and this can be preserved in what seems at first a hopeless state of neurological devastation" (1985:39). Lee (1981) demonstrated this potential in a summer day camp program for hospitalized elderly persons suffering from Korsakov syndrome and Alzheimer's disease who were awaiting nursing-home placement, and by Will (1950) in his treatment of hospitalized patients suffering from profoundly catatonic states over long periods of time.

Death and the Elderly

Some of the literature on death and dying implies that the death of an elderly person is less difficult for the family to cope with because the social value of the elderly person is supposedly less, because her or his roles are less critical to family functioning, and because death comes at the age-appropriate time. For the surviving spouse, however, the loss may be just as excruciating, after forty or more years of a loving and satisfying relationship (or even of a not-so-satisfying one), as it is for the younger person. Deaths of widowers within a year following the loss of the wife occur at a higher rate than the corresponding rate of deaths of widows within a year following the loss of the husband. It is thought that the loss of one's spouse is harder for men to cope with than for women, perhaps because men have less experience in coping with their own basic and household needs and because the social ties of couples are usually maintained by the wife.

Peak (1977) described three general types of responses to dying by elderly persons themselves:

1. Most elderly persons accept dying as part of being old. Their mastery implies that they feel in control of their situation, based on a minimal amount of denial. Many have worked out the acceptance of their inevitable death long before the terminal phase, and many have made plans for death or are ready to do so.

For some in this group, perhaps, the acceptance of dying is facilitated by memories of a life of some satisfaction. The apparently universal tendency of the elderly to recall earlier experiences, and to rework their memories in ways that develop a sense of continuity, integrity, and meaning to their life helps prepare them for the inevitability of death as part of life (Butler 1975). Religious beliefs, cultural patterns, and the love and caring of those held dear help ease the dying elderly person's transition to life's ending.

2. A small group of elderly persons appear to block out the idea of death completely. This reaction prevents their making the plans and preparations that might lead to a sense of closure and peace.

3. A still smaller group comprises those elderly who are greatly disturbed by ideas of death—their own or the death of those close to them. They spend time and energy avoiding the associated fears. It may be that among these two latter groups, the task of the acceptance of death as part of life is made more difficult as they look back upon an unhappy or disappointing past with anger or regrets. Pattison commented that those not ready to die "still question and doubt their existence. Death will be an intrusion unless and until they can affirm that their life was a unique existence to them, that allowed of no other existence" (1977b:26).

Kalish (1968) described a self-perceived social death, where an elderly person feels "as good as dead" and "may as well be dead." Such a self-perception may be precipitated by a terminal diagnosis, or by feelings of isolation and helplessness, or by anxiety over increasing dependence. The aged person's loss of statuses and roles, the many personal losses, or indignities imposed by an uncaring institution can lead to these feelings. Kalish also described a category of psychological death in which the comatose, completely drugged, or senile patient is no longer aware that she or he *is*. Since social death and psychological death are reversible in varying degrees, practitioners working with the elderly and the terminally ill need to know how to reverse these conditions and how to prevent them in the first place. What is needed are increased human interaction, cognitive stimulation, and opportunities to function as a mature and responsible adult in whatever ways are still possible: securing information about what is happening to one's physical self; making decisions, however modest in extent; participating in planning next steps; and so on.

Suicide

A serious public health problem is suicide by older persons. Those over 65 have the highest rate in the United States, and almost three fourths of the relatively rare double suicides in Western society are committed by elderly couples. Persons over 65 constitute 12 percent of the population, but 1989 figures reveal that their suicide rate is 21.6 per 100,000, reflecting a growing increase over the 1980s. In 1981, for example, the rate was 17.1. These government statistics are based on death certificates. Actual suicides are probably well above that rate, as older persons can easily cover up their suicides. They may stop visiting the physician, starve themselves, deliberately overdose on prescribed medications, or stop taking life-sustaining medications. Thus the cause of death may be listed as heart failure, diabetic complications, and so on. Older persons are more resolute in their desire to take their lives and succeed far more often than teenagers. Their success may indicate that the suicide is not a cry for help as it is in the teenager who fails in the attempt, but a determination to end what has come to be an unendurable condition.

Older suicidal individuals rarely seek help. For example, only 2 percent of the calls to a Washington, D.C., suicide and depression hotline came from persons 65 and older. Many are reluctant to seek therapeutic help, although if they can be persuaded to go once, many older persons do continue. The reasons for suicide among older persons, especially males, include the loss of the spouse, the loss of status and organizational affiliation, depression (estimated to be present in 15 to 20 percent of older persons and to underlie two thirds of older persons' suicides), financial problems, chronic or life-threatening illness, fear of eventual nursing-home placement, or hopelessness and alcoholism.

Situational depression may be helped by support from relatives and friends, supplemented by professional counseling in some instances, but chemically based depression responds best to medication, combined with other forms of therapy. In this connection, a study of suicides in a retirement community demonstrated that elderly married individuals, and not only the widowed, need to be involved in kin networks, friendships, and community organizations such as religious and fraternal groups. These social connections counteract the isolation of both widowed men and of married males who have no other social ties. While marriage is a restraining force against suicide, it must be reinforced by other connections if the suicide rate is to be reduced among older widowed and married persons (Bock 1972).

More preretirement counseling, bereavement groups, making sure that every elderly person has a telephone, and stricter gun laws (guns are the primary method of suicide in males) may help reduce the rate. Also, increased dissemination of information about suicide to professionals and the public, including the warning signs of depression (*Useful Information on Suicide* 1986), and educating older persons and families about improvements in nursing-home care (and further improving that care) are important preventive measures.

Elder Abuse

Another troubling health and social issue is elder abuse in families, nursing homes, psychiatric hospitals, board-and-care homes, and so on. Recognition of the seriousness and extent of elder abuse has been slow, although it is no newer a phenomenon than spousal and child abuse. It can be emotional in nature (verbal assaults and threats), physical (battering, shoving, shaking, tying to a bed or chair, or withholding physical care), medical (oversedating or failing to procure needed appliances such as walkers, glasses, or hearing aids), or financial (misuse of assets, exploitation, and scams). Accurate figures are difficult to obtain, but estimates suggest that one million of those 65 or older, or one out of twenty-five, suffer abuse. How many at the hands of institutions and nonfamily individuals and how many at the hands of family members is unknown, but one study reported slightly less than 10 percent of 404 clients attending a Cleveland Chronic Illness Center had been mistreated by a family member or a companion (Lau and Kosberg 1979).

The Federal Older Americans Act authorizes ombudsman programs in each state to investigate and act on complaints of abuse in long-term-care institutions. Most states now have laws requiring the reporting of elder abuse by individuals and institutions. In some areas, hospitals have formed interdisciplinary elder abuse teams. Matlaw and Mayer (1986) reported on complex practical, clinical, and ethical dilemmas that surface for social worker team members in the investigation and assessment of suspected elder abuse, neglect, and mistreatment by families or institutions and in the social consequences of the mandated reporting. It bears repeating that both respite services for family caregivers and day care programs for older persons help alleviate the intensive stress, frustration, and physical exhaustion many caregivers experience, which lead to abuse by a relatively few of them.

LONG-TERM INSTITUTIONAL CARE

While only 5 percent of the elderly are in long-term institutional care at any given time, it is estimated that 20 percent of the older population are likely to spend some time in a long-term facility (Monk and Dobrof 1978). Institutional care comprises several types, such as nursing homes (intermediate-care facilities), skilled-nursing facilities, homes for the aged or retirement homes, rehabilitation hospitals, and psychiatric hospitals. This section considers nursing homes that house the frail elderly (and the young chronically disabled), as the homes are an important focus of professional and public attention. To a lesser extent it considers also those homes for the aged that combine many types of services.

Most patients in nursing homes, but not all, are women. Most are over 80 years of age, many have lost their friends and relatives, and some have even outlived their children. Most frail elderly have multiple physical disabilities, and somewhat more than half suffer mental disability. Butler (1975) stated that the rates of organic brain diseases and functional disorders, such as some depressions and paranoic conditions, increase steadily each decade after the age of 60. Many older persons with such disorders were discharged from state psychiatric hospitals under the twin policies of deinstitutionalization and short-term treatment. Unable to maintain themselves in the community without appropriate supports, some have become part of the single-room-occupancy and homeless populations, and many others have ended up in nursing homes without any provision for in-house or outpatient rehabilitative mental health services. Professional social workers and other mental health practitioners are not found on the staffs of most nursing homes. However, the 1987 federal nursing home reform act requires that nursing homes with more than 120 beds have a full-time social worker with at least a BSW degree by 1990.

It is true that some residents without relatives may feel isolated and alone in the institution, except for possible visits from volunteers. As mentioned earlier, most families regard placement as a last resort when the parent's physical and/or mental impairments become severe and deplete the caregiver's emotional and physical resources. Most families visit their parents regularly; bring them home for a weekend or holiday, depending on their condition; take them for outings; and so on. It is harder for families who live at a distance to maintain closeness, but many keep in touch by telephone, cards and letters, and an occasional visit. Increasingly, family agencies and social workers in private practice offer geriatric services to families living at a distance from their relative. These include case management, monitoring of care, visiting the resident, and keeping the family informed.

A serious concern about nursing-home care is a financial one. The cost can range from $22,000 to $35,000 a year or more, which quickly exhausts the personal resources of middle-income persons, some in as little as three months. Half of the couples with one spouse in the nursing home are impoverished within six months. The only recourse is to apply for Medicaid, a means-tested welfare program, because Medicare does not reimburse the costs of long-term care (except in a skilled-nursing facility following hospitalization for an acute illness, if ordered by a physician, and then for only 100 days). In some states, Medicaid requires that all property or other assets must be used before aid is given.

A more rational response to the need for long-term care by the elderly is essential. Acute care is said to account for only 10 percent of the catastrophic health care costs of the elderly. Medicare reimbursement for home health care services, adult day care, and respite programs would provide a choice and would very likely prevent the premature institutionalization of many. Another criticism is that Medicaid was established to meet the health needs of poor children and adults of all ages, yet the present arrangement results in approximately 45 percent of Medicaid funds being used for long-term care of the elderly.

A second serious drawback of nursing-home care is environmental. In addition to feeling that placement is the final step before death itself, most elderly—unless they are totally disabled mentally—fear they will lose all sense of independence and self-direction in their lives. And, indeed, many nursing homes do fail to provide opportunities for self-regulation, action, decision making, and control over one's life situation to whatever degree the patient's condition permits. At the same time, the elderly also differ from other groups in that sensory, mental, and physical impairments make them more dependent on their environment for well-being than other adults. Yet, many nursing homes fail to provide stimulating physical and social settings that nourish the senses, the mind, the social interests, and the other capacities of their patients. The results are devastating, as the patients lose their sense of competence, their self-esteem, their self-direction, and their human relatedness (e.g., Vladek 1980).

In recent years, as a result of media attention and advocacy by families and the human service professions, including social work, some nursing homes have raised their standards of care. They provide recreation, crafts, reality-orientation programs, and outings and arrange to bring in pet dogs and cats to visit with the residents. Some have developed affiliations with nearby child care facilities for the exchange of visits for mutual pleasure and benefit. Some provide temporary respite care to relieve family caregivers, although it is expensive. Since 90 percent of nursing homes are for-profit institutions, the extent and rate of change have been limited. Federal standards, inspection, and sanctions have not been entirely successful in eliminating substandard care where it exists, although the ombudsman program and resident councils provide some leverage. With respect to social work, federal regulations do not require that social services be furnished by a professional social worker, but only that such a person serve as a consultant to the individual who does provide them. Such consultants cover many nursing homes, and some tend to define their role solely as that of supervisor of the consultee, and not as advocate and consultant to the administration for promoting improved care.

Wells, Singer, and Polgar (1986), Canadian social work educators and researchers, developed an effective model for residents' empowerment in nursing-home care. Its success has led to its spread across Canada. Their demonstration–research projects began in 1970 with a succession of student units in Toronto's municipal system of nursing homes. Working with strengths already in the system, the students achieved remarkable improvements in services and in organizational structures that support the changes (Singer and Wells 1981). By 1982, when that project ended, the links among the residents' kinship, friendship, formal caregiving, and mutual-aid networks had been developed and strengthened; inappropriate staff and resident attitudes about older people and their families had been modified; and policymakers in the institutions had been influenced to provide structures for the continuation of services after the students left (Wells and Singer 1985). Students had also succeeded in supporting residents during the potentially destructive relocation process when one home was closed and the residents were scattered among several others (Singer and Wells 1981). Although the seven homes had previously had no social workers, they obtained funding for social work personnel after the project ended.

Most recently, Wells, Singer, and Polgar developed an empowerment model that mobilizes the strengths of the residents, the staff, and the organization: "Engaging the clients themselves in the advocacy process helps to empower clients at the same time that it assures quality care" (1986:1). The model is designed to replace the medical and custodial models of long-term care, both of which are known to foster dependence and helplessness. It emerged out of a demonstration–action research project that was tested in two long-term institutions with a matched untreated pair of homes for comparison. Wells, Singer, and Polgar reported, "We were impressed by the capabilities that became evident in the elderly, despite their frailties and physical and mental impairments; we were impressed by the families' interest and dedication; we were impressed by the responsiveness and commitment of staff" (1986:3). The authors provided detailed guidelines for introducing into long-term facilities a process in which the elderly, their families, and the staff participate actively in policy and program development that enhance the well-being and quality of life of the residents and for creating a problem-solving structure to help the institution adapt to changes in the system and in the external environment.

In the United States, the long-term facilities that strive for quality of life, resident empowerment, and staff training tend to be the homes for the aged or home-and-hospitals. They are usually sponsored by religious or other nonprofit organizations. While they vary in their mission, the best provide an attractive and functional physical setting and an active social setting. They foster individual choice of programs and activities and avoid rigid routines to the degree possible. Some, certified for Medicaid and Medicare reimbursement, combine several levels of care: hospital (chronic illness) and both skilled-nursing and intermediate care. Some also offer community services such as adult day care and training in gerontology for the service professions, and most have professional social workers, allied health professionals, nurses, and physicians on staff. Some provide rehabilitative services and a rich variety of recreational and cultural programs and activities, including resident councils.

ADAPTATION REVISITED

Just as people are wonderfully diverse, so, too, are the adaptations they achieve in their passage through time. Simic and Myerhoff (1978) enriched our understanding of growing old under varying circumstances with their suggestion of three universal themes: continuity, sexual dichotomy, and aging as a career. These are inseparable aspects of a single, shared, deep structure of aging, from birth to old age.

Continuity has three aspects: Spatial continuity is people's attachment to certain real, imagined, or mythological spaces that become part of the self or one's identity. Social continuity is the permanency, frequency, and intensity in relationships as they shift over time; some are face-to-face and some are vicarious and symbolic in either life or death. Cultural continuity is contact with and access to a coherent and relatively stable body of ideas, beliefs, values, and symbols. Depending on the society and the culture, and on the exigencies of life, a person may experience more discontinuities or more continuities in life. For example, members of the El Senior Center (Cuellar 1978) in Los Angeles had been cut off from the experiences of their childhood by virtue of their migration from Mexico. They were separated from the culture in which they had been socialized. They were cut off to some extent from their Americanized children and thus had lost a sense of intergenerational continuity. But they found the continuity and strength to structure their old age by turning to each other in their voluntary association. Cultural continuity was restored and savored.

Sexual dichotomy is the disparity in the aging process of women and men, as well as the sex differences in the ways in which older individuals adapt to status and role transitions. In the El Senior Center, female roles appeared to be better defined than male roles. Enjoying the traditional prestige accorded grandmotherhood, the women members easily assumed managerial roles in the center. For the men, masculinity had been defined as physical prowess, now in decline, and was associated with work roles no longer available. Simic and Myerhoff (1978) noted that different kinds of power are lodged in male and female statuses and roles: "Power peaks at different times for men and women, and where power declines for one sex, leaving a vacuum, the other frequently steps in to fill it" (Simic and Myerhoff:240). This statement echoes Gutmann's hypothesis that as women age they become more active and dominant, and as men age they become more passive and nurturant.

Simic and Myerhoff (1978) view aging across the life course as a career, rather than as a series of losses. They emphasize "old age as a period of activity, participation, self-movement, and purposefulness: [Old age is a kind of work that requires] the constant expenditure of effort for sociocultural and physical survival. To live out each day with dignity, alertness, control over one's faculties, and mobility necessitates the output of tremendous energy" (1978:240). The notion of *career* also connotes long-term goals, and over the life course the individual "builds, or fails to build, a structure of relationships, achievements, affect, and respect that will give meaning and validation to one's total life at its close" (Simic and Myerhoff:740). Thus aging as a career represents a storing up of many kinds of resources. While there are inevitable losses, there are also accumulated gains.

As social workers well know, the gains and rewards are differently distributed in our society because of differing experiences and capacities and, more significantly, because of location in the social structure. Also, different cultures are likely to define success differently. A measure of success among the members of the El Senior Center was the skills they had developed in dealing with Anglo institutions and customs: literacy, bilingualism, and some awareness of the basic assumptions of the dominant society.

Thus old age as a career involves processes of construction and reconstruction, both psychologically and socially. Memories, the life story, narrative, autobiography, personal and family history—however such accounts are titled as they are told to others and oneself, they are significant parts of the creativity needed in the work of aging as a career. They are opportunities to relive, affirm, assess, and lend order to the variety of experiences, perceptions, feelings, actions, and relationships over the life course, and to reevaluate their significance. They, like myth and ritual, represent the less tangible aspects of continuity. It is no wonder, then, that reminiscence in the "life review" (Butler 1963) has such therapeutic potency in social work practice with older persons.

FAMILY TRANSFORMATIONS: YOUNG-OLD, OLD-OLD, AND VERY-OLD

The conclusion to be drawn from the data presented in this chapter is that the elderly are extremely diverse: "Because of longer life-histories, with their complicated patterns of personal and social commitments, adults are not only much more complex than children, but they are more different one from another, and increasingly different as they move from youth to extreme old age" (Neugarten 1969). In addition, there are strong cohort, historical period, and cultural effects at work in creating diversity among the old. For most old-old and very-old persons, the options for managing life events and transitions are apt to be limited because of diminished vigor and the likelihood of chronic illnesses, loss of spouse, dwindling income, and so on. Here the significance of the society and its social and health policies, the family and its capacity for love and caring, and the community and its sense of interconnectedness and communitas come to the fore.

Walsh (1980) pointed out that while these processes hold potential for loss and dysfunction, they also provide opportunities for transformation and growth. The transitions include retirement, chronic illness or impairment due to physical or mental disability of self or spouse, the death of the spouse and/or friends and consequent loneliness, and the draining of limited finances and even poverty. For some, one or more of these events and transitions may occur before the age of 75. For others, they may not occur until after that age. Although some of these transitions are expectable, probably many will be experienced by the older person and her or his adult children as second-order developments requiring difficult second-order changes. Because of the great diversity among older persons, it is difficult to generalize the form that the transformations among the three age groups may take. Instead, I present a living example of old-old and very-old people achieving successful transformations through a combination of individual, collective, and culturally based strengths as they managed many second-order developments. The example itself is a fitting conclusion to this chapter and to the book, for it is a celebration of life.

The example comes from an anthropological study of a group of Jewish old-old and very-old women and men, immigrants to America from Eastern Europe, carried out by Barbara Myerhoff (1978a). Numbering about three hundred, they lived in an urban ghetto in Venice, California, isolated from their assimilated, sophisticated adult children by geographic distance. They were poor, frail, lonely, and isolated. They suffered from communal and social neglect, and from even physical abuse at the hands of young thugs who roamed the neighborhood. As members of the dilapidated Aliyah Senior Citizen's Community Center, they transcended the perils of poverty, neglect, loneliness, poor health, substandard housing, and even physical danger through their culture-based personal and collective strengths. The account of their lives, their rituals and celebrations, and their serious troubles and how they managed them is unforgettably moving.

They had migrated to the east coast of America at the turn of the century, working mostly at unskilled and skilled labor. Most had liberal and socialist political beliefs, and many had been active in unions and various workers' movements. When retired, they moved as individuals or couples to California because of the climate and living conditions, leaving their more or less successful children behind. Aliyah's members suffered great discontinuities: Their eastern European *shtetl* (village) culture in which their identity was rooted had been wiped out by the Holocaust, along with the inhabitants. For them there was no way to reestablish the ties of their childhood, their children had not been socialized to the values and norms of the old culture, and even their treasured language, Yiddish, was threatened with extinction. Yet, as a collectivity in their voluntary association, the Aliyah Center, they found communitas—a spirit that enabled them to begin to repair the tragic ruptures in their lives. Together, they recreated the environment and the cultural values of their youth by reviving their common language and through culturally based myths and stories, through secular and sacred rituals and celebrations, and even through their sometimes disorderly rivalries and disagreements. Most of the members knew each other well as they had lived in this Yiddish ghetto for two or three decades. Most were in their mid-80's or older.

The subculture they created combined elements from their childhood beliefs and customs with modern urban American practices and attitudes, adapted to their present needs and circumstances and providing them with the essential sense of personal and ethnic worth (Myerhoff 1978b). In a sense, they could reconnect their old age to their childhood because of their common destiny "as poor outsiders and marginal members of society, a situation which did not prevail in their middle years" (Myerhoff 1978b:236). Indeed, their present circumstances recalled *shtetl* life for them. Myerhoff described in detail the incredible odds against which they struggled. Their successes included being able to get up each morning, prepare and pay for food, visit friends, and walk to the beach. These activities required skills of financial management in the face of dire poverty, knowledge of how to survive with little and of how to conserve declining physical energies, knowledge of the available services, and the ability to manipulate their obligations to friends or family.

Their continuing existence was a triumph: "They had outlived all their enemies—Cossacks, Nazis, anti-Semites—and successful defiance of those determined to extinguish them was a conspicuous source of pride" (Myerhoff 1978b:170). Myerhoff wrote of one 95-year-old man that he knew how to look at the inevitability of death without seeking to hasten it, and he knew how to bring the past into the present without remaining fixed on it or using it in negative comparisons with the present. He was able to substitute new standards and desires for himself as old ones were no longer attainable. He generated from within appropriate measures of self-worth in a continuous process of construction and reconstruction. He used thinking, talking, and writing his life story to stave off occasional depression, anxiety, and fear of senility. As the "elder" in their midst, he advised the members on the elements of a positive response to old age: "humor, perspective, the preservation of tradition, the necessity for continual learning, and adapting to change" (1978a:223). He was a symbol to the others of aging as an admirable career. In all these ways he organized his conception of himself and the meaning of his life, epito-mizing the integration of internal and external forces (Myerhoff 1978b).

Like the women at the El Senior Center, the women of Aliyah coped with their difficult circumstances better than did the men. Their skills in establishing social relationships with each other gave them a sense of their own power and meaning, in spite of the environment's nega-tive attitudes toward them and the powerlessness in the traditional female role in their culture. The men, severed from their economically based and intellectually oriented roles, had less adaptability and vi-tality in the present circumstances than they would have in the natu-ral course of aging in the original society.

Simic and Myerhoff commented on their collection of cross-cul-tural studies:

> We have encountered elderly survivors wending their way toward the culmination of life, sometimes following culturally desig-nated routes, and at others traversing terra incognita. For some, this task has met with satisfaction and success, for others it has resulted in misery and failure. Old age has not been the same for everyone. Some have built their future carefully while others have foundered along the way regardless of the cultural context. (1978:245)

At the close of this book, you, the reader, and I, the author, may join Simic and Myerhoff in their hope that, "With luck one day we, too, will find ourselves in old age" (1978:245).

The bird was formed by placing the hand of man in harmony with nature and the universe.

The interweaving of the bear, fish, insect and plant symbolizes the food chain. The star represents the heavens.

The symbol reminds us that all of life is inter-related and that each part is essential to form a whole.

FIGURE 13.1.

Appendix 1:
Stage Models of Development

Several theories of personality development based on invariant, universal, sequential stages are still used by many social workers and other professionals in the human services. These are briefly described here. Such brevity fails, inevitably, to do justice to the complexity and richness of the various ideas. Hence, additional readings for readers who desire to learn more about the theories, are provided at the end of this appendix.

SIGMUND FREUD (1856–1939)

The psychosexual stages of Freud constitute one part of what is perhaps the best known model, having entered American culture. The stages refer to the movement of libido (in a broad sense, the biologically based sexual drive) from one eroticized body zone to another during the first five years of life. It is a biologically based scheme in which tissue tension is aroused by libidinal needs, wishes, and fantasies. The organism seeks to meet the need and reduce the tension by means of an external object, usually human. Over the first year of life, the infant is dominated by oral needs and libidinal pleasures that center in the mouth and that are gratified by activities of sucking at the breast or bottle, thumb or finger, and by later mouthing of toys and other objects. In addition to the libidinal drive, Freud postulated an aggressive drive, although he did not work out a developmental framework for it as he did for the libidinal drive. However, aggression may be manifested in infancy by, for example, biting the nipple or spitting up. At this stage, the object that satisfies the libidinal oral drive is a part object, for example, the mother's breast, not the whole mother.

In the second year, at about the time that toilet training is usually introduced, the baby is dominated by libidinal needs and pleasures that center on the anus. This is a time when many babies show pleasure in expelling and/or smearing feces. The progression to the anal stage does not mean that oral behaviors and needs disappear. Rather, at each stage the drives and pleasures of the prior stages continue in some form but are less dominant than they were at the time of their ascendance. In adulthood they become part of sexual foreplay, or in a conflicted way, they may be transformed and may persist as character traits of a usually undesirable kind because of their infantile nature. The aggressive drive is observable in the anal stage when severe toilet training, for example, angers the baby. In retaliation, she or he may withhold feces or deposit them in places other than the bathroom. Since this is a stage when other forms of socialization are introduced as well, the aggressive drive is often aroused by restraints that may or may not be insensitive or inappropriate. In either case, temper tantrums and other difficult but often temporary behaviors may result. The anal stage is characterized by ambivalence (feeling love and hate toward the object at the same time), illustrated by the angry toddler's, "I hate you, Mommy." The object relations of the normal adult are expected to be relatively free of ambivalence, but where it persists, one of the feelings (usually the negative) is repressed because of anxiety and continues to influence functioning out of awareness.

The phallic stage and its Oedipus complex were of greatest interest to Freud and became central to the psychoanalytic theory of neurosis. Early in this stage, libidinal drives, interests, and pleasures shift from the anus to the external genitalia and are satisfied by masturbation and accompanying fantasies about adult sexuality and reproduction. The child begins to wish to replace the same-sex parent in such fantasied activity with the opposite-sex parent. This entry into the Odeipus complex is easier for the boy because he retains his primary love object (the mother). It is harder for the girl because she must give up her primary love object (the mother) in order to shift to the opposite-sex parent. Freud believed that this process in both the boy and the girl leads to the choice of a heterosexual object in adulthood, leaving an assumption that a homosexual choice is pathological. At about the same time the child also becomes aware of the anatomical differences between the sexes. Both the boy and the girl assume that the female child had a penis and that it was removed. The boy also assumes that he, too, could be castrated as punishment for his wish to replace his father and his fantasies about activities he will enjoy with his mother. The castration anxiety and guilt feelings mount to an unendurable peak, at which point he then represses (that is, renders unconscious) the entire Oedipus complex. In the process the boy identifies with his rival (the father), relinquishes his mother as a love object, and desires to become like his father and to find a woman "just like the girl who married dear old Dad." In identifying with his father, the young boy incorporates the father's prohibitions and culturally based rules of conduct as his own (in the superego).

The girl's experience takes a different course. She assumes that the mother was responsible for her not having a penis, a circumstance that serves to justify anger at the mother and disappointment in her. She thereupon can make the difficult shift from the mother to the father as her primary love object and fantasizes having a baby with him. Because she does not experience castration anxiety (assuming that she has already been castrated), her conflict is not as intense as the boy's, and the repression of the Oedipus conflict is correspondingly less complete. Hence, she may not relinquish her father entirely until adolescence. She may also identify partially with him and her brothers for a while, in the "tomboy" stage. Further, the girl's superego is said to be weaker than the boy's because it is not molded by intense (castration) anxiety and guilt and also because, in her relinquishment of the father, she identifies with the mother and the mother's superego, which is weak because of the very same processes in the mother's own childhood. Freud believed that the Oedipus complex is universal across all societies and cultures as a consequence of the human species' long infancy and dependence on parents who are also the first love objects. Further, it is reflected in the universality of the incest taboo.

Notably, oedipal forces do not dominate the child's mind all the time; children do continue to need, love, and enjoy both parents, while sometimes feeling rivalrous with one parent and wishing to have the other parent for themselves. For the most part, oedipal forces act as a spur to development rather than as an obstacle. The successful oedipal resolution produces a nonpunitive superego, satisfaction with one's sexual identity, and beginning capacity for nonambivalent object relations. Poor resolutions lead to the neuroses, while the psychoses originate in the unsuccessful negotiation of the preoedipal stages. Freud believed that the primitive libidinal and aggressive forces of infancy and early childhood subside following the oedipal resolution. The child enters a period of latency aided by repression and other defenses against old wishes and impulses and by ritualistic, obsessive, and compulsive behaviors. Latency frees the child to direct her or his sexual curiosity to formal learning and readiness for school, new interests, and a wider social world beyond the family. The drives were said to remain latent until reawakened by the storms of puberty and the associated weakening of defenses.

Freud also thought that how the child works out the preoedipal stages and the Oedipus complex helps shape the personality and determines behavior over the balance of her or his life. This conception is known as one of five or six psychic determinants of behavior. It is called the *genetic determinant.** A second psychic determinant, known as the *dynamic determinant,* arises from the operation of the pleasure principle and its infantlike, unconscious, drive-dominated thinking and impulsive action, which are characteristic of the id (the seat of the drives) and are termed the *primary process.* The pleasure principle and the primary process interact with the operation of the reality principle and its mature types of conscious, rational thinking and goal-directed action, which are characteristic of the ego (the executive part of the mind) and are termed the *secondary process.* A third, or *topographic,* determinant refers to the interplay among the conscious, unconscious, and preconscious (accessible to consciousness with a little effort) areas, which together constitute a metaphorical map of the mind.

A fourth, or *energic,* determinant refers to the nature of object cathexes (psychic energies attached to the mental images of objects that satisfy the drives), now of less significance in psychoanalytic theory. A fifth, or *structural,* determinant refers to the interactions among three metaphorical structures of the mind called *id, ego,* and *superego* (to be described in a moment). Later, with the work of Heinz Hartmann in ego psychology, the influence of the environment came to be viewed as a sixth, or *adaptive,* determinant, although attention to the environment was generally limited to the parents' influence on the child. *Psychic determinism,* as an early fundamental belief of psychoanalysis, refers to the notion that all behavior is determined by

* The word *genetic* in psychoanalytic theory refers to the historical development of the drives, and not to genes as in today's biological sciences, although Freud did believe that the drives were biologically based tissue tensions.

the interplay of these five (and later six) antecedent conditions or, put somewhat differently, that each determinant is necessary, and that together they are sufficient to understand behavior.

To understand Erikson's and Mahler's models, we must first consider Freud's view that the mind comprises three metaphorical structures:

1. The *id* is the seat of the drives (present at birth) and of later unacceptable thoughts, impulses, fantasies, wishes, and so on that are repressed (rendered unconscious) by the individual because of the anxiety they arouse. The id is entirely unconscious, although some of its content may erupt into consciousness during psychosis and, somewhat disguised, into dreams.

2. The *superego* arises during the oedipal resolution, although some precursors are present earlier, and it undergoes major changes in adolescence. It is mostly unconscious, although its conscious aspect is experienced as the conscience. The superego is not only the seat of internalized moral strictures and judgments but also the locus of self-esteem, that is, the feelings one has about oneself as a good or bad person.

3. The *ego* is the executive, synthesizing, and integrating aspect of the mind that seeks to mediate among the often conflicting demands of the other two structures and of the environment. The ego is partly conscious but mostly unconscious. More will be said of the ego in the next section.

HEINZ HARTMANN (1894–1970) AND ERIK H. ERIKSON (1902–   )

Heinz Hartmann

To understand Erikson's work fully requires an understanding of the earlier ideas of the psychoanalyst Heinz Hartmann as well as those of Freud. Hartmann's careful extension (1958) of Freud's ideas about the ego resulted in the elaboration of ego psychology as part of psychoanalytic theory. He did not wish to violate Freud's fundamental assumptions; rather, he wanted to supplement them with congenial ideas about adaptation to social reality. Freud had declared that the ego is born out of the id as the latter comes into conflict with the environment; he saw the ego as mainly defensive in nature but gradually came to acknowledge other functions. Hartmann, on the other hand, sought an independent base for the ego that would solve "the problem of adaptation" without departing from the drive-oriented, pleasure-seeking, tension-reduction model of Freud. Hartmann's solution was to suggest that a primary autonomous sphere of functioning (autonomous in the sense of being free of domination by the drives) exists within the ego at birth or shortly thereafter. That is, the baby is born with what Hartmann termed a "biological matrix," out of which both the id and the primary autonomous sphere of the ego arise. This sphere includes innate, unconflicted ego functions that equip babies for survival in the environment. They confer on the infant a state of preadaptedness to an average, expectable environment. Primary autonomous ego functions or capacities include crying, sucking, and the clinging and rooting reflexes; sensory-perceptual and intellectual capacities; physical structures (brain, tongue, and palate) for learning a language; skeletal and muscular structures for posture and movement; and memory and judgment. With biologists, Hartmann believed that the abilities had been built into the species' genetic structure over evolutionary time through gene mutations and selection by the evolutionary environment (Hartmann's average expectable environment).

Acquired (learned) functions of the ego, on the other hand, arise out of conflict between the baby's id wishes and the environment (the parents); hence they are dominated by id drives (libidinal and aggressive) at the outset. Normally, these conflicted functions gradually achieve freedom from the id drives through 1) identification with the loved and loving parents (and later with other admired adults), followed by 2) "neutralization" (a kind of purifying) of their drive elements, which facilitates 3) a change in function from serving the id to serving the ego. These previously conflicted (drive-dominated) functions now serve ego goals rather than id wishes. They comprise the secondary sphere of autonomy of the ego and include the following: the ability to distinguish between what is internal and what is external (reality testing); object (human) relationships; impulse control, or the ability to tolerate delay; adaptive defenses effective in coping with stress; and the self-concept and ego ideal. They are characterized by secondary-process thinking (logical and rational) and the reality principle. However, any one of these acquired functions may not achieve autonomy because of developmental obstacles that block positive identifications, the neutralization of drive elements, and changes in function. Such conflicted functions remain in the conflicted sphere of the ego, and they continue to be dominated by the drives, the pleasure principle, and primary-process thinking (unconscious, illogical, irrational, and impulsive). Nevertheless, through later identifications, neutralization, and change of function, they may leave the conflicted sphere and enter the sphere of secondary autonomy. They are then characterized by secondary-process thinking and the reality principle.

In contrast to the primary, innate, autonomous functions of the ego, which are largely immune to anxiety, its secondary acquired functions do remain vulnerable to anxiety. When the anxiety is severe enough, these functions may regress. They return to their former submission to drive components and primary-process thinking, because they are now once again in the conflict sphere of the ego. The conflict sphere also includes the ego function of anxiety (since anxiety is born of conflict). The anxiety is a signal to the ego to institute a defense against the painful feeling, so defenses are also located in the conflict sphere. Again, it must be kept in mind that these ego spheres, like the ego, the superego, and the id, are metaphorical. There is no region in the brain corresponding to them. *Ego spheres* and *ego functions* are simply names given to observable sets or clusters of human behaviors.

Erik Erikson

Building on Hartmann's concepts, Erikson (a nonphysician, psychoanalyzed in the late 1920s by Freud's daughter, Anna) presents a stage model of the development of the autonomous ego, or what he calls the healthy personality. His model parallels Freud's model of libidinal stages and, contrary to popular belief, is rooted in Freud's ideas, including those about female development. Erikson did not reject Freud's drive theory; he was bent on establishing a model of psychosocial development that would parallel Freud's framework of psychosexual development. In addition, however, Erikson carried his ideas of ego development beyond the childhood stages to include a stage in adolescence and three stages in adulthood, thus adding an optimistic assumption that development continues over the life course. This assumption is in contrast to Freud's pessimistic assumption that emotional development is largely completed by age 5. Freud did believe, however, that later additions or modifications were attainable through psychoanalysis and, in rare instances, through favorable life circumstances.

Each Eriksonian stage is a period of marked physical, social, and psychological change, and all are conceived of in terms of the embryological principle of epigenesis (Erikson 1964). In embryological development, each organ of the embryo has its critical period, in which certain aspects of its development must occur or the full development of the organ will never take place, or it will be severely damaged or missing altogether. Erikson maintains that, likewise, in psychosocial development the completion of one stage depends upon the successful completion of the prior stage; each stage successfully completed becomes the foundation for the next. Each has its unique time of dominance, though it continues as a life issue over the life course. Each stage has its stage-specific psychosocial task. Erikson calls them "normal crises," maintaining that all human beings experience them. The physical and mental characteristics of the person are the potentials, and the environment (family, community, and society) provides the opportunities for accomplishing each task. Erikson asserts that the baby has an inborn coordination with the environment, or preadaptedness in Hartmann's terms.

Each stage brings new drives and anxieties, new possibilities and limitations, and new achievements and frustrations. Possible outcomes are formulated in terms of more-or-less polar, though not necessarily opposite, positions. The successful outcome is reflected in the dominance of the positive position as a quality of the autonomous ego, together with an associated "virtue" or strength (Erikson 1964). The unsuccessful outcome reflects the dominance of the negative position as a quality of the ego within its conflicted sphere, and the corresponding "virtue" is missing or weak. While each stage has its time of ascendance and crisis, each persists to some degree throughout life. This assumption of persistence seems to suggest, despite the emphasis on the rigidity of epigenesis, that later opportunities may appear for the improved resolution of early poorly resolved stages. Erikson's works do not clarify this ambiguity.

As the centerpiece of Erikson's model, identity is rooted in the earlier achievement of trust, autonomy, initiative, and industry but has its ascendance in adolescence. After adolescence, ego identity incorporates elements derived from the later achievements of intimacy, generativity, and integrity. Like identity, each stage-specific quality is, according to Erikson, a functioning whole in which no part must have missed its original crisis, its further transformations, and its reintegration into each later stage. The matter of identity followed by intimacy presents an interesting issue. In Erikson's scheme, for example, the adaptive task for young adults, who have succeeded in the adolescent task of achieving identity, is to develop the capacity for establishing intimacy with another person. Erikson defines intimacy as mutuality or shared feeling, with a loved person of the opposite sex, with whom the individual is capable of coordinating the cycles of work, recreation, and procreation (Erikson 1959).

There are at least two difficulties in this position. One, a heterosexual bias, overlooks the adaptive task of the lesbian or gay young adult, whose need for intimacy is fulfilled by a person of the same sex. The other is a male bias. Until recently, and after being criticized by feminists, Erikson had asserted that women had no identity of their own but derived their identity first from their fathers and after marriage from their husbands.

Returning to Erikson's total-stages conception, each of the first three stages has a corresponding "organismic mode" (oral, anal, phallic) that, through identifications, neutralization, and change of function (as formulated by Hartmann), becomes a behavioral modality, presumably in the ego's secondary sphere of autonomy. For example, psychosexual orality becomes the psychosocial ability to take in and to receive and, reciprocally, to give, leading to trust in the self and others. Anality becomes the ability to hold on or to let go as appropriate in the struggle for autonomy and self-regulation. The intrusiveness of the phallic mode becomes the capacity for curiosity, creativity and imagination, and initiative. The behavioral modality of the latency period is learning in school, the family, and peer relations and thus achieving the ego quality of industry (versus inferiority).

Most social workers are familiar with Erikson's ideas, though not necessarily with their derivation. The ideas were welcomed as replacements for earlier emphases on the id and the drives. Erikson, like Hartmann, is concerned with the influence of the environment on development and functioning. His emphasis on age-specific tasks and on the reciprocal provision of needed resources by the environment seemed to fit the aims of social work very well. Today, however, the assumption of universality is faulted for not taking account of cultural diversity. The sequential and epigenetic aspects and gendered assumptions have also come into question.

MARGARET MAHLER (1897–1986)

Mahler, trained as a pediatrician and psychoanalyst, is best known for her work that delineates the developmental stages of infancy and toddlerhood. She, too, was an ego psychologist, having been deeply influenced by Hartmann's ideas as well as by her own observations of infants and their mothers in the therapeutic nursery she established in New York City. She is also more widely known as an object relations theorist. The underlying assumption of her model is that human beings "hatch out" from initial undifferentiation and total dependence on the mother to differentiation-separateness and mature object relations, a process she called "separation-individuation." While Mahler moved away from the centrality of drive satisfaction to the centrality of object relations, Freud's drive model was still very much her theoretical foundation. She did, however, reset the mainspring of development back from the Oedipus complex to an earlier time—to the preoedipal years, when object relations have their beginning. Her developmental model consists of three stages: normal autism, normal symbiosis, and separation-individuation. The latter has three subphases: differentiation, practicing, and rapprochement. When the stages have been traversed successfully, they culminate in identity formation and object constancy.

Mahler believed that the infant is born into the world in an objectless state that she called "normal autism." The primary sphere of ego autonomy is not yet operational. For approximately one month, the baby is his world; * he has no awareness of any external agency in the meeting of his needs. To the baby, his cries produce the nipple and milk. He is an omnipotent magician in need meeting. If the baby's needs are met optimally during this early period, then he will be ready to move to the next stage of *normal symbiosis*. This stage begins during the second month and ends about the fifth or sixth month. Now the sensory apparatus comes in to play, leading to a dawning awareness of the mother as an outside object. But the baby now experiences the mother and himself as being in a state of oneness. He is not yet able to tell where the mother ends and he begins. The earlier sense of his own omnipotence now yields to the omnipotence of the dual unity, and then to the mother's omnipotence.

At the peak of the symbiotic stage, at about the fourth or fifth month, *differentiation* from the object begins as the first step in separation-individuation. Mahler viewed emerging-from-oneness as "hatching out," or what she later called the "psychological birth" of the infant. Some acquired ego functions (the secondary sphere of ego autonomy) begin to appear: The baby can perceive internal sensations and those received from the environment. He now recognizes the mother as a separate object; he plays with her hair and face as part of the environment and learns that she has a mouth and eyes and that he does, too. The relationship deepens, and by the eighth to tenth month, the mother becomes a special and irreplaceable person. The

* In order to avoid being confused with the mother, the baby is designated by the masculine pronoun. In the discussion of Piaget's ideas later in this appendix, the child is designated by the feminine pronoun to avoid being confused with the male psychologist.

baby may now experience "stranger anxiety," especially if the symbiosis stage did not go well. If it did go well, he is more apt to regard
the stranger with interest, especially while in the mother's presence.
The baby's perception of himself is molded by the attitudes of the
mother toward the baby as lovable or not lovable. Other acquired ego
functions come into existence through the interaction of the baby and
the caregiver, in which the latter begins gradually to shift from immediate gratification of need to periods of waiting. The baby's sensory
and muscular maturation now enables him to hear and see the mother
as she prepares the feeding he is waiting for. And because of her
consistent need meeting earlier, he learned that the mother is reliable,
and so he becomes increasingly tolerant of delay. It is the graduated
experiences of delay that lead to the gradual growth in impulse control and reality testing.

The second subphase of separation-individuation appears about
the ninth or tenth month and is called *practicing*. It appears to be
ushered in by the baby's growing locomotor abilities, such as pulling
himself to a standing position, sitting upright, and creeping. These
abilities enable exploration of the environment by vision, hearing,
touch, taste, and kinetic sense as well as by motility. He can now
move away from the mother but returns periodically for emotional
refueling and then sets out again. Interest in exploring his own body
now appears as well. The new abilities lead into the third subphase of
rapprochement at about 14 or 15 months, continuing into the third
year. Over this long period, muscular-postural abilities and mobility
increase, language and cognitive abilities develop, knowledge grows,
and the toddler's exploration in the environment becomes more ven-
turesome. He is exhilarated by his forays and abilities, and he likes to
share with the mother what he has found in the yard, or his discovery
of the thrilling noise he can make by dropping a plate.

And then a time arrives suddenly (it seems) when the toddler becomes acutely aware of his separateness, and this awareness leads to
a fear of object loss (Mahler's "rapprochement crisis"). Such fears
may be augmented by many other experiences of separateness, for
example, going to bed at night and being alone in the dark (commonly, this is the age of sleep disorders), or playing contentedly in the
sandbox and then turning around to discover that the mother is no
longer there. It is as though the toddler's mental image of the mother
is not yet firm, so when he is not in contact with her she is gone
forever. The awareness is not of physical separation but of psychological separateness from mother. It is accompanied by a loss of self-
esteem as the belief in the mother's omnipotence diminishes and

leaves the toddler with feelings of helplessness. The rapprochement crisis normally causes a behavioral change that can be painful to mother. Her previously busy baby, who granted her more independence, has now turned into a clinging, whining toddler, demanding continuous attention. To her this behavior feels like regression, and she may become impatient, rejecting his temporary need for closeness and reassurance, or intuitively she may recognize it as "only a stage" and accept the behavior while continuing to encourage independence with warmth and understanding. The latter response is more likely to lead to a happy outcome, while Mahler believed that the former, if persistent, can lay a base for later depression.

There is yet another feature of the rapprochement subphase that is difficult for most parents. Mahler called it "ambitendency." She observed that the toddler appears to have simultaneous wishes to reunite with the mother and to separate from her that reflect the beginnings of ambivalence. Alternations of love toward the giving mother and hate toward the restraining mother; temper tantrums and fights with mother over dressing, eating, and sleeping; and negativism (the momentous discovery of the word *no*)—all now appear. The shifts between love and hate reflect the toddler's immature perception of the object. The baby has split the object in two: a good mother and a bad mother. By the end of the separation-individuation stage, however, the split objects must be melded into one person and must be perceived and experienced as such if mature object relations are to develop. By the end of the third year, gains are consolidated. The child now has a comfortable sense of identity and individuality as a separate individual. He has also acquired a reasonable degree of object constancy; that is, the good and bad objects have been integrated into a single, whole mother. And the image of the mother can now be carried in the mind, so that the child no longer experiences the fear of loss when separated from her—at least most of the time.

Like Freud, Mahler was interested in the cause of psychopathology, but instead of the neuroses, her interest was in the psychoses, the personality disorders, and the borderline states, which she saw as being the consequences of failures in object relations during infancy and toddlerhood. The earlier the failure in development, the more severe the disorder. If the infant's needs are not met at an optimal level, or if the infant has an inborn defect in the potential for object relations, he will be unable to move into the symbiotic stage. Instead, he will remain autistic and objectless, suffering a grossly psychotic state called *infantile* or *childhood autism*. If failure in the relationship occurs early in the symbiotic stage, the infant is apt to regress to autism. If failure occurs somewhat later, the base will be laid for personality disorder. Still later, failure toward the end of the symbiotic stage is likely to result in symbiotic psychosis. In the psychotic adult or adolescent, there is often a loss of boundary between self and other, hallucinations, and delusions of omnipotence, as there are in normal infantile symbiosis. The acquired ego functions are at best conflicted and weak. During acute psychotic episodes, reality testing, object relations, self-concept, impulse control, coping, and even defense may be completely, if temporarily, lost.

Failures in the third stage of separation-individuation are linked by Mahler to the borderline and narcissistic conditions of adulthood and adolescence. Thus the core difficulty is the inability to integrate the good and the bad objects. The person has an insatiable yearning for the good symbiotic mother, while the ambivalently held mother is felt to be dangerous and must be warded off. All object relationships are split in this way and therefore are difficult to sustain. Other ego functions have developed, but in a distorted manner, and this distortion leaves a structural flaw in the personality or character structure. It has been said that the borderline state can be viewed as a psychotic character disorder without psychotic symptoms. The narcissistic disorder also represents failure to integrate the split object and is marked by inflated omnipotence and grandiosity. Because ego functions are assimilated into the grandiosity, they are not available for actual achievements that could build a healthy self-esteem. Object cathexes are attached to mental representations of the self, instead of being distributed between those of the self and others.

JEAN PIAGET (1896–1980)

The Swiss psychologist Piaget made significant contributions to the understanding of how children think and how they acquire knowledge about such matters as time, space, number, quantity, and causality. Prior to his work, most theorists, and people in general, assumed that children were merely small adults who knew less but thought in the same way that adults do. By posing questions to children, including his own three offspring, and by observing their common strategies of reasoning and the common errors they made, Piaget concluded that children think in totally different ways from adults. Beginning in the 1920s, and extending to the 1980s, Piaget conducted extensive research with children, taught at several distinguished European universities, and published over sixty books and even more articles and monographs. He is best known in the United States for his model of sequential stages of cognitive development in children. He regarded the stages and their sequencing as universal across cultures, with attainment of one stage providing the base for the next. Intellectual functioning is qualitatively and quantitatively different at each stage. Individual rates of progress through the stages, however, depend on the nature of the environment and individual potential.

For Piaget, intelligence is an adaptive process, and its development arises from the child's action in the environment. In the early weeks of life children acquire knowledge of their world through sucking and looking. That is, they learn through actions of mouthing objects and by visual scanning of their environment. The first motoric acts and sensory perceptions constitute the earliest intellectual activity. The stage from birth to 2 years, then, is called *sensorimotor intelligence*, and Piaget gave more attention to this stage than to any other. Piaget was particularly interested in how the very young child acquires the ability to construct or reconstruct an object. At first, the object does not have an existence independent of the observer; it is a case of out of sight, out of mind. The object's existence depends on the baby's sensory experience of it. For example, Piaget rolled a ball for the 5-month-old baby. If the ball rolled out of sight, she immediately lost interest, as though the ball no longer existed. Even at 8 months, a baby watching Piaget drop an object continued to look at his hand, rather than following the downward path of the object.

By 19 months, however, the toddler can reconstruct an object's position. For example, Piaget showed a baby a coin in his hand, placed his hand under a cover, left the coin there, and showed her his empty hand. Babies this age immediately look under the cover for the coin. This is a momentous development, for it means that they now understand that the object still exists even though it is not seen ("object permanence"). The baby can now imagine where it has gone.

The second stage is called *preoperational intelligence* and is characteristic of the preschool child 3 to 7 years of age. During this stage, the child develops the ability to represent things in the mind, demonstrated by the use of language, symbolic play (for example, a rock is used to represent a frog), drawing, painting, molding, and even nightmares. However, she is not yet able to reason about causality and transformations according to physical laws. For example, in a typically ingenious task, Piaget presented preoperational children with two glasses containing equal amounts of orange juice. He poured the juice from one glass into a tall, thin, glass. When asked which glass held the most juice, children under 6 years of age answer that there is more juice in the second glass. They still believe only in their sensory perceptions. By age 7, however, most children begin to think logically and answer that the amount is the same ("conservation of the object"). Thinking now comes from within instead of from sensory perceptions.

The third stage, called *concrete operational intelligence,* is typical of the school-aged child 7 to 11 years of age. She can now sort and classify objects. For example, when presented with a box of twenty white wooden beads and seven brown wooden beads and asked if there are more white or brown beads, the children answer that there are more white ones. However, when asked if there are more white or more wooden beads, they are nonplussed. They can only say that there are more white than brown beads. Space is viewed only as concrete places, not as abstract positions; hence persons or objects cannot be in two places at the same time.

The final stage, *formal operations,* begins to appear in puberty, from about 12 to 15 years of age. The youth can now think conceptually and abstractly. Teenagers can think about their own thoughts and ideas, accept ideas that are contrary to fact and reason from them, and understand metaphors. They can discuss assumptions and theories, make predictions, and test hypotheses. They are able to work with higher level symbols such as scientific formulae and mathematical equations, and to utilize formal systems of logic. Teenagers tend to be interested in "great questions" of religion, philosophy, science, and the origin and destiny of the universe, spinning out elaborate systems of ideas. But they can also be egocentric, imagining that everyone is as interested in their mental preoccupations as they are. They assume that no adult has suffered, or loved, or hated to the degree that they have, so that they cannot possibly be understood. It is not surprising that the defense of intellectualization appears first in adolescence.

Assuming there is sufficient interaction with an appropriately stimulating environment, Piaget believed that every normal child follows this sequences of stages. From total reliance on motor acts and sensory experience in the environment for thinking and knowledge acquisition, she moves in roughly twelve years to high-level operations within the mind; from the sensory and concrete, she moves to the abstract, while continuing to acquire knowledge from action and perceptual experiences in the environment. Piaget's general theory is also of interest. He suggested that environmental actions that comprise sensorimotor intelligence can be repeated and generalized into what he called a "schema," a cognitive structure or a kind of image.

Schemas are assimilated into already-existing ones, or they are accommodations to new actions. A child might have developed a schema that corresponds to what she sees when looking at a rattle and what she hears when he shakes it (accommodation). Later she is able to grasp the rattle, and a grasping schema is assimilated to the visual-auditory scheme as she now "grasps" what she sees or hears.

A prominent early schema is mouthing an object, but soon the baby will encounter an object too unwieldy or untasty to mouth. This object does not fit the mouthing schema. Therefore the baby accommodates by forming a new schema, perhaps a tactile schema in which she now feels the outlines of objects with her hands. In this way the cognitive structures or schemas grow in number and complexity. By the eighth month the baby has several schemas for the mother as a special person. A stranger enters the scene, but there is no existing schema by which she can be assimilated, so the baby must form a stranger schema by the process of accommodation. If the baby comes to know the stranger better, she may assimilate the stranger into the schema for the mother. Such an assimilation is not yet at the level of thought, although it is practical intelligence, and it is the beginning of what will later, in the operational stages, become thought at the level of internal representation.

For Piaget, assimilation and accommodation are complementary. The mind operates by finding a balance between them to eliminate inconsistencies and contradictions between the real and what is imagined; Piaget called this balance "equilibration." By analogy, we assimilate food to make it part of our existing muscles, blood, and organs, and we accommodate to the food by digesting (changing) it. In a similar way, the child changes her existing schemas to accommodate new information, but at the same time she assimilates the new learning into existing cognitive structures or schemas. By the end of the first year the baby has more and different cognitive and social interactions with a wider range of objects. She enjoys producing effects such as the clatter of dropped objects, splashes of water, and rolling a ball. She also enjoys inducing others to produce interesting spectacles. When exploration of the environment expands with creeping and walking, a great variety of new objects present themselves, leading to new acts, and to new experiences. And again, with language, new experiences come to the fore, and schemas become more elaborate and greater in number. By the end of the second year simple schemas for time, quantity, and space begin to form.

Piaget emphasized the necessity for continuous action and perceptual experiences in the environment as essential "aliments" for cognitive growth. In sterile, unstimulating, confusing, or punishing environments (both physical and social), the practice, consolidation, integration, and elaboration of cognitive structuring will be difficult or impossible for the baby, and later the child, to sustain. Despite the usefulness of some of Piaget's constructs, the notion of invariant stages, critical periods in social and psychological development, and brain plasticity casts some doubts on the model. Jerome Bruner, the foremost American cognitive psychologist, has long held that evolution granted human beings not only the advantage of brain plasticity but that of culture as well. Thus human beings have a wider range of possibilities than Piaget allowed for. Cross-cultural studies show that not all children pass through Piaget's universal invariant stages. Different cultures have different ways of knowing. Also, certain cognitive abilities that Piaget viewed as developing in later childhood are now known to be present in an early form at birth or shortly thereafter.

LAWRENCE KOHLBERG (1927–1989)

Kohlberg (1969), influenced by Piaget's ideas, developed a model of sequential stages of moral reasoning (moral judgments, not moral behaviors). Originally based on the study of eighty-four boys and their development over the next twenty years, the model proposes three sequential levels, each consisting of two successive stages. Kohlberg carried out the studies by posing a series of hypothetical moral dilemmas to children and youths. Recently he used a variety of moral issues in various cultural contexts and stated that his six sequential stages had been validated cross-culturally. These stages appear sequentially in childhood and youth, and they also represent various levels of moral reasoning found among adults.

At the first level, the young child acts in obedience to the parents' superior force and seeks to avoid punishment (stage 1). A little later in the first level, she or he obeys the parents in order to receive a reward or need satisfaction (stage 2). At the second level (termed conventional morality), normally attained between ages 10 and 13, the child follows a "good boy" morality, seeking to please parents and others through stereotyped "nice" behaviors and to gain social approval (stage 3). As children reach the teens, some begin conforming to rules for the sake of upholding authority and the social order of the peer group and wider social institutions (stage 4). Kohlberg, like Freud, believed that the female is incapable of advanced moral judgments, and that she remains at stage 3 through adolescence and adulthood. Some boys may remain at stage 4.

However, during middle and late adolescence, many boys move up to the third level (termed postconventional morality). Some remain at stage 5, conforming in order to respect the views of those holding impartial expectations for judging community welfare. These young men are capable of recognizing conflicts of interest and dilemmas in making rational choices. Some of them later may move up to stage 6 and conform to avoid self-condemnation. That is, decisions of conscience are made on the basis of their self-chosen ethical principles, rather than on the earlier grounds of cultural do's and don't's.

The model, while accepted by many professionals, has been attacked by others on several grounds. The controversial issues include the research instruments used (said to reflect hypothetical resolutions to hypothetical dilemmas without testing actual moral behaviors) and the model's view of women as being deficient in moral judgment when compared to men.

THEORIES OF ADULT DEVELOPMENT

After a long preoccupation with childhood and adolescence, developmental theorists began in the 1970s to consider adult development. The way had been opened by the earlier work of Erikson, who proposed three developmental stages in adulthood: intimacy (young adulthood), generativity (middle adulthood), and integrity (old age). Two theorists developed more elaborate stage models of male psychosocial development, based on longitudinal research (Levinson 1978; Vaillant 1977b). One theorist (Gould 1978) developed a model that is described as phasic.

Levinson's Model

Levinson, a psychologist, and his associates studied forty men from young adulthood over the life course. Ten men were selected in each of four occupational categories: hourly workers in industry, business executives, academic biologists, and novelists. Each man was interviewed five to ten times for a total of ten to twenty hours. His task was to tell his life story. One staff member secured histories from the families. This primary research base was supplemented by a review of mens' lives as depicted in biographies, autobiographies, novels, drama, and poetry from many societies and historical periods. Out of the work, Levinson developed a theoretical life structure consisting of the following eras: preadulthood (age zero to 22), early adulthood (age 17 to 45), middle adulthood (age 40 to 65), late adulthood (age 60 to 85), and late, late adulthood (age 80 and over). The shift from one era to another requires what Levinson called "transition periods" or "developmental steps" of about five years' duration. The basic task of each transition is to terminate the previous era and create a basis for the next, hence the overlaps in years. Thus, the midlife transition, for example, both contains and bridges early and middle adulthood.

The research aim was to understand the overall pattern of living (life structure) and its evolution over time. Focusing on midlife, Levinson (1978) wrote that at this stage the life structure previously constructed in young adulthood now comes into question, including its associated values, desires, work, life direction, and the meaning of relationships to wife and children. Eighty percent of the sample experienced the tumultuous struggles within the self and with the environment as a time of moderate or severe crisis. A man begins to realize that his life until now was based on illusions, and he faces a task of deillusionment, a painful process through which he is stripped of his most cherished beliefs and values. As in all developmental transitions, if he is to make changes in aspects of his life, he must rework the lifelong polarities of being young/old, masculine/feminine, destructive/creative, and attached/separate. The task of change is made more difficult by the reactivation of early psychic conflicts that block the development of a new life structure (Levinson 1978).

Some men do not make the midlife transition successfully, and the outcome is estrangement, cynicism, and an inability to believe in anything. These men face constriction and decline. Another outcome is finding the freedom to form more flexible values and to relate to others in a more genuine and more realistic way. If dissatisfied with his marriage, for example, the man is better able now than in his 30s to look at his own part in the difficulties. These men create a new life structure that enables them to fulfill their roles; it keeps them busy and doing what is necessary for themselves and others. But the new life structure is not connected well to the self. The best outcome of the transition is the creation of a successful structure of middle adulthood that is satisfying and fulfilling, despite any burdens that may present themselves. Men developing this structure are less driven by work and their impulses, have fewer illusions, and are more deeply attached to others—and yet more separate and more centered in the self.

In a later article, Levinson stated that the components of the life structure are "One's relationships: with self, other persons, groups, and institutions, with all aspects of the external world that have significance in one's life. . . . The life structure stems from the engagement of self with the world. . . . Adult development is the story of the evolving process of mutual interpenetration of self and world" (1980:278). Additionally, he conceived of the life structure as evolving through "a relatively orderly sequence of periods during the adult years. The essential character of the sequence was the same for all the men in our study" (1980:279). Levinson stated that his conception is age-linked but is not hierarchical as are the models of Kohlberg and Piaget. Rather, as a model of adulthood, not childhood, the age-linked periods are best understood as seasons in a year: each is necessary, each has its proper place in the total pattern, and each has its characteristic tasks and dilemmas, as in the models of Freud and Erikson. Levinson also stated that, in contrast to other models, his life structures have both inner and outer aspects. They stem from multiple biopsychosocial sources: "The basic form of the adult life, at this stage of evolution, is conjointly determined by the maturational unfolding of the human psyche and the human body, and by the basic features of human society (as it has existed for, say, the last five or ten thousand years)" (1980:288). Despite these various statements, the focus remains personalistic.

Vaillant's Model

Vaillant (1977a, 1977b), a psychiatrist and psychoanalyst, worked with a much larger sample: 268 Harvard College men rated tops by their classmates in health, self-reliance, achievement, and stability. They were selected for a study supported by William T. Grant that is known as the Grant Study. It started in 1938, and Vaillant began his association with the Grant men in the mid-1960s. While they were students and for the next thirty-five years they were interviewed, tested, and studied by psychologists, psychiatrists, and anthropologists. Most went on to illustrious careers, and a few failed to succeed in their professional or personal lives. Vaillant's book, *Adaptation to Life* (1977b), concentrates on 95 men, randomly selected by Vaillant from the original 268 subjects. They were from the 1942, 1943, and 1944 classes and, at the time of Vaillant's study, were then in their

50s. About 80 percent were Protestant, 10 percent Catholic, and 10 percent Jewish. Eighty-nine percent came from the northern part of the country, east of the Missouri River. They were a group of elite, white males, although many were of modest origins and were thus atypical. When Vaillant began with them at their twenty-fifth Harvard reunion, they were 46 years old. Based on his experience with the Grant men, Vaillant rejected the notion of a midlife crisis as a tabloid fable. Instead, he saw the development of these men as following the Eriksonian stages of intimacy, generativity, and integrity in adulthood. He interpreted much of their mature adaptation in terms of ego mechanisms of defense against intrapsychic conflict between ego and superego, id, or environment. To explain the operations of the ego in conflict, he used the metaphor of oysters building pearls as they manage an irritant presented by a grain of sand. In his judgment, ego defenses are healthy more often than they are pathological. They can lead to creative adaptations (pearls), especially Freud's "mature" defenses of altruism, sublimation, and suppression.

Both Levinson's work and Vaillant's work demonstrate the weakness of stage models of development: the assumption that all humans pass through predictable, fixed, universal, and sequential stages, though Levinson stated that they go through them in their own way. In addition, whether regarded as models or as theories of adult development, both are gender-biased (all male; Levinson is working on a parallel study of women), racially biased (all white), and class-biased (all elites except for Levinson's ten working-class men). Levinson's small sample of forty, although examined in depth, makes suspect any generalizations made from it. Both models reflect middle-class values and do not refer to differences in culture, to the effects of rapid social change, or to the impact of oppression. Vaillant's interpretations are filtered through a psychoanalytic lens as well. I believe it is a severely limiting view of humanness to consider altruism and sublimation passive defenses against the unacceptable, as Vaillant (like Freud) does, rather than as active strivings toward the desirable. Vaillant also declared that "recovery from mental illness is analogous to passing from adolescence to adulthood. The person is the same; no lesson has been learned; no tumor has been excised; but different defenses have been deployed" (1977a:107). It is as though life itself is an illness: ego defenses seem to be the centerpiece of life, health, and growth for Vaillant.

Gould's Model

Gould constructed his model based on observations of therapy groups, distinguished by age decades, and on questionnaires returned by 524 nonpatients. An interesting aspect of the model is the centrality of the concept of transformation: "We are continually transforming ourselves—within a community, out of the past into the future, with and within a complex mind, trying always to gain a little more liberty to be what we are becoming" (1980:237). Gould's conception of transformation is only moderately similar to Reiss' (1981) concept of family transformation and to Terkelsen's (1980) ideas of first- and second-order changes in family members that trigger family transformations. Reiss and Terkelsen's ideas are central throughout part 2 of this book. Gould's developmental model focuses on work and love, and on the transformations that are generated mainly by internal processes and also by the environments of work and significant others—especially spouse, children, parents, and bosses. There is an implied universality in the internal processes and a somewhat muted sense of their sequential progression and predictability in reference to five age-related stages of adult development. As each new decade is reached, the task is to achieve further liberation from the persevering ideas of childhood through transformational internal processes and changes in attitudes toward self and others.

While the model seems less rigid and limited than the models of Levinson and Vaillant, it does not take account of cultural diversity, the effects of disempowerment and oppression, cohort experiences, social change, and marked shifts in norms and values—at least not so far.

Appendix 2:
General Systems Theory

At an epistemological level, general systems theory (GST) was a response to 1) new ideas in the physical sciences that emphasize patterns, processes, relativity, and uncertainty over the earlier Newtonian, mechanistic laws thought to govern the physical world; the latter had explained many scientific observations but not newly discovered phenomena in the 1920s and beyond, and it emphasized the separateness of subject and object; 2) new ideas in the biological sciences, including evolutionary theory, that require a holistic understanding of living organisms rather than sole reliance on analyses that destroy their livingness and ignore the influence of environment in their development and functioning; and 3) new ideas in the philosophy of science that question the assumption of objectivity, recognize the operation of personal and society values in science, and acknowledge social constructions of reality (Germain 1971).

In GST, a system is construed as an organized whole, usually defined as a set of interacting parts enclosed within a boundary that separates the system from its environment. Some systems have boundaries that are evident: they have skins, membranes, or even environmental markers such as fences and partitions. Other systems may not be so clearly marked off, and their imaginary or metaphorical boundaries may be drawn differently by different observers or participants, or they may be different at different times or under different conditions (such as the boundary of a community or a family). In these instances a boundary serves to demarcate who and what are included in the system and who or what are excluded, with the environment regarded as everything and everyone outside the boundary. Thus the boundary of an organization or a family defines who and what is viewed as being inside and outside the organization or a family—depending on who is doing the defining. Membership requirements in a group form a boundary; so, too, does language, as in the instance of black English, known to group members and used to "keep out" whites, to whom it is unfamiliar (Draper 1979).

GST proposes that biological and social systems are open, in contrast to mechanistic or physical systems (such as machines), which are closed systems. Being open means that biological and social systems are in continuous exchange with their environments across their boundaries, thereby ensuring their survival and development. Open systems are characterized by the processes of input-transformation-output. Their inputs from the environment are defined in GST as information, matter, and energy. That is, open systems are made of matter and energy, and they exchange matter and energy with the environment. They are organized by information, and they exchange information with the environment. In ecological terms, such inputs would include all "nutriments" needed by human beings for survival and optimal growth and development physically, biologically, socially, and emotionally as the particular culture defines human needs.

GST further specifies that, having received environmental inputs, an open system then transforms them through processes characteristic of the particular system and exports outputs back to the environment. Such outputs from communities, families, and formal and informal support systems, for example, include goods, services, information, and people prepared for adaptive functioning in the society. These input–transformation–output processes illuminate another feature of open systems, namely, their nested nature. At one level, the individual is a complete biological system of interacting parts such as cells, tissues, and organs, each of which is a subsystem. But at the next level down, each of those subsystems is also a biological system in its own right and has its own interacting parts. At the next level up from the individual, however, she or he is a part or subsystem of various social systems, such as a family, and of formal organizations, such as schools, religious sects, workplaces, informal networks, and formed groups. At still the next level up, these "social" systems are themselves interacting parts or subsystems of the community.

At any level, each system has its own boundary, and so does each of its interacting parts, nesting upward from the parts of the cell to the society. Not only are open systems open to the environment, but they must be open to the interactions of their parts as well. The reason is that what happens in one part of a system reverberates through all its parts, influencing them all to some degree, whether this influence is detectable by a human observer or not. Sometimes boundaries between systems and their environments need to be firm, sometimes loose, but always they must be permeable to needed inputs and appropriate outputs. It is the quality of permeability that permits an open system to stave off entropy, which besets closed systems. *Entropy* refers to the fact that closed systems inevitably run down, become disorganized, and are then unable to transform energy, matter, and information, or to produce further work. Open systems, in contrast, can store up energy, matter, and information to stave off disorganization or death, as when we preserve or refrigerate food, save money, or store fat in our tissues. This ability, however, is limited by the characteristics of the particular open system.

This brings us to the GST concept of equilibrium. As they approach entropy, mechanistic systems move more and more toward a static equilibrium. By contrast, open systems grow, develop, and change over time and across space and, eventually, die in accordance with the limits of their particular kind of system. Within their life course, open systems maintain a dynamic or changing equilibrium, rather than a static one, by virtue of their continuous input–transformation–output processes. The equilibrium changes because of the oscillations due to changes or adjustments in those processes. To survive, however, an open system must keep these oscillations within the normal limits for its kind of system. So-called normal limits are often referred to as a system's characteristic steady state.

To keep within system limits, the system must draw on internal feedback processes to inform it about the relationship among its parts, and on external feedback processes to inform it about the environment and its own relationship with the environment. Internal feedback includes biological, physiological, and psychological processes. External feedback includes such processes as the verbal and nonverbal expressions, perceptions, attitudes, expectations, and behaviors of other individuals; the sanctions exerted positively and negatively by social systems, the reactions and responses of physical settings, and many other kinds of information.

Inputs from the environment influence, shape, or alter the system, and outputs from the system influence, shape, or alter the environment. This is a metaphor of the reciprocal, transactional life processes of human adaptation described in chapter 1, but at a much more abstract level. GST is necessarily abstract because its intent is to specify properties that are common across the tremendous range of open systems, from cells to societies to transnational and global systems, however diverse they might otherwise be. Despite the mechanistic language and their abstract nature, GST concepts are useful to the social worker who is seeking to understand the dynamics and "behaviors" of a social system, such as an organization, a community, or a family—either as the focus of professional activity or as an environmental context of other systems of focal concern.

Appendix 3:
Maturational Milestones

For the convenience of the reader a brief sketch of the motor maturational timetable is presented here:

Head control	3 months
Rolling over	3 months
Reaching for an object	6 months
Sitting erect	8 months
Crawling	10 months
Standing	12 months
Walking unaided	15 months

While these ages of motor abilities vary widely among normal babies, the order of their achievement usually does not. The development of the abilities is governed by the maturation of the nervous, muscular, and other bodily systems as part of the species' genetic heritage. Motor and skeletal processes rely much less on environmental influences than do other abilities, so most children achieve these milestones. Intelligence, sensory perception, language, and social development, however, are much more dependent on environmental influences, so achievement levels vary widely.

LANGUAGE MILESTONES (L. BLOOM 1975):

Approximately 12 months	Child utters first words
Approximately 18 months–24 months	Child combines two or three words
Approximately 2–3 years	Child speaks in sentences

The timetable ignores the continuous changes over time. For example, a 14-month-old child who is speaking single words without the use of syntax is very different from the 18-month-old child who is about to use syntax although she is still saying one word at a time (Bloom 1975:246).

DEFINITIONAL DISTINCTIONS

Maturation: Emergence of genetic potential as a bundle of potentialities or preprogrammed changes in structure, form, complexity, integrity, and function. Poor nutrition or illness may delay the processes, but good health and proper diet do not speed them up dramatically.

Development: Changes in the structure, thought, personality, or behavior of a person as a function of both biological growth (including psychological) and environmental processes. Development is usually progressive and cumulative, for example, increased size and increased motor, cognitive, and language capacities. Some aspects of development rest primarily on biological elements, and some primarily on environmental and cultural elements. For some aspects, the relative participation of either is still unknown.

Growth: Increase in size, function, and complexity up to the optimal point, similar to the concept of maturation.

Aging: Same as growth over the life course but ultimately goes beyond the optimal point.

Biology: Life processes of the organism in the environment.

Physiology: A branch of biology that refers to metabolic and chemical activities and processes, and to the functions of organs and parts as opposed to their anatomy.

Anatomy: The structural makeup of organs and parts, their position, relationships, and structure.

Physical: Skeletal and muscular systems.

Suggested Additional Readings

1. The Ecological Perspective

Cataldo, Charles. 1979. "Wilderness Therapy: Modern Day Shamanism."
In Carel B. Germain, ed. *Social Work Practice: People and Environments*,
pp. 46–73. New York: Columbia University Press.

Bateson, Gregory. 1979. *Mind and Nature, A Necessary Unity*. New York:
Dutton.

Gould, Stephen Jay. 1977. *Ever Since Darwin*. New York: Norton.

Rosenberg, Morris. 1979. *Conceiving the Self*. New York: Basic Books.

Sagan, Carl. 1977. *The Dragons of Eden*. New York: Random House.

2. The Community as Context

Brown, June H., Wilbur A. Finch Jr., Helen Northen, Samuel H. Taylor,
and Marie Weil, eds. 1982. *Child, Family, Neighborhood: A Master Plan
for Social Service Delivery*. New York: Child Welfare League of America.

Cox, Fred M. John L. Erlich, Jack Rothman, and John E. Tropman, eds.
1979. *Strategies of Community Organization*. 3d ed. Itaska Ill.: Peacock.

Gramick, Jeannine. 1983. "Homophobia: A New Challenge." *Social Work*
(March–April, 28:137–141.

Shapiro, Joan. 1971. *Communities of the Alone*. New York: Association
Press.

Solomon, Barbara B. 1976. *Black Empowerment: Social Work in Minority
Communities*. New York: Columbia University Press.

Taylor, Samuel H. and Robert W. Roberts, eds. 1985. *Theory and Practice of Community Social Work*. New York: Columbia University Press.
Weinberg, Nancy. 1983. "Social Equity and the Physically Disabled." *Social Work* (September/October), 28:365–369.

3. The Community: Support Systems

Biegel, David E. and Arthur J. Naparstek, eds. 1982. *Community Support Systems and Mental Health*. New York: Springer.
Brager, George and Stephen Holloway. 1978. *Changing Human Service Organizations: Politics and Practice*. New York: Free Press.
Gottleib, Benjamin J., ed. 1981. *Social Networks and Social Support*. Beverly Hills, Calif.: Sage.
Weissman, Harold, Irwin Epstein, and Andrea Savage. 1983. *Agency-Based Social Work: Neglected Aspects of Clinical Practice*. Philadelphia: Temple University Press.
Zaltman, Gerald, Robert Duncan, and Jonny Holbek. 1973. *Innovations and Organizations*. New York: Wiley.

4. The Family as a Community Subsystem

McGoldrick, Monica, John K. Pearce, and Joseph Giordano, eds. 1982. *Ethnicity and Family Therapy*. New York: Guilford Press.
Social Casework. 1974. Issue on "Contra Viento y Marea (Against the Stormy Seas)" (February), 55.
Social Casework. 1976. Issue on "Asian and Pacific Islander Americans: Heritage, Characteristics, Self-Image, Conflicts, Service Needs, Organization." (March), 57.
Social Casework. 1980. Issue on "The Phoenix from the Flame: The American Indian Today." (October), 61.
Social Work. 1982. Issue on "Social Work and People of Color." (January), 27.

5. The Family: A View from Within

McGoldrick, Monica, Carol M. Anderson, and Froma Walsh, eds. 1989. *Women in Families*. New York: Norton.
Pinderhughes, Elaine. 1982. "Black Genealogy: Self-Liberator and Therapeutic Tool." *Smith College Studies in Social Work* (March), 52:93–106.
Pinderhughes, Elaine. 1989. *Understanding Race, Ethnicity, and Power*. New York: Free Press.
Roy, Ranjan. 1982. "Marital and Family Issues in Patients With Chronic Pain: A Review." *Psychotherapy and Psychosomatics* 37:1–12.

6. Family Formation: Working, Becoming a Couple, and the Parenting Option

Cogswell, Betty E. and Marvin B. Sussman. 1972. "Changing Family and Marriage Forms: Complications for Human Service Systems." *The Family Coordinator* (October), 21:505–516.

Corbin, M., ed. 1978. *The Couple*. New York: Basic Books.

Lowenthal, Marjorie F. and Clayton Haven. 1968. "Interaction and Adaptation: Intimacy as a Critical Variable." *American Sociological Review* (February), 33:20–30.

Mayeroff, Milton. 1971. *On Caring*. New York: Harper & Row.

Pleck, Joseph. 1981. *The Myth of Masculinity*. Cambridge, Mass.: MIT Press.

Sontag, Lester W. 1966. "Implications of Fetal Behavior and Environment for Adult Personalities." *Annals New York Academy of Sciences* 134:782–786.

7. The Parenting Option Continued: More Choices

Butler, Adrienne B. 1983. "Compassionate Pediatrics. There Is Something Wrong with Michael: A Pediatrician-Mother's Perspective." *Pediatrics* (March), 71:446–448.

Conyard, Shirley, Muthuswamy Krishnamurthy, and Harvey Dosik. 1980. "Psychosocial Aspects of Sickle-Cell Anemia in Adolescents." *Health and Social Work* (February), 5:20–26.

Hartman, Ann. 1985. "Practice in Adoption." In Joan Laird and Ann Hartman, eds., *A Handbook of Child Welfare: Context, Knowledge, and Practice*, pp. 667–692. New York: Free Press.

Wikler, Lynn and Maryanne P. Keenan, eds. 1983. *Developmental Disabilities: No Longer a Private Tragedy*. Silver Spring, Md.: National Association of Social Workers.

8. Family Transformations in Infancy

Ainsworth, Mary D. Salter. 1983. "Patterns of Infant-Mother Attachment as Related to Maternal Care: Their Early History and Their Contribution to Continuity." In David Magnusson and Vernon L. Allen, eds., *Human Development: An Interactional Perspective*, pp. 35–57. New York: Academic Press.

Dunn, Judy. 1977. *Distress and Comfort*. Cambridge, Mass.: Harvard University Press.

Feldman, Ronald, Arlene Rubin Stiffman, and Kenneth G. Jung. 1987.

Children at Risk: in the Web of Mental Illness. New Brunswick, N.J.: Rutgers University Press.

Field, Tiffany. 1978. "Interaction Behaviors of Primary Versus Secondary Caretaker Fathers." *Developmental Psychology* 14:183–185.

Field, Tiffany and Martin Reite. 1985. "The Psychology of Attachment and Separation: A Summary." In Martin Reite and Tiffany Field, eds., *The Psychobiology of Attachment and Separation,* pp. 455–479. New York: Academic Press.

Rock, Maxine A. 1978. "Gorilla Mothers Need Some Help from Their Friends." *Smithsonian* (April), 9:58–63.

9. Family Transformations in the Pre-School Years

Bond, Lynne A. and James C. Rosen, eds. 1980. *Competence and Coping During Adulthood.* Hanover, N.H.: University Press of New England.

Dillard, J. L. 1977. *Lexicon of Black English.* New York: Seabury Press.

Garvey, Catherine. 1977. *Play.* Cambridge, Mass.: Harvard University Press.

Sacks, Oliver. 1989. *Seeing Voices: A Journey into the World of The Deaf.* Berkeley: University of California Press.

10. Family Transformations in the School Years

Akabas, Sheila H. and Paul A. Kurzman, eds. 1982. *Work, Workers, and Work Organizations: A View from Social Work.* Englewood Cliffs. N.J.: Prentice-Hall.

Briar, Katharine Hooper. 1988. *Social Work and the Unemployed.* Silver Spring, Md.: National Association of Social Workers.

Canada's Mental Health. 1984. Entire Issue, "In or Out of the Game: Work, Unemployment and Mental Health." (September), 32.

Constable, Robert T. John F. Flynn, and Shirley McDonald, eds. 1990. *School Social Work: Practice and Research Perspectives,* 2nd ed. Chicago: Lyceum Press.

Gore, Susan. 1978. "The Effects of Social Support in Moderating the Health Consequences of Unemployment." *Journal of Health and Social Behavior* (June), 19:157–165.

Maypole, Donald E. and Rosemarie Skaine. 1983. "Sexual Harassment in the Workplace." *Social Work* (September–October), 30:385–390.

11. Family Transformations: Divorce, Chronic Illness and Disability, and Death and Bereavement

Agee, James. 1971. *A Death in the Family.* New York: Bantam.

Black, Rita Beck and Joan O. Weiss. (in press), "Chronic Physical Illness and Disability." In Alex Gitterman, ed., *Handbook of Social Work Practice with Vulnerable Populations.* New York: Columbia University Press.

Goldstein, Eda G. 1973. "Social Casework and the Dying Patient." *Social Casework* (December), 54:601–608.

Hartman, Carl, Barry MacIntosh, and Beverly Englehardt. 1983. "The Neglected and Forgotten Sexual Partner of the Physically Disabled." *Social Work* (September–October) 28:370–374.

Trevino, Fern. 1979. "Siblings of Handicapped Children: Identifying Those at Risk." *Social Casework* (October), 60:488–493.

Vastola, Joyce, Amy Nierenberg, and Elizabeth H. Graham. 1986. "The Lost and Found Group: Group Work With Bereaved Children." In Alex Gitterman and Lawrence Shulman, eds., *Mutual Aid Groups and the Life Cycle*, pp. 75–90. Itaska, Ill.: Peacock.

12. Family Transformations in Adolescence

Ashkinazy, Steve. 1984. "Working with Gay and Lesbian Youth." *Practice Digest* (Summer), 7:21–23.

Gibbs, Jewelle Taylor. 1984. "Black Adolescents and Youth: An Endangered Species." *American Journal of Orthopsychiatry* (January), 54:6–21.

Rossi, Alice. 1980. "Parenthood in the Middle Years." In Paul B. Baltes and Orville G. Brim, Jr., eds., *Life Span Development and Behavior*, vol. 3, pp. 138–205. New York: Academic Press.

13. The Elderly Family and Its Transformations

Beauvoir, Simone de. 1964. *A Very Easy Death.* New York: Putnam.

Chatters, Linda M. and Robert Joseph Taylor. 1989. "Life Problems and Coping Strategies of Older Black Adults." *Social Work* (July), 34:313–322.

Goldberg, Gertrude S., Ruth Kantrow, Eleanor Kremen, and Leah Lauter. 1986. "Spouseless, Childless Elderly Women and Their Social Supports." *Social Work* (March–April), 31:104–112.

Hochschild, Arlie Russell. 1973. *The Unexpected Community.* Englewood Cliffs, N.J.: Prentice-Hall.

Manuel, Ron. 1983. *Minority Aging: Sociological and Psychological Issues.* Westport, Conn.: Greenwood Press.

Netting, F. Ellen, Cindy C. Wilson, and John C. New. 1987. "The Human-Animal Bond: Implications for Practice." *Social Work* (January–February), 32:60–64.

Sarton, May. 1984. *At Seventy, A Journal.* New York: Norton:

Taylor, Robert Joseph and Linda M. Chatters. 1986. "Patterns of Informal

Support to Elderly Black Adults: Family, Friends, and Church Members." *Social Work* (November–December), 31:432–438.

Appendix 1. Stage Models of Development

Brenner, Charles. 1973. *An Elementary Textbook of Psychoanalysis*, rev. ed. New York: International Universities Press.

Erikson, Erik H. 1964. "A Schedule of Virtues." In Erik Erikson, *Insight and Responsibility*, pp. 111–157. New York: W. W. Norton.

Freud, Sigmund. 1922. *A General Introduction to Psychoanalysis*. London: Allen & Unwin.

Gould, Roger L. 1980. "Transformations: During Early and Middle Adult Years." In Neil J. Smelser and Erik H. Erikson, eds., *Themes of Work and Love in Adulthood*, pp. 213–237. Cambridge, Mass.: Harvard University Press.

Kohlberg, Lawrence. 1969. "Stage and Sequence: the Cognitive-developmental Approach to Socialization." In D. A. Goslin, ed., *Handbook of Socialization Theory and Research*. New York: Rand McNally.

Bibliography

AARP News Bulletin. 1988. "New Focus on Minority Aging." (January) 29:6.

Achenbaum, W. Andrew. 1985. "Societal Perceptions of Aging and the Aged." In Robert H. Binstock and Ethel Shanas, eds., *Handbook of Aging and the Social Sciences*, 2d ed., pp. 129–148. New York: Van Nostrand Reinhold.

Adams, John E. and Erich Lindemann. 1974. "Coping with Long-Term Disability." In George V. Coelho, David A. Hamburg, and John E. Adams, eds., *Coping and Adaptation*, pp. 127–138. New York: Basic Books.

After the Harvest. 1987. A report examining the lives and prospects of older farm laborers, prepared jointly by the Housing Assistance Council and the American Association of Retired Persons.

AIDS and the Education of Our Children: A Guide for Parents and Teachers. 1988. 3d ed. Washington, D.C.: U.S. Department of Education.

Ainsworth, Mary D. and S. M. Bell. 1974. "Mother-Infant Interaction and the Development of Competence." In K. J. Connolly and Jerome Bruner, eds. *The Growth of Competence*, pp. 97–118. New York: Academic Press.

Ainsworth, Mary D. and M. C. Blehar. 1978. *Patterns of Attachment: A Psychological Study of the Strange Situation*. Hillsdale, N.J.: Erlbaum Associates.

Alan Gutmacher Institute. 1987. *Teenage Pregnancy in Developed Countries*. New Haven, Conn.: Yale University Press.

Alderette, Paula and Donald F. deGraffenried. 1986. "Nonorganic Failure-to-Thrive Syndrome and the Family System." *Social Work* (May/June) 31:207–211.

Allen-Meares, Paula, Robert O. Washington, and Betty L. Welsh. 1986. *Social Work Services in Schools.* Englewood Cliffs, N.J.: Prentice-Hall.

Altman, Irwin. 1975. *The Environment and Social Behavior.* Monterey, Calif.: Brooks/Cole.

Antonucci, Toni C. 1985. "Personal Characteristics, Social Support, and Social Behavior.' In Robert H. Binstock and Ethel Shanus, eds., *Handbook of Aging and the Social Sciences,* pp. 94–128. New York: Van Nostrand Reinhold.

Ashley, Allyson. "Social Workers Aid Harried Farm Families." 1985. Quoted in *NASW News* (May), 30:4.

Atchley, Robert C. 1976. *The Sociology of Retirement.* Cambridge, Mass.: Schenkman.

Attneave, Carolyn. 1976. "Social Networks as the Unit of Intervention." In Philip J. Guerin, Jr., ed., *Family Therapy: Theory and Practice,* pp. 220–231. New York: Gardner Press.

Attneave, Carolyn. 1982. "American Indians and Alaska Native Families: Emigrants in Their Own Homeland." In Monica McGoldrick, John H. Pearce, and Joseph Giordano, eds., *Ethnicity and Family Therapy,* pp. 55–83. New York: Guilford Press.

Bacon, Kenneth H. 1989. "Nearly 0.2% of College Students in U.S. Who Were Tested Carry the AIDS Virus." *The Wall Street Journal,* May 23, pp. B4.

Ball, Donald W. 1974. "The Family as a *Sociological* Problem: Conceptualization of the Taken-for-Granted as Prologue to Social Problems Analysis." *Social Problems* (Winter), 19:295–305.

Balswick, Jack. 1988. *The Inexpressive Male: A Study of Men Who Express Love Too Little.* Lexington, Mass.: Lexington Books.

Bank, Stephen P. and Michael D. Kahn. 1982. *The Sibling Bond.* New York: Basic Books.

Banta, William F. 1988. *AIDS in the Workplace: Legal Questions and Practical Answers.* Lexington, Mass.: Lexington Books.

Barbarin, Oscar A. 1981. "Community Competence: An Individual Systems Model of Institutional Racism." In Oscar A. Barbarin, Paul R. Good, Martin Pharr, and Judith A. Siskind, eds., *Institutional Racism and Community Competence,* pp. 6–19. Rockville, MD: NIMH Center for Minority Group Mental Health Programs, DHHS Publication No. (ADM) 81-907.

Barglow, Peter, Brian E. Vaughn, and Nancy Molitor. 1987. "Attachment in a Low-Risk Sample." *Child Development* 58:945–954.

Bartlett, Harriett M. 1958. "Toward Clarification and Improvement of Social Work Practice." *Social Work* (April), 3:3–9.

Bartlett, Harriett M. 1970. *The Common Base of Social Work Practice.* New York: National Association of Social Workers.

Beal, Edward W. 1980. "Separation, Divorce, and Single-Parent Families." In Elizabeth A. Carter and Monica McGoldrick, eds., *The Family Life Cycle: A Framework for Family Therapy*, pp. 241–264. New York: Gardner Press.

Beard, Bruce H. 1977. "Hope and Fear with Hemodialysis." In E. Mansell Pattison, ed., *The Experience of Dying*, pp. 268–279. Englewood Cliffs, N.J.: Prentice-Hall.

Beardslee, William and John Mack. 1982. "The Impact on Children and Adolescents of Nuclear Developments." In Rita Rogers, ed., *Psychosocial Aspects of Nuclear Developments*, (Task Force Report #20) pp. 64–93. Washington, D.C.: American Psychiatric Association.

Beatrice, Dory Krongelb. 1979. "Divorce: Problems, Goals, and Growth Facilitation." *Social Casework* (March) 60:157–165.

Beauvoir, Simone de. 1972. *The Coming of Age*. New York: G. P. Putnam's Sons.

Bell, Kanani. 1986. "Reflections of an Unremembered Past." (unpublished)

Bem, Sandra Lipsitz. 1983. "Gender Schema Theory and Its Implications for Child Development: Raising Gender-Aschematic Children in a Gender-Schematic Society." *Signs: Journal of Women in Culture and Society* (Summer), 8:598–616.

Berger, Bennett M., Bruce M. Hackett, and R. Mervyn Millar. 1974. "Child-Rearing Practices in the Communal Family." In Arlene and Jerome H. Skolnick, eds., *Intimacy, Family, and Society*, pp. 441–464. Boston: Little, Brown.

Berger, Peter L. and Thomas Luckmann. 1966. *The Social Construction of Reality*. New York: Doubleday.

Berger, Raymond M. 1982. "The Unseen Minority: Older Gays and Lesbians." *Social Work* (May), 27:236–242.

Berger, Raymond M. 1984. "Realities of Gay and Lesbian Aging." *Social Work* (January–February), 29:57-62.

Berini, Ruth Y. and Eva Kahn. 1987. *Clinical Genetics Handbook*. Oradell, N. J.: Medical Economics Books.

Berkman, Lisa F. and S. Leonard Syme. 1979. "Social Networks, Host Resistance, and Mortality: A Nine-Year Follow-Up Study of Alameda County Residents." *American Journal of Epidemiology* (February), 109:186–204.

Berman, Alan L. 1986. "Helping Suicidal Adolescents: Needs and Responses." In Charles A. Corr and Joan N. McNeil, eds., *Adolescence and Death*, pp. 151–166. New York: Springer.

Berman, Lauren C. 1986 Letter to the Editor, "Failure-to-Thrive Syndrome." *Social Work* (September–October), 31:415–416.

Bernal, Guillermo and Ana Isabel Alvarez. 1983. "Culture and Class in the Study of Families." In James C. Hansen, ed., *Cultural Perspectives in Family Therapy*, pp. 33–50. Rockville, Md.: Aspen Systems Corporation.

Berns, Jacqueline Heiber. 1980. "Grandparents of Handicapped Children." *Social Work,* 25:238–239.

Bettelheim, Bruno. 1976. *The Uses of Enchantment: The Meaning and Importance of Fairy Tales.* New York: Alfred A. Knopf.

Bianchi, Suzanne M. and Daphne Spain. 1984. *American Women: Three Decades of Change,* rev. ed. U.S. Bureau of the Census, Special Demographic Analyses, CDS-80-8. Washington, D.C.: U.S. Government Printing Office.

Birth Defects: Tragedy and Hope. 1977. The National Foundation/March of Dimes, Box 2000, White Plains, N.Y. 10602.

Black, Rita Beck. 1982. "Social Work Trends: Education in Genetics for Social Workers Moves Beyond the Basics." In D. Brantley and S. Wright, eds., *Coordinating Comprehensive Child Health Services: Service, Training, and Applied Research Perspectives,* proceedings of the 1981 Tri-Regional Workshop for Social Workers in Maternal and Child Health, Center for Developmental and Learning Disorders, University of Alabama in Birmingham.

Black, Rita Beck. 1983. "Genetics and Adoption: A Challenge for Social Work." In Miriam Dinerman, ed., *Social Work Practice in a Turbulent World,* pp. 193–208. Silver Spring, Md.: National Association of Social Workers.

Blanchard, Evelyn Lance. 1982. "Observations on Social Work with American Indian Women." In Ann Weick and Susan T. Vandiver, eds., *Women, Power, and Change,* pp. 96–103. Washington, D.C.: National Association of Social Workers.

Blanchard, Evelyn Lance and Steven Unger. 1977. "Editorial Notes: Destruction of American Indian Families." *Social Casework* (May), 58:312–314.

Bloch, Judith and Judith Margolis. 1986. "Feelings of Shame: Siblings of Handicapped Children" In Alex Gitterman and Lawrence Shulman, eds., *Mutual Aid Groups and the Life Cycle,* pp. 99–110. Itaska, Ill.: F. D. Peacock.

Bloom, Bernard L., William F. Hodges, and Robert A. Caldwell. 1983. "Marital Separation: The First Eight Months." In Edward J. Callahan and Kathleen A. McCluskey, eds., *Life-Span Developmental Psychology: Nonnormative Life Events,* pp. 217–239. New York: Academic Press.

Bloom, Lois, 1975. "Language Development." In Frances Degan Horowitz, ed., *Review of Child Development Research,* 4:245–303. Chicago: University of Chicago Press.

Bloom, Lois, 1983. "Tensions in Linguistics" (in a review of *Language Acquisition,* Eric Wanner and Lila R. Gleitman, eds., New York: Cambridge University Press. 1982), *Science* (May 20), 220:843–845.

Bloom, Martin. 1979. "Social Prevention: An Ecological Approach." In Carel B. Germain, ed., *Social Work Practice: People and Environments,* pp. 326–345. New York: Columbia University Press.

Bloom, Martin, ed. 1980. *Life Span Development: Bases for Preventive and Interventive Helping.* New York: Macmillan.

Blume, Sheila B. 1985. "Alcohol and the Older Woman." *Hot Flash* (Spring), 4:2,6.

Bock, E. Wilbur. 1972. "Aging and Suicide: The Significance of Marital, Kinship, and Alternative Relations." *The Family Coordinator,* January, pp. 71–79.

Borders, William. 1980. "Away-on-Work Husbands and Marital Strains." *New York Times,* November 10, p. B12.

Bott, Elizabeth. 1972. *Family and Social Network.* 2nd ed. New York: Free Press.

Bower, Tom G. R. 1976. *The Perceptual World of the Child.* Cambridge, Mass.: Harvard University Press.

Bowlby, John. 1969. *Attachment and Loss, vol. 1: Attachment.* New York: Basic Books.

Bowlby, John. 1973. "Affectional Bonds: Their Nature and Origin." In Robert S. Weiss, ed., *Loneliness: The Experience of Emotional and Social Isolation,* pp. 38–52. Cambridge, Mass.: MIT Press.

Boyer, Ernest L. 1984. "The Test of Growing Student Diversity." *New York Times,* November 11, Sect. 12. p. 63.

Brawley, Edward A. and Emilia Martinez-Brawley. 1982. "Teaching Social Work Students to Use the News Media for Public Education Purposes." *Journal of Education for Social Work* (Spring), 18:76–83.

Brazelton, T. Berry. 1979. "Behavioral Competence of the Newborn Infant." *Seminars in Perinatology* 3(42):35–44.

Brazelton, T. Berry. 1985. *Working and Caring.* Reading, Mass.: Addison-Wesley.

Brenner, Harvey. 1984. *Estimating the Effects of Economic Change on National Health and Social Well-Being: A Study Prepared for the Subcommittee on Economic Goals and Intergovernmental Policy of the Joint Economic Committee, U.S. Congress.* Washington, D.C.: U.S. Government Printing Office.

Briley, Michael. 1983. "Over 80 and Doing Fine." A report of the research of Laurence G. Branch and Alan M. Jette. *Modern Maturity* (October–November), 26:96–97.

Brody, Elaine, M. 1981. " 'Women in the Middle' and Family Help to Older People." *The Gerontologist* (May), 21:471–480.

Brody, Elaine. 1984. Report of an interview. *Modern Maturity* (January), 27:33.

Bronfenbrenner, Urie. 1972. Quoted without reference in *Reader's Digest* (March).

Brown, Shirley Vining. 1983. "The Commitment and Concerns of Black Adolescent Parents." *Social Work Research and Abstracts* (Spring), 19:27–34.

Bruner, Jerome. 1983. *Child Talk: Learning to Use Language.* New York: Norton.

Burt, Martha R. 1986. "Estimates of Public Costs for Teen-age Childbearing." Unpublished paper prepared for the Center of Population Options, Washington, D.C.

Butler, Robert N. 1963. "The Life Review: An Interpretation of Reminiscence in the Aged." *Psychiatry* 26:65–76.

Butler, Robert N. 1975. "Psychiatry and the Elderly: An Overview." *American Journal of Psychiatry* 132:893–900.

Butler, Robert N. and Marian Emr. 1982. "Alzheimer's Disease: An Examination." *TWA Ambassador* (November), pp. 69–71.

Callahan, Daniel. 1987. *Setting Limits: Medical Goals in an Aging Society.* New York: Simon & Schuster.

Callahan, Edward J., William S. Brasted, and Juan L. Granados. 1983. "Fetal Loss and Sudden Infant Death: Grieving and Adjustment for Families." In Edward J. Callahan and Kathleen A. McCluskey, eds., *Life-Span Developmental Psychology: Nonnormative Life Events*, pp. 145–166. New York: Academic Press.

Campbell, John D. 1964. "Peer Relations in Childhood." In Martin L. Hoffman and Lois Wladis Hoffman, eds., *Review of Child Development Research.* vol. 1, pp. 289–322. New York: Russell Sage Foundation.

Cantor, Marjorie H. 1979. "The Informal Support System of New York's Inner City Elderly: Is Ethnicity a Factor?" In Donald E. Gelfand and A. J. Ketzik, eds., *Ethnicity and Aging*, pp. 153–174. New York: Springer.

Caring About Kids: Talking to Children About Death. 1979. Rockville, Md.: National Institute of Mental Health, DHEW Publication No. (ADM) 79-838.

Carmody, Deirdre. 1988. "Head Start Gets Credit for Rise in Scores." *New York Times*, September 21, p. B9.

Carpenter, Edward M. 1980. "Social Services, Policies, and Issues." *Social Casework* (October), 61:455–461.

Chen, Pei N. 1979. "A Study of Chinese-American Elderly Residing in Hotel Rooms." *Social Casework* (February) 60:89–95.

Chess, Stella, P. Fernandez, and S. Korn. 1980. "The Handicapped Child and His Family: Consonance and Dissonance." *Journal of the American Academy of Child Psychiatry* 19:56–67.

Chess, Stella and Alexander Thomas. 1986. *Temperament in Clinical Practice.* New York: Guilford Press.

Cho, Susan, Edith Freeman, and Shirley Patterson. 1982. "Adolescents' Experiences with Death: Practice Implications." *Social Casework* (February), 63:88–94.

Chodrow, Nancy. 1978. *The Reproduction of Mothering: Psychoanalysis and the Sociology of Gender.* Berkeley: University of California Press.

Chomsky, Noam. 1965. *Aspects of the Theory of Syntax.* Cambridge, Mass.: MIT Press.

Christian, Susan. 1984. "Grandparent Anxiety." *Modern Maturity* (January), 27:32–35.

Clarke, Ann M. 1982. "Developmental Discontinuities: An Approach to Assessing Their Nature." In Lynne A. Bond and Justin M. Joffe, eds., *Facilitating Infant and Early Childhood Development*, pp. 58–77. Hanover, N.H.: University Press of New England.

Clarke-Stewart, Alison. 1980. "The Father's Contribution to Children's Cognitive and Social Development in Early Childhood." In Frank A. Pedersen, ed., *The Father-Infant Relationship: Observational Studies in the Family Setting*, pp. 111–146. New York: Praeger.

Clarke-Stewart, Alison. 1982. *Day Care*. Cambridge, Mass.: Harvard University Press.

Cobb, Sidney. 1976. "Social Support as a Moderator of Life Stress." *Psychosomatic Medicine* (September–October), 38:300–314.

Cochran, Moncreiff M. and Jane Anthony Brassard. 1979. "Child Development and Personal Social Networks." *Child Development* (September), 50:601–616.

Cole, Johnetta B., ed. 1986. *All American Women: Lines That Divide. Ties That Bind*. New York: Free Press.

Collins, Alice H. and Diane L. Pancoast. 1976. *Natural Helping Networks*. Washington, D.C.: National Association of Social Workers.

Collins, Glenn. 1984. "Children of Interracial Marriage." *New York Times*, June 20, pp. C1, C7.

Comer, James P. 1972. *Beyond Black and White*. New York: Quadrangle/New York Times Books.

Comer, James P. and Muriel E. Hamilton-Lee. 1982. "Support Systems in the Black Community." In David E. Biegel and Arthur J. Naparstek, eds., *Commuinty Support Systems and Mental Health: Practice, Policy, and Research*, pp. 121–136. New York: Springer.

Commonwealth Fund's Commission on Elderly People Living Alone. 1987. Data from a survey conducted by Louis Harris & Associates for the Commission.

Consortium for Longitudinal Studies. 1983. *As the Twig Is Bent: Lasting Effects of Preschool Programs*. Hillsdale, N.J.: Erlbaum.

Cooper, Clare. 1976. "The House as Symbol of the Self." In Harold M. Proshansky, William H. Ittelson, and Leanne G. Rivlin, eds., *Environmental Psychology*. 2d ed., pp. 435–448. New York: Holt, Rinehart & Winston.

Coppersmith, Evan Imber. 1983. "The Family and Public Service Systems." In Bradford P. Keeney, ed., *Diagnosis and Assessment in Family Therapy*, pp. 84–99. Rockville, Md.: Aspen Systems Corporation.

Corbin, Juliet M. and Anselm Strauss. 1988. *Unending Work and Care*. San Francisco: Jossey-Bass.

Cotman, Carl. 1987. From a paper presented in a conference, "The Promise of Productive Aging," Washington, D.C., and reported in *AARP News Bulletin* (September), 28:2.

Cottrell, Leonard. 1976. "The Competent Community." In Berton H. Kaplan, Robert N. Wilson, and Alexander H. Leighton, eds., *Further*

Explorations in Social Psychiatry, pp. 195–209. New York: Basic Books.

Coupey, Susan M. and Michael I. Cohen. 1984. "Special Considerations for the Health Care of Adolescents with Chronic Illnesses." *Pediatric Clinics of North America* (February), 31:211–219.

Cowan, Philip. 1978. *The First Child and Family Formation*. Chapel Hill: University of North Carolina Press.

Coward, Raymond T. and Robert W. Jackson. 1983. "Environmental Stress: The Rural Family." In Hamilton I. McCubbin and Charles R. Figley, eds., *Stress and the Family*, pp. 178–200. New York: Brunner/Mazel.

Cox, Tom. 1978. *Stress*. Baltimore, Md.: University Park Press.

Coyne, James A. and Kenneth Holroyd. 1982. "Stress, Coping, and Illness: A Transactional Perspective." In Theodore Millon, Catherine Green, and Robert Meagher, eds., *Handbook of Clinical Health Psychology*, pp. 103–127. New York: Plenum.

Coyne, James C. and Richard S. Lazarus. 1980. "Cognitive Style, Stress Perception, and Coping." In Irwin L. Kutash and Louis B. Schlesinger, eds., *Handbook on Stress and Anxiety*, pp. 144–158. San Francisco: Jossey-Bass.

Cromwell, Ronald E., Bradford P. Keeney, and Bert N. Adams. 1976. "Temporal Patterning in the Family." *Family Process* (September), 15:343–348.

Croog, Sydney H. 1970. "The Family as a Source of Stress." In Sol Levine and Norman A. Scotch, eds., *Social Stress*, pp. 19–53. Chicago: Aldine.

Crowley, Susan. 1988. Report of minority contributions to a Washington, D.C., Conference on the needs of the elderly. *AARP News Bulletin* (December), 29:2.

Cuellar, Jose. 1978. "El Senior Citizens Club: The Older Mexican-American in the Voluntary Association." In Barbara G. Myerhoff and Andrei Simic, eds., *Life's Career—Aging: Cultural Variations in Growing Old*, pp. 207–230. Beverly Hills, Calif.: Sage.

Cummerton, Joan M. 1982. "Homophobia and Social Work Practice with Lesbians." In Ann Weick and Susan T. Vandiver, eds. *Women, Power, and Change*, pp. 104–113. Washington, D.C.: National Association of Social Workers.

Cunningham, Walter. 1986. "Older Persons Stay Intellectually Sharp." *AARP News Bulletin* (October), 27:2.

Curriculum Policy Statement for the Master's Degree and Baccalaureate Degree Programs in Social Work Education. 1982 (effective July 1, 1983). New York: Council on Social Work Education.

Curtis, Patricia. 1981. "Animals Are Good for the Handicapped, Perhaps All of Us." *Smithsonian* (July), 12:49–57.

Dahl, Ann Sale, Kathryn Markhus Cowgill, and Rigmor Asmundsson. 1987. "Life in Remarriage Families." *Social Work* (January–February) 32:40–44.

Dana, Richard H. 1981. "Epilogue." In Richard H. Dana, ed., *Human Services for Cultural Minorities*, pp. 353–354. Baltimore, Md.: University Park Press.

Darling, Rosalyn Benjamin. 1979. *Families Against Society: A Study of Reactions to Children with Birth Defects*. Beverly Hills, Calif.: Sage.

Davis, Morris E. 1977. "Occupational Hazards and Black Workers." *Urban Health* (August), 6:16–18.

Day, Clarence. 1920. *This Simian World*. New York: Knopf. (Reprinted in 1957.)

DeJong, Gerben. 1979. "Independent Living: From Social Movement to Analytic Paradigm." *Archives of Physical Medicine and Rehabilitation* (October), 60:435–446.

Delgado, Melvin and Denise Humm-Delgado. 1982. "Natural Support Systems: Source of Strength in Hispanic Communities." *Social Work* (January), 27:83–89.

DeLone, Richard. 1979. *Small Futures: Children, Inequality, and the Limits of Liberal Reform*. New York: Harcourt Brace Jovanovich.

De Long, Alton J. 1970. "The Micro-Spatial Structure of the Older Person: Some Implications of Planning the Social and Spatial Environment." In Leon A. Pastalan and Daniel H. Carson, eds., *Spatial Behavior of Older People*, pp. 68–87. Ann Arbor: University of Michigan Press.

Demos, John. 1974. "The American Family in Past Time." *The American Scholar* (Summer), 43:422–446.

Dillard, J. L. 1975. "General Introduction: Perspectives on Black English." In J. L. Dillard, ed., *Perspectives on Black English*, pp. 9–32. The Hague: Mouton.

Displaced Homemakers Network. 1989. "A Status Report on Displaced Homemakers and Single Parents in the United States," a study by the Network, Washington, D.C. (July).

Dobrof, Rose and Eugene Litwak. 1977. *Maintenance of Family Ties of Long-Term Care Patients*. Washington, D.C.: U.S. Government Printing Office, DHEW Publication No. (ADM) 77-400.

Dobzhansky, Theodosius. 1973. *Genetic Diversity and Human Equality*. New York: Basic Books.

Dobzhansky, Theodosius. 1976. "The Myths of Genetic Predestination and Tabula Rasa." *Perspectives in Biology and Medicine* (January), 19:156–170.

Draper, Barbara Jones. 1979. "Black Language as an Adaptive Response to a Hostile Environment." In Carel B. Germain, ed., *Social Work Practice: People and Environments*, pp. 267–281. New York: Columbia University Press.

Dreyer, Cecily A. and Albert S. Dreyer. 1973. "Family Dinner Time as a Unique Behavior Habitat," *Family Process* (September), 12:291–301.

Drezen, Warren. 1985. "Psychotropic Drug Use in Midlife and Older Women." *Hot Flash* (Spring), 4:3.

Dubos, René. 1968. *So Human an Animal.* New York: Scribner's.

Dubos, René. 1978. "Health and Creative Adaptation." *Human Nature* (January), 1:74–82.

Dubos, René. 1981. *Celebrations of Life.* New York: McGraw-Hill.

Duncan R., and M. Weston-Smith, eds. 1984. *The Encyclopedia of Medical Ignorance: The Mind and Body in Health and Disease.* New York: Pergamon Press.

Dunn, Judy. 1985. *Sisters and Brothers.* Cambridge, Mass.: Harvard University Press.

Dye, Nancy Schrim. 1980. "History of Childbirth in America." *Signs: Journal of Women in Culture and Society* (Autumn), 6:97–108.

Dyer, E. D. 1963. "Parenthood as Crisis: A Re-Study." *Marriage and Family Living* 25:196–201.

Eastman, Peggy. 1988. Report of a Symposium at Georgetown University, Washington, D.C., on the plight of refugees. *AARP News Bulletin* (September), 29:1.

Egan, Timothy. 1988. "Despairing Indians Looking to Tradition to Combat Suicides." *New York Times,* March 19, pp. 1, 54.

Elkin, Mayer. 1987. "Joint Custody: Affirming That Parents and Families Are Forever." *Social Work* (January–February), 32:18–24.

Entine, Alan D. 1984. "Voluntary Mid-Life Career Change: Family Effects." In Stanley H. Cramer, ed., *Perspectives on Work and the Family,* pp. 72–80. Rockville, Md.: Aspen Publishers.

Erikson, Erik H. 1959. "Growth and Crises of the Healthy Personality." In Erik H. Erikson, *Identity and the Life Cycle, Selected Papers by Erik H. Erikson,* pp. 50–100. Psychological Issues, Monograph No. 1. New York: International Universities Press.

Etaugh, Claire. 1984. "Effects of Maternal Employment on Children: Implications for the Family Therapist." In Stanley H. Cramer, ed., *Perspectives on Work and the Family,* pp. 16–39. Rockville, Md.: Aspen Systems Corporation.

Evans, Ron L. and Lawrence K. Northwood. 1979. "The Utility of Natural Help Relationships." *Social Science and Medicine* 13A:789–795.

Ewalt, Patricia L. and Robert M. Honeyfield. 1981. "Needs of Persons in Long-Term Care." *Social Work* (May), 26:223–231.

Ewalt, Patricia and Lola Perkins. 1979. "The Real Experience of Death Among Adolescents." *Social Casework* (November), 60:547–551.

Fairchild, Betty and Nancy Hayward. 1979. *Now That You Know: What Every Parent Should Know About Homosexuality.* New York: Harcourt Brace Jovanovich.

Falicov, Celia Jaes. 1982. "Mexican Families." In Monica McGoldrick. John K. Pearce, and Joseph Giordano, eds., *Ethnicity and Family Therapy,* pp. 134–163. New York: Guilford Press.

Falicov, Celia Jaes and Lilyan Brudner-White. 1983. "The Shifting Family Triangle: The Issue of Cultural and Contextual Relativity." In Celia

Jaes Falicov, ed., *Cultural Perspectives in Family Therapy*, pp. 51–67. Rockville, Md.: Aspen Publishers.

Falicov, Celia J. and Betty M. Karrer. 1980. "Cultural Variations in the Family Life Cycle: The Mexican American Family." In Elizabeth Carter and Monica McGoldrick, eds., *The Familiy Life Cycle: A Framework for Family Therapy*, pp. 383–426. New York: Gardner Press.

Farb, Peter. 1974. *Word Play*. New York: Knopf.

Farquharson, Andy. 1978. "Self-Help Groups: A Health Resource." Victoria, British Columbia: University of Victoria, School of Social Work. Mimeo.

Farquharson, Andy. 1979. "Self-Help in the Provision of Child Welfare Services: The Stoney Creek Indian Band, British Columbia, Canada." Paper presented to Conference on Self-Help and Mutual Aid in Contemporary Society, Dubrovnik, Yugoslavia, September 10–15. Mimeo.

Fimbres, Martha Molina. 1982. "The Chicana in Transition." In Ann Weick and Susan T. Vandiver, eds., *Women, Power, and Change*, pp. 89–95. Washington, D.C.: National Association of Social Workers.

Fine, Michelle, Sheila H. Akabas, and Susan Bellinger. 1982. "A Culture of Drinking: A Workplace Perspective." *Social Work* (September), 27:436–440.

Finlayson, Angela. 1976. "Social Networks as Coping Resources: Lay Help and Consultation Patterns Used by Women in Husbands' Post-Infarction Career." *Social Science and Medicine* (February), 10:97–103.

Fiske, Edward B. 1988. "35 Pages That Shook the Educational World." *New York Times*, April 27, p. B10.

Folkenberg, Judy. "Suicide Highest Among the Elderly." *ADAMHA* (March), 12: not paginated.

Fraiberg, Selma. 1959. *The Magic Years*. New York: Scribner's.

Fraiberg, Selma. 1977. *Insights from the Blind*. New York: Basic Books.

Fraser, Mark and Nance Kohlert. 1988. "Substance Abuse and Public Policy." *Social Service Review* (March), 62:103–126.

Freeman. M. 1984. "History, Narrative, and Life-Span Development Knowledge". *Human Development* 27:1–19.

Freud, Sigmund. 1953. *Three Essays on the Theory of Sexuality, vol. 7: The Standard Edition of the Complete Psychological Works of Sigmund Freud*. London: Hogarth Press.

Fried, Marc. 1969. "Grieving for a Lost Home." In Leonard J. Duhl, ed., *The Urban Condition*, pp. 151–171. New York: Simon & Schuster.

Friedman, Erica, Aaron Katcher, James L. Lynch, and Sue Ann Thomas. 1980. "Animal Companions and One Year Survival of Patients After Discharge from a Coronary Care Unit." *Public Health Reports* (July–August), 95:307–312.

Fromm-Reichmann, Freida. 1959. "Loneliness." *Psychiatry* 22:1–15.

Furstenberg, Frank F., Jr., J. Brook Gunn, and S. Philip Morgan. 1987. "Adolescent Mothers and Their Children in Later Life." *Family Planning Perspectives* (July–August, 19:142–151.

Gamble, T. J., and E. Zigler. 1986. "Effects of Infant Day Care: Another Look at the Evidence." *American Journal of Orthopsychiatry* 56: 26–41.

Garcia-Preto, Nydia. 1982. "Puerto Rican Families." In Monica McGoldrick, John K. Pearce, and Joseph Giordano, eds. *Ethnicity and Family Therapy*, pp. 164–186. New York: Guilford Press.

Gardner, John W. 1961. *Excellence: Can We Be Equal and Excellent Too?* New York: Harper Colophon Books.

Garland, James A., Hubert E. Jones, and Ralph Kolodney. 1965. "A Model for Stages of Development in Social Work Groups." In Saul Bernstein, ed., *Explorations in Group Work: Essays in Theory and Practice*, pp. 21–30. Boston: Boston University School of Social Work.

Garrison, Vivian. 1978. "Support Systems of Schizophrenic and Non-Schizophrenic Puerto Rican Women in New York City." *Schizophrenia Bulletin* 4:561–596.

Gary, Lawrence E. 1980. "Role of Alcohol and Drug Abuse in Homicide." *Public Health Reports* (November–December), 95:553–554.

Gary, Lawrence E. and Bogart R. Leashore. 1982. "High-risk Status of Black Men." *Social Work* (January), 54:54–59.

Geist, William E. 1984. *About New York:* "The Professionals Keeping Lyman Place Alive." *New York Times*, November 3, p. 25.

Gelfand, Donald E. and Rebeca Bialik-Gilad. 1989. "Immigration Reform and Social Work." *Social Work* (January) 34:23–28.

Gelman, Sheldon R. 1983. "The Developmentally Disabled: A Social Work Challenge." In Lynn Wikler and Maryanne P. Keenan, eds., *Developmental Disabilities, No Longer A Private Tragedy*, pp. 12–14. Silver Spring, Md.: National Association of Social Workers (co-published with American Association on Mental Deficiency, Washington, D.C.).

Genetic Counseling. 1987. The National Foundation/March of Dimes, Box 2000, White Plains, N.Y. 10602.

Gerard, Dianne. 1985. "Clinical Social Workers as Primary Prevention Agents." In Carel B. Germain, ed., *Advances in Clinical Social Work Practice*, pp. 84–89. Silver Spring, Md.: National Association of Social Workers.

Germain, Carel B. 1971. *Casework and Science, A Study in the Sociology of Knowledge*. Doctoral dissertation, Columbia University School of Social Work.

Germain, Carel B. 1981. "The Physical Environment and Social Work Practice." In Anthony N. Maluccio, ed., *Promoting Competence in Clients*, pp. 103–124. New York: Free Press.

Germain, Carel B. 1984. *Social Work Practice in Health Care:* An *Ecological Perspective*. New York: Free Press.

Germain, Carel B. 1985. "The Place of Community Work Within an Ecological Approach to Social Work Practice." In Samuel H. Taylor and Robert W. Roberts, eds., *Theory and Practice of Community Social Work*, pp. 30–55. New York: Columbia University Press.

Gerstel, Naomi and Harriet Fross. 1985. *Commuter Marriage.* New York: Guilford Press.

Getzel, George S. and Rosemary Masters. 1985. "Social Work Practice With Families of Homicide Victims." In Carel B. Germain, ed., *Advances in Cinical Social Work Practice,* pp. 7–16. Silver Spring, Md.: National Association of Social Workers.

Gibran, Kahlil. 1923. *The Prophet.* New York: Alfred Knopf.

Giele, Janet Z. 1980. "Adulthood as Transcendence of Age and Sex." In Neil J. Smelser and Erik H. Erikson, eds., *Themes of Work and Love in Adulthood,* pp. 151–173. Cambridge, Mass.: Harvard University Press.

Gilchrist, Lewayne D. and Steven Paul Schinke. 1983. "Teenage Pregnancy and Public Policy." *Social Service Review* (June), 57:307–322.

Gilligan, Carol. 1982. *In a Different Voice.* Cambridge, Mass.: Harvard University Press.

Gilligan, Carol. 1986. "On *In a Different Voice:* An Interdisciplinary Forum." *Signs: Journal of Women in Culture and Society* (Winter), 11:304–333.

Gitterman, Alex. 1971. "Group Work in the Public School." In William Schwartz and Serapio R. Zalba, eds., *The Practice of Group Work,* pp. 45–72. New York: Columbia University Press.

Glaser, Barney and Anselm Strauss. 1968. *Time for Dying.* Chicago: Aldine.

Glass, Gene V. and Mary Catherine Ellwein. 1984. "Early Education," a review of *As the Twig Is Bent. Science* (January 20), 223:273–274.

Gliedman, John and William Roth. 1980. *The Unexpected Minority: Handicapped Children in America.* New York: Harcourt Brace Jovanovich.

Gold, D. and D. Andres. 1980. "Maternal Employment and Development of Ten-Year Old Francophone Children." *Canadian Journal of Behavioral Science* 12:233–240.

Goldner, Virginia. 1987. "Instrumentalism, Feminism, and the Limits of Family Therapy." *Journal of Family Psychology* 1(1):109–116.

Goldsmith, Jean. 1982. "The Postdivorce Family System." In Froma Walsh, ed., *Normal Family Processes,* pp. 297–330. New York: Guilford Press.

Goodman, Bernice. 1980. "Some Mothers Are Lesbian." In Elaine Norman and Arlene Mancuso, eds., *Women's Issues and Social Work Practice,* pp. 153–180. Itaska, Ill.: F. E. Peacock.

Gordon, William E. 1969. "Basic Constructs for an Integrative and Generative Conception of Social Work." In Gordon Hearn, ed., *The General Systems Approach: Contributions Toward an Holistic Conception of Social Work,* pp. 5–12. New York: Council on Social Work Education.

Gould, Roger L. 1978. *Transformations: Growth and Change in Adult Life.* Boston: Little, Brown.

Grinker, William J. 1988. "Annual Report of the Human Resources Administration, Special Services for Children, New York City." *New York Times,* April 1, pp. B-1, B-2.

Gross, Jane. 1988. "Cocaine and Aids in New York Add to Infant Deaths." *New York Times,* February 13, pp. 1, 30.

Grosser, Charles F. and Jacqueline Mondros. 1985. "Pluralism and Partic- ipation: The Political Action Approach." In Samuel H. Taylor and Robert W. Roberts, eds., *Theory and Practice of Community Social Work*, pp. 154–178. New York: Columbia University Press.

Guinness Book of World Records. 1990. Donald McFarlan, ed. New York: Bantam.

Gussow, Zachary and George S. Tracy. 1976. "The Role of Self-Help Clubs in Adaptation to Chronic Illness and Disability." *Social Science and Medicine* (July–August), 10:407–414.

Gutis, Philip S. 1987. "Homosexual Paents Winning Some Custody Cases." *New York Times*, January 21, pp. C1, C16.

Gutmann, David. 1977. "The Cross-Cultural Perspective: Notes Toward a Comparative Psychology of Aging." In James E. Birren and K. Warner Schaie, eds., *Handbook of the Psychology of Aging*, pp. 302–326. New York: Van Nostrand and Reinhold.

Hage, Jerald and Michael Aikin. 1970. *Social Change in Complex Organi- zations*. New York: Random House.

Hakuta, Kenji. 1988. *Mirror of Language: The Debate on Bilingualism*. New York: Basic Books.

Hall, Edward T. 1966. *The Hidden Dimension*. New York: Doubleday.

Hall, Edward T. 1973. *The Silent Language*. Garden City, N.Y.: Doubleday.

Hamburg, Beatrix A. 1974. "Early Adolescence: A Specific and Stressful Stage of the Life Cycle." In George V. Coelho, David A. Hamburg, and John E. Adams, eds., *Coping and Adaptation*, pp. 101–124. New York: Basic Books.

Hanley, Robert. 1988. 'Baby M's Mother Wins Broad Visiting Rights." *New York Times*, April 7, pp. A1, B5.

Harbor Area Geriatric Program Staff (Erich Lindemann Mental Health Center, Boston, Mass.). 1985 "Letter to the Editor." *Hospital and Com- munity Psychiatry* (November), 35:1152–1153.

Hare-Mustin, Rachel T. 1978. "A Feminist Approach to Family Therapy." *Family Process* (June), 17:181–194.

Hareven, Tamara K. 1982. "The Life Course and Aging in Historical Perspective." In Tamara K. Hareven and K. J. Adams, eds., *Aging and Life Course Transitions: An Interdisciplinary Perspective*, pp. 1–26. New York: Guildford Press.

Harrison, James B. 1978. "Men's Roles and Men's Lives." *Signs: Journal of Women in Society and Culture* (Winter), 4:324–336.

Hartford, Margaret E. 1972. *Groups in Social Work*. New York: Columbia University Press.

Hartford Courant. 1988. "His and Hers Panel Discussions." (February 14), p. C1.

Hartman, Ann. 1978. 'Diagrammatic Assessment of Family Relation- ships." *Social Casework* (October), 59:465–476.

Hartman, Ann and Joan Laird. 1983. *Family Centered Social Work Practice*. New York: Free Press.

Hartmann, Heinz. 1958. *Ego Psychology and the Problem of Adaptation.* New York: International Universities Press.

Hartup, Willard W. 1979. "Peer Relations and the Growth of Competence." In Martha Whalen Kent and Jon E. Rolf, eds., *Primary Prevention of Psychopathology, vol. 3: Social Competence in Children,* pp. 150–170. Hanover, N.H.: University Press of New England.

Harvard Medical School Health Letter. 1986. "Not in My Back Yard: Low-level Radioactive Waste and Health." (April), 11:4–6.

Hayes, Cheryl D. 1987. *Risking the Future: Adolescent Sexuality, Pregnancy and Childbearing,* vol. 1. National Research Council, Panel on Adolescent Pregnancy and Childbearing. Washington, D.C.: National Academy Press.

Healthy People: The Surgeon General's Report on Health Promotion and Disease Prevention. 1979. DHEW (PHS) Publication No. 79-55071.

Hechinger, Fred M. 1988. "Toward Educating the Homeless." *New York Times,* February 2, p. C11.

Henley, Nancy M. 1985. "Psychology and Gender." *Signs: Journal of Women in Culture and Society* (Autumn) 11:101–119.

Henry, Jules. 1973. *Pathways to Madness.* New York: Vintage Books.

Henshaw, Stanley K., and Elise F. Jones. 1988. "The Delivery of Family Planning Services in Ontario and Quebec." *Family Planning Perspectives* (March–April), 20:80–87.

Hetherington, E. Mavis, Martha Cox, and Roger Cox. 1982. "Effects of Divorce on Parents and Children." In Michael E. Lamb, ed., *Non-Traditional Families: Parenting and Child Development,* pp. 233–288. Hillsdale, N.J.: Erlbaum.

HEW Secretary's Task Force on Hospice. 1978. Office of the Secretary, U.S. DHEW (December).

Hill, Catherine J. 1984. "Caring for an Elderly Relative." *Canada's Mental Health* (March), 32:13–15.

Hill, Robert. 1972. *The Strength of Black Families.* New York: Emerson Hall.

Hirsch, Barton J. 1981. "Social Networks and the Coping Process: Creating Personal Communities." In Benjamin H. Gottlieb, ed., *Social Networks and Social Support,* pp. 149–170. Beverly Hills, Calif.: Sage.

HIV/AIDS Surveillance Report. 1990. (no vol. no.), p. 5. Atlanta: Centers for Disease Control (April).

Hobbs, D. F. 1965. "Parenthood as Crisis: A Third Study." *Marriage and Family Living* 27:367–372.

Hochschild, Arlie Russell. 1974. "Communal Life Styles for the Old." In Arlene and Jerome H. Skolnick, eds. *Intimacy, Family, and Society,* pp. 565–578. Boston, Mass.: Little, Brown.

Hoffman, Lois Wladis. 1984. "Work, Family, and the Socialization of the Child." In Ross Parke, ed., *Review of Child Development Research,* vol. 7, pp. 223–282. Chicago: University of Chicago Press.

Hoffman, Lynn, 1980. "The Family Life Cycle and Discontinuous Change."

In Elizabeth A. Carter and Monica McGoldrick, eds., *The Family Life Cycle: A Framework for Family Therapy*, pp. 53–68. New York: Gardner Press.

Holmes, Lewis. 1978. "How Fathers Can Cause the Down Syndrome." *Human Nature* (October), 1:70–72.

Holmes, Thomas H. and Richard H. Raye. 1967. "The Social Readjustment Rating Scale." *Journal of Psychosomatic Research* 11:213–218.

Hooyman, Nancy R. and Rosemary Cunningham. 1986. "An Alternative Administrative Style." In Nan Van Den Bergh and Lynn B. Cooper, eds., *Feminist Visions for Social Work*, pp. 163–186. Silver Spring, Md.: National Association of Social Workers.

Hot Flash: Newsletter for Middle and Older Women, editorial. 1984. (Spring), 3:1.

Houle, Jocelyne and Kiely, Margaret C. 1984. "Intimacy: a Little-Understood Stage of Development." *Canada's Mental Health* (March), 32:7–11.

Hunt, Vilma R. 1975. "Reproduction and 'Work.' " *Signs: Journal of Women in Culture and Society* (Winter), 1:543–552.

Hyde, Janet S. 1981. "How Large Are Cognitive Gender Differences?" *American Psychologist* (August), 36:892–901.

Hytten, F. E. 1976. "Metabolic Adaptation of Pregnancy in the Prevention of Handicap Through Antenatal Care." In A. C. Turnbull and F. P. Woodford, eds., *Review of Research Practice*, Vol. 18. Amsterdam: Elsevier.

Jackson, Jacquelyne Johnson. 1985. "Race, National Origin, Ethnicity, and Aging." In Robert H. Binstock and Ethel Shanas, eds., *Handbook of Aging and the Social Sciences*, 2d ed., pp. 264–303 New York: Van Nostrand Reinhold.

James, Frank E. 1988. "Office Pariahs." *Wall Street Journal*, April 22, pp. 3R, 14R (Section 3).

Jay, K. and A. Young. 1979. *The Gay Report*. New York: Summit Books.

Jennings, Jeanette. 1987. "Elderly Parents as Caregivers for Their Adult Dependent Children." *Social Work* (September–October), 32:430–433.

Jeppsson-Grassman, Eva. 1986a. *After the Fall of Darkness: Three Studies of Visual Impairment and Work*. Stockholm: Stockholm Studies in Social Work 3. School of Social Work, University of Stockholm, Sweden.

Jeppsson-Grassman, Eva. 1986b. *Work and New Visual Impairment: A Study of the Adaptive Process*. Stockholm Studies in Social Work 2. School of Social Work, Stockholm, Sweden.

Johnson, Harriette C. 1988. "Drugs, Dialogue, or Diet: Diagnosing and Treating the Hyperactive Child." *Social Work* (July–August), 33:349–355.

Kagan, Jerome. 1984. *The Nature of the Child*. New York: Basic Books.

Kahn, Arnold S. and Paula J. Jean. 1983. "Integration and Elimination or Separation and Redefinition: The Future of the Psychology of Women." *Signs: Journal of Women in Society and Culture* (Summer), 8:659–671.

Kahn, Robert L. and Toni C. Antonucci. 1980. "Convoys Over the Life Course: Attachment, Roles, and Social Support." In Paul B. Baltes and Orville G. Brim, Jr., eds. *Life-Span Development*, vol. 3. pp. 254–286. New York: Academic Press.

Kalish, Richard A. 1968. "Life and Death: Dividing the Indivisible." *Social Science and Medicine* 2:249–259.

Kanter, Rosabeth Moss. 1972. " 'Getting It All Together': Some Group Issues in Communies." *American Journal of Orthopsychiatry* (July), 42:632–643.

Kanter, Rosabeth Moss. 1978. "Work in a New America." *Daedalus* (Winter), 107:47–78.

Kantor, David and William Lehr. 1975. *Inside the Family*. San Francisco: Jossey-Bass.

Kasl, Stanislav V. and Sidney Cobb. 1982. "Variability of Stress Effects Among Men Experiencing Job Loss." In Leo Goldberger and Shlomo Breznitz, eds., *Handbook of Stress: Theoretical and Clinical Aspects*, pp. 445–465. New York: Free Press.

Katchadourian, Herant A. 1976. "Medical Perspectives on Adulthood." *Daedalus* (Spring), 105:29–56.

Katz, Alfred H. and Eugene I. Bender. 1976. *The Strength in Us: Self-Help in The Modern World*. New York: New Viewpoints.

Katz, Mary Maxwell and Melvin J. Konner. 1981. "The Role of the Father: An Anthropological Perspective." In Michael E. Lamb, ed., *The Role of the Father in Child Development*, pp. 155–186. New York: Wiley.

Kavanaugh, Robert E. 1977. "Humane Treatment of the Terminally Ill." In Rudolf H. Moos, ed., *Coping With Physical Illness*, pp. 413–420. New York: Plenum.

Keith, Jennie. 1985. "Age in Anthropological Research." In Robert H. Binstock and Ethel Shanas, eds., *Handbook of Aging and the Social Sciences*, pp. 231–263. New York: Van Nostrand Reinhold.

Kelly, Thaddeus E. 1986. *Clinical Genetics and Genetic Counseling*. 2d ed. Chicago: Year Book, Medical Publishers Catalog.

Keniston, Kenneth and The Carnegie Council on Children. 1977. *All Our Children*. New York: Harcourt Brace Jovanovich.

Kerber, Linda K., Catherine G. Greeno, Eleanor E. Maccoby, Zella Luria, Carol B. Stack, and Carol Gilligan. 1986. "On *In a Different Voice*: An Interdisciplinary Forum." *Signs: Journal of Women in Culture and Society* (Winter), 11:304–333.

Kerson, Toba Schwaber and Lawrence A. Kerson. 1985. *Understanding Chronic Illness: The Medical and Psychosocial Dimensions of Nine Diseases*. New York: Free Press.

Kett, Joseph F. 1977. *Rites of Passage: Adolescence in America, 1790 to the Present*. New York: Basic Books.

Kinzel, August. 1970. "Body Buffer Zone in Violent Prisoners." *American Journal of Psychiatry* (July), 127:59–64.

Kira, Alexander. 1966. *The Bathroom.* Ithaca, New York: Cornell University Center for Housing and Environmental Studies.

Kjellstrand, Carl M. 1988. "Age, Sex, and Race Inequality in Renal Transplantation." *Archives of Internal Medicine* (June), 148:1305–1309.

Klaus, Marshall H. and John H. Kennell. 1976. *Maternal-Infant Bonding.* St. Louis: C. V. Mosby. (Revised 1982.)

Kleiman, Dena. 1984. "When Abortion Becomes Birth: A Dilemma of Medical Ethics Shaken by New Advances." *New York Times,* February 15, pp. B1, B4.

Kloosterman, G. J. 1975. "Obstetrics in the Netherlands: A Survival or a Challenge?" A paper presented at Tunbridge Wells Meeting on Problems in Obstetrics organized by the Medical Information Unit of the Spastics Society.

Kohlberg. Lawrence. 1969. "Continuities and Discontinuities in Child and Adult Moral Development." *Human Development* (February) 12:93–120.

Korner, Anneliese F. and R. Grobstein. 1966. "Visual Alertness as Related to Soothing in Neonates: Implications for Maternal Stimulation and Early Deprivation." *Child Development* 37:867–876.

Kotelchuck, M. 1976. "The Infant's Relationship to the Father: Experimental Evidence." In Michael E. Lamb, ed., *The Role of the Father in Child Development,* pp. 329–344. New York: Wiley.

Kroeber, Theodore. 1963. "The Coping Functions of the Ego Mechanisms." In Robert W. White, ed., *The Study of Lives,* pp. 178–198. New York: Atherton Press.

Kübler-Ross, Elisabeth. 1969. *On Death and Dying.* New York: Macmillan.

Kuhl, Patricia K. and Andrew N. Meltzoff. 1982. "The Bimodal Perception of Speech in Infancy." *Science* (December 10), 218:1138–1141.

Ladner, Joyce A. 1971. *Tomorrow's Tomorrow: The Black Woman.* New York: Anchor Books.

Laird, Joan. 1984. "Sorcerers, Shamans, and Social Workers: The Use of Ritual in Social Work Practice," *Social Work* (March-April), 29:123–129.

Laird, Joan. 1989. "Women and Stories: Restorying Women's Self-Constructions." In Monica McGoldrick, Carol M. Anderson, and Froma Walsh, eds., *Women in Families,* pp. 428–451. New York: Norton.

Lamb, Michael E. 1977a. 'The Development of Mother-Infant and Father-Infant Attachments in the Second Year of Life." *Developmental Psychology* 13:637–649.

Lamb, Michael E. 1977b. "Father-Infant and Mother-Infant Interaction in the First Year of Life." *Child Development* 48:167–181.

Lamb, Michael E. 1981. "The Development of Father-Infant Relationships." In Michael E. Lamb, ed., *The Role of the Father in Child Development,* 2d ed., pp. 459–488. New York: Wiley.

Lane, Harlan. 1987. "Listen to the Needs of Deaf Children." *New York Times,* July 17, pp. 35 (Op-Ed).

Lasch, Christopher. 1977. *Haven in a Heartless World: The Familiy Besieged.* New York: Basic Books.

Lau, Elizabeth and Jordan Kosberg. 1979. "Abuse of the Elderly by Informal Care Providers: Practice and Research Issues." *Aging* (September/October), nos. 299–300, pp. 10–15.

Lauer, Jeanette C. and Robert H. Lauer. 1986. *Til Death Do Us Part: How Couples Stay Together.* New York: Haworth Press.

Lazarus, Richard S. and Raymond Launier. 1978. "Stress-Related Transactions Between Person and Environment." In Lawrence A. Pervin and Michael Lewis, eds., *Perspectives in Interactional Psychology,* pp. 287–327. New York: Plenum.

Leary, Warren E. 1989. "Campus AIDS Survey Finds Threat is Real but Not Yet Rampant." *New York Times,* May 23, p. 12.

Lebow, Grace. 1976. "Facilitating Adaptation to Anticipatory Mourning." *Social Casework* (July), 57:458–465.

Lee, Judith A. B. 1980. "The Helping Professional's Use of Language in Describing the Poor." *American Journal of Orthopsychiatry* (October), 50:580–584.

Lee, Judith A. B. 1981. "Human Relatedness and the Mentally Impaired Older Person." *Journal of Gerontological Social Work* (Winter), 4:5–15.

Lee, Judith A. B. 1986. "No Place to Go: Homeless Women." In Alex Gitterman and Lawrence Shulman, eds., *Mutual Aid Groups and the Life Cycle,* pp. 245–262. Itaska, Ill.: F. E. Peacock.

Lee, Judith A. B., ed. 1989. *Group Work with the Poor and Oppressed.* New York: Haworth Press.

Lee, Judith A. B. (in press). "Teaching Lesbian and Gay Identity Formation Content in Human Behavior and Methods Courses." In Natalie J. Woodman, ed., *Lesbian and Gay Lifestyles: A Guide for Counseling and Education.* New York: Irvington Press.

Lee, Judith A. B. and Danielle N. Park. 1978. "A Group Approach to the Depressed Adolescent Girl in Foster Care." *American Journal of Orthopsychiatry* (July), 48:516–527.

Lee, Judith A. B. and Carol Swenson. 1978. "A Community Social Service Agency: Theory in Action." *Social Casework* (June), 59:359–369.

Leichter, Hope Jensen. 1974. "Some Perspectives on the Family as Educator." In Hope Jensen Leichter, ed., *The Family as Educator,* pp. 1–43. New York: Teachers College Press.

Le Masters, E. E. 1957. "Parenthood as Crisis." *Marriage and Family Living* 19:352–355.

Lenrow, Peter B. and Rosemary Burch. 1981. "Mutual Aid and Professional Services: Opposing or Complementary?" In Benjamin H. Gottlieb, ed., *Social Networks and Social Support,* pp. 233–258. Beverly Hills, Calif.: Sage.

Lerner, Gerda. 1971. "Women's Rights and American Feminism." *The American Scholar* (Spring), 40:235–248.

Levine, Renee Shai, Diane Metzendorf, and Kathryn A. Van Boskirk. 1986.

"Runaway and Throwaway Youth: A Case for Early Intervention With Truants." *Social Work in Education* 8:93–105.

Levine, Richard. 1988. "More Infants Showing Signs of Narcotics." *New York Times*, April 1, pp. B1, B3.

Levinson, Daniel J. with Charlotte N. Darrow, Edward B. Klein, Maria H. Levinson, and Braxton Mckee. 1978. *The Seasons of a Man's Life*. New York: Knopf.

Levinson, Daniel J. 1980. "Toward a Conception of the Adult Life Course." In Neil J. Smelser and Erik H. Erikson, eds., *Themes of Work and Love in Adulthood*, pp. 265–290. Cambridge, Mass.: Harvard University Press.

Lewis, Michael, Candice Feiring, and Marsha Weinraub. 1981. "The Father as a Member of the Child's Social Network." In Michael E. Lamb, ed., *The Role of the Father in Child Development*, 2d ed., pp. 259–294. New York: Wiley.

Lichtenberg, Joseph. 1981. "Implications for Psychoanalytic Theory of Research on the Neonate." *International Review of Psycho-Analysis* 8:35–52.

Lieberman, Morton A. 1982. "The Effects of Social Supports on Responses to Stress." In Lee Goldberger and Shlomo Breznitz, eds., *Handbook of Stress: Theoretical and Clinical Aspects*, pp. 764–783. New York: Free Press.

Lin, Keh-Ming and Minoru Masuda. 1981. "Impact of the Refugee Experience: Mental Health Issues of Southeast Asian Refugees." In *Bridging Cultures: Southeast Asian Refugees in America*, pp. 32–54. Los Angeles, Calif.: Asian American Community Mental Health Training Center.

Lippitt, Ronald and Martin Gold. 1959. "Classroom Social Structure as a Mental Health Problem." *Journal of Social Issues* (January), 15:40–49.

Lisansky-Gomberg, Edith. 1981. "Alcohol and Drug Abuse," paper presented at the Stony Brook Conference, "Health Issues of Older Women," April 1981.

Litwak, Eugene, Henry J. Meyer, and C. David Hollister. 1977. "The Role of Linkage Mechanisms Between Bureaucracies." In Roland Liebert and A. W. Imershien, eds., *Power, Paradigms and Community Research*, pp. 121–152. London: Sage.

Litwak, Eugene and Ivan Szelenyi. 1969. "Primary Group Structures and Their Functions: Kin, Neighbors and Friends." *American Sociological Review* 34:465–481.

Livson, F. B. 1980. "Sex Typing Over the Life Span: His, Hers, and Theirs." Paper presented at the annual meeting of the Gerontological Society of America, San Diego.

Luepnitz, Deborah Anna. 1982. *Child Custody: A Study of Families After Divorce*. Lexington, Mass.: Lexington Books.

Luepnitz, Deborah Anna. 1989. *The Family Interpreted*. New York: Basic Books.

Luey, Helen Sloss. 1980. "Between Worlds: The Problems of Deafened Adults." *Social Work In Health Care* (Spring), 5:253–265.

Lynn, D. A. and A. R. Cross. 1974. "Parent Preference of Preschool Children." *Journal of Marriage and the Family* 36:555–559.

Maccoby, Eleanor and Carol Nagy Jacklin. 1974. *The Psychology of Sex Differences*. Stanford, Calif.: Stanford University Press.

McCluskey, Kathleen A., Jim Killarney, and Dennis R. Papini. 1983. "Adolescent Pregnancy and Parenthood: Implications for Development." In Edward J. Callahan and Kathleen A. McCluskey, eds., *Life-Span Developmental Psychology: Normative Life Events*, pp. 69–113. New York: Academic Press.

Macfarlane, Aidan. 1977. *The Psychology of Childbirth*. Cambridge, Mass.: Harvard University Press.

Mackenzie, Thomas B., Nancy M. Collins, and Michael E. Popkin. 1982. "A Case of Fetal Abuse?" *American Journal of Orthopsychiatry* (October), 52:609–703.

McKusick, Victor A. 1986. *Mendelian Inheritance in Man: Catalogs of Autosomal Dominant, Autosomal Recessive, and X-Linked Phenotypes*, 7th ed. Baltimore: Johns Hopkins Press.

McLaughlin, Steven D., Susan E. Pearce, Diane L. Manninen, and Linda D. Winges. 1988. "To Parent or Relinquish: Consequences for Adolescent Mothers." *Social Work* (July–August), 33:320–324.

Maguire, Lambert. 1979. "Natural Helping Networks and Self Help Groups." Paper presented to the Conference on Primary Prevention in Social Work Education: Implications for Mental Health Curriculum, sponsored by the Council on Social Work Education, Louisville, Ky., October. Mimeo.

Mahaffey, Maryann and John W. Hanks, eds. 1982. *Practical Politics: Social Work and Political Responsibility*. Silver Spring, Md.: National Association of Social Workers.

Mahler, Margaret S. 1979. "Autism and Symbiosis: Two Extreme Disturbances of Identity." In Margaret S. Mahler, ed., *Selected Papers*, Vol I, pp. 169–182. New York: Jason Aronson.

Mahler, Margaret S., Fred Pine, and Anni Bergman. 1975. *The Psychological Birth of the Human Infant*. New York: Basic Books.

Martyna, Wendy. 1980. "Beyond the 'He/Man' Approach: The Case for Non-Sexist Language." *Signs: Journal of Women in Culture and Society* (Spring), 5:482–493.

Massachusetts Human Services Coalition, Inc. 1983. "Up the Down Escalator: State and Federal Budgets—The Impact on Families." First edition (February).

Massachusetts Human Services Coalition, Inc. 1988, "Up the Down Escalator, State and Federal Programs—The Impact on Families 1984–1986." 3d ed. (October).

Matlaw, Jane R. and Jane B. Mayer. 1986. "Elder Abuse: Ethical and Practical Dilemmas for Social Work." *Health and Social Work* (Spring), 11:85–94.

Matlin, Margaret W. 1987. *The Psychology of Women*. New York: Holt, Rinehart & Winston.

Maxwell, Robert J. 1971. "Anthropological Perspectives." In Henri Yakers, Humphrey Osmund, and Frances Cheek, eds., *The Future of Time*, pp. 36–72. New York: Doubleday.

Mayer, John and Aaron Rosenblatt. 1964. "The Client's Social Context." *Social Casework* (November), 45:511–518.

Mead, Margaret. 1970. *Culture and Commitment*. New York: Doubleday.

Mechanic, David. 1974a. "Social Structure and Personal Adaptation." In George V. Coelho, David A. Hamburg, and John E. Adams, eds., *Coping and Adaptation*, pp. 32–46. New York: Basic Books.

Mechanic, David. 1974b. "Discussion of Research Programs on Relations Between Stressful Events and Episodes of Physical Illness." In Barbara Snell Dohrenwend and Bruce P. Dohrenwend, eds., *Stressful Life Events: Their Nature and Effects*, pp. 87–97. New York: Wiley.

Meeks, Donald E. 1989. "Substance Abuse Disorders." In Francis J. Turner, ed., *Child Psychopathology: A Social Work Perspective*, pp. 317–350. New York: Free Press.

Meltzoff, Andrew N. and M. Keith Moore. 1977. "Imitation of Facial and Manuel Gestures by Human Neonates." *Science* (October 7), 198:75–78.

Mendes, Helen A. 1976. "Single Fatherhood." *Social Work* (July), 21:308–312.

Middleman, Ruth R. 1981 "The Pursuit of Competence Through Involvement in Structured Groups." In Anthony N. Maluccio, ed., *Promoting Competence in Clients: A New/Old Approach to Social Work Practice*, pp. 185–210. New York: Free Press.

Middleman, Ruth R. 1968. *The Non-Verbal Method in Working with Groups*. New York: Association Press.

Miller, Irving and Renee Solomon. 1979. "The Development of Group Services for the Elderly." In Carel B. Germain, ed., *Social Work Practice: People and Environments*, pp. 74–106. New York: Columbia University Press.

Milunsky, Aubrey. 1977. *Know Your Genes*. New York: Houghton Mifflin.

Minuchin, Salvador. 1974. *Families and Family Therapy*. Cambridge, Mass.: Harvard University Press.

Mizio, Emelicia. 1974. "Impact of External Systems on the Puerto Rican Family." *Social Casework* (February), 55:76–83.

Modern Maturity, 1979. "More People Than Ever Reaching 100." (October–November), 22.

Moen, Phyllis. 1983. "The Two-Provider Family: Problems and Potentials." In Michael E. Lamb, ed., *Changing Families*, pp. 13–43. New York: Plenum.

Moen, Phyllis and D. Dempster-McClain. 1981. "Work Time Preferences of Parents of Preschoolers." Unpublished draft.

Money, John and Anke A. Ehrhardt. 1972. *Man and Woman, Boy and Girl.* Baltimore, Md.: Johns Hopkins University Press.

Monk, Abraham and Rose Dobrof. 1978. "Social Services for Older Persons: A Review of the Research." Paper prepared for the National Association of Social Workers and the National Institute of Mental Health Conference on the Future of Social Work Research, San Antonio, Texas, October.

Moore, Kristin A., Margaret C. Simms, and Charles L. Betsey. 1986. *Choice and Circumstance.* New Brunswick, N.J.: Rutgers University Press, Transaction Books.

Moore, W. E. 1963. *Man, Time, and Society.* New York: Wiley.

Moos, Rudolf H. 1976. *The Human Context.* New York: Wiley.

Moses, A. Elfin and Robert O. Hawkins. 1982. *Counseling Lesbian Women and Gay Men: A Life-Issues Approach.* St. Louis, Mo.: Mosby.

Motulsky, Arno G. 1974. 'Brave New World?" *Science* (August 23), 185:653–663.

Munoz, Faye Untalan. 1976. "Pacific Islanders—A Perplexed, Neglected Minority." *Social Casework* (March), 57:179–184.

Murphy, Lois B. 1974. "Coping, Vulnerability, and Resilience in Childhood." In George V. Coelho, David A. Hamburg, and John E. Adams, eds., *Coping and Adaptation,* pp. 69–100. New York: Basic Books.

Murphy, Lois Barclay and Alice E. Moriarty. 1976. *Vulnerability, Coping, and Growth: From Infancy to Adolescence.* New Haven Conn.: Yale University Press.

Myerhoff, Barbara G. 1978a. *Number Our Days: A Triumph of Continuity and Culture Among Jewish Old People in an Urban Ghetto.* New York: Simon & Schuster.

Myerhoff, Barbara G. 1978b. "A Symbol Perfected in Death: Continuity and Ritual in the Life and Death of an Elderly Jew." In Barbara G. Myerhoff and Andrei Simic, eds., *Life's Career—Aging: Cultural Variations on Growing Old.,* pp. 163–230. Beverly Hills, Calif.: Sage.

NASW News. 1985. "Job Site Hazards Imperil Workers' Health." 30:13, 16.

NASW News. 1987. "Single Moms View Selves as Strong and Resourceful." 32(2):1, 16.

NASW News. 1987. "Project Supports Family Caregivers' Role." 32(10):6.

NASW News. 1989. "Rural Hospitals Go Under Knife." 34(2):3.

National Commission on Excellence in Education. 1983. *Nation at Risk: The Imperative for Educational Reform.* Washington, D.C.: U.S. Government Printing Office.

National Institute on Drug Abuse. 1988a. *National Household Survey on Drug Abuse, Main Findings 1985.* Washington, D.C.: DHHS Publication No. (ADM) 88-1586.

National Institute on Drug Abuse. 1988b. *Illicit Drug Use, Smoking, and Drinking by America's High School Students, College Students, and Young*

Adults, 1975–1987. Washington, D.C.: DHHS Publication No. (ADM) 89-1602.

Neugarten, Bernice L. 1968. "The Awareness of Middle Age." In Bernice L. Neugarten, ed., *Middle Age and Aging*, pp. 93–98. Chicago: University of Chicago Press.

Neugarten, Bernice L. 1969. "Continuities and Discontinuities of Psychological Issues Into Adult Life." *Human Development* 12(2):121–130.

Neugarten, Bernice L. 1978. "The Future and the Young-Old." In L. F. Jarvik, ed., *Aging Into the 21st Century*, pp. 137–152. New York: Gardner Press.

Neugarten, Bernice L. and Gunhild O. Hagestad. 1976. "Age and the Life Course." In R. H. Binstock and E. Shanas, eds. *Handbook of Aging and the Social Sciences*, pp. 35–55. New York: Van Nostrand Reinhold.

Neugarten, Bernice L. and Karol K. Weinstein. 1968. "The Changing American Grandparent." In Bernice L. Neugarten, ed., *Middle Age and Aging*, pp. 280–285. Chicago: University of Chicago Press.

Newcomb, Michael and Peter Bentler. 1988. *Consequences of Adolescent Drug Use: Impact on the Lives of Young Adults.* Newbury Park, Calif.: Sage.

Newman, Oscar. 1972. *Defensible Space.* New York: Macmillan.

Newsweek. 1978. "Communes Live." May 15, 91: pp. 89–90.

Newton, Niles and Charlotte Modahl. 1978. "Pregnancy: The Closest Human Relationship." *Human Nature* (March), 1:39–49.

New York Times, October 14, 1984. "Baby Doe at Age 1: A Joy and a Burden," p. A56.

New York Times, February 11, 1985. "Half U.S. Couples Can't Have Babies," p. A12.

New York Times, March 7, 1985. "Decline in Divorce is First in 20 Years," p. C11.

New York Times, June 26, 1986. "Study Compares Incomes of Spouses," p. C7.

New York Times, April 9, 1987. "Lower Rate of Divorce Found," P. C9.

New York Times, September 8, 1987. "U.S. Fertility at Low and Life Expectancy at High," p. A6.

New York Times, January 28, 1988. "Twenty-four Percent of U.S. School Children Live with Just One Parent," p. C8.

New York Times, March 16, 1988. "Newborns in 30 Cities to be tested for presence of Aids antibodies," p. A20.

New York Times, December 12, 1988. "Study Finds Blacks Twice as Liable to School Penalties as Whites," p. A16.

New York Times, month and day unknown, 1988. "Letter to Editor," Editorial page.

NIDA Capsules. 1988. "Facts About Drugs in The Workplace." National Institute on Drug Abuse, Rockville, Md.

Nieto, Daniel S. 1982. "Aiding the Single Father." *Social Work* (November), 27:473–478.

Noble, Dorinda N. and Adrianne K. Hamilton. 1983. "Coping and Complying: A Challenge in Health Care." *Social Work* (November–December), 28:462–466.

Nobles, Wade. 1974. "Africanity: Its Role in Black Families." *The Black Scholar* (June), 9:10–17. Reprinted in Robert Staples. ed., *The Black Family: Essays and Studies*, 2d ed., pp. 19–25. Belmont, Calif.: Wadsworth, 1978.

Norman, Michael. 1988. "Lessons: American Indians seek better schools and more control over the education of their children." *New York Times*, April 6, p. B-9.

Notman. Malkah. 1981. Abstract of a lecture on menopause reported in *Hot Flash* (Fall), 1:3.

Nowak, Carol A. and Gary C. Brice. 1984. "The Process of Retirement: Implications for Late-Life Counseling." In Stanley H. Cramer, ed., *Perspectives on Work and the Family*, pp. 108–123. Rockville, Md.: Aspen Systems Corp.

Nuckolls, Katherine B., John Cassel, and Berton H. Kaplan. 1972. "Psychosocial Assets, Life Crises, and the Prognosis of Pregnancy." *American Journal of Epidemiology* 95:431–441.

Oakley, Ann. 1979. "A Case of Maternity: Paradigms of Women as Maternity Cases." *Signs: Journal of Women in Culture and Society* (Summer), 4:607–631.

O'Barr, William M. 1984. "Asking the Right Questions About Language and Power." In Cheris Kramarae, Muriel Schulz, and William M. O'Barr, eds., *Language and Power*, pp. 260–280. Los Angeles, Calif.: Sage.

O'Connell, Patricia. 1972. "Developmental Tasks of the Family," *Smith College Studies in Social Work* (June), 42:203–210.

Offer, Daniel and J. B. Offer. 1975. *From Teenage to Young Manhood: A Psychological Study*. New York: Basic Books.

Offer, Daniel, Eric Ostrov, and Kenneth I. Howard. 1981. *The Adolescent: A Psychological Self-Portrait*. New York: Basic Books.

Offer, Daniel, Eric Ostrov, Kenneth I. Howard, and Robert Atkinson. 1988. *The Teenage World: Adolescents' Self-Image in Ten Countries*. New York: Plenum.

O'Neil, James M. 1982. "Gender-Role Conflict and Strain in Men's Lives: Implications for Psychiatrists, Psychologists, and Other Human-Service Providers." In Kenneth Solomon and Norman Levy, eds., *Man and Transition*, pp. 5–44. New York: Plenum.

Opie, Iona and Peter Opie. 1969. *Children's Games in Street and Playground*. Oxford: Oxford University Press.

Owan, Tom C. 1978. "Improving Productivity in the Public Sector Through Bilingual-Bicultural Staff." *Social Work Research and Abstracts* (Spring), 14:10–18.

Owen, M. T., M. A. Easterbrooks, L. Chase-Sandole, and W. A. Goldberg. 1984. "The Relation Between Maternal Employment Status and the

Stability of Attachments to Mother and Father." *Child Development* 55:1894–1901.

Pancoast, Diane. 1980. "Finding and Enlisting Neighbors to Support Families." In James Garbarino and S. Holly Stocking, eds., *Protecting Children from Abuse and Neglect*, pp. 109–132. San Francisco: Jossey-Bass.

Parke, Ross D. 1981. *Fathers.* Cambridge, Mass.: Harvard University Press.

Parke, Ross D. and S. E. O'Leary. 1976. "Father-Mother Infant Interaction in the Newborn Period." In Karl Riegel and J. Meacham, eds., *The Developing Individual in a Changing World, vol. 2: Social and Environmental Issues*, pp. 653–663. The Hague: Mouton.

Parke, Ross D. and D. B. Sawin. 1976. "The Father's Role in Infancy: A Re-evaluation." *The Family Coordinator* 25:365–371.

Parke, Ross D.and Barbara R. Tinsley. 1981. "The Father's Role in Infancy: Determinants of Involvement in Caregiving and Play." In Michael E. Lamb, ed., *The Role of the Father in Child Development*, pp. 429–458. New York: Wiley.

Patterson, Shirley L. 1987. "Older Rural Natural Helpers: Gender and Site Differences in the Helping Process." *The Gerontologist* (May), 27:639–644.

Patterson, Shirley and Eileen Brennan. 1983. "Matching Helping Roles With the Characteristics of Older Natural Helpers." *Journal of Gerontological Social Work* 5(4):55–66.

Patterson, Shirley, Eileen Brennan, Carel B. Germain, and Jay Memmot. 1988. "The Effectiveness of Rural Natural Helpers." *Social Casework* (May), 69:272–279.

Pattison, E. Mansell. 1977a. "The Dying Experience." In E. Mansell Pattison, ed., *The Experience of Dying*, pp. 303–316. Englewood Cliffs, N.J.: Prentice-Hall.

Pattison, E. Mansell. 1977b. "Death Throughout the Life Cycle." In E. Mansell Pattison, ed., *The Experience of Dying*, pp. 18–27. Englewood Cliffs, N.J.: Prentice-Hall.

Paul, Maureen, Cynthia Daniels, and Robert Rosofsky. 1988. "A Study of Employers' Practices and Reproductive Health." Massachusetts Department of Health and the University of Massachusetts Occupational Health Program.

Peak, Daniel T. 1977. "The Elderly Who Face Dying and Death." In David Barton, ed., *Dying and Death: A Clinical Guide for Caregivers*, pp. 210–219. Baltimore: Williams & Wilkins.

Pedersen, Frank A. 1980. "Overview: Answers and Reformulated Questions." In Frank A. Pedersen, ed., *The Father-Infant Relationship: Observational Studies in the Family Setting*, pp. 147–179. New York: Praeger.

Pedersen, Frank A., B. J. Anderson, and R. L. Cain. 1980. "Parent-Infant and Husband-Wife Interactions Observed at Age Five Months." In Frank A. Pedersen, ed., *The Father-Infant Relationship: Observational Studies in the Family Setting*, pp. 71–86. New York: Praeger.

Pedersen, Frank A., Judy L. Rubenstein, and Leon J. Yarrow. 1979. "Infant Development in Father-Absent Families." *Journal of Genetic Psychology* 135:51–61.

Penney, Bobby. 1976. In an interview reported in "Seniors Gain Happier, Healthier Lives at MZ Center." *Mount Zion Bulletin* (Summer), nos. 6–7.

Perrin, Ellen C. and P. Susan Gerrity. 1984. "Development of Children with a Chronic Illness." *Pediatric Clinics of North America* (February), 31:19–31.

Perrin, James M. 1985. "Introduction." In Nicholas Hobbs and James M. Perrin, eds., *Issues in the Care of Children with Chronic Illness*, pp. 1–10. San Francisco: Jossey-Bass.

Perry, Helen Swick. 1982. *Psychiatrist of America: The Life of Harry Stack Sullivan*. Cambridge, Mass.: Harvard University Press.

Petersen, Anne and Ralph Spiga. 1982. "Adolescence and Stress." In Leo Goldberger and Shlomo Breznitz, eds., *Handbook of Stress: Theoretical and Clinical Aspects*, pp. 515–528. New York: Free Press.

Pfeffer, Cynia R. 1987. "Families of Suicidal Children." In René F. W. Diekstra and Keith Hawton, eds. *Suicide in Adolescence*, pp. 137–138. Hingham, Mass.: Kluwer Academic Publishers.

Philipp, Connie and Kristine Siefert. 1979. "A Study of Maternal Participation in Preschool Programs for Handicapped Children and Their Families." *Social Work in Health Care* (Winter), 5:165–175.

Phillips, D. and Ross D. Parke. 1979. "Father and Mother Speech to Prelinguistic Infants." University of Illinois, unpublished manuscript.

Piaget, Jean and Barbel Inhelder. 1969. *The Psychology of the Child*. New York: Basic Books.

Pilisuk, Marc and Charles Froland. 1978. "Kinship, Social Networks, Social Support and Health." *Social Science and Medicine* 12B(4):273–280.

Pinderhughes, Elaine. 1979. "Teaching Empathy in Cross-Cultural Social Work." *Social Work* (July), 24:312–316.

Pinderhughes, Elaine. 1983. "Empowerment for Our Clients and for Ourselves." *Social Casework* (June), 64:331–38.

Pleck, Joseph H. 1986. Interview reported in *Realia*. (March), 4. Wellesley, Mass.: Wellesley College.

Pless, I. Barry. 1984. "Clinical Assessment: Physical and Psychological Functioning." *Pediatric Clinics of North America* (February), 31:33–45.

Pless, I. Barry and James M. Perrin. 1985. "Issues Common to a Variety of Illnesses." In Nicholas Hobbs and James M. Perrin, eds., *Issues in the Care of Children with Chronic Illness*, pp. 41–60. San Francisco, Jossey-Bass.

Polit, Denise, Cozette Morrow White, and Thomas D. Morton. 1987. "Sex Education and Family Planning Services for Adolescents in Foster Care." *Family Planning Perspectives* (January–February), 19:18–23.

Pollack, Otto. 1960. "A Family Diagnosis Model." *Social Service Review* (March), 34:1–50.

Practice Digest. 1979. "Reaching Senior Citizens in Ten Rural Counties." (June), 2:19–20.

Practice Digest. 1983. Issue on "The New Arrivals." (March), 5.

Practice Digest. 1984. Issue on "Working with Gay and Lesbian Clients." (Summer), 7.

Profile of Older Americans. 1986. Administration on Aging and American Association of Retired Persons (brochure).

Provence, Sally and Rose C. Lipton. 1962. *Infants in Institutions: A Comparison of Their Development with Family-Reared Infants During the First Year of Life.* New York: International Universities Press.

Queralt, Magaly. 1984. "Understanding Cuban Immigrants: A Cultural Perspective." *Social Work* (March–April), 29:115–121.

Radin, Norma. 1976. "The Role of the Father in Cognitive, Academic, and Intellectual Development." In Michael E. Lamb, ed., *The Role of the Father in Child Development,* 2d ed., pp. 379–428. New York: Wiley.

Rando, Therese A. 1985. "Bereaved Parents: Particular Difficulties, Unique Factors, and Treatment Issues." *Social Work* (January–February), 30:19–23.

Raske, Kenneth E. 1986. "Letter to the Editor" from the President of the Greater New York Hospital Association, *New York Times,* December 29, p. A20.

Rasky, Susan F. 1988. "Fort Apache Journal: What's in a name? For Indians, Cultural Survival." *New York Times,* August 4, p. A12.

Rebecca, Meda, Robert Heffner, and Barbara Oleshansky. 1976. "A Model of Sex-Role Transcendence." *Journal of Social Issues* 32(3):197–206.

Red Horse, John G. 1980. "Family Structure and Value Orientation in American Indians." *Social Casework* (October), 61:462–467.

Reichard, Suzanne, Florine Livson, and Paul G. Petersen. 1968. "Adjustment to Retirement." In Bernice L. Neugarten, ed., *Middle Age and Aging,* pp. 178–180. Chicago: University of Chicago Press.

Reiss, David. 1981. *The Family's Construction of Reality.* Cambridge, Mass.: Harvard University Press.

Reiss, David. 1982. "The Working Family: A Researcher's View of Health in the Household." *American Journal of Psychiatry* (November), 139:1412–1420.

Reiss, David and Mary Ellen Oliveri. 1983. "Family Stress as Community Frame." In Hamilton I. McCubbin, Marvin B. Sussman, Joan M. Patterson, eds., *Advances and Developments in Family Stress Theory and Research,* pp. 61–83. New York: Haworth Press.

Research Dialogues. 1989. "Long-Term Care: A National Issue." TIAA/CREF (April), no. 24, p. 9.

Rhodes, Sonya. 1977. "A Developmental Approach to the Life Cycle of the Family." *Social Casework* (May), 58:301–311.

Riccardi, Vincent. 1977. *The Genetic Approach to Human Disease.* New York: Oxford University Press.

Rice, Dorothy. 1980. "Homicide from the Perspective of NCHS Statistics on Blacks." *Public Health Reports* (November–December), 95:550–552.

Richards, M. P. M., J. F. Dunn, and B. Antonis. 1977. "Caretaking in the First Year of Life: The Role of Fathers, and Mothers' Social Isolation." *Child: Care, Health and Development* 3:23–26.

Riessman, Catherine K. 1989. "From Victim to Survivor: A Woman's Narrative Reconstruction of Marital Sexual Abuse." *Smith College Studies in Social Work* (June), 59:232–251.

Riley, Mathilda W. 1978. "Aging, Social Change, and the Power of Ideas.' *Daedalus* (Fall), 107:39–52.

Riley, Mathilda W. 1985a. "Women, Men, and the Lengthening Life Course." In Alice S. Rossi, ed., *Gender and the Life Course*, pp. 333–347. New York: Aldine.

Riley, Matilda White. 1985b. "Age Strata in Social Systems." In Robert H. Binstock and Ethel Shanas, eds., *Handbook of Aging and the Social Sciences*, 2d ed., pp. 369–411. New York: Van Nostrand Reinhold.

Rist, Ray C. and Jan E. Harrel. 1982. "Labeling the Learning Disabled Child: The Social Ecology of Educational Practice." *American Journal of Orthopsychiatry* (January), 52:146–160.

Ritvo, Edward, B. J. Freeman, Anne Mason-Brothers, Amy Mo, and Anne M. Ritvo. 1985. 'Concordance for the Syndrome of Autism in 40 Pairs of Afflicted Twins." *The American Journal of Psychiatry* (January), 142: 74–77.

Rosen, Sumner M., David Fanshel, and Mary E. Lutz, eds. 1987. *Face of the Nation 1987, Statistical Supplement to the 18th Edition of the Encyclopedia of Social Work*. Silver Spring, Md.: National Association of Social Workers.

Rotman, Patricia. 1983. "Shaping Industrial Policy: An Expanding Arena for Social Work Practice." Abstract of paper presented at the National Association of Social Workers Symposium, Washington, D.C., November (unpublished).

Royer, Terry D. and Richard P. Barth. 1984. "Improving the Outcome of Pregnancy." *Social Work* (September–October), 29:470–475.

Rubin, Joan. 1984. "Planning for Language Change in the United States: The Case of Monolingual Spanish Speakers." In Cheris Kramarae, Muriel Schulz, and William M. O'Barr, eds., *Language and Power*, pp. 154–175. Los Angeles, Calif.: Sage.

Rubin, Lillian. 1976. *Worlds of Pain: Life in the Working-Class Family*. New York: Basic Books.

Rubin, Zick. 1980. *Children's Friendships*. Cambridge, Mass.: Harvard University Press.

Rutter, Michael. 1972. *Maternal Deprivation Reassessed*. Harmondsworth, U.K.: Penguin Books.

Rutter, Michael. 1979a. "Protective Factors in Children's Responses to Stress and Disadvantage." In Martha Whalen Kent and Jon E. Rolf, eds., *Primary Prevention of Psychopathology*, pp. 49–74. Hanover, N.H.: University Press of New England.

Rutter, Michael. 1979b. *Changing Youth in a Changing Society*. London: Nuffield Provincial Hospitals Trust.

Ryan, Angela Shen. 1982. "Asian-American Women: A Historical and Cultural Perspective." In Ann Weick and Susan T. Vandiver, eds., *Women, Power, and Change*, pp. 78–88. Washington, D.C.: National Association of Social Workers.

Ryerson, Diane M. 1987. "ASAP—an Adolescent Suicide Awareness Programme." In René F. W. Diekstra and Keith Hawton, eds., *Suicide in Adolescence*, pp. 173–190. Hingham, Mass.: Kluwer Academic Publishers.

Sacks, Oliver. 1985. *The Man Who Mistook His Wife for a Hat*. New York: Harper & Row.

Saghir, M. and E. Robins. 1973. *Male and Female Sexuality: A Comprehensive Investigation*. Baltimore: Williams and Wilkens.

Salcido, Ramon M. 1979. "Problems of the Mexican-American Elderly in an Urban Setting." *Social Casework* (December), 60:609–616.

Sander, Joelle Hevesi and Jacqueline L. Rosen. 1987. "Teenage Fathers: Working with the Neglected Partner in Adolescent Childbearing." *Family Planning Perspectives* (May–June), 19:107–110.

Sander, L. W. 1980. "New Knowledge About the Infant from Current Research: Implications for Psychoanalysis." *Journal of the American Psychoanalytic Association* 28:181–198.

Santa-Barbara, Jack. 1984. "Employee Assistance Programs: An Alternative Resource for Mental Health Service Delivery." *Canada's Mental Health* (September), 32:35–38.

Sarri, Rosemary C. and Maeda J. Galinsky. 1967. "A Conceptual Framework for Group Development." In Robert D. Vinter, ed., *Readings in Group Practice*, pp. 72–94. Ann Arbor, Mich.: Campus Publishers.

Schafer, Alice T. and Mary W. Gray. 1981. "Sex and Mathematics." *Science* (January 16), 216:231.

Schaffer, H. Rudolph. 1977. *Mothering*. Cambridge, Mass.: Harvard University Press.

Schaffer, H. Rudolph and Peggy E. Emerson. 1964. "The Development of Social Attachments in Infancy." *Monographs of Social Research in Child Development*, vol. 29, no. 94.

Schaie, K. Warner, Stan Orchowsky, and Iris A. Parham. 1982. "Measuring Age and Sociocultural Change: The Case of Race and Life Satisfaction." In Ron Manuel, ed., *Minority Aging, Sociological and Social Psychological Issues*, pp. 223–230. Westport, Conn.: Greenwood Press.

Schermerhorn, Richard A. 1970. *Comparative Ethnic Relations: A Framework for Theory and Research*. Chicago: University of Chicago Press.

Scherz, Frances H. 1967. "The Crisis of Adolescence in Family Life." *Social Casework* (April), 48:209–215.

Schild, Sylvia and Rita Beck Black. 1984. *Social Work and Genetics*. New York: Haworth Press.

Schlesinger, Benjamin, Audrey Danaher, and Carol Robert. 1984. "Dual Career, Delayed Childbearing Families: Some Observations." *Canada's Mental Health* (March) 32:4–6.

Schmeck, Harold M. Jr. 1985. "Life, Death and the Rights of Handicapped Babies." *New York Times*, June 18, pp. C1, C3.

Schmitt, Eric. 1987. "Ordeal for Homeless Students in Suburbs." *New York Times*, November 16, pp. B-1, B-2.

Schneider, Keith. 1988. "Energy Department Faulted on Dealing with Nuclear Waste." *New York Times*, June 7, pp. A-24.

Schowalter, John E. 1977. "The Adolescent with Cancer." In E. Mansell Pattison, ed., *The Experience of Dying*, pp. 195–202. Englewood Cliffs, N.J.: Prentice-Hall.

Schwartz, P. 1983. "Length of Day-Care Attendance and Attachment Behavior in Eighteen-Month-Old Infants." *Child Development* 54:1073–1078,

Schwartz, William. 1961. "Private Troubles and Public Issues: One Social Work Job or Two?" *Social Welfare Forum, 1961*, pp. 146–177. New York: Columbia University Press.

Schwartz, William. 1971. "On the Use of Groups in Social Work Practice." In William Schwartz and Serapio R. Zalba, eds., *The Practice of Group Work*, pp. 3–24. New York: Columbia University Press.

Searles, Harold F. 1960. *The Non-Human Environment*. New York: International Universities Press.

Shabecoff, Philip. 1981. "Toxic Chemicals Loom as Big Threat to the Nation's Supply of Safe Water." *New York Times*, August 13, pp. C-6.

Shabecoff, Philip. 1988. "Military Is Accused of Ignoring Rules on Hazardous Waste." *New York Times*, June 14, pp. C-4.

Shanker, Renee. 1983. "Occupational Disease, Workmen's Compensation, and the Social Work Advocate." *Social Work* (January–February), 28:24–30.

Shapiro, Constance Hoenck. 1981. *Adolescent Pregnancy Prevention: School-Community Cooperation*. Springfield, Ill.: Charles C Thomas.

Shernoff, Michael J. 1984. "Family Therapy for Lesbian and Gay Clients." *Social Work* (July–August), 29(4):393–396.

Shipp, E. R. 1985. "More Married Women Choosing Sterilization." *New York Times*, July 5, pp. A1, B5.

Shneidman, Edwin. 1980. *Voices of Death*. New York: Harper & Row.

Shon, Steven P. and Y. Ja Davis. 1982. "Asian Families." In Monica McGoldrick, John K. Pearce, and Joseph Giordano, eds., *Ethnicity and Family Therapy*, pp. 208–228. New York: Guilford Press.

Shulman, Lawrence. 1967. "Scapegoats, Group Workers, and Preemptive Interventions." *Social Work* (April), 12:37–43.

Sibley, Charles and Jon E. Ahlquist. 1984. "The Phylogeny of the Hominoid Primates as Indicated by DNA-DNA Hybridization." *Journal of Molecular Evolution* (February), 20:2–15.

Siever, L. J. 1982. "Genetic Factors in Borderline Personalities." *Psychiatry 1982*, pp. 437–456. Washington, D.C.: American Psychiatric Association Press.

Simic, Andrei and Barbara Myerhoff. 1978. "Conclusion." In Barbara G. Myerhoff and Andrei Simic, eds., *Life's Career—Aging: Cultural Variations on Growing Old*, pp. 231–246. Beverly Hills, Calif.: Sage.

Singer, Carolyn and Lilian M. Wells. 1981. "The Impact of Student Units on Services and Structural Change in Homes for the Aged." *Canadian Journal of Social Work Education.* 7(3):11–27.

Sinnott, J. D., 1986. *Sex Roles and Aging: Theory and Research from a Systems Perspective.* Farmington, Conn.: S. Karper.

Skolnick, Arlene and Jerome Skolnick, eds. 1974. *Intimacy, Family, and Society.* Boston: Little Brown.

Sluzki, Carlos E. 1983a. "The Sounds of Silence: Two Cases of Elective Mutism in Bilingual Families." In James D. Hansen, ed., *Cultural Perspectives in Family Therapy*, pp. 68–77. Rockville, Md.: Aspen Systems Corporation Publication.

Sluzki, Carlos E. 1983b. "Process, Structure and World Views: Toward an Integrated View of Systemic Models in Family Therapy." *Family Process* (December) 22:469–476.

Smitherman, Geneva. 1984. "Black Language as Power." In Cheris Kramarae, Muriel Schulz, and William H. O'Barr, eds., *Language and Power*, pp. 101–115. Los Angeles: Sage.

Social Work Education Reporter. 1985. "Infusing Genetic Content into Social Work Education Curriculum." (Spring), 53:11.

Solomon, Barbara Bryant and Helen A. Mendes. 1979. "Black Families: A Social Welfare Perspective." In Virginia Tufte and Barbara Myerhoff, eds., *Changing Images of the Family*, pp. 271–295. New Haven, Conn.: Yale University Press.

Sommer, Robert. 1969. *Personal Space.* Englewood Cliffs, N.J.: Prentice-Hall.

Sonenstein, Freya L., Joseph H. Pleck, and Leighton C. Ku. 1989. "At Risk of Aids: Behaviors, Knowledge and Attitudes Among a National Sample of Adolescent Males." Paper presented at the Annual Meeting of the Population Association of America, March 31, Baltimore. Mimeo.

Sotomayer, Marta. 1977. "Language, Culture, and Ethnicity in Developing Self-Concept." *Social Casework* (April), 58:195–203.

Spiegel, David. 1982. "Self-Help and Mutual-Support Groups: A Synthesis of the Recent Literature." In David E. Biegel and Arthur J. Naparstek, eds., *Community Support Systems and Mental Health*, pp. 98–118. New York: Springer.

Spiegel, John P. and Florence Kluckhohn. 1954. "Integration and Conflict in Family Behavior." *Report No. 27, The Group for the Advancement of Psychiatry* (April).

Spinetta, John J., David Rigler, and Myron Karon. 1974. "Personal Space as a Measure of a Dying Child's Sense of Isolation." *Journal of Consulting and Clinical Psychology* (December), 42:751–756.

Spivack, Mayer. 1973. "Archetypal Place." In Wolfgang F. E. Preisner, ed., *Environmental Design Research*, vol. 1, pp. 33–46. Stroudsburg, Pa.: Dowden, Hutchinson & Ross.

Sroufe, L. Alan. 1978. "Attachment and the Roots of Competence." *Human Nature* (October), 1:50–57.

Stack, Carol B. 1974. *All Our Kin: Strategies for Survival in a Black Community*. New York: Harper Colophon.

Staples, Robert. 1978. "Masculinity and Race: The Dual Dilemma of Black Men." *Journal of Social Issues* 34(1):169–183.

State of Families 1985. New York: Family Association of America.

Stein, Ruth. 1983. "Growing Up with a Physical Difference." *Children's Health Care* (February), 12:53–61.

Stellman, Jeanne M. and Susan M. Daum. 1973. *Work Is Dangerous to Your Health*. New York: Pantheon Books.

Stern, Daniel. 1977. *The First Relationship*. Cambridge, Mass.: Harvard University Press.

Stern, Daniel. 1985. *The Interpersonal World of the Human Infant*. New York: Basic Books.

Stewart, William A. 1969. "On the Use of Negro Dialect in the Teaching of Reading." In Joan Baratz and Roger W. Shuy, eds., *Teaching Black Children to Read*, pp. 156–219. Washington, D.C.: Center for Applied Linguistics.

Strauss, Anselm L. and Barney G. Glaser. 1975. *Chronic Illness and The Quality of Life*. St. Louis: Mosby.

Stringham, Jean G., Judith Hothan Riley, and Ann Ross. 1982. "Sient Birth: Mourning a Stillborn Baby." *Social Work* (July), 27:322–327.

Sullivan, Harry Stack. 1953. *The Interpersonal Theory of Psychiatry*. New York: Norton.

Surgeon General's Report on Acquired Immune Deficiency Syndrome. 1988. Washington, D.C.: U.S. Department of Health and Human Services.

Sussman, Marvin B. 1985. "The Family Life of Old People." In Robert H. Binstock and Ethel Shanas, eds., *Handbook of Aging and the Social Sciences*, 2nd ed. pp. 415–449. New York: Van Nostrand Reinhold.

Szinovacz, M. E. 1982. *Women's Retirement: Policy Implications of Recent Research*. Beverly Hills: Sage.

Szinovacz, M. E. 1983. "Beyond The Hearth: Older Women and Retirement." In E. W. Markson, ed., *Older Women: Issues and Prospects*, pp. 93–120. Lexington, Mass.: Lexington Books.

Taggart, Morris. 1985. "The Feminist Critique in Epistemological Perspective: Questions of Context in Family Therapy." *Journal of Marital and Family Therapy* 11(2):113–126.

Taggart, Morris. 1989. "Epistemological Equality as the Fulfillment of

Family Therapy." In Monica McGoldrick, Froma Walsh, and C. Anderson, eds., *Women in Families*, pp. 97–116. New York: Norton.

Terkelsen, Kenneth G. 1980. "Toward a Theory of the Family Life Cycle." In Elizabeth A. Carter and Monica McGoldrick, eds., *The Family Life Cycle: A Framework for Family Therapy*, pp. 21–52. New York: Gardner Press.

Thomas, Alexander. 1975. "A Longitudinal Study of Three Brain-Damaged Children." *Archives of General Psychiatry* 32:457–465.

Thomas, Alexander. 1981. "Current Trends in Developmental Theory." *American Journal of Orthopsychiatry* (October), 51:580–609.

Thomas, Alexander and Stella Chess. 1977. *Temperament and Development*. New York: Brunner/Mazel.

Thomas, Alexander and Stella Chess. 1984. *Origins and Evolution of Behavioral Disorders*. New York: Brunner/Mazel.

Thomas, Lewis. 1974. *Lives of a Cell*. New York: Viking.

Tolman, Richard M., Donald D. Mowry, Linda E. Jones, and John Brekke. 1986. "Developing a Profeminist Commitment Among Men in Social Work." In Nan Van Den Bergh and Lynn B. Cooper, eds., *Feminist Visions for Social Work*, pp. 61–79. Silver Springs, Md.: National Association of Social Workers.

Tou-fou, Vang. 1981. "The Hmong of Laos." In *Bridging Cultures: Southeast Asian Refugees in America*, pp. 73–82. Los Angeles: Asian American Community Mental Health Training Center.

Toupin, Elizabeth Sook Wah Ahn. 1981. "Counseling Asians: Psychotherapy in the Context of Racism and Asian-American History." In Richard H. Dana, ed., *Human Services for Cultural Minorities*, pp. 295–306. Baltimore, Md.: University Park Press.

Trela, James E. and Jay H. Sokolovsy. 1979. "Culture, Ethnicity, and Policy for the Aged." In Donald E. Gelf and Alfred J. Kutzik, eds., *Ethnicity and Aging, Theory, Research, and Policy*, pp. 117–136. New York: Springer.

Triandis, Harry C. 1988. "Commentary." In Daniel Offer, Eric Ostrov, Kenneth I. Howard, and Robert Atkinson. *The Teenage World: Adolescents' Self-Image in Ten Countries*, pp. 127–128. New York: Plenum.

Trost, Cathy. 1988. "Occupational Hazard." *Wall Street Journal*, April 22, p. 25R–26R.

Turner, Victor. 1982. "Introduction." In Victor Turner, ed., *Celebration, Studies in Festivity and Ritual*, pp. 11–30. Washington, D.C.: Smithsonian Institution Press.

U.S.B.C. (United States Bureau of the Census). 1989. *Statistical Abstracts of the United States*. Washington, D.C.: GPO.

Table 13. "Total Population by Age and Sex, 1960 to 1987," p. 13.

Table 67. "Family Groups with Children Under 18, by Race and Type, 1970 to 1987," p. 50.

Table 70. "Family Households with Own Children Under Age 18, by

Type of Family, 1970 to 1987, and by Age of Householder, 1987," p. 51.

Table 93. "Births to Unmarried Women, by Race of Child and Age of Mother, 1970 to 1986," p. 66.

Table 106. "Expectations of Life at Birth," 1950 to 1987," p. 71.

Table 125. "Suicide Rates by Sex, Race, and Age Group, 1970 to 1986." p. 84.

Table 680. "Workers Killed or Disabled on the Job, 1960-1987, and by Industry Group, 1987," p. 413.

Useful Information on Suicide. 1986. Rockville, Md.: DHHS Publication No. (ADM) 86-1489.

Vaillant, George E. 1977a. "How the Best and Brightest Came of Age." *Psychology Today* (September), 11:34–41, 107–108, 110.

Vaillant, George E. 1977b. *Adaptation to Life.* Boston: Little, Brown.

Valentine, Betty Lou. 1978. *Hustling and Other Hard Work.* New York: Free Press.

Valentine, Charles A. and Betty Lou Valentine. 1970. "Making the Scene, Digging the Action, and Telling It like It is: Anthropologists at Work in a Dark Ghetto." In Norman E. Whitten and John F. Szwed, eds. *Afro-American Anthropology*, pp. 403–418. New York: Free Press.

Vladeck, Bruce. 1980. *Unloving Care.* New York: Basic Books.

Vogel, Ezra F. and Norman W. Bell. 1968. "The Emotionally Disturbed Child as the Family Scapegoat." In Norman W. Bell and Ezra F. Vogel, eds., *A Modern Introduction to the Family*, pp. 412–427. New York: Free Press.

Wald, Esther. 1981. *The Remarried Family: Challenge and Promise.* New York: Family Service Association of America.

Walker, Lou A. 1987. *A Loss for Words: The Story of Deafness in a Family.* New York: Harper & Row.

Wallerstein, Judith S. 1984. "Children of Divorce: Preliminary Report of a Ten-Year Follow-Up of Young Children." *American Journal of Orthopsychiatry* (July), 54:444–458.

Wallerstein, Judith S. 1985. "The Overburdened Child: Some Long-Term Consequences of Divorce." *Social Work* (March–April), 30:116–123.

Wallerstein, Judith S. and Joan Berlin Kelly. 1980. *Surviving the Breakup.* New York: Basic Books.

Wallerstein, Judith S. and Sandra Blakeslee. 1989. *Second Chances: Men, Women, and Children a Decade After Divorce.* New York: Ticknor & Fields.

Walsh, Froma. 1980. "The Family in Later Life." In Elizabeth A. Carter and Monica McGoldrick, eds., *The Family Life Cycle: A Framework for Family Therapy*, pp. 197–220. New York: Gardner.

Walsh, Froma. 1983. "Normal Family Ideologies: Myths and Realities. In James D. Hansen, ed., *Cultural Perspectives in Family Therapy*, pp. 2–14. Rockville, Md.: Aspen Systems Corporation Publication.

Waltner, James D. 1988. Report of a lecture given at the 1988 Annual meeting of the American Society on Aging. *Modern Maturity* (June–July) 31:17.

Warren, Roland. 1963. *The Community in America*. Chicago: Rand McNally.

Warshak, Richard A. and John W. Santrock. 1983. "Children of Divorce: Impact of Custody Disposition on Social Development." In Edward J. Callahan and Kathleen A. McClusky, eds., *Life Span Developmental Psychology: NonNormative Life Events*, pp. 241–263. New York: Academic Press.

Washington Post. 1985. "Religious Leaders Champion Parent's Right in Decision Making for Handicapped Newborns." July 24, pp. A 20.

Wattenberg, Esther. 1986. "The Fate of Baby Boomers and Their Children." *Social Work* (January–February), 31:20–28.

Weber, Gwen K. 1980. "Preparing Social Workers for Practice in Rural Social Systems." In H. Wayne Johnson, ed., *Rural Human Services*, pp. 203–214. Itaska, Ill.: F. E. Peacock.

Weeks, J. R. and J. B. Cuellar. 1981. "The Role of Family Members in the Helping Networks of Older People." *The Gerontologist* (April), 21:388–394.

Weikart, David P. 1984. *Changed Lives: The Effects of the Perry Preschool Program on Youths Through Age 19*. Monographs of High-Scope, Educational Research Foundation: No. 8.

Weiss, Robert S. 1982. "Attachment in Adult Life." In Colin M. Parkes and Joan Stevenson-Hinde, eds., *The Place of Attachment in Adult Life*, pp. 171–183. New York: Basic Books.

Weiss, Robert S. 1973. *Loneliness, the Experience of Emotional and Social Isolation*. Cambridge: MIT Press.

Weitzman, Lenore J. 1985. *The Divorce Revolution: The Unexpected Social and Economic Consequences for Women and Children in America*. New York: Free Press.

Weitzman, Michael. 1984. "School and Peer Relations." *Pediatric Clinics of North America* (February), 31:59–69.

Wells, Lilian M. and Carolyn Singer. 1985. "A Model for Linking Networks in Social Work Practice with the Institutionalized Elderly." *Social Work* (July–August), 30:318–322.

Wells, Lilian M., Carolyn Singer, and Alex T. Polgar. 1986. *To Enhance Quality of Life in Institutions. An Empowerment Model in Long Term Care: A Partnership of Residents, Staff and Families*. Toronto: Faculty of Social Work, University of Toronto and University of Toronto Press.

Wertz, Richard W. and Dorothy C. Wertz. 1977. *Lying-In*. New York: Free Press.

Westhoff, Charles F. 1988. "Unintended Pregnancy in America and Abroad." *Family Planning Perspectives* (November–December), 20:254–261.

Wetzel, Janice Wood. 1978a. "Depression and Dependence Upon Unsustaining Environments." *Clinical Social Work Journal* 6(2):75–89.

Wetzel, Janice Wood. 1978b. "The Work Environment and Depression." In John Hanks, ed., *Toward Human Dignity,* pp. 236–245. Washington, D.C.: National Association of Social Workers.

White, Robert W. 1959. "Motivation Reconsidered: The Concept of Competence." *Psychological Review* (September), 66:297–333.

White, Robert W. 1971. "The Urge Towards Competence." *American Journal of Occupational Therapy* (September), 25:271–274.

White, Robert W. 1974. "Strategies of Adaptation: An Attempt at Systematic Description." In George V. Coelho, David A. Hamburg, and John E. Adams, eds., *Coping and Adaptation,* pp. 47–68. New York: Basic Books.

White, Robert W. 1979. "Competence as an Aspect of Personal Growth." In Martha Whalen Kent and Jon. E. Rolf, eds., *Primary Prevention of Psychopathology,* pp. 5–22. Hanover, N.H.: University Press of New England.

Wilkerson, Isabel. 1988. "Farms, Deadliest Workplace, Taking the Lives of Children." *New York Times,* September 26, pp. A1, A21.

Wilkinson, Gerald Thomas. 1980. "On Assisting Indian People." *Social Casework* (October), 61:451–454.

Will, Otto A. 1959. "Human Relatedness and the Schizophrenic Reaction." *Psychiatry* (August), 22:205–223.

Williams, Juanita. 1983. *Psychology of Women: Behavior in a Biosocial Context,* 2d ed. New York: Norton.

Williams, Lena. 1987. "Race Bias Found in Location of Toxic Dumps." *New York Times,* April 16, p. A20.

Williams, Leon F. 1987. "Under the Nuclear Umbrella." *Social Work* (May–June), 32:246–249.

Wilson, Edward O. 1978. *On Human Nature.* Cambridge, Mass.: Harvard University Press.

Winick, Myron, Knarig Katchadurian Meyer, and Ruth C. Harris. 1975. "Malnutrition and Environmental Enrichment by Early Adoption." *Science* (December 19) 190:1173–1175.

Winters, Wendy Glasgow and Freda Easton. 1983. *The Practice of Social Work in the Schools, An Ecological Perspective.* New York: Free Press.

Wong, Janlee. 1981. "Appropriate Mental Health Treatment and Service Delivery for Southeast Asians." In *Bridging Cultures: Southeast Asian Refugees in America,* pp. 195–223. Los Angeles: Asian American Community Mental Health Training Center.

Wood, John. 1987. "Labors of Love." *Modern Maturity* (August–September), 30:28–34, 90–94.

Wortman, Camille B. and Roxane Cohen Silver. 1989. "The Myths of Coping with Loss." *Journal of Consulting and Clinical Psychology* (June), 57:349–357.

Yahraes, H. 1978. *Genes and Mental Health: The Mechanics of Heredity in Major Mental Illneses.* Rockville, Md.: Science Reports, National Institute of Mental Health, DHEW Pub. no. (ADAMHA) 78-640.

Yamamoto, Kaoru, Abdalla Soliman, James Parson, and O. L. Davies, Jr. 1988. "Voices in Unison: Stressful Events in the Lives of Children in Six Countries." *Journal of Child Psychology and Psychiatry* (March), 28:855–864.

Yancey, William L. 1971. "Architecture, Interaction, and Social Control: The Case of a Large-Scale Public Housing Project." *Environment and Behavior* (March), 3:3–18.

Yarrow, Andrew L. 1987. "Divorce at a Young Age: The Troubled Twenties." *New York Times*, January 12, p. A19.

Yarrow, Leon J. 1964. "Separation from Parents During Early Childhood." In Martin L. Hoffman and Lois Wladis Hoffman, eds., *Review of Child Development Research*, 1:89–136. New York: Russell Sage.

Yogman, M., S. Dixon, E. Tronick, H. Als, and T. B. Brazelton. 1977. "The Goals and Structure of Face-to-Face Interaction Between Infants and Fathers." Paper presented at the Biennial Meeting of the Society for Research in Child Development, New Orleans (March).

Young, Michael and John Ziman. 1971. "Cycles in Social Behavior." *Nature* (London) (January 8), 229:91–95.

Figure Credits

Figure 1.2 From Irwin Altman, *The Environment and Social Behavior*, p. 71. Reprinted with permission of the publisher. New York: Brooks/Cole, 1975.

Figure 3.1. Reprinted with permission of Dr. Andy Farquharson.

Figure 3.2. Reprinted from Toni C. Antonucci, "Personal Characteristics, Social Support, and Social Behavior." In Robert H. Binstock and Ethel Shanas, eds., *Handbook of Aging and the Social Sciences*, p. 100. 2d ed. New York: Van Nostrand Reinhold, 1985.

Figures 7.1–7.3. Reprinted from *Genetic Counseling*, with permission of the publisher. White Plains, N.Y.: March of Dimes Birth Defects Foundatino, 1987, pp. 12, 14, 15.

Figure 7.4. Reprinted from *Genetic Counseling*, with permission of the publisher. White Plains, N.Y.: March of Dimes Birth Defects Foundation, 1987, p. 16.

Figure 13.1. Reprinted with the permission of The Science Museum of Connecticut, Roaring Brook Nature Center.

515

Author Index

Subject Index

Able-ism, 54-56; *see also* Chronic illness; Disability; Genetics

Adaptation and adaptedness, 17-18; *see also* Transaction

Adolescents, 351-92; abuse, neglect, and throwaway youth, 384; and accidents and injury, 364; adaptive tasks of teens, 354-55; and childbearing and child rearing, 169, 375-81, 391-92; as a cultural phenomenon, 353; death rates of, 364; and disability and chronic illness, 356, 367-69, 388-89; delinquent, 355; disturbed, 355-56; as a first-order development, 382-84; homicide, 367; normative views of, 354-57; and peers, 377, 382, 383; policy and services implications, 367, 386, 387, 389; racial differences in sexual activity and unintended pregnancy, 375-76, 391-92; and school, 358-59; as a second-order develop-ment, 384-92; sexual orientation and coming out, 361-63, 385-86; and societal issues, 357-58; statistics on teenage pregnancy, abortions, and births, 375-76; and substance abuse, 371-73, 389-90; suicide, 364-67; teenage fathers, 379-81; terminal illness and dying, 369-70; worries, 359-61; *see also* AIDS; Family transformations; Puberty; Sexuality

Adoption, 183, 378-79; and genetic disease, 191; of minority children, 183; of malnourished Korean children, 231

Adult development: community participation and social learning, 310; community roles in mid-adulthood, 382; Erikson's model of, 447; Gould's model of, 462; Levinson's model of, 458-60; tasks of middle adulthood, 382-84, 395-405; tasks of

527